ELEVENTH EDITION

EDUCATIONAL TESTING AND MEASUREMENT:
Classroom Application and Practice

TOM KUBISZYN
University of Houston

GARY BORICH
The University of Texas at Austin

WILEY

VICE PRESIDENT & DIRECTOR	George Hoffman
EXECUTIVE EDITOR	Christopher Johnson
ASSISTANT	Wauntao Matthews
SENIOR DIRECTOR	Don Fowley
PROJECT MANAGER	Gladys Soto
PROJECT SPECIALIST	Nichole Urban
PROJECT ASSISTANT	Anna Melhorn
ASSISTANT MARKETING MANAGER	Puja Katariwala
ASSOCIATE DIRECTOR	Kevin Holm
SENIOR CONTENT SPECIALIST	Nicole Repasky
PRODUCTION EDITOR	Sangeetha Rajan
PHOTO RESEARCHER	Nicholas Olin
COVER PHOTO CREDIT	© Christopher Futcher/Getty Images

This book was set in 10/12pt TimesLTStd by SPi Global, Chennai and printed and bound by Markono Print Media Pte Ltd.

Founded in 1807, John Wiley & Sons, Inc. has been a valued source of knowledge and understanding for more than 200 years, helping people around the world meet their needs and fulfill their aspirations. Our company is built on a foundation of principles that include responsibility to the communities we serve and where we live and work. In 2008, we launched a Corporate Citizenship Initiative, a global effort to address the environmental, social, economic, and ethical challenges we face in our business. Among the issues we are addressing are carbon impact, paper specifications and procurement, ethical conduct within our business and among our vendors, and community and charitable support. For more information, please visit our website: www.wiley.com/go/citizenship.

ISBN: 978-1-119-23915-4 (PBK)
ISBN: 978-1-119-22934-6 (EVALC)

Library of Congress Cataloging in Publication Data:

Kubiszyn, Tom, author.
  Educational testing and measurement : classroom application and practice / Tom Kubiszyn, Gary Borich. — Eleventh edition.
      pages cm
  Includes bibliographical references and index.
  ISBN 978-1-119-23915-4 (paperback)
  1. Educational tests and measurements— United States. I. Borich, Gary D., author. II. Title.
  LB3051.K8 2015
  371.260973— dc23

                                    2015024256

Printing identification and country of origin will either be included on this page and/or the end of the book. In addition, if the ISBN on this page and the back cover do not match, the ISBN on the back cover should be considered the correct ISBN.

Printed in Singapore

10 9 8 7 6 5 4 3 2 1

PREFACE

Welcome to the eleventh edition of *Educational Testing and Measurement: Classroom Application and Practice*, an up-to-date, practical, reader-friendly resource that will help you navigate today's seemingly ever changing and complex world of educational testing, assessment, and measurement. Since the last edition was published, the intensity of the controversy surrounding educational testing and assessment has not diminished. Of course, this makes it tempting to "take sides" and advocate for one position or another. However, as we have in all earlier editions of this text, our approach for this edition has been to present a balanced perspective, informed by developments and the ever increasing research base. By presenting both sides of controversial testing and measurement issues our hope has always been to enable you to be informed enough to form your own opinions. We continue this approach in this edition.

As with all previous editions of *Educational Testing and Measurement*, we continue to present complex test and measurement content in a friendly, nonintimidating, and unique manner, and to relate this content in meaningful ways to important developments in educational measurement and assessment. In completing this revision, we have kept our primary audience—classroom teachers—fully in mind. We have striven to present often abstract and sometimes difficult concepts and procedures in an up-to-date and accurate, but accessible, manner. Rather than overwhelm students with jargon and statistical theory, we continue to use a friendly, conversational style and many classroom-based examples to enhance our emphasis on the application of theory. At the same time, we provide sufficient theoretical background to ensure that students will understand the foundations of measurement and avoid an oversimplified approach to measurement. Thus, we expect that both new and long-time users of the text should feel comfortable with the eleventh edition of the text. To facilitate accommodation to the eleventh edition, we will provide a review of the revisions we have made since the tenth edition.

Many of the changes to this edition were driven by feedback we received from students and instructors. We do value that feedback, and we encourage you to continue to let us know what you think about our text. Other changes were made to reflect recent national or state policy, practice, and political developments that affect testing and assessment practice. We include these to inform readers about the complex and changing educational testing landscape, as it exists today, and as it can be expected to evolve in the future.

Importantly for past users of the text, the sequence of the chapters has not changed from the tenth edition. Two chapter titles (Chapters 2 and 4) and some headings and subheadings have been changed. Chapter 2 has been re-titled to "National Developments: Impact on Classroom Testing and Measurement" to reflect a shift in emphasis away from the prior edition's emphasis on "High-Stakes Testing." To better reflect the chapter's primary focus on decision making, the title of Chapter 4 was changed to "Testing and Educational Decision-Making" instead of "The Purpose of Testing."

Our primary goals for this edition were fourfold. First, we shortened the book to reduce costs. To do so, we abbreviated several sections of the text and moved most of the appendices, the Suggested Readings, and several large sections of text (e.g., much of the high-stakes testing information previously included in Chapter 2) to the book's companion website. We have attempted to migrate sections carefully and have indicated where we have done so in each relevant section of the book. To facilitate student access to our companion website, we have provided links to the website in each instance where we have moved text from the tenth or earlier editions. The Instructor's Manual and Test Bank continue to be found on the companion website and they have also been updated to align with the changes to the text.

Second, as we have in the past, we hope to inform our readers about the latest testing and assessment changes and challenges, including legislative initiatives and requirements that drive testing policy and practice. However, the highly polarized political gridlock that has character-ized national politics for the last several years has not abated and appeared to have intensified as we completed this revision in 2015. We describe some of the reasons for the political gridlock in Washington, DC, and the test and assessment implications of the gridlock (e.g., the failure to reau-thorize long overdue national legislative initiatives that have been highly influential in educational testing and assessment policy, such as the No Child Left Behind (NCLB) Act, which was sched-uled for reauthorization in 2009, and the Individuals with Disabilities Education Improvement Act (IDEIA), which was scheduled for reauthorization in 2011).

Third, we expanded our presentation of recent state and national educational reforms to inform readers about the way those reforms have influenced testing and assessment practice. In the tenth edition, we described the development of the Common Core State Standards (CCSS) and considered the implications of the CCSS for educational testing in the context of other educational reforms, such as the NCLB, IDEIA, and high-stakes testing (HST). In this edition, we describe how the CCSS have evolved since the last edition and we integrate the state-sponsored CCSS with the national Race-to-the-Top (RTT) voluntary initiative and the RTT-sponsored multistate assessment consortia (i.e., the Smarter Balanced Assessment Consortium and the Partnership for the Assess-ment of Readiness for College and Careers, or PARCC). Although those reforms were initially embraced widely across the nation and across political parties, support began to erode in 2014 and as we prepared this revision the futures of the CCSS and RTT were unclear.

Fourth, to help students focus on key points we added Learning Outcomes to the beginning of Chapters 1–20 to preview the primary topics and concepts we cover in each chapter. Clarifications are also provided within almost every chapter to help ensure that recent developments are integrated with content in other chapters. As with all prior revisions, we have added recent research findings and updated references where relevant. The popular step-by-step summaries included at the end of each chapter have been expanded and updated, as have the practice items and discussion questions. The discussion and practice questions and exercises help students learn how to apply the concepts presented in the chapter, and exercises marked with an asterisk continue to have answers listed in Appendix B for this edition. The popular Math Skills Review continues to be included in the text (in Appendix A) for those with math anxiety or in need of a math skills refresher.

Past users of the text will notice that Chapters 1, 2, and 19 were the most heavily revised chapters. We reduced the length of Chapter 1 while also adding a section to clarify what we mean about the specific purposes of testing (i.e., academic content areas, such as mathematics, science, or social studies) and the general purposes of testing (formative, interim, and summative), that differ primarily based on intent and timing.

Compared to the tenth edition, Chapter 2 has a new title and is now shorter and more focused on relevant national testing/assessment developments (e.g., NCLB, IDEIA CCSS, and RTT). New material includes the development by multistate consortia of two CCSS-aligned, on-line standard-ized assessments, the controversies that have recently evolved around those developments, and their current status in a politically gridlocked U.S. Congress. Other updates cover recent findings from international testing programs that compare U.S. students with students from both indus-trialized and nonindustrialized nations, and the competency testing for teachers section has been expanded to include the growing and controversial use of student test scores, in part, to evaluate teachers. To maintain accessibility to the HST history and controversies, that information from the tenth edition was moved to the companion website, along with the American Educational Research Association (AERA) position statement about HST and our recommendations for teachers that can help students prepare for HST.

Chapter 19 now clarifies the relationships among standardized, summative tests, the CCSS, RTT assessment consortia, and the RTT-sponsored Common Core-aligned tests, including Common Core-aligned performance assessments. We describe recent court cases that underscore the importance of adhering to standardized administration and scoring procedures, and the risks educators may face if they violate those requirements. Recent research that addresses the fairness of accommodations and alternative assessments has been included, and we provide a companion website reference for the supplemental section that discusses accommodations and alternative assessments in the context of IDEIA and SLD determination. A new, fictitious norms table and related interpretive exercises now follow the converted scores section to enhance the student's ability to apply what they have learned about converted scores into a norms table. The emphasis on the importance of evaluating the match between your class and the norm group before making performance comparisons based on the norm group has been enhanced. We also moved a second parent conference interpretation example to the companion website to reduce the text's length. New sample test reports from a test publisher and the NY State Department of Education and new interpretive scenarios replace the reports and scenarios from prior editions.

Throughout the text, we have integrated the CCSS and RTT initiatives into the presentation. For example we have described the role of the RTT and CCSS in educational decision making in Chapter 4, clarified the linkages among the CCSS and instructional objectives and how they relate to norm- and criterion-referenced tests in Chapters 5 and 6. In Chapter 7, we explain how teacher-made test items can be better aligned with the CCSS, and the PARCC and Smarter Balanced Common Core consortium tests, and provide links to their respective websites. Chapter 8 explains why well-constructed classroom essay, knowledge organization, and open-book tests align with the higher-order thinking skills emphasized by the CCSS and some state-specific academic standards. We also replaced four older examples of the assessment of knowledge organization with two new examples. Chapter 9 discusses the inclusion of performance assessments in the web-based CCSS-aligned PARCC and Smarter Balanced tests and Chapter 10 describes how the classroom assessment of CCSS-aligned higher-order thinking skills can be enhanced with portfolios.

Two appendices associated with Chapter 13 were moved to the companion website. Those tenth edition appendices were Appendix C (Determining the median with multiple tied middle scores) and Appendix E (Statistics and measurement tests). Appendix D from the tenth edition (Pearson product–moment correlation) is also now located on the companion website.

Chapter 20 encourages students to visit relevant websites (test publisher, Smarter Balanced or PARCC consortia, or state education agencies) to access relevant resources. It also distinguishes between formative, interim/benchmark, and summative standardized tests, provides selected standardized test updates, and adds summaries of three new standardized tests.

For Chapter 21, we moved the lengthy interpretive section that followed the dialog in earlier editions to the companion website to reduce the text's length. The dialog itself was updated to incorporate recent CCSS- and RTT-related developments.

Appendix A is unchanged and Appendix B has been updated with answers to several new practice questions. All other appendices from the tenth edition have been migrated to the book's companion website (go to http://www.wiley.com/college/kubiszyn and click on the link to the Student Companion Site).

We hope that you will agree that the eleventh edition is a timely and comprehensive revision that captures the realities of educational testing and assessment today. We have tried to select traditional and contemporary topics and provide examples that help the teacher, especially the beginning teacher, deal with practical, day-to-day issues related to the testing and assessment of students and measuring their behavior, in the context of NCLB, state HST programs, IDEIA, RTI, the CCSS, and the RTT initiative. The topics we have chosen, their natural sequences and linkage to the real-life tasks of teachers, the learning outcomes and step-by-step summaries of major topics and concepts, and our discussion and practice questions and exercises, all work, we believe, to make this text a valuable tool and an important resource for observing, measuring, and understanding life in today's changing classroom. We hope that our approach helps ensure that these important activities are sensitive to the increasing accountability requirements today's educators face.

ACKNOWLEDGMENTS

We would like to express our appreciation to the following instructors for their constructive comments regarding this text over the years: Neal Schnoor, University of Nebraska–Kearney; Molly Jameson, Ball State University; Janet Carlson, University of Nebraska–Lincoln; Barry Morris, William Carey University; Lenore Kinne, Northern Kentucky University; Christopher Maglio, Truman State University; and Michael Trevisan, Washington State University. Thanks also to W. Robert Houston, University of Houston; Alice Corkill, University of Nevada—Las Vegas; Robert Paugh, University of Central Florida; Priscilla J. Hambrick, City University of New York; Pam Fernstrom, University of North Alabama; Bill Fisk, Clemson University; Lilia Ruban, University of Houston; David E. Tanner, California State University at Fresno; Gregory J. Cizek, University of Toledo; Thomas J. Sheeran, Niagara University; Jonathan A Plucker, Indiana University; Aimin Wang, Miami University; William M. Bechtol, late of Southwest Texas State University; Deborah E. Bennett, Purdue University; Jason Millman, Cornell University; David Payne, University of Georgia; Glen Nicholson, University of Arizona; Carol Mardell-Czudnowski, Northern Illinois University; and James Collins, University of Wyoming for their constructive comments on earlier revisions. Also, thanks to Marty Tombari for his contributions to Chapters 9 and 10 and other examples, illustrations, and test items in this volume, and to Ann Schulte for her contributions to Chapter 18. Finally, thanks to Natalie Raff, a doctoral candidate at the University of Houston, for her conscientious help in reviewing and refining both the tenth and eleventh editions.

—Tom Kubiszyn and Gary Borich

CONTENTS

AN INTRODUCTION TO CONTEMPORARY EDUCATIONAL TESTING AND MEASUREMENT

LEARNING OUTCOMES

After completing this chapter, the student will be able to:

1. Explain why tests are only tools that can be used appropriately or inappropriately.
2. Explain why test scores are fallible.
3. Distinguish between formative, interim or benchmark, and summative assessment.
4. Describe how technical adequacy, test user competency, and the extent to which a test aligns with its intended purpose can limit or enhance a test's usefulness.
5. Describe how educational test usefulness is affected by diversity considerations.
6. Explain why a single test score alone should not be used for important educational decision making.
7. Compare and contrast testing, assessment, and the assessment process.
8. Compare and contrast the various types of educational tests and assessments.
9. Explain why testing and assessment skills are vital to today's classroom teacher.

CHANCES ARE that some of your strongest childhood and adolescent memories include taking tests in school. More recently, you probably remember taking a great number of tests in college. If your experiences are like those of most of the students who come through our educational system, you probably have very strong or mixed feelings about tests and testing. Indeed, some of you may swear that you will never test your students when you become teachers, unless of course you are required by law to do so! If so, you may think that test results add little to the educational process and fail to reflect learning, that testing may turn off students, or that tests do not measure what they are supposed to measure. On the other hand, others may believe that tests are necessary and vital to the educational process, and are critical for accountability purposes. For you, tests may represent irrefutable evidence that learning has occurred and that goals and objectives are being met. Rather than viewing tests as deterrents that turn off students, you may see them as motivators that stimulate students to study and provide both students and decision makers with vital and objective feedback about student achievement.

Between those who feel positively about tests and those who feel negatively about them lies a third group. Within this group, which includes the authors of this textbook, are those who see tests as tools that can make important contributions to the process of evaluating pupils, curricula, and teaching methods, but who question the status and power too often given to individual tests and test scores. We are concerned that test users and consumers of test results (e.g., teachers, parents, the media, administrators, policy makers, and other decision makers) often uncritically accept test scores without careful consideration of how useful the test scores may actually be for whatever decision may be at hand.

Whatever your feelings may be about educational testing, it is critical that prospective teachers be aware of important recent developments that have altered significantly the testing landscape at national, state, district, and local levels. In Chapter 2, we will review these developments to give you an historical context that we hope will enable you to understand how today's testing picture has developed over the last several decades. Before we review those developments, we will clarify what our perspective is about the utility of educational tests, assessment, and the broader assessment process in this chapter. We then discuss briefly the specific and general purposes of educational testing, and the various types of educational tests that exist. We conclude this chapter with a discussion of the impact of educational testing on the general education classroom teacher.

TESTS ARE ONLY TOOLS; THEIR USEFULNESS CAN VARY

One of the driving reasons we originally decided to write this textbook was the concern we had at that time about some common misconceptions. These included the ideas that many teachers, administrators, parents, and other decision makers had about the utility of tests and test scores, and especially the uncritical acceptance of individual test scores for important educational decision making. Uncritical acceptance of test scores by decision makers concerned us for five reasons. First, tests are only tools, and tools can be appropriately used, unintentionally misused, and intentionally abused. Second, tests, like other tools, can be well designed or poorly designed. Third, both poorly designed and well-designed tools in the hands of ill-trained or inexperienced users can be dangerous. Fourth, the usefulness of a well-designed tool, even in the hands of a competent user, can be limited if the tool, or test, is used for an unintended purpose or population. In other words, just as there is no "one-size-fits-all" tool (not even the venerable Swiss army knife!), no single test is appropriate for all purposes and all persons. Fifth, even when a test is well designed and is appropriately used by a competent examiner (i.e., for the purpose and populations it was designed for), the test can only provide us with *some* of the information we may want or need to make the best possible educational decision about a student.

"Wait a minute!" you may say. "All this makes it sound like you are saying that tests are not useful for educational decision making, even if they are well constructed and properly used." Not so! We are *not* saying test results are useless, unimportant, or unhelpful. We *are* saying that it *is important* to recognize that the usefulness of tests, like the usefulness of all tools, depends on a variety of factors. Let us explore some of these factors next.

WHY WE DEVELOPED THIS TEXT: ENHANCING TEST USEFULNESS

By helping you learn to design and use tests and test results appropriately, we hope you will be less likely to misuse tests and their results and be better able to recognize and avoid using poorly designed tests with questionable technical accuracy. We also hope that you will become mindful of how the purpose of testing and the population to be tested can affect a test's usefulness. Finally, we hope that you will grasp the importance of considering multiple sources of information obtained from multiple informants *along with* test results to make important educational decisions about students. Let us turn to a more detailed explanation of how each of these points can affect the usefulness of a test for educational decision making.

Technical Adequacy

A critically important factor that affects a test's usefulness is its technical adequacy. Today's teachers must not only administer tests developed or required by their state or federal requirements (e.g., the No Child Left Behind Act, or NCLB), but also develop their own tests to inform day-to-day instructional decision making. Much of this text is devoted to helping you develop teacher-constructed (or teacher-made) tests with good technical adequacy and to help you understand how to use the results of teacher-made tests to evaluate instructional effectiveness and to provide data to help teachers complement and adjust instruction. We also intend to help you learn to evaluate the technical adequacy of commercial or state-mandated tests (i.e., developed by test publishers) required for accountability purposes so that you know how to use the results from those tests, when appropriate, to evaluate and inform instruction and educational decision making.

The technical adequacy of a test includes evidence of its validity (see Chapter 15) and its score reliability (see Chapter 16). Validity evidence helps us determine whether the test is measuring what it is intended to measure, and score reliability indicates the extent to which test scores are consistent and stable. In general, we strive to use tests with the strongest validity and score reliability evidence. However, contrary to common wisdom, these factors are *not fixed* characteristics of a test, even if the test is well established, widely used, and respected. This is because a test's validity and score reliability can be affected by many factors, including the competency of the test user, whether the test is being used for the purpose it was developed, the person or population it is used with, and even the testing conditions (e.g., noisy rooms, poor lighting, and timing errors) (see Chapters 15–19).

This is why we said before that no test, even one with well-established reliability and validity, is a "one-size-fits-all" test that is equally useful for all test users, purposes, and populations. Thus, it is inappropriate to speak of the "validity of a test" or the "reliability of a test," as though validity and reliability are permanent, unchanging characteristics of the test. Nevertheless, this is exactly what many test users believe. Because test usefulness can vary, it is most appropriate to speak of the evidence of a test's validity and score reliability *for a particular use and with a particular population, when administered by a competent test user.* The need to consider test user competency, a test's intended use, and the intended population when discussing the test's technical adequacy and usefulness emerged from deliberations among measurement experts from the American Educational Research Association (AERA), the American Psychological Association (APA), and the National Council on Measurement in Education (NCME) over several years when they developed the third edition of the *Standards for Educational and Psychological Testing* (American Educational Research Association, American Psychological Association & National Council on Measurement in Education, 1999). Often referred to as the *Standards*, the importance of those factors was reinforced when the fourth edition was released (American Educational Research Association, American Psychological Association & National Council on Measurement in Education, 2014). The *Standards* are widely regarded as one of the most authoritative and influential guidelines in the testing, measurement, and assessment arena. Next, let us consider several examples that should help you understand why it is so important to consider the competency of a test user and a test's validity and reliability evidence within the context of a test's intended use and the intended population.

Test User Competency

Evidence of a test's usefulness can vary depending upon the competency of the people administering, scoring, and interpreting the test. An electric drill (the corded type, not the battery-powered ones that always seem to need recharging) can be very useful in the hands of a competent electrician who is skilled in carefully drilling holes in a wall while avoiding the electrical and water lines behind the wall. The same drill may be far less useful, and even dangerous, in the hands of a child or in the hands of an adult who acts like a child! Does this mean that a child or an incompetent adult could not drill a hole in the wall? Of course not; it simply means that the competent tool user will make better use of the tool, just as a competent test user will likely make better use of a test. Could a child use the drill to drill holes in the wall? Probably. Could the child avoid all the electrical and water lines behind the wall? And could the child avoid drilling a hole in its hand or electrocuting itself? We can only hope! In short, an electric drill's, or a test's usefulness, varies depending upon the competency of the person using it.

Matching the Test's Intended Purpose

A screwdriver is intended to be used to drive screws. Nonetheless, who has not used a screwdriver as an ice pick, a lever or pry bar, a chisel, a paint mixing stick, a means to poke an older sibling in the eye, or for some other purpose? Did it work? Probably. Did it work as well as an ice pick, a lever or pry bar, a chisel, or a sharp stick would have? Probably not. In short, the screwdriver's usefulness depends on whether you are using it for its intended purpose. It also is important to know whether the purpose of testing is specific or more general.

Specific Purposes Like other tools, tests have been designed for many specific measurement purposes (achievement in various academic content areas, intellectual and personality functioning, vocational aptitudes, etc.). Like other tools, a test's usefulness (i.e., the evidence of its validity and reliability) can vary, depending upon how well the current purpose of testing matches the specific purpose for which the test was developed. A test designed to identify individuals with above-average ability to quickly and accurately recognize typographical errors in a document may have excellent validity and score reliability when it is used to predict a potential employee's ability to quickly and accurately recognize typographical errors in a book manuscript. On the other hand, the validity of the same test may be substantially lower if the test is used to predict a person's ability to actually write a book (a very different skill, believe us!), or to predict a person's ability to program a video game. In those cases, the test's usefulness is more limited; it was not designed to assess writing or programming ability. This does not mean it is useless for this purpose, but there may be better tools … oops, we mean tests, that would be more useful.

General Purposes: Formative, Interim, and Summative Assessment In addition to being designed for a wide variety of specific content areas (e.g., assessing reading vocabulary, comprehension, spelling, mathematics, algebra, and general science), educational tests also can be designed to be administered at different times over the school year. The timing of test administration refers to the more general purposes of testing: *formative* (any time), *interim* (two to three times per year), and *summative* (end of year or semester) assessment. Historically, summative tests/assessments have been considered to be the most important tests in education, although their utility for day-to-day instructional decision making is limited. In recent years, formative and interim assessments have rapidly gained popularity in classroom testing.

Summative tests are administered after some period of instruction is completed (this can vary widely, e.g., a unit on vertebrates in biology, a semester of physics, or a year of algebra). Summative tests are intended to provide a measure or gauge of student learning following the *completion* of a unit of instruction. Summative tests are lengthy and are used to meet annual state and federal accountability requirements, to assign grades, to evaluate curriculum effectiveness, and to compare annual year-to-year performance among students, schools, and districts. Summative tests/assessments can be very useful if the purpose of testing is to inform us about broad achievement trends *after* instruction has been completed. However, summative tests/assessments may not be very useful if the purpose of testing is to evaluate acquisition of specific skills after a lesson, or the effectiveness of instruction on a day-to-day basis. Summative tests are simply not designed to be sensitive to small, day-to-day specific changes in achievement; rather, they are designed to measure larger and broader changes in achievement.

Formative tests/assessments are intended to assess the effectiveness of instruction on an ongoingbasis (e.g., have specific skills been acquired?), and to inform day-to-day instructional decision making (e.g., move on to the next step in the curriculum, review or re-present the content using a different approach/medium, or provide instruction in a different setting). Formative assessments are intentionally brief (e.g., from one to several minutes) and are intended to be administered frequently, unlike summative tests that are typically administered annually or every few years.

In the past, most formative assessments were constructed by classroom teachers to support the learning process and inform instruction on a classroom by classroom basis. However, over the last decade, the adoption of the Response to Intervention (RTI) model, which we will describe in Chapter 3 and more recently, and the Common Core State Standards (CCSS), which will be discussed in detail in Chapter 2, have prompted a surge in formative assessment products developed by commercial test developers. However, questions have been raised about the validity, quality, and utility of recent, commercially developed formative assessments (Molnar, 2014).

Interim assessments reside between summative and formative assessments. They are longer than formative assessments but not as long as summative assessments. They are intended to be administered at more than one point during the academic year, at regular intervals (e.g., fall, winter, and spring). They are not intended to be as comprehensive as summative assessments, nor are they intended to be as narrowly focused as formative assessments. They are intended to measure student growth or progress over time and can be useful in differentiating instruction and evaluating instructional program effectiveness (i.e., both special education and general education programs). When they are used to identify students at risk for poor performance on an annual summative test, they are referred to as benchmark tests.

Matching Diverse Test-Takers to the Test

The U.S. population has become increasingly diverse in recent years, and there is no reason to expect that this trend will diminish any time soon. A wide range of cultural, linguistic, and academic backgrounds are common in today's classrooms (Banks & Banks, 2013). Yet, the technical adequacy of many educational tests and assessments was established based on test development samples that included primarily, if not entirely, Caucasian, Hispanic American, and African-American students. Would we expect the technical adequacy of these tests to be the same when used with populations from different cultural, linguistic, and academic backgrounds (e.g., Middle Eastern and

Indonesian learners, limited English-speaking learners, and both higher and lower socioeconomic learners)? Before you answer this question, let us return to the example of the electric drill.

Did you ever try to drill a hole in metal with a drill bit designed for drilling into wood? If you did, you will not make that mistake again! Specialized drill bits have been developed to enhance usefulness when drilling into diverse surfaces (e.g., wood, metal, concrete, and ceramic). Thus, a wood bit works best for drilling into wood, a metal bit for drilling into metal, and so on. Would we expect that one bit would work equally well for all diverse surfaces? Of course not. To be most useful, the drill bit must match the surface into which you are drilling the hole.

Things are no different with tests. For example, a test may be designed to measure certain characteristics for a particular group. We would expect the test to be most useful when used for similar groups, but like a single drill bit, we would not expect the test to be equally useful for all groups. Let us consider a multiple-choice test used to assess end-of-year achievement in a tenth-grade American History class (quick, is this a formative or a summative test?). The class is composed largely of two groups: native English-speaking U.S. children who have taken many multiple-choice tests and recent immigrants from Nicaragua who speak little English and have had little formal schooling. Excellent evidence may exist for the test's technical adequacy (e.g., reliability and validity) when it is used to assess achievement for the English-speaking students. However, evidence for the same test's reliability and validity may be less impressive (or even non-existent) when used to assess achievement for the limited English proficient (LEP), recently emigrated students from Nicaragua. In this case, linguistic (lack of familiarity with the English language) and cultural (lack of experience with multiple-choice tests in their native Nicaragua) factors may seriously limit the usefulness of the test. This consideration does not necessarily mean the test should not be used at all with this population. It does mean we should always be thoughtful and try to select the test that is most useful for the population we are testing—if there is one available—and to be very careful in interpreting results.

Although using a test that is not a great "fit" is not ideal, it is a matter of practicality. We simply lack tests that have strong evidence for their validity and usefulness with all populations and for all purposes for which tests are used. For example, school children in the Houston, Texas, public schools speak almost 200 different languages and have a similarly wide range of cultural backgrounds. Because of the diverse cultural, linguistic, and academic backgrounds of these students, it follows that the usefulness of the tests used to evaluate these diverse children will vary. This leads us to our next point.

Even though we should always strive to select the test that is *most* appropriate for the group(s) to be tested, we cannot always achieve this goal. When we cannot match the purpose and the group, we should try to be *especially* thoughtful and careful in interpreting test results. What else can we do?

Test Results and Diversity Considerations

What should you do when the group being tested does not match the characteristics of the sample used in its development? Depending on whom you ask, you will get a variety of suggestions. Here are ours. In such situations, the results of a single test administered at a single point in time should *never* be used alone to make important decisions—even when the technical adequacy, test user competency, and purpose criteria we have just described have been met. Instead, we recommend that testing should be part of a thoughtful, multifaceted approach to assessment, with input provided over time by multiple informants (i.e., teachers and other trained personnel). Simply put, in our diverse society there can be no "one-size-fits-all" test or assessment, and this applies to summative, interim, and formative tests.

That, as they say, is the theory (or perhaps wishful thinking on our part). Reality is very different. For more than two decades now, promotion, graduation, and other high-stakes educational decisions (e.g., ranking of schools as exemplary, acceptable, or in need of improvement) are commonly made based entirely, or primarily, on summative test scores obtained at a single point in time, in spite of the increasingly diverse nature of our society. This phenomenon is largely attributable to the rapid spread of the high-stakes testing (HST) movement since the mid-1990s and the passage of the No Child Left Behind Act (NCLB) (discussed in detail in Chapter 2).

That said, efforts have been undertaken to make accommodations for culturally, linguistically, and academically diverse test-takers (Flanagan, Ortiz & Alfonso, 2013). In some cases, tests have been translated or otherwise modified in an effort to better align them with diverse populations (Malda, van de Vijver & Temane, 2010). Nevertheless, the technical adequacy and appropriateness of these tests after such modifications, as well as the impact on results of the use of interpreters, and variations in examiner and situational variables have all proven difficult to determine (American Educational Research Association, American Psychological Association & National Council on Measurement in Education, 1999). In view of our nation's increasing diversity, further study of the impact of such modifications is clearly needed. Fairbairn and Fox (2009) provide a summary of the relevant issues, and they also offer test development suggestions for English-language learners.

TESTS ARE ONLY TOOLS: A VIDEO BEATS A PHOTO

The importance of making decisions based on more than a single test result is not a concern limited to testing with diverse populations. Even when a test has technical adequacy, the test user is competent, and the purpose and population are appropriate, we *still* do not recommend making important educational decisions based on a single test administered at a single point in time. Instead of relying on such a limited "snapshot" or photograph (or JPEG) of student achievement for important decision making, we recommend that test results should be considered to be part of a broader "video" or process of measurement called assessment. We will describe the process of assessment in the next section and also distinguish between testing and assessment. See Box 1-1 about the Waco, Texas, public schools for an example of the controversial use of test results from a single test at a single point in time to make important educational decisions.

The situation described in Box 1-1 is not unusual. Well-intended educators and others continue to rely solely or primarily on test results from a single point in time to make important, high-stakes educational decisions. At times, they may have little choice because federal, state, or district requirements mandate "one-size-fits-all" policies that are tied to scores from a specific, "approved" test, without regard for the extent to which the validity and reliability of the scores from this test may vary for diverse populations of students, or for a different purpose than the one for which the test was developed.

To sum up, our position is that tests are only tools that can be appropriately used, abused, or misused. To minimize inappropriate test use, it is important to carefully consider the (1) evidence of a test's technical adequacy, (2) competency of the test users, (3) extent to which the purpose of testing matches the purpose for which the test was developed, and (4) degree to which the test-takers match the group that was used to establish the technical adequacy of the test. Furthermore, we encourage you to consider additional background, historical, and observational data, especially when the test is administered to a group that differs from the test's development sample, and when the test is used to make high-stakes educational decisions (Rhodes, Ochoa & Ortiz, 2005). In short, these situations call for a thoughtful and comprehensive assessment process rather than simply a testing/assessment snapshot.

BOX 1-1

*WACO, TEXAS, SCHOOLS USE STANDARDIZED TEST SCORES ALONE TO MAKE
PROMOTION DECISIONS*

Concerned with possible negative effects of social promotion, the Waco, Texas, public schools decided to utilize standardized test scores as the basis for promotion decisions beginning with first graders in 1998. As a result, the number of students retained increased from 2 percent in 1997 to 20 percent in 1998 (The Waco Experiment, 1998). The Waco schools are not alone in curtailing social promotion. The Chicago public schools, in the midst of a wide-ranging series of educational reform initiatives, retained 22,000 students in 1994, with 175,000 retained in 1998 (*Newsweek*, June 22, 1998).

Social promotion is a practice that purports to protect student self-esteem by promoting students to the next grade so that they may stay with their classmates even when they are not academically ready for promotion. Educational, psychological, political, fiscal, cultural, and other controversies are all associated with social promotion. What has come to be known by some as the "Waco Experiment" also raised a number of measurement-related issues.

Even though the Waco schools' decision was doubtless well intended, their policy may have overlooked the fact that the utility of test scores varies with age, with test results for young children being less stable and more prone to error than those for older children. A relatively poor score on a test may disappear in a few days, weeks, or months after additional development has occurred, regardless of achievement. In addition, older children are less susceptible to distractions and, with years of test-taking experience under their belts, are less likely to be confused by the tests or to have difficulty completing tests properly. All these factors can negatively affect a student's score and result in a score that underrepresents the student's true level of knowledge.

Furthermore, a single standardized test score provides only a portion of a child's achievement over the school year, regardless of the grade level. As we will see when we consider the interpretation of standardized test results in Chapter 19, a number of student-related factors (e.g., illness and emotional upset) and administrative factors (e.g., allowing too little time and failing to read instructions verbatim) can negatively affect a student's performance on the day the test was taken. Thus, making a decision that so substantially affects a child's education based on a single measure obtained on a single day rather than relying on a compilation of measures (tests, ratings, observations, grades on assessments and portfolios, homework, etc.) obtained over the course of the school year seems ill-advised.

On the other hand, using data collected on a single day and from a single test to make what otherwise would be complex, time-consuming, and difficult decisions has obvious attraction. It appears to be expedient, accurate, and cost-effective and to be addressing concerns about the social promotion issue. However, it also may be simplistic and shortsighted if no plan exists to remediate those who are retained. As noted in a June 12, 1998, editorial in the *Austin American-Statesman*, "Failing students who don't meet a minimum average score, without a good plan to help them improve, is the fast track to calamity." Nevertheless, this trend has not diminished since we first reported on it in our sixth edition. Indeed, reliance on the use of test scores to make high-stakes promotion decisions has increased across the nation. Several states have now adopted versions of Florida's retention policy, enacted by then Governor Jeb Bush in 2002–2003 to combat social promotion. In these states, students who do not pass the states' high-stakes test must be retained, although there are often several "good cause" exemptions from this policy that soften this practice (Robelen, 2012).

THE DIFFERENCE BETWEEN TESTING/ASSESSMENT AND THE ASSESSMENT PROCESS

Today, the terms *tests* and *assessments* are commonly used interchangeably. Indeed, some seem to have eliminated the word "testing" from their vocabularies and replaced it with the word "assessment" because they believe that use of the word "assessment" is less evaluative, threatening, or negative than use of the word "testing." In any case, we too will consider the terms *testing* and *assessment* to be synonymous. However, we believe a clear distinction needs to be made between tests and assessments and the *assessment process*.

Tests and Assessments

The terms *tests* and *assessments* typically refer to single measures that yield results at a single point in time. There are exceptions, and some of these will be discussed in Chapters 9 and 10 (i.e., performance and portfolio assessments that combine multiple types of measures into a single aggregated rating). It is from the results of tests and assessments that we attempt to measure learning or to quantify some attribute or characteristic (e.g., intellectual ability and level of anxiety). Educational tests/assessments may be either formative, interim, or summative, depending upon whether they are used to measure day-to-day changes in learning (i.e., formative), over the course of months or a semester (i.e., interim), or learning over a more extended time frame (i.e., summative).

Assessment Process

The assessment *process* may span days, weeks, an entire semester, the entire school year, or longer. Formative, interim, and summative assessments are typically part of this broad assessment process, but are *not end points*. The assessment process is a means to an end, a comprehensive evaluation made up of many testing and assessment components and relevant background and contextual information. A comprehensive assessment process may include the following:

a. Traditional (i.e., summative and interim) test results from one or more multiple-choice, true-false, matching, or essay tests, or performance/portfolio assessments.

b. Progress monitoring (i.e., formative) results from less-traditional tests, such as curriculum-based measurement (CBM) or other brief, repeated measures.

c. A variety of other measurement procedures (e.g., observations, checklists, rating scales—included in the supplemental chapters on the textbook website at http://www.wiley.com/college/kubiszyn).

d. The findings from all these assessments are integrated with relevant background and contextual information (e.g., language proficiency and cultural considerations—also covered later in the text, as well as the five factors that can affect a test's usefulness that we described at the beginning of this chapter) to help ensure that educational decisions are as appropriate and as valid as possible.

Therefore, you can see that from our perspective, testing is only one part (i.e., like a snapshot or photograph) of the *process* of assessment that may include multiple photographs or segments (i.e., like a slide show, movie, or video) that reflect multiple types of information obtained from multiple informants at multiple points in time. Taken together, these components can provide us with a far richer and, we believe, more valid and accurate description of the individual than we can possibly obtain from any of the individual components alone. Figure 1.1 further clarifies the distinction between testing/assessment, and the assessment process. To avoid confusion later, be sure to understand the distinction we make between testing/assessment (as components of the assessment process) and the broader and richer assessment process itself, as depicted in Figure 1.1.

For an introductory chapter, we have exposed you to a lot of terms and concepts. If you are having any trouble absorbing all of this material, do not despair, but do take the time to review

Testing/Assessment

1. Tests (or assessments) are developed or selected, administered to the class, and scored.
2. Test results may then be used to make decisions about a pupil (assign a grade, recommend for an advanced program), instruction (repeat, review, move on), curriculum (replace, revise), or other educational activities.

An Assessment Process

1. Information is collected from tests and *other measurement instruments* (portfolios and performance assessments, rating scales, checklists, and observations).
2. This information is critically evaluated and integrated with relevant background and contextual information, including the five factors that can affect a test's or assessment's usefulness.
3. The integration of critically analyzed test results and other information results in a decision about a pupil (assign a grade, recommend for an advanced program), instruction (repeat, review, move on), curriculum (replace, revise), or other educational factors.

FIGURE 1.1 The distinction between testing/assessment and the assessment process.

and master what we have covered so far because these terms and concepts are important to your success as we go forward. Here are some of the main points we have made:

- Tests/assessments are only tools that can be well or poorly designed.
- Even well-designed tests can be misused or abused.
- Competent test users are less likely to misuse or abuse tests (we want you to become one of these!).
- The usefulness of tests/assessments can vary depending upon the purposes of testing.
- The usefulness of tests/assessments can vary depending upon the characteristics of the persons who are being tested, or assessed.
- Obtaining multiple forms of assessment information from multiple informants at multiple time points enriches our understanding of pupils.
- Important educational decisions should not be made based on a single test taken at a single point in time.
- A test/assessment is only one part of a much broader and more comprehensive process of assessment. Today, this process increasingly includes formative and interim data as well as summative assessment data.

Next, we will build on this foundation by introducing you to the various types of tests/assessments used in education and explaining how they differ from each other.

TYPES OF TESTS/ASSESSMENTS

So far, we have clarified the notion that tests are only tools, and we have described some of the factors that can affect the usefulness of these tools. Then we distinguished among formative, interim, and summative tests, and between tests/assessments and the much broader assessment process.

Next, we clarify some technical test-related terminology. The terms we introduce here will be referred to over and over again in the text. Even though it is important to understand as many of these terms as you can at this point, if you are like most students, you will need to return to this section repeatedly as you work your way through the text.

"You can't tell the players without a scorecard." Yes, this is an old baseball expression, so you are probably wondering what it is doing in a testing textbook. A baseball team has many players, and the scorecard, or roster, helps you to identify the players and the positions they play (or what purpose the players are best used for). Similarly, you will be introduced to many types of tests and assessments over the remainder of the text, and the next section of the chapter will serve as a "scorecard," or reference, to help you identify and distinguish among the various types of tests and their best uses. In almost every case, the various types of tests and assessments will be discussed in much more detail later in the text. We should also note that these types of tests are used for formative, interim, summative, or in some cases for all three general assessment purposes. For now, our intention is only to highlight the major differences among objective, essay, and performance/portfolio assessments; standardized and teacher-made tests; norm-referenced and criterion-referenced tests; and the newest entry into classroom testing, curriculum-based measurements (CBMs).

Objective, Essay, and Performance/Portfolio Tests/Assessments

The distinctions among these three types of tests have to do with the types of responses produced by test-takers, and how consistently, objectively, and reliably these responses can be scored. Tests that include item response formats that can be scored consistently and objectively are referred to as objective tests. Objective tests include multiple-choice, true-false, and matching formats, and student responses are typically limited to "bubbling in" electronically scanned answer sheets, or circling or underlining on test booklets. Even though objective test items can be used to measure higher-order learning and thinking (see Chapter 7), too often they are written to measure only factual knowledge.

Responses to essay test items vary in length from a single paragraph to several pages. For this reason, they are more difficult to score consistently and objectively. However, enabling students to respond in flexible and creative ways can make essay items well suited to measure analytic, composition, and higher-order thinking skills. A third item response format is the completion item. These items may require the test-taker to supply a word or phrase. Even though completion items are generally scored more consistently than essay items, completion items may not be able to be as objectively scored as objective test items. Completion items tend to measure factual knowledge.

Performance and portfolio examinations are intended to reduce pressures to test solely for factual knowledge and to provide a stimulus to introduce more extended thinking and reasoning activities into the curriculum (Borich, 2015; Borich & Tombari, 2004). Responses may be products, processes, collections, or other combinations of activities. They may include having students videotape portions of their own projects, conducting interviews with the student in order to probe for understanding and thinking abilities, or making a visual inspection of a product in order to determine whether it has the required characteristics for successful operation. The intent is usually for the learner to carry out the activities actually used in the real world (such as measuring the tensile strength of a building material, estimating the effects of pollutants on aquatic life, designing circuitry for a microprocessor, or assembling a folder or portfolio of "works in progress" to reflect growth in critical or integrative thinking or other skills over the course of a semester or school year). As with essay tests, these measures can be difficult to score consistently, objectively, and reliably. They will be considered in depth in Chapters 9 and 10.

Teacher-Made and Standardized Tests

Teacher-made tests are developed, administered, and scored by teachers, and often consist of completion, true-false, matching, multiple-choice, and essay items. Teacher-made tests are often flexible, or variable, in terms of their administration and scoring procedures, and in the amount of attention given to their construction. Different teachers may be more or less careful in constructing their tests, may allow more or less time for the test to be taken, and may be more or less stringent in grading the test. Even though teachers may use the same test repeatedly, they may also make modifications to the test each time they use it. In the latter case, the usefulness of performance comparisons over time would be reduced.

Standardized tests (described in more detail in Chapters 19 and 20) are typically developed by test construction professionals over lengthy intervals and at considerable expense to standardized test publishers, and state education agencies. The developmental process typically includes pilot testing, and then multiple drafts of the test are evaluated over several years to enhance item quality and the overall quality of the test. Standardized tests are called so because they *must* be administered and scored in a consistent manner, no matter who administers them, or where or when they may be administered. Standardized test users are specifically trained to follow exactly the same administration procedures, and scorers also are trained to always follow the exact same scoring procedures. Standardized achievement tests often include multiple-choice, matching, and true-false items. Essay items are also increasingly common in standardized tests.

Norm-Referenced Tests (NRTs) and Criterion-Referenced Tests (CRTs)

Norm-referenced tests (NRTs) are typically standardized tests developed by commercial test publishers (e.g., the SAT), sometimes in conjunction with state education agencies. They are designed to enable us to compare the performance of students who currently take the test with a sample of students who completed the test when it was being developed. The sample of students who completed the test in the past is called a norm group (or normative group or sample). NRTs tend to measure broad educational goals and are usually lengthy (hours long in duration). If the purpose of the NRT is to enable current student performance to be compared to national averages, or norms, the normative sample must be carefully selected to proportionately represent the key characteristics of the national population (e.g., age, gender, ethnicity, parental income, and geographic region). However, current student performance may also be compared to local or state norms. In these cases, the samples may or may not be similar to national norms, depending on how closely local or state samples compare to key characteristics of the national population. Where local or state norms differ significantly from national norms, it is possible that current student performance may be above average when compared to national norms, for example, but below average compared to local norms (e.g., if the local norms come from an unusually high-achieving school or district). In any case, for an NRT, the meaning given to a student's performance is always *relative* to that of the norm group (e.g., "Marie is above average" or "Joel is well below average," where average refers to the norm group's performance). NRTs will be discussed more fully in Chapters 5, 19, and 20.

CRTs may be standardized or teacher made, and enable a different kind of comparison. Compared to NRTs, CRTs are typically shorter in length and narrower in focus. Instead of comparing current student performance to other students (i.e., the norm group), CRTs enable comparisons to an *absolute* standard or criterion. CRTs help us to determine what a student can or cannot do. Rather than stating that "Marie is above average," CRTs enable us to make judgments about a student's (or group of students') level of proficiency or mastery over a skill or set of skills (e.g., "Marie is able to spell the words in the third-grade spelling list with greater than 80% accuracy," or "Joel is less than 10% accurate when subtracting two-digit numbers with borrowing."). For this reason, and because they are shorter than NRTs, scores from a CRT are more likely to be useful for formative, day-to-day instructional decision making than scores from an NRT would be. CRTs are described more fully in Chapter 5.

Curriculum-Based Measurements (CBMs)

Although relatively new to the regular education classroom, brief, formative, CBMs (commonly referred to as CBM probes) have been in use in special education programs since the early 1980s (Deno, Mirkin & Chang, 1982). CBM probes may be standardized or teacher made. CBM probes are designed to be sensitive to small changes in learning. This makes CBM probes suitable to monitor day-to-day progress in reading (CBM-R), math (CBM-M), writing (CBM-W), and spelling (CBM-S), which in turn facilitates day-to-day instructional decision making. Commercial CBM probes are commonly norm referenced and may include national, state, and/or local norms. However, unlike commercial NRTs, the national norm groups may not be carefully selected to match key characteristics of the population. Instead, commercial CBM norm groups typically are "convenience" samples, developed from large numbers of students tested with CBMs over time without the intent to match population characteristics.

CBM probes, or other brief formative assessment measures, are now crucial to the progress monitoring and data-based decision making components of the response to intervention (RTI) model required by the 2004 Individuals with Disabilities Education Improvement Act (IDEIA). We will discuss RTI and its significance for the regular education teacher in detail in Chapter 3. For now, suffice it to say that brief, formative assessments like CBM will be increasingly used to monitor the progress of both regular and special education students in the regular education curriculum, as required by the IDEIA.

EFFECTS ON THE CLASSROOM TEACHER

As we said earlier, we believe that a firm grounding in testing and assessment practice is vital to today's classroom teacher. However, teachers traditionally have not been well trained in test construction and use or in assessment. Many teachers see no need for training in testing and assessment because they believe these activities are supplemental or peripheral to the instructional process. Indeed, many prospective teachers have been heard to say things like, "If I need to know about tests, I'll go to the counselor!" Perhaps the trend toward seemingly ever-increasing "specialists" in education has fostered or reinforced such beliefs. Nevertheless, regardless of how a teacher feels about the relationship of tests and assessments to instruction, it is frequently the classroom teacher who must administer and then organize and interpret state-mandated high stakes and teacher-constructed test and assessment data, including performance and portfolio data, to curious and sometimes hostile parents and other concerned parties. Under IDEIA, regular classroom teachers will also collect and interpret these kinds of data to the parents of children with disabilities, and their advocates. Figure 1.2 depicts many sources of pressure influencing a teacher's use of tests. It is intended to convince you of the seriousness with which you should consider your knowledge or lack of knowledge of testing and assessment. After years of consulting and teaching experience in the public schools, we have concluded that discussing test results with parents is frequently an anxiety-provoking experience for teachers. Lacking appropriate training, some teachers are tempted to try to avoid

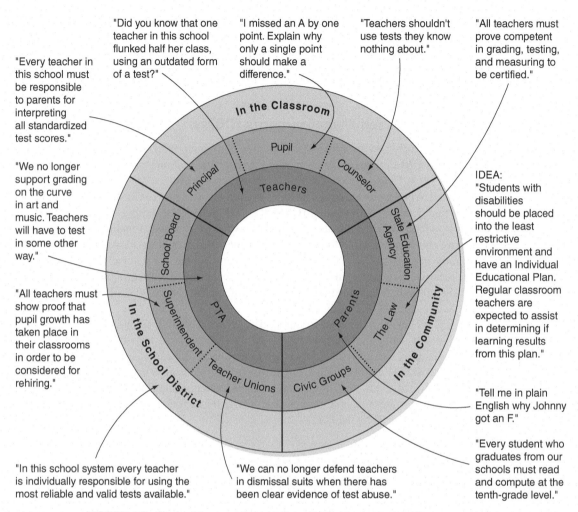

"Did you know that one teacher in this school flunked half her class, using an outdated form of a test?"

"I missed an A by one point. Explain why only a single point should make a difference."

"Teachers shouldn't use tests they know nothing about."

"All teachers must prove competent in grading, testing, and measuring to be certified."

"Every teacher in this school must be responsible to parents for interpreting all standardized test scores."

"We no longer support grading on the curve in art and music. Teachers will have to test in some other way."

"All teachers must show proof that pupil growth has taken place in their classrooms in order to be considered for rehiring."

IDEA: "Students with disabilities should be placed into the least restrictive environment and have an Individual Educational Plan. Regular classroom teachers are expected to assist in determining if learning results from this plan."

"Tell me in plain English why Johnny got an F."

"Every student who graduates from our schools must read and compute at the tenth-grade level."

"In this school system every teacher is individually responsible for using the most reliable and valid tests available."

"We can no longer defend teachers in dismissal suits when there has been clear evidence of test abuse."

FIGURE 1.2 Some of the many forces influencing the teacher's use of tests.

interpretation entirely by dismissing test data as unimportant or inaccurate, not realizing that such data are often very important and thought to be quite accurate by parents. The following dialogue occurred when one of the authors had a conference with his son's second-grade teacher.

TEACHER: Hi, I'm Jeff's second-grade teacher. What can I do for you so early in the year?

AUTHOR: Jeff says he's in the low reading group, and I am curious about why he is. Could you explain that to me?

TEACHER: Oh, don't worry—we don't label kids at this school. I think that would be a terrible injustice.

AUTHOR: I see, but could you explain why Jeff is in the "Walkers" instead of the "Runners"?

TEACHER: Oh, those are just names, that's all.

AUTHOR: Are both groups at the same level in reading?

TEACHER: They're both at the first-grade level, yes.

AUTHOR: I'm beginning to catch on. Are they reading in the same level books in the same reading series?

TEACHER:	Of course not! Some children are further along than others—that's all—but the kids don't know.
AUTHOR:	Let me guess, the "Runners" are further ahead?
TEACHER:	Yes, they're in Book 9.
AUTHOR:	And the "Walkers" are in ...
TEACHER:	Book 5. But they are only grouped for instructional purposes—I have 25 students, you know!
AUTHOR:	I'm confused. Jeff's reading scores on the California Achievement Test last May were above the 90th percentile.
TEACHER:	(*Chuckles to herself*) I can understand your confusion. Those test scores are so hard to understand. Why, even we professionals can't understand them.
AUTHOR:	A score at the 90th percentile means the score was higher than the scores of 90% of the students who took the test all across the country.
TEACHER:	Oh, really? (*Blushing*) It is very complicated. As I said, even professional educators don't understand testing.
AUTHOR:	Some do, Mrs B.

Had the teacher understood the data she was dealing with, an embarrassing situation might have been avoided. Unfortunately, many classroom teachers have similar experiences. Another often overheard statement is, "I don't even have time to teach. How can I learn about test construction and interpretation?" We are well aware that paperwork and bureaucratic requirements increasingly burden teachers and most other professionals.

Educational testing has increased over the last few decades, primarily to meet the accountability requirements included in state and federal legislation (i.e., state high-stakes testing and the NCLB act). We discuss those and other testing developments in detail in Chapter 2. Although there has been resistance to increased testing demands, we continue to anticipate high levels of test and assessment use in the future. The public will be keeping a watchful eye on the collectors and users of test data. Teachers of the future will continue to need to be adequately trained in formative, interim, and summative testing and assessment practice. Ignoring or denying the need for proper training in this area will not make the watchful eye of the public, administrators, or other decision makers go away. Given the time constraints under which the average teacher must operate, it appears wiser to seek such training now, before you begin teaching. The alternative may be to attend what might seem like an endless series of workshops later on, while you also have to attend to your class of students and all the related responsibilities.

In short, it looks like tomorrow's teachers will continue to be regularly exposed to student test and assessment data and will need to explain and interpret those data to parents and others. Public pressure for accountability, coupled with the formative, interim, and summative testing requirements driven by state and federal education reform initiatives, suggests that the average teacher will not be able to get ahead or even get by without a good working knowledge of test and assessment practice. We sincerely hope that this text will help you acquire such knowledge and the skills necessary to construct good tests and use test data knowledgeably and professionally.

ABOUT THE TEXT

When you talk to teachers who have completed courses in testing and assessment, you often find that they are somewhat less than inspired by their courses. In fact, talking with such veterans may have made you a little reluctant to register for this course. Nevertheless, here you are! The authors have taught testing and assessment courses for many years and, quite frankly, are accustomed to hearing the course content described as "dry, but necessary." Too many times, however, we have heard, "The course is dry, but necessary—I think!" Since a fair amount of straightforward, technical information is presented, we could understand calling a course in testing and assessment "dry." Indeed, this is almost how we feel about some of the content when we teach it! Thus, hearing "dry, but necessary" from students did little more than confirm our own feelings. But, to hear "dry, but necessary—I think!" made us think and led us to evaluate our courses to determine the cause for this uncertainty. Remember, we stated earlier that we think knowledge of testing and assessment practice is vital to today's teacher, yet somehow this was not coming across to some of our students.

We concluded that what was needed to engage readers with the material we present was a text that (1) emphasizes the application of formative, interim, and summative test and assessment practices and concepts to real-world situations and (2) provides new teachers with an understanding of the political, philosophical, pedagogical, and other factors that affect the educational testing, assessment, and measurement landscape today. With this aim in mind we wrote, and have once again recently revised, this text. Only you can tell whether we have succeeded. We invite your comments and suggestions.

WHAT IF YOU ARE "NO GOOD IN MATH"?

Since tests yield numerical scores and test theory is based on statistical principles, it is no surprise that many who feel weak in math have great reservations about being able to succeed in a course in testing and assessment. If you fall into this category, rest assured that many of your fears are groundless or exaggerated. In our experience, fewer than 1% of the students who have completed the testing and assessment courses we have taught have done poorly solely because of a weak math background.

Naturally, knowledge of the basic mathematical functions—addition, subtraction, multiplication, and division—is a necessity. Mix these with fractions, decimals, and a sprinkling of algebra and you are all set! If you are still doubtful, work your way through the review of math skills provided in Appendix A. That review and accompanying self-check test should also prove useful to you if you feel a little rusty in math—a fairly common experience in this age of calculators and personal computers. All operations necessary to complete the calculations in this text are covered in the review. We think you will agree that our review of math skills in Appendix A will be all that is needed.

SUMMARY

In this chapter, we have introduced you to issues related to educational testing and measurement and have described the orientation of the text. Its major points are as follows:

1. Tests are only tools, and like all tools, poor design, unintentional misuse, and intentional abuse can impair their usefulness.

2. Several factors can affect the usefulness of any test. These factors include the following:
   a. The technical adequacy of the test.
   b. The competency of the test user.
   c. The extent to which the purpose the test is being used for matches the purpose for which the test was developed.

    d. The extent to which the population being tested matches the population the test was developed on.

    e. Whether additional sources of information also are considered, especially with culturally, linguistically, and academically diverse students.

3. Summative assessments are used when the purpose of testing is to evaluate the extent of student achievement after some period of instruction. They typically are lengthy and administered at the end of the school year or semester.

4. Formative assessments are used when the purpose of testing is to inform the instructor about whether students are learning while the curriculum is being delivered, which enables ongoing instructional adjustments to be made. Formative assessments are also considered to be useful for assessing student responsiveness to instruction and tend to be brief. Interim assessments are administered two to three times per year (e.g., fall, winter, and spring) to indicate whether progress over time is occurring. When interim assessments are used to identify students at risk for failure on a summative tests they are called benchmark tests.

5. Because there is no "one-size-fits-all" test, important educational decisions should not be made based entirely on test results from a single point in time (i.e., like a photo). Important decisions should also consider information from multiple sources obtained over multiple time points (i.e., like a video).

6. Tests and assessments are terms that typically refer to single measures that yield results at a single point in time.

7. Testing and assessment should be considered to be only a part of an assessment *process* that includes testing/assessment and the use of other measurement techniques (e.g., performance and portfolio assessments, rating scales, checklists, and observations) along with relevant background and contextual information in a critical, integrated way to make educational decisions.

8. Tests, because they have no preconceived or biased notions about test-takers, can provide objective data that can be helpful in educational decision making and can minimize bias and subjectivity that may characterize decisions based on subjective data.

9. Test use (i.e., both formative and summative) is more likely to increase than decrease in the foreseeable future.

10. There are many different types of tests and assessments, including objective, essay, and performance and portfolio tests/assessments; teacher-made and standardized tests; norm-referenced tests and criterion-referenced tests; and curriculum-based measurements (CBMs).

11. The classroom teacher who is trained in educational testing procedures will be able to use test results more efficiently and effectively and will be less likely to misuse or abuse test results.

12. This text is oriented toward the sound application of measurement principles to real-world situations.

FOR DISCUSSION AND PRACTICE

1. Thinking back to your own high school days, what were some of the factors that turned you off about tests?

2. Were these factors connected with the tests themselves, or were they the result of how the tests were used?

*3. You ask an experienced fellow teacher, "How do you decide which tests to use for your students?" She responds, "That's easy. Just pick one. They are all about the same and equally useful." On the basis of what you've read in the text, how would you respond?

*4. Noting that you have results from teacher-made tests, the district's standardized high-stakes tests, formative CBM probes, last year's grades, and a variety of other information in front of you, Mr. Quick asks "What is all that for?" You respond, "I am assigning my final grades for the semester, so I'm using all the information I have to try to be as fair as possible." "There is no need for all that," asserts Mr. Quick, "I just use the scores from the high-stakes test to assign my grades. It only takes a minute." What, if anything, might be wrong with Mr. Quick's approach to grading?

*5. Distinguish between what the authors call the specific purposes and general purposes of educational testing in the classroom.

6. Compare and contrast formative assessments with interim and summative assessments.

7. At lunch, you mention to another teacher that you are planning to start using CBM probes to determine how responsive your students are to the new research-based instructional approach you are implementing. She says, "What on earth are CBM probes?" How do you respond?

*8. Differentiate testing/assessment from the assessment process.

9. Imagine the modern U.S. high school 20 years from now. Identify several ways in which testing and measurement will have changed since the time you were attending high school.

*Answers for these questions appear in Appendix B.

CHAPTER 2

NATIONAL DEVELOPMENTS: IMPACT ON CLASSROOM TESTING AND MEASUREMENT

LEARNING OUTCOMES

After completing this chapter, the student will be able to:

1. Compare and contrast the recent educational reforms that have strongly influenced educational testing and assessment in the last two decades, including the No Child Left Behind (NCLB) Act; the Individuals with Disabilities Education Improvement Act (IDEIA); the standards-based reform movement that evolved into the Common Core State Standards (CCSS); recent Race to the Top (RTT) initiatives; and the growth of online, computer-adaptive testing for use with the CCSS-aligned tests.

2. Name the report that began the education reform movement.

3. Explain what Adequate Yearly Progress (AYP) means.

4. Explain why permitting each state to select its own annual summative assessment prohibited true comparison across states and within states, districts, and schools over time.

5. Define high-stakes testing (HST).

6. Compare and contrast the *No Child Left Behind* (NCLB) Act and state high-stakes testing programs.

7. Describe the broad impact high-stakes testing can have on students, teachers, administrators, schools, and the community.

8. Explain why the federal government made waivers available to states that were not able to meet certain NCLB requirements.

9. Compare and contrast the regular and special education reform movements.

10. Compare and contrast standards-based reform, the Common Core State Standards (CCSS) and performance standards.

11. Describe the Race to the Top (RTT) initiative.

12. Explain how the RTT initiative promoted the development of CCSS-aligned tests.

13. Explain why the future of NCLB, IDEIA, CCSS, and RTT became so politically polarized by January 2015.

14. Compare and contrast the pros and cons of conventional testing and computer-adaptive testing.

15. Compare the findings from the most recent Trends in International Mathematics and Science Study (TIMSS) and Program for International Student Assessment (PISA) international tests with prior results.

16. Describe the history of competency testing for teachers.

17. Explain what value-added models (VAM) means as it is applied to the evaluation of teachers.

18. Explain why national organizations have become increasingly interested in educational testing and assessment in recent years.

OVER THE last three decades, multiple national- and state-level education reform initiatives and other related developments have had significant impact on educational testing and assessment policy and practice. Regardless of when reforms have been implemented, they have been complex and controversial, and their actual impact on educational reform has been difficult to determine. Both Republicans and Democrats have accused each other of playing politics around educational reform, contributing to the increasingly polarized political environment that we have endured for several years now. The implications of this political polarization are not trivial. For example, the revision and reauthorization of both the 2002 No Child Left Behind (NCLB) Act and the 2004 Individuals with Disabilities Education Act (IDEIA) are now several years overdue. Both NCLB and IDEIA are landmark pieces of federal legislation that have significantly influenced educational testing for more than a decade, but they were supposed to be revised after 7 years. Each party has blamed the other for the gridlock in Washington DC around these, and many other, important pieces of legislation.

Yet, as this text goes to press, the polarization between the two political parties has deepened and the reauthorization of these important federal initiatives remains uncertain. Because of this uncertainty, we cannot predict how these reform initiatives may change or affect educational testing policy and practice in the future. What we can do is describe the history and current status of the educational testing components of the NCLB, IDEIA, and several other recent reform initiatives and developments. We do our best to do so in a balanced manner so that readers may come to their own conclusions about the value and benefits of these legislative initiatives rather than attempting to sway readers one way or the other.

In this chapter, we review the implications of several recent educational reforms and developments and their implications for testing. These reforms and developments include the high-stakes testing (HST) movement that has been incorporated into the NCLB Act, the IDEIA, the standards-based reform movement that evolved into the Common Core State Standards (CCSS), recent Race to the Top (RTT) initiatives, and the growth of online, computer-adaptive testing for use with the CCSS-aligned tests. We also consider the impact of globalization and the latest findings with regard to the international competitiveness of American students on international tests; competency testing for teachers; the use of student test scores in the evaluation of teachers (i.e., based on value-added models, or VAM); and the increased interest shown in these developments by national professional associations.

We know that seems like an awful lot to cover, and it is. Nevertheless, we firmly believe that providing you with an understanding of these developments, their importance, and how highly politicized they have become in recent years will help you understand the inevitable changes that will affect educational testing and measurement policy and practice in the future. Onward!

EDUCATION REFORM

Many efforts to change, or reform, our education system were launched over the last 30 years or so, with varying degrees of impact. In this section, we discuss reform efforts within the regular education system, including passage of the NCLB and HST, followed by a discussion of the impact of the IDEIA on special education reform and the extent to which NCLB and IDEIA have affected both the general and special education teachers.

Regular Education Reform

The regular education reform movement arose in response to the National Commission on Excellence in Education's release of *A Nation at Risk: The Imperative for Educational Reform* in 1983. This report documented multiple shortcomings of the U.S. public education system at that time. Since then a number of regular education reform initiatives have been implemented in an effort to overcome the deficiencies. These efforts have typically been included in one of the multiple reauthorizations of the *Elementary and Secondary Education Act* (ESEA). The last reauthorization of the ESEA is more commonly known as the *No Child Left Behind* (NCLB) *Act*. Historically, regular education reform initiatives have included raised expectations for individuals and groups of students (e.g., English-language learners and special education students); development of statewide academic and performance standards; HST and increased accountability, along with incentives for improved performance, improved teacher salaries; local or site-based management and decision making; and innovations in teacher training.

NCLB As controversial as most of what we will describe in the remainder of this chapter is, almost everyone would agree that the NCLB reauthorization influenced educational testing the most. It required that public "report cards" be issued annually describing the performance of subgroups of students on the annual HST required under NCLB. The reports were required to disaggregate or break down test performance to identify differences among economically disadvantaged students, ethnic minorities, limited English proficient (LEP) students, and students with disabilities. These report cards also are used to rank schools under NCLB, into categories that range from "low performing" to "exceptional," based on whether student achievement meets state-specified proficiency levels. These proficiency levels are more often described as whether a school has made "Adequate Yearly Progress" or AYP. States were allowed to set their own academic proficiency criteria under NCLB, but the 2002 law clearly stated that all state criteria had to specify that 100% of students who take the annual assessment were to be academically proficient by the 2013–2014 school year. For much of the last decade, the criteria set by the states typically were increased each year as states attempted to reach the 100% proficiency NCLB goal. Under NCLB, if a school fails to meet the state's AYP criteria two or more years in a row, the state must impose increasingly serious consequences on the school. Those steps have included shutting down schools and reconstituting school staff (i.e., replacing existing staff with new teachers and administrators).

States were free to use different tests to measure AYP. Some chose to develop state-specific tests, while other states chose "off-the-shelf" commercially developed standardized tests. Furthermore, states were able to change the criteria for passing the test (e.g., a failing score one year might be a passing score the next), and change the AYP criteria from year to year (e.g., an AYP criterion of 70% of students must pass the summative high-stakes test could be raised or lowered the following year). Multiple tests and variable criteria made reliable comparisons of student performance and AYP across states or within a state from year to year were difficult, at best. This conclusion was highlighted by an analysis completed by the nonpartisan Thomas B. Fordham Institute. That study compared how well 36 actual elementary and middle schools from different states would fare when evaluated according to differing NCLB requirements across 28 states. The study concluded that a school's proficiency rating under the NCLB depends as much on location (i.e., the state) as on actual student performance (Finn, Petrilli & Winkler, 2009). The following language is from the report's Executive Summary:

> Almost all our sampled schools failed to make AYP in some states, and nearly all of these same schools made AYP in others … Same kids, same academic performance, same schools—different states, different cut scores, different rules, and very different results. (p. 2).

NCLB Waivers   Over time, it became clear that the 100% proficiency goal from NCLB was unattainable. As we reported in the last edition of this text (Kubiszyn & Borich, 2013), by 2011 both Democratic President Obama and his Secretary of Education, Arnie Duncan, acknowledged that 100% proficiency criterion would never be met. Thus, to prevent states from violating federal law after the 2013–2014 school year, they began to offer waivers from certain NCLB requirements to the states, including the 100% proficiency goal and the requirement that states provide free tutoring to struggling students. In return for the waivers, states were required to emphasize attainment of college and career readiness standards, focus academic improvement efforts on the lowest performing 15% of schools, and develop *teacher* evaluation plans that are based in part on *student* test performance. Even though the waivers were controversial, 26 states and the District of Columbia applied for waivers by March 2012, joining 11 states granted waivers in 2011. By December 2014, waivers were granted to 43 out of 45 states and the District of Columbia that applied for NCLB waivers (U.S. Department of Education, 2014). States that chose not to apply for the waivers were to be held to the goals established by NCLB, according to the president's plan (McNeil, 2012).

High-Stakes Testing (HST)   HST is the use of a summative test or an assessment (i.e., a test designed to measure student achievement after a period of instruction has been completed) to make decisions that are of prominent educational, financial, or social impact. Thus, the NCLB requirements we discussed in the last section reflect some of the HST decisions that test data have been used for.

Before NCLB was enacted in 2002, states established their own proficiency criteria. State HST programs began with a minimum competency testing program in Florida in the 1970s, but it was the 1990 appearance of the Texas Assessment of Academic Skills (TAAS) that heralded today's HST movement (Amrein & Berliner, 2002; Wright, 2007). By 2002, HST programs had spread to all 50 states and the District of Columbia (Doherty, 2002). By contrast, NCLB and its HST requirements did not exist until 2002. Because state HST programs existed before NCLB, the architects of NCLB, for both practical and political reasons, gave states the authority to select the tests and assessments that would be used to meet federal NCLB accountability requirements. In many cases, states opted to use the same measures they were already using for their HST programs to meet NCLB accountability requirements, effectively "killing two birds with one stone." However, because HST tests and performance criteria vary so much across states, the findings from the Fordham Institute study we highlighted earlier with regard to NCLB criteria (Finn et al., 2009) also apply to HST tests and performance criteria. Whether a student who passed the New York State HST was achieving comparably to a student who passed the Alabama HST was unable to be determined. Yet, passing a state HST meant that a student fulfilled a critical NCLB criterion, even if that student's actual achievement was not comparable to that of another student in a different state. Furthermore, because states change their passing criteria from year to year, it was also impossible to measure HST growth or improvement over time.

After NCLB was enacted, a number of states employed performance criteria of their own in addition to NCLB requirements for HST and decision making, or employed criteria that exceeded NCLB requirements. For example, some state HST programs required that certain levels of proficiency were necessary for students to be promoted to the next grade (see Box 1-1,Chapter 1), or for high school graduation. Zabala et al. (2008) reported that 26 states required an exit test for graduation, compared to 18 states in 2002 (Amrein & Berliner, 2002). HST results were also used to determine whether educators receive salary increases or bonuses, or, similar to NCLB, whether states take over schools or reassign school staff to other schools. Even though controversy regarding the use of tests to make decisions about promotion, retention, and financial incentives or penalties for school staff is often attributed to NCLB, these are not NCLB requirements—they arose from state HST program requirements (Hursh, 2008).

The topic of HST has been confusing and very controversial for decades. The controversies have included educators altering test scores or coaching students to change incorrect answers, which has resulted in penalties ranging from relatively small fines (Martinez, 2002) to the recent criminal trial of 12 Atlanta, Georgia educators, including five teachers and a principal (Faucet, 2014). That trial resulted in the conviction of 11 of 12 educators on racketeering charges, with sentences ranging from 1 to 7 years in prison, fines of $1,000 to $25,000, and probation after prison terms were completed. Other concerns include narrowing of the curriculum, teaching to the test, additional stress on teachers and pupils, and excessive time spent on test preparation at the expense of classroom instruction. Kubiszyn and Borich (2013) recently provided a detailed history and summary of these and other HST controversies. For this edition, we have moved our 2013 discussion of the many issues and controversies that surround HST to the textbook companion Website (go to http://www.wiley.com/college/kubiszyn). On that Website Supplement Ch. 2.1 reviews many additional issues and controversies and Supplement 2.2 reviews the reactions of the respected American Educational Research Association (AERA) to HST and recommendations to help you and your students prepare for HST.

Special Education Reform

A somewhat less-visible reform movement has also been evident within special education circles over the last quarter century or so. Children with special needs were guaranteed a free and appropriate public education (FAPE) for the first time with passage of the *Education of All Handicapped Children Act* (EAHC) in 1975 (P.L. 94–142). Before passage of this law, many children with special needs were denied services within the regular education system. To help ensure that all special needs children were identified and enrolled in school, a special education system evolved, largely separate from the regular education system. In contrast to the regular education system, special education had different laws and rules; different funding streams; different administrators and professional staff; and different time lines, procedures, and other requirements. Looking back, it is clear that this separate system was successful in ensuring that special needs children had access to FAPE, but with that success came an unanticipated negative outcome.

Even though special education law required that special needs children should receive FAPE in what was known as the least restrictive environment (LRE), or "mainstreamed," this requirement often was overlooked. Special needs pupils typically received instruction from special education staff in segregated (e.g., resource and self-contained) settings; were excluded from, or only minimally included with, their regular education peers in nonacademic activities; received only annual progress reports instead of six- or nine-week grade reports; and were excluded from the annual districtwide assessments that would have enabled their progress to be compared to their regular education counterparts. Furthermore, culturally, linguistically, and academically diverse learners receiving services from the separate special education system often were stigmatized and ostracized, and fell further and further behind their regular education peers; as a result, many remained in special education throughout their school years, never catching up with their regular education peers.

IDEA and IDEIA Recognition of these unanticipated consequences prompted the special education reform that began with passage of the *Individuals with Disabilities Education Act* (IDEA) in 1990, intensified with the reauthorization of this act in 1997 (IDEA-97), and expanded with the most recent reauthorization of this act as the *Individuals with Disabilities Education Improvement Act* (IDEIA) in 2004. These reform initiatives have diminished the long-standing separation between regular education and special education systems. Even though they continue to receive services from special education professionals, children with disabilities must now be instructed as much as possible by qualified regular education teachers within the general curriculum. Whenever possible, their progress within the general curriculum must also be assessed regularly with formative and interim assessments and, except where a multidisciplinary team can justify accommodations or an alternate assessment, all students with disabilities must participate in the same annual academic assessment required for their nondisabled peers. In summary, the special education reform movement now ensures that children with special needs will increasingly be served within the regular education curriculum, classroom, and accountability system.

Merging Regular and Special Education Reform: IDEIA and NCLB

To help integrate the regular and special education reform, the 2004 IDEIA was intentionally crafted to be integrated with the 2002 NCLB. These laws may be best viewed as complementary pieces of federal education legislation, rather than as regular education or special education legislation. IDEIA also complements the primary intention of NCLB: to improve educational outcomes for all students through increased accountability and the use of research-based practices. Both IDEIA and NCLB emphasize the use of scientifically based instruction, and both emphasize academic achievement for *all* students. Both laws also emphasize the *ongoing* formative and interim monitoring of the progress of all students in the regular education curriculum. This has come to be known as progress monitoring, or PM, using brief, repeated formative tests or assessments and is used to enable early identification of learning problems and the provision of increasingly specialized and/or intensified instruction to students identified as struggling. These brief, formative assessments are part of what has come to be known as the response-to-intervention (RTI) model (also known as response to instruction). The primary components of RTI include universal screening of all students at the beginning of school, progress monitoring (PM) of all students utilizing curriculum-based measurement (CBM) probes or other brief formative assessments, and data-based decision making to identify as early on as possible those students in need of more intensive or specialized instruction. To help you become familiar with these approaches, we discuss them in detail, along with this paradigm shift in regular and special education classroom testing, in Chapter 3.

IDEIA also has had an impact on regular education teachers with regard to the role of the regular teacher in specific learning disability (SLD) identification. In the eighth edition of this text, we indicated that the IDEIA included a dramatic shift in the way SLDs could be identified, and we predicted that the regular education teacher would play a larger role in SLD identification than was the case previously. Additional information about the IDEIA and SLD identification can be found on the textbook Website (go to http://www.wiley.com/college/kubiszyn). Finally, with the exception of the lowest performing 3% of students, IDEIA requires that *all* students must be exposed to the regular education curriculum as much as is possible, and that special education students must be evaluated with the same statewide high-stakes tests and assessments that are used for regular education students. In summary, IDEIA and NCLB both served to raise expectations for special education students and to reduce the segregation of special education students from the general education mainstream. IDEIA ensured that regular education teachers would have regular contact with all but the most severely disabled special education students.

Even though it has been more than a decade since the passage of both NCLB and IDEIA, it should be noted that their implementation has been uneven across the country. Indeed, even as this eleventh edition goes to press, there remain areas around the country where the requirements of NCLB and IDEIA are not being fully met. Like all federal legislation, both NCLB and IDEIA were scheduled for reauthorization after 7 years. Yet, as this edition goes to press, neither piece of legislation has been reauthorized, a reflection of the controversies and polarizing political vortex that both NCLB and IDEIA have been drawn into. Nevertheless, one fact is clear; the impact of both NCLB and IDEIA on regular education teachers has been significant.

Standards-Based Reform

A "standards-based reform" movement arose in response to the release of *A Nation at Risk* in 1983. Standards-based reform evolved into two general themes or strands: academic standards and performance standards. We review these two strands next.

Academic Standards In an effort to strengthen their curricula, several states began to integrate and improve the objectives of instruction for pupils in each academic subject across the elementary, middle, and high school years after *A Nation at Risk* was released. These learning objectives were intended to be sequential and hierarchical and came to be known as academic standards. However, for a variety of practical, philosophical, and political reasons, the development of uniform and universal academic standards at the national level was too controversial for consensus to emerge. Many conservatives supported state-based standards but considered national standards to be an unwanted and even illegal intrusion of the federal government into what has traditionally been considered the domain of the individual states.

In spite of their efforts, progress toward development of acceptable standards was inconsistent and uneven across the states. For example, according to *Making Standards Matter 2001, the Annual Report of the American Federation of Teachers* (American Federation of Teachers, 2001), all states and the District of Columbia had in place some form of academic standards in 2001. However, only 29 states and the District had strong (i.e., clear and specific) standards in math, English, and science at the elementary, middle, and high school levels. Improvements were slow to bear fruit. A five-year follow-up AFT report found that by 2006 a majority of states had standards at each grade level, although these standards were not uniformly strong. In fact, only 18 states were judged to have strong standards in all subjects, and only 53% of the states' reading standards were considered to be strong (American Federation of Teachers, 2006).

Similarly, a 2006 report from the Fordham Institute compared current state standards to those in existence in 2000 (Finn, Petrilli & Julian, 2006). The report found that most states had strengthened their reading or English standards, with 20 states receiving grades of A or B for their reading or English standards, and 8 states receiving grades of D or F, with deficiencies particularly noted at the high school level. On the other hand, the report found that math standards in most states remained problematic across all grade levels. The report also found that 40 states replaced or revised their math standards since 2000, but only 6 states received an A or B rating, with 29 states receiving a D or F. The overall grade assigned to state standards was a C−, the same grade the Fordham Institute assigned in 2000.

The Common Core State Standards (CCSS) In response to the disappointing and uneven efforts of individual states to develop strong academic standards, in 2009 the National Governors' Association and the Council of Chief State School Officers began a year-long process to identify the Common Core State Standards, or CCSS (Common Core State Standards Initiative, 2010). Separate sets of standards were developed for English/Language Arts and Mathematics to foster critical and integrative thinking, problem-solving, metacognition (i.e., thinking about thinking), and other "higher-order" thought processes. Even though participation in the CCSS was voluntary for each state, the CCSS were intended to apply to all participating states, and to identify the knowledge and skills that would better position high school graduates for success in college and careers, and in today's increasingly global society and marketplace. The standards were developed with input from 48 states, the District of Columbia, two territories, public comment, and included standards already in place and from top-performing countries around the world.

By 2013, only Texas, Nebraska, Virginia, and Alaska had not yet formally adopted the CCSS, and Minnesota only adopted the English/Language Arts component. However, Indiana, Oklahoma, and South Carolina withdrew from the CCSS and reverted to their state academic standards during 2014, illustrating growing controversy among the states around the CCSS. The CCSS have been criticized by some as an inappropriate overreach of the federal government into education, which traditionally has been under local and state control. Given how controversial the CCSS have become, it is worth noting that it was state leaders that developed and promoted this education reform; the CCSS were not developed or required by the federal government, although federal funding was made available for states to pursue this initiative.

So, how well do the CCSS compare to state academic standards? Similar to what it did with state standards in 2000 and 2006, the Fordham Institute critically evaluated the strength of the CCSS in 2011. Their report (Fordham Institute, 2011) gave the English/Language Arts CCSS a grade of B+ and gave the Mathematics CCSS a grade of A−. The Fordham Institute concluded that the CCSS exceeded state standards in both English/Language Arts and Mathematics in 33 states, 39 states in math only, and 37 states in English/Language Arts. On the other hand, it concluded that in English/Language Arts, the state standards in California, the District of Columbia, and Indiana exceeded the CCSS. In math, the CCSS were comparable to state standards in 11 states.

Performance Standards In order to determine whether academic standards (and later the CCSS) were attained, it was necessary to establish performance standards. To do so, committees identified appropriate levels of performance for each standard that would indicate that the objective, or standard, was met. Generally, whether a student passed a test section (e.g., reading, math, and writing) or the entire test depended on whether the student met or surpassed the performance standard for proficiency on a majority of the standards. The intention of performance standards is to raise expectations enough to raise achievement but not to raise expectations so high that students, teachers, and others fail to take them seriously because they are unattainable. "Hmmm," you might say, "What were they thinking when they set the NCLB standards at 100% proficiency?" We have often wondered about that too! An assumption that underlies performance standards reform is that all children can meet high expectations. Regardless of whether all children can meet high expectations, performance standards reform arose from the realization that achievement expectations for economically disadvantaged and minority students have generally been lower than for other students. Thus, many believe that setting high performance standards for all students will especially enhance achievement for low-income and minority students. Indeed, increasing achievement in economically disadvantaged youth was a primary intent of NCLB.

Performance standards often are controversial, with definitions of accomplishment sometimes very different for educators and for noneducators (e.g., parents, businesspersons, politicians, and others), or even within the same person or group over time. Does any of this sound familiar? It should!

Even though we did not call them performance standards when we described the wide variability in NCLB and HST passing criteria from state to state (and within states over time), we were talking about variability in performance standards. Because performance standards have been so different from state to state, and even within states over time, what separates "acceptable, unacceptable, proficient, and exceptional" performance has been a "moving target," varying both across states and within states over time. This lack of consistency did not go unnoticed by the federal government.

Race to the Top (RTT)

President Barack Obama, a Democrat, and Secretary of Education Arnie Duncan announced the $4.35 billion RTT federal grant program in July 2009. This initiative was part of the much broader American Recovery and Reinvestment Act of 2009 (ARRA), which followed the Great Recession, and was intended to stimulate the economy, support job creation, and invest in critical sectors, including education. The RTT initiative was intended to support innovative strategies that would lead to improved achievement for all subgroups of students (e.g., disabilities, cultural, socioeconomic, and English proficiency), and to increase the extent to which high school graduates are prepared for colleges and careers, as well as to support a variety of other educational outcomes.

Like participation in the CCSS, participation by states in the RTT competition was voluntary, and four states chose not to do so. The voluntary competition was overseen by the U.S. Department of Education. Tennessee and Delaware were the first two states awarded RTT grants in 2010 and by March 2014, 20 states and the District of Columbia were awarded grants. Even though the total RTT funding was less than 1% of all education spending in the U.S. during that period, the funding enabled state and local leaders, educators, and communities to implement various reforms that would otherwise not have been possible.

More specifically, the RTT gave states the opportunity to compete for grants intended to spur innovation and reforms to facilitate compliance with the Common Core State Standards (CCSS), increase college preparation and participation (especially in science, technology, engineering, and mathematics, also known as the STEM disciplines), develop performance-based standards for teachers and principals based in part on *student* test scores, enable the establishment of more charter schools, and improve low-performing schools. One of the RTT components, the RTT Assessment Competition, funded two state-based consortia in 2010 to develop assessments aligned with the CCSS that each state in each consortium would agree to use. One assessment consortium was the Partnership for Assessment of Readiness for College and Careers (PARCC). The following states were PARCC members: Arkansas, Colorado, District of Columbia, Illinois, Louisiana, Maryland, Massachusetts, Mississippi, New Jersey, New Mexico, New York, Ohio, and Rhode Island. The second assessment consortium was the Smarter Balanced Assessment Consortium (Smarter Balanced). The following states were Smarter Balanced members: California, Connecticut, Delaware, Hawaii, Idaho, Iowa, Maine, Michigan, Missouri, Montana, Nevada, New Hampshire, North Carolina, North Dakota, Oregon, South Dakota, Vermont, Washington, West Virginia, Wisconsin, and Wyoming.

In this way, the RTT supported adoption of the CCSS, while also moving the states away from reliance on a wide range of state-developed and commercial tests (and differing criteria for proficiency), and toward the two CCSS-aligned tests developed by the RTT-supported assessment consortia. The two consortium developed tests were originally scheduled for implementation by the states within each consortium by 2013–2014, but that goal was not met. If fully implemented in the future, the use of only two tests aligned with the CCSS across all the states in each consortium would enable stable and meaningful performance comparisons of across states and within states over time for the states that use the CCSS-aligned tests. For those states, the wide variability in NCLB, AYP, and HST outcomes that we described earlier in this chapter would be reduced if not eliminated (Cavanagh, 2013).

RTT was not limited to general education reform, however. As another example of the integration of education and special education reform, RTT was also intended to include development of common accommodation policies for implementation of technological innovations (e.g., computer-adaptive testing) and development of tests to ensure access of special education students to grade-level curricula and assessments.

How effective has the initiative been? As you might expect by now, there is no single answer to this question. The RTT initiative has been awash in controversy since its inception, and the controversy has only grown since then. Conservative Republicans have branded the RTT as an example of federal overreach into states' rights (education has traditionally been the purview of state governments). Others welcomed its emphasis on teaching students critical thinking skills and movement away from the "teaching to the test" that many felt characterized the HST movement and especially after NCLB.

The Future: NCLB, RTT, CCSS, and the CCSS-Aligned Tests

At the time of publication of this text, the futures of NCLB, the RTT, and the CCSS and its aligned tests were all unclear. This was especially true for the HST-related requirements that were championed by Republican President George W. Bush when NCLB was enacted in 2002. The 114th Congress convened in January 2015 with Republicans holding the majority in both the House and the Senate on the one hand, and Democratic President Obama holding the authority to veto any legislation passed by the House and Senate. To say their positions are polarized may be an understatement.

Interestingly, as the old expression goes, "Politics makes strange bedfellows." For example, many civil rights and disabilities groups (typically Democratic) and the business community (typically Republican) remain in strong support of the CCSS and the use of CCSS-aligned tests for accountability purposes. However, in the face of growing Republican political opposition to federal education K-12 initiatives over the last few years, some supporters of the CCSS-aligned tests are wavering. For example, sensing that the Republican dominated 114th Congress may provide the best opportunity to reduce the numbers of tests required for teachers, the National Education Association (NEA), a long-standing ally of the Democrats, has aligned with influential Republicans in an effort to reduce or eliminate the testing requirements that accompanied the passage of the NCLB (Klein & Camera, 2015).

Almost immediately after Congress convened in January 2015, Republicans launched efforts to reduce or eliminate the number of tests required under federal legislation, or to turn over all testing authority to the states. In Texas, the number of tests required was reduced from 15 to 5 in 2013. Yet, many of the states may not want any reduction in testing requirements. Representing the states, the Council of Chief State School Officers (also predominantly Republican) issued a statement in January 2015 that supported an increase in state authority for school improvement and accountability, but also supported maintenance of testing requirements. The last point is contrary to what conservative Republicans (primarily) have argued that the states wanted (Klein & Camera, 2015).

In the face of this confusing and contradictory polarized political picture, the future of NCLB, RTT, and CCSS and their aligned tests are all unclear as we prepare this edition of this textbook. Furthermore, even though there is evidence both for and against the success of the RTT and CCSS, the evidence is not compelling on either side. Citing the success of the RTT Advanced Placement (AP) initiative, intended to increase the percentage of students who are prepared for college success, a report issued by the White House in 2014 indicated that 1.8 million more students took AP tests than in 2011 (a 13.2% increase). Of those, 1.1 million more students (16.1%) qualified for college credits by taking AP tests (White House, 2014). Suggesting that RTT has fostered improved federal-state collaboration, a report from the Fordham Institute noted that the progress under RTT is attributable to collaboration between the U.S. Department of Education and state leadership (Fordham, 2014). An earlier report by the nonpartisan Center for American Progress (Boser, 2012) investigated implementation of RTT grants on a state-by-state basis. That report concluded that "although a lot of work remains to be done, RTT has sparked significant school reform efforts and shows that significant policy changes are possible (p. 3)."

Opponents of the RTT and CCSS and their aligned tests argue that there is no chance of long-term success, and that the RTT and CCSS are primarily intended to increase federal influence over state and local education policies. The initiatives also have come under fire because they have been associated with significantly increased revenue for test publishers. For example, Fortune magazine reported a 57% growth in commercial testing through high school between 2011 and 2014 (Reingold, 2015). Much of that growth in revenue has been driven by the development of formative assessments, especially those aligned with the CCSS (Allen, 2011; Cavanagh, 2013; FairTest, 2009; Ravitch, 2010). Reflecting the extent of dissatisfaction with RTT in some quarters, a legislative effort to defund the initiative was launched for the 2015 congressional year.

Even though congressional opposition to RTT was initially divided along party lines, with Republicans providing the most opposition, congressional Democrats have become increasingly critical as well (Ravitch, 2014). Several states have begun to back away from the commitments they made to use CCSS-aligned tests when they joined the RTT Assessment consortia. For example, Tennessee, one of the first states to obtain RTT funding, decide to leave the PARCC and abandoned its plans to use the new CCSS-aligned test developed by the PARCC for 2015. Instead that state is revising the Tennessee Comprehensive Assessment Program (TCAP) test it has administered in the past. The new test will be called TNReady, with its launch scheduled for the 2015–2016 school year (Spears, 2014). In addition, parents are increasingly exercising their right to "opt-out", refusing to allow their children to take the CCSS-aligned tests. In New York State over 200,000 students have opted out from the CCSS-aligned PARCC test by their parents, with large numbers of primarily high school students also opting out in Colorado, New Jersey and California (Straus, 2015). If participation in CCSS-aligned states drops below 95% federal funding for education could be reduced as a penalty. As the expression goes, we live in interesting times! Hopefully, there will be some resolution to these controversial issues soon.

Other Trends: Computer-Adaptive Achievement Testing

Computer-adaptive achievement testing recently has generated considerable interest along assessment professionals and educators. Computer-adaptive tests use software to adjust item difficulty levels based on student responses to previous items. For example, if an incorrect answer is selected, the next item the computer selects will be from a pool of easier items. If a correct answer is selected the next item will be selected from a pool of more difficult items. In either case, the items are selected from pools of items that are expected to be valid measures of the content area or domain in question.

Even though all assessments provide estimates of student achievement, advocates argue that computerized adaptive tests provide results that are more accurate, both as snapshots of student achievement and as measures of growth over time than are "one-size-fits-all" paper-and-pencil standardized tests. Advocates also argue that computerized adaptive testing is more accurate for all students, from those who are struggling to those who are advanced. Proponents also claim that computer-adaptive tests, since they are administered online, provide real-time feedback for students and teachers and reduce the amount of time spent completing and scoring assessments. This feature enables the use of computer-adaptive tests for formative and interim assessments in addition to summative assessment, and increases test security since other students do not see the same test items used by peers.

Computer-adaptive testing also has proven attractive to and adopted by the two state assessment consortia funded by the RTT initiative, the Smarter Balanced Assessment Consortium and the PARCC. Both consortia have relied heavily on computer-adaptive online testing for their CCSS assessments. In addition, both consortia have developed substantial online resources to help teachers, parents, and others adjust to and prepare for this testing format, and the CCSS-aligned online tests that the consortia have developed. Proponents of computer-adaptive testing also argue that they are cost-effective and objective and that they standardize grading, minimizing grading errors and inconsistencies among scorers (Great Schools Partnership, 2014). Critics argue that this technology is too new to be used for important decision making purposes, and that further study of the reliability and validity of computer-adaptive tests is needed. Because computers and reliable Internet access are necessary, low-income schools and students may be disadvantaged by this approach compared to the use of traditional paper-and-pencil measures. And, as we all know, technological advances that are heavily dependent on computers and the Internet all require extensive technical support capacities, which may be beyond means of many school districts (Great Schools Partnership, 2014). In any case, the debate about the utility computer-adaptive testing will continue for the foreseeable future.

Globalization and International Competitiveness

The rapid technological advances of the last decade and the emergence of the global economy, coupled with growing concerns about the ability of U.S. students to compete in the global marketplace, have only stimulated increased interest in educational reform and accountability. Because we have come to rely so heavily on summative test results for accountability purposes and because formative and interim assessments have become increasingly popular, the continued use of tests and other assessments in the classroom seems assured. But are our students able to hold their own in international competition? The most recent comparative international studies reveal a mixed picture.

Trends in International Mathematics and Science Study U.S. fourth and eighth graders scored above the international average in science and mathematics on the 2011 Trends in International Mathematics and Science Study (TIMSS). The 2011 TIMSS included 57 countries in the fourth-grade assessment and 56 for the eighth-grade assessment. In general, U.S. students lagged behind Asian students in both science and mathematics, and behind some European countries in science. U.S. students also lagged behind Russian Federation students in fourth- and eighth-grade science and eighth-grade math for the first time. In both math and science, fourth graders performed better than eighth graders when compared to their international counterparts. There were no measurable differences in the average performance of U.S. students in 2011 compared to TIMMS results from the prior administration in 2007 in eighth-grade math or science, or fourth-grade science. In math, fourth graders scored 12 points higher (541 vs. 529) in 2011 than in 2007. The TIMSS was scheduled to be readministered in 2015, but results were not available at the time of this revision.

Program for International Student Assessment The findings from the 2012 Program for International Student Assessment (PISA) were similar (Kelly et al., 2013). The PISA is coordinated by the Organization for Economic Cooperation and Development (OECD). It has been administered every three years since 2000. The PISA evaluates the mathematics, science, and reading literacy of 15-year-olds across 62 countries. The 2012 results indicated that U.S. students scored below the international average in mathematics (13 points) and science (4 points) and higher in reading (2 points), although none of the differences were considered to be of statistical significance. The PISA study indicated that, overall, U.S. 15-year-olds scored lower on average than their peers in nine Asian countries, eight European countries, and Canada. Results from the 2015 PISA administration were not available at the time of this revision.

Competency Testing for Teachers

In the early 1980s, a number of states passed legislation requiring teachers to pass paper-and-pencil competency tests of teaching. Concurrent with these trends was the development of professional teaching standards. The National Board for Professional Teaching Standards (NBPTS) for advanced certification was formed in 1987 with three major goals:

1. To establish high and rigorous standards for what effective teachers should know and be able to do.
2. To develop and operate a national, voluntary system to assess and certify teachers who meet these standards.
3. To advance related education reforms for the purpose of improving student learning in U.S. schools.

During the same year, the Interstate New Teacher Assessment and Support Consortium (INTASC) was formed to create "board-compatible" standards that could be reviewed by professional organizations and state agencies as a basis for licensing beginning teachers (Miller, 1992). The INTASC standards were written as 10 principles, which were then further described in terms of teacher knowledge, dispositions, and performances—in other words, what a beginning teacher should know and be able to do.

In 2011, the Council of Chief State School Officers (CCSSO) updated the INTASC Core Teaching Standards, making them applicable to the growth and development of all, not just beginning, teachers. These updated standards were also written to be compatible with the Common Core State Standards for students in math and language arts, thereby providing a single coherent system by which teachers can be prepared, supported, and licensed.

Much controversy still surrounds the use of tests aligned with these teacher competency standards. No one wants to see poorly trained teachers in the classroom. However, the development of a cost-effective, valid, and reliable paper-and-pencil method of measuring the complex set of skills and traits that go into being an effective classroom teacher remains elusive. Currently, such tests are not ordinarily used to prohibit a teacher from teaching or to terminate an experienced teacher. Instead, they are used on a preemployment basis to document minimum levels of competency in various content areas (Holmes Group, 1986; Miller, 1992). An example of such a test that is widely used across the United States is the PRAXIS Series. To give you an idea of what such a test looks like, we provide a description of the Praxis Series, sample questions, and answers to those questions in Ch. 2 Supplement 2.3 on the companion Website for this text (go to http://www.wiley.com/college/kubiszyn).

Even though many teacher preparation programs now require that their students pass tests as a condition for graduation and for licensure recommendations, passing rates have been around 96% since 1998, and this finding has led many to question whether the tests are rigorous enough (Sawchuck, 2012). Furthermore, Goldhaber (2007) found that performance on teacher licensing tests was weakly and inconsistently related to student performance. For these reasons, there has been increased interest in the use of performance and portfolio assessments (see Chapters 9 and 10) for teachers in hopes that they may provide for a more valid assessment of teaching competency than paper-and-pencil measures alone for both preservice and in-service teachers. Currently, 24 states are in various stages of development of these assessment systems, either as replacements for their current teacher licensing tests or as supplements to them.

Nevertheless, interest in the use of paper-and-pencil tests to evaluate teacher competency has continued. In 1998, the Higher Education Act required teacher training programs in colleges and universities to report their students' scores on teacher licensing tests. By 2001, 42 states and the federal government relied heavily on test scores to judge teacher quality and the quality of teacher preparation programs (Blair, 2001). Yet, a report from the National Research Council (2000) cautioned that there are many limitations in reliance on tests as a sole measure of teacher competence. Recently, the Educational Testing Service (ETS) announced that it is pursuing development of assessments for teachers that focus on whether teachers know how students tackle questions, common mistakes they make, and how to check for understanding (Njuguna, 2011).

Teacher Evaluation Based on Student Test Scores: Value-Added Models (VAM)

Perhaps in part because of the challenges associated with reliance on paper-and-pencil tests to evaluate teacher competency, interest has increased dramatically over the last five years in evaluating teachers based, in part, on student test scores. In 2014, 35 states and the District of Columbia required that student achievement must be a significant, or the most significant factor, in teacher evaluations (Layton, 2014). Systems that include student achievement test scores in teacher evaluation (along with other factors) have come to be referred to as "value-added models," or VAM. States are increasingly using teacher evaluation systems like this because teacher evaluation systems were requirements for the RTT funding competition sponsored by the federal government in 2009. In many cases, personnel decisions about teachers (e.g., hiring, termination, and compensation adjustments) have been affected by VAM ratings.

Yet, a recent study of 327 fourth- and eighth-grade mathematics and English-language arts teachers from six school districts in the East and Midwest by Polikoff and Porter (2014) revealed little to no correlation (see Chapter 14) between ratings of teachers based on VAM ratings and ratings of quality of teaching. Legal challenges to similar VAM systems have arisen in Tennessee, Florida, and Texas. In 2014, the American Statistical Association recommended that states and school districts refrain from using VAM systems to make important personnel decisions. They concluded that based on recent studies, teachers accounted for a maximum 14% of a student's score with a minimum of 86% of student score variability attributable to nonteacher, systemic factors (American Statistical Association, 2014). Clearly, the issues around the utility (and legality) of VAM models remains unsettled, so stay tuned for further developments!

Increased Interest from Professional Groups

In addition to the American Statistical Association's 2014 statement about VAM use, several national professional organizations have been increasingly interested in educational testing and assessment developments in recent years. This interest appears to be driven by the dramatic increase in the number and kinds of tests and assessments that are used in the schools. Individually and in collaboration, professional organizations have established high-level committees to study the broad implications of NCLB, IDEIA, the assessment-related provisions of the RTT, HST, use of growth versus status models for decision making, performance, and portfolio assessment, diversity and equity issues in testing, modification of tests for students with disabilities, required participation of students with disabilities in the same annual assessments given to regular education students, new assessment options for students with specific learning disabilities, culturally sensitive and language-appropriate assessment, computer-adaptive tests and interpretations, and several specific IDEIA innovations (e.g., technical adequacy of universal screening, progress monitoring, CBM, and response-to-intervention RTI cutoff scores and decision making rules). There is also increased interest in the development of competency standards for all test users (American Psychological Association, 2000) and in the fair use of test results, as reflected in the Code of Fair Testing Practices in Education (Joint Committee on Testing Practices, 2004). If these professional organizations are able to influence policy as they historically have, the issues they raise with regard to educational testing and assessment may become even more prominent in the future. Next, we describe a novel partnership between two national professional associations and a book publisher that reflects growing public and private interest in testing and assessment.

A Professional Association–Book Publisher Information Initiative

Recognizing that consumers can be easily overwhelmed by the complex, technical nature of testing and assessment information, John Wiley & Sons, the publisher of this textbook, and two public national organizations, the Joint Committee on Testing Practices (JCTP) and the National Council on Measurement in Education (NCME), have collaborated to make available to purchasers of this textbook a "plain English" video entitled *The ABCs of School Testing*. The video provides a lively and informative introduction to parents' most frequently asked questions about school testing. Various types of tests and their appropriate uses in the school setting are illustrated, and aptitude and achievement tests are also discussed. Even though the video was originally designed for lay audiences, it has proven helpful to professional educators as well.

The video previously was available for purchase only from JCTP and NCME. Now, the video has been made available for free in streaming video format on the Wiley Website (go to http://www.wiley.com/college/kubiszyn and click on the link to the Student Companion Site). In addition, the JCTP and Wiley have also agreed to make the *Code of Fair Testing Practices in Education* available for downloading at the Wiley Website. The Code was initially developed by JCTP in 1988 to clarify the primary obligations that professionals who develop or use educational tests have toward test-takers. It was revised in 2004. Even though designed primarily for professionals who develop and use tests, it provides information helpful to consumers as well and is appropriate for both lay and professional audiences. JCTP resources may be found at its Website (click on http://www.apa.org/science/jctpweb.html). Resources and other information about NCME may be found at the NCME Website (click on http://www.ncme.org).

SUMMARY

In this chapter, we have introduced you to issues related to educational testing and measurement and have described the orientation of the text. Its major points are as follows:

1. Recent educational reforms that have strongly influenced educational testing and assessment include the No Child Left Behind (NCLB) Act; the Individuals with Disabilities Education Improvement Act

(IDEIA); the standards-based reform movement that evolved into the Common Core State Standards (CCSS); recent Race to the Top (RTT) initiatives; and the growth of online, computer-adaptive testing for use with the CCSS-aligned tests.

2. Annual Yearly Progress (AYP) is an NCLB requirement that is measured with annual, summative tests and assessments. Schools that fail to demonstrate sufficient AYP face consequences including staff reassignment, ineligibility for salary increases, and possible closure.

3. Historically, each state decided which summative standardized test to use to measure AYP, which compromised attempts to compare AYP across states and over time.

4. High-stakes testing (HST), which is the use of a summative standardized test for important educational decision making, began as a state initiative in the 1970s. With the enactment of NCLB, HST became a requirement under federal law.

5. The impact of HST extends beyond education, also influencing property values, community demographics, businesses, and political agendas.

6. Under NCLB, enacted in 2002 under Republican President George W. Bush, all schools were required to demonstrate that 100% of students met academic proficiency standards by the end of the 2013–2014 academic year, or face federally mandated consequences.

7. Under Democratic President Barack Obama, the federal government began to grant states waivers from the 100% requirement and other NCLB provisions in exchange for increased emphasis on achieving college and career readiness standards, especially for the lowest performing schools, and developing teacher evaluation plans based in part on student test performance.

8. Even though regular education and special education reforms were initially separate, they were integrated with the enactment of the NCLB in 2002 and the IDEIA in 2004.

9. Standards-based reforms began with individual state academic and performance standards. This movement evolved into the CCSS to standardize academic standards across states.

10. The CCSS was a state-initiated movement. It was not mandated by the federal government.

11. The Race to the Top (RTT) initiative was a voluntary part of the much broader federal American Recovery and Reinvestment Act of 2009 (ARRA). The intent of RTT was to increase the extent to which high school graduates from all subgroups of students (e.g., disabilities, cultural, socioeconomic, and English proficiency) are prepared for colleges and careers.

12. RTT was a voluntary federal grant competition intended to facilitate compliance with the CCSS, increase college preparation and participation (especially in science, technology, engineering and mathematics, also known as the STEM disciplines), develop performance-based standards for teachers and principals based in part on student test scores, enable the establishment of more charter schools and improve low-performing schools.

13. One of the RTT components, the Race to the Top Assessment Competition, funded two state-based consortia in 2010 to develop assessments aligned with the CCSS that each state in each consortium would agree to use.

14. Even though they initially enjoyed widespread support across the states, both the RTT and the CCSS became increasingly controversial and politicized between 2011 and 2014, and their futures were uncertain by early 2015.

15. Conservative Republicans asserted that RTT and CCSS represented an attempt by the Obama administration to exert federal control over education in the states, although RTT was voluntary and CCSS was a state and not a federal initiative.

16. In an unusual development, by early 2015, support for and opposition against both initiatives was mixed, emerging from both Republicans and Democrats.

17. Proponents of computer-adaptive testing argue that such tests are more accurate, secure, efficient, and cost effective than paper-and-pencil tests. Critics argue that further study of the reliability and validity of computer-adaptive tests is needed and that their technology requirements exceed the capacities of many schools and districts, especially in economically disadvantaged areas.

18. Recent evidence from international assessments indicates that students from the United States may not be as competitive as we would like with students from other countries.

19. Competency testing for teachers continues to evolve, with recent efforts focused on assessment of competencies of both new and experienced teachers.

20. RTT has prompted increased usage of student summative test performance into annual teacher evaluations. This development, which has been very controversial, has been called a value-added model (VAM).

21. As test use, importance and controversy have increased, many national professional organizations have become increasingly involved in educational testing and assessment in recent years.

FOR DISCUSSION AND PRACTICE

1. This chapter reviewed several regular and special education reform initiatives. Compare and contrast each of these with each other, including dates of enactment, primary impact on classroom testing and measurement, and their current status.

2. By referring to the chapter and especially the textbook's companion Website, discuss the history and the pros and cons of high-stakes testing.

3. Discuss the possible reason(s) why the NCLB goal of 100% proficiency was not realistic when enacted in 2002. Given that it was unrealistic, speculate about why it was enacted, and why NCLB waivers began to be granted in 2011.

4. Alignment of a high-stakes test with state academic standards or the CCSS is critical for a test to demonstrate evidence of its content validity—the most important technical consideration of an achievement test. NCLB also requires that annual academic assessments should be based on state standards. When would a state test developed to measure the state's standards be more likely to be aligned with the state standards than an off-the-shelf, nationally standardized test?

*Answers for these questions appear in Appendix B.

5. If a state-developed test is more likely to be aligned with state standards, why do you think some states use a nationally standardized test that may not be as well aligned?

6. Discuss why the CCSS, a state-sponsored initiative, and the RTT, a voluntary initiative, have both been criticized as attempts by the federal government to take direct control over education policy and practice in the states.

7. Discuss the implications of U.S. pupil performance on the TIMMS and PISA, given that our world has become increasingly global and technologically sophisticated.

8. As a new teacher, you learn that VAM will be used to evaluate your future performance. Identify potential costs and benefits of VAM from the perspective of teachers, students, parents, and politicians.

9. Point out some societal trends (e.g., changing demographics, increased population, or global competition for jobs) occurring in your city, state, or region that will likely make testing and measurement in our schools more complicated and important in the future.

CHAPTER 3

RESPONSE TO INTERVENTION (RTI) AND THE REGULAR CLASSROOM TEACHER

LEARNING OUTCOMES

After completing this chapter, the student will be able to:

1. Define response to intervention (RTI).
2. Explain why RTI applies to both regular and special education.
3. Describe the various tiers in the RTI model and indicate the approximate percentages of students to whom each tier applies.
4. Explain the role of curriculum-based measurement (CBM) in RTI.
5. Give examples of the ways in which the RTI model may facilitate the early identification of students struggling with reading or math.
6. Explain why RTI implementation has been uneven around the country.
7. Explain why NCLB, IDEIA, and RTI represent the merger of regular education reform and special education reform.
8. Compare and contrast summative and formative assessments.
9. Define and give examples of universal screening, progress monitoring, data-based decision making, and research-based instruction.
10. Compare and contrast the assessment, progress monitoring, instructional processes, and educators involved in Tiers 1, 2, and 3.
11. Compare and contrast universal screening and benchmark tests.
12. Explain the concept and process involved in progress monitoring.
13. Define data-based decision making.
14. Provide examples of data-based decision making.
15. Graphically illustrate progress-monitoring data to distinguish between struggling learners and those achieving at expectancy.
16. Distinguish between the standard protocol (SP) and problem-solving (PS) RTI models.
17. Explain why the RTI approach is characterized by both promise and controversy.

RESPONSE TO Intervention (RTI) is a recent education reform initiative that has been phased into regular education classrooms around the country over the last several years. In some parts of the country, the RTI model is referred to as response to *instruction* rather than as response to *intervention*, but both phrases refer to the RTI model. For the sake of consistency, we will use RTI to refer to response to intervention throughout this text.

WHAT IS RTI?

RTI is a tiered system designed to integrate assessment, research-based instruction, and data-based decision making to improve educational outcomes for all students in both regular and special education classrooms. The first tier is implemented in the regular education classroom and involves screening and high-quality instruction in the regular education curriculum for all students. Academic progress is monitored through universal screening of all students at the beginning of the year and once or twice over the school year through interim or benchmark assessments (see Chapter 1). Those students in need of additional instructional intervention are served within the second tier of services (usually about 15% of students). Instruction may be provided in the regular classroom, a special education classroom, after school, or in another setting. The responsiveness of these students to more intensive instruction is monitored on an ongoing (e.g., weekly) basis with brief, formative assessments, such as curriculum-based measurement, or CBM (see Chapter 1). Instructional adjustments may be made depending on whether students respond to the more intensive instruction/intervention. Only those students who do not respond to second tier, intensive instruction are referred for even more intensive third tier instruction and support (usually about 5%). Those students receive more specialized services to address their challenges, typically coordinated or delivered by special education teachers and related professionals (e.g., speech or occupational therapists and school psychologists). Tier 3 students may also be referred for a comprehensive, multidisciplinary evaluation to determine their eligibility for special education services, as required by the IDEIA. In some states, the RTI model includes four tiers.

In the end, the RTI system holds promise to foster better and earlier identification and more effective intervention with academic difficulties than was previously the case. As a result, RTI may be best viewed as supporting improved achievement for all students, the major objective of both regular education and special education reform movements (see Chapter 2). In some states, RTI may also be used to identify pupils with specific learning disabilities (SLD), as we discussed in previous editions of this text. Readers interested in this more limited, and more controversial RTI application are referred to the special education chapters that are now available on this textbook's accompanying website (go to http://www.wiley.com/college/kubiszyn and click on the link to the Student Companion Site).

WHAT IF YOU HAVE NOT HEARD OF RTI BEFORE?

Depending on where you live, your familiarity with RTI may be considerable, only limited, or nonexistent. It would not surprise us at all to learn that you have never heard of RTI or that your understanding of this approach is limited. But how can this be if it was mandated by federal law?

The answer is twofold. First, in most states RTI is a recent concept and one that did not exist prior to 2006. Second, implementation of RTI around the country has grown consistently but is still uneven (Global Scholar Spectrum K12, 2011). We will describe the uneven implementation of RTI more fully later in this chapter.

HOW NEW IS RTI?

It was not evident that RTI would need to be implemented in all regular education classrooms until the final regulations for the *Individuals with Disabilities Education Improvement Act* (IDEIA) were released in October 2006. In many states, it was not until one or more years after those regulations were released that state education agencies adopted implementing regulations that specifically defined the RTI model and approach required in each state. Those regulations may also have changed since their first release. Thus, it is entirely possible that educators in your state may have been "in the dark" about RTI and its requirements until sometime in 2008, 2009, or even later. On the other hand, those of you who live in Iowa, Minnesota, Pennsylvania, South Carolina, and a smattering of other locations may be more familiar with RTI because in some of these states this model has been in place for 20 years, or longer, even though it was not required by federal law.

WHY DO REGULAR EDUCATION TEACHERS NEED TO KNOW ABOUT RTI?

All teachers must now learn about RTI. Why? RTI is now required under federal law, and RTI has significant potential educational benefit. If properly implemented, RTI can enhance the early identification and remediation of academic difficulties in the regular classroom by utilizing frequent formative assessment results to directly inform instructional decision making to the potential benefit of students, teachers, schools, and society.

To date, RTI's impact on regular education teachers has varied from state to state and school to school, but there is little doubt that RTI eventually will have a significant impact on all teachers. In fact, demonstrating that RTI is more than just a special education initiative, RTI implementation is being led by collaborations between regular and special education in 81% of school districts across the country (Spectrum K12, 2011). The following scenario captures (with a hint of exaggeration) several conversations the authors have had with teachers in the last several years with regard to RTI and its overlap with NCLB, IDEIA, AYP, and the new Common Core-aligned tests (please review Chapters 1 and 2 if any of these terms are unclear to you). Of course, the names have been changed to protect the innocent! This conversational introduction prepares you for the more detailed consideration of RTI that follows. After the scenario, we will explain what RTI is in more detail, describe its various components, and discuss its implementation across the country. Finally, we will consider some of the controversies that have arisen around RTI.

AN RTI SCENARIO

"Hi Mr. Past," said Ms. Future as she stepped through the doorway of Mr. Past's regular education classroom. "In addition to being the special ed coordinator, I'm now the school's response-to-intervention, or RTI, coordinator too. Hard to believe the new school year is

beginning already isn't it?" "Sure is," said Mr. Past. "I wish the vacation was about a month longer. What did you say about RT and your eye?" he asked. "Not my eye, silly, RTI!" she said while smiling. "One of my responsibilities is to remind all the regular ed teachers about the mandatory RTI implementation meeting tomorrow afternoon. We will discuss universal screening and the new CBM progress monitoring probes that teachers will administer and score. I'm sure you are ready to go, but we want to make sure all regular ed teachers hit the ground running on the first day of classes next week," said Ms. Future.

"RTI, CBM? Is that what they're calling high-stakes testing now?" asked Mr. Past. "No!" exclaimed Ms. Future. "We hope RTI will help us meet the NCLB accountability requirements, but we adopted RTI last year to meet the requirements of the IDEIA. You know, the Individuals with Disabilities Education Improvement Act. We discussed IDEIA and RTI several times last year at our faculty meetings, and at the mandatory in-service training last week, weren't you there?" she asked. "Hold on now, Ms. Future. I may not know what RTI is, or whatever this BM or BS screening and monitoring stuff is, but I DO know that IDEIA is a special ed law, and I know I'm a regular ed teacher, so don't try to BS me or get me involved in special ed requirements on top of all the NCLB stuff I have to keep up with. And by the way, I did attend that special ed in-service on RTI last week, but I had to prepare my lesson plans for the new Common Core State Standards based textbook series the district just adopted, so I may have missed something." said an annoyed Mr. Past.

"Wait! You are terribly mistaken!" stated Ms. Future emphatically. "This is NOT a special education meeting. It's a mandatory meeting for ALL regular and special education teachers. IDEIA, NCLB, RTI, CBM, universal screening, and progress monitoring are now requirements for both regular and special education teachers. The principal told me that any teachers who missed this meeting will receive a disciplinary write up," said Ms. Future.

"Don't you dare threaten me!" stated an irritated Mr. Past. "I've been teaching for 30 years, you know. I don't have time for this. Classes begin next week, I have the Common Core tests and a new textbook to deal with, and the first benchmark assessment for the state high-stakes test is at the end of the month! I need to start getting my 28 kids ready from day one. And by the way, six of those kids are special ed kids who, as you know, are now fully included in my classroom because of that IDEIA law. They will take the same state high-stakes test that my other kids take, even though they're way behind. So please don't try to waste my time with this RTI special ed stuff!" said Mr. Past, raising his voice.

Just then, Ms. Indamiddle, the school's principal, appeared. Both Ms. Future and Mr. Past took a step back from each other and simultaneously said "Good morning," with forced smiles on both of their faces.

"I couldn't help but overhear your ... ahem ... , discussion," said the stern-faced principal. "I can see you are both frustrated, and I think I know why. Mr. Past, you are absolutely right about the Common Core Standards based textbook and the NCLB requirements, but Ms. Future is also absolutely right about the RTI approach, including the use of universal screening for ALL students, at least weekly CBM probes for progress monitoring of our research-based instruction, and data-based decision making," she emphasized. "Mr. Past, IDEIA and NCLB can no longer be considered to be separate special ed and general ed laws. They are intended to complement and reinforce each other. They are the result of the merger of more than 25 years of general and special education reform initiatives, and they are intended to unify our educational system to improve educational outcomes for ALL students. By the way, all this was explained at the required in-service RTI training last week." she said, looking directly at Mr. Past.

"But Ms. Indamiddle," said Mr. Past. "More meetings and all these new RTI requirements will take time away from high-stakes test preparation. You don't want us to fail to make AYP because my class is not prepared for the Common Core aligned tests, do you?" asked Mr. Past.

"I think you know the answer to that, don't you, Mr. Past?" glared Ms. Indamiddle. "I also don't think you get it, Mr. Past. It is precisely the implementation of the RTI model with all students that we are counting on to help us meet the NCLB AYP requirements on the new

Common Core tests. As a result of RTI, we expect that more of our students will improve their skills and help us excel in meeting AYP under NCLB," said Ms. Indamiddle confidently.

Then Ms. Future chimed in, "To make it work, our RTI plan calls for us to administer universal screening assessments to all of our students at least three times per year to identify those who are at risk academically in spite of receiving the same research-based instruction that all our kids get. In the RTI model this is referred to as Tier 1 instruction. The first of these universal screenings is scheduled to take place at the end of the first week of classes. When the universal screenings identify a student as being at risk academically, the student receives more intense research-based instruction, either individually or in small groups in the classroom or on a pull-out basis, and he or she will be progress monitored on at least a weekly basis with CBM probes that classroom teachers like you will administer and score. This is known as Tier 2. If the student has received at least eight weeks of Tier 2 instruction and still is not progressing, we may provide even more intense scientifically based instruction for another eight weeks, or we may refer the student for a comprehensive full and individual special-education evaluation. This is known as Tier 3, and it is only at this point in the RTI process that special education becomes a possibility," concluded Ms. Future.

Ms Indamiddle added, "So, as you can see, our RTI plan requires serious involvement from regular education teachers in Tier 1 and Tier 2 instruction and progress monitoring of that instruction using the CBM probes the district has selected for you to administer and score. Furthermore, regular ed teachers may continue to be involved in Tier 3 because we practice full inclusion in our district, which is why you have six special education pupils in your regular education classroom," concluded Ms. Indamiddle. "As I have said, and as Ms. Future said, RTI is NOT a special education initiative, and it is NOT optional. The district has adopted this RTI approach, and we WILL implement it next week!" stated Ms. Indamiddle emphatically while Ms. Future nodded enthusiastically.

"Okay, okay, I guess I just didn't take this RTI stuff seriously. I thought it was just another fad or change for the sake of change. You know what I mean?" asked Mr. Past quietly. When no one responded, he said, "Well, anyway, I have all the materials from last week's in-service training. I'll review them and I will be prepared for tomorrow's meeting." "That will be most appreciated," said Ms. Indamiddle. "Yes indeed, thank you for understanding, Mr. Past," said Ms. Future with a wink.

Does this scenario seem far-fetched? Out of touch? Inaccurate? If it does, then you, like Mr. Past, may not be aware of the dramatic changes in testing and assessment in the regular classroom that have been prompted by the IDEIA and RTI and how RTI overlaps with NCLB. If so, no problem! This chapter is intended to bring you up to speed.

HOW IMPORTANT IS RTI TO REGULAR EDUCATION TEACHERS?

In our opinion, it would not be an exaggeration to say that RTI represents a "sea change" in our educational system, driven by the merger of regular education and special education reform initiatives (e.g., NCLB and IDEIA). Sea change is a term typically reserved for significant, systemwide changes that have the potential to undo practices or policies that may have been in place for years, decades, or generations. We believe RTI can be characterized as a sea change because it:

- is a systemwide initiative intended to improve educational outcomes for *all* students by integrating assessment, instruction, and data-based decision making;
- utilizes repeated, brief, formative assessments (e.g., CBM) rather than one-time summative assessments to assess student responsiveness to research-based instruction and to inform adjustments to instruction;

- incorporates lessons learned from decades of regular and special education reform movements and research-based practices;
- reflects the recent merger of regular education reform (NCLB) with special education reform (IDEIA).

We mentioned earlier that RTI implementation is being led by collaborating regular and special educators in 81% of school districts across the country (Spectrum K 12, 2011). Taken together, IDEIA, NCLB, and RTI are expected to drive even greater integration of regular and special education in the future. Regular education teachers must be prepared for this change. The handwriting is on the wall: all teachers in training must learn at least the basics of the RTI approach to formative and interim assessment and should understand how it differs from and complements traditional summative assessment approaches. This is what we intend to do with this chapter.

HOW IS RTI SUPPOSED TO HELP STUDENTS AND SCHOOLS?

After years of regular and special education reform, and after hearing testimony from nationally known researchers and other experts between 2001 and 2003, Congress concluded that RTI held the most promise for achieving the goal of improved educational outcomes for all students. Congress was convinced that 30 years of experience with the prior special education model that relied on infrequent, summative assessments (e.g., aptitude-achievement discrepancy to identify students with specific learning disabilities, or SLDs) and referrals to special education to assist struggling learners was ineffective and inefficient. Indeed, some critics referred to that model as the "wait to fail" model (Fletcher, Denton, & Francis, 2005). It was so-called because most struggling learners typically were unable to qualify for special education services until they were in the third grade, after the learners had experienced years of failure and lacked foundational skills needed to remedy deficits. We discuss aptitude–achievement discrepancies in detail in Chapter 18, and interested readers can find out more about the application of the aptitude–achievement discrepancy model to SLD identification at this textbook's accompanying website (go to http://www.wiley.com/college/kubiszyn and click on the link to the Student Companion Site).

RTI advocates convinced Congress that the RTI model was not only a solution to the "wait to fail" SLD identification model but that RTI also was a way to apply a research-based problem-solving model to identify struggling regular education pupils earlier and more effectively, and to provide them with research-based instruction. The use of universal screening measures (described later in this chapter) with all students enables early identification of struggling learners in regular education classes. Once struggling learners are identified, Congress concluded that it would be best to continuously monitor student responsiveness to research-based instruction (i.e., formative assessment) to determine whether changes to instruction are needed on an ongoing basis. In this way, Congress believed that more serious difficulties could be prevented, special education would be more effective, and that overall educational outcomes for all students would be improved. In addition, advocates argued that referrals for expensive special education services would be reduced, occurring only for those students who had failed to respond to multiple interventions. Stated differently, the RTI model came to be viewed by Congress as "an ounce of prevention instead of a pound of cure."

Testing and assessment under RTI is very different from the traditional summative approach to educational decision making. Summative assessments are administered at a single point in time (e.g., end of unit/semester/year teacher-made tests or annual standardized high-stakes tests). Typically, summative assessments are also not sensitive to the small, incremental improvements in learning that can characterize academic skill development. At the same time, RTI approaches were not intended to replace the summative, high-stakes testing approaches that are required by the *No Child Left Behind Act* (NCLB). Instead, RTI, required by the IDEIA, was intended to complement and reinforce the accountability requirements of the NCLB.

Although limited at this point, evidence is beginning to emerge that formative CBM assessments used in most RTI approaches can be used effectively to identify struggling students much earlier than previously was possible (Shapiro et al., 2006) and that CBM can be used to predict performance on state high-stakes tests up to 2 years later (Keller-Margulis, Shapiro, & Hintze, 2008). Murray, Woodruff, and Vaughn (2010) found that the implementation of RTI was associated with a 47% reduction in first-grade retention, but they were not able to determine the extent to which RTI findings were considered in the retention decisions (i.e., other factors may have been responsible).

RTI DEFINITIONS, COMPONENTS, AND APPROACHES

Thus far in this chapter, we have explained what RTI is, why awareness of RTI can vary across the country, the evolution of RTI, why RTI is important to regular education teachers, and how RTI can help improve outcomes for all students. In this section, we get down to the "nuts and bolts" of RTI and describe the definitions, components, and implementation approaches associated with RTI. Before we begin, you should know that, even though RTI is federally mandated, there can be many variations in the way the RTI is defined and implemented across the country. We will only introduce you to the most commonly agreed-on components and implementation approaches. Although we will provide you with a solid RTI foundation, in some cases, you may need to modify and build on this foundation to adjust to the way that RTI may be implemented in the district in which you eventually will work. However, that is down the road a bit (hopefully not too far!).

RTI Definitions

Space limitations preclude us from listing all the different definitions of RTI that exist. In reviewing these definitions, we have concluded that the differences typically reflect the orientation or philosophy of the organization, its constituents, and differences in levels of specificity. Two examples of definitions offered by prominent national organizations illustrate these different emphases. According to the RTI Action Network, a national organization interested in the education of all students, "Response to Intervention (RTI) is a multi-tiered approach to help struggling learners. Students' progress is closely monitored at each stage of intervention to determine the need for further research-based instruction and/or intervention in general education, in special education, or both" (RTI Action Network, 2008). According to the National Center for Research on Learning Disabilities (NCRLD), an organization most interested in children with learning disabilities, "Responsiveness to intervention is an education model that promotes early identification of students who may be at risk for learning difficulties" (National Center for Research on Learning Disabilities, 2007).

Regardless of the definition, it is important to understand that RTI is about much more than just testing or assessment. RTI is an *integrated* assessment–instruction–decision making system. When properly implemented, RTI links assessment to research-based instruction and data-based decision making by utilizing multiple but brief, frequent assessments (i.e., *formative* assessments) to evaluate student responsiveness to instruction (i.e., progress monitoring). The progress-monitoring data from these assessments inform educational decision making in ways that are not possible with traditional *summative* assessments, including annual high-stakes tests, or even benchmark tests.

RTI Components

Although definitions may vary, there is considerable agreement about the key RTI components. These components include a tiered, integrated, research-based intervention system; universal screening; progress monitoring with frequent and brief formative assessments; and data-based decision making (Brown-Chidsey & Steege, 2010). We will describe each of these components in turn.

A Tiered, Integrated, Research-Based Prevention System
Most RTI systems are based on a three-tier model of increasingly intensive research-based instruction to prevent future problems for those students with increasingly greater instructional needs. The largest and most common component of the three-tier model is sometimes referred to as primary prevention (Tier 1). The next level is called secondary prevention (Tier 2), and the third level is called tertiary prevention (Tier 3). Although four-tier and even five-tier systems exist, they are variations of the three-tier model and should be readily understood by anyone who comprehends the basic three-tier model. For our purposes, we will limit our discussion to the three-tier model illustrated in Figure 3.1.

As Figure 3.1 indicates, the three tiers can be differentiated from each other by the proportion of students involved and the type or intensity of intervention or instruction provided. Within this model, about 80% of students will receive Tier 1 instruction (primary prevention), about 15% of students will receive Tier 2 instruction (secondary prevention), and about 5% of students will receive Tier 3 instruction (tertiary prevention). Note that the percentage of students within each tier may vary dependent on resource availability and need.

Within Tier 1 (primary prevention), all students receive high-quality, research-based instruction from their regular classroom teachers in general education classrooms. It is anticipated that approximately 80% of all regular education students will remain at Tier 1 throughout their academic careers.

Within Tier 2 (secondary prevention), those students who have been identified through universal screening (to be described in the next section) as being nonresponsive to Tier 1 instruction (i.e., at risk for academic failure) are provided with more intensive research-based Tier 2 instruction. This is usually about 15% of the school population. To help ensure that a student's lack of responsiveness to Tier 1 instruction is about the student, rather than simply poor-quality instruction,

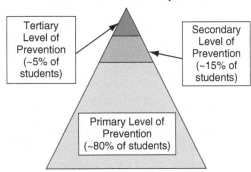

FIGURE 3.1 A multi-level prevention system.
Source: National Center on Response to Intervention (June 2012). *RTI Implementer Series: Module 1: Screening—Training Manual.* Washington, DC: U.S. Department of Education, Office of Special Education Programs, National Center on Response to Intervention.

most RTI approaches require that a student be provided with Tier 2 instruction only if the majority of the student's classmates have made adequate progress with Tier 1 instruction. If the majority of students in a classroom failed to respond to Tier 1 instruction, a change in the teacher or method of Tier 1 instruction may be indicated before Tier 2 instruction is provided to the students. This is one of the ways that RTI models guard against mischaracterizing teaching deficits as student deficits.

Compared to Tier 1 instruction, Tier 2 instruction may be more individualized, intensive, or delivered in small groups. Because Tier 2 instruction is more intensive or specialized, it may not be able to be provided effectively in the regular education classroom and may be provided on a pullout basis, or after school. Tier 2 instruction may be provided by the regular classroom teacher or a specialist (such as the school interventionist). It is anticipated that approximately 15% of students will require Tier 2 instruction at some point(s) in their academic careers. Typically, students continue with Tier 2 instruction for about 8–12 weeks, and their responsiveness to Tier 2 instruction is regularly progress monitored (i.e., at least weekly) with brief CBM probes typically administered and scored by classroom teachers. At the end of this period of Tier 2 instruction, the progress-monitoring data is reviewed. At this point, the student may

- be moved back into Tier 1 instruction, if the student has made sufficient progress;
- continue with more of the same Tier 2 instruction for another 8–12 weeks, if the progress has been made but is not yet sufficient to warrant a return to Tier 1 instruction;
- be provided with a second phase of Tier 2 research-based instruction that is more frequent, individualized, and/or intense than was provided during the initial period of Tier 2 instruction.

The student's progress-monitoring data is again reviewed at the end of the second phase (8 to 12 weeks) of Tier 2 instruction, and this data then drives decision making. At this point, the student may

- return to Tier 1 instruction, if he or she has made sufficient progress;
- continue with the same intensity, or a reduced intensity of Tier 2 instruction if progress has been made but is not sufficient to warrant a return to Tier 1;
- be referred to Tier 3, if the progress-monitoring data indicate that the student has not responded to increasingly intensive Tier 2 research-based instruction.

Tier 3 (tertiary prevention) can vary depending on the model adopted in a particular state. In some states, if a student fails to progress under appropriate Tier 2 instruction, the student may be referred for a full, comprehensive special education evaluation to determine whether the student qualifies for special education services as a student with a specific learning disability (SLD). In other states, failure to respond to Tier 2 instruction is considered the primary or only criterion for a student to qualify for special education services as a student with an SLD, as long as other factors can be ruled out (e.g., frequent absences, ineffective teaching, limited English proficiency). In 2010 these states included Colorado, Connecticut, Louisiana, Rhode Island, and West Virginia (Zirkel & Thomas, 2010). In those states, screening measures rather than full measures may be used to comply with the federal IDEIA requirement for a comprehensive evaluation. The use of RTI for SLD identification has been highly controversial; interested readers are referred to this textbook's accompanying website for further discussion of these controversies (go to http://www.wiley.com/college/kubiszyn and click on the link to the Student Companion Site).

Universal Screening Typically, universal screening of *all* students in the school is completed two to three times per year, beginning early in the fall term. In some states, standardized commercial or state-developed tests are used for universal screening. In some cases, winter and spring interim or benchmark tests associated with the state's high-stakes test may be employed, and in other cases, brief screening measures are used.

Whichever measure or timing is used, the purpose of universal screening is to identify those students in Tier 1 instruction who may not be sufficiently responsive to that instruction. Typically, about 25% of the lowest scoring all students on the universal screening (or interim/benchmark) measure are considered to be potentially at risk for academic difficulty, although the proportion may be higher or lower in different states. Students who score in the at-risk range are typically considered for Tier 2 research-based instruction, and they are progress monitored with frequent and ongoing CBM probes or other brief formative measures. Universal screening (or benchmark testing) is often repeated with all students again in late fall and in spring, and again the lowest scoring 25% or so of students are considered for Tier 2 instruction. When used as benchmarks, the percentage referred to Tier 2 may vary from year to year. This is because the proportion of students who score at or above a "target" score may change from year to year. A target score typically is the score below which about 80% of test-takers are predicted to fail to achieve proficiency scores on the summative, end-of-year high-stakes test. By repeatedly screening for a lack of responsiveness to Tier 1 instruction, the hope is that students at risk for academic difficulty will be identified early enough that their deficiencies can be efficiently remediated by Tier 2 instruction. This would enable their prompt return to Tier 1 instruction, potentially reduce referrals for Tier 3, or special education, and lead to improved performance on annual, summative tests.

Astute readers may wonder why the lowest scoring 25% (or the percentage who score below the benchmark target score) on the screening measure are considered for Tier 2 instruction when the three-tier model illustrated in Figure 3.1 indicates that only 15% of students are expected to need Tier 2 intervention. The answer is that screening measures in education, like those in health and other fields, tend to be brief, and the accuracy of brief screening measures is often less than is desirable. To compensate for this relative lack of accuracy, we err on the side of overidentifying potentially at-risk students by including about 5% more students (i.e., 25% minus about 15% in Tier 2 and about 5% in Tier 3) than actually need it. By doing so, we hope to provide needed instruction to those who would likely continue to fall further behind until the next universal screening. Those students who are incorrectly identified to be at risk will, at worst, obtain Tier 2 instruction until progress monitoring indicates that they were incorrectly placed. Universal screening measures include a wide variety of measures with varying degrees of accuracy. Interested readers are referred to Jenkins, Hudson, and Johnson (2007) for a review of the accuracy of several common universal screeners. A more comprehensive web-based resource from the National Center for Response to Intervention (NCRTI) compares multiple screening measures and ratings of their technical adequacy (http://www.rti4success.org/resources/tools-charts/screening-tools-chart).

Progress Monitoring The IDEIA requires that student responsiveness to Tier 2 or Tier 3 instruction be repeatedly monitored. This requirement has come to be known as progress monitoring. Progress monitoring of student responsiveness to instruction typically means daily or weekly monitoring with brief, *formative* assessments administered and scored by teachers (such as the CBM that we discussed in Chapter 1). Although CBM is probably the most commonly used progress-monitoring tool, a variety of other research-based progress-monitoring tools are available. Examples of CBM for different academic content areas can be found on the website of the U.S. Department of Education-sponsored National Center for Student Progress Monitoring (http://www.studentprogress.org/weblibrary.asp). Other progress-monitoring tools with established technical adequacy may also be compared on another page at that website (http://www.studentprogress.org/chart/chart.asp). CBM or other formative progress-monitoring data are collected on a repeated, frequent basis rather than in simple pre- or post-test manner. Thus, instead of measuring a student's skill acquisition at only one or two points in time, the child is assessed on an ongoing and regular basis over the course of instruction to evaluate the effect of an instructional intervention.

The collection of multiple data points for formative assessments such as CBM also helps compensate for the limited reliability that characterizes brief tests and assessments (see Chapter 17). When sufficient data points are used, the reliability of formative assessments can be comparable to traditional norm-referenced, standardized tests (Francis et al., 2005). CBM shifts the focus for progress monitoring from a summative evaluation perspective (e.g., determining what a student has learned *after* instruction) to a formative evaluation perspective (e.g., determining what the student is continuously learning *during* instruction).

Continuous progress monitoring means that these formative assessments continue to be collected across multiple points in time (i.e., weeks and months) for as long as the Tier 2 or Tier 3 instruction is being provided. By regularly reviewing the results of these formative assessments, those students who are not responsive to instruction can be quickly identified, and more frequent, focused, and/or intensive research-based instruction may be provided. Alternatively, progress monitoring can also indicate which students are responsive to instruction, enabling the return of the students to Tier 1 instruction, if sufficient progress has been made. In summary, the progress-monitoring process provides the teacher with the information needed for informed data-based instructional decision making, enabling the classroom teacher to quickly adjust the level of instruction (or intervention) provided to students.

Data-Based Decision Making Within the RTI model data-based decision making occurs often, ranging from universal screening through special education eligibility determination (Kowaleski & Mahoney, 2008). For universal screening, data-based decision making is relatively straightforward, once cutoff scores are agreed upon. Typically, a score on the screening measure that identifies the lowest performing 25% of students is used to determine which students are referred for Tier 2 instruction.

Once a student has entered Tier 2 (or Tier 3) instruction, data from CBM or other progress-monitoring tools are typically collected at least weekly for regular and continuous progress-monitoring purposes. To illustrate data-based decision making, we will use CBM reading fluency (CBM-R) probes in our examples to illustrate one way in which CBM data can be used to inform data-based decision making. It is important to recognize that the examples we present are illustrative only; there can be many variations to this approach to data-based decision making we have illustrated. We believe that you will be able to adapt to any variation that your district may use, once you understand this approach.

Typically, CBM-R probes are straightforward to administer and score and are only 1 minute in duration. They are administered in groups of three probes at a time, but only one score, the median or numerical middle score (see Chapter 13), is used for progress-monitoring and data-based decision making purposes. The highest and lowest scores are disregarded. In spite of their ease of use and brevity, CBM-R probes have been demonstrated to be reliable and valid enough for screening purposes and for measuring reading progress in the regular curriculum (Deno et al., 2001; Fuchs & Fuchs, 2002), although the reliability of math and writing CBM probes is not as well established (Amato & Watkins, 2011), especially at the secondary education level for students with low achievement levels (Masterson, 2009).

Because CBM probes are designed to be sensitive to small changes in learning, CBM scores enable data-based decisions to be made about how responsive students are to their research-based interventions. Thus, CBM probes may be ideally suited to monitor day-to-day responsiveness to

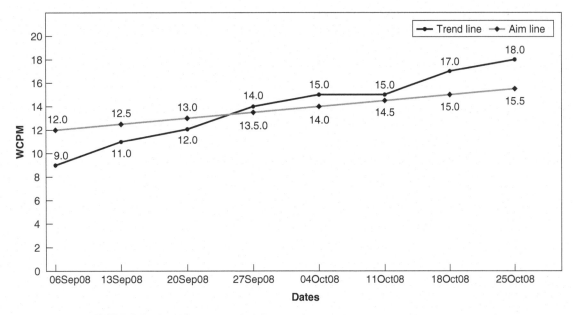

FIGURE 3.2 A student responds to intervention.

Tier 2 or Tier 3 instruction, which in turn facilitates day-to-day instructional decision making. Next, we provide two examples that illustrate how CBM-R probes can inform data-based decision making.

Figure 3.2 illustrates how CBM-R data can be graphically organized to reflect learning level and slope of learning improvement in response to instruction. Because a "picture is worth a thousand words," simple graphs like the one shown in Figure 3.2, as well as more complex graphs available from commercial test publishers, have proven invaluable in organizing CBM data to inform data-based decision making. Each circular data point in Figure 3.2 represents the median number of words read correctly per minute (WCPM) by an at-risk learner on a given day while exposed to a Tier 2 reading intervention. Dates for Figure 3.2 and Figure 3.3 are listed on the horizontal axis and WCPM on the vertical axis. For both figures, Tier 2 instruction began on September 6, 2008 (far left in both graphs). The lines connecting the circles indicate the trend or the actual rate of progress under the Tier 2 intervention. The line connecting the diamonds is known as the "aim line" or the expected level of performance or growth over time in WCPM for a typical child. The expected level of performance is a goal that is based on previously collected data that indicate how typical students in the same, or similar, grade improve in WCPM on a weekly basis with Tier 1 instruction. The difference between the student's trend line and the aim line is what is used to determine whether the student is making adequate progress in the Tier 2 intervention.

Notice that at the beginning of Tier 2 instruction the trend line was below the aim line, indicating that the student's level of performance in WCPM was lower than expected. As the Tier 2 instruction was delivered, however, the gap between the trend line and the aim line closed, then the trend line crossed the aim line and continued to increase until the end of the Tier 2 instruction. This graph indicates that not only has this student responded to the Tier 2 instruction but also the rate of improvement (i.e., the slope of the trend line) was actually greater than expected for Tier 1 students (i.e., the slope of the aim line). All other factors being equal, these data suggest that this student should be dismissed from Tier 2 instruction and returned to the regular classroom for Tier 1

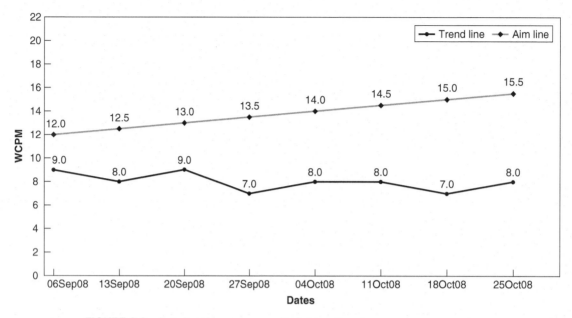

FIGURE 3.3 A student does not respond to intervention.

instruction. If the student maintained the gains while receiving Tier 1 instruction, as indicated by the next universal screening, the student would remain at Tier 1 but could always return to Tier 2 if indicated by the next universal screening.

Figure 3.3 illustrates just the opposite. In Figure 3.3, the student's trend line begins below the aim line, and the difference between the trend line and the aim line increases over the course of the Tier 2 instruction. In this case, the graphed data would lead us to conclude that the Tier 2 instruction delivered to this student has been ineffective. As a result, a decision would need to be made about whether to switch to a different Tier 2 instruction method, to deliver the same intervention with more frequency or duration, or to move this student to Tier 3, where a comprehensive evaluation would be considered in order to determine whether the student qualifies for special education services as a student with an SLD.

Progress-monitoring data are also used to inform decision making regarding SLD identification for special education eligibility purposes. Interested readers can learn more about this more controversial process on the textbook's accompanying webpage (go to http://www.wiley.com/college/kubiszyn and click on the link to the Student Companion Site).

RTI Approaches

Although there are variations, two approaches to the implementation of RTI predominate. They are known as the standard protocol (SP) approach and the problem-solving (PS) approach (Shapiro, 2009). As we will see, the differences between these approaches are most evident at Tier 2.

Standard Protocol Approach (SP) The SP approach to RTI includes the delivery of one clearly specified Tier 2 research-based intervention appropriate for the identified academic difficulty. Decisions are made according to clearly specified guidelines, and the instruction is also delivered according to clearly specified guidelines and procedures. The intervention is closely monitored to help ensure the fidelity of the treatment (i.e., that the instruction is delivered according to a research-based protocol). The same intervention is used for all struggling learners, which presents both advantages and disadvantages. Because the same intervention approach is used with all students, teachers and others who implement the intervention can become skilled and efficient in doing so with fidelity, potentially maximizing student learning. Training new teachers to implement SP RTI is also easier for the same reasons. Because the same intervention is used for all students, this approach also lends itself well to ongoing research and evaluation. On the other hand, individual differences in learning styles or learners may be given little if any consideration within SP approaches. Thus, the intervention may be more successful for some than for others who may require differentiated instruction (Tomlinson, 2004). Although SP approaches have considerable research support (see Torgeson et al., 2001) and have the advantage of quality control (Fuchs et al., 2003), whether the interventions can be implemented as effectively in the classroom by busy classroom teachers as opposed to dedicated research assistants has been controversial. SP approaches may also be limited in addressing the unique learning needs of children who are experiencing more severe deficits (Fuchs, 2003).

Problem-Solving Approach (PS) The problem-solving (PS) approach to RTI utilizes a team approach to the identification and analysis of a learning problem. The team then develops or identifies, implements, and evaluates an individualized intervention to address the learning problem. Thus, different students in the same classroom would typically have different instructional interventions (Tomlinson & McTighe, 2006).

Although the PS approach has the advantage of individualizing interventions to match the individual characteristics of each of the students, this benefit may be offset by the challenges inherent in this approach. Because many different interventions may be necessary within the same classroom, it is unlikely that the teacher will be equally skilled in all interventions. Obviously, having to learn multiple interventions rather than a single, standardized intervention will also be more challenging for new teachers. PS procedures may also lack specificity, allowing for flexibility across sites and also resulting in considerable variability in instructional decision making and in the implementation of the intervention. For these reasons, PS approaches are susceptible to difficulties with implementation integrity, a significant obstacle to large-scale RTI implementation (Burns, Vanderwood, & Ruby, 2005). Nevertheless, when implemented with integrity, PS approaches can be effective in improving student learning (Burns & Symington, 2002; Burns, Wiley, & Viglietta, 2008).

Table 3.1 compares and contrasts the PS and SP approaches to RTI implementation. As you can see, the main differences are evident at Tier 2.

Which Approach Is Best? At this point, there appears to be no right or wrong answer to this question. In large part, this is because the outcomes obtained under either the SP or PS approaches depend highly on the quality, or integrity, with which either approach is implemented. In other words, the choice of approach is probably less important than the accuracy and quality, integrity, and fidelity of the screening, the instructional interventions, the progress monitoring, and the decision making. We could spend the rest of this chapter, or an entire new chapter on the complexities associated with each of these issues in the implementation of RTI. We will not do so, however, because these are issues for policy makers, administrators, and researchers to fret over, rather than teachers in training.

TABLE 3.1 Comparing Problem Solving and Standard Protocol Approaches to RTI

Comparison of RTI Approaches

	Problem Solving	Standard Treatment Protocol
Universal screening	Class-wide assessment/universal screening is administered to identify students who are potentially struggling.	
Tier 1	All students receive high-quality instruction. Frequent progress monitoring is conducted to assess struggling students' performance levels and rates of improvement.	
Tier 2	Students whose progress in Tier 1 is not adequate receive additional support. 1. A team makes instructional decisions based on an individual student's performance. The team identifies the academic problem; determines its cause; and then develops, implements, and evaluates a plan to address the problem. 2. Students are presented with a variety of interventions, based on their unique needs and performance data. 3. Interventions are flexible and individualized to meet a student's needs.	Students whose progress in Tier 1 is not adequate receive additional support. 1. The person delivering the intervention makes instructional decisions following a standard protocol. 2. Students with similar needs are presented with one standard, research-validated intervention. 3. The intervention is delivered in a predetermined format that may address multiple skill sets. This allows for greater quality control (i.e., treatment fidelity is easier to monitor given the ease of implementing a single intervention).
Tier 3	Students whose progress is still insufficient in Tier 2 may receive even more intensive intervention. Depending on a state's or district's policies, some students may qualify for special education services based on their progress monitoring data. In some states or districts, they may receive either an abbreviated or comprehensive evaluation for the identification of a learning disability.	

Materials Created by The Iris Center (http://Iris.Peabody.Vanderbilt.Edu) for The National Association Of State Directors of Special Education's Idea Partnership, Sponsored by The U.S. Department Of Education, Office of Special Education Programs, 2007.

HOW WIDELY IS RTI BEING IMPLEMENTED?

Although RTI has now been adopted widely, RTI implementation across the nation has been uneven historically, as may be expected for a major reform initiative. Next, we will report the results of three surveys, two published in 2008 and another in 2011, to see how widely and well RTI is being implemented.

In August 2008, Hoover, Baca, Wexler-Love, and Saenz administered a survey to state special education directors in all 50 states and the District of Columbia, and 44 responses were received.

All reported that they are either currently implementing or are considering implementing some form of an RTI model, with 16 states (36%) in the planning stages and 28 states (64%) already implementing some form of RTI. Respondents also commented about the extent of implementation among individual schools within districts in their states. Seventeen indicated that less than 10% of the districts in their states were currently using an RTI model. Eleven respondents indicated that 10–25% of their districts were using an RTI model, four reported that 26–50% of their districts were using an RTI model, and only one respondent indicated that over 75% had implemented an RTI approach. A critical aspect of successful RTI implementation is training for current teachers and other personnel. Forty-one of the 44 respondents reported that training efforts were underway in their states, but 3 respondents reported that there were no statewide RTI training efforts in place. However, the survey did not attempt to assess the quantity or the quality of the training efforts that were in progress.

The results of a December 2008 informal online survey posted on the website of the RTI Action Network, an organization created to disseminate information about RTI, portrayed a different picture. More than 80% of the close to 800 people who responded rated their knowledge of RTI as "minimal to none." About 70% of respondents to the web survey reported working in schools that are planning to or just beginning to implement RTI. A little more than a third reported that their school districts have never offered professional development related to RTI, and another 17% said training was offered only once a year.

A more recent web-based survey of 1,390 respondents was completed in April 2011 by Global Scholar/Spectrum K12 School Solutions (2011), in collaboration with several respected national organizations, the American Association of School Administrators (AASA), Council for the Advancement and Support of Education (CASE), National Association of Departments of Special Education (NASDSE), and the RTI Action Network. According to this survey, RTI implementation has grown, with 68% of respondents indicating that their districts were either fully implementing RTI with integrity (24%) or were in the process of districtwide implementation (44%). However, when asked what percentage of individual schools within districts were fully implementing RTI with fidelity, the picture changed. Only 7% indicated that all schools were fully implementing RTI with fidelity and another 41% indicated that 50–99% of schools within districts were doing so. In short, more than half of the individual schools were not fully implementing RTI in 2011. Forty-four percent of districts did not yet have a formal RTI implementation plan, 5% of districts were still investigating RTI, and 1% were not yet considering RTI.

SOME BENEFITS OF RTI

Throughout this chapter, we have discussed many of the potential benefits of RTI, and we will only summarize those briefly here. Because RTI emphasizes early identification and effective, research-based instruction, it may benefit all children, including struggling learners who enter school with limited literacy and language proficiency, as well as children with disabilities. RTI integrates the following: (1) universal screening of all learners two to three times per year; (2) brief, repeated formative assessments with tiered instruction through data-based decision making; and (3) frequent, ongoing monitoring of student progress and instructional effectiveness for students receiving Tier 2 and Tier 3 instructions. To reduce the influence of measurement error that is associated with brief assessments and assessments administered at a single point in time, RTI requires the consideration of multiple data points (i.e., at least eight) for data-based decision making. In this way, a more accurate picture of the student may be possible since multiple data points allow for both current level of performance and growth over time to be considered. Interested readers are referred to this textbook's accompanying website for discussion of the potential advantages of RTI for the SLD identification process (go to http://www.wiley.com/college/kubiszyn and click on the link to the Student Companion Site).

RTI: THE PROMISE AND SOME CONTROVERSIES

The promise of RTI is that, when fully implemented with fidelity, general education teachers will be able to enhance learning for all students. Under properly implemented RTI, teachers can more quickly and accurately identify struggling learners and provide them with early research-based instruction and reduce costly referrals to special education. Along with the promise of RTI, however, comes controversy. Although some of the controversy parallels what might be expected from any attempt at systems change, other controversies reflect RTI-specific issues that will only be addressed by future research, and research-informed dissemination and implementation.

Technical Issues: Reliability, Validity, and Fairness

Various controversies related to the technical adequacy of universal screening measures (Jenkins, Hudson, & Johnson, 2007) and CBM progress monitoring await resolution. With regard to CBM, Christ and Ardoin (2009) concluded, "It is time to reexamine the evidence-base with regard to the technical and psychometric characteristics of CBM. The simplistic conclusion that CBM is valid and reliable is too broad and should be evaluated with reference to the particular decisions, purpose, and interpretation" (p. 72). After studying CBM writing probes for eighth-grade students, Amato and Watkins (2011) concluded that the probes offer promise, but that this promise may be limited to the elementary grades.

Controversy also exists around the overall RTI process as well. Fletcher (2008) noted the importance of evaluating the reliability and validity of the RTI decision making process. Braden, Kubiszyn, and Ortiz (2007) emphasized that further study was needed to determine whether the RTI process meets the reliability, validity, and fairness requirements of the *Standards for Educational and Psychological Tests* (American Educational Research Association, American Psychological Association, National Council on Measurement in Education, 1999). Orosco et al. (2007) noted that the lack of emphasis on culturally responsive RTI may have significant, potentially negative, long-term impacts on decision making for culturally and linguistically diverse learners throughout our schools.

Implementation Issues

As we noted earlier, although RTI implementation has increased substantially, implementation remains uneven. The National Joint Committee on Learning Disabilities (NJCLD) encouraged further study of RTI implementation "in order to guide its thoughtful implementation, advance the field of special education, and enhance the academic outcomes and life success of all students, including students with learning disabilities" (National Joint Committee on Learning Disabilities, 2005, p. 258). Jimerson, Burns, and VanDerHeyden (2007) concluded that although RTI shows considerable promise, "implementation integrity will be the most significant obstacle to overcome when implementing RTI on a national level" (p. 7).

The feasibility of evidence-based, differentiated instruction (Tomlinson, 2014) in the general education classroom is another issue. Interventions that are research-based but not feasible are not likely to be implemented with fidelity, which would undercut the validity of RTI decision making. Durability of response is another issue. If a student responds to relatively intensive but short-term Tier 2 research-based instruction, the assumption under RTI is that a disability has been ruled out. Although this may be true for many students, the difficulty may reemerge for others when the intensive instruction ceases. Finally, since RTI implementation requires a paradigm shift for many professionals, uncertainty, frustration, and resistance to change should all be expected as RTI implementation continues to increase across the country (Richards et al., 2007).

SUMMARY

This chapter introduced readers to the response-to-intervention (RTI) model. Its most important points were as follows:

1. Response to intervention (RTI) is a relatively new education reform initiative that is being rapidly phased into regular education classrooms.

2. RTI is a tiered system designed to integrate assessment, research-based instruction, and data-based decision making to improve educational outcomes for all students.

3. A three-tier model is most common, with each tier characterized by increasingly intensive, focused instruction delivered in smaller and smaller groups or even individually. Four-tier and five-tier models also exist but are much less common.

4. On average, approximately 80% of students would be expected to receive Tier 1 instruction, 15% Tier 2 instruction, and 5% Tier 3 instruction.

5. For Tier 2 and Tier 3 students, responsiveness to instruction is monitored on an ongoing (e.g., weekly) basis with brief, formative assessments such as curriculum-based measurement, or CBM.

6. RTI holds promise for earlier identification and more effective intervention with academic difficulties than has occurred previously.

7. Although controversial, RTI may also be used to facilitate identification of pupils with specific learning disabilities (SLD).

8. RTI may be a new concept to many because RTI did not exist in most states prior to release of the final regulations for the *Individuals with Disabilities Education Improvement Act* (IDEIA) in 2006; RTI implementation around the country has been increasing in recent years but remains uneven.

9. To date, the impact of RTI on regular education teachers has been varied, but RTI will likely have a significant impact on all teachers over time.

10. One type of a formative assessment, curriculum-based measurement (CBM), tends to be brief (e.g., 1-minute reading probes), can be administered and scored by regular teachers, and has adequate technical characteristics when used to progress monitor student responsiveness to instruction on an ongoing, weekly basis.

11. Unlike summative assessments, such as end-of-semester or annual tests, which are typically not sensitive to the small, incremental improvements in learning, curriculum-based measurement (CBM), and

other formative assessments are designed to be sensitive to such small incremental improvements in learning.

12. Although RTI definitions may vary, there is considerable agreement about the common components of RTI, which include universal screening; tiered, integrated research-based instruction; progress monitoring; and data-based decision making.

13. Tier 1 research-based instruction takes place in the regular classroom and is delivered to all students. Tier 1 is also known as primary prevention.

14. Tier 2 research-based instruction may take place in the regular classroom or a different location, may be delivered by the regular education teacher or a specialist, and is typically more intensive, focused, and delivered in different modalities than Tier 1 instruction. Tier 2 instruction may be delivered for one or more 8- to 12-week periods and is also known as secondary prevention.

15. Tier 3 research-based instruction tends to be even more intensive, focused, and frequent than Tier 2 instruction. Although it may be provided in the regular classroom, Tier 3 instruction is often delivered by special education staff and is often synonymous with what we traditionally considered to be special education. Tier 3 is also known as tertiary prevention.

16. Universal screening is another RTI component. Such screenings are administered two or more times per year to identify students at risk for academic difficulty. Commercial or state-developed screening instruments, benchmark tests, or other measures are all used for universal screening.

17. Progress monitoring is another important RTI component. Students receiving Tier 2 or Tier 3 instruction are progress monitored, usually on at least a weekly basis using formative assessments such as curriculum-based measurement (CBM) or other progress-monitoring tests to determine whether students are responding to the instruction provided. Although CBM is the most popular progress-monitoring tool, a variety of alternatives also exist.

18. Data-based decision making is another critical RTI component. Data-based decisions may be made using data from universal screening and/or progress monitoring. When CBM is used for progress monitoring, data-based decision making is enhanced by graphing the data points over time and comparing the student's actual CBM performance to expected CBM performance for the student's grade level. Decisions about responsiveness to intervention usually involve consideration of the level of skill development, as well as the rate of improvement in the academic skill.

19. There are two primary approaches to RTI implementation: standard protocol (SP) and problem solving (PS).

20. Standard protocol (SP) approaches require that the same research-based intervention be administered at Tier 2 for all students with academic difficulties. These approaches are less flexible than PS approaches, but tend to be easier to implement and have better research support.

21. Problem-solving (PS) approaches rely on a team approach to develop individualized interventions for each student with an academic difficulty. Although more flexible than SP approaches, they tend to be more difficult to implement and have less research support than SP approaches.

22. As with any innovation, RTI has great promise, but it has also generated much controversy around technical and implementation issues.

FOR DISCUSSION AND PRACTICE

1. While shopping at the local mall, you run into Ashley King, a former teacher at your school who moved to an adjacent district. When you ask whether things are different there from your district, she says, "Not all that much. The rumor is we're supposed to start something called RTI next year. All I know is that it's some sort of new testing requirement, probably has something to do with all the NCLB testing requirements." How would you reply to her? In your reply, be sure to

distinguish between general and special education reform and IDEIA and NCLB, and explain why RTI is about much more than simply testing or assessment.

*2. After attending an RTI implementation workshop, a fellow teacher asks you to distinguish between formative, interim, and summative assessment. (a) How would you respond? He then asks how widely RTI has been implemented across the country. (b) How would you respond?

3. Compare and contrast the primary RTI components: universal screening, tiered research-based instruction, progress monitoring, and data-based decision making.

*4. While visiting with your parents, both of whom are retired special education teachers, you mention that the new IDEIA is responsible for the school-wide RTI approach that

your district has recently adopted. In unison, they state, "You are mistaken. Federal special education legislation exists for the protection of special education students and has nothing to do with regular education students or teachers." How would you respond?

5. The use of brief, ongoing, formative assessments such as curriculum-based measurement (CBM) for progress monitoring to evaluate student responsiveness to instruction is a key component of RTI. What are the potential advantages of using formative assessments such as CBM probes for this purpose, and are there any potential disadvantages?

6. Compare and contrast the standard protocol and problem-solving approaches to RTI implementation.

*Answers to these questions appear in Appendix B.

CHAPTER 4

TESTING AND EDUCATIONAL DECISION MAKING

LEARNING OUTCOMES

After completing this chapter, the student will be able to:

1. Describe the primary reason we administer tests and assessments.
2. Explain why classroom teachers must be concerned with accountability demands.
3. Describe how the IDEIA has changed the role of the regular education teacher today compared to a couple of decades ago.
4. Compare and contrast the types of educational decisions outlined in the text.
5. Give examples of each type of decision.
6. Discriminate between how and what we measure.
7. Compare and contrast the various types of tests used in education and their appropriate uses.

IN THE CLASSROOM, decisions are constantly being made. As a teacher, you may decide:

John, Don, Marie, and Jeri are ready to advance to level 7 in reading, but Chris and Linda are not.

Keisha receives an A; Mary receives a C.

Ed has difficulty discriminating between long and short vowel sounds.

My teaching method is not effective for this group of students.

Mike's attitude toward school has improved.

Pablo should be moved to a higher reading group.

Mrs. Morrison's class is better at math concepts than my class.

Donna has not responded to Tier 2 instruction in our response-to-intervention approach.

On what basis do teachers make decisions such as these? In some cases, the teacher relies solely on personal judgment. In other cases, the teacher relies solely on measurement data obtained through the assessment process. In still other cases, the teacher combines measurement data with judgment or subjective data. Which approach is best?

Antitest advocates suggest that testing should be done away with. Unfortunately, tests or no tests, decisions will still have to be made. Teachers, as human beings, are subject to good and bad days, biases, student and parent pressures, faulty perceptions, and a variety of other influences. In other words, relying solely on a teacher's judgment means relying on a subjective decision making process. Naturally, no teacher would intentionally make a "wrong" decision about a student. However, all of us make mistakes.

Tests represent an attempt to provide objective data that can be used along with background and other contextual information (i.e., through the assessment process described in Chapter 1) with subjective impressions to make better, more defensible educational decisions. This is the reason we test in education: to make informed and defensible educational decisions. Tests are not subject to the ups and downs or other influences that affect teachers. Subjective impressions can often place in perspective important aspects of a decision making problem for which no objective data exist. Thus, it seems likely that a combination of subjective judgments and objective data obtained through the assessment process will result in more appropriate rather than less appropriate decisions. Reliance on test data alone can even prove to be detrimental to decision making. Although test data are objective, we must remember that they are only estimates of a student's behavior. Test data are never 100% accurate!

In summary, we test to provide objective information, which we combine with background and contextual information and our subjective, commonsense impressions to make better informed, data-based educational decisions. However, suggesting that combining objective measurement data and subjective impressions results in better educational decisions assumes that:

- Measurement data are valid.
- The teacher or individual interpreting such data understands the uses and limitations of such data.

Unfortunately, too often one or both of these assumptions are violated in the decision making process. Obviously, when this happens, the resultant educational decisions may be less valid than we would like.

TESTING, ACCOUNTABILITY, AND THE CLASSROOM TEACHER

It is no longer surprising to say that some Americans have become disenchanted with U.S. education. Reduced school budgets, defeated bond issues, and the elimination of special programs are common occurrences, especially during difficult economic times. The reasons for this disenchantment are many and complex, but at least some can be traced to poor decision making in our schools—decision making not just at the classroom level, but at the grade, school, district, state, and national levels as well. Nevertheless, the most frequently made decisions are the everyday decisions of the classroom teacher, which also form the cornerstone for other decisions at higher levels of the educational structure. If the cornerstone is weak, the structure itself cannot be sound.

At the classroom level, the extent to which unsound educational decision making occurs is not yet known. However, the everyday decisions of classroom teachers are coming under ever closer scrutiny. Classroom teachers are increasingly being asked questions such as the following:

PARENT: On what grounds was Jane moved to the lower reading group?

PRINCIPAL: Are your students well prepared for the Common Core aligned high-stakes test next week?

COUNSELOR: How is it that you've determined Tom's behavior exceeds normal limits?

PARENT: Is Billie performing at a level in math that will help us make Adequate Yearly Progress (AYP)?

RTI COORDINATOR: How many of your students are below the 25th percentile on our universal screening test?

Today, teachers are faced with an even wider range of decisions than was the case a decade ago. We describe how federal legislation has expanded the regular classroom teacher's reach into the once largely separate realm of special education. Then we describe the different types of educational decisions that are often based on tests results and an informed assessment process.

Special Learners, the Regular Curriculum, and Annual Assessments

Once it was the case that regular classroom teachers had only limited contact with special education students. In Chapters 1 through 3, we described some of the responsibilities of classroom teachers under the *No Child Left Behind* (NCLB) *Act*, the *Individuals with Disabilities Education Improvement Act* (IDEIA), and the Race to the Top (RTT) initiative. Regular education teachers are now expected to help both regular and special education students make Adequate Yearly Progress (AYP) under NCLB and to frequently monitor the progress of students receiving Tier 2 or 3 instruction, where RTI has been implemented (see Chapter 3). Regular education teachers are also required to be members of the special education Individual Educational Plan (IEP) teams. Teachers now have to include and assess students with disabilities in the regular curriculum to help the IEP team determine performance and progress and to provide parents with regular reports of progress. While special education staff may assist in this task, it is regular, not special education, teachers who are experts in the regular curriculum. As a result, regular education teachers may now expect to hear questions such as the following:

SPECIAL ED TEACHER: We need weekly progress monitoring results to make a data-based decision about whether Billie's responding to instruction for the IEP team meeting next week. What do you have?

PRINCIPAL: The annual CTBS [i.e., a standardized test battery] testing is next month. Based on what you know from testing Billie in the regular classroom, do we need to recommend special accommodations for him to take it?

IDEIA also extends the teacher's involvement with students with disabilities to require participation in behavior plan development, implementation, and evaluation when behavior impedes progress in the general curriculum. As a result, classroom teachers can now expect to hear these kinds of questions:

PARENT: What evidence do you have that Billie's behavior plan is working?

SCHOOL PSYCHOLOGIST: Is Billie's behavior plan working in the regular classroom? What about his attitude? Attitudes can affect behavior, so it would be nice to know whether his attitude toward being in the regular class has changed.

To respond to questions about behavior, teachers will need more than data about achievement, they will also have to collect data about the student's behavior. On the textbook's accompanying webpage (go to http://www.wiley.com/college/kubiszyn and click on the link to the Student Companion Site), we describe a number of measures, both teacher-made and standardized, that classroom teachers can use to collect classroom-based achievement, behavioral, social, and attitudinal information. This information can be invaluable to the IEP team (including the regular education teacher) in developing and evaluating progress in the general curriculum and behavior plans.

Clearly, the requirements of IDEIA and the implementation of RTI will place increased demands on the regular education teacher's time and skill. What does the teacher do? Give up? Complain? Yearn for the "good old days"? We hope not! Yet, the answers to these and many other questions need to be provided if the educational achievement of all learners is to improve.

Fortunately, in passing IDEIA Congress recognized that regular education teachers must be given support to achieve the goals of the new law. Like NCLB before it, IDEIA (and RTI) require increased staff development resources and support for regular education teachers to meet their demands. And the task may not be as overwhelming as it may appear at first glance. Many of the techniques that regular education teachers currently use to assess regular education students are readily applicable to the assessment of special learners. A good working knowledge and understanding of testing and measurement—what you will have on successful completion of this course—will help you meet the requirements of IDEIA, NCLB, and RTI.

The successful regular education teacher of tomorrow will have to report formative, interim, and summative test and assessment data to parents, principals, counselors, academic review committees, and even the courts. In addition to reporting those data, teachers also will have to interpret test data and be fully aware of the uses and limitations of such data. One of the first steps toward acquiring the ability to interpret test data is to understand the different types of educational decisions that are made based on test and measurement data.

Types of Educational Decisions

Measurement data enter into decisions at all levels of education from those made by the individual classroom teacher to those made by the U.S. Department of Education. There are several ways of categorizing these decisions. We have found the following classification approach, suggested by Thorndike (2004), useful for understanding the various types of decisions that can be made in schools. The categories range from specific everyday in-class decision making to much less frequent administrative decisions. The categories of decisions discussed here are instructional, grading, diagnostic, selection, placement, counseling and guidance, program or curriculum, and administrative policy.

Instructional Decisions Instructional decisions are the nuts-and-bolts types of decisions made by all classroom teachers. In fact, these are the most frequently made decisions in education. Examples of such decisions include the following:

Spending more time in math class on addition with regrouping.

Skipping the review you planned before the test.

Making a referral for Tier 3 instruction or special education evaluation.

Sticking to your instructional plan.

Since educational decisions at classroom levels have a way of affecting decisions at higher levels, it is important that these types of decisions be sound ones. Deciding that more time should be spent on addition with regrouping when it doesn't need to be wastes valuable instructional time and also may have negative effects on achievement in other areas or on classroom behavior. Students may get turned off, tune you out, or act up. You may expect similar detrimental effects when you present material too quickly. Moving too quickly almost invariably results in skill deficiencies in some students. The introduction of RTI, with its ongoing progress-monitoring requirement, holds promise to enhance decision making in cases like these.

Today, instructional decisions are also linked to NCLB accountability requirements and progress toward achievement of Common Core Standards (in states that have adopted them). If students do not do well on valid classroom tests or on formative progress-monitoring measures (such as curriculum-based measurement, or CBM), they are likely to do poorly on benchmark and annual academic assessments.

Grading Decisions To assign grades, the classroom teacher also makes educational decisions but much less frequently than instructional decisions. Grades, or marks (see Chapter 12), are usually assigned about every 6–9 weeks, and the teacher often considers test scores and other data in making decisions about who gets As, Bs, and so on. If test data are used, naturally it is important that such data be acquired from appropriate tests, including performance and portfolio assessments, which will be described in detail in Chapters 9 and 10. Teacher-made tests are usually the most appropriate for grading decisions, although data from brief, frequent formative assessments may be used as well.

Other factors such as attendance, ability, attitude, behavior, and effort are sometimes graded as well. A common mistake is to combine one or more of these factors with achievement data to decide on grades. Although each factor represents an area of legitimate concern to classroom teachers, and assigning grades for one or more of these factors is perfectly acceptable, these grades should be kept separate from grades for achievement. These issues will be discussed at length in Chapter 12. Methods used to measure nonachievement factors are presented on this textbook's accompanying webpage (go to http://www.wiley.com/college/kubiszyn and click on the link to the Student Companion Site).

Grade inflation—or the tendency for teachers to assign higher grades today than in the past for the same level of performance—has become a matter of considerable public concern. Annual academic assessments under NCLB, Common Core tests, and state high-stakes testing programs that are used to make decisions about student promotion and graduation have helped bring grading concerns to the public's attention. Consequently, it will be no surprise if grading decisions and policies come under increasing public scrutiny and accountability in the future.

For most students, grading decisions may be the most influential decisions made about them during their school years. All students are familiar with the effects grades have on them, their peers, and their parents. Given all the attention and seriousness afforded to grades today, it is advisable for teachers to invest extra care and time in these important decisions, since they may be called on to defend their decisions more frequently in the future. The teacher who is most likely to be able to defend the grades that are assigned will be the teacher who (1) adheres to an acceptable grading policy; (2) uses data obtained through multiple, appropriate measurement instruments; and (3) knows the uses and limitations of such data.

Diagnostic Decisions Diagnostic decisions are those made about a student's strengths and weaknesses and the reason or reasons for them. For example, a teacher may notice in teacher-made or formative, interim, or summative test results that Ryan can successfully subtract four-digit numbers from four-digit numbers, but not if borrowing is involved. Given this information, the teacher decides that Ryan does not fully understand the borrowing process. The teacher has made a diagnostic decision based, at least in part, on information yielded typically by an informal, teacher-made test or a formative assessment. Such decisions can also be made with the help of a standardized test, but because they are administered at the end of the semester or year, they tend to be too infrequent to inform day-to-day instructional decision making.

Because diagnostic decisions are of considerable importance, we believe that objective test data should always be used along with the teacher's subjective judgment to make such decisions. In the past, important diagnostic decisions often have been delegated to specialists. Under IDEIA, however, the regular education teacher is increasingly expected to make diagnostic decisions to facilitate the progress of struggling learners in the general curriculum. This increased emphasis on diagnostic decision making results from the inclusion of students with disabilities in the regular classroom and the increasing implementation of response-to-intervention (RTI) approaches across the country (see Chapters 1 and 3).

The three types of decisions listed—instructional, grading, and diagnostic—are types of educational decisions every classroom teacher must make. The five remaining types of decisions are made by specialists, administrators, or committees composed of teachers, specialists, and administrators. Historically, these decisions were typically based on summative, standardized tests rather than teacher-made tests. Although teachers are not directly involved in decisions based on standardized test data, parents often turn to teachers to explain and interpret standardized test results and other tests that may be in a student's cumulative file. Standardized testing and score interpretation to parents will be discussed in detail in Chapters 19 and 20. The extent to which formative assessments such as CBM and the RTI process play a role in these types of decisions varies from state to state (see Chapter 3), depending on the extent to which states have implemented the RTI process. For now, let's get familiar with the types of decisions in which standardized tests play the most prominent role.

Selection Decisions Selection decisions involve test data used in part for accepting or rejecting applicants for admission into a group, program, or institution. The SAT or ACT that you probably took before being admitted to college and the Graduate Record Examination (GRE) that you will be required to take if you intend to go to graduate school are examples of standardized tests that are used to help make selection decisions. At the elementary and secondary school level, teachers are often asked to assist with testing pupils for selection into private schools or remedial programs that are designed to improve educational opportunities for economically disadvantaged students.

Placement Decisions Placement decisions are made after an individual has been accepted into a program. They involve determining where in a program someone is best suited to begin work. For example, you may have had to take an English test prior to freshman college registration to determine whether you were ready for first-year college English courses, needed remedial work, or were ready for intermediate or advanced courses. Standardized achievement test data are often used in elementary and secondary schools for placing students in courses that match their current level of functioning.

Counseling and Guidance Decisions Counseling and guidance decisions involve the use of test data to help recommend programs of study that are likely to be appropriate for a student. For example, in your junior or senior year in high school, you may have taken the Differential Aptitude Test (DAT) or some similar aptitude test battery. Partly on the basis of your scores, your guidance counselor may have recommended that you consider one or more career paths or apply to a particular set of colleges.

Program or Curriculum Decisions Program or curriculum decisions are usually made at the school district level after an evaluation study comparing two or more programs has been completed. Your district's decision to abandon a traditional math program in favor of a new math program is an example of a program or curriculum decision. Teachers are often required to participate in these studies and even to help collect test data for them.

Administrative Policy Decisions Administrative policy decisions may be made at the school, district, state, or national level. These decisions tend to be strongly influenced by measurement data. Such decisions, for example, may determine the amount of money to be channeled into a school or district; whether a school or district is entitled to special funding; or what needs to be done to improve a school, district, or the nation's achievement scores. In Chapter 2 we discussed NCLB, Common Core Standards and tests aligned with them, and state high-stakes testing programs and the types of decisions with which they are now associated. Typically, these decisions have the most impact on students or on school staff. The decisions that have the most direct impact on students are the following:

Promotion decisions—whether a student's score is at or above the cutoff established to allow the student to be promoted to the next grade, whether the student will be offered an opportunity for remedial instruction, or whether the student is retained and must repeat the year.

Graduation decisions—whether a student's score is at or above the cutoff established to allow the student to obtain a high school diploma, or whether the student must retake the test.

The decisions that have the most direct impact on school staff include the following:

Reconstitution—if a class, school, or district's performance on a high-stakes test is unacceptably low, or fails to make Adequate Yearly Progress (AYP), a teacher, principal, or some or all school staff may be replaced or "reconstituted" in an effort to break a pattern of low achievement.

Recognition—if a class, school, or district's performance on a high-stakes test is high enough the class, teacher, school, principal, district, or superintendent may qualify for financial or other incentives, including recognition at local, state, and national gatherings designed to recognize exemplary or high-performing classes, school, and districts.

Thus far, we have considered why we test, and the types of decisions we make based on test results. Next, let's consider two other aspects of educational measurement: how we measure and what we measure. To introduce you to the issues, we take a short trip into the kitchen and then into the classroom.

A Pinch of Salt

Jean-Pierre, the master French chef, was watching Marcel, who was Jean-Pierre's best student, do a flawless job of preparing the master's hollandaise sauce. Suddenly, Jean-Pierre began pummeling Marcel with his fists. "Fool!" he shouted. "I said a pinch of salt, not a pound!" Jean-Pierre was furious. He threatened to pour the sauce over Marcel's head, but before he could, Marcel indignantly emptied the whole salt container into the pot.

"There, you old goat, I only added a pinch to begin with, but now there is a pound of salt in the sauce—and I'm going to make you eat it!"

Startled by his student's response, Jean-Pierre regained his composure. "All right, all right. So you didn't add a pound, but you certainly added more than a pinch!" Still upset, Marcel shouted, "Are you senile? You were watching me all the time and you saw me add only one pinch!" Marcel pressed his right thumb and index finger together an inch from the master's nose to emphasize his point. "Aha! You see! There you have it!" Jean-Pierre said. "That is not the way to measure a pinch. Only the tips of the thumb and index finger make contact when you measure a pinch!"

Marcel looked at the difference between his idea of a "pinch" of salt and the master's. Indeed, there was quite a difference. Marcel's finger and thumb made contact not just at the fingertips, but all the way down to the knuckle. At Jean-Pierre's request, they both deposited a "pinch" of salt on the table. Marcel's pinch contained four or five times as much salt as Jean-Pierre's.

Who is correct? Is Marcel's pinch too much? Is Jean-Pierre's pinch too little? Whose method would you use to measure a pinch of salt? Perhaps relying on an established standard will help.

Webster's New Collegiate Dictionary defines a pinch this way: "As much as may be taken between the finger and the thumb." If *Webster's* is our standard of comparison, we may conclude that both Jean-Pierre and Marcel are correct. Yet, we see that Marcel's pinch contains a lot more salt than Jean-Pierre's. It seems we have a problem. Until Marcel and Jean-Pierre decide on who is correct and adopt a more specific or standard definition of a "pinch," they may never resolve their argument. Furthermore, if we were to try to match the recipes they develop for their culinary masterpieces, we might never succeed unless we know which measuring method to use.

This measurement problem resulted from the lack of a clear, reliable, unambiguous method of measurement. Who is to say Jean-Pierre's method is better than Marcel's or vice versa? In Jean-Pierre's eyes, his method is correct, and Marcel's is not. In Marcel's eyes, his method is correct, and Jean-Pierre's is not. According to *Webster's*, both are correct. A clear and unambiguous method of measuring a "pinch" would resolve the problem. It seems reasonable to suggest that any time measurement procedures—that is, how we measure—are somewhat subjective and lack specificity, similar interpretive problems may arise.

"Pinching" in the Classroom

Mr. Walsh assigns his history grades based entirely on his monthly tests and a comprehensive final examination. He takes attendance, comments on homework assignments, encourages classroom participation, and tries to help his students develop positive attitudes toward history, but none of these is considered in assigning grades. Mr. Carter, another history teacher, assigns grades in the following manner:

Monthly tests 20%

Comprehensive final 20%

Homework 10%

Attendance 20%

Class participation 15%

Attitude 15%

Both teachers assign roughly the same numbers of As, Bs, Cs, Ds, and Fs each semester. Does an A in Mr. Walsh's class mean the same thing as an A in Mr. Carter's class? Obviously, Mr. Walsh "pinches" more heavily when it comes to test data than does Mr. Carter (100% vs 40%). On the other hand, Mr. Carter "pinches" more heavily on attendance and participation in assigning grades than does Mr. Walsh (35% vs 0%).

Which method is correct? In interpreting grades earned in each class, would you say that students who earn As in either class are likely to do equally well on history tests constructed by a third teacher? Should Mr. Walsh "pinch," that is, assign grades, more like Mr. Carter, or should Mr. Carter assign grades more like Mr. Walsh? Obviously, there are no easy answers to these questions. The differences in how chefs Jean-Pierre and Marcel measure a pinch of salt result from the lack of a clear, unambiguous definition of a pinch. Similarly, the differences in how Mr. Walsh and Mr. Carter measure learning in history result from the lack of a clear, unambiguous definition of what constitutes a grade. As a result, their grades represent somewhat different aspects of their student's performance. The way they "pinch" or how they measure differs.

For Jean-Pierre and Marcel, there is a relatively easy way out of the disagreement. Only their method of measurement or how they measure is in question, not what they are measuring. It would be easy to develop a small container, a common standard, that could then be used to uniformly measure pinches of salt. In the classroom, the task is more difficult for Mr. Walsh and Mr. Carter. What is in question is not only their measurement method, or how they weight components of a grade, but what they are measuring.

Much of what we measure or attempt to measure in the classroom is not clearly defined. For example, think of how many different ways you have heard learning, intelligence, or adjustment defined. Yet, we constantly attempt to assess or measure these traits. Furthermore, the methods we use to measure these often ill-defined traits are not very precise. But even good methods cannot accurately measure ill-defined or undefined traits.

Only when both what to measure and how to measure have been considered, specified, and clearly defined can we hope to eliminate the problems involved in measuring and interpreting classroom information. The task is formidable. We cannot hope to solve it entirely, but we can minimize the subjectivity, the inaccuracy, and the more common interpretative errors that are often inherent in classroom measurement. Achieving these goals will go far toward helping us "pinch" properly. Sound measurement practice will benefit you professionally. Moreover, it will benefit mostly those unwitting and captive receptors of measurement practice, your students.

The examples presented are intended to alert you to two general problems encountered in classroom measurement:

1. Defining what it is that you want to measure.
2. Determining how to measure whatever it is that you are measuring.

WHAT TO MEASURE

Defining what to measure may, at first glance, not appear like much of a problem but consider the following example:

> Mrs. Norton taught first-year math in a small high school with high-achieving students. She prided herself on her tests, which stressed the ability to apply math concepts to real-life situations. She did this by constructing fairly elaborate word problems. When she moved to another part of the state, she went to work in another more heterogeneous high school teaching an introductory math skills course. Realizing that her new students were not nearly as "sharp" as her other students, she "toned down" her tests by substituting simpler computations in her word problems. Even with this substitution, 29 of her 31 students failed the "easier" test. Dejected, she substituted even simpler computations into her next test, only to have 30 out of 31 fail. She concluded that her students "totally lack even basic math skills," and applied for a transfer.

Think about these questions:

Do you agree with Mrs. Norton's conclusion? If so, why? If not, why not?

Are there any possible alternative conclusions?

What might she have done differently?

We disagree with Mrs. Norton. While it may be that some of her students lack or are weak in basic math skills, there seems to be little conclusive evidence that all, or even most, lack these skills. There may be another explanation for her students' poor performance.

Her tests were originally designed to measure the ability of her high-achieving students to apply their skills to real-life situations. This is what she wanted to measure. In her more heterogeneous school assignment, what Mrs. Norton wanted to measure was a bit different. What she wanted to measure was not the ability to apply skills (at least not at first) but whether the skills were ever acquired. How she measured must also be considered. Her tests consisted of fairly elaborate word problems. They may have been tests of reading ability as much as tests of math applications. Their reading level may have been appropriate for her "bright" students but too advanced for her new students. Since her tests measured skill application and reading ability rather than skill acquisition, how Mrs. Norton measured also was not appropriate. Assuming you are convinced that it is important to define what you are measuring, let's look in more detail at what we mean by determining how to measure.

HOW TO MEASURE

Mrs. Norton got into trouble mainly because she wasn't sure what she was measuring. At least by giving a written test she had the right idea about one aspect of how to measure basic math skills . . . . Or did she? How else could basic math skills be measured? An oral test, you say? But in a class of 31 students? Any other ideas? What about a questionnaire without any math problems, just questions about math skills to which students respond yes or no to indicate whether they believe they have acquired a certain skill? How about simply observing your students in the process of completing a math problem? Or how about requiring your students to complete a practical project requiring math skills? The techniques mentioned are all possible measurement methods, some for measuring basic math skills, others for measuring attitudes toward math. Questionnaires, oral responses, observation, and projects are common methods of measurement. These and a variety of performance assessment techniques, including portfolios, will be discussed in Chapters 9 and 10. For now, simply be aware that there are alternatives to written tests and that how we measure is often determined by what we measure. Let's return to Mrs. Norton and the most commonly used form of measurement, the written test.

Written Tests

The test Mrs. Norton used was heavily verbal, which suggests that it relied almost exclusively on words to ask questions. Although the answers to her questions may have been numerical, the questions themselves were word problems. While there is probably no better way to measure basic math skills than through a written test, was the written test that Mrs. Norton used the best type of written test? We would say no and suggest that her test should have looked more like the following instead of consisting of only word problems:

$$(1)\quad \begin{array}{r} 1431 \\ +\ 467 \end{array} \qquad (2)\quad \begin{array}{r} 798 \\ -\ 581 \end{array} \qquad (3)\quad \begin{array}{r} 125 \\ \times\ 7 \end{array} \qquad (4)\quad 21 \div 11 =$$

The advantages of a basic math skills test with items similar in format to those here include the following:

- The items do not rely on reading ability.
- Basic skills are measured directly.
- More items can be included in the same amount of test time.

TABLE 4.1 Types of Written Tests.

Type of Written Test	Description
Verbal	Emphasizes reading, writing, or speaking. Most tests in education are verbal tests.
Nonverbal	Does not require reading, writing, or speaking ability. Tests composed of numerals or drawings are examples.
Objective	Refers to the scoring of tests. When two or more scorers can easily agree on whether an answer is correct or incorrect, the test is an objective one. True–false, multiple-choice, and matching tests are the best examples.
Subjective	Also refers to scoring. When it is difficult for two scorers to agree on whether an item is correct or incorrect, the test is a subjective one. Essay tests are examples.
Teacher-made	Tests constructed entirely by teachers for use in the teachers' classrooms.
Standardized	Tests constructed by measurement experts over a period of years. They are designed to measure broad, national objectives and have a uniform set of instructions that are adhered to during each administration. Most also have tables of norms, to which a student's performance may be compared to determine where the student stands in relation to a national sample of students at the same grade or age level.
Power	Tests with liberal time limits that allow each student to attempt each item. Items tend to be difficult.
Speed	Tests with time limits so strict that no one is expected to complete all items. Items tend to be easy.

All these points are important. The first two points help ensure that the test measures what it is supposed to measure (i.e., the test's validity, see Chapter 16). The last point improves the test's score reliability (see Chapter 17), or the consistency of the scores it yields over time. Furthermore, inspecting a student's written work on such a test can help you diagnose errors in the process used by students to arrive at an answer.

So, you see, there can be different types of written tests. The point of our discussion about Mrs. Norton is simply that how you measure must always match what you measure. Whether you give word problems, use number formats, or provide real-world examples depends on whether you are measuring problem-solving ability, knowledge of facts or processes, application, and so on. Table 4.1 defines some common types of written tests.

In this section, we have considered the importance of knowing what we want to measure and how we want to measure. We also saw that determining what and how may not be as simple as it appears. However, both considerations are vitally important in classroom measurement, since failing to be clear about them is likely to result in invalid measurement.

SUMMARY

This chapter has introduced you to why we test, what we test, and how we test. Its major points are as follows:

1. The primary reason why we test in education is to collect objective information that may be used in conjunction with subjective information to make better educational decisions.

2. In our age of increasing demands for accountability, it has become imperative that teachers be able to understand and demonstrate the role that test data can play in educational decision making.

3. Classroom teachers are responsible for the bulk of educational decision making, such as everyday instructional decisions, grading decisions, and diagnostic decisions. Such decisions are often based, or ought to be based, on information obtained from teacher-made tests and brief formative assessments like CBM. With the passage of NCLB and IDEIA, regular education teachers increasingly will be required to include students with disabilities in classroom testing as well.

4. Other, less frequent kinds of educational decisions are usually made by administrators or specialists other than the classroom teacher. These include decisions about selection, placement, counseling and guidance, programs and curriculum, and administration. Such decisions are usually based on information obtained from annual summative, standardized tests.

5. Measurement problems may be expected any time testing procedures lack definition or specificity, or when we fail to clearly specify the trait we are measuring.

6. Specifying or defining what we want to measure often determines how the trait should be measured.

FOR DISCUSSION AND PRACTICE

1. Identify some of the ways we measure "pinches" of achievement, intelligence, and classroom conduct.

2. Make a list of all the different kinds of behaviors you will need to measure, formally or informally, during your first month of teaching. Identify two different ways of measuring each of these behaviors.

3. List some of the instructional, grading, and diagnostic decisions you will be expected to make during your first month of teaching. Identify which category each decision represents.

4. Using Mrs. Norton's problem as a guide, make up some examples in your own subject area that illustrate mismatches between what is being tested and how it is being tested.

5. Think about our discussion about the effects of different populations on a test's usefulness in Chapter 1. How does this apply to Mrs. Norton's problem?

CHAPTER 5

NORM-REFERENCED AND CRITERION-REFERENCED TESTS AND CONTENT VALIDITY EVIDENCE

LEARNING OUTCOMES

After completing this chapter, the student will be able to:

1. Distinguish between norm- and criterion-referenced tests.
2. Explain why it is necessary to decide on the type of information desired before deciding on the type of test to administer.
3. Compare and contrast the advantages and disadvantages of norm- and criterion-referenced tests.
4. Explain how a test may be used for both norm- and criterion-referenced purposes.
5. Identify the reasons why linguistic and cultural sensitivities are important in administering and interpreting tests.
6. Explain why specialized norms tables may be useful adjuncts to national norms when interpreting results from diverse student populations.
7. Define content validity.
8. Explain why content validity is most important for classroom achievement tests.
9. Describe the three-stage classroom measurement model and give examples of each stage.
10. Explain why mastery is less certain with norm-referenced tests than with criterion-referenced tests.
11. Describe the process by which broad, general goals become specific instructional objectives.
12. Compare and contrast goals, program objectives, and instructional objectives.
13. Discriminate between specific instructional or behavioral objectives and general or expressive objectives.
14. Explain how instructional objectives can make a teacher's job easier.

IN CHAPTER 4, we stated that the primary reason for educational testing is to provide objective data that can be used along with subjective impressions to make better educational decisions. In this chapter, we begin by discussing norm-referenced and criterion-referenced tests. These types of tests give us different types of information. Both inform us about how well students are performing, but they are based on different approaches to testing (i.e., "how" we measure). We will then discuss how our ability to clarify "what" we want to measure can help us decide "how" we measure to ensure that our test measures what we intend it to (i.e., that the test has evidence of its content validity).

DEFINING NORM-REFERENCED (NRT) AND CRITERION-REFERENCED (CRT) TESTS

One type of information tells us where a student stands compared to other students. In other words, certain kinds of test data help us determine a student's "place" or "rank." This is accomplished by comparing the student's performance to a norm or an average of performances by other, similar students. A test that yields this kind of information is called a *norm-referenced test* (NRT). Such information is useful only for certain types of decisions, which we will discuss later in this chapter.

A second type of information provided by tests tells us about a student's level of proficiency in or mastery of some skill or set of skills. This is accomplished by comparing a student's performance to a standard of mastery called a criterion. A test that yields this kind of information is called a *criterion-referenced test* (CRT) because the information it conveys refers to a comparison with a criterion or an absolute standard. Such information helps us decide whether a student needs more or less work on some skill or set of skills. It says nothing about the student's place or rank compared to other students, and, hence, it too is useful only for certain types of decisions. Figure 5.1 illustrates the relationship of NRTs and CRTs to the purpose of testing.

As you may have guessed, it is important to identify the type of information you need before you administer a test. If you fail to do so, you may have test data but be unable to use the data to make necessary decisions. Too often teachers, parents, and others report that they know little or

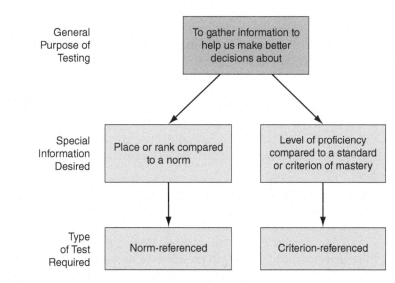

FIGURE 5.1 Relationships among the purpose of testing, information desired, and the type of test required.

nothing more about students after testing than before. This can result when decision makers fail to clearly identify the purpose of testing before selecting and administering a test. In such cases, teachers, parents, and others may be quick to denounce or blame the test, not recognizing that this frustrating outcome may be the result of a failure to identify the purpose of testing prior to testing. Attempts to use existing test data may be equally frustrating if test users are not clear about the kinds of information NRTs and CRTs yield. Consider the following:

> *Pat, the counselor, was checking her records when she heard a knock at the door. It was Mary, a sixth-grade teacher.*

PAT: Come in. What can I do for you?

MARY: I just stopped by to get the latest test information you have on Danny. As you know, he's going to be in my class this year after being in remedial classes for the last 5 years. Mrs. French, his teacher last year, said you have all the test information on him.

PAT: Well, I'd be glad to help out. In fact, I was just reviewing his folder.

MARY: Great! Can I see it?

PAT: Well, his Math Cluster score on the Woodcock-Johnson is at the sixth percentile, and his Reading Cluster is at the first percentile. Good luck with him.

MARY: Boy, he sure is low. I guess that's why he's been in the remedial classroom for so long.

PAT: You're right.

MARY: Okay. That's about what I was expecting. Now what about his skill levels?

PAT: What do you mean?

MARY: You know, his academic skill levels.

PAT: Oh, his grade levels! Now let's see, his math grade equivalent is 2.6, and his reading grade equivalent is even lower, 1.7.

MARY: That's not really what I need to know. I know he's way below grade level, but I'm wondering about his skills—specific skills, that is. You know, like what words he can read, what phonetic skills he has, whether he can subtract two-digit numbers with regrouping… things like that.

PAT: (*Becoming a bit irritated*) Mary, what more do you need than what I've given you? Don't you know how to interpret these scores? Perhaps you should have taken a tests and measurements course in college.

MARY: (*Beginning to get frustrated*) Pat, I have taken a tests and measurements course and I do know what those scores mean, but they only compare Danny to other students. I'm not interested in that. I want to know what he can and can't do, so I can begin teaching him at the proper skill level.

PAT: (*Shaking her head*) Look, he's at a first-grade level in reading and second-grade level in math. Isn't that enough?

MARY: But what level of mastery has he demonstrated?

PAT: Mastery? He's years behind! He has mastered very little of anything.

MARY: This has been a very enlightening conversation. Thank you for your time.

It appears that there is a communication gap between Mary and Pat. Pat has provided a lot of test data to Mary, yet Mary doesn't seem to care about it. Pat is frustrated, Mary is frustrated, and little that may be of help to Danny has resulted. Why? Just what is the problem? Is it Pat or is it Mary? Or is it something else?

Take another look at the situation. Do you think Mary was being unreasonable? Why did Pat seem satisfied that she had provided the necessary data? Should Mary's course in tests and measurements have helped her "understand" the test data better? What if Danny's mother were asking the questions instead of Mary—would the outcome have been different? Finding answers to these questions may help us. Let's consider each of these in turn.

Was Mary being unreasonable? Mary's questions were specific: Does he have phonetic skills? Can he subtract two-digit numbers with regrouping? Certainly these are not unreasonable questions. She was probably expecting answers that were fairly specific. Maybe something like "yes" or "no" or maybe something like "about 80% of the time" or "about 20% of the time." Responses like these would have helped her plan instruction for Danny. She would know which skills he had mastered, which he was a little deficient in, and which would require a lot of work. However, the grade-equivalent and percentile scores that Pat reported provided her with none of this information. No wonder she was frustrated.

Then why was Pat reporting these scores? Obviously, they were close at hand, and she probably thought she was conveying useful information. Actually, she was conveying useful information; it just wasn't very useful in this particular case. She may have thought she was answering Mary's questions by relaying this information.

Does Mary need another course in tests and measurements? Maybe, but we don't really know. Mary seems to have a perfectly adequate understanding of the information that grade-equivalent scores convey. If we agree that her questions were reasonable, is it necessarily a lack of understanding of test scores that prevented her from making use of the data Pat provided? Or could it be that the information provided failed to answer her questions? The latter explanation appears most satisfactory. Indeed, as you will discover shortly, it seems that it is Pat, not Mary, who would benefit most from a tests and measurements course.

Would things be different if a parent were doing the questioning? Maybe. Teachers may respond differently to other teachers than to parents. In some cases, inquisitive parents can be intimidated by authoritative-sounding test scores and jargon. But is a parent–teacher conference supposed to cloud or sidestep issues, rather than deal with them directly? We think not. If a parent were as concerned as Mary was about certain skills, that parent would probably end up feeling as frustrated as Mary. While Mary might go home and complain to a friend or husband, a parent might complain to a principal or a superintendent!

Mary's questions, whether raised by her or a parent, are legitimate. Pat probably could answer these questions if she thought about them. However, she seems to think that the test scores she reported are acceptable substitutes for direct answers to questions about specific skills.

Then what is the problem? The problem appears to be Pat's, not Mary's. Mary's questions refer to competencies or mastery of skills. Referring back to Figure 5.1, we can conclude that Mary was interested in information about Danny's level of proficiency. Pat's answers refer to test performance compared to other students, which, according to Figure 5.1, means information about Danny's place or rank compared to others. Answers to Mary's questions can come only from a test designed to indicate whether Danny exceeded some standard of performance taken to indicate mastery of some skill. If a test indicated that Danny could subtract two-digit numbers with regrouping, he would probably be considered to have "mastered" this skill, at least if, say, 80% or more correct was the standard for having attained mastery. In other words, he would have exceeded the standard or criterion of "80% mastery of subtraction of two-digit numbers with regrouping." Recall that a CRT is a test designed to measure whether a student has mastered a skill, where the definition of mastery depends on the level or criterion of performance set.

The information Pat was providing was normative or comparative rather than mastery information. Grade-equivalent scores only allow you to make decisions involving comparisons between a child's performance and that of the typical or average performance of a child in a "norm" group. Danny's grade-equivalent score of 1.7 in reading indicates that his reading ability is equivalent to that of the average first grader after 7 months in the first grade (technically, this is not completely accurate as we will see when we discuss misconceptions about grade equivalents in Chapter 19). It says nothing about which words he knows, gives no information about the process he uses to read new words and does not indicate how long it takes Danny to comprehend what he reads or to learn the meaning of new words. All this score indicates is that his ability to read is below that of the average fifth grader and roughly equivalent to that of an average first grader after 7 months of school. In short, grade-equivalent scores, and a variety of other scores obtained from standardized NRTs, allow one to make only general, comparative decisions, not decisions about mastery of specific skills. Unfortunately, situations as the one described occur every day. Only by becoming knowledgeable about the information yielded by CRTs and NRTs can we avoid these situations.

Recall that in the previous chapter we talked about eight types of decisions for which test data are used. Of these eight we decided that for instructional and grading decisions, teacher-made tests or formative assessments (which can be teacher-made or commercially developed) were most appropriate. We said that both teacher-made and standardized tests are useful in diagnostic decisions and that standardized tests are most appropriate for selection, placement, counseling and guidance, program or curriculum evaluation, and administrative policy decisions. Most teacher-made tests should be of the mastery type, since these are most useful for instructional decisions—the type of decisions most frequently made.

Mary's questions were related to instructional decisions. She was interested in Danny's skill levels. The information Pat was providing came from a norm-referenced, standardized test. If Mary had been interested in where Danny stands compared to national norms, then Pat's information would have been perfectly appropriate. However, she was apparently not all that interested in his position relative to others; she was interested in what he knew or what he had mastered. Although we are constantly reminded of where our class, school, or district stands in comparison to state or national norms, on a day-to-day basis these reminders are usually of secondary importance to the classroom teacher. Of prime importance in the classroom is whether our students are reaching the goals and objectives set for them. Daily decisions to reteach, review, or push ahead depend on whether mastery is occurring. What better way to measure whether our students have mastered an objective or a Common Core Standard than to test them to see if they can perform the learning outcome specified, under the conditions or with the materials specified, and at or above the standard of performance specified for them.

COMPARING NRTs AND CRTs

As you may have guessed, CRTs must be very specific if they are to yield information about individual skills. This is both an advantage and a disadvantage. Using a very specific test enables you to be relatively certain that your students have mastered or failed to master the skill in question. The major disadvantage of CRTs is that many such tests would be necessary to make decisions about the multitude of skills typically taught in the average classroom.

Norm-referenced tests (NRTs), in contrast, tend to be general. They measure a variety of specific and general skills at once but are not designed to measure them thoroughly. Thus, you are not as sure as you would be with a CRT that your students have mastered the individual skills in question. On the other hand, you get an estimate of ability in a variety of skills in a much shorter time than you could through a battery of CRTs. Since there is a trade-off in the uses of criterion- and norm-referenced measures, there are situations in which each is appropriate. Determining the appropriateness of a given type of test depends on the purpose of testing. Finally, the difficulty of

TABLE 5.1 Comparing Norm-Referenced and Criterion-Referenced Tests

Dimension	NRT	CRT
Average number of students who get an item right	50%	80%
Compares a student's performance	The performance of other students.	Standards indicative of mastery.
Breadth of content sampled	Broad, covers many objectives.	Narrow, covers a few objectives.
Comprehensiveness of content sampled	Shallow, usually one or two items per objective.	Comprehensive, usually three or more items per objective.
Variability	Since the meaningfulness of a norm-referenced score basically depends on the relative position of the score in comparison with other scores, the more variability or spread of scores, the better.	The meaning of the score does not depend on comparison with other scores: It flows directly from the connection between the items and the criterion. Variability may be minimal.
Item construction	Items are chosen to promote variance or spread. Items that are "too easy" or "too hard" are avoided. One aim is to produce good "distractor options."	Items are chosen to reflect the criterion behavior. Emphasis is placed on identifying the domain of relevant responses.
Reporting and interpreting considerations	Percentile rank and standard scores used (relative rankings).[*]	Number succeeding or failing or range of acceptable performance used (e.g., 90% proficiency achieved, or 80% of class reached 90% proficiency).

[*]For a further discussion of percentile rank and standard scores, see Chapters 13 and 14.

items in NRTs and CRTs also differs. In the NRT, items vary in level of difficulty from those that almost no one answers correctly to those that almost everyone answers correctly. In the CRT, the items tend to be equivalent to each other in difficulty. Following a period of instruction, students tend to find CRT items easy and answer most correctly. In a CRT, about 80% of the students completing a unit of instruction are expected to answer each item correctly, while in an NRT about 50% are expected to do so. Table 5.1 illustrates differences between NRTs and CRTs.

DIFFERENCES IN THE CONSTRUCTION OF NRTs AND CRTs

In the following chapters, we will describe in detail test planning, construction, and evaluation procedures. The procedures outlined in the test planning and test construction phases are, for the most part, equally appropriate whether you are using an NRT or a CRT. However, because of differences in the difficulty level of the items and the amount of variability in student scores, different evaluation procedures must be used in selecting test items. These will be described further in Chapter 11. At this point, we will simply describe some of the general differences in the construction of these two items, which are designed to measure a student's knowledge about the Gulf War in 2003:

> *Item 1*. During the War against Terror in Afghanistan and Iraq, which of the following were employed against U.S. soldiers?
> **a.** Biological weapons
> **b.** Nuclear weapons
> **c.** Roadside bombs
> **d.** Naval bombardment

Item 2. During 2003, more Iraqi tanks were destroyed by this aircraft than by all other aircraft combined.
- **a.** F14 Tomcat
- **b.** F16 Hornet
- **c.** A6 Intruder
- **d.** A10 Thunderbolt

What are the correct answers? Most would answer Item 1 correctly (i.e., Roadside bombs), and probably only military buffs would answer Item 2 correctly (i.e., A10 Thunderbolt). The second item involves a subtle point that is probably of interest only to military professionals and historians. Such an item might prove useful in discriminating among individuals who have mastery of specific details of the second Gulf War, such as in a class in military history at a military academy. For a high school or junior high unit on American history, however, this level of specificity likely would be unnecessary. Item 1, which assesses common knowledge about the second Gulf War, would be most appropriate for a CRT, since it measures a common fact about the war. Item 2 would be most appropriate for an NRT or a more advanced course, since it attempts to make more subtle distinctions among the facts. Owing to the difficulty and specificity of Item 2, few junior or senior high students would answer Item 2 correctly, even if they showed mastery of other aspects of the unit.

Let's complicate matters, however: Item 2 might be included in a CRT in a military history class. Students of military history might be expected to be familiar with the intricacies and specifics of weaponry employed during the War against Terror. In such a class, we would expect the content of the item to represent basic knowledge extensively addressed in text and lecture. In other words, test items are not norm-referenced or criterion-referenced by nature. They need to be considered in terms of the instructional context and the audience for whom they are being prepared.

NRTs, CRTs, AND LINGUISTIC AND CULTURAL DIVERSITY

NRTs compare a student's performance to a norms table based on a nationally representative sample, called a norm group or normative sample, of students in the same grade and a similar age. The resultant scores or rankings tell us how a student compares to this national sample. Such comparisons are appropriate when the student's cultural, language, economic, family, and other characteristics are comparable to those of the students in the normative sample.

The appropriateness of NRT results can be compromised when comparisons are made for children whose language, cultural, socioeconomic, or other important characteristics differ importantly from those of the norm group. For example, let's consider the case of Svetlana, a recent Russian immigrant, and Diana, a recent immigrant from England. Which student would you expect to score higher on the verbal portion of the Scholastic Assessment Test (SAT)? Of course, Diana would most likely outscore Svetlana, assuming Svetlana's English-language skills are weak and all other factors are equal. Does this mean that Diana is brighter than Svetlana or that Diana will necessarily fare better in college over the next 4–5 years than Svetlana? You probably answered "Not necessarily" to these last two questions, illustrating your sensitivity to the effect language proficiency can have on test performance. Similarly, other factors such as poverty, the importance placed on achievement in the family, and various differences across cultures (e.g., assertiveness, competitiveness, and compliance with authority figures) can affect performance on tests that reflect primarily the majority culture in our country.

Ideally, test publishers would include in their large, nationally representative norm groups sufficient numbers of pupils representative of our nation's diversity to enhance NRT comparability for all students, or develop separate norms tables representative of the nation's language, cultural, and socioeconomic diversity. There has been movement in those directions. Test publishers have been sensitive to our nation's growing diversity, and increased norm group diversity is being sought as tests are periodically restandardized or as new tests are developed. And although it is expensive for test publishers to develop them, we are now beginning to see specialized norm tables for students for whom English is a second language, for students in low-achieving schools, and for students from low socioeconomic backgrounds. Other specialized norms tables also may be available, although their samples will be smaller than the nationally representative sample. Therefore, unless the publisher confirms that the specialized norms are nationally representative, we must not be overconfident about the comparability of the conclusions drawn from specialized and nationally representative norms tables. So what should we do when interpreting NRT performance for diverse minority groups?

There is no single or simple answer to that question, and any answer is likely to be controversial. Our suggestion is that a two-pronged approach be adopted. First, where a student's background is not comparable to a test's norm group, the weight given to the score obtained by comparing the student to the norm group should be reduced or even eliminated in some cases. Second, where a student is not from the majority culture, additional attention should be given to the effects of the student's cultural and socioeconomic context when interpreting NRT scores. The factors to consider in interpreting NRT scores are many and complex, even for students from the majority culture. We will review these factors in Chapter 18 when we consider standardized tests in more depth.

What about CRTs? Do the same considerations apply? Because CRTs do not utilize comparisons to norm groups to obtain scores, differences between a pupil's background and that of the students in the norm group are not as relevant. Use of CRTs with pupils from diverse backgrounds may be more appropriate—but only if a CRT is appropriate for the purpose of testing! Nevertheless, language, cultural, and socioeconomic contextual variability can also affect performance on CRTs and should always be considered in administering and interpreting CRTs. Some students cannot read English, have been acculturated not to ask authority figures questions, have never seen or been expected to complete an essay question before, or have not eaten breakfast. These, and a variety of other factors, will negatively affect test performance, regardless of whether it is an NRT or a CRT.

NRTs, CRTs, AND VALIDITY EVIDENCE

Thus far in this chapter, we have discussed some important aspects of how we measure. We have distinguished between NRTs and CRTs and have discussed the importance of sensitivity to language, culture, and social diversity issues for both NRTs and CRTs. In the remainder of this chapter and in the next, we will consider how to determine whether we are actually measuring what we intend to measure. If we can demonstrate that a test measures what it is intended to measure, we have accumulated evidence of the test's *validity*. As we will learn in Chapter 16, the validity evidence supporting a test's use is the single most important characteristic that determines whether a test's use is appropriate.

To help us determine whether a test does what we intend it to, we will present a model for classroom measurement that links instructional objectives (or the Common Core State Standards, or CCSS), instructional methods, and test items. We will help you learn to write specific, measurable instructional objectives in Chapter 6, but for now let's simply keep in mind that all teachers have some objectives in mind (or on paper!) when they teach. As we noted in Chapter 2, since the passage of NCLB and the adoption of the CCSS external standards may be included in these objectives. For now, we need not be concerned about this issue. Instead, it is important to recognize that all teachers must have objectives in mind when they teach. Usually, these are both long- and short-term objectives. An example of a long-term objective is as follows.

The student will master all phases of addition.

With this long-term objective come several short-term objectives, which might include such goals as

The student will correctly add one-, two-, three-, and four-digit numbers without regrouping.

The student will correctly add two-digit numbers with regrouping.

The student will correctly add three-digit numbers with regrouping.

Regardless of whether we are talking about long- or short-term objectives, it is important to know when your students have mastered your objectives. Remember Mrs. Norton (see Chapter 4)? One of her objectives was probably "The student will master basic math skills." Like any good teacher, she tried to determine through a test whether her students mastered this objective. The problem was that her test did not measure mastery of basic math skills. It measured the ability to apply math skills and to read and to comprehend word problems.

In short, she knew what she wanted to measure, but her test did not actually measure that content. This is another way of saying that her test lacked validity evidence as a measure of her students' mastery of basic math skills. More specifically, it lacked evidence of content validity. In the classroom, evidence of content validity is of utmost importance. Simply stated, content validity evidence is the extent to which a test actually measures the teacher's instructional objectives or the CCSS. Later in this chapter, we will introduce procedures for examining a test to determine whether it has evidence of its content validity. Since most day-to-day instructional decisions are based on classroom achievement tests, we cannot overemphasize the importance of constructing tests that have adequate evidence of content validity. If the tests you construct have evidence that they are content valid, you will be on your way to making sound instructional decisions and having valid evidence to support your decisions should they ever be questioned.

A THREE-STAGE MODEL OF CLASSROOM MEASUREMENT

Most classroom instruction takes place with some teacher developed, state, or CCSS objective in mind. One way to determine whether the objective has been reached is through a test. The three-stage classroom measurement model in Figure 5.2 depicts these relationships. We will illustrate this model by describing how a CRT is constructed.

The first stage in the model is the first step in constructing a CRT. It is also the first step in sound instructional planning. For our purposes, we will use as examples only a few of the many possible objectives in a unit on writing instructional objectives. Some of these objectives might be as follows:

The student will discriminate learning activities from learning outcomes.

The student will discriminate observable learning outcomes from unobservable learning outcomes.

The student will construct well-written instructional objectives.

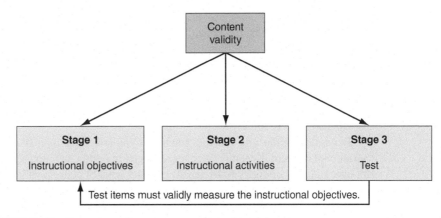

FIGURE 5.2 The three-stage classroom measurement model.

Each of these objectives would fit in Stage 1 of the model.

In Stage 2, instructional activities designed to develop student mastery of these objectives would be implemented. For example,

Objective. The student will discriminate learning activities from learning outcomes.

Instructional Activity. Define and provide examples of learning activities and learning outcomes. Point out similarities and differences between the two.

Naturally, the instructional procedures will vary depending on the content and type of learning outcomes desired. Courses in teaching methods are most concerned with the structure of the procedures in Stage 2 of this model. For our purposes, however, we are more concerned with determining the effectiveness of the procedures, not necessarily the nature of the procedures themselves. Thus, Stages 1 and 3 will be of most interest to us.

In constructing a CRT, our task is made easier if we develop or have available clear and measurable instructional objectives or standards. In Chapter 6, we will learn how to develop measureable instructional objectives. Once we have measurable instructional objectives, our task is to construct several items to validly measure each objective. Typically, this means about three to ten items per objective. Furthermore, we normally define mastery not as perfect performance but as 70%, 80%, or 90% correct performance. A student who answers correctly four of five or eight of ten items that validly measure an objective generally is considered to have mastered the objective. The following is an example of a five-part test item to measure the first objective.

Objective. The student will discriminate learning activities from learning outcomes.

Test Item. Indicate which terms in the following list are learning activities by placing an A in the space to the left of the term and indicate which are learning outcomes by placing an O in the space.

_____ **1.** Practice multiplication tables.
_____ **2.** List the parts of a carburetor.
_____ **3.** Recall the main events in a story.
_____ **4.** Listen to a foreign language tape.
_____ **5.** Memorize the names of the first five U.S. presidents.

Answers: 1. A; 2. O; 3. O; 4. A; 5. A.

These response alternatives are content-valid measures of the objective because they ask the student to do exactly what the objective requires. There are certainly other equally valid ways of measuring this objective, but the response alternatives listed are appropriate. If a student answers four of five or five of five correctly on this CRT, the teacher could feel reasonably secure in concluding that the student has mastered the objective. These types of tests are called criterion-referenced because a specific level of acceptable performance called the criterion is established directly from the instructional objectives. As we shall see, we are less confident of the mastery of specific objectives when an NRT is employed.

Regardless of the type of achievement test you select, the issue of content validity evidence is of paramount concern. Keep the three-stage model in mind when you select or develop an achievement test, and you are likely to be sensitive to the issue of content validity.

Now that we have an overall framework for thinking about classroom measurement, let's get into test construction itself. Keep in mind that any good classroom test begins with your objectives, Stage 1 of our three-stage measurement model. Much of the remainder of this chapter and the next will be devoted to considering instructional objectives and ways of ensuring the content validity of items intended to measure instructional objectives.

WHY OBJECTIVES? WHY NOT JUST WRITE TEST ITEMS?

What if you don't believe that instructional objectives are necessary? What if you feel that they are a waste of time? What if you don't think you will need to use or construct instructional objectives in your teaching career? Many believe that objectives for classroom instruction are unnecessary, limiting, too time-consuming, and mechanistic. If you agree, then learning to write instructional objectives may be a frustrating, difficult task. If we told you they're necessary and you're better off learning to write them, you probably would not believe us. We do think it is important for teachers to be able to write measurable instructional objectives, but we also understand and respect your right to hold another opinion. You should, however, take the time to consider the place of instructional objectives, or state standards or the CCSS in the overall instructional process. Consider the situation described next and then decide whether it's worthwhile to take the time to learn to write instructional objectives to guide your teaching.

Two Schools: Their Objectives

As Maude got off the bus, she was immediately taken by the name of the first of the two schools she was about to visit: the Center for Self-Actualization and Humanistic Experiences. Maude was awestruck. At last she would see what education really should be about—free from dry, mechanical methods and curricula and characterized by the teachers' loving acceptance and excitement and the students' sense of freedom. To her surprise, the door was open, so Maude walked in and was greeted with a warm smile and hug from the "facilitator."

"Is that another name for teacher?" Maude asked.

"Heavens, no!" said the facilitator. "I only facilitate learning, I don't teach. For your information, use of the words teacher and educator are forbidden here at the Center; we are all facilitators." Maude was confused, but decided not to press the issue.

The students were engaged in a variety of activities or lack of activities. One was reading a book; another worked with an abacus; a third was asleep on a couch; others were talking, playing, and generally having what appeared to Maude to be a pretty good time. Maude was encouraged by the facilitator to "experience" the students. Almost unanimously the students felt the Center was "fun." One said, "You never have to do nuthin' around here."

Concerned, Maude questioned the facilitator about this comment. The facilitator's reply was that freedom of choice is strongly encouraged at the Center. All students are free to choose what to do or not to do. "After all, reality is only a construct!" he said. "But are they learning anything?" Maude asked.

"They are learning that they are free and independent human beings, capable of personally or socially constructing their own realities," said the facilitator. "When they are ready, they will choose to learn on their own. Now, if you'll excuse me, I have an appointment with my aroma therapist." At a loss for words and feeling troubled, Maude said goodbye and left the Center for Self-Actualization and Humanistic Experiences.

The Center for Accelerated Education was Maude's next stop. After knocking on the door, she was greeted by a rather stern-faced, middle-aged man who was wearing a "Better Living Through Behaviorism" button on his lapel. He called himself a "behavioral engineer." He said hello and handed Maude a list of "behaviors" that the students would be engaging in for the next 30 minutes or so and told her to feel free to "collect data." He then picked up a box of plastic strips—"tokens," he called them—muttered something about a "reinforcement schedule" and "consequating appropriate behaviors," and walked off toward his "subjects."

The students at the Center for Accelerated Education sat in individual cubicles or carrels. Each student had a contract specifying what was expected of him or her. Privileges, such as free time, and rewards from the "reinforcement menu" were earned by performing on-task behavior (like sitting quietly in a cubicle, working on a worksheet, or reading from an iPad). The behavioral engineer circulated around the room, periodically "reinforcing" on-task behaviors he referred to as "operants" with tokens and also providing tokens for each completed worksheet. Students demonstrating off-task and disruptive behavior relinquished tokens or, in extreme cases, were required to spend several minutes in the time-out room. The time-out room was "devoid of all potential reinforcers," according to the behavioral engineer. In other words, it was a barren room—no windows, tables, books, iPads, or anything interesting.

When Maude asked whether the pupils were learning, the behavioral engineer pointed to the stacks of completed worksheets almost filling a large storeroom. He said, "We also have tons more stored on the Cloud."

"Let's see you get that much learning from the kids at the Center for Self-Actualization and Humanistic Experiences," chuckled the behavioral engineer.

More confused and concerned than she had been before she entered, Maude decided not to press the issue and instead to engage in some exiting behaviors.

As you probably guessed, both the Center for Self-Actualization and Humanistic Experiences and the Center for Accelerated Education are, we hope, exaggerations. They represent extremes in educational theory. On the one hand, the "hands-off" approach is characteristic of nondirective, discovery approaches to learning. On the other hand, the regimented approach is characteristic of a directive, guided approach to learning. Which approach is better for every student? We don't know, and probably no one knows. Fortunately, most educational institutions operate with some combination of directive and nondirective approaches.

Instruction is not a rigid, easily defined procedure. It tends to be different things to different people. No one will ever be completely happy with any one approach to instruction since no one approach is really a single method but a combination of methods. As a result, specific educational goals and objectives are unlikely to be approved or supported by everyone. So where do the goals and objectives come from, and who decides on the goals and objectives or standards for education? The answer is that society, government, school boards, school administration, teachers, students, and parents all, to some extent, set educational goals and objectives.

Where Do Goals Come From?

Educators must be responsive to societal needs and pressures. This is especially true for public school educators, since the purse strings that make public education a reality are controlled by all who make up our society. If a superintendent or school board implements educational policies or procedures that are too far removed from what the community wants and needs or that may be required by state or national law, the superintendent may find himself or herself looking for work elsewhere, and board members may not be reelected.

We frequently make the mistake of thinking that it is the administration that is completely responsible for the curriculum implemented in a given school or district. This is only partially true. Ultimately, it is the general public, or society, through elected state and federal officials and the legislation and rules that they pass, that sets the goals for public education. We reviewed several developments in Chapters 1 and 2 that illustrate this point. Those developments included the

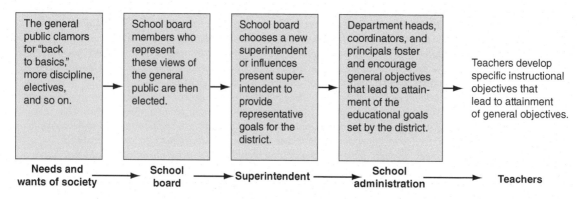

FIGURE 5.3   Back to basics: the flow of goals to objectives.

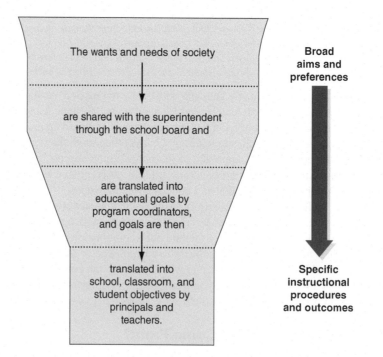

FIGURE 5.4   The funneling of societal wants into objectives.

passage of NCLB in 2002, the explosion of interest in high-stakes testing over the last decade, standards-based reform and the subsequent adoption of the CCSS by all but four states in 2010, and the acceptance of funding through the Race to the Top initiative in 20 states in 2011. The state standards and the CCSS may define for each grade and each subject area what pupils are expected to master. In some states, achievement of these standards is necessary for students to qualify for promotion to the next grade or to graduate, and the annual academic assessments required by NCLB and states high-stakes testing programs may also be linked to these standards. Figure 5.3 uses a specific example to illustrate the flow from goals to objectives in public education. This illustration shows how, for example, public pressure for a back-to-basics movement can reach the classroom.

We may also view this process as a funneling or narrowing of focus, with the often ambiguous wants and needs of society gradually translated into manageable "bits" called instructional objectives, as shown in Figure 5.4. Instructional objectives are part and parcel of the CCSS. State academic standards, because they still represent a "work in progress" in the states that have not adopted the CCSS, may at times resemble either broad goals or more specific objectives.

Are There Different Kinds of Goals and Objectives?

What do you think are the instructional goals and objectives of the schools Maude visited? Well, you probably can't say precisely, but you could probably look at a list of objectives and decide which would be acceptable to the Center for Self-Actualization and Humanistic Experiences or to the behaviorist Center for Accelerated Education. Look at the objectives in the following exercise and indicate the school with which they would most likely be associated.

EXERCISE: *Write H for humanistic or B for behavioristic in the blank to the left of each objective to indicate which school they would probably be associated with*

_____ **1.** With 80% accuracy, subtract two-digit numbers from three-digit numbers without borrowing.
_____ **2.** Identify initial consonant sounds correctly 90% of the time when listening to an audiocassette.
_____ **3.** Enjoy the beauty of nature.
_____ **4.** Interpret *The Lion, the Witch, and the Wardrobe*.
_____ **5.** Type at least 25 words per minute with no more than two errors, using a manual typewriter.
_____ **6.** Visit the zoo and discuss what was of interest.
_____ **7.** Be creative.
_____ **8.** Be spontaneous.
_____ **9.** List the days of the week in proper order, from memory, with 100% accuracy.

This exercise points out the difference between two types of educational objectives: behavioral (specific, or measureable) and expressive (general, often not measureable). A behavioral objective is a precise statement of the behavior to be exhibited; the criterion by which mastery of the objective will be judged; and a statement of the conditions under which the behavior must be demonstrated. Objectives 1, 2, 5, and 9 are examples. As you can see, they are specific statements or "bits" of observable behavior with specific conditions under which the behavior is to be observed and the level of performance attained. Using these objectives, two or more observers would likely agree about whether a student was, for example, able to list the days of the week in proper order, from memory, with 100% accuracy.

An expressive objective is somewhat different. Behaviors are not usually specified, and a criterion performance level is generally not stated. What is stated in an expressive objective is the experience or educational activity to be undertaken. The outcome of the activity is not detailed in specific terms, but in general terms such as interpret or analyze. Examples of expressive objectives include items 4 and 6 from the list. They specify an activity or experience and a broad educational outcome.

Now you might ask, "What about items 3, 7, and 8?" They do not describe a specific observable behavior, conditions, or criterion level of performance, and they do not describe an educational activity or experience. What do they describe? They describe broad, hard-to-define, and subjective entities. We would have little agreement among individuals trying to define enjoyment, creativity, and spontaneity. These may be best classified as broad goals rather than objectives because they are the end result of perhaps a complete educational program.

Educational goals reflect the general needs of society. As a result, most goals, if stated in general terms, tend to be accepted or adopted by most educators and educational institutions. Regardless of whether a program is directive or nondirective, behavioral or humanistic, rigid or flexible, various general goals will be held in common. When we get more specific, often at the local school level, disagreements over methods used to reach these goals arise. For example, the two schools described would probably agree that creativity is an important goal for education but disagree as to how creativity should be fostered or developed. One school may say creativity is best developed through structured experiences. Another school may say creativity is best developed in an open, unstructured environment.

As a result, sometimes different methods are employed to reach the same goal. But it is important to realize that, in addition to having a goal, any method must also have some implicit or explicit steps thought necessary to achieve the goal. Such steps may vary in specificity but are present in any logically constructed instructional program. For example, in the Center for Self-Actualization and Humanistic Experiences, the facilitators most certainly had some steps in mind in trying to foster creativity. It is unlikely that they expected creativity to develop without any guidance. If they did, why would they see a need for their Center? The expressive objectives mentioned might be one of the steps they would use. Others might include the following:

Welcome students each morning.

Encourage students to try out new activities and methods of expression.

Encourage students to express all ideas, regardless of how inappropriate they may seem.

Statements such as these help define the atmosphere or philosophy of the Center but are they instructional objectives? Some would say yes, and some would say no. We would say no, since they do not meet our criteria for instructional objectives. That is, they do not specify a single observable and measureable student behavior, nor do they specify a criterion performance level or the conditions under which the behavior must be demonstrated. Determining whether a behavior is observable or measureable is often challenging. To test whether a behavior is observable or measureable, consider whether two independent observers would agree as to the presence or absence of the student behavior in question. Would two or more observers agree that "expression of student ideas is warmly encouraged?" Some probably would agree and some would not. This statement would not qualify as an instructional objective according to our criteria. But consider this statement: "During each period the students will write an alternative ending to each assigned short story." Here it seems more likely that observers would agree as to whether students displayed this behavior. It is student oriented, and it is easily observed or measured.

Thus far, we have discussed the difference between specific instructional objectives and general expressive objectives. Objectives tend to reflect a school's educational philosophy. We have also mentioned general goals that tend to reflect the overall needs of society. From this point on, we

TABLE 5.2 Goals, Program Objectives, and Instructional Objectives

Category	Description	Examples
Goals	Broad statements of very general educational outcomes that: do not include specific levels of performance. tend to change infrequently and in response to societal pressure.	Become a good citizen. Be competent in the basic skills areas. Be creative. Learn problem solving. Appreciate art. Develop high-level thinking skills.
General educational program objectives	More narrowly defined statements of educational outcomes that: apply to specific educational programs. may be formulated on an annual basis. are developed by program coordinators, principals, and other high school administrators.	By the end of the academic year, students receiving remedial reading program services will realize achievement gains of at least 0.8 of a grade level, as measured by the Iowa Test of Basic Skills.
Instructional objectives	Specific statements of learner behavior or outcomes that are expected to be exhibited by students after completing a unit of instruction. A unit of instruction, for example, can mean: a 6-week lesson on foreign culture. a 1-week lesson on deciduous trees. a class period on "Subtracting with Borrowing." a 5-minute lesson on "Cursive Letters: Lowercase b." These objectives are often included in teacher manuals, and more and more frequently instructional objectives are also being included for specific lessons. Unfortunately, they are not always well written and do not always fit a particular class or style. Instructional objectives often have to be formulated by classroom teachers to fit their individual classrooms.	By Friday, the students will be able to recite the names of the months in order. The student will be able to take apart and correctly reassemble a disk drive with the tools provided, within 45 minutes.

will focus on specific instructional objectives, but we will also consider another type of objective called a general or program objective. Although these are usually formulated at the state education agency or school district level, they are sometimes confused with classroom instructional objectives. Table 5.2 illustrates the differences among educational goals, program objectives, and instructional objectives.

Since the average classroom teacher will have little input into the formulation of either educational goals or general educational program objectives, we will not concern ourselves further with these. For the remainder of this chapter and in the next, we will focus on those objectives that classroom teachers must formulate themselves. In other words, we will concentrate on instructional objectives. Instructional objectives can make a teacher's day-to-day job easier, save time, and result in more effective instruction.

HOW CAN INSTRUCTIONAL OBJECTIVES MAKE A TEACHER'S JOB EASIER?

When we were first learning about goals and objectives, we also wondered how instructional objectives could make a teacher's job easier. How can something that takes time to prepare actually save time, and how does that make a teacher's job easier?

You've probably heard the old saying that it takes money to make money. It's true. An equally relevant but far less popular expression is that it takes time to save time. In other words, taking time to plan and to organize will save you time in the long run. Planning your lessons, getting organized, and being efficient all take time but can save time later.

Nevertheless, writing good instructional objectives does take time and skill. We will help you develop the skill in Chapter 6, but we can't do much about time! Fortunately, personal computers and tablets are now so common in schools that they can help. Beginning with this chapter, we will include sidebars that will show how computers or tablets can help with a variety of measurement tasks. Visit the sidebar for this chapter titled "Computers and Instructional Objectives" to learn how PCs or tablets can help with this important task (Box 5-1). Your state legislature and state education agency may also help. If you teach in a state where the state education agency has developed academic standards for each grade level and for each subject as part of its high-stakes testing and accountability program, you may find that some of the state standards can be adopted as is or modified to provide you with your instructional objectives. Finally, if you teach in a state that has adopted the CCSS, you will have online access to those standards, and those standards are the same in all states that have adopted that CCSS.

BOX 5-1

COMPUTERS AND INSTRUCTIONAL OBJECTIVES

One of the measurement tasks teachers find to be time consuming is writing instructional objectives. Educational software will not diminish the necessary skills and time initially needed to construct good instructional objectives. However, word processing programs enable teachers to retain and modify their objectives from year to year to reflect changing state academic standards, educational trends, and goals. A file of instructional objectives on a computer's hard drive, flash drive, CDs, or on a "cloud computing" web-based storage site can enable teachers to develop a "bank" of instructional objectives that may be drawn on as educational needs change over time. Such a file also can minimize the amount of time a teacher spends writing and rewriting instructional objectives each year. As a result, teachers may find they have increased amounts of time available for instructional or other measurement tasks. Storing instructional objectives also facilitates analysis of objectives and sharing of well-written objectives among teachers at the same grade level, thus saving still more time and leading to better written objectives, thereby improving measurement practice. Finally, printing the objectives and distributing them to your students (or posting them to your instructional webpage, if you have one), especially in the secondary grades, will help students focus on the most relevant content areas.

Research has identified several factors that are associated with effective, successful teaching. Among these are organization and clarity, which typically go hand in hand. While it is possible to be clear without being organized, and vice versa, it is unlikely. In education, we have historically spent a lot of time "spinning our wheels" because we do not have clear objectives for our students. In other words, we often don't know where we're going so we don't know when we get there. Using instructional objectives, whether constructed by the teacher, state or in the form of the CCSS, helps minimize this floundering by clearing the way. The result is increased efficiency and effectiveness in teaching and learning.

SUMMARY

This chapter introduced you to norm-referenced and criterion-referenced tests, content validity evidence considerations, and educational goals and objectives. Its major points are as follows:

1. A norm-referenced test (NRT) indicates how a pupil's performance compares to that of other pupils.

2. A criterion-referenced test (CRT) indicates how a pupil's performance compares to an established standard or criterion thought to indicate mastery of a skill.

3. The type of test you use depends on the purpose of the testing, which should be determined before you administer the test.

4. Information from NRTs is usually not as useful for classroom decision making as information from CRTs.

5. In addition to differing in regard to what a pupil's performance is compared to NRTs and CRTs differ in the following dimensions:
   - Item difficulty
   - Content sampling (breadth and depth)
   - Variability of scores
   - Item construction
   - Reporting and interpreting considerations.

6. Because NRTs compare a student's performance to the norm group to establish a student's score, language, culture, and socioeconomic differences between the student and the norm group can affect the student's score.

7. For this reason, it may be appropriate in such cases to reduce the weight given an NRT score and to give additional attention to the factors that influence NRT scores when interpreting NRT scores.

8. Although CRT scores do not require a comparison to a norm group, performance on CRTs also can be negatively affected by language, cultural, and socioeconomic factors.

9. Content validity evidence describes the extent to which a test measures or matches the teacher's instructional objectives, or aligns with state academic standards.

10. There are three stages involved in classroom measurement:
    - Constructing instructional objectives.
    - Implementing instructional activities.
    - Testing to measure the attainment of the instructional objectives.

    Each of these stages must match with the others for measurement to be valid.

11. Instructional activities tend to vary across educational institutions, and they range from flexible to rigid.

12. These instructional activities tend to be determined by instructional objectives, which tend to be derived from educational goals and state academic standards or the Common Core State Standards (CCSS), which tend to reflect societal attitudes and values.

13. One type of instructional objective is the behavioral objective. It specifies a single observable, measurable behavior to be exhibited, the conditions under which it is to be exhibited, and the criterion for mastery.

14. Another type of instructional objective is the expressive objective. It specifies an educational activity but does not specify the particular outcome of the activity.

15. Instructional objectives help the teacher clarify and organize instruction, enabling the teacher to save time in the long run.

16. Unlike the Common Core State Standards (CCSS), which were adopted by most states when this edition was revised, state academic standards can vary from state to state both in terms of their academic content and in terms of their specificity.

FOR DISCUSSION AND PRACTICE

1. Identify five characteristics that distinguish a norm-referenced from a criterion-referenced test.

2. Describe several testing decisions for which you would want to use a norm-referenced test and several situations in which you would want to use a criterion-referenced test.

3. A parent calls you and wants to set up a conference to discuss Johnny's potential for getting into the college of his choice. Which type of test score, NRT or CRT, should you be prepared to discuss first? Why?

4. Another parent calls and wants to discuss why Brittany received a D in math this grading period. Which type of test score, NRT or CRT, should you be prepared to discuss first? Why?

5. Imagine that you have been randomly chosen to be evaluated by your school district's Office of Evaluations. They ask you for your students' scores on an achievement test. What type of test scores, NRT or CRT, would be most indicative of your success as a teacher?

6. Think back to the last NRT and CRT that you took. Describe how your performance on each test would have been affected if

• You were not fluent in English.
• This was the first time you were asked to take this kind of test.
• You came from a culture that seldom used tests to make important decisions.
• You and your parents believed that your future success depended on your performance on this test.

7. Now, try to imagine that the conditions described in item 6 apply to you. Describe your thoughts and feelings related to taking an NRT and a CRT.

8. Compare and contrast the following:

• Behavioral and expressive objectives
• Program objectives and instructional objectives
• Educational goals and instructional objectives

9. A teacher is complaining about having to write instructional objectives. He just cannot see any benefit they may have and thinks they are too time-consuming. Role-play with another student and describe how well-written objectives can make teaching more effective.

*Answers to these to questions appear in Appendix B.

*10. Identify which of the following are expressive (E) and which are behavioral (B) objectives.

_____ **a.** Properly use and adjust a microscope without a checklist.

_____ **b.** Develop an appreciation for the nature of plant growth.

_____ **c.** Enjoy driving a car.

_____ **d.** Appreciate the role of physics in everyday life.

_____ **e.** Be able to divide fractions with 80% accuracy.

_____ **f.** Be able to dissect a starfish using only a scalpel.

_____ **g.** Value the importance of eating the right foods.

_____ **h.** List the parts of the abdomen from memory with 100% accuracy.

11. Convert the following goals in to general objectives:

• Become a good citizen.
• Be creative.
• Appreciate art.
• Know math.
• Develop musical ability.

*12. Match the following general objectives to the most content-valid method of testing.

_____ **1.** From memory, describe the main figures in classical music.

_____ **2.** Match the classical composers with their compositions.

_____ **3.** Identify the titles and composers of the classical pieces discussed in class, after listening to no more than 2 minutes of each piece.

_____ **4.** Play two classical compositions on the piano by the end of the semester.

a. Copy by hand at least two classical compositions.

b. Associate the composers listed with their compositions.

c. Chronicle the lives of three European composers who lived between 1500 and 1875.

d. After listening to this tape, identify the composer.

e. Play two classical selections of your choice.

MEASURING LEARNING OUTCOMES

LEARNING OUTCOMES

After completing this chapter, the student will be able to:

1. Describe the components of a well-written instructional objective.
2. Differentiate between learning outcomes and learning activities.
3. Differentiate between observable and unobservable learning outcomes.
4. Specify for an instructional objective the conditions under which learning must be demonstrated.
5. Specify for an instructional objective the criterion performance levels by which performance is to be evaluated.
6. Explain why test items must match instructional objectives.
7. Differentiate between items that match and fail to match instructional objectives.
8. Compare and contrast the six levels of Bloom's taxonomy.
9. Differentiate among objectives written at different levels of the Taxonomy of Educational Objectives—Cognitive Domain.
10. Write objectives at different levels of the taxonomy.
11. Describe the levels of the affective taxonomy.
12. Describe the levels of the psychomotor taxonomy.
13. Describe the advantages of using a test blueprint for instructional planning and test construction.
14. Differentiate among the terms content outline, categories, number of items, and functions, as they apply to test blueprints.
15. Construct a test blueprint for a given unit of instruction, according to the guidelines provided.

IN CHAPTER 5, we considered the differences between norm-referenced and criterion-referenced tests, the important concepts of content validity, various types of goals and objectives, and some reasons why instructional objectives are helpful to the teacher, whether constructed by the teacher or in the form of the Common Core State Standards. Next, we will describe methods for writing instructional objectives, matching test items to objectives, and using a test blueprint to ensure balanced classroom tests that include items measuring higher-level thinking.

WRITING INSTRUCTIONAL OBJECTIVES

An instructional objective should be a clear and concise statement of the skill or skills that your students will be expected to perform after a unit of instruction. It should include the level of proficiency to be demonstrated and the special conditions under which the skills must be demonstrated. Furthermore, an instructional objective should be stated in observable, behavioral terms, in order for two or more individuals to agree that a student has or has not displayed the learning outcome in question. In short, a complete instructional objective includes the following:

- An observable behavior (action verb specifying the learning outcome).
- Any special conditions under which the behavior must be displayed.
- The performance level considered sufficient to demonstrate mastery.

The following series of exercises should help you become familiar with each of these components. With practice, they should lead to your mastery in writing instructional objectives.

Identifying Learning Outcomes

An instructional objective must include an action verb that specifies a learning outcome. However, not all action verbs specify learning outcomes. Learning outcomes are often confused with learning activities. Try to determine which of the following examples represent learning outcomes and which represent learning activities:

1. By the end of the semester, the child will identify pictures of words that sound alike.
2. The child will demonstrate an appreciation of poetry.
3. The student will subtract one-digit numbers with 80% accuracy.
4. The student will show a knowledge of correct punctuation.
5. The student will practice the multiplication tables.
6. The student will sing "The Star-Spangled Banner."

In the first four objectives, the action words *identify, demonstrate, subtract*, and *show* all point to outcomes or end products of units of instruction. However, practice, the action word in objective 5, only implies an activity that will lead to a learning outcome. Thus, objective 5 has no learning outcome; it is a learning activity. The means rather than the end is identified.

Objective 6 is a little troublesome, too. Is *sing* an outcome or an activity? It's hard to say without more information. If your goal is to have a stage-frightened pupil sing in public, this may be a learning outcome. If singing is only practice for a later performance, however, it is a learning activity. The following exercise should help you discriminate between learning outcomes and learning activities. Look at the examples of outcomes and activities, then work through the exercise and check your answers.

Learning Outcomes (Ends)	*Learning Activities (Means)*
identify	study
recall	watch
list	listen
write	read

EXERCISE: *Distinguish learning outcomes from learning activities by marking an O next to outcomes and an A next to activities.*

_____ **1.** Fixing a car radio.
_____ **2.** Reciting the four components of a good essay.
_____ **3.** Adding signed numbers correctly.
_____ **4.** Practicing the violin.
_____ **5.** Recalling the parts of speech.
_____ **6.** Outlining the main theme in *The House of the Seven Gables*.
_____ **7.** Reciting the alphabet.
_____ **8.** Punctuating an essay correctly.

Answers: 1. O; 2. O; 3. O; 4. A; 5. O; 6. O; 7. A; 8. O.

If an activity implies a specific product or result, we have considered it an outcome. What we want our instructional objective to include is the end product of the instructional procedure. It is on this end product that we will base our test item. If you find that your objective includes a learning activity (means) and not an outcome (end), rewrite it so that the product of the intended activity is stated. Next, let's consider two types of learning outcomes: those that are observable and directly measurable and those that are not.

Identifying Observable and Directly Measurable Learning Outcomes

At this stage, your task is to determine whether the outcome is stated as a measurable, observable behavior or an unmeasurable, unobservable behavior. That is, would two or more individuals observing a student agree that the student had demonstrated the learning outcome? Sometimes, we need to replace the unobservable behavior with an observable indicator of the learning outcome. For example, if our objective is:

The student will show a knowledge of punctuation.

then the learning outcome, "show a knowledge of punctuation," is unmeasurable. How would we know whether knowledge was shown? Ask the student? Would we assume that if a student was present for a lecture or read the appropriate section of a text, knowledge followed? Probably not. Instead we would need some indication that would demonstrate evidence of knowledge. For example, to indicate knowledge of punctuation, a student would have to "insert commas where appropriate" in sentences, "list the rules governing the use of colons or semicolons," and so on. Instructional objectives are specific, measurable statements of the outcomes of instruction that indicate whether instructional intents have been achieved (add two-digit numbers with regrouping, independently pick up a musical instrument and play it, and so on).

Let's practice identifying observable learning outcomes. Study the following examples of observable and unobservable outcomes, work through the exercise, and then check your answers.

Observables	*Unobservables*
list	value
recite	appreciate
build	know
draw	understand

EXERCISE: *Distinguish observable learning outcomes from unobservable outcomes by marking O next to observables and U next to unobservables.*

_____ 1. Circle the initial sound of words.

_____ 2. Be familiar with the law.

_____ 3. Add two-digit numbers on paper.

_____ 4. Understand the process of osmosis.

_____ 5. Enjoy speaking French.

_____ 6. Change the spark plugs on an engine.

_____ 7. Recite the names of the characters in *Tom Sawyer*.

_____ 8. Really understand set theory.

_____ 9. Appreciate art deco.

_____ 10. Recite a short poem from memory.

Answers: 1. O; 2. U; 3. O; 4. U; 5. U; 6. O; 7. O; 8. U; 9. U; 10. O.

Stating Conditions

An instructional objective describes any special conditions in which the learning will take place. If the observable learning outcome is to take place at a particular time, in a particular place, with particular materials, equipment, tools, or other resources, then the conditions must be stated explicitly in the objective, as the following examples show:

Given a calculator, multiply two-digit numbers, correct to the nearest whole number.

Given a typed list, correct any typographical errors.

Given a list of six scrambled words, arrange the words to form a sentence.

EXERCISE: *Write conditions for the following learning outcomes.*

_____ 1. Given _____, change the oil and oil filter.

_____ 2. Given _____, identify the correct temperature.

_____ 3. Given _____, add three-digit numbers.

Possible answers: 1. a foreign automobile; 2. a thermometer; 3. an electronic calculator.

Stating Criterion Levels

An instructional objective indicates how well the behavior is to be performed. For any given objective, a number of test items will be written. The criterion level of acceptable performance specifies how many of these items the student must get correct to have attained the objective. The following are examples of objectives with the criterion stated:

Given 20 two-digit addition problems, the student will compute all answers correctly.

Given 20 two-digit addition problems, the student will compute 90% correctly.

EXERCISE: *Write criterion levels of acceptable performance for the following objectives.*

_____ 1. Given 10 words, circle those that contain a silent "e" with _____ percent accuracy.

_____ 2. The student will swim freestyle for 100 yards in less than _____.

_____ 3. The good student must be able to leap tall buildings _____.

Possible answers: 1. 80; 2. 60 seconds; 3. in a single bound.

Remember, criterion levels need not always be specified in terms of percentages of items answered correctly. They may also be stated as follows:

- Number of items correct.
- Number of consecutive items correct (or consecutive errorless performances).
- Essential features included (as in an essay question or paper).
- Completion within a prescribed time limit (where speed of performance is important).
- Completion with a certain degree of accuracy.

Now that you have worked through the exercises, you have some idea of what is necessary for a complete instructional objective. The following are examples of complete instructional objectives:

> With a ballpoint pen, write your name, address, birth date, telephone number, and grade with 100% accuracy.

> Without reference to class notes, correctly describe four out of five alternative sources of energy discussed in class.

> The student will reply in grammatically correct French to 95% of the French questions spoken orally during an examination.

> Given a human skeleton, the student will identify at least 40 of the bones correctly.

To this point, we have shown you how to

- discriminate learning outcomes from learning activities,
- discriminate observable/measurable learning outcomes from unobservable/unmeasurable learning outcomes,
- state conditions, and
- state criterion levels.

Before moving on to our next topic, let's consider one more issue related to the construction of instructional objectives.

Keeping It Simple and Straightforward

We often make the mistake of being too complicated in measuring learning outcomes. As a result, we often resort to indirect or unnecessarily complex methods to measure learning outcomes. If you want to know whether students can write their name, ask them to write their name—but not blindfolded! Resist the temptation to be tricky. Consider the following examples:

> The student will show his or her ability to recall characters of the book *Tom Sawyer* by painting a picture of each.

> Discriminate between a smart phone and laptop computer by drawing an electrical diagram of each.

> Demonstrate that you understand how to use Wikipedia by identifying the URL location for a specific topic.

In the first example, painting a picture would likely allow us to determine whether the pupils could recall the characters in *Tom Sawyer* but isn't there an easier (and less time-consuming) way to measure recall? How about asking the students to simply list the characters? If your objective is to determine recall, listing is sufficient.

For the second example, another unnecessarily complex task is suggested. Instead, how about presenting students with two illustrations, one of a smartphone, the other of a laptop computer, and simply ask them to tell you (orally or in writing) which is which?

Finally, the third example is on target. The task required is a simple and efficient way of measuring whether someone can use Wikipedia to find specific information.

The next step is to practice writing objectives on your own. Return to the exercises when you have trouble and be sure you include the three components in each objective. Remember, the three components are

- observable learning outcome,
- conditions,
- criterion level.

Once you have written an instructional objective, it is always a good idea to analyze it to make sure that the necessary components are included. Determining whether an observable learning outcome has been stated is usually the initial step. The checklist for written objectives in Figure 6.1 addresses this point and provides you with a step-by-step method to analyze and improve written objectives. We are now ready to consider the third stage of the classroom measurement model introduced in Chapter 5—matching a test item to the instructional objective.

MATCHING TEST ITEMS TO INSTRUCTIONAL OBJECTIVES

There is one basic rule to keep in mind when matching test items to instructional objectives: The learning outcome and conditions specified in the test question must match the learning outcome

	Yes	No
1. Are the objectives composed of only learning outcomes, and not learning activities? **a.** If yes, go to Step 2. **b.** If no, eliminate the learning activities or replace them with the learning outcomes.	____	____
2. Are the learning outcomes stated in overt observable terms? **a.** If yes, go to Step 3. **b.** If no, replace the unobservable outcomes with indicators of the outcomes. Remember, because this almost always results in more specific objectives, you may have to write several overt objectives to adequately "sample" the covert learning outcome.	____	____
3. Now that you have all overt learning outcomes listed, are they the simplest and most direct ways to measure the learning outcomes? **a.** If yes, you now have a useful list of instructional objectives that will serve as a basis for a content-valid test. **b.** If no, rewrite the indirect or complicated means of measurement so that they are as simple and direct as possible. Once you have done so, you have the basis for a content-valid test.	____	____

FIGURE 6.1 Checklist for written objectives.

and conditions described in the objective. This rule will ensure that the test you are developing will have content validity. Because content validity is so important, let's go through some exercises to be sure we can actually match correctly.

The following exercises illustrate the two steps involved in matching items to objectives.

Step 1: Identify the learning outcome called for by the objective. Check to determine if your item requires the same learning outcome.

EXERCISE: *For the following, employ Step 1 and decide whether the learning outcomes match.*

	Match?	
	Yes	*No*
1. *Objective*: Recall the names of the capitals of all 50 states. *Test item*: List the capitals of Texas, New York, California, and Rhode Island.	_____	_____
2. *Objective*: Discriminate fact from opinion in the President's most recent State of the Union address. *Test item*: Given a text of the State of the Union address, list three examples of facts and three examples of opinion.	_____	_____
3. *Objective*: The student will write complete instructional objectives, including behavior, conditions, and criteria. *Test item*: Describe why instructional objectives must contain an observable behavior, conditions, and criteria.	_____	_____
4. *Objective*: Using your text as a reference, recognize the names of the various components of the central nervous system. *Test item*: From memory, list the various components of the central nervous system.	_____	_____
5. *Objective*: Given a written story, list the main events in chronological order. *Test item*: From the story provided, list the main events in chronological order.	_____	_____

Answers: Items 1, 2, and 5 have learning outcomes that match; items 3 and 4 do not have learning outcomes that match.

Step 2: Identify the learning conditions that are called for by the objective. Check to determine if your item requires the same learning conditions.

EXERCISE: *For the following, assume that Step 1 has been performed. Employ Step 2.*

	Match?	
	Yes	*No*
1. *Objective*: Using your map as a guide, make a freehand drawing of Australia. *Test item*: Without using your map, draw the continent of Australia.	_____	_____

2. *Objective*: Given a complete instructional objective, write a test item   _____ _____
that matches the objective's learning outcome and conditions.
Test item: Write an item that matches the learning outcome and
conditions of the following objective: "The student will add on paper 10
two-digit numbers without regrouping within 1 minute with 80%
accuracy."

3. *Objective*: Given a list of words, the student will circle the nouns with   _____ _____
90% accuracy.
Test item: Give 10 examples of nouns and 10 examples of verbs.

4. *Objective*: Using their own nondigital watches, the students will tell   _____ _____
time to the quarter hour with 90% accuracy.
Test item: Look at the digital clock on my desk and write down the
correct time when I ask.

5. *Objective*: The student will sing "The Star-Spangled Banner" in front of   _____ _____
the class with the aid of a record.
Test item: Sing "The Star-Spangled Banner" in front of the class.

Answers: Item 2 has matching conditions; items 1, 3, 4, and 5 do not have matching conditions.

In summary, ensuring that content validity is as simple as making sure that both the learning outcomes and the conditions called for by your test items match the learning outcomes and conditions called for by your instructional objectives. Remember, your goal is to measure achievement, not to trick your students or to have them guess what kind of answer you are looking for. The best way to measure achievement is to ask your students to demonstrate mastery of a skill under the conditions you specify in your instructional objectives. With time, Steps 1 and 2 will become second nature. Until then, subject your items to these steps to ensure their content validity.

TAXONOMY OF EDUCATIONAL OBJECTIVES

We've now considered methods not only to analyze objectives already written but also to write instructional objectives and to match test items to instructional objectives. In the rest of this chapter, we will consider different levels of complexity at which objectives and test items may be written and a method for test construction that will help us write items at these levels to ensure that our classroom tests measure higher-level thinking skills. Writing test items that measure higher-level thinking is especially important to help your students prepare for success on tests aligned with the Common Core State Standards, because of their emphasis on higher-order thinking, such as problem-solving and integrative and critical thinking.

Cognitive Domain

The level of an objective refers to the cognitive, mental, or thought complexity called for by the objective. For example, the objective "The student will list from memory the names of at least three of the last four U.S. presidents" is a relatively straightforward cognitive task. It involves only recall of the information. Such an objective would be considered lower level. On the other hand, an objective such as "Given an eyewitness account of an event, separate fact from opinion with at least

75% accuracy" is a relatively complex cognitive task. It requires the ability to analyze an eyewitness account and to apply some criteria in determining whether statements are observable and objective or subjective and based on inference. Such an objective would be considered higher level.

One method of categorizing objectives according to cognitive complexity was devised by Bloom et al. (1984). It is a taxonomy of educational objectives for the cognitive domain and delineates six levels of cognitive complexity ranging from the knowledge level (simplest) to the evaluation level (most complex). As illustrated in Figure 6.2, the levels are presumed to be hierarchical. That is, higher-level objectives are assumed to include, and be dependent on, lower-level cognitive skills. Each level of the taxonomy has different characteristics. Each of these levels is described next with examples of action verbs that are usually indicative of the different levels.

Knowledge   Objectives at the knowledge level require the students to remember. Test items ask the student to recall or recognize facts, terminology, problem-solving strategies, or rules. Some action verbs that describe learning outcomes at the knowledge level are the following:

define	list	recall
describe	match	recite
identify	name	select
label	outline	state

Some example objectives:

The student will recall the four major food groups without error by Friday.

From memory, the student will match each U.S. general with his most famous battle with 80% accuracy.

Comprehension   Objectives at the comprehension level require some level of understanding. Test items require the student to change the form of a communication (translation), to restate what has been read, to see connections or relationships among parts of a communication

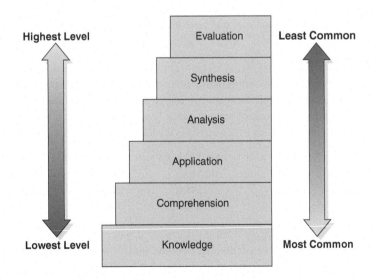

FIGURE 6.2   Taxonomy of educational objectives: cognitive domain.

(interpretation), or to draw conclusions or consequences from information (inference). Some action verbs that describe learning outcomes at the comprehension level are as follows:

convert	explain	infer
defend	extend	paraphrase
discriminate	estimate	predict
distinguish	generalize	summarize

Some example objectives:

By the end of the semester, the student will summarize the main events of a story in grammatically correct English.

The student will discriminate between the "realists" and the "naturalists," citing examples from the readings with 80% accuracy.

Application   Objectives written at the application level require the student to use previously acquired information in a setting other than that in which it was learned. Application differs from comprehension in that questions requiring application present the problem in a different and often applied context. Thus, the student can rely on neither the question nor the context to decide what prior learning information must be used to solve the problem. Some action verbs that describe learning outcomes at the application level are the following:

change	modify	relate
compute	operate	solve
demonstrate	organize	transfer
develop	prepare	use
employ	produce	

Some example objectives:

On Monday, the student will tell the class what he or she did over the holiday, without using notes.

Given fractions not covered in class, the student will multiply them on paper with 85% accuracy.

Analysis   Objectives written at the analysis level require the student to identify logical errors (e.g., point out a contradiction or an erroneous inference) or to differentiate among facts, opinions, assumptions, hypotheses, or conclusions. Questions at the analysis level often require the student to draw relationships among ideas or to compare and contrast. Some action verbs that describe learning outcomes at the analysis level are the following:

break down	distinguish	point out
deduce	illustrate	relate
diagram	infer	separate out
differentiate	outline	subdivide

Some example objectives:

Given a presidential speech, the student will be able to point out the positions that attack an individual rather than his or her program, with at least 90% accuracy.

Given absurd statements (e.g., "A man had flu twice. The first time it killed him. The second time he got well quickly."), the student will be able to point out the contradiction more than 60% of the time.

Synthesis   Objectives written at the synthesis level require the student to produce something unique or original. Questions at the synthesis level require students to solve some unfamiliar problem in a unique way or to combine parts to form a unique or novel whole. Some action verbs that describe learning outcomes at the synthesis level are the following:

categorize	create	formulate
compile	design	rewrite
compose	devise	summarize

Some example objectives at the synthesis level:

> Given a short story, the student will write a different but plausible ending within 15 minutes.

> Given a problem to be solved, the student will design on paper a scientific experiment to address the problem, without using any reference materials.

Evaluation   Instructional objectives written at the evaluation level require the student to form judgments about the value or worth of methods, ideas, people, or products that have a specific purpose. Questions require the student to state the basis for his or her judgments (e.g., what external criteria or principles were drawn upon to reach a conclusion). Some action verbs that describe learning outcomes at the evaluation level are the following:

appraise	criticize	interpret
compare	defend	support
contrast	justify	validate
conclude		

Some example objectives at the evaluation level:

> Given a previously unread paragraph, the student will judge its value according to the five criteria discussed in class.

> Given a description of a country's economic system, the student will defend it, basing arguments on principles of socialism, described in your text.

Anderson and Krathwohl (2001) have prepared an updated version of the Bloom et al. (1984) taxonomy of educational objectives from a cognitive learning perspective that helps teachers identify and assess not only the outcomes they desire but also the thinking processes their students must use to achieve those outcomes. Their edited volume explores curricula from three perspectives—the cognitive learning perspective, the teaching perspective, and the assessment perspective—providing a useful framework for writing objectives that connect all three perspectives. Their extensions to the original taxonomy emphasize the distinctions among factual (declarative), conceptual, procedural, and metacognitive knowledge when writing objectives and selecting a teaching strategy that can most effectively achieve those objectives.

Affective Domain

The affective taxonomy, which describes objectives that reflect underlying emotions, feelings, or values rather than cognitive or thought complexity, has been developed by Krathwohl, Bloom, and Masia (1999). This taxonomy describes a process by which another person's, group's, or society's ideas; beliefs; customs; philosophies; attitudes; and so on are gradually accepted and internalized by a different person, group, or society. This process usually begins with a minimal, partial, or incomplete acceptance of an alternative point of view and culminates with the complete integration of this point of view into an individual's personal belief system.

For example, an individual who naively believed in early 1985 that the return of Halley's Comet in 1986 would cause the end of life on Earth may at first have found it difficult even to listen to, *receive*, or *attend* to information that indicated that the comet's return would have no significant or lasting effect on life on Earth. Instead, the individual may have ignored such information, attempting instead to convince others of Earth's impending doom. However, with the passage of time throughout the year, and with increased media and educational reports about the event, the individual may have increasingly listened to such information and even considered, discussed, or *responded* to explanations regarding Earth's safety due to the comet's distance from Earth, its lack of mass, and the protection afforded by Earth's atmosphere, for example. Eventually, the individual likely began to *value* the argument that the comet would have little or no effect on life on Earth and ceased preaching Earth's demise. Finally, after trying unsuccessfully even to see the comet on numerous occasions during its closest approach to Earth, the individual may have accepted and *organized* the arguments against the total destruction of the human race to the extent that these arguments have come to be internalized and now *characterize* the individual's *value complex*. This would be evident by the individual's calm acceptance of near approaches by celestial bodies in the future and efforts to reassure others of their safety in the face of such events.

The preceding italicized words indicate the five categories or levels of the affective domain. Each of these levels is described further under the following heads, and sublevels within each of these levels are also italicized. As with the cognitive taxonomy, the levels and sublevels are generally considered to be hierarchical.

Receiving (Attending) Responses at the receiving level require that a student have at least an *awareness* of some stimulus. Once this has occurred, a *willingness* at least to listen or attend to the stimulus must be present (i.e., tolerance). A student will next be able to *attend selectively* to various aspects of the context within which the stimulus exists, differentiating those that are relevant to the stimulus from those that are not.

Responding Student responses at the responding level indicate more than passive listening or attending; they require active participation. In the most basic form of responding, a student will at least *acquiesce* to a teacher's or other's request, although given a choice, the student might choose some other activity. More complete responding would be indicated by a student's *willingness* to engage in an activity, even when allowed a choice. The highest level within this category is indicated by *satisfaction* after engaging in a response. Not only does the student participate, but it is evident that the student enjoys the activity.

Valuing At the valuing level, students judge an activity as to its worthiness and tend to do so consistently enough that the pattern is recognizable to others. The most basic sublevel involves the *acceptance* of a belief, idea, attitude, and the like. The individual may not be willing to publicly defend the idea but has internalized it. When a student actively pursues an idea, he or she is demonstrating a *preference* for it, the next sublevel of valuing. Finally, after becoming convinced of the validity of an idea, a student expresses *commitment* to the idea. At this point, the student demonstrates conviction by pursuing the goal or idea diligently.

Organization As ideas are internalized, they become increasingly interrelated and prioritized. That is, they become organized into a value system. This requires first that a student *conceptualize* a value by analyzing interrelationships and drawing generalizations that reflect the valued idea. It may be noted that such an activity is cognitive. However, it is classified here because such conceptualizing would only be undertaken after an idea or philosophy was valued. Next, values that have been conceptualized are subject to the *organization of a value system*. That is, the valued ideas are arranged to foster their consistency and compatibility with one another.

Characterization by a Value or Value Complex Students operating at the value level behave in a way that is consistent with their value system, avoiding hypocrisy and behaving consistently with an underlying philosophy "automatically." The first sublevel is characterized by a *generalized set*. This means that the individual is predisposed to perceive, process, and react to a situation in accordance with an internalized value system. The next level, *characterization*, is evident in the consistency between an individual's thoughts and behaviors. Such individuals would never say "Do as I say, not as I do."

Now that you are familiar with the affective taxonomy you may ask, "What do I do with it in the classroom?" First of all, it is probably unrealistic to expect a classroom teacher to structure experiences over a 1-year period that would lead a student through all five levels. Indeed, many would argue that few human beings ever reach a point in their lives where they function at the fifth, or even the fourth, level. Nonetheless, this taxonomy has important implications for instructional activities and for methods to evaluate instructional activities.

Let's look at an example. Suppose most of the children in your class say they hate history and avoid all stimuli related to history. Asking those students to write a paper describing the importance of history courses in the public-school curriculum would likely be a frustrating experience for them and for you, since those students are not even at the receiving or attending level when it comes to history. You might spend a good deal of time developing a reliable scoring scheme for such a paper and grading the papers only to find that the students failed to see any value in history courses in general or in the topic of the paper. It would be more appropriate, given this example, to develop activities and ways to evaluate those activities aimed initially at the receiving or attending level. Students would progress to the responding level only after demonstrating their willingness to consider history as an important part of the curriculum and after demonstrating the ability to attend selectively to history when distracting stimuli are present. They would progress to the valuing level only after demonstrating their willingness to deal objectively with history and/or their satisfaction with history as a subject. The affective taxonomy provides you with a framework that allows you to better assess "where your students are" regarding various topics. This should help you keep your expectations for the class realistic and keep you from pushing for too much too soon, perhaps frustrating yourself and the class in the process.

The Psychomotor Domain

In addition to the cognitive and affective taxonomies, taxonomies of psychomotor behaviors have been developed by Dave (1970), Harrow (1977), and Moore (1992). This domain includes virtually all behaviors: speaking, writing, eating, jumping, throwing, catching, running, walking, driving a car, opening a door, dancing, flying an airplane, and so on. The psychomotor domain has proved most difficult to classify into taxonomic levels since all but the simplest reflex actions involve cognitive, and often affective, components. Nonetheless, a taxonomy is presented because it does again provide a framework within which to consider the design of instructional activities and methods to evaluate the activities. This taxonomy may prove especially useful to teachers in the lower elementary grades and teachers of physical education, dance, theater, and other courses that require considerable movement. The psychomotor taxonomy listed under the following headings ranges from the lowest level of observable reflexive behavior to the highest level, representing the most complex forms of nonverbal communication.

Reflex Movements Reflex movements are involuntary movements that are either evident at birth or develop with maturation. Sublevels include *segmental reflexes*, *intersegmental reflexes*, and *suprasegmental reflexes*.

Basic Fundamental Movements Basic fundamental movements are inherent in more complex or skilled motor movements. Sublevels include *locomotor movements, nonlocomotor movements,* and *manipulative movements.*

Perceptual Abilities Perceptual abilities refer to all the abilities of an individual that send input to the brain for interpretation, which in turn affects motor movements. Sublevels include *kinesthetic, visual, auditory, tactile discrimination,* and *coordinated abilities.*

Physical Abilities Physical abilities are the characteristics of an individual's physical self, which, when developed properly, enable smooth and efficient movement. Sublevels include *endurance, strength, flexibility,* and *agility.*

Skilled Movements Skilled movements are the result of learning, often complex learning. They result in efficiency in carrying out a complex movement or task. Sublevels include *simple, compound,* and *complex adaptive skills.*

Nondiscursive Communication Nondiscursive communication is a form of communication through movement. Such nonverbal communication as facial expressions, postures, and expressive dance routines are examples. Sublevels include *expressive movement* and *interpretive movement.*

THE TEST BLUEPRINT

Thus far, we've devoted a good deal of time to writing and analyzing objectives and showing you how to match test items to objectives. We also need to spend some time discussing a technique to help you remember to write objectives and test items at different levels to ensure our tests include items that measure higher-level thinking. As we have noted, this is particularly important now that most states have adopted the Common Core Standards, with their emphasis on higher-level thinking. This technique is referred to as a *test blueprint.* Much like a blueprint used by a builder to guide building construction, the test blueprint used by a teacher guides test construction. The test blueprint is also called a *table of specifications.*

The blueprint for a building ensures that the builder will not overlook details considered essential. Similarly, the test blueprint ensures that the teacher will not overlook details considered essential to a good test. More specifically, it ensures that a test will sample whether learning has taken place across the range of (1) content areas covered in class and readings and (2) cognitive processes considered important. It ensures that your test will include a variety of items that tap different levels of cognitive complexity. To get an idea of what a test blueprint helps you avoid, consider the following:

> Joan was nervous. She knew she had to do very well on the comprehensive final in order to pass American History: 1945–2015. To make matters worse, her teacher was new and no one knew what his final exams were like.
>
> "Well," she told herself. "There's really no point in worrying. Even if I don't do well on this test, I have learned to analyze information and think critically—the discussions were great. I've studied the text and lessons very hard and managed to cover every topic very thoroughly beginning with the end of World War II in 1945 through the reelection of President Barack Obama. I realize I missed the class dealing with the late 1960s and early 1970s, but that stuff only covered a few pages in the text anyway, and we only spent one class on it!"
>
> Feeling more relaxed and confident, Joan felt even better when she saw that the entire final was only one page long. After receiving her copy, however, Joan began shaking. Her test is reproduced here.

American History: 1945–2005
Name: _____   Date:_____
It has been a long year and you have been good students. This short test is your reward.

1. *On what date did American soldiers first begin to fight in Vietnam?_____*
2. *How many years did Americans fight in Vietnam?_____*
3. *What was the capital of South Vietnam?_____*
4. *On what date did Richard Nixon become president?_____*
5. *Who was Richard Nixon's vice president during his second administration?_____*
6. *What is Vietnam's largest seaport?_____*
7. *Who was the president of South Vietnam?_____*
8. *On what date did Americans begin to leave Vietnam?_____ Have a good summer!*

We wish we could safely say that things like this never happen, but they do! Chances are you have had a similar experience—perhaps not as extreme, but similar. This test items do not comprehensively sample important events in American History between 1945 and 2015 and their consequences. It focuses entirely on events that occurred during the Vietnam War. It fails to representatively sample content presented in the text and it omits most content presented in class, except for one class. Finally, it fails to tap any higher-level thinking processes. Each question requires rote memorization at the knowledge level. A test blueprint, as shown in Table 6.1, helps us avoid falling into this or similar traps in test construction.

TABLE 6.1   Test Blueprint for a Unit on Instructional Objectives

Content Outline	Knowledge	Comprehension	Application	Analysis	Total	Percentage (%)
			(Number of Items)			
1. Role of objectives						
a. The student can state purposes for objectives in education.	4				4	12
b. The student can describe a classroom system model and the role of objectives in it.	1				1	3
2. Writing objectives						
a. Given a general educational goal, the student will write an instructional objective that specifies that goal.		5			5	14
b. The students can match instructional objectives with their appropriate level in the cognitive domain.		5			5	14
c. The student can identify the three parts of an objective: behavior, conditions, criteria.		5			5	14
d. The student can distinguish learning activities from learning outcomes when given examples of each.		10			10	29
3. Decoding ready-made objectives						
a. Given instructional objectives in need of modification, the student will rewrite the objective so that it is a suitable instructional objective.				5	5	14
Total	4	21	5	5	35	
Percentage	12%	60%	14%	14%	100%	

A test blueprint is essential to good test construction. It not only ensures that your test will sample all important content areas and processes (levels of cognitive complexity) but is also useful in planning and organizing instruction. The blueprint should be assembled before you actually begin a unit. Table 6.1 illustrates a test blueprint appropriate for a unit on instructional objectives being taught in an education course. Let's consider each component of the blueprint. Once we understand how the components are interrelated, the significance of a test blueprint will become clearer.

Content Outline

The content outline lists the topic and the important objectives included under the topic. It is for these objectives that you will write test items. Try to keep the total number of objectives to a manageable number. No more than four are normally needed for any one unit.

Categories

The categories serve as a reminder or a check on the "cognitive complexity" of the test. Obviously, many units over which you want to test will contain objectives that do not go beyond the comprehension level. However, the outline can suggest that you try to incorporate higher levels of learning into your instruction and evaluations. In the cells under these categories, report the number of items in your tests that are included in that level for a particular objective. For example, five items are to be constructed to measure comprehension level objective 2b in Table 6.1.

Number of Items

Fill in the cells in Table 6.1 using the following procedure:

1. Determine the classification of each instructional objective.
2. Record the number of items that are to be constructed for the objective in the cell corresponding to the category for that objective.
3. Repeat Steps 1 and 2 for every objective in the outline.
4. Total the number of items for the instructional objective and record the number in the total column.
5. Repeat Steps 1 through 4 for each topic.
6. Total the number of items falling into each category and record the number at the bottom of the table.
7. Compute the column and row percentages by dividing each total by the number of items in the test.

Functions

The information in Table 6.1 is intended to convey to the teacher the following:

- How many items are to be constructed for which objectives and content topics.
- Whether the test will reflect a balanced picture of what was taught.
- Whether all topics and objectives will be assessed and their level of cognitive complexity.

Seldom can such "balance" be so easily attained. The extra time required to construct such a blueprint for your test (and your instruction!) will quickly repay itself. You will not only avoid constructing a bad test, but you will have to make fewer and less extensive revisions of your test.

TABLE 6.2 Test Blueprint for a Unit on Subtraction without Borrowing

Content Outline	Categories (Number of Items): Knowledge	Comprehension	Application	Total	Percentage (%)
1. The student will discriminate the subtraction sign from the addition sign.	1			1	4
2. The student will discriminate addition problems from subtraction problems.	2			2	8
3. The student will discriminate correctly solved subtraction problems from incorrectly solved subtraction problems.		4		4	16
4. The student will correctly solve single-digit subtraction problems.			6	6	24
5. The student will correctly solve subtraction problems with double-digit numerators and single-digit denominators.			6	6	24
6. The student will correctly solve double-digit subtraction problems.			6	6	24
Total	3	4	18	25	
Percentage	12%	16%	72%	100%	

You will also have a sense of satisfaction from realizing you've constructed a representative test that has content validity, the most important criterion for an achievement test.

Since test blueprints are so important to test construction (not to mention instructional planning), we have included a second example of a test blueprint in Table 6.2. This table illustrates a test blueprint appropriate for an elementary unit on subtraction without borrowing.

Clearly, constructing test blueprints requires some time and effort. This will be time and effort well spent, we believe, because it will serve you and your students well by improving the content validity and appropriateness of your test. Nevertheless, we realize that time is of the essence. For some tips on how a computer can help save time in revising test blueprints see the sidebar (Box 6-1).

BOX 6-1

COMPUTERS AND TEST BLUEPRINTS

If instructional objectives have been saved in a word processing file, it is relatively simple to use your word processing program's cut-and-paste functions to transfer the objectives to the content outline section of a test blueprint outline in a separate word processing file. A spreadsheet file can be established that will automatically sum and convert in to percentages the cell totals for the rows and columns. If the word processing program is compatible with a spreadsheet program or is part of an integrated suite of related programs, you can also use the cut-and-paste functions to transfer the spreadsheet file into the cell space in the word processing file. Once you have done so, you can make modifications to the combined word processing and spreadsheet file as needed for future revisions of the test.

This concludes our introduction to test planning and instructional objectives. In the next two chapters, we'll consider the actual process by which objective and essay test items are constructed. Soon you'll be able to construct not just a representative test but a good representative test!

SUMMARY

Chapter 6 introduced you to the first two steps in test construction, writing instructional objectives and preparing a test blueprint. Its major points are as follows:

1. A complete instructional objective includes the following:
   a. an observable learning outcome,
   b. any special conditions under which the behavior must be displayed, and
   c. a performance level considered to be indicative of mastery.

2. Learning outcomes are ends (products); learning activities are the means (processes) to the ends.

3. Objectives may be analyzed to determine their adequacy by
   a. determining whether a learning outcome or learning activity is stated in the objective,
   b. rewriting the objective if a learning outcome is not stated,
   c. determining whether the learning outcomes are stated in measurable or unmeasurable terms, and
   d. determining whether the objective states the simplest and most direct way of measuring the learning outcome.

4. Learning outcomes and conditions stated in a test item must match the outcomes and conditions stated in the objective if the item is to be considered a content valid measure of or match for the objective.

5. The taxonomy of educational objectives for the cognitive domain helps categorize objectives at different levels of cognitive complexity. There are six levels: knowledge, comprehension, application, analysis, synthesis, and evaluation.

6. The affective taxonomy describes objectives that reflect emotions, feelings, or values rather than cognitive complexity. There are five levels of the affective taxonomy: receiving (attending), responding, valuing, organization, and characterization by a value complex.

7. The psychomotor taxonomy describes increasingly complex behaviors rather than cognitive or affective complexity. Its levels include reflex movements, basic fundamental movements, perceptual abilities, physical abilities, skilled movements, and nondiscursive communication.

8. A test blueprint, including instructional objectives covering the content areas to be covered and the relevant cognitive processes, should be constructed to guide item writing and test construction.

9. The test blueprint conveys to the teacher the number of items to be constructed per objective, their level of cognitive complexity in the taxonomy, and whether the test represents a balanced picture based on what was taught.

FOR DISCUSSION AND PRACTICE

1. For the same content area, make up two objectives each at the knowledge, comprehension, application, analysis, synthesis, and evaluation levels of the taxonomy of cognitive objectives. Select verbs for each level from the lists provided. Try to make your objectives cover the same topic.

2. Exchange the objectives you have just written with a classmate. Have him or her check each objective for (a) an observable behavior, (b) any special conditions under which the behavior must be displayed, and (c) a performance level considered sufficient to demonstrate mastery. Revise your objectives if necessary.

3. Now take your list of objectives and arrange them into the format of a test blueprint (Table 6.1). To construct a test blueprint, determine some general content headings under

which your specific objectives can be placed. List these with your objectives vertically down the left side of the page. Next, across the top of the page, indicate the levels of behavior at which you have written your objectives. In the cells of the table, place the number of items you would write for each objective if you were to prepare a 100-item test over this content. Total the items and compute percentages as indicated in Table 6.1.

***4.** Column A contains instructional objectives. Column B contains levels of cognitive learning outcomes. Match the levels in Column B with the most appropriate objective in Column A. Write the letter that indicates the highest level of cognitive outcome implied in the space next to the numbers in Column A. Column B levels can be used more than once.

Column A

_____ **1.** Given a two-page essay, the student can distinguish the assumptions basic to the author's position.

_____ **2.** The student will correctly spell the word *mountain*.

_____ **3.** The student will convert the following English passage into Spanish.

_____ **4.** The student will compose new pieces of prose and poetry according to the classification system emphasized in lecture.

_____ **5.** Given a sinking passenger ship with 19 of its 20 lifeboats destroyed, the captain will decide who is to be on the last lifeboat on the basis of perceptions of their potential worth to society.

Column B

a. Knowledge

b. Comprehension

c. Application

d. Analysis

e. Synthesis

f. Evaluation

*Answers to these questions appear in Appendix B.

***5.** Using the following test blueprint or table of specifications for a unit on mathematics, answer the following questions:

a. How many questions will deal with long division at the comprehension, application, and analysis levels?

b. What percentage of the test questions will deal with multiplication and division?

Major Area	Minor Area	Knowledge	Comprehension	Application	Analysis	Synthesis	Evaluation	Total	Percentage (%)
Addition	Whole numbers	2	1	2				5	
	Fractions	1	1	2	1			5	20
Subtraction	Whole numbers	1	1	2	1			5	
	Fractions	1	1	2	1			4	20
Multiplication	Tables	2	2					4	
	Whole numbers				2	2	1	5	
	Fractions	1	1	2	1	1		6	30
Division	Long division	1	2	1				4	
	Whole numbers	1	1	2	1			5	
	Fractions	1	2	2	1			6	30

CHAPTER 7

WRITING OBJECTIVE TEST ITEMS

LEARNING OUTCOMES

After completing this chapter, the student will be able to:

1. Determine the type of item format most appropriate for different objectives.
2. Differentiate between well-written and poorly written objective test items (true–false, matching, multiple-choice, and completion).
3. Correct the faults in poorly written objective items.
4. Describe ways to minimize the effects of guessing on true–false items.
5. Identify the suggestions for writing true–false items.
6. Describe ways to minimize the effects of guessing on matching items.
7. Identify the suggestions for writing matching items.
8. Recognize item faults specific to multiple-choice items.
9. Develop multiple-choice items at higher levels of cognitive complexity (i.e., Bloom's taxonomy).
10. Identify the suggestions for writing multiple-choice items.
11. Explain why scoring time is increased when completion items are employed.
12. Identify the suggestions for writing completion items.
13. Explain ways to avoid gender and racial bias in objective test items.
14. Compare and contrast the advantages and disadvantages for each item format.
15. Write fault-free objective test items that match their instructional objectives.

THUS FAR we have discussed how to establish general goals for instruction and how to develop instructional objectives derived from those goals. We have also discussed using the test blueprint to ensure both an adequate sampling of the content area and accurate matching of test items to instructional objectives, as well as to guarantee that our test measures higher-level thinking skills. We are now ready to put some "meat" on this test "skeleton." In this chapter, we will discuss objective test items and how to construct them. Objective test items include items with the following formats: true–false, matching, multiple choice, and completion or short answer. The essay item, because of its special characteristics and scoring considerations, will be treated in Chapter 8, along with methods to measure the way students organize knowledge and suggestions for open-book exams.

WHICH FORMAT?

Once you have reached the item-writing stage of test construction, you will have to choose a format or combination of formats to use for your test. Although your choice can be somewhat arbitrary at times, this is not always the case. Often your decision has already been made for you, or, more correctly, you may have at least partially made the decision when you wrote the objective or objectives. In many instances, however, you will have a choice among several item formats. For example, consider the following objectives and item formats.

Objective 1. Given a story, the student can recognize the meaning of all new words.

Test Items. Circle the letter that represents the correct meaning of the following words:

1. intention
   a. desire
   b. need
   c. direction
   d. command
2. crisis
   a. feeling
   b. message
   c. pending
   d. critical

Objective 2. The student can associate the characteristics of leading characters with their names.

Test Item. The first column is a list of the names of the main characters in *Huckleberry Finn*. Descriptions of the main characters are listed in the second column. In the space provided, write the letter of the description that matches each character.

Character	*Description*
_____ 1. Tom	a. Cruel
_____ 2. Becky	b. Always by himself, a loner
_____ 3. Jim	c. Popular, outgoing, fun loving
_____ 4. Huck	d. Always critical
_____ 5. Mrs. Watson	e. Sneaky, lying, scheming
	f. Kind, gentle, loving
	g. Dull, slow moving

Objective 3. The student can write a plausible alternative ending to a story.

Test Item. You have just read the story *Huckleberry Finn*. In 40 words, write a different ending to the story that would be believable.

Objective 4. The students will recognize whether certain events occurred.

Test Item. Here is a list of incidents in *Huckleberry Finn*. Circle T if it happened in the story and F if it did not.

1. The thieves were killed in the storm on the river.	T	F
2. Jim gained his freedom.	T	F
3. Tom broke his leg.	T	F

Objective 1 was measured using a multiple-choice format. We might also have tested this objective using a true–false or matching format. Similarly, objective 2 lends itself to a multiple-choice as well as a matching format. In many circumstances, alternative item formats may be appropriate, so the choice between them will be made on the basis of other considerations. For example, time constraints or your preference for, or skill in, writing different types of items will undoubtedly influence your choice of item format.

Objective 3, however, requires an essay item. There is no way this objective can be measured with an objective item. Objective 4 lends itself almost exclusively to a true–false format. Perhaps other formats would work, but the true–false format certainly does the job. In short, at times our objectives tell us which format to use. At other times, we must consider other factors. Let's look more closely at the different item formats.

TRUE–FALSE ITEMS

True–false items are popular probably because they are quick and easy to write, or at least they seem to be. Actually, true–false items do take less time to write than good objective items of any other format, but *good* true–false items are *not* that easy to write. Consider the following true–false items. Use your common sense to help you determine which are good items and which are poor.

> **EXERCISE: *Put a G in the space next to the items you believe are good true–false items and a P next to the items you feel are poor.***
>
> _____ **1.** High-IQ children always get high grades in school.
> _____ **2.** Will Rogers said, "I never met a man I didn't like."
> _____ **3.** If a plane crashed on the Mexican–U.S. border, half the survivors would be buried in Mexico and half in the United States.
> _____ **4.** The use of double negatives is not an altogether undesirable characteristic of diplomats and academicians.
> _____ **5.** Prayer should not be outlawed in schools.
> _____ **6.** Of the objective items, true–false items are the least time consuming to construct.
> _____ **7.** The trend toward competency testing of high school graduates began in the late 1970s and represents a big step forward for slow learners.
>
> *Answers*: 1. P; 2. G; 3. P; 4. P; 5. P; 6. G; 7. P

In item 1, the word *always* is an absolute. To some extent, true–false items depend on absolute judgments. However, statements or facts are seldom completely true or completely false. Thus, an alert student will usually answer "false" to items that include *always*, *all*, *never*, or *only*.

To avoid this problem, avoid using terms such as *all*, *always*, *never*, or *only*. Item 1 could be improved by replacing always with a less absolute term, perhaps *tend*. Thus item 1 might read:

High-IQ children tend to get high grades in school.

Item 2 is a good one. To answer the item correctly, the students would have to know whether Will Rogers made the statement. Or do they? Consider the following situation:

Mrs. Allen, a history teacher and crusader against grade inflation, couldn't wait to spring her latest creation on her students. She had spent weeks inserting trick words, phrases, and complicated grammatical constructions into her 100 item true–false test. In order to ensure low grades on the test, she allowed only 30 minutes for the test. Although her harried students worked as quickly as they could, no one completed more than half the items, and no one answered more than 40 items correctly. No one, that is, except Tina. When Tina handed her test back to Mrs. Allen after two minutes, Mrs. Allen announced, "Class, Tina has handed in her test! Obviously, she hasn't read the questions and will earn a zero!" When she scored the test, however, Mrs. Allen was shocked to see that in fact Tina had answered 50 items correctly. She earned the highest score on the test without even reading Mrs. Allen's tricky questions. Confused and embarrassed, Mrs. Allen told the class they would have no more true–false tests and would have essay tests in the future.

This points to the most serious shortcoming of true–false items: With every true–false item, regardless of how well or poorly written, the student has a 50% chance of guessing correctly even without reading the item! In other words, on a 50-item true–false test, we would expect individuals who were totally unfamiliar with the content being tested to answer about 25 items correctly. However, this doesn't mean you should avoid true–false items entirely, since they are appropriate at times. Fortunately, there are ways of reducing the effects of guessing. Some of these are described next, and another will be presented in Chapter 11.

1. Encourage all students to guess when they do not know the correct answer. Since it is virtually impossible to prevent certain students from guessing, encouraging all students to guess should equalize the effects of guessing. The test scores will then reflect a more or less equal "guessing factor" plus the actual level of each student's knowledge. This will also prevent testwise students from having an unfair advantage over nontestwise students.

2. Require revision of statements that are false. With this approach, space is provided for students to alter false items to make them true. Usually, the student also underlines or circles the false part of the item. Item 1 is revised here along with other examples.

T	F	High-IQ children *always* get high grades in school. *tend to*
T	F	Panama is *north* of Cuba. *south*
T	F	*September* has an extra day during leap year. *February*

With such a strategy, full credit is awarded only if the revision is correct. The disadvantage of such an approach is that more test time is required for the same number of items and scoring time is increased.

Item 3 is a poor item, but Mrs. Allen would probably like it because it is a trick question. "Survivors" of a plane crash are not buried! Chances are that you never even noticed the word *survivors* and probably assumed the item referred to fatalities. Trick items may have a place in tests of critical reading or visual discrimination (in which case they would no longer be trick questions), but seldom are they appropriate in the average classroom test. Rewritten, item 3 might read:

If a plane crashes on the Mexican–U.S. border, half the fatalities would be buried in Mexico and half in the United States.

Item 4 is also poor. First of all, it includes a double negative—*not* and *undesirable*. Items with a single negative are confusing enough. Negating the first negative with a second wastes space and test-taking time and also confuses most students. If you want to say something, say it positively. The following revision makes this item slightly more palatable.

The use of double negatives is an altogether desirable trait of diplomats and academicians.

We said slightly more palatable because the item is still troublesome. The word altogether is an absolute, and we now know we should avoid absolutes, since there usually are exceptions to the rules they imply. When we eliminate altogether, the item reads as follows:

The use of double negatives is a desirable trait of diplomats and academicians.

However, the item is still flawed because it states an opinion, not a fact. Is the item true or false? The answer depends on whom you ask. To most of us, the use of double negatives is probably undesirable, for the reasons already stated. To some diplomats, the use of double negatives may seem highly desirable. In short, true–false statements should normally be used to measure knowledge of factual information. If you must use a true–false item to measure knowledge of an opinionated position or statement, state the referent (the person or group that made the statement or took the position), as illustrated in the following revision:

> According to the National Institute of Diplomacy, the use of double negatives is a desirable trait of diplomats and academicians.

Item 5 further illustrates this point. It is deficient because it states an opinion. It is neither obviously true nor obviously false. This revision includes a referent that makes it acceptable.

> The American Civil Liberties Union (ACLU) has taken the position that prayer should *not* be outlawed in schools.

Notice the word *not* in Item 5. When you include a negative in a test item, highlight it in italics, underlining, or uppercase letters so that the reader will not overlook it. Remember that, unlike Mrs. Allen, you intend to determine whether your students have mastered your objective, not to ensure low test scores.

Item 6 represents a good item. It measures factual information, and the phrase "Of the objective items" qualifies the item and limits it to a specific frame of reference.

The last item is deficient because it is double barreled: It is actually two items in one. When do you mark true for a double-barreled item? When both parts of the item are true? When one part is true? Or only when the most important part is true? The point is that items should measure a single idea. Double-barreled items take too much time to read and comprehend. To avoid this problem, simply construct two items, as we have done here:

> The trend toward competency testing of high school graduates began in the late 1970s.

> The trend toward competency testing represents a big step forward for slow learners.

Better? Yes. Acceptable? Not quite. The second item is opinionated. According to whom is this statement true or false? Let's include a referent.

> According to the Office of Education, the trend toward competency testing of high school graduates is a big step forward for slow learners.

Whose position is being represented is now clear, and the item is straightforward?

Suggestions for Writing True–False Items

1. The desired method of marking true or false should be clearly explained before students begin the test.
2. Construct statements that are definitely true or definitely false, without additional qualifications. If opinion is used, attribute it to some source.
3. Use relatively short statements and eliminate extraneous material.
4. Keep true and false statements at approximately the same length, and be sure that there are approximately equal numbers of true and false items.
5. Avoid using double-negative statements. They take extra time to decipher and are difficult to interpret.

6. Avoid the following:
   a. Verbal clues, absolutes, and complex sentences.
   b. Broad general statements that are usually not true or false without further qualifications.
   c. Terms denoting indefinite degree (e.g., large, long time, and regularly) or absolutes (e.g., never, only, and always).
   d. Placing items in a systematic order (e.g., TTFF, TFTF, and so on).
   e. Taking statements directly from the text and presenting them out of context.

MATCHING ITEMS

Like true–false items, matching items represent a popular and convenient testing format. Just like good true–false items, though, good matching items are not as easy to write as you might think. Imagine you are back in your tenth-grade American History class and the following matching item shows up on your test. Is it a good matching exercise or not? If not, what is wrong with it?

Directions: Match A and B

A		*B*
1. Lincoln	**a.**	President during the twentieth century
2. Nixon	**b.**	Invented the telephone
3. Whitney	**c.**	Delivered the Emancipation Proclamation
4. Ford	**d.**	Recently resigned from office
5. Bell	**e.**	Civil rights leader
6. King	**f.**	Invented the cotton gin
7. Washington	**g.**	Our first president
8. Roosevelt	**h.**	Only president elected for more than two terms

See any problems? Compare the problems you have identified with the list of faults and explanations below.

Faults Inherent in Matching Items

As you will see, matching items can be subject to a wide range of potential faults. We describe these next.

Lack of homogeneity The lists are not homogeneous. Column A contains names of presidents, inventors, and a civil rights leader. Unless specifically taught as a set of related public figures or ideas, this example represents too wide a variety for a matching exercise. To prevent this from happening, you might title your lists (e.g., "U.S. Presidents"). This will help keep irrelevant or filler items from creeping in. If you really want to measure student knowledge of presidents, inventors, and civil rights leaders, then build three separate matching exercises. Doing so will prevent implausible options from being eliminated by the student. When students can eliminate implausible options, they are more likely to guess correctly. For example, the student may not know a president who resigned from office but may know that Washington and Lincoln were presidents and that neither was recent. Thus, the student could eliminate two options, increasing the chance of guessing correctly from one out of eight to one out of six.

Wrong Order of Lists The lists should be reversed; that is, Column A should be Column B, and Column B should be Column A. This is a consideration that will save time for the test-taker. We are trained to read from left to right. When the longer description is in the left-hand column, the student only reads the description once and glances down the list of names to find the answer. As the exercise is now written, the student reads a name and then has to read through all or many of the lengthier descriptions to find the answer—a much more time-consuming process.

Easy Guessing There are equal numbers of options and descriptions in each column. Again, this increases the chances of guessing correctly through elimination. In the preceding exercise, if a student did not know who invented the cotton gin but knew which of the names went with the other seven descriptions, the student would arrive at the correct answer through elimination. If there are at least three more options than descriptions, the chances of guessing correctly in such a situation are reduced to one chance in four. Alternatively, the instructions for the exercise may be written to indicate that each option may be used more than once.

Poor Directions Speaking of directions, those included were much too brief. Matching directions should specify the basis for matching. For example,

> **Directions.** Column A contains brief descriptions of historical events. Column B contains the names of presidents. Indicate which man was president when the historical event took place by placing the appropriate letter to the left of the number in Column A.

The original directions also do not indicate how the matches should be shown. Should lines be drawn? Should letters be written next to numbers, or numbers next to letters? Failure to indicate how matches should be marked can greatly increase your scoring time.

Too Many Correct Responses The description "President during the twentieth century" has three defensible answers: Nixon, Ford, and Roosevelt. You say you meant Henry Ford, inventor of the Model T, not Gerald Ford! Well, that brings us to our final criticism of this matching exercise.

Ambiguous Lists The list of names is ambiguous. Franklin Roosevelt or Teddy Roosevelt? Henry Ford or Gerald Ford? When using names, always include first and last names to avoid such ambiguities.

Now that we have completed our analysis of this test item, we can easily conclude that it needs revision. Let's revise it, starting by breaking the exercise into homogeneous groupings.

> **Directions.** Column A describes events associated with U.S. presidents. Indicate which name in Column B matches each event by placing the appropriate letter to the left of the number of Column A. Each name may be used only once.

Column A	*Column B*
_____ **1.** A president not elected to office	**a.** Abraham Lincoln
_____ **2.** Delivered the Emancipation Proclamation	**b.** Richard Nixon
_____ **3.** Only president to resign from office	**c.** Gerald Ford
_____ **4.** Only president elected for more than two terms	**d.** George Washington
_____ **5.** Our first president	**e.** Franklin Roosevelt
	f. Theodore Roosevelt
	g. Thomas Jefferson
	h. Woodrow Wilson

We can make one more clarification. It is a good idea to introduce some sort of order—chronological, numerical, or alphabetical—to your list of options. This saves the reader time. Students usually go through the list several times in answering a matching exercise, and it is easier to remember a name's or date's location in a list if it is in some sort of order. We can arrange the list of names in alphabetical order to look like this:

Column A	*Column B*
_____ **1.** A president not elected to office	**a.** Gerald Ford
_____ **2.** Delivered the Emancipation Proclamation	**b.** Thomas Jefferson
_____ **3.** Only president to resign from office	**c.** Abraham Lincoln
_____ **4.** Only president elected for more than two terms	**d.** Richard Nixon
_____ **5.** Our first president	**e.** Franklin Roosevelt
	f. Theodore Roosevelt
	g. George Washington
	h. Woodrow Wilson

Our original exercise contained two items relating to invention. If we were determined to measure only knowledge of inventors through a matching exercise, we would want to add at least one more item. Normally, at least three items are used for matching exercises. Such an exercise might look like the following:

Directions. Column A lists famous inventions and Column B famous inventors. Match the inventor with the invention by placing the appropriate letter in the space to the left of the number in Column A. Each name may be used only once.

Column A	*Column B*
_____ **1.** Invented the cotton gin	**a.** Alexander Graham Bell
_____ **2.** One of his inventions was the telephone	**b.** Henry Bessemer
_____ **3.** One of his inventions was the telephone	**c.** Thomas Edison
	d. Guglielmo Marconi
	e. Eli Whitney
	f. Orville Wright

Notice that we have complete directions, there are three more options than descriptions, the lists are homogeneous, and the list of names is alphabetically ordered. But what about the final item remaining from our original exercise? Let's say we want to determine whether our students know that Martin Luther King, Jr., was a civil rights leader. We can construct another matching exercise with one column listing the names of civil rights leaders and another listing civil rights accomplishments. However, an alternative would be simply to switch item formats. Usually, single items that are removed from matching exercises because of their lack of homogeneity are easily converted into true–false, completion, or, with a little more difficulty, multiple-choice items. For example,

True–False

T   F   Martin Luther King, Jr., was a civil rights leader.

Completion

The name of the black civil rights leader assassinated in 1968 is _____.

Multiple Choice

Which one of the following was a civil rights leader?
  a. Jefferson Davis
  b. Martin Luther King, Jr.
  c. John Quincy Adams
  d. John Wilkes Booth

Suggestions for Writing Matching Items

1. Keep both the list of descriptions and the list of options fairly short and homogeneous—they should both fit on the same page. Title the lists to ensure homogeneity and arrange the descriptions and options in some logical order. If this is impossible, you're probably including too wide a variety in the exercise. Try two or more exercises.

2. Make sure that all the options are plausible distractors for each description to ensure homogeneity of lists.

3. The list of descriptions should contain the longer phrases or statements and should be on the left, while the options in the right column should consist of short phrases, words, or symbols.

4. Each description in the list should be numbered (each is an item), and the list of options should be identified by letter.

5. Include more options than descriptions. If the option list is longer than the description list, it is harder for students to eliminate options. If the option list is shorter, some options must be used more than once. Always include some options that do not match any of the descriptions, or some that match more than one, or both.

6. In the directions, specify the basis for matching and whether options can be used more than once.

MULTIPLE-CHOICE ITEMS

Another popular item format is the multiple-choice question. Practically everyone has taken multiple-choice tests at one time or another, but probably more often in high school and college than in elementary school. This doesn't mean that multiple-choice items are not appropriate in the elementary years; it suggests only that one needs to be cautious about using them with younger children.

Multiple-choice items are unique among objective test items because, contrary to popular opinion, they enable you to measure behavior at the higher levels of the taxonomy of educational objectives. Our discussion of multiple-choice items will be in two parts. The first part will consider the mechanics of multiple-choice item construction applied to knowledge-level questions. The second part will deal with the construction of higher-level multiple-choice items. As before, let's start by using common sense to identify good and poor multiple-choice items in the following exercise.

EXERCISE: *Place a G in the space next to a good item and a P next to a poor item.*

_____ **1.** U.S. Grant was an
   a. president
   b. man
   c. alcoholic
   d. general

_____ **2.** In what year did humans first set foot on the Moon?
   a. 1975
   b. 1957
   c. 1969
   d. 1963

_____ **3.** The free-floating structures within the cell that synthesize protein are called
   a. chromosomes
   b. lysosomes
   c. mitochondria
   d. free ribosomes

_____ **4.** The principal value of a balanced diet is that it
   a. increases your intelligence
   b. gives you something to talk about with friends
   c. promotes mental health
   d. promotes physical health
   e. improves self-discipline

_____ **5.** Some test items
   a. are too difficult
   b. are objective
   c. are poorly constructed
   d. have multiple defensible answers

_____ **6.** Which of the following are not associated with pneumonia?
   a. quiet breathing
   b. fever
   c. clear chest X-ray
   d. a and c
   e. b and c

_____ **7.** When 53 Americans were held hostage in Iran,
   a. the United States did nothing to try to free them.
   b. the United States declared war on Iran.
   c. the United States first attempted to free them by diplomatic means and later attempted rescue.
   d. the United States expelled all Iranian students.

_____ **8.** The square root of 256 is
   a. 14
   b. 16
   c. 4×4
   d. both a and c
   e. both b and c
   f. all of the above
   g. none of the above

_____ **9.** When a test item and the objective is intended to measure match in learning outcome and conditions, the item

    a. is called an objective item
    b. has content validity
    c. is too easy
    d. should be discarded

Go over the exercise again. Chances are you'll find a few more problems the second time. Here's the answer key, and a breakdown of the faults found in each item follows in the text.

Answers: 1. P; 2. G; 3. P; 4. P; 5. P; 6. P; 7. P; 8. P; 9. G.

Most students would probably pick up on the grammatical clue in the first item. The article "an" eliminates options a, b, and d immediately, since "U.S. Grant was an man," "an president," or "an general" are not grammatically correct statements. Thus, option c is the only option that forms a grammatically correct sentence. Inadvertently providing students with grammatical clues to the correct answer is very common in multiple-choice items. The result is decreased test validity. Students can answer items correctly because of knowledge of grammar, not content.

Replacing "an" with "a/an" would be one way to eliminate grammatical clues in your own writing. Other examples would be "is/are," "was/were," "his/her," and so on. As an alternative, the article, verb, or pronoun may be included in the list of options, as the following example illustrates:

Poor. Christopher Columbus came to America in a

    a. car
    b. boat
    c. airplane
    d. balloon

Better. Christopher Columbus came to America in

    a. a car
    b. a boat
    c. an airplane
    d. a balloon

Let's return to the first item and replace "an" with "a/an":

U.S. Grant was a/an

    a. president
    b. man
    c. alcoholic
    d. general

There! We've removed the grammatical clue, and we now have an acceptable item, right? Not quite. We now have an item free of grammatical clues, but it is still seriously deficient. What is the correct answer?

This item still has a serious flaw: multiple defensible answers. In fact, all four options are defensible answers! U.S. Grant was a president, a man, a general, and, as historians tell us, an alcoholic. Including such an item on a test would contribute nothing to your understanding of student knowledge. But what can you do when you have an item with more than one defensible answer? The answer, of course, is to eliminate the incorrect but defensible option or options.

Let's assume that item 1 was written to measure the following objective:

The student will discriminate among the U.S. presidents immediately before, during, and immediately after the U.S. Civil War.

We could modify item 1 to look like this:

U.S. Grant was a
   a. general
   b. slave
   c. pirate
   d. trader

This item is fine, from a technical standpoint. The grammatical clue has been eliminated and there is but one defensible answer. However, it does not match the instructional objective; it is not very valuable as a measure of student achievement of the objective.

We could also modify the item to look like this:

Of the following, who was elected president after the Civil War?
   a. U.S. Grant
   b. Andrew Johnson
   c. Abraham Lincoln
   d. Andrew Jackson

This item is technically sound, and all response alternatives are relevant to the instructional objective. It meets the two main criteria for inclusion in a test: The item is technically well constructed, and it matches the instructional objectives.

We said item 2 was good, but it can still stand some improvement. Remember when we recommended arranging lists for matching items in alphabetical or chronological order? The same holds true for multiple-choice items. To make a good item even better, arrange the options in chronological order. Revised, the item should look like this:

In what year did humans first set foot on the Moon?
   a. 1957
   b. 1963
   c. 1969
   d. 1975

The major deficiency in item 3 is referred to as a "stem clue." The statement portion of a multiple-choice item is called the stem, and the correct answer and incorrect choices are called options or response alternatives. A stem clue occurs when the same word or a close derivative occurs in both the stem and options, thereby clueing the test-taker as to the correct answer. In item 3, the word *free* in the option is identical to *free* in the stem. Thus, the wise test-taker has a good chance of answering the item correctly without mastery of the content being measured. This fault can be eliminated by simply rewording the item without the word *free*.

The structures within the cell that synthesize protein are called
   a. chromosomes
   b. lysosomes
   c. mitochondria
   d. ribosomes

Item 4 is related to the "opinionated" items we considered when we discussed true–false items. Depending on the source, or referent, different answers may be the "right" answer. To Person X, the principal value may be to promote physical health; to Person Y, the principal value may be to improve self-discipline. As stated earlier, when you are measuring a viewpoint or opinion, be sure to state the referent or source. To be acceptable, the item should be rewritten to include the name of an authority:

The USDA says that the principal value of a balanced diet is that it
   a. increases your intelligence
   b. gives you something to talk about
   c. promotes mental health
   d. promotes physical health
   e. improves self-discipline

Item 5 is, of course, meaningless. It has at least two serious faults. To begin with, the stem fails to present a problem, and it fails to focus the item. What is the item getting at? The test-taker has no idea what to look for in trying to discriminate among the options. The only way to approach such an item is to look at each option as an individual true–false item. This is very time consuming and frustrating for the test-taker. Be sure to focus your multiple-choice items by presenting a problem or situation in the stem.

Like item 1, item 5 also has more than one defensible answer. However, option d seems to control this problem. But if more than a single option is defensible, how can you mark as incorrect someone who chooses a, b, or c and not d? Sometimes, however, you may wish to construct items that have two defensible answers. Is there any way to avoid the problem just mentioned? Fortunately, there is a way to avoid the problem, as illustrated in item 6:

Which of the following are not associated with pneumonia?
   a. quiet breathing
   b. fever
   c. clear chest X-ray
   d. a and c
   e. b and c

Where the possibility of more than one answer is desirable, use an option format such as that just shown. This approach avoids the wording problems we ran into in item 5. We would caution, however, that "a and b," "b and c," and so on should be used sparingly.

Now, how about the rest of item 6; is it okay? No; again a grammatical clue is present. The word *are* indicates a plural response is appropriate. Options a, b, and c can automatically be eliminated, leaving the test-taker with a 50% chance of guessing correctly. This fault can be corrected by using the same approach we used with item 1, where we substituted "a/an" for "an." Of course, in this instance, we would substitute "is/are" for "are." Rewritten, the item looks like this:

Which of the following is/are not associated with pneumonia?
   a. quiet breathing
   b. fever
   c. clear chest X-ray
   d. a and c
   e. b and c

All set? Not yet! Remember what we said about negatives? Let's highlight the "not" with uppercase letters, italics, or underlining to minimize the likelihood of someone misreading the item. After this revision, we have an acceptable multiple-choice item.

Two very common faults in multiple-choice construction are illustrated by item 7. First, the phrase "the United States" is included in each option. To save space and time, add it to the stem. Second, the length of options could be a giveaway. Multiple-choice item writers have a tendency to include more information in the correct option than in the incorrect options. Testwise students take advantage of this tendency, since past experience tells them that longer options are more often than not the correct answer. Naturally, it is impossible to make all options exactly the same length but try to avoid situations where correct answers are more than one-and-a-half times the length of incorrect options. After eliminating the redundancies in the options and condensing the correct option, we have the following:

When 53 Americans were held hostage in Iran, the United States
- **a.** did nothing to try to free them.
- **b.** declared war on Iran.
- **c.** undertook diplomatic and military efforts to free them.
- **d.** expelled all Iranian students.

Item 8 has some problems, too. First, let's consider the use of "all of the above" and "none of the above." In general, "none of the above" should be used sparingly. Some item writers tend to use "none of the above" only when there is no clearly correct option presented. Students, however, can quickly catch on to such a practice and guess that "none of the above" is the correct answer without knowledge of the content being measured.

As far as "all of the above" goes, we cannot think of any circumstances in which its use may be justified. We recommend avoiding this option entirely.

The use of "both a and c" and "both b and c" was already discussed in relation to item 6. In that item, their use was appropriate and justifiable, but here it is questionable.

Again, let us see just what it takes to arrive at the correct choice, option e. Presumably, the item is intended to measure knowledge of square roots. However, the correct answer can be arrived at without considering square roots at all! A logical approach to this item, which would pay off with the right answer for someone who doesn't know the answer, might go something like this:

Sure wish I'd studied the square root table. Oh well, there's more than one way to get to the root of the problem. Let's see, 14 might be right, 16 might be right, and 4 × 4 might be right. Hmmm, both a and c? No, that can't be it because I know that 4 × 4 = 16 and not 14. Well, both b and c have to be it! I know it's not "none of the above" because the teacher never uses "none of the above" as the right answer when she uses "both a and c" and "both b and c" as options.

When using "both a and c" and "both b and c," be on the alert for logical inconsistencies that can be used to eliminate options. Naturally, this problem can be minimized by using such options sparingly. Also try to monitor your item construction patterns to make sure you're not overusing certain types of options.

Finally, we come to a good item. Item 9 is free of the flaws and faults we've pointed out in this section. There are a lot of things to consider when you write test items, and keeping them all in mind will help you write better multiple-choice questions. But it's virtually impossible for anyone to write good items all the time. So, when you've written a poor item, don't be too critical of yourself. Analyze it, revise or replace it, and learn from your mistakes.

Higher-Level Multiple-Choice Questions

Good multiple-choice items are the most time-consuming kind of objective test items to write. Unfortunately, most multiple-choice items are also written at the knowledge level of the taxonomy of educational objectives. As a new item writer (and, if you're not careful, as an experienced item writer), you will have a tendency to write items at this level. In this section, we will provide you with suggestions for writing multiple-choice items to measure higher-level thinking. With the increased emphasis on higher-level, critical thinking called for by the Common Core State Standards (CCSS) and other state standards, greater inclusion of higher-level objective items in teacher-made tests will help stimulate your students and potentially enhance performance on the CCSS aligned tests or your state high stakes test.

The first step is to write at least some objectives that measure comprehension, application, analysis, synthesis, or evaluation to ensure that your items will be at the higher than knowledge level—if your items match your objectives! The following objectives measure behavior at the knowledge level:

The student will name, from memory, the first three presidents of the United States by next Friday.

Given a color chart, the students will identify each of the primary colors.

Objectives such as those will generate multiple-choice items that will measure only memorization. By contrast, the following objectives measure behavior at higher than the knowledge level:

Given a copy of the President's State of the Union address, the student will be able to identify one example of a simile and one of a metaphor.

The student will be able to correctly solve three-digit addition problems without regrouping.

With objectives such as those, higher-level multiple-choice items would have to be constructed to match the objectives. Some suggestions for other approaches to measuring at higher than the knowledge level follow.

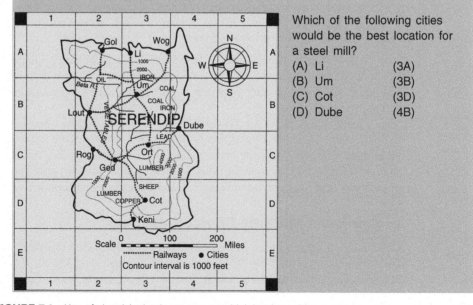

In the following questions you are asked to make inferences from the data which are given you on the map of the imaginary country, Serendip. The answers in most instances must be probabilities rather than certainties. The relative size of towns and cities is not shown. To assist you in the location of the places mentioned in the questions, the map is divided into squares lettered vertically from A to E and numbered horizontally from 1 to 5.

Which of the following cities would be the best location for a steel mill?

(A) Li   (3A)
(B) Um   (3B)
(C) Cot   (3D)
(D) Dube   (4B)

FIGURE 7.1 Use of pictorial stimulus to measure high-level cognitive processes.
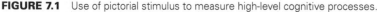

Use Pictorial, Graphical, or Tabular Stimuli Pictures, drawings, graphs, tables, and so on require the student to think at the application level of the taxonomy of educational objectives and may involve even higher levels of cognitive processes. Also, the use of such stimuli can often generate several higher-level multiple-choice items rather than a single higher-level multiple-choice item, as Figure 7.1 illustrates. Other items based on the map in Figure 7.1 could be as follows:

1. Approximately how many miles is it from Dube to Rog?
   a. 100 miles
   b. 150 miles
   c. 200 miles
   d. 250 miles

2. In what direction would someone have to travel to get from Wog to Um?
   a. northwest
   b. northeast
   c. southwest
   d. southeast

A variation on the same theme is to include several pictorial stimuli to represent options and build several stems around them. The following items would be appropriate for a plane geometry class:

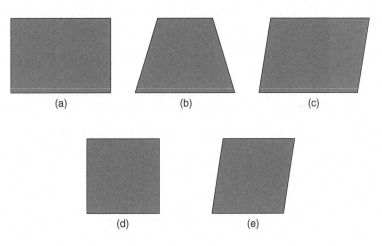

(a)   (b)   (c)

(d)   (e)

1. Which of the figures is a rhombus?
2. Which of the figures is a square?
3. Which of the figures is a trapezoid?

Naturally, it is important to include several more stimulus pictures than items in order to minimize guessing.

Use Analogies That Demonstrate Relationships among Terms To answer analogies correctly, students must not only be familiar with the terms but also be able to understand how the terms relate to one another, as the following examples show.

1. Man is to woman as boy is to
   a. father
   b. mother
   c. girl
   d. boy

2. Physician is to humans as veterinarian is to
   a. fruits
   b. animals
   c. minerals
   d. vegetables

Require the Application of Previously Learned Principles or Procedures to Novel Situations

To test whether students really comprehend the implications of a procedure or principle, have the students use the principle or procedure with new information or in a novel way. This requires that the student do more than simply "follow the steps" in solving a problem. It asks the student to demonstrate an ability to go beyond the confines within which a principle or procedure was originally learned.

1. In class we discussed at length Darwin's notion of the "survival of the fittest" within the animal world. Which of the following best describes how this principle applies to the current competitive residential construction industry?
   a. Those builders in existence today are those who have formed alliances with powerful financial institutions.
   b. Only those builders who emphasize matching their homes to the changing structure of the family will survive in the future.
   c. The intense competition for a limited number of qualified home buyers will eventually "weed out" poorly managed construction firms.
   d. Only those home builders who construct the strongest and most durable homes will survive in the long term.

2. (*Follows a lesson on division that relied on computation of grade point averages as examples.*) After filling up his tank with 18 gallons of gasoline, Mr. Watts said to his son, "We've come 450 miles since the last fill-up. What kind of gas mileage are we getting?" Which of the following is the best answer?
   a. 4 miles per gallon.
   b. 25 miles per gallon.
   c. Between 30 and 35 miles per gallon.
   d. It can't be determined from the information given.

These examples are intended to stimulate your creativity—they are by no means exhaustive of the many approaches to measuring higher-level cognitive skills with multiple-choice items. Rather than limit yourself to pictorial items and analogies, use them where appropriate and also develop your own approaches. Remember the main point: Be sure your items match your objectives. Do not write higher-level items if your objectives are at the knowledge level. Doing so will impair your test's content validity. Instead change your objectives so that they are written at higher levels and then develop items accordingly. All this will help stimulate higher-order thought among your students and bring your teacher-made tests into alignment with the CCSS tests. In Chapter 9, we will consider another way you can measure higher-level thinking skills, called performance-based assessment, and we cover yet another, called portfolio assessment, in Chapter 10.

Suggestions for Writing Multiple-Choice Items

Here are some guidelines for writing multiple-choice tests:

1. The stem of the item should clearly formulate a problem. Include as much of the item as possible, keeping the response options as short as possible. However, include only the material needed to make the problem clear and specific. Be concise—don't add extraneous information.

2. Be sure that there is one and only one correct or clearly best answer.

3. Be sure wrong answer choices (distractors) are plausible. Eliminate unintentional grammatical clues, and keep the length and form of all the answer choices equal. Rotate the position of the correct answer from item to item randomly.

4. In most cases, it is more important for the student to know what a specific item of information is rather than what it is not. So, only use negative questions or statements if the knowledge being tested requires it, and be sure to italicize or somehow highlight the negative(s).

5. Include from three to five options (two to four distractors plus one correct answer) to optimize testing for knowledge rather than encouraging guessing. It is not necessary to provide additional distractors for an item simply to maintain the same number of distractors for each item. This usually leads to poorly constructed distractors that add nothing to test validity and reliability.

6. To increase the difficulty of a multiple-choice item, increase the similarity of content among the options.

7. Use the option "none of the above" sparingly and only when the keyed answer can be classified unequivocally as right or wrong. Don't use this option when asking for a best answer.

8. Avoid using "all of the above." It is usually the correct answer and makes the item too easy for students with partial information.

Thus far, we have considered true–false, matching, and multiple-choice items. We have called these items objective items, but they are also referred to as recognition items. They are recognition items because the test-taker needs only to "recognize" the correct answer. Then compare recognition formats with "recall" or "supply" formats such as essays and completion items. With essays and completion items, it is much more difficult to guess the right answer than with true–false, matching, or multiple-choice items.

Nevertheless, we will classify completion items with true–false, matching, and multiple-choice items. We call items written in these formats objective items because of the way they are scored, which tends to be fairly straightforward and reliable. This is in contrast to essays, which we will call subjective, because their somewhat less reliable scoring makes them more prone to bias.

COMPLETION ITEMS

Like true–false items, completion items are relatively easy to write. Perhaps the first tests classroom teachers construct and students take are completion tests. Like items of all other formats, though, there are good and poor completion items. Work through the following exercise, again relying on your common sense to identify good and poor items. After having worked through the three previous exercises, you are probably now adept at recognizing common item-writing flaws.

The first item probably reminds you of many you have seen. It is a good rule to avoid using more than one blank per item. The item writer had a specific evolutionary theorist in mind when writing this item, but the final form of the item is not at all focused toward one single theorist. There are a variety of possible correct answers to this item. Not only are such items disturbing and confusing to test-takers, they are very time consuming and frustrating to score. An acceptable revision might look like this:

The evolutionary theory of Darwin is based on the principle of [survival of the fittest].

EXERCISE: *Put a G in the space next to the items you feel are good and a P next to the items you feel are poor*

_____ **1.** The evolutionary theory of [Darwin] is based on the principle of [survival of the fittest].
_____ **2.** Columbus discovered America in [1492].
_____ **3.** The capital of Mexico is [Mexico City].
_____ **4.** In what year did William J. Clinton become president of the United States? [1992]
_____ **5.** [Too many] blanks cause much frustration in [both test-takers and test-scorers].
_____ **6.** [Armstrong] was the first American to [walk on the moon].

Answers: 1. P; 2. P; 3. P; 4. G; 5. P; 6. P.

If you marked item 2 with a G, you were probably in the majority. This is a standard type of completion item that is frequently used. It is also the kind of item that can generate student–teacher conflict. Granted, "1492" is probably the answer most students who studied their lesson would write. But how would you score a response like "a boat" or "the fifteenth century" or "a search for India"? These may not be the answers you wanted, but they are correct answers.

This illustrates the major disadvantage of completion items and gives you some idea on a much smaller scale of the kinds of difficulties encountered in scoring essay items as well. Unless you take pains to be very specific when you word completion items, you will come across similar situations frequently. In general, it's better to be very specific in writing completion items. Item 2 could be made specific by adding the words "the year," as illustrated here:

Columbus discovered America in the year [1492].

In this form, the item leaves little to be interpreted subjectively by the student. The test-taker doesn't spend time thinking about what the question is "really" asking, and the test-scorer doesn't spend time trying to decide how to score a variety of different, but correct, answers. For once everybody's happy.

Item 3 is a similar case. Consider the following dialogue as heard by one of the authors in a teachers' lounge at an elementary school:

Ms. RIGIDITY: (*To no one in particular*) Smart-aleck kids nowadays! Ask them a simple question and you get a smart-aleck answer. Kids today don't give you any respect.

Ms. FEELINGS: I hear some frustration in what you're saying. Anything I can do?

Ms. RIGIDITY: No, there's nothing you can do, but listen to this. On the last test, one of the questions was "The largest city in Puerto Rico is _____." Simple enough, right? Well, not for Mitch! Instead of answering "San Juan," he answered "the capital city." Smart-aleck kid. We'll see how smart he feels when he gets no credit for that ridiculous answer.

Ms. FEELINGS: What I hear you saying is that you feel Mitch may not have known that San Juan is the largest city in Puerto Rico.

MS. RIGIDITY: Of course he doesn't know—otherwise he would have given the correct answer. That's the whole point!

AUTHOR: (*Never known for his tactfulness*) He did give a correct answer. Your question wasn't specific enough.

MS. RIGIDITY: I've been using this same test for years, and there are always one or two kids who give me the same answer Mitch did! And they are always kids who lack respect!

AUTHOR: How do you know they lack respect?

MS. RIGIDITY: Because they always argue with me when they get their tests back. In fact, they say the same thing you did! You're as bad as they are!

MS. FEELINGS: I'm hearing some frustration from both of you.

How could this have been avoided? Let's look at Ms. Rigidity's item again.

The largest city in Puerto Rico is _____.

Since San Juan is the largest city in Puerto Rico and is the capital city of Puerto Rico as well, then "the largest city in Puerto Rico is the capital city." There are at least two defensible answers. Just as in true–false, matching, and multiple-choice items, we should strive to avoid multiple defensible answers in completion items. But how can this be avoided? Again, be specific. Made more specific, Ms. Rigidity's item looks like this:

The name of the largest city in Puerto Rico is [San Juan].

Of course, you could have students who carry things to an extreme. For example, some might claim the following is a defensible answer:

The name of the largest city in Puerto Rico is [familiar to many people].

Only you, as the classroom teacher, can determine which answers are defensible and which are not. Your job will be to determine which responses are logical derivations of your test item and which responses are creative attempts to cover up for lack of mastery of content. Keep an open mind, and good luck! Don't be like Ms. Rigidity!

We can clean up item 3 in much the same manner as we did Ms. Rigidity's item. Revised in this way, item 3 looks like this:

The name of the capital city of Mexico is [Mexico City].

Adding "name of the" to the original item minimizes your chances of students responding that the capital of Mexico is "a city," "very pretty," "huge," "near central Mexico," and so forth.

Item 4 is an example of a well-written completion item. It is specific, and it would be difficult to think of defensible answers other than "1992."

Both the fifth and sixth items illustrate a case of having too many blanks, which prevents the item from taking on any single theme. Blanks are contagious—avoid using more than one.

Suggestions for Writing Completion Items

1. If at all possible, items should require a single-word answer, or a brief and definite statement. Avoid statements that are so indefinite that they may be logically answered by several terms.
   a. Poor item: World War II ended in _____.
   b. Better item: World War II ended in the year _____.

2. Be sure that the question or statement poses a problem to the examinee. A direct question is often more desirable than an incomplete statement (it provides more structure).

3. Be sure that the answer that the student is required to produce is factually correct. Be sure that the language used in the question is precise and accurate in relation to the subject matter area being tested.

4. Omit only key words; don't eliminate so many elements that the sense of the content is impaired.
   a. Poor item: The _____ type of test item is usually more _____ than the _____ type.
   b. Better item: The completion type of test item is usually graded less objectively than the _____ type.

5. Word the statement such that the blank is near the end of the sentence rather than near the beginning. This will prevent awkward sentences.

6. If the problem requires a numerical answer, indicate the units in which it is to be expressed.

You've now used common sense and an increased level of "test-wiseness" to analyze and think about different types of objective test items. In Chapter 8, we will extend our discussion to essay items. Before we move on to essays, however, let's consider one more topic related to item writing, one that applies equally to objective and essay items. This topic is gender and racial bias in test items.

GENDER AND RACIAL BIAS IN TEST ITEMS

An important but often overlooked aspect of item writing involves gender or racial bias. Over the last decades, most of us have become increasingly aware of, and sensitive to, such issues. Professional item writers take great care to eliminate or minimize the extent to which such biases are present in their test items. The classroom teacher would be wise to follow their lead.

One example of gender bias is the exclusive use of the male pronoun *he* in test items. Since the item writer may use it unconsciously, it does not necessarily follow that the item writer is biased. However, this does not prevent the practice from offending a proportion of the population. Similarly, referring exclusively in our items only to members of a single ethnic group will likely be offensive to individuals of different ethnicity. Again, such a practice may be almost unconscious and may not reflect an ethnic bias, but this will not prevent others from taking offense to it.

To avoid such bias, you should carefully balance your references in items. That is, always check your items to be sure that fairly equal numbers of references to males and females are made. Obviously, equal care and time should be devoted to ensure that ethnic groups are appropriately represented in your items. Such considerations are especially relevant when items are being written at higher than the knowledge level. Since such items often are word problems involving people, gender and racial bias can easily creep in. The test assembly checklist in Chapter 11 (Figure 11.1) will help remind you to be on the watch for such bias.

Remember, our goal is to measure learning in as valid and reliable a manner as possible. When emotions are stimulated by gender-biased items or racially biased items, these emotions can interfere with valid measurement, leaving us with results that are less useful than they would be otherwise. Given all the care and time we have taken to learn to develop good tests, it makes good sense to take just a bit more to avoid racial and gender bias in our items.

GUIDELINES FOR WRITING TEST ITEMS

In this chapter, we have provided you with a good deal of information related to item writing. Much of this information is condensed in the summary, and some general guidelines for item writing are also included. Following these guidelines, you will find a summary of the advantages and disadvantages of various item formats. This section should help you make decisions about the type of format to use for your test items. Remember, you will write poor items until the recommendations we have provided become second nature, which comes only with practice. Finally, review the sidebar (Box 7-1) for some suggestions on how a computer can save item-writing time and—with appropriate item-writing software—actually help improve the quality of the items you write.

1. Begin writing items far enough in advance that you will have time to revise them.
2. Match items to intended outcomes at the proper difficulty level to provide a valid measure of instructional objectives. Limit the question to the skill being assessed.
3. Be sure that each item deals with an important aspect of the content area and not with trivia.
4. Be sure that the problem posed is clear and unambiguous.
5. Be sure that each item is independent of all other items. The answer to one item should not be required as a condition for answering the next item. A hint to one answer should not be embedded in another item.
6. Be sure that the item has one correct or best answer on which experts would agree.
7. Prevent unintended clues to the answer in the statement or question. Grammatical inconsistencies such as *a* or *an* give clues to the correct answer to those students who are not well prepared for the test.
8. Avoid replication of the textbook in writing test items; don't quote directly from textual materials. You're usually not interested in how well the student memorized the text. In addition, taken out of context, direct quotes from the text are often ambiguous.
9. Avoid trick or catch questions in an achievement test. Don't waste time testing how well the students can interpret your intentions.
10. Try to write items that require higher-level thinking.

BOX 7-1

COMPUTERS, THE WEB, AND TEST ITEMS

Computers can help save item-writing time through word processing functions and item-writing software. With a word processing program, you can easily make minor or major modifications to test items or even whole tests. You can also reorder the items or change the order of distractors for multiple-choice items much more quickly than you could without a word processing program. This could be a major time saver when it is important to develop alternate forms of a test. Sharing of well-written items is facilitated if they are stored on a flash drive, CD, a hard drive, or the "cloud" and are made available to all teachers, either by sharing flash drives or other portable media, through a local area network (LAN), or over the Web.

Commercial software is also available that can assist the teacher in constructing test items. By indicating the common faults of a test item, these programs minimize the chances that you will construct and use poor items.

Programs are also available that will generate alternate forms of tests according to instructional objectives and difficulty levels. Given a pool of test items and their difficulty levels, the computer could be instructed to make a number of shorter tests based on common objectives and at prespecified difficulty levels, thereby ensuring that different tests would be comparable. With the passage of NCLB and IDEIA, regular classroom teachers will play a greater role in evaluating the progress of special learners in the general education curriculum. Because the range of achievement of special learners may vary considerably, and because a variety of accommodations may be needed because of their disabilities, a wider range of item difficulties and formats may be required for special learners than for regular education pupils. The computer may be helpful in this regard, allowing easier and more accurate item storage, modification, and incorporation into tests and assessments of varying lengths and difficulties. Being able to use a computer to efficiently "customize" tests designed for a classroom of regular education students to fit the needs of the special learners will enable you to devote more time to instructional activities. This may minimize the frustration of having to "start from scratch" with each new addition to your class, and may also reduce frustration in special learners and enhance the validity of your assessments of their progress in the general education curriculum.

Finally, both CCSS test consortia have placed sample test items and a variety of other learning and assessment resources online. These can provide you with examples of the types of higher-level skills the CCSS are designed to stimulate, and the kinds of test items that are used in the CCSS aligned tests to measure those skills. The URL for the Smarter Balanced Assessment Consortium is http://www.smarterbalanced.org/ and the URL for the Partnership for the Assessment of Readiness for College and Careers (PARCC) is http://parcconline.org/.

ADVANTAGES AND DISADVANTAGES OF DIFFERENT OBJECTIVE ITEM FORMATS

True–False Tests

Advantages

Because true–false questions tend to be short, more material can be covered than with any other item format. Thus true–false items tend to be used when a great deal of content has been covered.

True–false questions take less time to construct but avoid taking statements directly from the text and modifying them slightly to create an item.

Scoring is easier with true–false questions but avoid having students write "true" or "false" or a "T" or "F." Instead, have them circle "T" or "F" provided for each item.

Disadvantages

True–false questions tend to emphasize rote memorization of knowledge, although sometimes complex questions can be asked using true–false items.

True–false questions presume that the answer to the question or issue is unequivocally true or false. It would be unfair to ask the student to guess at the teacher's criteria for evaluating the truth of a statement.

True–false questions allow for and sometimes encourage a high degree of guessing. Generally, longer examinations are needed to compensate for this.

Matching Tests

Advantages

Matching questions are usually simple to construct and to score.

Matching items are ideally suited to measure associations between facts.

Matching questions can be more efficient than multiple-choice questions because they avoid repetition of options in measuring associations.

Matching questions reduce the effects of guessing.

Disadvantages

Matching questions sometimes tend to ask students trivial information.

They emphasize memorization.

Most commercial answer sheets can accommodate no more than five options, thus limiting the size of any particular matching item.

Multiple-Choice Tests

Advantages

Multiple-choice questions have considerable versatility in measuring objectives from the knowledge to the evaluation level.

Since writing is minimized, a substantial amount of course material can be sampled in a relatively short time.

Scoring is highly objective, requiring only a count of the number of correct responses.

Multiple-choice items can be written so that students must discriminate among options that vary in degree of correctness. This allows students to select the best alternative and avoids the absolute judgments found in true–false tests.

Since there are multiple options, effects of guessing are reduced.

Multiple-choice items are amenable to item analysis (Chapter 11), which permits a determination of which items are ambiguous or too difficult.

Disadvantages

Multiple-choice questions can be time consuming to write. If not carefully written, multiple-choice questions can sometimes have more than one defensible correct answer.

Completion Tests

Advantages

Construction of a completion question is relatively easy.

Guessing is eliminated since the question requires recall.

Completion questions take less time to complete than multiple-choice items, so greater amounts of content can be covered.

Disadvantages

Completion questions usually encourage a relatively low level of response complexity.

The responses can be difficult to score since the stem must be general enough so as not to communicate the correct answer. This can unintentionally lead to more than one defensible answer.

The restriction of an answer to a few words tends to measure the recall of specific facts, names, places, and events as opposed to more complex behaviors.

SUMMARY

This chapter introduced you to four types of objective test items: true–false, matching, multiple choice, and completion. The major points are as follows:

1. Choice of item format is sometimes determined by your instructional objectives. At other times, the advantages and disadvantages of the different formats should influence your choice.

2. True–false items require less time to construct than other objective items, but they are most prone to guessing, as well as a variety of other faults. These include absolutes in wording, double negatives, opinionated and double-barreled statements, excessive wordiness, and a tendency to reflect statements taken verbatim from readings.

3. Matching items are fairly easy to construct but tend to be subject to the following faults: lack of clarity and specificity in directions, dissimilar and nonordered lists, and reversal of options and descriptions.

4. Multiple-choice items are the most difficult of the objective items to construct. However, higher-order multiple-choice items lend themselves well to measuring higher-level thinking skills. They are subject to several faults, including grammatical cues or specific determiners, multiple defensible answers, unordered option lists, stem clues, opinionated statements, failure to state a problem in the stem, redundant wording, wordiness in the correct option, use of "all of the above," and indiscriminate use of "none of the above."

5. Completion items rival true–false items in ease of construction. Since answers must be supplied, they are least subject to guessing. On the other hand, they require more scoring time than other objective formats. Common faults include too many blanks, lack of specificity (too many potential responses), and failure to state a problem.

6. To avoid gender and/or racial biases in test items, avoid using stereotypes and be sure to make equal reference to both males and females and to various ethnic groups.

FOR DISCUSSION AND PRACTICE

1. Write a behavioral objective in some area with which you are familiar. Using this objective as your guide, write a test item using each of the four test item formats (true–false, matching, multiple-choice, and completion) discussed in this chapter.

2. Exchange your test items with a classmate. Have him or her check the appropriateness of each of your items for a match with the appropriate objective and against the criteria and guidelines given in this chapter for each test item format. List and correct any deficiencies.

*3. Each of the following items is defective in some way(s). Identify the principal fault or faults in each item and rewrite the item so that it is fault-free.

a. *The Time Machine* is considered to be a
   a. adventure story
   b. science fiction story
   c. historical novel
   d. autobiography

b. Thaddeus Kosciusko and Casimer Pulaski were heroes in the Revolutionary War. What was their country of origin?
   a. Great Britain
   b. Poland
   c. France
   d. Italy

c. The use of force to attain political goals is never justifiable. (T F)

d. The personal computer was invented in _____.

e. _____ spent his life trying to demonstrate that _____.

f.
   1. Discovered the Zambezi River   a. Webb
   2. First female governor   b. Armstrong
   3. Invented the cotton gin   c. Minuit
   4. First to swim the English   d. Livingstone
      Channel   e. Whitney
   5. Purchased Manhattan Island   f. Edison
   6. First to walk on the Moon   g. Cortez
                                         h. Keller
                                         i. Rhodes

*Answers to Question 3 appear in Appendix B.

CHAPTER 8

WRITING ESSAY TEST ITEMS

LEARNING OUTCOMES

After completing this chapter, the student will be able to:

1. Explain what an essay item is.
2. Differentiate between objective and essay items.
3. Identify the types of learning outcomes for which essays are best suited.
4. Differentiate between extended and restricted response essay items.
5. Differentiate between poorly written and well-written essay items.
6. Identify the advantages and disadvantages of essay items.
7. Describe the suggestions for writing essay items.
8. Explain why essay items are difficult to score reliably.
9. Recall suggestions for improving scoring reliability.
10. Apply a detailed scoring scheme, including scoring for content, process, and organization, to an extended response essay item.
11. Construct a complete restricted response essay item including a content-oriented scoring scheme.
12. Construct a complete extended response essay item, including a detailed scoring scheme that considers content, organization, and process criteria.
13. Provide examples of the suggestions for facilitating knowledge organization in the classroom.
14. Differentiate between the way we assess knowledge organization and the way we assess concepts.
15. Describe situations appropriate for open-book questions and exams.
16. Compare and contrast open-book (or open resource) and closed-book exams.
17. Describe the item-writing guidelines for essays, knowledge organization, and open-book questions and exams.

9 a.m., Tuesday, October 20

"I can't believe it! I just can't believe it!" Donna thought to herself. "How can he do this to us?" Donna was becoming more and more upset by the second, as were many of the other students in Mr. Smith's government class. They were taking the midterm exam, on which 50% of their grade would be based. Before the exam, the students spent only two classes discussing this issue. All other classes that semester dealt with a rather mechanical review of the federal government. The exam consisted of a single essay item:

Why should presidents be limited or not be limited to two consecutive terms in office?
   (100 points)

DOES THIS ring a bell? Test questions that do not reflect what was taught can frustrate test-takers. "How could he do it?" Well, there are probably several answers to this question, but we can only speculate about Mr. Smith's reasons. Just as we could generate a variety of explanations for Mr. Smith's test item, students could generate a variety of answers to his question! Let's look at his question again.

Why should presidents be limited or not be limited to two consecutive terms in office? (100 points)

What answer is he looking for? Again, only Mr. Smith knows for sure. "Come on," some of you may say. "He's not looking for any specific answer—he wants you to take a position and defend it, to test your knowledge and writing ability, that's all!" Well, if that's the case, why didn't he phrase the test item something like this:

In class and in your assigned readings, arguments both for and against giving presidents the opportunity to complete more than two consecutive terms in office were presented. Take a stand either for or against two consecutive terms in office. Use at least three points made in class or in your readings to support your position. Both the content and organization of your argument will be considered in assigning your final grade. Use no more than one page for your answer. (28 points)

This item focuses the task for the student—he or she has a clearer idea of what is expected, and, therefore, how he or she will be evaluated. Remember, your goal is not to see whether students can correctly guess what you are expecting as an answer. Your goal is to measure learning—to determine whether your instructional objectives have been met.

In the remainder of this chapter, we will discuss various aspects of essay item construction. While this will go far in helping you avoid writing poor essay items, we will also discuss several other equally important issues related to essay items. We will begin with a general discussion of what an essay item is, describe the two major types of essay items and their relationships to instructional objectives, identify the major advantages and disadvantages of essay items, provide you with suggestions for writing essay items, and discuss various approaches to scoring essays.

Then, we will show how you can apply your knowledge of essay item writing to several other types of measures, including the open-book exam and dialectical and interpretative questions. By appropriately using these measures, you can ensure that your tests challenge your learners to engage in higher levels of critical thinking, problem solving, and decision making. With this comprehensive treatment, we hope to increase your awareness of classroom assessment techniques beyond just objective test items.

WHAT IS AN ESSAY ITEM?

An essay item is one for which the student supplies, rather than selects, the correct answer. The student must compose a response, often extensive, to a question for which no single response or pattern of responses can be cited as correct to the exclusion of all other answers. The accuracy and quality of such a response can often be judged only by a person skilled and informed in the subject area being tested.

Essay Items Should Measure Complex Cognitive Skills or Processes

Like objective test items, essay items may be well constructed or poorly constructed. The well-constructed essay item aims to test the complex, higher-level cognitive skills that are included in the Common Core State Standards (CCSS) and individual state standards. To do so, essay items require the student to organize, analyze, integrate, and synthesize knowledge, to use information to solve novel problems, or to be original and innovative in problem solving. The poorly constructed essay item may require the student to do no more than recall information as it was presented in the textbook or lecture. Worse, the poorly constructed essay may not even let the student know what is required for a satisfactory response, like our initial example in this chapter.

The potential of the essay item as an evaluation device depends not only on writing appropriate questions that elicit complex cognitive skills but also on being able to structure the student's response so that other factors do not obscure your ability to evaluate whether the student is applying the complex cognitive skills you are trying to measure. For example, differences in knowledge of factual material can be hidden by differences in ability to use and organize those facts. The time pressures of a test situation, student anxiety, and deficiencies in writing ability (which does not necessarily mean that there are corresponding cognitive deficits!) can all interfere with a student's ability to demonstrate mastery of complex cognitive skills. A well-constructed essay item will clearly indicate the cognitive skills or process that should be employed to formulate the answer, clarify ambiguous details, and set appropriate page or time limits. A well-constructed essay makes it easier for you to evaluate accurately the student's response.

Consider the following essay item:

Question 1. What methods have been used in the United States to prevent industrial accidents?

What learning outcomes are being tested? To provide an acceptable answer, a student need only recall information. The item is at the knowledge level; no higher-level mental processes are tapped. It would be easy and much less time consuming to score a series of objective items covering this same topic. This is not abuse of the essay item, but it is a misuse. Now consider a second question:

Question 2. Examine the data provided in the table on causes of accidents. Explain how the introduction of occupational health and safety standards in the United States accounts for changes in the number of industrial accidents shown in the following table. Be sure to consider at least three specific occupational health and safety standards in your response. Limit your response to one-half page.

Causes of Accidents and Rate for Each in 1980 and 2000

	Accident Rate per 100,000 Employees	
Cause of accident	*1980*	*2000*
1. Defective equipment	135.1	16.7
2. Failure to use safety-related equipment	222.8	36.1
3. Failure to heed instructions	422.1	128.6
4. Improper training for job	598.7	26.4
5. Medical or health-related impairment	41.0	13.5

This question requires that the student recall something about the occupational health and safety standards. Then, the student must relate these standards to such things as occupational training programs, plant safety inspections, the display of warning or danger signs, equipment manufacturing, codes related to safety, and so forth, that may have been incorporated in industrial settings between 1980 and 2000.

The second question clarifies considerably what you are expecting from the student. In short, the student must use higher-level mental processes to answer the question successfully. The student must be able to analyze, infer, organize, apply, and so on. These are all examples of complex processes that are at the highest levels of Bloom's cognitive taxonomy (see Chapter 6). No objective item or series of items would suffice. This is an appropriate use of the essay item. However, not all essays are alike. We will consider two types of essay items: extended response and restricted response items.

Essay Items: Extended or Restricted Response

Essay items can vary from lengthy, open-ended end-of-semester term papers or take-home tests that have flexible page limits (e.g., 10–12 pages, or no more than 20 pages) to essays with responses limited or restricted to one page or less. These essay types are referred to, respectively, as extended response essay items and restricted response essay items. Essays may be used to measure general or specific outcomes of instruction. The restricted response item is most likely to be used to assess knowledge, comprehension, and application types of learning outcomes. An extended response essay is more appropriate to assess the ability to evaluate, synthesize, analyze, organize, and select viewpoints.

Extended Response Essays   An essay item that allows the student to determine the length and complexity of response is called an extended response essay item. This type of essay is most useful at the synthesis or evaluation levels of the cognitive taxonomy. When we are interested in determining whether students can organize, integrate, express, and evaluate information, ideas, or knowledge, the extended response essay may be the best option. The extended response item also is useful for assessing written communication ability. The following is an example of an extended response essay.

> **EXAMPLE:** Identify as many different ways to generate electricity as you can. Give the advantages and disadvantages of each and how each might be used to provide the electrical power requirements of a medium-sized city. Your response will be graded on its accuracy and your evaluation of how practical each source of electricity would be, if implemented. Your response should be 12–15 pages in length and will be evaluated based on the scoring criteria distributed in class. For maximum credit, be sure that your response addresses each of the scoring criteria components.

To respond to this essay, the students must be able to assemble relevant information, critically analyze the information and apply the information to a novel situation, and synthesize and evaluate potential outcomes. Obviously, you would not expect students to be able to respond to this complex task in a single class period, or without access to suitable reference materials. Nevertheless, this may be an important set of skills that you need to evaluate. If so, the extended range essay can work well.

Keep in mind, however, that a complex item such as this one will take time to develop and will be even more time consuming to score. It is also difficult to score extended response essays objectively. For both of these reasons, it is important to use extended range essays only in those situations where you have adequate time to develop the extended response item and specific scoring criteria for it, and when your students have adequate time and resources to devote to their responses. Later in this chapter, we will provide you with a variety of suggestions that you can use to develop and score both extended and restricted response items.

Restricted Response Essays An essay item that poses a specific problem for which the student must recall proper information, organize it in a suitable manner, derive a defensible conclusion, and express it within the limits of the posed problem, or within page or time limits, is called a restricted response essay item. The statement of the problem specifies response limitations that guide the student in responding and provide evaluation criteria for scoring.

> **EXAMPLE:** List the major political similarities and differences between U.S. participation in the Korean War and in World War II. Limit your answer to one page. Your score will depend on accuracy, organization, and clarity.

Typically, a restricted response essay item may supplement a test that is otherwise objective, or there may be several (e.g., 5–7) restricted response items in an essay test designed to be completed during a class period. When several essay items are used, students may be expected to respond to them with or without various resources, depending on your instructional objectives. The typical classroom teacher will use restricted response essays far more often than extended response essays. Thus, in the next section, we will focus primarily on suggestions to help you develop and score restricted range essays. Nevertheless, you will find that almost all these suggestions will also be applicable should you choose to use extended range essays. We will consider several examples of restricted range essays next.

Examples of Restricted Response Essays

> **EXAMPLE:** The Learning to Like It Company is proposing profit sharing for its employees. For each 1% increase in production compared to the average production figures over the last 10 years, workers will get a 1% increase in pay. In no more than one page:
>
> **1.** List the advantages and disadvantages to the workers of this plan.
> **2.** List the advantages and disadvantages to the corporation of this plan.

> **EXAMPLE:** Now that we've studied about the Gold Rush, imagine you are on a wagon train going to California. Write a one-page letter to your relatives back home telling them of some of the (1) hardships you have suffered and (2) dangers you have experienced.

To demonstrate that they know the advantages and disadvantages of profit sharing and the hardships and dangers of traveling West by wagon train during the Gold Rush, your learners must do two things: They must respond in their own words and not simply recall what their text said, or what they copied from an overhead, and they must give original examples. If they can do this, then you can correctly say that your learners have acquired the concept of profit sharing or understood the difficulties of traveling West during the Gold Rush.

When Should Restricted Response Essays Be Considered? The following describes some of the conditions for which restricted response questions are best suited.

- The instructional objectives require supplying information rather than simply recognizing information. These processes often cannot be measured with objective items.

- Relatively few areas of content need to be tested. If you have 30 students and design a test with six restricted response questions, you will spend a great deal of time scoring. Use restricted responses when class size is small, or use them in conjunction with objective items.

- Test security is a consideration. If you are afraid multiple-choice test questions will be passed on or told to other students, it is better to use a restricted response question. In general, a good restricted response essay test takes less time to construct than a good objective test.

Some learning outcomes and example content for which restricted response questions may be used include the following:

- Analyze relationships.

    EXAMPLE: The colors blue and gray are related to cool temperatures. What are some other colors related to? What effect would these colors have on a picture you might draw?

- Compare and contrast positions.

    EXAMPLE: Compare and contrast two characters from stories you have read to understand how the characters responded differently to conditions in the stories.

- State necessary assumptions.

    EXAMPLE: When Columbus landed on San Salvador, what did he assume about the land he had discovered? Were his assumptions correct?

- Identify appropriate conclusions.

    EXAMPLE: What are some of the reasons for and against building a landfill near homes?

- Explain cause-and-effect relations.

    EXAMPLE: What might have caused early Americans to travel West in the 1780s? Choose one of the pioneers we have studied (like Daniel Boone) and give some of the reasons he or she traveled West.

- Formulate hypotheses.

    EXAMPLE: What can you predict about a coming storm by observing clouds? Explain what it is about the clouds that helps you predict rain.

- Organize data to support a viewpoint.

    EXAMPLE: On the board you will find the number of new homes built and autos purchased for each month over the past year. Use these data to support the viewpoint that our economy is growing either larger or smaller.

- Point out strengths and weaknesses.

    EXAMPLE: What is either a strength or a limitation of the following musical instruments for a marching band: oboe, trumpet, tuba, violin?

- Integrate data from several sources.

    EXAMPLE: Imagine you are celebrating your birthday with nine of your friends. Two pizzas arrive but each is cut into four pieces. What problem do you have? What method would you choose for seeing that everyone gets a piece of the pizza?

- Evaluate the quality or worth of an item, product, or action.

    EXAMPLE: What should be considered in choosing a balanced meal from the basic food groups?

PROS AND CONS OF ESSAY ITEMS

We've already mentioned some of the benefits of using essay items, and the following list summarizes the advantages of essays over objective items.

Advantages of the Essay Item

Most Effective in Assessing Complex Learning Outcomes   To the extent that instructional objectives require the student to organize information constructively to solve a problem, analyze and evaluate information, or perform other high-level cognitive skills, the essay test is an appropriate assessment tool.

Relatively Easy to Construct   Although essay tests are relatively easy to construct, the items should not be constructed haphazardly; consult the table of specifications, identify only the topics and objectives that can best be assessed by essays, and build items around those.

Emphasize Essential Communication Skills in Complex Academic Disciplines   If developing communication skills is an instructional objective, it can be tested with an essay item. However, this assumes that the teacher has spent time teaching communication skills pertinent to the content area, including special vocabulary and writing styles, as well as providing practice with relevant arguments for and against controversial points.

Guessing Is Eliminated   Since no options are provided, the student must supply rather than select the proper response.

Naturally, there is another side to the essay coin. These items also have limitations and disadvantages.

Disadvantages of the Essay Item

Difficult to Score   It is tedious to wade through pages and pages of student handwriting. Also, it is difficult not to let spelling and grammatical mistakes influence grading or to let superior abilities in communication cover up for incomplete comprehension of facts.

Scores Are Unreliable   It is difficult to maintain a common set of criteria for all students. Two persons may disagree on the correct answer for any essay item; even the same person will disagree on the correctness of one answer read on two separate occasions.

Limited Sample of Total Instructional Content   Fewer essay items can be attempted than any objective type of item; it takes more time to complete an essay item than any other type of item. Students become fatigued faster with these items than with objective items.

Bluffing   It is no secret that longer essays tend to be graded higher than short essays, regardless of content! As a result, students may bluff.

The first two limitations are serious disadvantages. Fortunately, we do have some suggestions that have been shown to make the task of scoring essays more manageable and reliable. These will be discussed shortly. First, however, we will consider several suggestions to help you write good essay items.

SUGGESTIONS FOR WRITING ESSAY ITEMS

Here are some suggestions to keep in mind when preparing essay questions:

1. Have clearly in mind what mental processes you want the student to use before starting to write the question. Refer to the mental processes we have discussed previously and the various levels of the Bloom's taxonomy of educational objectives for the cognitive domain described in Chapter 6 (e.g., comprehension, application, analysis, synthesis, and evaluation). For example, if you want students to apply what they have learned, determine what mental processes would be needed for students to demonstrate that they can do so.

> Poor item: Describe the escape routes considered by Mark and Alisha in the story "Hawaiian Mystery."

> Better item: Consider the story about Mark and Alisha. Remember the part where they had to escape over the volcanic ridge? Compare the advantages of Mark's plan of escape with that of Alisha's. Which provided the least risk to their safety, and which plan of escape would get them home the quickest? Which would you have chosen, and why?

> Poor item: Criticize the following speech by our President.

> Better item: Consider the following presidential speech. Focus on the section dealing with economic policy and discriminate between factual statements and opinions. List these statements separately, label them, and indicate whether each statement is or is not consistent with the President's overall economic policy.

2. Write the question to clearly and unambiguously define the task to the student. Tasks should be explained (1) orally, (2) in the overall instructions preceding the questions, and/or (3) in the test items themselves. Indicate whether spelling and grammar will be counted and whether organization of the response will be an important scoring element. Also, indicate the level of detail and supporting data required.

> Poor item: Discuss the choices Mark and Alisha had to make in the story "Hawaiian Mystery."

> Better item: Mark and Alisha had to make three decisions on their journey home. Identify each of them and indicate if you disagree with any of these decisions and why you disagree. Organize your response into three or four paragraphs and check your spelling so you do not lose credit for misspelled words.

> Poor item: What were the forces that led to the outbreak of the Civil War?

> Better item: Compare and contrast the positions of the North and South at the outbreak of the Civil War. Include in your discussion economic conditions, foreign policies, political sentiments, and social conditions. Also, to avoid losing points be sure to spell all words correctly, use proper grammar, and your answer should not exceed one double-spaced page.

3. Start essay questions with such words or phrases as *compare, contrast, give reasons for, give original examples of, predict what would happen if*, and so on. Do not begin with such words as *what, who, when*, and *list*, because those words generally lead to tasks that require only recall of information.

> Poor item: In the story "Hawaiian Mystery," who made the decision to take the path by the sea?

Better item: Give three reasons why, in the story "Hawaiian Mystery," Alisha decided to take the path by the sea and predict what would have happened if they had stayed on the mountain for another night.

Poor item: List three reasons behind America's military withdrawal from Iraq in 2012.

Better item: After almost 10 years of military involvement, the United States withdrew from Iraq in 2012. Subsequently, there was an increase in insurgent violence in Iraq. Predict what would have happened if the United States had not withdrawn its troops in 2012 and instead increased troop levels. Speculate about the impact of an increased U.S. military presence after 2012 on both Iraq and the United States.

4. A question dealing with a controversial issue should ask for and be evaluated in terms of the presentation of evidence for a position rather than the position taken. It is not defensible to demand that a student accept a specific conclusion or solution, but it is reasonable to assess how well the student has learned to use the evidence on which a specific conclusion is based.

Poor item: What laws should Congress pass to improve the medical care of all citizens in the United States?

Better item: Some feel that the cost of all medical care should be borne by the federal government. Do you agree or disagree? Support your position with at least three arguments.

Poor item: Provide arguments for the support of laws to speed up the economic development of a community.

Better item: Some local laws work to slow the economic development of a community while others are intended to speed it up. Discuss the advantages and limitations of each point of view for (1) the homeowner and (2) the business community and decide which you would support if you were on the City Council.

5. Establish reasonable time and/or page limits for each essay question to help the student complete the question and to indicate the level of detail for the response you have in mind. Indicate such limits orally and in the statement of the question.

6. Use essay questions with content and objectives that cannot be satisfactorily measured by objective items.

7. Avoid using optional items. That is, require all students to complete the same items. Allowing students to select three of five, four of seven, and so forth decreases test validity and decreases your basis for comparison among students.

8. Be sure each question relates to an instructional objective.

Not all of the suggestions may be relevant for each item you write. However, it is worthwhile to go over the suggestions after you've written items, as a means of checking and, when necessary, modifying your items. With time you will get better and more efficient at writing essay items.

SCORING ESSAY QUESTIONS

Restricted response questions are difficult to score consistently across individuals. That is, the same answer may be given an A by one scorer and a B or C by another scorer. The same answer may even be graded A on one occasion but B or C on another occasion by the same scorer!

To understand the difficulties involved in scoring essays reliably, it is necessary to consider the difficulty involved in constructing good essay items. As you saw earlier, the clearer your instructional objective, the easier the essay item is to construct. Similarly, the clearer the essay item in terms of task specification, the easier it is to score reliably. Make sense? If you're not sure, look at the next two examples of essay items and decide which would likely be more reliably scored.

EXAMPLE 1: Some economists recommend massive tax cuts as a means of controlling inflation. Identify at least two assumptions on which such a position is based, and indicate the effect that violating each assumption might have on inflation. Limit your response to one-half page. Organize your answer according to the criteria discussed in class. Spelling, punctuation, and grammar will be counted in your grade. (8 points)

EXAMPLE 2: What effect would massive tax cuts have on inflation? (100 points)

Which did you select? If you chose the first one, you are catching on. Example 2 is a poor question. It is unstructured and unfocused; it fails to define response limits; and it fails to establish a policy for grammar, spelling, and punctuation. Thus, depending on the scorer, a lengthy answer with poor grammar and good content might get a high grade, a low grade, or an intermediate grade. Different scorers would probably all have a different idea of what a "good" answer to the question looks like. Questions like this trouble and confuse scorers and invite scorer unreliability. They do so for the same reasons that they trouble and confuse test-takers. Poorly written essay items hurt both students and scorers.

But the first example is different. The task is spelled out for the student; limits are defined; and the policy on spelling, punctuation, and grammar is indicated. The task for the scorer is to determine whether the student has included (1) at least two assumptions underlying the proposition and (2) the likely effect on inflation if each assumption is violated. Granted, there may be some difficulty agreeing how adequate the statements of the assumptions and effects of violating the assumptions may be, but there is little else to quibble over. Thus, there are fewer potential sources of scorer error or variability (i.e., unreliability) in this question than in the second. Remember, essay scoring can never be as reliable as scoring an objective test, but it doesn't have to be little better than chance.

What can you do to avoid such scoring problems?

1. Write good essay questions. Poorly written questions are one source of scorer inconsistency. Questions that do not specify response length are another. Depending on the grade, long (e.g., three-page) responses generally are more difficult to score consistently than shorter responses (say, one page). This is due to student fatigue and subsequent clerical errors as well as to a tendency for grading criteria to vary from response to response, or for that matter from page to page or paragraph to paragraph within the same response.

2. Instead of using a single comprehensive extended response question, use several shorter, more specific, and detailed restricted response questions. This will provide greater focus within each question, offer a greater variety of criteria to respond to, and thus give students a greater opportunity to more reliably demonstrate their learning.

3. Prepare a rubric (i.e., a scoring plan or scheme) that identifies the criteria for a correct or an acceptable response to each of your questions. All too often, questions are graded without the scorer having specified in advance the criteria for a "good" answer. If you do not specify the criteria beforehand, your scoring consistency will be greatly reduced. If these criteria are not readily available (written down) for scoring each question, the criteria themselves

TABLE 8.1 **An Essay Item Appropriate for a Tenth-Grade American Government Course, Its Objective, and a Simple Scoring Scheme**

Scoring Scheme	Description
Objective	The student will be able to name and describe at least five important conditions that contributed to the Industrial Revolution, drawn from among the following: Breakdown of feudal ideas and social boundaries (rise of ordinary people) Legitimization of individualism and competition Transportation revolution, which allowed for massive transport of goods (first national roads, canals, steamboats, railroads, etc.) New forms of energy (e.g., coal) that brought about factory system Slow decline of death rates due to improved hygiene and continuation of high birth rates resulted in rise in population Media revolution (printing press, newspapers, telegraph, etc.) Migration to urban areas
Test item	Name and describe five of the most important conditions that made the Industrial Revolution possible. Please ensure that your response includes appropriate spelling, grammar, and punctuation, although these elements will not affect your grade. (10 points)
Scoring criteria	1 point for each of the seven factors named, to a maximum of 5 points 1 point for each appropriate description of the factors named, to a maximum of 5 points No penalty for spelling, punctuation, or grammatical error No extra credit for more than five factors named or described Extraneous information will be ignored

may change (you may grade harder or easier after scoring several papers, even if the answers do not change). Or your ability to keep the criteria in mind will be influenced by fatigue, distractions, frame of mind, and so on.

What do such criteria look like? Scoring criteria, or rubrics, may vary from fairly simple checklists to elaborate combinations of checklists and rating scales. How elaborate your scoring scheme is depends on what you are trying to measure. If your essay item is a restricted response item simply assessing mastery of factual content, a fairly simple listing of essential points will suffice. Table 8.1 illustrates this type of scoring scheme. For many restricted response items, a similar scoring scheme may suffice. However, when items are measuring higher-level cognitive skills such as synthesis and evaluation, more complex schemes are necessary. This is true whether the item is a restricted or an extended range essay. Borich and Tombari (2004) and Stiggins (2011) have identified key components useful in scoring high-level essay items: content, organization, and process. We will consider this approach and another method called the rating method in the following section.

Scoring Extended Response and Higher-Level Questions

Remember that an extended range essay item is best employed when we are measuring at the synthesis or evaluation levels of the cognitive taxonomy. Thus, extended response essays often take the form of a term paper or a take-home assignment. As you might imagine by now, the breadth and depth of material extended response essays can cover poses a real challenge to scoring consistency (i.e., reliability). Using a checklist or similar simple scoring rubric is not likely to work well for these measures. Fortunately, this daunting task is made manageable if you use the following recommendations. Let's consider this approach, which assigns ratings for three key elements: content, organization, and process. Table 8.2 illustrates the application of these three criteria to an extended response essay item.

TABLE 8.2   An Essay Item Appropriate for a High School American History Course, Its Objectives, and a Detailed Scoring Scheme

Objectives	The student will be able to explain the forces that operated to weaken Southern regional self-consciousness between the Civil War and 1900. The student will consider these forces and draw an overall conclusion as to the condition of Southern self-consciousness at the beginning of the twentieth century.
Test item	The Civil War left the South with a heritage of intense regional self-consciousness. In what respects and to what extent was this feeling weakened during the next half century, and in what respects and to what extent was it intensified? Your answer will be graded on content and organization; on the accuracy, consistency, and originality of your conclusion; and on the quality of your argument in support of your conclusion. Be sure to identify at least seven weakening factors and seven strengthening factors. Although spelling, punctuation, and grammar will not be considered in grading, do your best to consider them in your writing. Limit your answer to two (2) pages. (32 points)
Detailed scoring Criteria	**A. Content (14 pts possible)**

A. Content (14 pts possible)

1 point for each weakening factor mentioned, to a maximum of 7 points

1 point for each strengthening factor mentioned, to a maximum of 7 points—all factors must come from the following lists:

Forces weakening Southern regional self-consciousness:
Growth of railroads and desire for federal subsidies
Old Whigs join Northern businessmen in Compromise of 1877
Desire for Northern capital to industrialize the South
Efforts of magazines and writers to interpret the South
The vision of the New South
Aid to Negro education by Northern philanthropists
New state constitutions stressing public education
Supreme Court decisions affecting Negro rights
Tom Watson's early Populist efforts
Booker T. Washington's "submissiveness"
The Spanish–American War
The "white man's burden"
After 1890, new issues did not conform to a North–South political alignment
World War I

Forces strengthening Southern regional self-consciousness:
Destruction caused by the war and its long-range effects
Reconstruction policy of Congress
One-crop economy, crop-lien system, and sharecropping
Carpetbaggers, Ku Klux Klan, Redshirts
Waving the bloody shirt
Memories of the lost cause
Glorifying the prewar tradition
Continuing weakness of Southern education compared with the rest of the Union Populism
Jim Crow laws after 1890
Solid South

14 points possible

B. Organization (6 pts possible)

0 to 6 points assigned, depending on whether the essay has an introduction, body, and conclusion.

6 points possible

TABLE 8.2 (*Continued*)

C. Process (12 pts possible)

1. Solution: 0 to 6 points depending on whether the solution is
   a. Accurate (0 to 2 points)
      Does the solution/conclusion fit?
   b. Internally consistent (0 to 2 points)
      Does the solution/conclusion flow logically?
   c. Originality/creativity (0 to 2 points)
      Is the solution/conclusion novel or creative?
2. Argument: 0 to 6 points, depending on whether the argument is
   a. Accurate (0 to 2 points) Dependent on whether the argument fits the situation.
   b. Internally consistent (0 to 2 points) Is the argument logical?
   c. Original/creative (0 to 2 points) Is the argument unique or novel in its approach?

12 points possible

Maximum score of 32 points possible for this item overall

Content Although essays often are not used to measure factual knowledge as much as thinking processes, the information included in an essay—its content—can and should be scored specifically for its presence and accuracy. In other words, in addition to grading for application, analysis, synthesis, and the like, your assessment should include whether the student has acquired the prerequisite knowledge and content needed to demonstrate any higher-level behaviors that may be required by your question. A scoring rubric for content similar to those illustrated in Tables 8.1 and 8.2 would improve scoring reliability for the presence and accuracy of content. Alternatively, a rating scale similar to the one portrayed in Figure 8.1 may be used, depending on the type of content called for by the item.

Scale	Description
5	Firm command of basic concepts Uses all terminology correctly Identifies most important principles
4	Shows nearly complete understanding of concepts Most terms used correctly Has identified a majority of important principles
3	Has only tentative grasp of concepts Relevant terminology used inconsistently Some inference evident, but most important principles are missed
2	Lacks command of most of the important concepts Uses little relevant terminology Little evidence of ability to abstract important principles
1	Shows no understanding of basic concepts No attempt to use relevant terminology No evidence of abstraction or inference of important principles
Points _____	

FIGURE 8.1 Rating scale for scoring an essay for knowledge of basic concepts.

Organization   Does the essay have an introduction, body, and conclusion? Let the students know that you will be scoring for organization to minimize rambling. Beyond the three general organizational criteria mentioned, you may want to develop specific criteria for your class. For example, are recommendations, inferences, and hypotheses supported? Is it apparent which supporting statements go with which recommendation? Do progressions and sequences follow a logical or chronological development? You should also decide on a spelling and grammar policy and develop these criteria, alerting the students before they take the test. Table 8.2 illustrates how organization will be scored in the sample essay.

Process   If your essay item tests at the application level or above, the most important criteria for scoring are usually those that reflect the extent to which these processes have been carried out. Each process (application, analysis, synthesis, and evaluation) results in a solution, recommendation, or decision and some reasons for justifying or supporting the final decision, and so on. Thus, the process criteria should attempt to assess both the adequacy of the solution or decision and the reasons behind it. In Table 8.2, the process component is broken down into two components, solution and argument, and each of those in turn is broken down into three subparts: accuracy, internal consistency, and originality/creativity. Whenever you require your students to develop or synthesize a solution or conclusion as part of the assessment, we recommend that you evaluate the solution or conclusion according to those criteria to enhance scoring reliability. Some additional clarification of the criteria are as follows.

> **Accuracy and Reasonableness.** Will the solution or conclusion work? Have the correct analytical dimensions been identified? Scorers must ultimately decide for themselves what is accurate but should be prepared for unexpected, but accurate, responses.
>
> **Completeness and Internal Consistency.** To what extent does the solution or conclusion sufficiently deal with the problem presented? Again, the scorer's judgment will weigh heavily, but points should be logically related and cover the topics as fully as required by the essay item. The solution or conclusion should not include contradictory statements, arguments, or conclusions that are not explained or reconciled.
>
> **Originality and Creativity.** Again, it is up to the scorer to recognize the unexpected and give credit for it, as long as it applies to the question. That is, the scorer should expect that some students will develop new ways of conceptualizing questions, and credit should be awarded for such conceptualizations when appropriate.

As the scorer reads through each response, points are assigned for each of the three major criteria of the scoring scheme. As you can probably guess, this approach has some disadvantages. It is likely to be quite laborious and time consuming. Furthermore, undue attention may be given to superficial aspects of the answer. When used properly, however, such a scoring scheme can yield reliable scores for extended range essay answers. Another advantage of this approach is that constructing such a detailed scoring scheme before administering the test can often alert the teacher to such problems in the item as unrealistic expectations for the students or poor wording. A third advantage is that discussion of a student's grade on such an item is greatly facilitated. The student can see what aspects of his or her response were considered deficient.

Keep in mind that Table 8.2 represents a scoring scheme for an extended response essay item. When reliability is crucial, such a detailed scheme is vital. Scoring schemes for restricted response items would be less complex, depending on what components of the answer the teacher felt were most critical. The point we have been making is that using some kind of scoring scheme is helpful in improving the reliability of essay scoring.

Your criteria should be made known to students. This will maximize their learning experience. Knowing how you are going to score the test, students will be able to develop better and more defensible responses. In addition, we would also like to refer you to the item development and scoring rubric (i.e., scoring criteria) suggestions provided in Chapter 9, Performance-Based Assessment, for additional help with extended response items. The suggestions provided in Chapter 9 have direct applicability because extended response essays actually represent one form of performance assessment. Next, we will consider another essay scoring method called the rating method.

The Rating Method With the rating method, the teacher generally is more interested in the overall quality of the answer than in specific points. Rating is done by simply sorting papers into piles, usually five, if letter grades are given. After sorting, the answers in each pile are scanned, and an attempt is made to ensure that all the A papers are of comparable quality (i.e., that they do not include B and C papers) and so forth. This step is important, since the problem of the scoring criteria changing during grading is always present in rating answers. It helps minimize the likelihood, for example, that an A paper gets sorted into the C pile because it was graded early while the teacher was maintaining "strict" criteria.

This method is an improvement over simply reading each answer and assigning a grade based on some nebulous, undefined rationale. However, this method is still subject to the problem of unintentionally changing the criteria if they have not been written beforehand.

General Essay Scoring Suggestions

In addition to the specific suggestions we have offered for restricted and extended response essays, several other suggestions apply regardless of the type of essay that is used. Some of these we have already mentioned. Do you remember our first three suggestions?

1. Write good essay items that structure the task for students.
2. Use mostly restricted response rather than extended response items, for in-classroom assessments.
3. *Always* use a predetermined scoring scheme.
   Now let's consider several other suggestions to improve essay-scoring reliability.
4. Use the scoring scheme consistently. In other words, don't favor one student over another or get stricter or more lax over time. How can you do this?
5. Remove or cover the names on the papers before beginning scoring (e.g., with sticky notes). In this way, you are more likely to rate papers on their merits, rather than on your overall impression of the student.
6. Score each student's answer to the same question before going on to the next answer. In other words, do all of the answers to the first question before looking at the answers to the second. Why? First, you want to avoid having a student's score on an earlier question influence your evaluation of his or her later questions; and second, it is much easier to keep scoring criteria for one question in mind than it is to keep scoring criteria for all the questions in mind.
7. Try to keep scores for previous items hidden when scoring subsequent items, for the same reason already mentioned.
8. Try to reevaluate your papers before returning them. When you come across discrepant ratings, average them.

Well, there you have it! Eight suggestions for improving the reliability of essay scoring. If you use essay items, try to incorporate as many of these suggestions as possible. Next, we will turn to our final topics for this chapter: essay items you can use to assess student ability to organize knowledge or information and open-book exams.

ASSESSING KNOWLEDGE ORGANIZATION

The mind spontaneously organizes information as it is learned. As students attend and listen to your presentations and discussions, watch online videos, or read from their books or online resources, they link this new information with prior learning, and this linking helps them to learn concepts, principles, and to make generalizations. Over time, as their knowledge base grows, it becomes increasingly organized in a hierarchical manner. Even though learners construct this organization on their own, teachers can facilitate it in these ways.

1. At the start of a lesson, you can ask questions that get learners to recall previous learning.

2. During the lesson you can ask questions and provide activities that help learners see similarities and differences and to detect patterns and relationships among the pieces of information that they are hearing or reading.

3. You can also construct outlines or other schematics that visually remind learners of how new information is organized and relates to previously learned information.

Figure 8.2 represents a visual plan constructed by a teacher for an interdisciplinary thematic unit about Attention Deficit Hyperactivity Disorder, or ADHD. This important tool helped the teacher organize knowledge for instruction and assess it in ways that emphasize the interrelationships that build to more important themes and concepts.

Thus, knowledge organization is an important goal of instruction because an organized knowledge base helps students acquire new information, learn it in a meaningful way, remember it, and better solve problems that require it. Assuming that knowledge organization is a goal for your learners, what are some of the ways you can assess it?

First of all, the assessment of knowledge organization differs from the assessment of concepts. The assessment procedures previously discussed let you determine understanding of ADHD

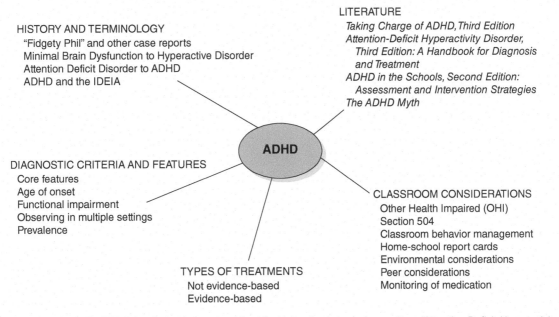

FIGURE 8.2 A visual representation of a high school psychology unit on "Attention Deficit Hyperactivity Disorder" (ADHD).

features, the disorder's history, considerations for the classroom, and types of treatments, usually in isolation from each other. But they don't tell you much about how well the student understands the relationships among those terms or concepts. It is these connections that you will want to assess when you evaluate your learners' knowledge organization.

The connections between and among terms and concepts represent the student's knowledge and understanding of rules, principles, and generalizations. Now the learner has moved from simple knowledge (recall and recognition) to simple understanding (the learner can give examples, tell how a term is different from and similar to other terms and expressions, and explain what it means in his or her own words) to the organization of knowledge (not only does the learner know the pieces but also how the pieces are connected to one another and ordered hierarchically). For example, the learner knows not only about the condition known as ADHD, but also the various terms that preceded the adoption of the term ADHD, diagnostic criteria, types of treatments, classroom implications, and some of the relevant literature. In other words, students must construct concepts, principles, and generalizations that connect the disorder known as ADHD to its history, diagnosis, treatment, and the classroom and relevant literature, all of which represent knowledge organization.

Learners construct connections, concepts, principles, and generalizations as a result of your instruction and the supporting print and electronic resources that allow them to explore similarities and differences and to establish relationships and connections. Learners of all ages spontaneously organize information and form orderly knowledge bases in this way.

Thus, assessing for knowledge organization requires identifying the connections among concepts, or the sets and subsets of knowledge. But how can learners display their organization of knowledge—of cause-and-effect relationships, similarities and contrasts, or problems and solutions? Traditional outlines in which major topics and subtopics are grouped in a I, II, III, or A, B, C order may not reveal knowledge organization. Some educators (Goetz, Alexander, & Ash, 1992) believe such outlines emphasize categories of things over relationships that can impose a structure that differs from the way knowledge should actually be organized for deep understanding.

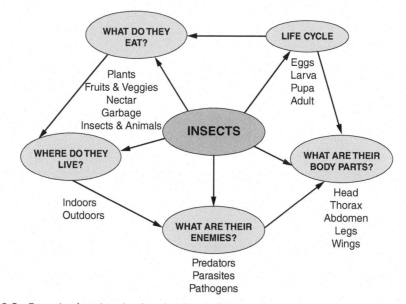

FIGURE 8.3 Example of student-developed web to indicate relationships important to insects for a middle school science class.

Dansereau (1988) urged teachers to model alternate strategies to help learners when they listen to presentations or read from books or online sources, which, in turn, can be used to assess the depth of understanding and organization of their knowledge base. He advocates that you assess your learners' understanding and organization of their knowledge with graphic outlines displayed as webs, much like the visual interdisciplinary thematic unit plan about five domains of interest for a unit about insects shown in Figure 8.3, but this time prepared by your students. Webbing is a free-form outline technique that learners can use to display their level of understanding of class discussions or textbook content, as displayed in Figure 8.3. The following are some rules for communicating to your learners how to construct webs, networks, or maps for study and for assessment:

- Display only essential information or big ideas or concepts.
- Assign the central idea or concept to a central location.
- Draw arrows from the main ideas to show relationships.
- Label the arrows with key words or code letters to describe their relationship.

OPEN-BOOK QUESTIONS AND EXAMS

Having selected a topic area and identified the cognitive outcomes that you wish to assess, you have the choice to give the questions you want your learners to answer in an open-book format. Ideas for these questions can come not only from the text but also from online sources, newspapers, news programs, technical reports, and journals related to your curriculum, and your experiences with a variety of real-life situations in which the behaviors you want to assess are used. Your open-book questions may ask students or collaborative groups of students to prepare an outline of a presentation to a supervisory board using reference material from the text, simulate an experiment or laboratory task using data from resource tables, develop specifications for a product using a published list of industry standards, or develop a mass transit plan, given maps and budgetary information. You can get started on developing open-book questions by asking yourself the following questions:

What do the jobs of professionals who make their living as mathematicians, electronic technicians, journalists, food processing supervisors, and so on look and feel like?

Which of the projects and tasks of these professionals can be adapted to the knowledge and skills required by your curriculum?

Which of these skills are enhanced by being able to refer to existing data, resources, tables, charts, diagrams, and the like, without having to memorize them?

Once you answer these questions, a host of ideas arise. The task then becomes one of developing the open-book exam questions. The following examples illustrate different types of open-book questions.

Some Open-Book Techniques

Here is an example open-book question with explicit directions:

On pages 146–149 of your text you will find a description of a static electricity experiment. Read the description carefully. Then, using your understanding of the experiment and the principles of the electroscope in Table 5.1 in your text, answer the following questions:

1. What would happen to the leaves of the electroscope as the charged ruler is brought closer or farther away from it? Explain why this happens.
2. What would happen to the leaves when you touch the electroscope with the charged ruler and then touch it with your finger? Explain why this happens.
3. What would happen when you pass the charged ruler close to the leaves but do not make contact with them? Explain why this happens.
4. What would happen to the charged leaves when you heat the air next to them with a match? Explain why this happens.

For each question:

a. Make a prediction about what would happen.
b. State what you would observe.
c. Assess whether your prediction could be supported.

Since you want the answer to show evidence of particular reasoning strategies, be sure to include explicit cues to learners to show evidence of the strategy they are using or the thinking and reasoning they went through on the way to solving the problem. Reminders such as "Show all work" and "Be sure to list the steps involved" will allow you to better assess both cognitive and metacognitive strategies.

Quellmalz and Hoskyn (1997) and Quellmalz (1991) recommend that, particularly with questions that assess analysis and comparison, you include the question, "So what?" Rather than simply list elements in an analysis or develop a laundry list of similarities and differences, learners should be asked to explain the significance of the analysis or points of comparison. Thus, questions should explicitly cue learners to explain why the various aspects of the analysis or comparison are important (e.g., "Why should the reader care about the things you analyzed?" or "Why are the similarities and differences that you discussed important for an understanding of this event?"). Today, most students can readily access a wealth of factual information through online resources, such as Wikipedia. With such ready access to factual information today, asking "So what?" may be even more important to assess whether students see connections and their implications today than was the case a few years ago.

One very effective way of encouraging and assessing higher-level thinking skills with open-book exams is through dialectical journals. The word *dialectical* comes from a method of argumentation originating with the ancient Greeks. This process involves the art of examining opinions or ideas logically, often by the method of question and answer so as to determine their validity. It was the practice of Socrates and his followers to conduct this process through oral discourse, but many of the same positive results can be achieved by implementing this structure into a written or online journal form.

In a sense, the dialectical journal is a conversation with oneself over the concepts of a given text. Here is one suggested format. Divide your examination in half vertically and title two columns as follows:

Quotation, Summary, or Paraphrase	*Reaction, Prediction, or Analysis*
(From text)	(From student)

A quotation, summary, or paraphrase from the text or related reading (e.g., relevant online, magazine, or newspaper article) is chosen by you. A reaction, prediction, or analysis to your quotation, summarization, or paraphrasing is written by the student in the column on the right. Just like the professional on the job, your students are allowed to consult the text or other sources to find material to formulate a response.

This journal format should be modeled with examples and practiced with students before using it for assessment purposes. Initially, students unfamiliar with this procedure may make shallow or superficial comments, often thinking that simple explication or explanation is what is wanted. Encourage students to use what is presented in the text as a *starting* point rather than the end point for their responses. Learning to use the text or other sources in this manner can increase the accuracy and depth of responses and encourage higher-level cognition.

The dialectical procedure can be practiced in the initial stages of a new topic or unit to encourage active reading, at midpoint to see if early ideas were valid, and at the conclusion, as an open-book exam where new perspectives and deep understanding can be assessed. A good rule is to use the early dialectical journals for modeling and feedback, or to generate the exchange of ideas, and for assessment of deep understanding at the conclusion of a topic or unit. Here are some sample dialectical entries in the form of an open-book exam.

Dialectical Open-Book Questions

Quotation, paraphrase, or summary	*Student reaction, prediction, or analysis*
"Scientists have determined that the height of a deep-water wave cannot exceed one-seventh of its wavelength if the wave's structure is to support its crest." (from a trigonometry text)	
Does the same principle apply to radio waves? Using examples from the text, what other factors such as wind velocity or atmospheric pressure might influence this formula?	

Quotation, paraphrase, or summary	*Student reaction, prediction, or analysis*
"The reflection symmetry of living creatures like the lizard and butterfly is often called bilateral symmetry." (from an art text)	
Symmetry has favorable and practical physical attributes as well as aesthetic ones. Because of this symmetry, the butterfly can soar through the air and the lizard can crawl in a straight line, or variations of one. From examples in the text show how we tend to lean toward symmetry in aesthetics because of its inherent usefulness.	

Quotation, paraphrase, or summary	*Student reaction, prediction, or analysis*
"The strength of triangular bracing is related to the SSS Postulate, which tells us that a triangle with given sides can have only one shape. A rectangle formed by four bars joined at their ends can flatten into a parallelogram, but the structural triangle cannot be deformed except by bending or stretching the bars." (from a geometry text)	

From the pyramids of ancient Egypt to the Eiffel Tower in France, extending to the modest tripod of photography, or the tallest of radio towers, we see the ever-present tower. Using examples from the text or the class website, what other building or structural uses can be made of the simple triangle?

Quotation, paraphrase, or summary	*Student reaction, prediction, or analysis*
"Never read feverishly, never read as though you were racing against time—unless you wish to derive neither pleasure nor profit from your reading" (from a literature text)	
Could it be that pleasure and profit are connected? Do we remember things more if we take the time to enjoy them? How important are emotions to learning? According to this author, the conventional advice to read faster and more efficiently may not be so good. Can you show from any of the stories you have read that slowing down and enjoying what you are doing can increase your understanding and ability to apply what you have read?	

Since the student self-selects the material to answer the question from the text, there is already inherent interest in the content and meaning for the student.

This journal technique may be refined to meet the individual instructor's needs. For example, students may be asked to choose entries that relate to a single theme or concept, such as the application of conservation practices, future uses of known scientific principles, or analysis of a historical event.

Here is another type of dialectical question. This one reverses the process by asking the student to find a quotation, paraphrase, or summary from the text that exhibits a certain principle or concept provided by you.

Directions: Read the following passage from your text and choose five quotations, paraphrases, or summaries from any chapter we have studied that supports its theme.

Machines and tools have always been created in the image of man. The hammer grew from the balled fist, the rake from the hand with fingers, outstretched for scratching, the shovel from the hand hollowed to scoop. As machines became more than simple tools, outstripping the creators in performance, demanding and obtaining increasing amounts of power, and acquiring superhuman speed and accuracies, their outward resemblance to the natural model disappeared; only the names of the machines' parts show vestiges of the human origin. The highly complex machinery of the industrial age has arms that swing, fingers that fold, legs that support, and teeth that grind. Machines feed on material, run when things go well, and spit and cough when they don't.

Quotation, paraphrase, or summary from text	*Page*
1.	
2.	
3.	
4.	
5.	

Now that we've studied ways of writing good essay questions in the form of extended and restricted response questions, knowledge organization, open-book exams, and dialectical journals, let's summarize with some guidelines that can help you write good test items in all of these formats.

GUIDELINES FOR PLANNING ESSAYS, KNOWLEDGE ORGANIZATION, AND OPEN-BOOK QUESTIONS AND EXAMS

1. Make clear the requirements for answering your questions, but not the solution itself. While your questions should be complex, learners should not have to question whether they are finished, or whether they have provided what you want. They should, however, have to think long and hard about how to answer a question. As you refine your questions, make sure you can visualize what an acceptable answer looks like and identify the skills you can infer from it.

2. The questions should represent a valid sample from which you can make generalizations about the learner's knowledge, thinking ability, and attitudes. What essay tests lack in breadth of coverage, they make up in depth. In other words, they get your students to exhibit higher-order thinking behavior in a narrow domain or skill. Thus, the type of questions you choose should be complex enough and rich enough in detail to allow you to draw conclusions about transfer and generalization to other tasks. In other words, they should be representative of other important skills that assess the essential performance outcomes you wish your learners to achieve (Borich, 2015; Shavelson & Baxter, 1992).

3. The questions should be complex enough to allow for multiple correct answers. Most assessment tends to depend on a single right answer. Essays, open-book exams, assessments of knowledge organization, and dialectical journals, however, are designed to allow learners to demonstrate learning through a variety of paths. In science, for example, a student might choose to answer a question by emphasizing the results of an experiment from the text, showing the solution by explaining how laboratory equipment would be used to arrive at it, or by simulating data and conclusions from an experiment that would answer the question. Allowing for multiple paths to the correct answer will be more time consuming than a multiple-choice test, but it will provide unique information about your learners' achievement untapped by other assessment methods. Shavelson and Baxter (1992) have shown that examination procedures that allow teachers to draw different conclusions about a learner's problem-solving ability lead to more analysis, interpretation, and evaluation behavior than do multiple-choice tests or restricted response essay tests. Because higher-level cognitive skills are now part of the CCSS and many state standards, development, and assessment of those skills have become increasingly important to help ensure college and career readiness.

4. The questions should yield multiple solutions where possible, each with costs and benefits. Essay questions are not a form of practice or drill. They should involve more than simple tasks for which there is one solution. Essays and the other assessments we have discussed should be nonalgorithmic (the path of action is not fully specified in advance) and complex (the total solution cannot be seen from any one vantage point), and they should involve judgment and interpretation.

5. The questions should require self-regulated learning. The questions or assignments should require considerable mental effort and place high demands on the persistence and determination of the individual learner. The learner should be required to use self-generated cognitive

strategies to arrive at a solution rather than depend on memorized or online content at various points in the assessment process.

6. The questions should have clear directions, and should be complex, require higher-level thinking, assess multiple goals, and permit considerable latitude about how to reach these goals. Nevertheless, your questions should leave no doubt in the minds of learners about what is expected. While your students need to think long and hard about how to answer the question, they should be clear about what a good answer looks like. In other words, they should be able to explain exactly what you expect them to submit when the exam or assessment is over.

SUMMARY

This chapter introduced you to the major issues related to the construction and scoring of essay items and other assessments of higher-order thinking. Its major points are as follows:

1. Each of the assessments we covered in this chapter (essay items, knowledge organization assessments, open-book exams, and dialectical journals) requires that the students supply rather than select a response. The length and complexity of the response may vary, and these items lend themselves best to the assessment of higher-level cognitive skills.

2. There are two main types of essay items that are differentiated by length of response: extended response and restricted response essay items.
   a. The extended response item usually requires responses more than a page in length and may be used to assess synthesis and evaluation skills. It is usually appropriate for term papers and end-of-semester reports.
   b. The restricted response item is usually answered in a page or less. It is often used to measure comprehension, application, and analysis.

3. The type of item written is determined by the cognitive skills called for in the instructional objective.

4. Suggestions for writing essay items include the following:
   a. Identify the cognitive processes you want the student to use before you write the item.
   b. State the task clearly (i.e., focus the item), including any criteria on which the essay will be graded.
   c. Avoid beginning essay items with *what*, *who*, *when*, and *list*, unless you are measuring at the knowledge level.
   d. Ask for presentation of evidence for a controversial position, rather than ask the student simply to take a controversial position.
   e. Avoid using optional items.
   f. Establish reasonable time and/or page limits for each item.
   g. Use essays to measure learning outcomes that cannot be adequately measured by objective items.
   h. Be sure the item matches the instructional objective.

5. Advantages of essay items over objective items include the following:
   a. Essays enable you to assess complex learning outcomes.
   b. Essays are relatively easy to construct.
   c. Essays enable you to assess communication skills.
   d. Essays eliminate student guessing.

6. Disadvantages of essay items include the following:
   a. Longer scoring time is needed.
   b. Scoring can be unreliable.
   c. Essays sample limited content.
   d. Answers are susceptible to bluffing.

7. Essay items should be used when:
   a. Objectives specify higher-level cognitive processes and objective items are inappropriate.
   b. Few tests or items are necessary.
   c. Test security is in question.

8. Essay scoring reliability may be improved by the following:
   a. Writing good essay items.
   b. Using restricted range rather than extended range essays whenever appropriate.
   c. Using a predetermined scoring scheme.
   d. Implementing the scoring scheme consistently with all students.
   e. Removing or covering names on papers to avoid scoring bias.
   f. Scoring all responses to one item before scoring the next item.
   g. Keeping scores from previous items hidden when scoring subsequent items.
   h. Rescoring all papers before returning them and averaging discrepant ratings.

9. Essays may be scored according to the following:
   a. Simple scoring schemes that assign credit for content.
   b. Detailed scoring schemes that assign credit for content, organization, process, and any other factors that the scorer deems desirable.
   c. The rating method, in which grades are assigned on the basis of a global impression of the whole response.

10. A type of assessment for measuring the organization of knowledge in which the learner makes connections among concepts or subsets of knowledge is called webbing.

11. Open-book exams are ideal for questions that use tabular data, charts, and graphs that come from the text, online resources, or newspapers, magazines, and reports related to your curriculum and that ask students to think about and apply information that comes from real-life situations in which the behaviors you want to assess are used.

12. One way of encouraging and assessing higher-level thinking skills with an open-book exam is with dialectical journals, which involve examining the opinions or ideas of others logically, often by the method of question and answer so as to determine their validity.

FOR DISCUSSION AND PRACTICE

1. Write essay test items using both an extended response format and a restricted response format. Your extended response question should be targeted to measure a synthesis or evaluation objective, while your restricted response question should be targeted to measure a comprehension, application, or analysis objective.

2. Prepare a scoring guide for your restricted response essay item using the format shown in Table 8.1.

3. Describe five scoring procedures from among those discussed in this chapter that will help ensure the reliability of scoring your essay question.

4. Give some pros and cons of the rating method, in which grades are assigned on the basis of global impressions of the whole response.

5. Prepare an open-book exam question requiring the use of specific reference material from the text or an online source (e.g., data, graphs, tables).

CHAPTER 9

PERFORMANCE-BASED ASSESSMENT

After completing this chapter, the student will be able to:

1. Describe the circumstances for which performance tests may be more appropriate than objective or essay tests.

2. Explain why performance test may improve both instruction and learning.

3. Explain why performance assessments have been included in the tests aligned with Common Core Sate Standards.

4. Differentiate among the four steps involved in constructing a performance assessment.

5. Compare and contrast the kinds of skills necessary to acquire and organize and use information that are suited to performance assessments.

6. Suggest appropriate ways to evaluate each of these skills.

7. Describe the five criteria intended to help refine the performance assessment context.

8. Explain why a scoring rubric is necessary for a performance assessment.

9. Develop a scoring rubric for a performance assessment.

10. Define primary trait scoring.

11. Develop a primary trait scoring scheme.

12. Compare and contrast rating scales and checklists regarding the types of performances each is best/least suited for.

13. Explain how holistic scoring is used.

14. Identify the primary constraints that must be decided on when developing a performance measure.

IN CHAPTER 6 (in the Writing Instructional Objectives section), you learned that children acquire a variety of skills in school. Some of these skills require learners to acquire information by memorizing vocabulary, multiplication tables, and dates of historical events. Other skills involve learning action sequences or procedures to follow when performing mathematical computations, dissecting a frog, focusing a microscope, handwriting, or typing. In addition, you learned that students must acquire concepts, rules, and generalizations that allow them to understand what they read, analyze and solve problems, carry out experiments, write poems and essays, and design projects to study historical, political, or economic problems.

Some of these skills are best assessed with paper-and-pencil tests. But other skills—particularly those involving independent judgment, critical thinking, and decision making—are best assessed with performance tests. Traditionally, paper-and-pencil tests have been the principal means of assessing these more complex cognitive outcomes, in this chapter, we will study other ways of measuring them in more authentic contexts. The two state assessment consortia that have developed the online tests aligned with the Common Core State Standards (CCSS) represent examples of the extent to which such measures are now increasingly included in high-stakes summative tests.

PERFORMANCE TESTS: DIRECT MEASURES OF COMPETENCE

In earlier chapters, you learned that many educational tests measure learning indirectly. That is, they ask questions, the responses to which indicate or suggest that something has been learned or mastered. Performance tests, on the other hand, use direct measures of learning rather than indirect measures that simply suggest cognitive, affective, or psychomotor processes have taken place. In the field of athletics, diving and gymnastics are examples of performances that judges rate directly. Their scores are pooled and used to decide who, for example, earns a medal, wins first, second, and third, or qualifies for district or regional competition. Likewise, at band contests, judges directly see and hear the competence of trombone or violin players and pool their ratings to decide who makes the state or district band and who gets the leading chairs.

Teachers can use performance tests to assess complex cognitive learning, as well as attitudes and social skills in academic areas such as science, social studies, or math (National Research Council, 2001). When doing so, they establish situations that allow them to observe and to rate learners directly as they analyze, problem-solve, experiment, make decisions, measure, cooperate with others, present orally, or produce a product. These situations simulate real-world activities, as might be expected in a job, in the community, or in various forms of advanced training—for example, in the military, at a technical institute, during on-the-job training, or in college.

Performance tests also allow teachers to observe achievements, mental habits, ways of working, and behaviors of value in the real world that conventional tests may miss and in ways that an outside observer would be unaware that a "test" is going on. Performance tests can include observing and rating learners as they carry out a dialogue in a foreign language, conduct a science experiment, edit a composition, present an exhibit, work with a group of other learners in designing a student attitude survey, or use equipment. In other words, the teacher observes and evaluates student abilities to carry out complex activities that are used and valued outside the immediate confines of the classroom.

PERFORMANCE TESTS CAN ASSESS PROCESSES AND PRODUCTS

Performance tests can be assessments of processes or products, or both. For example, at the Darwin School in Winnipeg, Manitoba, teachers assess the reading process of each student by noting the percentage of words read accurately during oral reading, the number of sentences read by the learner that are meaningful within the context of the story, and the percentage of story elements that the learner can talk about in his or her own words after reading.

At the West Orient School in Gresham, Oregon, fourth-grade learners assemble a portfolio of their writing products. These portfolios include rough as well as final drafts of poetry, essays, biographies, and self-reflections. Several math teachers at Twin Peaks Middle School in Poway, California, require their students to assemble math portfolios that include the following products of their problem-solving efforts: long-term projects, daily notes, journal entries about troublesome test problems, written explanations of how they solved problems, and the problem solutions themselves.

Social studies learning processes and products are assessed in the Aurora, Colorado Public Schools by having learners engage in a variety of projects built around the following question: "Based on your study of Colorado history, what current issues in Colorado do you believe are the most important to address, what are your ideas about the resolutions of those issues, and what contributions will you make toward the resolutions?" Learners answer these questions in a variety of ways involving individual and group writing assignments, oral presentations, and exhibits.

PERFORMANCE TESTS CAN BE EMBEDDED IN LESSONS

The examples of performance tests given above involve performances that occurred outside the context of a lesson and that are completed at the end of a term or during an examination period. But many teachers use performance tests as part of their lessons, to stimulate the kind of higher-level thinking that are called for in the CCSS and recently upgraded state standards in states that have not adopted the CCSS. In fact, some proponents of performance tests hold that the ideal performance test is a good teaching activity. Viewed from this perspective, a well-constructed performance test can serve as a teaching activity as well as an assessment.

During a performance assessment activity, the teacher observes the activity and rates the learners on the method they used to solve the problem, the care with which they measured, the manner of recording results, and the correctness of the final solution. This type of assessment provides immediate feedback on how learners are performing, reinforces hands-on teaching and learning, and underscores for learners the important link between teaching and testing. In this manner, it moves the instruction toward higher-order thinking and behavior.

Some examples of lesson-embedded performance tests might include observing and rating the following activities as they are actually happening: typing, preparing a microscope slide, reading out loud, programming a calculator, giving an oral presentation, determining how plants react to certain substances, designing a questionnaire or survey, solving a math problem, developing an original math problem and a solution for it, critiquing the logic of an editorial, or graphing information.

PERFORMANCE TESTS CAN ASSESS AFFECTIVE AND SOCIAL SKILLS

Teachers across the country are using performance tests to assess not only higher-level cognitive skills but also noncognitive outcomes, such as self-direction, ability to work with others, and social awareness (Costa & Kallick, 2013; Marzano, Pickering, & Heflebower, 2010). This concern for the affective domain of learning reflects an awareness by educators that the skilled performance of complex tasks involves more than the ability to recall information, form concepts, generalize, and problem-solve. It also includes the mental and behavioral habits or characteristics evident in individuals who successfully perform such complex tasks, also known as habits of mind, and interpersonal or social skills (Costa & Kallick, 2008).

For example, the Aurora Public Schools in Colorado developed a list of learning outcomes and their indicators for learners in grades K-12. These are shown in Figure 9.1. For each of these 19 indicators, a four-category rating scale has been developed to serve as a guide for teachers who are unsure of how to define "assumes responsibility" or "demonstrates consideration." While observing learners during performance tests in social studies, science, art, or economics, teachers are alert to recognize and rate those behaviors that suggest learners have acquired the outcomes.

Teachers in the Aurora Public Schools are encouraged to use this list of outcomes when planning their courses. They first ask themselves, "What key facts, concepts, and principles should all learners remember?" In addition, they try to fuse this subject area content with the five district outcomes by designing special performance tests. For example, a third-grade language arts teacher who is planning a writing unit might choose to focus on indicators 8 and 9 to address district

A self-directed learner

1. Sets priorities and achievable goals.
2. Monitors and evaluates progress.
3. Creates options for self.
4. Assumes responsibility for actions.
5. Creates a positive vision for self and future.

A collaborative worker

6. Monitors own behavior as a group member.
7. Assesses and manages group functioning.
8. Demonstrates interactive communication.
9. Demonstrates consideration for individual differences.

A complex thinker

10. Uses a wide variety of strategies for managing complex issues.
11. Selects strategies appropriate to the resolution of complex issues and applies the strategies with accuracy and thoroughness.
12. Accesses and uses topic-relevant knowledge.

A quality producer

13. Creates products that achieve their purpose.
14. Creates products appropriate to the intended audience.
15. Creates products that reflect craftsmanship.
16. Uses appropriate resources/technology.

A community contributor

17. Demonstrates knowledge about his or her diverse communities.
18. Takes action.
19. Reflects on his or her role as a community contributor.

FIGURE 9.1 Learning outcomes of Aurora Public Schools.

outcomes related to "collaborative worker," indicator 1 for the outcome of self-directed learner, and indicator 13 for the outcome "quality producer." She would then design a performance assessment that allows learners to demonstrate learning in these areas. She might select other indicators and outcomes for subsequent units and performance tests.

In summary, performance tests represent an addition to the measurement practices reviewed in previous chapters. Paper-and-pencil tests are the most efficient, reliable, and valid instruments available for assessing knowledge, comprehension, and some types of application. But when it comes to assessing complex thinking skills, habits of mind, and social skills, performance tests can, if properly constructed, do a better and more comprehensive job than most paper-and-pencil tests. On the other hand, if not properly constructed, performance assessments can have some of the same problems with scoring efficiency, reliability, and validity as traditional approaches to testing, and essay testing in particular. This chapter will guide you through a process that will allow you to properly construct performance tests in your classroom.

DEVELOPING PERFORMANCE TESTS FOR YOUR LEARNERS

As we learned in the previous section, performance assessment has the potential to improve both instruction and learning. But as we have also learned, there are both conceptual and technical issues associated with the use of performance tests that teachers must resolve before these assessments can be effectively and efficiently used. In this chapter, we will discuss some of the important considerations in planning and designing a performance test and how to score performance tests to help ensure scoring reliability, including student portfolios. In Chapter 12, we will describe how you can integrate scores from performance tests into your six-week and semester grades.

Step 1: Deciding What to Test

The first step in developing a performance test is to create a list of objectives that specifies the knowledge, skills, habits of mind, and indicators of the outcomes that will be the focus of your instruction.

There are three general questions to ask when deciding what to teach:

- What knowledge or content (i.e., facts, concepts, principles, and rules) is essential for learner understanding of the subject matter?
- What intellectual skills are necessary for the learner to use this knowledge or content?
- What habits of mind are important for the learner to successfully perform with this knowledge or content?

Instructional objectives that come from answering the first question are usually measured by paper-and-pencil tests (discussed in Chapters 7 and 8). Objectives derived from answering questions 2 and 3, though often assessed with objective- or essay-type questions, can be more appropriately assessed with performance tests. Thus, your assessment plan for a unit should include both paper-and-pencil tests to measure mastery of content and performance tests to assess skills and habits of mind. Let's see what objectives for the latter outcomes might look like.

Performance Objectives in the Cognitive Domain
Designers of performance tests usually ask the following questions to help guide their initial selection of objectives:

- What kinds of essential tasks, achievements, or other valued competencies am I missing with paper-and-pencil tests?

- What accomplishments of those who practice my discipline (historians, writers, scientists, and mathematicians) are valued but left unmeasured by conventional tests?

Two categories of performance skills are typically identified from such questions:

1. Skills related to acquiring information.
2. Skills related to organizing and using information.

Figure 9.2 contains a suggested list of skills for acquiring, organizing, and using information. As you study this list, consider which skills you might use as a basis for a performance test in your area of expertise.

The following are some example objectives for performance tests from a consideration of the performance skills described in Figure 9.2.

1. Write a summary of a current controversy drawn from school life and tell how a courageous and civic-minded American you have studied might decide to act on the issue.

Skills in acquiring information	Skills in organizing and using information
Communicating	**Organizing**
Explaining	Classifying
Modeling	Categorizing
Demonstrating	Sorting
Graphing	Ordering
Displaying	Ranking
Writing	Arranging
Advising	
Programming	**Problem solving**
Proposing	Stating questions
Drawing	Identifying problems
	Developing hypotheses
Measuring	Interpreting
Counting	Assessing risks
Calibrating	Monitoring
Rationing	
Appraising	**Decision making**
Weighing	Weighing alternatives
Balancing	Evaluating
Guessing	Choosing
Estimating	Supporting
Forecasting	Electing
Defending	Adopting
Investigating	
Gathering references	
Interviewing	
Using references	
Experimenting	
Hypothesizing	

FIGURE 9.2 Skills for acquiring, organizing, and using information.

2. Draw a physical map of North America from memory and locate 10 cities.

3. Prepare an exhibit showing how your community responds to an important social problem of your choice.

4. Construct an electrical circuit using wires, a switch, a bulb, resistors, and a battery.

5. Describe two alternative ways to solve a mathematics word problem.

6. Identify the important variables that affected recent events in our state, and forecast how these variables will affect future events.

7. Design a free-standing structure in which the size of one leg of a triangular structure must be determined from the other two sides.

8. Program a calculator to solve an equation with one unknown.

9. Design an exhibit showing the best ways to clean up an oil spill.

10. Prepare a visual presentation to the city council requesting increased funding to deal with a problem in our community.

Performance Objectives in the Affective and Social Domain Performance assessments require curriculum not only to teach thinking skills but also to develop positive dispositions and "habits of mind." Habits of mind include such behaviors as constructive criticism, tolerance of ambiguity, respect for reason, flexibility, appreciation for the significance of the past, and recognition of the contextual limitations of application of the past to the present. Performance tests are ideal vehicles for assessing habits of mind and social skills (e.g., cooperation, sharing, and negotiation). In deciding what objectives to teach and measure with a performance test, you should give consideration to affective and social skill objectives. Following are some key questions to ask for including affective and social skills in your list of performance objectives:

- What dispositions, habits of mind, or values characterize successful individuals in the community who work in your academic discipline?

- What are some of the qualities of mind or character traits that good scientists, writers, reporters, historians, mathematicians, musicians, and so on have?

- What will I accept as evidence that my learners have or are developing these qualities?

- What social skills for getting along with others are necessary for being successful as a journalist, weather forecaster, park ranger, historian, economist, mechanic, and so on?

- What evidence will convince my learners' parents that their children are developing these skills?

Figure 9.3 displays some examples of habits of mind in checklist form that could be the focus of performance assessments in science, social studies, and mathematics. Once you have completed Step 1, you will have identified the important knowledge, skills, and habits of mind that will be the focus of your instruction and assessment. The next step is to design the task or context in which those outcomes will be assessed.

Step 2: Designing the Assessment Context

The purpose of Step 2 is to create a task, simulation, or situation that will allow learners to demonstrate the knowledge, skills, and attitudes that they have acquired. Ideas for these tasks may come from newspapers, popular books, or interviews with professionals as reported in the media (e.g., an oil tanker runs aground and creates an environmental crisis, a drought occurs in an underdeveloped

In Science

☐ Values lifelong learning. Shows ongoing interest in knowledge acquisition.

☐ Values the role of science in lifelong learning. Demonstrates the application of problem-solving and the scientific method in approaching problems.

☐ Is skeptical. Appropriately questions authoritarian statements, preconceived conclusions, and self-assured conclusions.

☐ Employs data-based decision making. Collects, organizes, and uses data to inform decision making.

☐ Comfort with ambiguity. Accepts and understands that data and conclusions often are only suggestive and can be unexpected.

☐ Values flexibility in self and others. Acknowledges that opinions and conclusions may change in the face of new data.

☐ Values collaboration and collegiality. Acknowledges that solutions to complex problems require teamwork and integration.

☐ Values honesty. Accepts data and conclusions that are contradictory to previously held beliefs and biases.

In Social Studies

☐ Comprehends the influence of past events on the individual and society.

☐ Demonstrates the capacity to differentiate relevant and irrelevant data in developing strategies, conclusions, and judgments.

☐ Acceptance of the complexity of most social challenges, how resistant they are to change, and the need to be persistent in addressing those challenges.

☐ Appreciates the contextual limitations of the applications of historical data, conclusions, and solutions to contemporary issues and challenges.

In Mathematics

☐ Appreciates that the solution of many complex real-world problems is facilitated through mathematics.

☐ Values mathematics as a problem-solving tool, while recognizing that some may view mathematics as a mystery or impediment. Engages with others to help them comprehend the potential benefits of mathematics.

☐ Is flexible in approaching problems. Appreciates that there are often multiple paths to a conclusions and pursues them.

FIGURE 9.3 Examples of habits of mind in performance assessment.

country causing famine, a technological breakthrough presents a moral dilemma). The tasks should center on issues, concepts, or problems that are important to your content area. In other words, they should be the same issues, concepts, and problems that important people who are working in the field face every day.

The tasks you create may involve debates, mock trials, presentations to a city commission, reenactments of historical events, science experiments, job responsibilities (e.g., a travel agent, weather forecaster, and park ranger), and the like. Regardless of the specific context, they should present the learner with a challenge.

For example, consider the following social studies performance test item:

Imagine that you and your group have been assigned to plan a two week to trip to Brazil for the 2016 Olympic Games. The trip will be for a co-ed group of elite high-school track athletes. Your final product should be an extensive brochure, an itinerary, and behavioral expectations for the high-school athletes as they travel to and from the Games, and during the games. In addition to the itinerary and behavioral expectations, be sure to address what you consider to be the most important among the following: transportation needs, international travel and health requirements and considerations, weather, accommodations, clothing requirements, communications with caretakers, language issues, cultural differences, safety concerns and considerations, smart phone/tablet and computer usage and limits, voltage converters, curfews, consequences for inappropriate behavior, currency conversions, spending money, souvenirs, the costs, and other information necessary for families to decide if they want their children to participate.

Notice that this example presents learners with the following:

1. A hands-on exercise or problem to solve that produces

2. An observable outcome or product (typed business letter, a map, graph, piece of clothing, multimedia presentation, poem, etc.), so that the teacher

3. Can observe and assess not only the product but also the process used to get there.

Designing the content for a performance test involves equal parts of inspiration and perspiration. While there is no formula or recipe to follow that guarantees a valid performance test, the following criteria can help guide you in revising and refining the task.

The Requirements for Task Mastery Should Be Clear Without Revealing the Solution

Although your tasks should be complex, the final product should be clear. Learners should not have to question whether they are finished or whether they have provided what you want. They should, however, have to think long and hard about how to complete the task. As you refine the task, make sure you can visualize what mastery of the task looks like and identify the skills that can be inferred from it.

The Task Should Represent a Specific Activity from Which Generalizations about the Learner's Knowledge, Thinking Ability, and Habits of Mind Can Be Made

What performance tests lack in breadth of coverage, they make up in depth. In other words, they allow you to observe a wide range of behavior in a narrow domain of skill. The type of tasks you choose should be complex enough and rich enough in detail to allow you to draw conclusions about transfer and generalization to other tasks. Ideally, you should be able to identify about 8 to 10 important performance tasks for an entire course of study (one or two a unit) that assess the essential performance outcomes you wish your learners to achieve.

The Tasks Should Be Complex Enough to Allow for Multimodal Assessment

Most assessment tends to depend on the written word. Performance tests, however, are designed to allow learners to demonstrate learning through a variety of modalities. In science, for example, one could make direct observations of students while they investigate a problem using laboratory equipment, have students give oral explanations of what they did, require them to record procedures and conclusions in notebooks, prepare an exhibit of their project, and solve short-answer paper-and-pencil problems. This approach will be more time consuming than a multiple-choice test but will provide unique information about your learners' achievement untapped by other assessment methods. Shavelson and Baxter (1992) have shown that performance tests allow teachers to draw different conclusions about a learner's problem-solving ability than do higher-order multiple-choice tests or restricted response essay tests that ask learners to analyze, interpret, and evaluate information.

The Tasks Should Yield Multiple Solutions Where Possible, Each with Costs and Benefits Performance testing is not a form of practice or drill. It should involve more than simple tasks for which there is one solution. Performance tests should be nonalgorithmic (the path of action is not fully specified in advance) and complex (the total solution cannot be seen from any one vantage point) and should involve judgment and interpretation.

The Tasks Should Require Self-Regulated Learning Performance tests should require considerable mental effort and place high demands on the persistence and determination of the individual learner. The learner should be required to use cognitive strategies to arrive at a solution rather than depend on coaching at various points in the assessment process.

Step 3: Specifying the Scoring Rubrics

One of the principal limitations of performance tests is the time required to score them. Just as these tests require time and effort on the part of the learner, they demand similar commitment from teachers when scoring them. True–false, multiple-choice, and short-answer questions are significantly easier to score than projects, portfolios, or performances. In addition, projects, portfolios, or performances force teachers to make difficult choices over how much qualities such as effort, participation, and cooperation count in the final score.

Given the challenges confronting teachers who use performance tests, there is a temptation to limit the scoring criteria to those qualities of performance that are easiest to rate rather than the most important required for doing an effective job. Resorting to scoring what is easiest or least controversial can turn an authentic and well-thought-out performance test into an inaccurate one. Your goal when scoring performance tests is to do justice to the time spent developing them and the effort expended by students taking them. You can accomplish this goal by developing carefully constructed scoring systems, called rubrics.

By giving careful consideration to rubrics, you can develop a scoring system for performance tests that minimizes the arbitrariness of your judgments while holding learners to high standards of achievement. Here are some of the important considerations in developing rubrics for a performance test.

Develop Rubrics for a Variety of Accomplishments In general, performance tests require four types of accomplishments from learners:

Products	Poems, essays, charts, graphs, exhibits, drawings, maps, and so on.
Complex cognitive processes	Skills in acquiring, organizing, and using information (see Figure 9.2).
Observable performance	Physical movements as in dance, gymnastics, or typing; oral presentations; use of specialized equipment as in focusing a microscope; following a set of procedures as when dissecting a frog, bisecting an angle, or following a recipe.
Habits of mind and social skills	Mental and behavioral habits (such as persistence and cooperation) and recognition skills.

As the list suggests, the effect of your teaching may be realized in a variety of ways.

Choose a Scoring System Best Suited for the Type of Accomplishment You Want to Measure In general, there are three categories of rubrics to use when scoring performance tests: checklists, rating scales, and holistic scoring. Do those terms sound familiar? They should; we introduced you to them in Chapter 8 when we discussed ways to score essays more reliably, and those rubrics can help score performance assessments more reliably too. Each has certain strengths and limitations, and each is more or less suitable for scoring products, cognitive processes, performances, and social skills.

Checklists Checklists contain lists of behaviors, traits, or characteristics that can be scored as either present or absent. They are best suited for complex behaviors or performances that can be divided into a series of clearly defined, specific actions. Dissecting a frog, bisecting an angle, balancing a scale, making an audiotape recording, or tying a shoe are behaviors that require sequences of actions that can be clearly identified and listed on a checklist. Checklists are scored on a yes/no, present or absent, 0 or 1 point basis and should provide the opportunity for observers to indicate that they had no opportunity to observe the performance. Some checklists also include frequent mistakes that learners make when performing the task. In such cases, a score of +1 may be given for each positive behavior, −1 for each mistake, and 0 for no opportunity to observe. Figures 9.4 and 9.5 show checklists for using a microscope and a calculator.

No opportunity to observe	Observed	
☐	☐	Wipes slide with lens paper
☐	☐	Places drop or two of culture on slide
☐	☐	Adds a few drops of water
☐	☐	Places slide on stage
☐	☐	Turns to low power
☐	☐	Looks through eyepiece with one eye
☐	☐	Adjusts mirror
☐	☐	Turns to high power
☐	☐	Adjusts for maximum enlargement and resolution

FIGURE 9.4 Checklist for using a microscope.

No opportunity to observe	Observed	
☐	☐	Knows how to turn calculator on
☐	☐	Can "key in" 10 numbers consecutively, without hitting adjacent keys
☐	☐	Can quickly add three 2-digit numbers, without error
☐	☐	Knows how to position keyboard and to rest arm and elbow for maximum comfort and accuracy
☐	☐	Knows how to reposition display screen to reduce reflection and glare, when necessary
☐	☐	Pushes keys with positive, firm motions
☐	☐	Can feel when a key touch is insufficiently firm to activate calculator

FIGURE 9.5 Checklist for using an electronic calculator.

Rating Scales   Rating scales are typically used for those aspects of a complex performance that do not lend themselves to yes/no or present/absent type judgments. The most common form of a rating scale is one that assigns numbers to categories of performance. Figure 9.6 shows a rating scale for judging elements of writing in a term paper. This scale focuses the rater's observations on certain aspects of the performance (accuracy, logic, organization, style, etc.) and assigns numbers to five degrees of performance.

Most numerical rating scales use an analytical scoring technique called *primary trait scoring* (Sax, 1989). This type of rating requires that the test developer first identify the most salient characteristics or primary traits of greatest importance when observing the product, process, or performance. Then, for each trait, the developer assigns numbers (usually 1–5) that represent degrees of performance.

Figure 9.7 displays a numerical rating scale that uses primary trait scoring to rate problem solving (Szetela & Nicol, 1992). In this system, problem solving is subdivided into the primary

Quality and accuracy of ideas		
1 2	3 4	5
Very limited investigation; little or no material related to the facts.	Some investigation and attention to the facts are apparent.	Extensive investigation; good detail and representation of the facts.
Logical development of ideas		
1 2	3 4	5
Very little orderly development of ideas; presentation is confusing and hard to follow.	Some logical development of ideas, but logical order needs to be improved.	Good logical development; ideas logically connected and built upon one another.
Organization of ideas		
1 2	3 4	5
No apparent organization. Lack of paragraphing and transitions.	Organization is mixed; some of the ideas not adequately separated from others with appropriate transitions.	Good organization and paragraphing; clear transitions between ideas.
Style, individuality		
1 2	3 4	5
Style bland and inconsistent, or "borrowed."	Some style and individuality beginning to show.	Good style and individuality; personality of writer shows through.
Words and phrasing		
1 2	3 4	5
Wording trite; extensive use of clichés.	Some word choices awkward.	Appropriate use of words and phrasing work to sharpen ideas.

FIGURE 9.6   Rating scale for themes and term papers that emphasizes interpretation and organization.

Understanding the problem

0	–	No attempt
1	–	Completely misinterprets the problem
2	–	Misinterprets major part of the problem
3	–	Misinterprets minor part of the problem
4	–	Complete understanding of the problem

Solving the problem

0	–	No attempt
1	–	Total inappropriate plan
2	–	Partially correct procedure but with major fault
3	–	Substantially correct procedure with major omission or procedural error
4	–	A plan that could lead to a correct solution with no arithmetic errors

Answering the problem

0	–	No answer or wrong answer based on an inappropriate plan
1	–	Copying error, computational error, and partial answer for problem with multiple answers; no answer statement; and answer labeled incorrectly
2	–	Correct solution

FIGURE 9.7 Analytic scale for problem solving.

traits of understanding the problem, solving the problem, and answering the problem. For each trait, points are assigned to certain aspects or qualities of the trait. Notice how the designer of this rating scale identified both characteristics of effective and ineffective problem solving.

Two key questions are usually addressed when designing scoring systems for rating scales using primary trait scoring:

1. What are the most important characteristics that show a high degree of the trait?

2. What are the errors most justifiable for achieving a lower score?

Answering those questions can prevent raters from assigning higher or lower scores on the basis of performance that may be trivial or unrelated to the purpose of the performance test, such as the quantity rather than the quality of a performance. One advantage of rating scales is that they focus the scorer on specific and relevant aspects of a performance. Without the breakdown of important traits, successes, and relevant errors provided by these scales, a scorer's attention may be diverted to aspects of performance that are unrelated to the purpose of the performance test.

Holistic Scoring Holistic scoring is used when the rater is more interested in estimating the overall quality of the performance and assigning a numerical value to that quality than assigning points for the addition or omission of a specific aspect of performance. Holistic scoring is typically used in evaluating extended essays, term papers, or some artistic performances such as dance or musical creations.

For example, a rater might decide to score an extended essay question or term paper on an A–F rating scale. In this case, it is important for the rater to have a model paper that exemplifies each score category. After having created or selected these models from the set to be scored, the rater again reads each paper and then assigns each to one of the categories. A model paper for each category (A–F) helps ensure that all the papers assigned to a given category are of comparable quality.

Holistic scoring systems can be more difficult to use for performances than for products. For the former, some experience in rating the performance, for example, dramatic rendition, oral interpretations, and debate may be required. In these cases, audiotapes or videotapes from past classes can be helpful as models representing different categories of performance.

Combining Scoring Systems As suggested, good performance tests require learners to demonstrate their achievements through a variety of primary traits, for example, cooperation, research, and delivery. Several ratings, therefore, may need to be combined from checklists, rating scales, and holistic impressions to arrive at a total assessment. Figure 9.8 shows how scores across several traits for a current events project might be combined to provide a single performance score.

Comparing the Three Scoring Systems Each of the three scoring systems has its particular strengths and weaknesses. Table 9.1 serves as a guide in choosing a particular scoring system for a given type of performance, according to the following criteria:

1. **Ease of construction** refers to the time involved in generating a comprehensive list of the important aspects or traits of successful and unsuccessful performance. Checklists, for example, are particularly time consuming, while holistic scoring is not.

Checklist (Assign 1 or 0 points)   Total points (5)

— Interviewed four people
— Cited current references
— Typed
— No spelling errors
— Included title and summary page

Rating (Circle numbers which best represent quality of the presentation.)

Total points (9)

Persuasiveness

1	2	3
Lacks enthusiasm	Somewhat unanimated	Highly convincing

Delivery

1	2	3
Unclear, mumbled a lot	Often failed to look at audience, somewhat unclear	Clear, forceful delivery

Sensitivity to audience

1	2	3
Rarely looked at or noticed audience	Answered some questions, not always aware when audience didn't understand	Encouraged questions, stopped and clarified when saw that audience didn't understand

Holistic rating Total points (3)

What is your overall impression of the quality of the project?

1	2	3
Below average	Average	Clearly outstanding

Total Points (17)

FIGURE 9.8 Combined scoring rubric for current events project.

TABLE 9.1   The Strength of Three Performance-Based Scoring Systems According to Five Measurement Criteria

	Ease of construction	Scoring efficiency	Reliability	Defensibility	Feedback	More suitable for
Checklists	Low	Moderate	High	High	High	Procedures
Rating scales	Moderate	Moderate	Moderate	Moderate	Moderate	Attitudes, products, and social skills
Holistic scoring	High	High	Low	Low	Low	Products and processes

2. **Scoring efficiency** refers to the amount of time required to score various aspects of the performance and sum these scores into an overall score.

3. **Reliability** refers to the likelihood of two raters independently coming up with a similar score, or the likelihood of the same rater coming up with a similar score on two separate occasions.

4. **Defensibility** refers to the ease with which you can explain your score to a student or parent who challenges it.

5. **Quality of feedback** refers to the amount of information that the scoring system gives to learners or parents concerning strengths and weaknesses of the learner's performance.

Limit the Number of Points   Limit the number of points that the assessment or component of the assessment is worth to that which can be reliably discriminated. For example, 25 points assigned to a particular product or procedure assumes that the rater can discriminate 25 degrees of quality. When faced with more degrees of quality than can be detected, a typical rater may assign some points arbitrarily, reducing the reliability of the assessment.

On what basis should points be assigned to a response on a performance test? On one hand, you want a response to be worth enough points to allow you to differentiate subtle differences in response quality. On the other hand, you want to avoid assigning too many points to a response, the complexity of which does not lend itself to complex discriminations. Assigning one or two points to a math question requiring complex problem solving would not allow you to differentiate among outstanding, above-average, average, and poor responses. Yet, assigning 30 points to this same answer would seriously challenge your ability to distinguish a rating of 15 from a rating of 18. Two considerations can help in making decisions about the size and complexity of a rating scale.

The first is that a scoring model can be prepared wherein the rater specifies the exact performance—or examples of acceptable performance—that corresponds with each scale point. The ability to successfully define distinct criteria can then determine the number of scale points that are defensible. A second consideration is that, although it is customary for homework, paper-and pencil-tests, and report cards to use a 100-point (percent) scale, scale points derived from performance assessments do not need to add up to 100. In Chapter 12, we will explain how to assign marks to performance tests and how to integrate them with other aspects of an overall grading system (e.g., homework, paper-and-pencil tests, classwork, and student portfolios).

Step 4: Specifying Testing Constraints

Should performance tests have time limits? Should learners be allowed to correct their mistakes? Can they consult references or ask for help from other learners? If these were questions asked on a multiple-choice test, most test developers would respond negatively without much hesitation. But performance tests confront the designer with the following dilemma: If performance tests are designed to confront learners with real-world challenges, why shouldn't they be allowed to tackle these challenges as real-world people do?

In the world outside of the classroom, mathematicians make mistakes and correct them, journalists write first drafts and revise them, weather forecasters make predictions and change them. These workers can consult references and other resources to help them solve problems and consult with colleagues. Why then shouldn't learners who are working on performance tests that simulate similar problems be allowed the same working (or testing) conditions? But even outside the classroom, professionals have constraints on their performance, such as deadlines, limited office space, and outmoded equipment. So how does a teacher decide which conditions to impose during a performance test? Before examining this question, let's look at some of the typical conditions imposed on learners during tests.

The following are among the most common forms of test constraints:

1. *Time.* How much time should a learner have to prepare, rethink, revise, and finish a test?

2. *Reference/resource material.* Should learners be able to consult online or print dictionaries, textbooks, notes, and other material, as they take a test?

3. *Other people.* May learners ask for help from peers, teachers, or experts as they take a test or complete a project? Can those requests be through social media, online, or only in person?

4. *Equipment.* May learners use computers, smart phones, calculators, and other devices to help them solve problems?

5. *Prior knowledge of the task.* How much information on what they will be tested should learners receive in advance?

6. *Scoring criteria.* Should learners know the standards by which the teacher will score the assessment?

To determine the constraints appropriate for the performance assessment, consider the following three points:

1. Identify the constraints under which the performance you are assessing would have to be demonstrated in the real world. Include these constraints in your assessment to ensure that the assessment is authentic.

2. Suggest that students pay particular attention to those constraints that may support the highest levels of performance on the assessment.

3. Consider what the most appropriate time limits may be on the availability of resources needed to complete the assessment and clarify those time limits

Objective tests, by the nature of the questions asked, require numerous constraints during the testing conditions. Performance tests, on the other hand, are direct forms of assessment in which real-world conditions and constraints play an important role in demonstrating the competencies desired.

A FINAL WORD

Performance assessments create challenges that objective and even essay tests do not. Performance grading requires greater use of judgment than do true–false or multiple-choice questions. These judgments will be more indicative of your learners' performance if (1) the performance to be judged (process and product) is clearly specified, (2) the ratings or criteria in making the judgments are determined beforehand, and (3) more than a single rater independently grades the performance and an average is taken.

Using videotapes or audiotapes can enhance the validity of performance assessments when direct observation of performance is required. Furthermore, performance assessments need not take place at one time for the whole class. Learners can be assessed at different times, individually or in small groups. For example, learners can rotate through classroom learning centers and be assessed when the teacher feels they are acquiring mastery.

Finally, don't lose sight of the fact that performance assessments are meant to serve and enhance instruction rather than being simply an after-the-fact test given to assign a grade. When tests serve instruction, they can be given at a variety of times and in as many settings and contexts as instruction requires. Some performance assessments can sample the behavior of learners as they receive instruction or be placed within ongoing classroom activities rather than consume extra time during the day.

SUMMARY

This chapter introduced you to performance-based assessment. Its main points are as follows:

1. The four steps to constructing a performance assessment are deciding what to test, designing the assessment context, specifying the scoring rubrics, and specifying the testing constraints.

2. Some questions to ask in designing the performance assessment context are (1) what does the "doing" of math, history, and so on, look and feel like to professionals, (2) what projects and tasks are performed by these professionals, and (3) what roles—or habits of mind—do professionals assume?

3. A good performance assessment includes a hands-on exercise or problem, an observable outcome, and a process that can be observed.

4. A performance test can require five types of accomplishments from learners: products, complex cognitive processes, observable performance, habits of mind, and social skills. These performances can be scored with checklists, rating scales, or holistic scales.

5. Rubrics are scoring standards composed of model answers that are used to score performance tests. They are samples of acceptable responses against which the rater compares a student's performance.

6. Primary trait scoring is a type of rating that requires that the test developer first identify the most relevant characteristics or primary traits of importance.

7. Checklists contain lists of behaviors, traits, or characteristics that can be scored as either present or absent. They are best suited for complex behaviors or for performances that can be divided into a series of clearly defined, specific actions.

8. Rating scales assign numbers to categories representing different degrees of performance. They are typically used for those aspects of a complex performance, such as attitudes, products, and social skills, which do not lend themselves to yes/no or present/absent type judgments.

9. Holistic scoring estimates the overall quality of a performance by assigning a single numerical value to represent a specific category of accomplishment. They are used for measuring both products and processes.

10. Constraints that must be decided on when constructing and administering a performance test are amount of time allowed, use of online or print reference material, help from others (including social media), use of specialized equipment, prior knowledge of the task, and scoring criteria.

FOR DISCUSSION AND PRACTICE

*1. Compare and contrast some of the reasons given to explain why we give conventional tests with those reasons given to explain why we give performance assessments.

*2. In your own words, explain how performance assessment can be a tool for instruction.

*3. Using an example from your teaching area, explain the difference between a direct and an indirect measure of behavior.

4. Describe some habits of mind that might be required by professionals working in your teaching area and their importance in the workplace.

*5. Describe how at least two school districts have implemented performance assessments. Indicate the behaviors they assess and by what means they are measured.

6. Would you agree or disagree with this statement: "An ideal performance test is a good teaching activity?" With a specific example in your teaching area, illustrate why you believe as you do.

7. Provide at least two learning outcomes and how you would measure them in your classroom that could indicate that a learner is (a) self-directed, (b) a collaborative worker, (c) a complex thinker, (d) a quality producer, and (e) a community contributor.

*8. Describe what is meant by a "scoring rubric."

9. In your own words, how would you answer a critic of performance tests who says they do not measure generalizable thinking skills outside the classroom?

10. Identify several habits of mind and/or social skills for a unit you will be teaching that will be important to use in the real world.

11. Create a performance test of your own choosing that (a) requires a hands-on problem to solve and (b) results in an observable outcome for which (c) the process used by learners to achieve the outcome can be observed.

12. For the previous performance assessment, describe and give an example of the accomplishments—or rubrics—you would use in scoring the assessment.

13. For that same assessment, compose a checklist, rating scale, or holistic scoring method by which a learner's performance would be evaluated. Explain why you chose the scoring system you did, which may include a combination of the previously listed methods.

14. For your performance assessment, describe the constraints you would place on your learners pertaining to the time to prepare for and complete the activity; references that may be used; people who may be consulted, including other students (and whether they must be in person, over the phone, online or through social media); equipment allowed; prior knowledge about what is expected; and points or percentages you would assign to various degrees of their performance.

*Answers to these questions appear in Appendix B.

CHAPTER 10

PORTFOLIO ASSESSMENT*

LEARNING OUTCOMES

After completing this chapter, the student will be able to:

1. Describe the situations most appropriate for portfolio assessments in the classroom.
2. Compare and contrast validity, representativeness, rubrics, and relevance as they apply to portfolios.
3. Describe the seven steps recommended for developing portfolio assessments.
4. Compare and contrast the cognitive skills that are better suited for assessment by student portfolios, compared to essay or objective items.
5. Compare and contrast purpose, skill and disposition, planning, and ownership and the portfolio's link to instruction.
6. Explain why scoring rubrics are necessary for reliable portfolio evaluation.
7. Construct the criteria to use in judging the extent to which the purposes for portfolios are achieved.
8. Develop a procedure to aggregate portfolio ratings into a single portfolio grade.
9. Average portfolio grades with other grades for an overall mark for the grading period.
10. Plan a final conference with learners and parents to discuss what the portfolio says about the learner's development and achievement.
11. Complete a portfolio development checklist to ensure the quality of the portfolio.
12. Identify the pitfalls that can undermine the validity of portfolio assessment.

AS WE SAW in the last chapter, performance assessment is a type of demonstration by which learners show their critical thinking ability and deep understanding of a particular area of learning. This demonstration is like a snapshot that captures what a learner has accomplished at a particular point in the academic year. But as we know from our discussion of photos and videos for assessments from Chapter 1, snapshots or photos may be too limited in what they can tell us about student learning. There is another type of performance assessment, called portfolio assessment, that is more like a video than a one-time picture of what a learner has accomplished. The principal purpose of a portfolio assessment is to tell a story of a learner's growth in proficiency over time, long-term achievement, and significant accomplishments in a given academic area. The portfolio

*This chapter was written with Martin L. Tombari. See Tombari, M. & Borich, G. (1999). *Authentic Assessment in the Classroom: Applications and Practice*. Upper Saddle River, NJ: Prentice-Hall/Merrill.

is a measure of deep understanding and critical thinking, like the performance assessments covered earlier. In addition, it shows growth in competence and understanding across the term or school year (Adams-Bullock & Hawk, 2010; Johnson, Mims-Cox, & Doyle-Nichols, 2009; Lightfoot, 2006). Our definition of a portfolio is as follows:

> *a planned collection of learner achievement that documents what a student has accomplished and the steps taken to get there. The collection represents a collaborative effort among teacher and learner, to decide on portfolio purpose, content, and evaluation criteria.*

Portfolio assessment is based on the idea that a collection of a learner's work throughout the year is one of the best ways to show both final achievement and the effort put into getting there. You are probably already familiar with the idea of a portfolio. Painters, fashion designers, artisans, and writers assemble portfolios that embody their best work. Television and radio announcers compile videotaped and audiotaped excerpts of their best performances that are presented when interviewing for a job. A portfolio is their way of showing what they can really do.

Classroom portfolios serve a similar purpose. They show off a learner's best writing, artwork, science projects, historical thinking, or mathematical achievement. They also show the steps the learner took to get there. They compile the learner's best work, but they also include the works in progress: the early drafts, test runs, pilot studies, or preliminary trials. Thus, they are an ideal way to assess final mastery, effort, reflection, and growth in learning that tell the learner's "story" of achievement over time (Reynolds & Davis, 2013).

The idea of classroom portfolio assessment has gained considerable support and momentum in recent years. Many school districts use portfolios and other types of exhibitions to help motivate effort and show achievement and growth in learning. While the reliability and validity of a classroom teacher's judgments are always a matter of concern, they are less so when the teacher has multiple opportunities to interact with learners and numerous occasions to observe their work and confirm judgments about their capabilities.

In this section, we will first clarify what portfolio assessment is. Then, we will cover the most significant design considerations: deciding on the purpose of the portfolio; the cognitive outcomes to be assessed; who will plan it; what products to include; the criteria for assessing outcomes; the data that need to be collected to document progress, effort, and achievement; the logistics of where the products are kept; and, finally, how collaborative feedback will be given.

RATIONALE FOR THE PORTFOLIO

We believe that a portfolio's greatest potential is for showing teachers, parents, and learners a richer array of what students know and can do than paper-and-pencil tests and other "snapshot" assessments. If designed properly, portfolios can show a learner's ability to think and to solve problems, to use strategies and procedural-type skills, and to construct knowledge. In addition, they also tell something about a learner's persistence, effort, willingness to change, skill in monitoring his or her own learning, and ability to be self-reflective. One purpose for a portfolio is to give a teacher the information about a learner's growth over time that no other measurement tool can provide.

There are other reasons for using portfolios. Portfolios are also means to communicate to parents and other teachers the level of achievement that a learner has reached. Report card grades give us some idea of this, but portfolios supplement grades by showing parents, teachers, and learners the supporting evidence.

Portfolios are not an alternative to paper-and-pencil tests, essay tests, or performance tests. Each of those tools possesses validity for a purpose not served by a different tool. If you want to assess a learner's factual knowledge base (as discussed in Chapter 7), then objective-type tests are appropriate. If you are interested in a snapshot assessment of how well a learner uses a cognitive strategy, there are ways to do this that don't involve the work required for portfolio assessment. But if you want to assess both achievement and growth in an authentic context, portfolios are a tool that you should consider.

Finally, portfolios are a way to motivate learners to higher levels of effort. They provide a seamless link between classroom teaching and assessment in a way that is consistent with modern cognitive theories of learning and instruction.

Ensuring Validity of the Portfolio

Let's say that one of the goals you have for the portfolio is to assess how well learners can communicate to a variety of audiences. However, you collect only formal samples of writing of the type you would submit to a literary journal. Or you want your math portfolio to assess growth in problem-solving ability. Yet, your evaluation criteria place too heavy an emphasis on the final solution. These are some of the pitfalls that can undermine the validity of the portfolio. In general, you need to address three challenges to validity: representativeness, rubrics, and relevance.

Representativeness   The best way to ensure representativeness is to be clear at the outset about the cognitive learning skills and dispositions that you want to assess and to require a variety of products that reflect these. You want the samples of writing, scientific thinking, mathematical problem solving, or woodworking to reflect the higher-order thinking skills, procedural skills, or dispositions that you want the portfolio to measure.

Rubrics   You have already had practice at designing rubrics in Chapters 8 and 9. The same considerations for designing clear criteria to assess complex essay items, performances, or demonstrations also apply to assessing portfolios. You will want criteria for assessing both individual entries and the portfolio as a whole. You can accomplish this by developing carefully articulated scoring systems, called *rubrics* (Burke, 2010). By giving careful consideration to rubrics, you can develop a scoring system that minimizes the arbitrariness of your judgments while holding learners to high standards of achievement. We will look at some important considerations for developing portfolio rubrics shortly.

Relevance   Assembling the portfolio shouldn't demand abilities of the learner extraneous to the ones you want to assess. A second-grade geography portfolio whose purpose is to reflect skill in map making shouldn't demand fine motor skills beyond what you would expect a 7-year-old to possess. Likewise, a junior high school science portfolio designed to reflect problem solving shouldn't require the reading of scientific journals that are beyond the ability of a ninth grader to understand. Measurement devices often fail to measure what they intend to measure (i.e., lack validity) because they require learner skills that are extraneous to those the instrument was built to measure.

DEVELOPING PORTFOLIO ASSESSMENTS

Now that you've given some consideration to validity, let's get started on building a system for portfolio assessment for your teaching area.

Step 1: Deciding on the Purposes for a Portfolio

Have your learners think about their purpose in assembling a portfolio. Having learners identify for themselves the purpose of the portfolio is one way to increase the authenticity of the task. We encourage you to use this as part of your teaching strategy. However, your learners' purposes for the portfolio (e.g., getting a job with the local news station) won't necessarily coincide with yours (e.g., evaluating student learning and your teaching). In this section, we discuss how to be clear about your purposes at the outset of portfolio design.

Classroom-level purposes that portfolios can achieve include the following:

- Monitoring student progress or growth over time.
- Communicating what has been learned to parents.
- Passing on information to subsequent teachers.
- Evaluating how well something was taught.
- Showing off what has been accomplished.
- Assigning a course grade.

Step 2: Identifying Cognitive Skills and Dispositions

Portfolios, like performance assessments, are intended to be measures of deep understanding and genuine achievement. They can measure growth and development of competence in areas like knowledge construction (e.g., knowledge organization), cognitive strategies (analysis, interpretation, planning, organizing, and revising), procedural skills (clear communication, editing, drawing, speaking, and building), and metacognition (self-monitoring and self-reflection) as well as certain dispositions—or habits of mind—such as flexibility, adaptability, acceptance of criticism, persistence, collaboration, and desire for mastery. The Common Core State Standards, or CCSS (or state academic standards in states that do not adopt the CCSS), identify outcomes that leaders have identified as important for your grade. The CCSS-aligned tests are designed to assess for those outcomes. This text also has provided you with practice in specifying different types of cognitive outcomes and in planning to assess them. As part of your teaching strategy, you will want to discuss all of those outcomes with your learners.

Step 3: Deciding Who Will Plan the Portfolio

When deciding who will plan the portfolio, consider what's involved in preparing gymnasts or skaters for a major tournament. The parent hires a coach. The coach, pupil, and parent plan together the routines, costumes, practice times, music, and so on. They are a team whose sole purpose is to produce the best performance possible. The gymnast or skater wants to be the best that he or she can be. He or she also wants to please parents and coaches and wants to meet their expectations. The atmosphere is charged with excitement, dedication, and commitment to genuine effort.

That is the atmosphere you are trying to create when using portfolios. You, the learner, and parents are a team for helping the student to improve writing, math reasoning, or scientific thinking and to assemble examples of this growing competence. Learners want to show what they can do and to verify the trust and confidence that you and their family have placed in them. The portfolio is their recital, their tournament, their competition. The principal stakeholders in the use of the portfolio are you, your learners, and their parents. Involve parents by sending home an explanation of portfolio assessment and, in addition, by asking that parents and students discuss its goals and content.

Step 4: Deciding Which Products to Put in the Portfolio and How Many Samples of Each Product

Two key decisions need to be considered: ownership and the portfolio's link with instruction. Ownership refers to your learners' perception that the portfolio contains what they want it to. You have considered this issue in Step 3. By involving learners and their parents in the planning process, you enhance their sense of ownership. You also do this by giving them a say in what goes into the portfolio. The task is to balance your desire to enhance ownership with your responsibility to see that the content of the portfolio measures the cognitive skills and dispositions that you identified in Step 3.

Both learners and their parents need to see that your class instruction focuses on teaching the skills necessary to fashion the portfolio's content. You don't want to require products in math, science, or social studies that you didn't prepare learners to create. If it's a writing portfolio, then your instructional goals must include teaching skills in writing poems, essays, editorials, or whatever your curriculum specifies. The same holds for science, math, geography, or history portfolios. In deciding what you would like to see included in your learners' portfolios, you will have to ensure that you only require products that your learners were prepared to develop.

The best way to satisfy learner needs for ownership and your needs to measure what you teach is to require certain categories of products that match your instructional purposes and cognitive outcomes and to allow learners and parents to choose the samples within each category. For example, you may require that an eighth-grade math portfolio contains the following categories of math content (Lightfoot, 2006):

1. *Number and operation*, in which the learner demonstrates understanding of the relative magnitude of numbers, the effects of operations on numbers, and the ability to perform those mathematical operations.

2. *Estimation*, in which the learner demonstrates understanding of basic facts, place value, and operations; mental computation; tolerance of error; and flexible use of strategies.

3. *Predictions*, in which the learner demonstrates ability to make predictions based on experimental probabilities; to systematically organize and describe data; to make conjectures based on data analyses; and to construct and interpret graphs, charts, and tables.

Learners and their parents would have a choice of which assignments to include in each of the categories listed. For each sample, the learner includes a brief statement about what it says about his or her development of mathematical thinking skills.

Another example could be a high-school writing portfolio. The teacher requires that the following categories of writing be in the portfolio: persuasive editorial, persuasive essay, narrative story, autobiography, and dialog. Learners choose the samples of writing in each category. For each sample, they include a cover letter that explains why the sample was chosen and what it shows about the learner's development as a writer.

You will also have to decide how many samples of each content category to include in the portfolio. For example, do you require two samples of persuasive writing, one of criticism, and three of dialogue? Shavelson, Gao, and Baxter (1991) suggest that at least eight products or tasks over different topic areas may be needed to obtain a reliable estimate of performance from portfolios.

Step 5: Building the Portfolio Rubrics

In Step 2, you identified the major cognitive skills and dispositions that your portfolio will measure. In Step 4, you specified the content categories that your portfolio will contain. Now you must decide what good, average, and poor performance look like for each entry in the portfolio and for the portfolio as a whole.

You already have experience with rubrics from Chapters 8 and 9. You will follow the same process here. First, list the primary traits or characteristics that you think are important for each cognitive learning outcome. Do this for each content category in the portfolio. Next, construct a rating scale that describes the range of student performance that can occur for each trait. Figures 10.1 and 10.2 show how this was done for the essay writing content area.

Essay Portfolio Rating Form.

_____ First Draft
_____ Second Draft
_____ Final Draft

To be completed by student:

1. Date submitted: _____

2. Briefly explain what this essay says about you._____

_____

3. What do you like best about this piece of writing?_____

_____

4. What do you want to improve on the next draft? _____

_____

5. If this is your final draft, will you include this in your portfolio and why? _____

_____

To be completed by teacher:

1. Quality of reflection

Rating   Description
  5   States very clearly what he or she likes most and least about the essay. Goes into much detail about how to improve the work.
  4   States clearly what he or she likes and dislikes about the essay. Gives detail about how to improve the work.
  3   States his or her likes and dislikes but could be clearer. Gives some detail about how the work will be improved.
  2   Is vague about likes and dislikes. Gives few details about how essay will be improved.
  1   No evidence of any reflection on the work.

2. Writing conventions

Rating   Description
  5   The use of writing conventions is very effective. No errors evident. These conventions are fluid and complex: spelling, punctuation, grammar usage, and sentence structure.

FIGURE 10.1 Essay portfolio rating form.

4	The use of writing conventions is effective. Only minor errors evident. These conventions are nearly all effective: punctuation, grammar usage, sentence structure, and spelling.
3	The use of writing conventions is somewhat effective. Errors don't interfere with meaning. These conventions are somewhat effective: punctuation, grammar usage, sentence structure, and spelling.
2	Errors in the use of writing conventions interfere with meaning. These conventions are limited and uneven: punctuation, grammar usage, sentence structure, and spelling.
1	Major errors in the use of writing conventions obscure meaning. Lacks understanding of punctuation, grammar usage, sentence structure, and spelling.

3. Organization

Rating	Description
5	Clearly makes sense.
4	Makes sense.
3	Makes sense for the most part.
2	Attempted but does not make sense.
1	Does not make sense.

4. Planning (first draft only)

Rating	Description
5	Has clear idea of audience. Goals are very clear and explicit. An overall essay plan is evident.
4	Has idea of audience. Goals are clear and explicit. Has a plan for the essay.
3	Somewhat clear about the essay's audience. Goals are stated but somewhat vague. Plan for whole essay somewhat clear.
2	Vague about who the essay is for. Goals are unclear. No clear plan evident.
1	Writing shows no evidence of planning.

5. Quality of revision (second draft only)

Rating	Description
5	Follows up on all suggestions for revision. Revisions are a definite improvement.
4	Follows up on most suggestions for revision. Revisions improve on the previous draft.
3	Addresses some but not all suggested revisions. Revisions are a slight improvement over earlier draft.
2	Ignores most suggestions for revision. Revisions made do not improve the earlier draft.
1	Made only a minimal attempt to revise, if at all.

Sum of ratings _____

_____

Average of ratings: _____

_____

Comments: _____

_____
_____
_____
_____
_____

FIGURE 10.1 *continued.*

Essay Cumulative Rating Form.

(Attach to each completed essay)

_____ Essay Sample One
_____ Essay Sample Two

Student _____

Draft 1		*Draft 2*		*Final Draft*	
Criteria	**Rating**	**Criteria**	**Rating**	**Criteria**	**Rating**
Reflection	3	Reflection	4	Reflection	3
Conventions	3	Conventions	4	Conventions	4
Organization	4	Organization	5	Organization	5
Planning	4	Planning	4	Planning	3
Average	3.5	Average	4.25	Average	3.75

Teacher: Comments on final essay development _____

_____

Student: Comments on final essay development _____

_____

Parent: Comments on final essay development _____

_____

Included in portfolio: _____ Yes
_____ No

FIGURE 10.2   Essay cumulative rating form.

Figures 10.3 and 10.4 show examples from a math portfolio under the content category of problem solving. The teacher wants to measure the cognitive outcomes of knowledge base, cognitive strategies, communication, and reflection.

Once you design rubrics for each entry in the portfolio, you next design scoring criteria for the portfolio as a whole product. Some traits to consider when developing a scoring mechanism for the entire portfolio are the following:

thoroughness

variety

growth or progress

overall quality

self-reflection

flexibility

organization

appearance

Choose among these traits or include others and build five-point rating scales for each characteristic.

The key to Step 5 is to do the following:

1. For each cognitive skill and disposition in each content area, build your scoring rubrics.

2. Put these on a form that allows you to include ratings of early drafts.

3. Prepare a rating for the portfolio as a whole.

Math Problem-Solving Portfolio Rating Form.

Content categories:

_____ Problem solving	_____ Problem One
_____ Numbers and operations	_____ Problem Two
_____ Estimation	_____ Final Problem
_____ Predictions	

To be completed by student:

1. Date submitted: _____

2. What does this problem say about you as a problem solver? _____
_____

3. What do you like best about how you solved this problem? _____
_____

4. How will you improve your problem-solving skill on the next problem? _____
_____

To be completed by teacher:

1. Quality of reflection

Rating   Description

5   Has excellent insight into his or her problem-solving abilities and clear ideas of how to get better.

4   Has good insight into his or her problem-solving abilities and some ideas of how to get better.

3   Reflects somewhat on problem-solving strengths and needs. Has some idea of how to improve as a problem solver.

2   Seldom reflects on problem-solving strengths and needs. Has little idea of how to improve as a problem solver.

1   Has no concept of himself or herself as a problem solver.

2. Mathematical knowledge

Rating   Description

5   Shows deep understanding of the problems, math concepts, and principles. Uses appropriate math terms and all calculations are correct.

4   Shows good understanding of math problems, concepts, and principles. Uses appropriate math terms most of the time. Few computational errors.

3   Shows understanding of some of the problems, math concepts, and principles. Uses some terms incorrectly. Contains some computation errors.

2   Errors in the use of many problems. Many terms used incorrectly.

1   Major errors in problems. Shows no understanding of math problems, concepts, and principles.

3. Strategic knowledge

Rating   Description

5   Identifies all the important elements of the problem. Reflects an appropriate and systematic strategy for solving the problem; gives clear evidence of a solution process.

4   Identifies most of the important elements of the problem. Reflects an appropriate and systematic strategy for solving the problem and gives clear evidence of a solution process most of the time.

FIGURE 10.3   Math problem-solving portfolio rating form.

Rating	Description
3	Identifies some important elements of the problem. Gives some evidence of a strategy to solve the problems but process is incomplete.
2	Identifies few important elements of the problem. Gives little evidence of a strategy to solve the problems and the process is unknown.
1	Uses irrelevant outside information. Copies parts of the problem; no attempt at solution.

4. Communication

Rating	Description
5	Gives a complete response with a clear, unambiguous explanation; includes diagrams and charts when they help clarify explanation; presents strong arguments that are logically developed.
4	Gives good response with fairly clear explanation, which includes some use of diagrams and charts; presents good arguments that are mostly but not always logically developed.
3	Explanations and descriptions of problem solution are somewhat clear but incomplete; makes some use of diagrams and examples to clarify points but arguments are incomplete.
2	Explanations and descriptions of problem solution are weak; makes little, if any, use of diagrams and examples to clarify points; arguments are seriously flawed.
1	Ineffective communication; diagrams misrepresent the problem; arguments have no sound premise.

Sum of ratings: _____

Average of ratings: _____

Comments: _____
_____
_____

FIGURE 10.3 *continued.*

Math Problem-Solving Cumulative Rating Form.

(Attach to problem-solving entries)

_____ Problem One
_____ Problem Two
_____ Final Problem

Student _____

Problem 1		Problem 2		Final Problem	
Criteria	**Rating**	**Criteria**	**Rating**	**Criteria**	**Rating**
Reflection	3	Reflection	4	Reflection	3
Knowledge	2	Knowledge	3	Knowledge	3
Strategies	2	Strategies	2	Strategies	2
Comm	2	Comm	2	Comm	2
Average	2.5	Average	2.75	Average	2.5

Teacher: Comments on problem-solving ability and improvement: _____
_____

Student: Comments on problem-solving ability and improvement: _____
_____

Parent: Comments on problem-solving ability and improvement: _____
_____

FIGURE 10.4 Math problem-solving cumulative rating form.

Step 6: Developing a Procedure to Aggregate All Portfolio Ratings

For each content category that you include in the portfolio, learners will receive a score for each draft and the final product. You will have to decide how to aggregate these scores into a final score or grade for each content area and, then, for the portfolio as a whole. Figures 10.2 and 10.4 are examples of a cumulative rating form in two content areas (essay and math) for one student. You will have one of these forms for each content area identified in Step 4. If you want a writing portfolio to include five areas of content (persuasive writing, dialogue, biography, criticism, and commentary), you will have five rating forms, each of which rates drafts and final product.

As you can see in Figures 10.2 and 10.4, the teacher averaged the ratings for the two preliminary drafts and the final one. The next step is to develop a rule or procedure for combining these three scores into an overall score. One procedure would be to compute a simple average of three scores. This method gives equal importance in the final score to the drafts and final product. Another procedure would be to assign greatest importance to the final product, lesser importance to the second draft, and least importance to the first draft. This is called weighting. If and how you weight scores is up to you. You might seek input from learners and parents, but there is no hard and fast rule about whether or which products in an area should be given more weight.

If you should decide to assign different importance or weight to the products in a content area, do the following:

1. Decide on the weight in terms of a percentage (e.g., first draft counts 20%, second draft counts 30%, and final draft counts 50% of final score). Make sure the percentages add up to 100%.

2. Take the average score for each product and multiply that by the weight. In our example as shown in Figure 10.2, this would involve the following calculations:

$$
\begin{array}{lll}
\text{Draft 1:} & 3.50 \times 0.2 = 0.7 \\
\text{Draft 2:} & 4.25 \times 0.3 = 1.3 \\
\text{Final:} & 3.75 \times 0.5 = 1.9
\end{array}
$$

3. Add up the products to get an overall score (e.g., $0.7 + 1.3 + 1.9 = 3.9$ for the content area of essay writing). We will consider the meaning of this value shortly. (Had you not weighted, the average score would have been 3.8.)

Follow this same procedure for each content area. If you have five content areas in the portfolio, you will have five scores. Let's say that these scores are as follows:

Content Area	Score
Essay	3.9
Dialogue	4.0
Criticism	2.5
Biography	3.8
Commentary	2.0

The next step is to decide how to aggregate these scores. Again, you can choose to weight or not to weight. You may decide to involve learners and their parents in this decision. If you decide not to weight, the average rating for all the content areas is 3.2 (rounded to one decimal place).

Finally, assign a rating to the portfolio as a whole. Let's say that the rating came out to be a 4.5. Now you must decide how to include this rating in the overall portfolio grade. If you take an unweighted average, you assign as much importance to that one rating as you did to all the separate content ratings. That's probably not a good idea. Your average grade of 3.2 for the portfolio areas taken separately is a more reliable rating than your one rating of 4.5 for the whole portfolio. We recommend that you assign more weight to the former score than the latter—let's say 90% versus 10%:

$$3.2 \times 0.9 = 2.88$$
$$4.5 \times 0.1 = 0.45$$
$$\text{Final grade} = 2.88 + 0.45 = 3.33$$

This gives a final grade of 3.33, versus 3.85 if you had not weighted.

Now, let's consider what 3.33 (or 3.3 rounded) means in terms of the quality of the overall portfolio. In other words, how good is a 3.3 in indicating the competence of the learner? Making this decision involves evaluation.

Here is one way to assign meaning to our measurement of 3.3. Schools usually assign the following values to grades:

Grading Schemes			Meaning
90–100	A	E	Outstanding
80–89	B	S+	Above average
70–79	C	S	Average
60–69	D	S−	Below average
below 60	F	N	Failure, not at standard, etc.

When using 5-point rating scales, we usually consider 3 as average, 1 as below standard, and 5 outstanding. Similarly, if you use a 7-point scale, a 3.5 would be average, ratings between 1 and 2 are below standard, and ratings between 6 and 7 are outstanding. One way to assign value to a 3.3 would be to link the traditional grading systems and their conventional meanings to scores on the rating scale. Select a range of rating scale values that correspond to a letter or numerical grade in your school and link the two:

Average Rating	Grade
1.0–1.9	F, 50–59
2.0–2.5	D, 60–69
2.6–3.6	C, 70–79
3.6–4.3	B, 80–89
4.4–5.0	A, 90–100

If we use this chart, a 3.3 would represent a C grade, a numerical grade somewhere between 70 and 79, or a grade of satisfactory plus (S+). Depending on factors that we will discuss in Chapter 12, you may want to add plus and minus to your grading system. Or you may decide that a C gets a grade of 75, C− gets a grade of 70, and C+ a grade of 79. Making those decisions before you begin grading the portfolios and evaluating each portfolio using the same criteria helps minimize subjectivity.

Step 7: Determining the Logistics

So far, you have accomplished these aspects of portfolio design:

1. Specified the purpose of the portfolio.
2. Identified the cognitive skills it will reflect.

3. Decided who will help plan it.

4. Decided what and how many products go in it.

5. Specified the rubrics by which to score it.

6. Developed a rating and grading scheme.

There are just a few details left.

Time Lines   Your learners and their parents need to know exact dates when things are due. Point this need out to your learners. This reinforces in your learners' minds the link between your teaching and what's required in the portfolio. Be prepared to revise some of your requirements. You may find that there's not enough time in the school year and not enough hours in a week for you to read all the drafts and products and get them back to your learners in a timely manner.

How Products Are Turned in and Returned   Decide how, when, and where you want your learners to turn in their products. At the start of class? Placed in an "In" basket? Secured in a folder or binder? Returned in an "Out" basket? How will late assignments be handled? How do absent learners submit and get back assignments? Will there be penalties for late assignments?

Where Final Products Are Kept   Decide where the final products will be stored. Will it be the learners' responsibility to keep them safely at home? Or do you want to store them so that they can be assembled easily for a final parent conference and passed on to other teachers? Remember that the products may include videotapes or audiotapes, so a manila folder might not work. You may need boxes, filing cabinets, or closets.

Who Has Access to the Portfolio?   Certainly you, learners, and parents have a right to see what's in it. But do other students, current and future teachers, or administrators? You might want learners (and their parents) to help make those decisions.

Plan a Final Conference   Plan to have a final conference at the end of the year or term with individual learners and, if possible, their parents to discuss the portfolio and what it says about your learners' development and final achievement. Your learners can be responsible for conducting the conference, with a little preparation from you on how to do it. This final event can be a highly motivating force for your learners to produce an exemplary portfolio.

The following checklist will help you as you design and revise your portfolio assessment program. Consider it carefully when planning your portfolio assignment.

Portfolio Development Checklist

1. What purpose(s) will your portfolio serve? (Check any that apply.)

   ☐ Prepare a sample of best work for future teachers to see.
   ☐ Communicate to parents what's been learned.
   ☐ Evaluate my teaching.
   ☐ Assign course grades.
   ☐ Create collections of favorite or best work.
   ☐ Document achievement for alternative credit.
   ☐ To submit to a college or employer.
   ☐ To show growth in skill and dispositions.
   ☐ Other (specify) _____

2. What cognitive skills will be assessed by the individual entries?
   - ☐ Cognitive strategies (specify) _____
   - ☐ Deep understanding (specify) _____
   - ☐ Communication (specify) _____
   - ☐ Metacognition (specify) _____
   - ☐ Procedural skills (specify) _____
   - ☐ Knowledge construction (specify) _____
   - ☐ Other (specify) _____

3. What dispositions do you want the entries to reflect?
   - ☐ Flexibility
   - ☐ Persistence
   - ☐ Collaboration
   - ☐ Acceptance of feedback
   - ☐ Other (specify) _____

4. What criteria or rubrics will you use to judge the extent to which these skills and dispositions were achieved?

   _____
   _____

5. In rating the portfolio as a whole, what things will you look for?
   - ☐ Variety of entries.
   - ☐ Growth in reflection.
   - ☐ Growth in skill or performance.
   - ☐ Organization.
   - ☐ Presentation.

6. What kind of scale will you construct to rate the overall portfolio?

   _____
   _____

7. How will you combine all your ratings into a final grade?

   _____
   _____

8. Who will be involved in the planning process?
   - ☐ Learners
   - ☐ Teacher
   - ☐ Parents

9. What content categories are included in the portfolio?

   _____
   _____

10. Will learners have a choice over content categories?
    - ☐ Yes
    - ☐ No

11. Who decides what samples to include in each content area?
    - ☐ Learner
    - ☐ Teacher
    - ☐ Parents

12. How many samples will be included in each area?

   □ One
   □ Two
   □ More than two (specify) _____

13. Have you specified deadlines for the entries?

   □ Yes
   □ No

14. Have you developed forms to rate and summarize ratings for all drafts and final products?

   □ Yes (specify) _____
   □ No

15. What are your instructions for how work gets turned in and returned?

   _____
   _____

16. Where will the portfolios be kept, and who has access to them?

   □ Who (specify) _____
   □ Where (specify) _____
   □ When (specify) _____

17. Who will plan, conduct, and attend the final conference?

   □ Learner
   □ Other teachers
   □ Parents
   □ Others (specify) _____

SUMMARY

This chapter introduced you to the major issues related to the construction and scoring of portfolios. Its major points are as follows:

1. A portfolio is a planned collection of learner achievement that documents what a student has accomplished and the steps taken to get there.

2. Portfolios are a means of communicating to parents, learners, and other teachers the level of learning and performance that a learner has achieved. Portfolios can measure growth and development of competence in areas such as knowledge construction (e.g., knowledge organization), cognitive strategies (analysis, interpretation, planning, organizing, revising), procedural skills (clear communication, editing, drawing, speaking), and metacognition (self-monitoring and self-reflection), as well as certain habits of mind—such as flexibility, adaptability, acceptance of criticism, persistence, collaboration, and desire for mastery.

3. Portfolios are not substitutes for paper-and-pencil tests, essay tests, or performance tests. Each of those assessment tools possesses validity for a purpose not served by a different tool.

4. By utilizing actual tasks—such as projects, scripts, essays, research reports, demonstrations, and models—the learner applies knowledge and understanding to exhibit the level of deep learning that has been acquired from your instruction.

5. Ownership refers to your learners' perception that the portfolio contains what they want it to. Having learners identify for themselves, the purpose of the portfolio is one way to increase ownership.

6. Portfolio assessment is often the best and sometimes the only method for gauging your learners' level of deep learning. Planning and designing a portfolio assessment must be as systematic and methodical as constructing an objective test or essay exam.

7. Each cognitive skill and disposition for each portfolio content area should be identified, and scoring rubrics should be developed.

8. Some traits to consider when developing a scoring mechanism for the entire portfolio are thoroughness, variety, growth or progress, overall quality, self-reflection, flexibility, organization, and appearance.

FOR DISCUSSION AND PRACTICE

1. Identify three threats to the validity of a portfolio and indicate what you would do in the design of your portfolio to minimize these threats.

2. Plan a real portfolio by answering each of the questions on the Portfolio Development Checklist. Check the boxes that apply and provide the necessary details where requested.

3. Develop a portfolio rating form and cumulative rating form for the entries in your portfolio using Figures 10.1 and 10.2 as guides. Be sure to include definitions for all the scale alternatives (e.g., 1 to 5) being rated, as illustrated in Figure 10.1.

4. Describe the procedure you will use to aggregate scores for all the portfolio ratings. By providing hypothetical ratings for the entries on your rating form, indicate, with actual numbers and averages, how you will (a) calculate weights, (b) take the average score for each entry, (c) add up all the entries to get an overall score, and (d) assign a grade symbol (e.g., A–F) to the average score.

CHAPTER 11

ADMINISTERING, ANALYZING, AND IMPROVING THE TEST OR ASSESSMENT

LEARNING OUTCOMES

After completing this chapter, the student will be able to:

1. Explain why the test assembly suggestions are important to consider.
2. Explain why the test administration suggestions are important to consider.
3. Explain why maintaining a realistic attitude for test-taking is important.
4. Explain why the test-scoring suggestions are important to consider.
5. Discriminate between quantitative and qualitative item analyses.
6. Compute item difficulty levels and discrimination indices.
7. Analyze multiple-choice options to determine need for modification, given quantitative item analysis data.
8. Identify multiple-choice items, likely to be ambiguous, miskeyed, or subject to guessing, given quantitative item analysis data.
9. Identify acceptable ranges for item difficulty levels and discrimination indices.
10. Explain why unmodified norm-referenced item analysis procedures are inappropriate for criterion-referenced tests.
11. Compute quantitative item analysis data for criterion-referenced tests using the modified norm-referenced procedures described in the text.
12. Interpret these data to assess the appropriateness of criterion-referenced test items.
13. Recall suggestions to facilitate emotional detachment during test debriefing.
14. Give examples of the steps in the process of evaluating classroom achievement.

OVER THE LAST several chapters, we have discussed various aspects of test planning and item construction. If you have written (or been provided with) instructional objectives that include higher-level thinking, constructed a test blueprint, and written items or constructed performance or portfolio assessments that match your objectives, then more than likely you will have a good test or assessment. All the raw material will be there. However, sometimes the raw material, as good as it may be, can be rendered useless because of poorly assembled and administered paper-and-pencil tests. By now you know it requires a substantial amount of time to write objectives, put together a test blueprint, write items, and develop assessments. It is worth a little more time to properly assemble or package your test or assessment so that your efforts will not be wasted. Our goal for this chapter is to provide some suggestions to help you avoid common pitfalls in test and assessment assembly, administration, and scoring. Later in the chapter, we will discuss considerations and techniques of test analysis. First, let's consider test assembly.

ASSEMBLING THE TEST

At this point, let's assume you have:

1. Written measurable instructional objectives, or they have been provided by your state or local education agency in the form of academic standards,
2. Prepared a test blueprint, specifying the number of items for each content and process area, and
3. Written test items or assessments that match your instructional objectives.

In Chapters 9 and 10, we described several issues to consider when administering, collecting, and scoring performance and portfolio assessments; they will not be repeated in this chapter. For paper-and-pencil classroom tests, once you have completed the three activities we mentioned above you are ready to:

1. Package the test;
2. Reproduce the test.

These components constitute what we are calling test assembly. Let's consider each a little more closely.

Packaging the Paper-and-Pencil Test

There are several packaging guidelines worth remembering, including grouping together items of similar format, arranging test items from easy-to-hard, properly spacing items, keeping items and options on the same page, placing illustrations near the descriptive material, checking for randomness in the answer key, deciding how students will record their answers, providing space for the test-taker's name and the date, checking test directions for clarity, and proofreading the test before you reproduce and distribute it.

Group Together All Items of Similar Format   If you have all true–false items grouped together, all completion items together, and so on, the students will not have to "switch gears" to adjust to new formats. This will enable them to cover more items in a given time than if item formats were mixed throughout the test. Also, by grouping items of a given format together, only one set of directions per format section is necessary, which is another time saver, and also a paper saver.

Arrange Test Items from Easy to Hard   Arranging test items according to level of difficulty should enable more students to answer the first few items correctly, thereby building confidence and, it is hoped, reducing test anxiety.

Space the Items for Easy Reading   If possible, try to provide enough blank space between items so that each item is distinctly separate from others. When items are crowded together, a student may inadvertently perceive a word, phrase, or line from a preceding or following item as part of the item in question. This may be especially important for children with visual disabilities, most of whom are now required to participate in the regular curriculum and regular summative assessments under the 2004 IDEIA. A visually impaired student's capacity to demonstrate his or her true ability will be compromised if that student cannot clearly see test items or other stimuli.

Keep Items and Options on the Same Page   There are few things more aggravating to a test-taker than to have to turn the page to read the options for multiple-choice or matching items or to finish reading a true–false or completion item. To avoid this awkwardness, do not begin an item at the bottom of the page unless you have space to complete the item. Not only will this eliminate having to carry items over to the next page, it will also minimize the likelihood that the last line or two of the item will be cut off when you reproduce the test.

Position Illustrations Near Descriptions   Place diagrams, maps, or other supporting material immediately above the item or items to which they refer. In other words, if items 9, 10, and 11 refer to a map of South America, locate the map above items 9, 10, and 11—not between 9 and 10 or between 10 and 11 and not below them. Also, if possible, keep any such stimuli and related questions on the same page to save the test-taker time, and be sure to indicate which item(s) the map or other material refers to.

Check Your Answer Key   Be sure that the correct answers follow a fairly random pattern. Avoid true–false patterns such as T F T F, or T T F F, and multiple-choice patterns such as D C B A D C B A. At the same time, check to see that your correct answers are distributed about equally between true and false and among multiple-choice options.

Determine How Students Record Answers   Decide whether you want to have students record their answers on the test paper or a separate answer sheet. In the lower elementary grades, it is generally a good idea to have students record answers on the test papers themselves. In the upper elementary and secondary grades, separate answer sheets can be used to facilitate scoring accuracy and cut down on scoring time. Also, in the upper grades, learning to complete separate answer sheets will make students familiar with the process they will use when taking standardized interim or benchmark, and summative tests.

Provide Space for Name and Date   Be sure to include a blank on your test booklet and/or answer sheet for the student's name and the date. This may seem an unnecessary suggestion, but it is not always evident to a nervous test-taker that a name should be included on the test. Students are much more likely to remember to put their names on tests if space is provided (and if you remind them to do so!).

Check Test Directions   Check your directions for each item format to be sure that they are clear. Directions should specify the following:

1. The numbers of the items to which they apply.
2. How to record answers.
3. The basis on which to select answers.
4. Criteria for scoring.

Test Assembly Checklist

Put a check in the blank to the right of each statement after you've checked to see that it applies to your test.

	Yes	No
1. Are items of similar format grouped together?	_____	_____
2. Are items arranged from easy-to-hard levels of difficulty?	_____	_____
3. Are items properly spaced?	_____	_____
4. Are items and options on the same page?	_____	_____
5. Are diagrams, maps, and supporting material above designated items and on the same page with items?	_____	_____
6. Are answers random?	_____	_____
7. Will an answer sheet be used?	_____	_____
8. Are blanks for name and date included?	_____	_____
9. Have the directions been checked for clarity?	_____	_____
10. Has the test been proofread for errors?	_____	_____
11. Do items avoid racial and gender bias?	_____	_____

FIGURE 11.1 Test assembly checklist.

Proofread the Test Proofread for typographical and grammatical errors before reproducing the test and make any necessary corrections. Having to announce corrections to the class just before the test or during the test will waste time and is likely to inhibit the test-takers' concentration.

Before reproducing the test, it's a good idea to check off these steps. The checklist in Figure 11.1 can be used for this purpose.

Reproducing the Test Most test reproduction in the schools is done on photocopying machines. As you well know, the quality of such copies can vary tremendously. Regardless of how valid and reliable your test might be, poor copies will make it less so. If someone else will do the reproducing, be sure to specify that the copies are for an important test and not simply an enrichment exercise. Ask the clerk or aide to randomly inspect copies for legibility while running the copies and to be alert for blank or partially copied pages while collating, ordering, and stapling multipage tests.

ADMINISTERING THE TEST

The test is ready. All that remains is to get the students ready and hand out the tests. Here is a series of suggestions to help your students psychologically prepare for the test, whether it is formative, interim, or summative.

Maintain a Positive Attitude Try to create a realistic, but positive test-taking attitude. It helps to keep the main purposes of classroom testing in mind—to evaluate achievement and to provide feedback to yourself and your students. Too often tests are used to punish ("Well, it's obvious the class isn't doing the readings, so we'll have a test today") or are used indiscriminately ("It's Tuesday, I guess I may as well give my class a test") or inappropriately ("I need a good evaluation from the principal; I'll give my class an easy test"). To the extent that you can avoid falling victim to such testing traps, you will be helping to create and maintain a positive test-taking atmosphere.

Maximize Achievement Motivation Try not to minimize the achievement aspect of the test. While you do not want to immobilize your students with fear, you do want them to try to do their best on the test. Encourage them to do so. If a student's grade will be influenced, avoid making comments such as, "We're just going to have an easy little quiz today; it's no big deal." Such an approach will probably minimize anxiety in very nervous test-takers, which might improve their performance, but it may also serve to impair the test performance of students who need to take tests seriously in order to be motivated enough to do their best. In your class you will likely have both types of students. Keep your general statement about the test accurate. The test is something to be taken seriously, and this should be clear to the class. Remember, you can always make reassuring or motivational comments individually to students.

Equalize Advantages Try to equalize the advantages testwise students have over nontest-wise students. Since you are interested in student achievement, and not how testwise a student is (unless you are teaching a course in test-taking skills), the results will be more valid if the advantages of testwiseness are minimized. You can do so by instructing the class when it is best to guess or not guess at an answer and remind them about general test-taking strategies (for example: "Don't spend too much time on difficult items," "Try all items, then return to those you are unsure of," "Cross off options you've ruled out on matching or multiple-choice items," "Check your answers for accuracy before turning in the test").

You may even want to take guessing into consideration when scoring the test. If time allows each student to attempt every item, a total score that is equal to the number of right answers may be perfectly adequate. In this case, students should be told to make an "educated" guess, even if they are not certain of the answer. However, different students may attempt different numbers of items. This most often occurs when the test has a strict time limit, which may prevent some students from finishing. In this situation you may want to discourage guessing, that is, discourage the random filling out of unfinished answers seconds before the time limit is up.

A correction-for-guessing formula can be used to deter students from randomly answering test questions. A student's score that has been corrected for guessing will be equal to the number of questions answered incorrectly divided by the number of answer choices for an item minus 1 and, then, this amount subtracted from the total number of right answers.

$$\text{Score} = \text{Total right} - \frac{\text{Total wrong}}{\text{Number of answer choices} - 1}$$

For example, in a 50-item multiple-choice test where there are 4 possible answers and a student gets 44 answers correct, the student's score would be $44 - 6/3 = 42$. The student's score, corrected for guessing, is 42. When this formula is used, students should be encouraged to make educated guesses and to avoid randomly selecting answers.

Avoid Surprises Be sure your students have sufficient advance notice of a test. "Pop" quizzes have little beneficial effect on overall academic achievement. They are especially problematic in junior high school and high school where students have five or six different teachers. If each teacher gave pop quizzes, students would be hard pressed to be well prepared for each class each day. This is not to say that you should avoid frequent quizzes, however. When students are tested frequently, learning or study takes place at more regular intervals rather than massed or crammed the night before a test. Retention is generally better following spaced rather than massed learning.

Clarify the Rules Inform students about time limits, restroom policy, and any special considerations about the answer sheet before you distribute the tests. Students often tune out the instructor after they receive their tests and may miss important information.

Rotate Distribution   Alternate beginning test distribution at the left, right, front, and back of the class. This way, the same person will not always be the last one to receive the test.

Remind Students to Check Their Copies   After handing out the tests, remind students to check page and item numbers to see that none has been omitted, and remind them to put their names on their papers.

Monitor Students   Monitor students while they are completing their tests. While it would be nice to trust students not to look at one another's papers, it is not realistic. Inform students about penalties for cheating, and implement the penalties when cheating occurs. After students learn they can't get away with it, there should be little need for the penalties.

Minimize Distractions   Try to keep noise and distractions to a minimum, for obvious reasons.

Give Time Warnings   Give students a warning 15, 10, and 5 minutes before the time limit is up, so they are not caught by surprise at the deadline.

Collect Tests Uniformly   Finally, have a uniform policy on collecting the tests. Indicate whether you want all papers or only some returned, where they are to be placed, and so forth. This not only saves time but minimizes instances of lost papers.

SCORING THE TEST

We discussed specific scoring recommendations for various types of objective test formats in Chapter 7 and for essay items in Chapter 8, and scoring of performance and portfolios was discussed in Chapters 9 and 10. Following are some general suggestions to save scoring time and improve scoring accuracy and consistency.

Prepare an Answer Key   Prepare your answer key in advance, which will save time when you score the test and will help you identify questions that need rewording or need to be eliminated. Also, when constructing the answer key, you should get an idea of how long it will take your students to complete the test and whether this time is appropriate for the time slot you have allocated to the test.

Check the Answer Key   If possible, have a colleague check your answer key to identify alternative answers or potential problems.

Score Blindly   Try to score "blindly." That is, try to keep the student's name out of sight to prevent your knowledge about, or expectations of, the student from influencing the score.

Check Machine-Scored Answer Sheets   If machine scoring is used, check each answer sheet for stray marks, multiple answers, or marks that may be too light to be picked up by the scoring machine.

Check Scoring   If possible, double check your scoring. Scoring errors due to clerical error occur frequently. There is no reason to expect that you will not make such errors.

Record Scores   Before returning the scored papers to students, be sure you have recorded their scores in your record book! (Forgetting to do this has happened at least once to every teacher.)

ANALYZING THE TEST

Just as you can expect to make scoring errors, you can expect to make errors in test construction. No test you construct will be perfect—it will include inappropriate, invalid, or otherwise deficient items. In the remainder of this chapter, we will introduce you to a technique called *item analysis*. Item analysis can be used to identify items that are deficient in some way, thus paving the way to improve or eliminate them, with the result being a better overall test. We will make a distinction between two kinds of item analyses, quantitative and qualitative. *Quantitative item analysis* is likely to be something new. But as you will see, *qualitative item analysis* is something with which you are already familiar. Finally, we will discuss how item analysis differs for norm- and criterion-referenced tests (CRTs), and we provide you with several modified norm-referenced analysis methods to use with CRTs.

Quantitative Item Analysis

As mentioned, quantitative item analysis is a technique that will enable us to assess the quality or utility of an item. It does so by identifying *distractors* or response options that are not doing what they are supposed to be doing. How useful is this procedure for a completion or an essay item? Frankly, it is not very useful for these types of items, but qualitative item analysis is. On the other hand, quantitative item analysis is ideally suited for examining the usefulness of multiple-choice formats. The quantitative item analysis procedures that we will describe are most appropriate for items on a norm-referenced test (NRT). As you now know, we are interested in spreading out students, or discriminating among them, with an NRT. When dealing with a CRT, qualitative and modified quantitative item analysis procedures are most appropriate. We describe some of these later in this chapter.

There is some terminology or jargon associated with quantitative item analysis that must be mastered. Figure 11.2, Item Analysis Terminology, defines these terms. Study the definitions in the box and refer to them throughout this section.

Difficulty Index Now that you have reviewed the terms and definitions, let's see how they apply to multiple-choice items for an NRT. Consider the following example. Suppose your students chose the options to a four-alternative multiple-choice item the following numbers of times: Three students chose option A; none chose B; 18 chose the correct answer, C (marked with an asterisk); and 9 chose D.

A	B	C*	D
3	0	18	9

How does that help us? We can see immediately that B was not a very good option or distractor, because no one chose it. We can also see that more than half the class answered the item correctly. In fact, by employing the following formula, we can compute p, the item's difficulty index, which is the first step in item analysis.

$$p = \frac{\text{Total number of students selecting correct answer}}{\text{Total number of students attempting the item}}$$

$$p = \frac{18}{30} = 0.60$$

Quantitative item analysis	A numerical method for analyzing test items employing student response alternatives or options.
Qualitative item analysis	A non-numerical method for analyzing test items not employing student responses, but considering test objectives, content validity, and technical item quality.
Key	Correct option in a multiple-choice item.
Distractor	Incorrect option in a multiple-choice item.
Difficulty index (*p*)	Proportion of students who answered the item correctly.
Discrimination index (*D*)	Measure of the extent to which a test item discriminates or differentiates between students who do well on the overall test and those who do not do well on the overall test.
	There are three types of discrimination indexes:
	1. *Positive discrimination index:* Those who did well on the overall test chose the correct answer for a particular item more often than those who did poorly on the overall test.
	2. *Negative discrimination index:* Those who did poorly on the overall test chose the correct answer for a particular item more often than those who did well on the overall test.
	3. *Zero discrimination index:* Those who did well and those who did poorly on the overall test chose the correct answer for a particular item with equal frequency.

FIGURE 11.2   Item analysis terminology.

From this information, we learn that the item was moderately difficult (60% of the class got it right) and that option B ought to be modified or replaced. This is useful information, but we can learn (and need to know) more about this item. Were the students who answered it correctly those who did well on the overall test? Were the distractors chosen by those who did well or poorly on the test? The answers to those questions are important because they tell us whether the item discriminated between students who did well and those who did not do well on the overall test. A little confused? Let's look at it another way:

QUESTION: Why do we administer tests?
ANSWER: To find out who has mastered the material and who has not (i.e., to discriminate between the two groups).
QUESTION: Will a test discriminate between the groups better if each item on the test discriminates between those who did and did not do well on the test overall?
ANSWER: Absolutely! If more students who do well on the test overall answer an item correctly—positive discrimination index—that item helps the overall discrimination ability of the test. If this is true for all items (they are all positively discriminating), the test will do a good job of discriminating between those who know their stuff and those who don't. To the extent that students who do poorly on the overall test answer individual items correctly—negative discrimination index—the test loses its ability to discriminate.

QUESTION: How can I tell whether the key for any question is chosen more frequently by the better students (i.e., the item is positively discriminating) or the poorer students (i.e., the item is negatively discriminating)?

ANSWER: Follow the procedure described next.

Discrimination Index To determine each item's discrimination index (D), complete the following steps:

1. Arrange the papers from highest to lowest score.

2. Separate the papers into an upper group and a lower group based on total test scores. Do so by including half of your papers in each group.

3. For each item, count the number in the upper group and the number in the lower group that chose each alternative.

4. Record your information for each item in the following form (the following data are from the previous example; again the asterisk indicates the keyed option):

Example for Item X (Class Size = 30)

Options	A	B	C*	D
Upper	1	0	11	3
Lower	2	0	7	6

5. Compute D, the discrimination index, by plugging the appropriate numbers into the following formula:

$$D = \frac{\left(\begin{array}{c}\text{Number who got item} \\ \text{correct in upper group}\end{array}\right) - \left(\begin{array}{c}\text{Number who got item} \\ \text{correct in lower group}\end{array}\right)}{\begin{array}{c}\text{Number of students in either group (if group} \\ \text{sizes are unequal, choose the higher number)}\end{array}}$$

Plugging in our numbers, we arrive at

$$D = \frac{11 - 7}{15} = 0.267$$

Our discrimination index (D) is 0.267, which is positive. More students who did well on the overall test answered the item correctly than students who did poorly on the overall test. Now, let's put it all together for this item.

$$\text{Difficulty index}(p) = 0.60$$
$$\text{Discrimination index}(D) = 0.267$$

An item with $p = 0.60$ and $D = 0.267$ would be considered a moderately difficult item that has positive (desirable) discrimination ability for an NRT. When NRT p levels are less than about 0.25, the item is considered relatively difficult. When NRT p levels are above 0.75, the item is considered relatively easy. Test construction experts try to build tests that have most items between p levels of 0.20 and 0.80, with an average p level of about 0.50. All other factors being equal, the NRT test's discrimination ability is greatest when the overall p level (difficulty) is about 0.50. How high is a "good" discrimination index? Unfortunately, there is no single answer. Some experts insist that D should be at least 0.30, while others believe that as long as D has a positive value, the NRT item's discrimination ability is adequate. Further complicating the issue is the fact that D is related to p. Just as a test tends to have maximum discrimination ability when p is around 0.50, so too does an individual item. It can be difficult to obtain discrimination indices above 0.30 when items are mostly easy or difficult.

Naturally, you want your items to have as high a discrimination index as possible, but our recommendation is that you seriously consider any item with a positive D value. Based on this information, we would conclude that, in general, the item is acceptable. But we must also look at the item analysis data further to see if any distractors need to be modified or replaced.

We noted earlier that B would need to be replaced, since no one chose it. But what about A and D? Are they acceptable? The answer is yes but can you figure out why? The answer is because more people in the lower group chose them than did people in the upper group. This is the opposite of what we would want for the correct answer, and it makes sense. If we want more students who do well on the overall test to choose the correct answer, then we also want more students who do poorly on the overall test to choose the distractors.

Let's look at the responses for another item.

Example for Item Y (Class Size = 28)

Options	A*	B	C	D
Upper	4	1	5	4
Lower	1	7	3	3

The following questions will help guide us through the quantitative item analysis procedure.

1. What is the difficulty level?

$$p = \frac{\text{Number selecting correct answer}}{\text{Total number taking the test}}$$

$$p = \frac{5}{28} = 0.176$$

2. What is the discrimination index?

$$D = \frac{\text{Number correct (upper)} - \text{Number correct (lower)}}{\text{Number in either group}}$$

$$D = \frac{4-1}{14} = 0.214$$

3. Should this item be eliminated? No, since it is positively discriminating. However, it is a difficult item; only about 18% of the class got it right.

4. Should any distractor be eliminated or modified? Yes; distractors C and D have attracted more students who did well on the test overall. If these distractors are modified or replaced, a good item will be made even better. Remember, in order for an item to discriminate well, more students who do well on the test should choose the correct answer than students who do poorly (the correct answer should be positively discriminating) and fewer students who do well on the test should choose each distractor than those who do poorly (the distractors should be negatively discriminating).

Example for Item Z (Class Size = 30)

Options	A	B*	C	D
Upper	3	4	3	5
Lower	0	10	2	3

Again, let's ask the four basic questions to analyze item Z:

1. What is the difficulty level?

$$p = \frac{\text{Number selecting correct answer}}{\text{Total number taking test}}$$

$$p = \frac{14}{30} = 0.467 \text{ (moderately difficult)}$$

2. What is the discrimination index?

$$D = \frac{\text{Number correct (upper)} - \text{number correct (lower)}}{\text{Number in either group}}$$

$$D = \frac{4 - 10}{15} = \frac{-6}{15} = -0.40 \text{ (negatively discriminating)}$$

3. Should this item be eliminated? Yes! The item is moderately difficult (approximately 47% of the class got it right), but it discriminates negatively ($D = -0.40$). Remember, one reason for testing is to discriminate between those students who know their stuff and those who do not. On this item more students who knew their stuff (who did well on the overall test) chose the incorrect options than the correct answer. If the test were made up mostly of or entirely of items like this, the students who scored high on the test, who answered the most items correctly, might be those who did not know their stuff. This is clearly what we want to avoid. An item that discriminates negatively should be eliminated.

4. Should any distractor(s) be modified or eliminated? Since we have already decided to eliminate the item, this is a moot question. However, let's look at the distractors anyway. In the case of options A, C, and D, more students who did well on the test chose each of these options than students who did poorly on the test. Each distractor discriminates *positively*. We want our distractors to discriminate *negatively*. Thus, this item has nothing going for it, according to our quantitative item analysis. The correct answer, which should discriminate positively, discriminates negatively. The distractors, which should discriminate negatively, discriminate positively!

In addition to helping us decide which items to eliminate from a test before it is again administered, quantitative item analysis also enables us to make other decisions. For example, we can use quantitative item analysis to decide whether an item is miskeyed, whether responses to the item are characterized by guessing, or whether the item is ambiguous. To do so, we need to only consider the responses of students in the upper half of the class. Let's see how.

Miskeying When an item is miskeyed, most students who did well on the test will likely select an option that is a distractor, rather than the option that is keyed. Consider the following miskeyed item:

Which of the following social media applications preceded Facebook?

a. Instagram

b. Snapchat

c. Myspace

*d. Twitter

Analyzing the responses for the *upper* half of the class, we find the following distribution:

	A	B	C	D*
Upper half	1	1	9	2

Any time most students in the *upper* half of the class fail to select the keyed option, consider whether your item is miskeyed (the correct answer is option C). Remember, just as you are bound to make scoring errors, you are bound to miskey an item occasionally.

Guessing When guessing occurs, students in the *upper* half of the class respond in more or less random manner. This is most likely to occur when the item measures content that is (1) not covered in class or the text, (2) so difficult that even the upper half students have no idea what the correct answer is, or (3) so trivial that students are unable to choose from among the options provided. In such cases, each alternative is about equally attractive to students in the upper half, so their responses tend to be about equally distributed among the options. The following choice distribution would suggest that guessing occurred:

	A	B	C*	D
Upper half	4	3	3	3

Ambiguity So far, we have discussed using quantitative item analysis to identify miskeying and guessing. We did so by looking at response distributions for the *upper* group. With miskeying, the *upper* group chooses a distractor more frequently than the key. With guessing, each option is chosen with about equal frequency. Ambiguity is suspected when, among the *upper* group, one of the distractors is chosen with about the same frequency as the correct answer. The following distribution suggests that an item is ambiguous:

	A	B	C	D*
Upper half	7	0	1	7

In this item, students who do well on the test but miss the item are drawn almost entirely to one of the distractors. However, quantitative item analysis data can only suggest ambiguity. In the preceding item, there is no way for us to tell whether the "good" students chose distractor A because the item is deficient, or whether it was because they were distracted by an option that was plausible, but not as correct as the key.

The only way to determine whether the root of the problem is lack of mastery or a poorly written item is through qualitative item analysis, to which we turn next. Before leaving quantitative item analysis, however, a final point should be made. As you are by now aware, a teacher can invest considerable time and effort in quantitative item analysis. As a result, some teachers will be turned off by this method and will fail to use this very useful test analysis tool. Fortunately, with the advent of personal computers and item analysis software, the actual time the teacher spends in quantitative item analysis may now be significantly reduced; see the sidebar (Box 11-1) to see how.

We will turn to qualitative item analysis next. However, first review what we have learned about the application of quantitative item analysis by studying Figure 11.3, the Quantitative Item Analysis Checklist.

BOX *11-1*

COMPUTERS AND TEST ASSEMBLY AND ANALYSIS

Commercial software is available that will guide the classroom teacher through the entire test construction process from writing instructional objectives to matching items to objectives to assembling and analyzing the test. It is in this last area, test and item analysis, that such software may prove most beneficial. Programs to compute item difficulty levels and discrimination indices are available, and quantitative item analyses of objective test items are now a reality for the busy classroom teacher. Programs that enable the teacher to determine the reliability (see Chapter 17) of classroom tests are also available. Statistical packages and data management programs make it possible for classroom teachers to keep accurate and comprehensive records of student performances over the course of the year and over several years. This enables the teacher to compare classes, tests, and curricula; to identify discrepancies; and to evaluate the effects of new instructional techniques on test performance. By utilizing these resources, the classroom teacher can objectively and scientifically analyze data from classroom tests without all the hand calculation that otherwise would be necessary. These data can enhance instruction and increase the satisfaction of pupils, parents, and administrators with the measurement process.

Qualitative Item Analysis

As noted earlier, you already know something about qualitative item analysis. It's something you can and ought to do with items of all formats. Essentially, when we talk about qualitative item

Quantitative item analysis checklist

1. Item number _____

2. Difficulty level: _____

$$p = \frac{\text{Number correct}}{\text{total}} =$$

3. Discrimination index: _____

$$D = \frac{\left(\begin{array}{c}\text{Number correct}\\ \text{(upper)}\end{array}\right) - \left(\begin{array}{c}\text{Number correct}\\ \text{(lower)}\end{array}\right)}{\text{Number of students in either group}}$$

4. Eliminate or revise item? Check.

   (a) Does key discriminate positively? _____
   (b) Do distractors discriminate negatively? _____
   If you answer yes to both a and b, no revision may be necessary.
   If you answer no to a *or* b, revision is necessary. If you answer no to a *and* b, eliminate the item.

5. Check for miskeying, ambiguity, or guessing. Among the choices for the upper group *only*, was there evidence of:

   (a) miskeying (more chose distractor than key)? _____
   (b) guessing (equal spread of choices across options)? _____
   (c) ambiguity (equal number chose one distractor and the key)? _____

FIGURE 11.3 Quantitative item analysis checklist.

analysis, we are talking about matching items and objectives and editing poorly written items. These are activities we've discussed in Chapters 6–8 in relation to improving the content validity of a test. We refer to them again simply because it is appropriate to edit or rewrite items and assess their content validity after a test, as well as before a test.

Let's face it. In spite of our best intentions, we often end up pressed for time as the day for the test approaches. What do we do? Probably we work more quickly to assemble the test—overlooking such things in our items as grammatical cues, specific determiners, double negatives, multiple defensible answers, and items that fail to match instructional objectives.

As a result, these faults creep into the final version of the test. It would be nice if quantitative item analysis pointed out such problems, but it does not. Quantitative item analysis is useful but limited. It points out items that have problems but doesn't tell us what the problems are. It is possible that an item that fails to measure or match an instructional objective could have an acceptable difficulty level, an answer that discriminates positively, and distractors that discriminate negatively. In short, quantitative item analysis is fallible. To do a thorough job of test analysis, one must use a combination of quantitative and qualitative item analyses, and not rely solely on one or the other. In other words, there is no substitute for carefully scrutinizing and editing items and matching test items with objectives.

Item Analysis Modifications for the Criterion-Referenced Test

The statistical test analysis method discussed earlier, called quantitative item analysis, applies most directly to the NRT. We know from Chapter 5, however, that the classroom teacher will typically use CRTs rather than NRTs. Well, then, we can just use these same procedures for our teacher-made CRTs. Right? Wrong!

As we will discover in later chapters, variability of scores is crucial to the appropriateness and success of norm-referenced quantitative item analysis procedures. In short, these procedures depend on the variability or spread of scores (i.e., low to high) if they are to do their jobs correctly. In a typical teacher-made CRT, however, variability of scores would be expected to be small, assuming instruction is effective and the test and its objectives match. Thus, the application of quantitative item analysis procedures to CRTs may not be appropriate, since by definition most students will answer these items correctly (i.e., there will be *minimal* variability or spread of scores). In this section, we will describe several ways in which these procedures can be modified when a criterion-referenced, mastery approach to test item evaluation is employed. As you will see, these modifications are straightforward and easier to use than the quantitative procedures described earlier.

Using Pretest and Post-Test as Upper and Lower Groups   The following approaches require that you administer the test as a pretest prior to your instruction and as a post-test after your instruction. Ideally, in such a situation, the majority of students should answer most of your test items incorrectly on the pretest and correctly on the post-test. By studying the difference between the difficulty (p) levels for each item at the time of the pre- and post-tests, we can tell if this is happening. At pretest, the p level should be low (e.g., 0.30 or lower), and at post-test, it should be high (e.g., 0.70 or higher). In addition, we can consider the pretest results for an item as the lower group (L) and post-test results for the item as the upper group (U), and then we can perform the quantitative item analysis procedures previously described to determine the discrimination direction for the key and the distractors.

EXAMPLE: *Analyze the following results*

Numbers of students choosing option ($n = 25$)

Option	At Pretest (Lower or L)	At Post-Test (Upper or U)
A	9	1
B	7	1
C	3	2
D* (key)	6	21

Step 1: Compute *p* levels for both tests.

	Pretest	Post-Test
Number choosing correctly/total number	$\dfrac{6}{25} = 0.24$	$\dfrac{21}{25} = 0.84$

This is what we would hope for in a CRT; most students should answer the item *incorrectly* on the pretest and *correctly* on the post-test. In this case, it was an improvement from 24% to 84%.

Step 2: Determine the discrimination index (*D*) for the key.

$$D = \frac{\text{Number correct (post)} - \text{number correct (pre)}}{\text{Number in either group}}$$

$$D = \frac{21 - 6}{25} = \frac{15}{25} = 0.60$$

This indicates that the keyed correct option has a positive discrimination index, which is what we want.

Step 3: Determine whether each option discriminates *negatively*.

$$\text{Option A: } D = \frac{1 - 9}{25} = \frac{-8}{25} = -0.32$$

Option A discriminates *negatively*, which is what we want; more students chose this option on the pretest (L) than the post-test (U).

$$\text{Option B: } D = \frac{1 - 7}{25} = \frac{-6}{25} = -0.24$$

Option B also discriminates *negatively*.

$$\text{Option C: } D = \frac{2 - 3}{25} = \frac{-1}{25} = -0.04$$

Option C also discriminates *negatively*, albeit weakly.

In summary, our modified quantitative item analysis procedures indicate the following:

1. There was a sizeable increase in *p* value from pretest to post-test.
2. The *D* index for the key was positive.
3. The distractors all discriminated negatively.

If a CRT item manifests these features, it has passed our "test" and probably is a good item with little or no need for modification. Contrast this conclusion, however, with the following item from the same test.

EXAMPLE: *Analyze the results in the following table*

Numbers of students choosing option ($n = 25$)

Option	At Pretest (L)	At Post-Test (U)
A*	23	24
B	1	1
C	1	0
D	0	0

For this item, the pretest p level was 0.92 and the post-test level was 0.96—an increase by only 0.04, hardly an increase at all. In addition, the majority of students answered this item *correctly* on the pretest. We want *most* students to answer *incorrectly* at the pretest and correctly at the post-test!

Furthermore, the D index for the key is only 0.04:

$$D = \frac{24 - 23}{25} = \frac{1}{25} = 0.04$$

While this index is positive and *might* be acceptable in an NRT, it is not acceptable for a CRT.

Okay, so what D value is acceptable? Unfortunately, there is no easy answer to this question. We would suggest, however, that you look for D values of 0.40 or greater. This would mean that almost twice as many students are answering the item correctly on the post-test than on the pretest.

Finally, let's investigate our distractors. The D values for both options B and D are 0.00.

$$\text{Option B: } D = \frac{1 - 1}{25} = \frac{0}{25} = 0.00$$

$$\text{Option D: } D = \frac{0 - 0}{25} = \frac{0}{25} = 0.00$$

Neither of these options is useful; they both fail to differentiate between pre- and post-test. These options require modification or elimination.

Let's look at option C.

$$\text{Option C: } D = \frac{0 - 1}{25} = \frac{-1}{25} = -0.04$$

This option does discriminate negatively but weakly. Modifications to this option may increase its ability to discriminate negatively.

To evaluate this item overall, let's subject it to our three-step analysis:

1. Is there a substantial increase in p value (0.40 or more) between pre- and post-test?
   p increased from 0.92 to 0.96, hardly substantial.
2. Was D greater than 0.40 for the key?
   D was only 0.04.
3. Did all distractors discriminate negatively?
   Options B and D had zero discrimination ability; option C discriminated negatively, but only weakly.

Thus, the item in Example 2 failed all the tests. Rather than modify the item, it is probably more efficient to replace it with another.

Less technical variations of modified quantitative item analysis procedures for CRTs follow. The next two methods also have the advantage of applying to true–false, matching, and completion tests rather than to just multiple-choice tests.

***Comparing the Percentage Answering Each Item Correctly on Both Pre-
and Post-Test*** If your test is sensitive to your objectives (and assuming you teach to your
objectives), the majority of learners should receive a low score on the test prior to your instruction
and a high score afterward. This method can be used to determine whether this is happening.

Subtract the percentage of students passing each item before your instruction from the percentage of students passing each item after your instruction. The more positive the difference, the
more you know the item is tapping the content you are teaching. This method is similar to the first
step as described in the preceding section.

For example, consider the following percentages for five test items:

Item	*Percentage Passing Pretest*	*Percentage Passing Post-Test*	*Difference*
1	16	79	+63%
2	10	82	+72%
3	75	75	0%
4	27	91	+64%
5	67	53	−14%

Notice that item 3 registers no change in the percentage of students passing from before to after
instruction. In fact, a high percentage of students got the item correct without any instruction! This
item may be eliminated from the test, since little or no instruction pertaining to it was provided *and*
most students already knew the content it represents.

Now, look at item 5. Notice that the percentage is negative. That is, 14% of the class actually
changed from getting the item *correct* before instruction to getting it *wrong* after. Here, either the
instruction was not related to the item or it actually confused some students who knew the correct
answer beforehand. A revision of the item, the objective pertaining to this item, or the related
instruction is in order.

***Determining the Percentage of Items Answered in the Expected Direction
for the Entire Test*** Another, slightly different approach is to determine whether the entire test
reflects the change from fewer to more students answering items correctly from pre- to post-test.
This index uses the number of items each learner failed on the test prior to instruction but passed
on the test after instruction. Here is how it is computed:

Step 1: Find the number of items each student *failed* on the pretest, *prior* to instruction, but *passed*
on the post-test, *after* instruction.

Item	*Bobby at Pretest*	*Bobby at Post-Test*
1*	Incorrect	Correct
2	Correct	Correct
3*	Incorrect	Correct
4	Correct	Incorrect
5	Incorrect	Incorrect

The asterisks indicate that the two items Bobby answered incorrectly on the pretest and correctly
on the post-test. This count is then repeated for each student.

Step 2: Add the counts in Step 1 for all students and divide by the number of students.

Step 3: Divide the result from Step 2 by the number of items on the test.

Step 4: Multiply the result from Step 3 by 100.

Let's see how this would work for a 25-item test given to five students before and after instruction.

Step 1: Find the number of items that students answered incorrectly prior to instruction but correctly after instruction.

Mary	18
Carlos	15
Sharon	22
Amanda	20
Charles	13

Step 2: Add counts and divide by the number of students.

$$\frac{18 + 15 + 22 + 20 + 13}{5} = \frac{88}{5} = 17.6$$

Step 3: Divide by number of test items.

$$\frac{17.6}{25} = 0.70$$

Step 4: Multiply by 100. $0.70 \times 100 = 70\%$.

Seventy percent of the items on the test registered a positive change after instruction, where a positive change is defined as failing an item before instruction and passing it afterward. The greater the overall positive percentage of change, the more your test is likely to match your instruction and to be a content-valid test.

Limitations of These Modifications   One limitation of these modified quantitative item analysis procedures is that it is difficult, especially at first, to write items that virtually everyone will be successful on only after a unit of instruction. Thus, you may find that in your initial efforts, 40% of your students answer an item correctly on the pretest and only 60% answered an item correctly on the post-test. This is less than optimal, but it may be a good "first try."

Another limitation is that if the unit of instruction is brief, there may be some contamination of the post-test by a student's recollection of responses made during the pretest. A third limitation is that we are taking a procedure that was developed for a single administration of an NRT and applying it to a CRT administered to the same group at two different times. Finally, these modifications require two test administrations (pre and post), which will reduce the amount of time you devote to instruction.

In conclusion, it would be a mistake to uncritically apply the quantitative item analysis procedures appropriate for NRTs to CRTs. At the same time, it would be a mistake to reject their utility. Their utility is probably strongest when tests or test items are in their early stages of use and development, and when the methods are used along with qualitative item analysis.

We have discussed quantitative and qualitative item analyses, how they apply to NRTs, and how these procedures must be modified to apply more specifically to the typical classroom test. What's left is returning the test to the students, something we like to call debriefing.

DEBRIEFING

Take a moment to think back to the times a test on which you did well was returned. Remember the happy, satisfied feeling you had? You felt good about yourself, your teacher, and the test. Of course, it was a good test because it proved that you knew your stuff. Now take a minute to think back to the times a test on which you did poorly was returned. Remember the unhappy, unsatisfied feeling you had? Were you angry or resentful? It's likely you weren't feeling very fond of yourself, your teacher, or the test—especially the test. Any time you give a test, it's likely that some students will do poorly and feel unhappy or angry as a result.

Teachers adopt their own ways of coping with complaints about a test. These range from "Your score is final, and that's it" to "I'll give everybody 10 extra points so that no one fails." We feel that neither of these positions is defensible. The first position denies or ignores reality. It is not just possible, but *probable*, that your test has deficiencies. Refusing to examine the test with your students robs you of the opportunity to get feedback that you can use to improve or fine-tune your test before you use it again.

Furthermore, such an approach serves to antagonize and alienate students. Awarding extra credit or a makeup test may calm the angry students who did poorly but may be unfair to those who did well. As with the first approach, it robs you of the opportunity to get feedback on, and make appropriate modifications to, your test. Instead, we advocate having genuine concern for the quality of your test and showing this concern by going over the test with your students each time you use it. Your students can actually save your time and effort by screening your test and identifying those items that are worth subjecting to the time-consuming processes of quantitative and qualitative item analyses.

If you are truly interested in improving the validity and reliability of your test, you can subject each item to both kinds of item analyses. Your reward will be a better test. Or you can find out which items your students found problematic and subject only those few items to analysis. Again, your reward will be a better test. The choice is yours, but, of course, we hope you choose to go over the test with your students later. Should you do so, consult the following suggested debriefing guidelines.

Debriefing Guidelines

Before handing back answer sheets or grades, you should do the following.

Discuss Problem Items Discuss any items you or your students found to be problematic in scoring the test. This sets the stage for rational discussion and makes for more effective consideration of the item(s) in question. Also, you are more likely to have the attention of the students than you would if they were looking over their answer sheets or thinking about the grades they received.

Listen to Student Reactions Ask for student reactions to your comments and listen to their reactions. Again, you are setting the stage for rational discussion of the test by letting the students know you are interested in their feedback. Remember, your goal is to improve the validity and reliability of your test by improving on its weaknesses. When you or your students begin to respond emotionally, defensiveness is likely to replace listening, and issues of power and control replace rational discussion. In short, improving the test may seem less important than asserting your authority. You will have plenty of opportunities to assert your authority and few opportunities to improve your test. Try to keep these issues separate, and use the few opportunities you do have for test improvement as advantageously as you can.

Avoid on-the-Spot Decisions Tell your students that you will consider their comments, complaints, and suggestions, but you will not make any decisions about omitting items, partial credit, extra credit, and so forth until you have had time to study and think about the test data. If necessary, you may want to make it clear that soliciting their comments is only for the purpose of preparing the next test, not for reconsidering grades for the present test.

Be Equitable with Changes If you decide to make changes, let your students know that any changes in scoring will apply to all students, not just those who raise objections. After handing back answer sheets or grades, do the following.

Ask Students to Double-Check Ask students to double check your arithmetic and ask any who think clerical errors have been made to see you as soon as possible. Here you are presenting yourself as human by admitting that you can make errors.

Ask Students to Identify Problems If time permits, ask students to identify the items they find problematic and why. Make note of the items and problems. Such items may then be discussed or worked into some new instructional objectives. We have been suggesting that you use the time you spend returning your test as an opportunity to improve your test. To the extent that you can elicit relevant and constructive feedback from your class, you will be likely to reach this goal. In trying to remain nondefensive and emotionally detached from your test, it is useful to keep a few points in mind:

1. Your test will include at least some items that can be improved. You are human!

2. Students are criticizing your skill as a test constructor, not you as a person. Admittedly, though, frustrated students can get too personal. When this happens, try to remember what's behind it—frustration with your test.

3. The quality of an item is not necessarily related to the loudness with which complaints are made. At times, items that students loudly protest are indeed poor items. At other times, they are simply difficult or challenging items. Use quantitative item analysis to determine which is the case.

4. When it appears necessary to rescore a test or award credit, keep in mind that research has shown that rescoring tends to be highly related to the original scoring. Thus, although some individual scores may change, one's rank in relation to others is not likely to change much. For all their protest, students seldom really gain much other than letting off steam.

5. Finally, keep in mind that the most important objectives for debriefing are to improve your test, to gain insight into the effectiveness and thoroughness of your instruction, and to plan new objectives that can address the problems students had in learning the test content.

THE PROCESS OF EVALUATING CLASSROOM ACHIEVEMENT

Figure 11.4 summarizes all of the important components of achievement testing that we have discussed thus far. If you've studied and worked at these chapters, you are ahead in the test construction game. What that means for you is better tests that cause fewer students and parents to complain and tests that are more valid and reliable measurements of achievement.

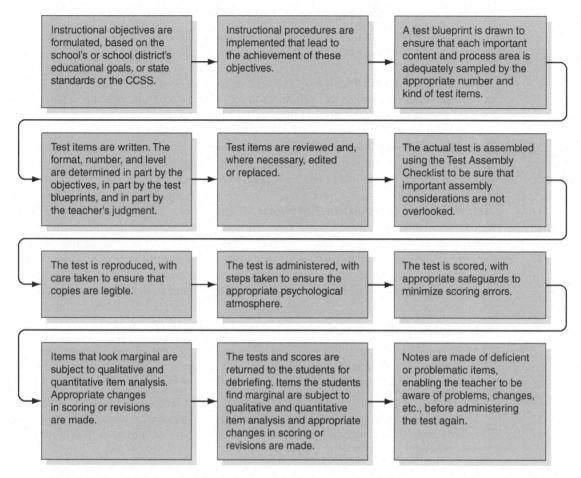

FIGURE 11.4 The process of measuring achievement in the classroom.

SUMMARY

This chapter covered many issues related to test assembly, administration, scoring, and analysis. Major points mentioned are as follows:

1. When assembling a test:
   a. Group all items of same or similar formats together.
   b. Arrange items so that item difficulty progresses from easy to hard.
   c. Space items to eliminate overcrowding.
   d. Keep items and options on the same page.
   e. Place contextual material above the items to which they refer.
   f. Arrange answers in a random pattern.
   g. Decide how students are to record answers.
   h. Be sure to include a space for the student's name.

     i. Be sure that directions are specific and accurate.

     j. Proofread your master copy before reproducing it.

     k. Check items for race or gender bias.

2. Care must be taken in reproducing the test to avoid illegible copies that would impair test validity.

3. In administering a test, make an effort to do the following:

     a. Induce a realistic, but positive test-taking attitude.

     b. Maximize the achievement nature of the test.

     c. Equalize the advantages testwise students have over nontestwise students.

     d. Avoid surprise tests.

     e. Provide special instructions before the tests are actually distributed.

     f. Alternate your test distribution procedures.

     g. Have students check that they have the entire test.

     h. Keep distractions to a minimum.

     i. Alert students to the amount of time left toward the end of the test.

     j. Clarify test collection procedures before handing out the test.

4. In scoring the test, try to do the following:

     a. Have the key prepared in advance.

     b. Have the key checked for accuracy.

     c. Score blindly.

     d. Check for multiple answers if machine scoring is used.

     e. Double-check scores, if scored by hand.

     f. Record scores before returning the tests.

5. Quantitative item analysis is a mathematical approach to assessing an item's utility that is best suited for norm-referenced multiple-choice tests.

6. An item's difficulty level (p) is computed by dividing the number of students who answered correctly by the total number of students who attempted the item.

7. An item's discrimination index (D) is computed by subtracting the number of students who answered correctly in the low-scoring half of the class from the number of students who answered correctly in the high-scoring half of the class, and dividing the remainder by the number of students in the upper or lower group.

8. Keyed correct options should discriminate positively (positive D value), and incorrect options should discriminate negatively (negative D value).

9. Quantitative item analysis helps us decide whether to retain or eliminate an item, which distractor(s) should be modified or eliminated, whether an item is miskeyed, whether guessing occurred, and whether ambiguity is present.

10. Qualitative item analysis is a nonmathematical approach to assessing an item's utility. It is appropriate for both norm- and criterion-referenced tests.

11. Qualitative item analysis is performed by checking an item's content validity and inspecting it for technical faults, as outlined in Chapters 6–8.

12. Do not apply the quantitative item analysis procedures that have been developed and proved using norm-referenced tests to criterion-referenced tests without appropriate caution and modification.

13. Several modifications of traditional norm-referenced item analysis procedures appropriate for criterion-referenced tests were discussed; they vary in their complexity.

14. These modifications to the usual quantitative item analysis procedures should be coupled with the qualitative item analysis procedures discussed in Chapters 6–8 to properly evaluate the criterion-referenced teacher-made test.

15. After the test has been scored, but before you give students their scores:
    a. Discuss any items considered to be problematic.
    b. Listen to student concerns and try to stay unemotional.
    c. Let students know you will consider their comments but will not make any decisions affecting their scores until you have had time to reflect on their comments.
    d. Let students know that any changes made will apply equally to all students.

16. After the students are given their scores, ask them to check for clerical errors.

FOR DISCUSSION AND PRACTICE

*1. Compute p, the difficulty index, for the following items. Interpret your results. (The asterisk indicates the correct option.)

a. Options	A	B*	C	D
	10	5	8	0

b. Options	A	B	C*	D
	4	2	16	3

*2. Compute D, the discrimination index, for the following items. Interpret your results.
(Class size = 40)

a. Options	A	B	C	D*
Upper half	3	0	7	10
Lower half	5	4	9	2

(Class size = 30)

b. Options	A*	B	C	D
Upper half	3	5	7	0
Lower half	8	5	1	1

*3. Identify which of the following items are likely to be miskeyed, which are likely to be susceptible to guessing, and which are probably ambiguous.

a. Options	A*	B	C	D
Upper half	8	0	7	2

b. Options	A	B	C*	D
Upper half	10	2	4	3

c. Options	A	B*	C	D
Upper half	3	11	3	10

d. Options	A*	B	C	D
Upper half	9	8	11	9

e. Options	A*	B	C	D
Upper half	0	1	6	2

*4. Do a complete item analysis for the following item data. Use the Quantitative Item Analysis Checklist (Figure 11.3) as your guide, answering each of the questions indicated.
(Class size = 20)

a. Options	A*	B	C	D
Upper half	3	2	3	2
Lower half	2	3	1	4

5. A number of test assembly and administration suggestions were offered to improve your classroom test. Think back to the tests you took in school. What percentage of those tests do you think actually were assembled with those suggestions in mind? If less than 100%, why do you think suggestions like those were not followed.

*Answers for these questions appear in Appendix B.

CHAPTER 12

MARKS AND MARKING SYSTEMS

LEARNING OUTCOMES

After completing this chapter, the student will be able to:

1. Describe the primary purpose of a mark, according to the authors.
2. Identify the most important factor to be reflected in a mark.
3. Explain why mixing factors other than achievement into marks is problematic.
4. Compare and contrast the five marking systems presented in the text.
5. Identify the marking system recommended by the authors.
6. Explain the reasons for their recommendations.
7. Take a position in defense of a different marking system, compare and contrast this system with the one recommended by the authors to support your position.
8. Compare and contrast the different symbol systems presented in the text.
9. Explain how checklists can be a useful adjunct to letter or numerical symbol systems.
10. Describe why simply weighting component scores differentially may result in distortions of a composite mark.
11. Describe the procedure suggested (i.e., equate before you weight) in the text to minimize the likelihood that such distortions will affect final marks.
12. Compare and contrast front-end and back-end equating systems.
13. Use front-end and back-end equating procedures used to combine performance measures and traditional measures into a single mark.

AFTER YOU have administered your test, you score it and assign a grade to the test. This grade is not what we will be referring to in this chapter. In this chapter, we will discuss several issues related to the assignment of *marks*—cumulative or final grades that reflect academic achievement at the end of a 6- or 9-week marking period, semester, or school year.

WHAT IS THE PURPOSE OF A MARK?

Marks are assigned to provide feedback about student *achievement*. We will reiterate this point several times in this chapter, not because it is so difficult, but because it is so often forgotten. All too often, marks have been assigned as rewards and punishments, or have been affected by nonachievement factors we will discuss in this chapter. This is not what they are intended for.

Why Be Concerned about Marking?

Marks have become an accepted and expected aspect of our culture. Students come to realize very early in their educational careers that they will be graded or marked depending on their performance in school. Parents of students, having been graded themselves, realize that the marks a student receives affect their child's educational, occupational, and financial status by opening or closing various opportunities. Parents know that children are compared with each other through their marks. Marks are also considered by college and graduate admissions officers and committees. Thus, marks have considerable meaning for the child and parent, and school to which a child may apply.

Educators also are strongly influenced by marks, often relegating pupils to faster or slower tracks, depending on their marks. Since marks carry a great deal of importance for many people, it seems sensible that care and objectivity be exercised in assigning marks. Unfortunately, this is often not the case. Rather than being assigned accurately, in hopes of presenting as valid a picture of student achievement as possible, marks are sometimes assigned in haste, or according to nebulous, undefined, and little understood "marking systems." Different marking systems have different advantages and disadvantages—some of which the average teacher often does not know. We will acquaint you with various marking systems so that you may choose the system that best fits your situation. In general, such systems compare students with other students or with established standards of knowledge, or are based on aptitude, effort, and improvement.

What Should a Mark Reflect?

What a mark should reflect depends on the subject or topic being marked. We generally talk about marks in relation to reading, math or science achievement, and so on. However, marks are also assigned in areas such as conduct, study skills, and responsibility. When marks are related to academic subjects, marks should reflect *academic achievement* and nothing more!

Marks are assigned to provide feedback about academic achievement in order for students to be compared according to their achievement. If marks reflect only academic achievement and are assigned consistently according to a system, such marks may be compared with considerable validity (as long as the system according to which the marks are assigned is made clear). But when a single mark represents a hodgepodge of factors beyond achievement (e.g., attitude, attendance, punctuality, or conduct) or systems (e.g., comparisons with other students, comparisons with standards of effort, or improvement), interpretation or comparison of such marks becomes a hopeless task.

Unfortunately, the latter case characterizes some marking practices today. Different schools employ different marking systems and weigh various nonachievement factors in assigning marks, making direct and meaningful comparisons of grades from different difficult at best.

We are not suggesting that information about nonachievement factors, such as conduct and punctuality, should be unreported or is unimportant. We *are* suggesting that such information should not be mixed with test scores and other indicators of academic achievement in a single grade. In other words, don't mix apples with oranges in a single mark for an academic subject. All this may seem perfectly obvious, but strange things happen when marks are assigned. It's all too tempting to use marks as vehicles to reach, or try to reach, other ends. Consider the following dialog:

PARENT: Mr. Stokes, Jack got a D in reading these 6 weeks, but he had A's in reading all year. I don't understand. He seems to be reading better all the time, but I'm no teacher. What can I do to help him?

TEACHER: One thing you can do is tell him to stop looking out the window during oral reading. Some of these third graders seem to think that what is going on outside is more important than reading!

PARENT: Do you mean Jack is being disruptive in class?

TEACHER: Yes, he looks out the window, then the next thing you know another one does, then another …

PARENT: Have you asked him why he's doing it?

TEACHER: Of course, but it's always the same excuse—"I'm bored listening to the others read aloud what I've already read to myself."

PARENT: I see, but what about his reading ability—has it declined?

TEACHER: Oh, no! Jack's one of the top readers in the class—there's nothing he can't read.

PARENT: So he's a top reader, but he got a D in reading for not paying attention—is that it?

TEACHER: Mrs. Burns! What do you think I am? I grade on achievement—not on conduct!

PARENT: Why *did* he get the D, then? It sounds as though he was punished for not paying attention.

TEACHER: You've got it wrong. He failed to turn in two homework assignments. That's an automatic D in all my classes. Someone's got to teach these kids responsibility.

PARENT: Mr. Stokes, I know that Sarah Smith failed to turn in two homework assignments, and she got an A.

TEACHER: That's different; she pays attention during oral reading. It's obvious that she's getting more out of the class. She also tries harder, even though she's not as smart as Jack.

PARENT: Mr. Stokes, you certainly are an exceptional teacher.

TEACHER: Thank you, Mrs. Burns, but it won't work—Jack's D still stands.

Unfortunately, this type of dialogue is not uncommon. We agree with the parent in that grades should be based on achievement, not conduct. However, it is quite clear that Jack's D is unrelated to reading achievement. By the teacher's own admission, Jack is reading well, but his classroom *behavior* is not congruent with Mr. Stokes's expectations, and he failed to turn in some homework assignments—another behavioral deficiency that Mr. Stokes equates with poor reading achievement, based on his grade of D. To what is Mr. Stokes comparing Jack's reading achievement? We can't be sure, although effort and aptitude were mentioned.

It appears that the main function of the marks in this case is punishment. Rather than providing feedback to the student about *reading* achievement, Mr. Stokes is punishing Jack for off-task behavior during class and for less than perfect compliance with his homework expectations. The major problem we see here is that the main function of grades—to provide feedback about achievement—has been lost in Mr. Stokes's zeal to change Jack's behavior. In too many cases, a single grade is used to report achievement, conduct, homework compliance, tardiness, and so on. This would be less of a problem if it were done consistently across schools. However, different schools weight each of these differently. The real point is that as long as grades continue to be based on factors other than achievement, we are robbing ourselves of the effective use of the main purpose of grading—evaluating achievement. Let's consider the different marking systems employed in schools.

MARKING SYSTEMS

Various types of marking systems have been used in the schools. They may be considered along two dimensions:

1. Type of comparison involved.
2. Type of symbol used.

Types of Comparisons

Often, the type of symbol a teacher uses is determined at the school or district level—the teacher has little to say about whether an A–F; E, G, S, U; or a numerical marking system is employed. However, the classroom teacher often has more flexibility and autonomy in deciding how to assign the marks. That is, teachers often have considerable control over how they decide who gets an A or B. As mentioned earlier, marks are based on comparisons, usually from among comparisons of students with:

1. other students;
2. established standards;
3. aptitude;
4. actual versus potential effort;
5. actual versus potential improvement.

Each of these systems has advantages and limitations. Our aim is to acquaint you with these, so that you may choose wisely. Whichever system you choose to employ, be sure to indicate it on the report card. Remember, the function of marking is to provide feedback on achievement. However, a grade of B based on effort versus a grade of B based on comparisons to established standards can reflect very different absolute levels of achievement. Clarifying the basis for comparison of your marking system will minimize potential misinterpretation of student achievement.

Comparisons with Other Students   Certainly you have had instructors who have graded "on the curve." It almost sounds illegal, shady, or underhanded. At times, it seems that this is some mysterious method by which test grades are transformed into semester marks. Basically, all that the expression "grading on the curve" means is that your grade or mark depends on how your achievement compares with the achievement of other students in your class. You may recall from Chapter 5 that such an approach may also be considered to be *norm-referenced*. Certain proportions of the class are assigned A's, B's, and so on, regardless of their absolute level of performance on a test. In such a system, a student who misses 50% of the items on a test might get an A, F, or any other grade on the test depending on how his or her score of 50% compared with the scores of the other students in the class. Sometimes, districts or schools encourage grading on the curve by specifying the percentages of students who will be assigned various grades. The following distribution is an example:

Grade	Percentage of Students
A	10
B	25
C	40
D	20
F	5

The main advantage of such a system is that it simplifies marking decisions. With clear-cut decision-making guidelines, there is no apparent need for teachers to deliberate or agonize over what cutoff scores should determine student grades; the student is either in the top 10% or he or she doesn't get an A.

However, such a system has several disadvantages. First, this type of marking system fails to consider differences due to the overall ability level of the class. Imagine the disappointment that would result if such a system were imposed on a class of intellectually gifted students, none of whom had ever earned less than a B. Suddenly 65% would be transformed into C through F students. Regardless of achievement, in such a system, some students will always get A's while others will get F's. Another problem involves the percentages—why not 5% A's or 15% A's? The percentages may be set rather arbitrarily. Furthermore, what does it mean when a student gets an A? Has the student mastered all course content? Or was the student lucky enough to be in a class of low-performing learners? Such a system says nothing about absolute achievement, which makes comparisons across grades and schools difficult.

Finally, consider the teacher in such a system. No matter how well or poorly the teacher teaches, his or her students always get the same percentage of grades. As a result, a teacher may not feel quite as motivated to improve.

Comparison with Established Standards   In a marking system using comparison with established standards, it is possible for all students to get A's or F's or any other grade in between. How much the rest of the students in the class achieve is irrelevant to a student's grade. All that is relevant is whether a student attains a defined standard of achievement or performance. We labeled this approach *criterion-referenced* in Chapter 4. In such a system, letter grades may be assigned based on the percentage of test items answered correctly, as the following distribution illustrates:

Grade	Percentage of Items Answered Correctly
A	85
B	75
C	65
D	55
F	Less than 55

Thus, a student who answers 79% of the test items correctly earns a B, regardless of whether the rest of the class did better, worse, or about the same. Obviously, such a system requires some prior knowledge of the difficulty of the test and what level of achievement or performance is reasonable to expect.

There are several advantages to such a system. First, it is possible, in theory, for all students to obtain high grades if they put forth sufficient effort (assuming that the percentage cutoffs are not unreasonably high). Second, assignment of grades is simplified. A student either has answered 75% of the items correctly or has not. As with comparison with other students, there is no apparent need to deliberate or agonize over assigning grades. Finally, assuming that the ability levels of incoming students remain fairly constant and that tests remain comparable in validity and difficulty, teachers who work to improve teaching effectiveness should see improvement in grades with the passage of time. Presumably, this would help motivate teachers to continue working to improve their effectiveness.

As you might expect, such a system also has its drawbacks. Establishing a standard is no small task. Just what is reasonable for an A may vary from school to school and from time to time, as a result of ability levels, societal pressures, and curriculum changes. Furthermore, should the same standards be maintained for a gifted or a special education class as for an average class? Another problem is that the public and administrators often have difficulty "adjusting" to a marking system that potentially allows everyone to make an A. It is a curious fact of life that everyone presses for excellence in education, but many balk at marking systems that make attainment of excellence within everyone's reach.

Comparisons with Aptitude   Aptitude is another name for potential or ability. In aptitude-based marking systems, students are compared neither to other students nor to established standards. Instead, they are compared to themselves. That is, marks are assigned depending on how closely to their potential students are achieving. Thus, students with high aptitude or potential who are achieving at high levels would get high grades, since they would be achieving at their potential. Those with high aptitude and average achievement would get lower grades, since they would be achieving below their potential. But students with average aptitude and average achievement would get high grades, since they would be considered to be achieving at their potential. Such a system sounds attractive to many educators. However, serious problems exist, as Table 12.1 shows.

Table 12.1 shows that the concept of assigning grades based on the congruence of a student's achievement with the student's aptitude is quite sensible for high-aptitude students. Look at what happens for the low-aptitude students, however. If a student's aptitude is low enough, the student would have a hard time achieving below his or her potential. Thus, the student always would be achieving at or above the expected level. Would this be fair to the moderate- and high-ability students? Perhaps more important, can you see how such a system would greatly complicate interpreting grades? For example, a C for a high-aptitude student might indicate 70% mastery, while for an average-aptitude student, it might indicate 60%, and perhaps 50% mastery, or less, for the low-aptitude student. The same grade may mean very different things in terms of absolute achievement.

Other drawbacks of such a system relate to statistical considerations beyond the scope of this text that affect the reliability of such comparisons. Another is the tendency for the achievement scores of slow learners to increase and the achievement scores of fast learners to decrease when tested again. Technically, this phenomenon is called the *regression toward the mean effect*—the more extreme an achievement score, the more it can be expected to "regress" or fall back toward the average or mean of all students at another testing. Finally, such a system requires more complex record keeping than the first two systems discussed. Such a system, as appealing as it is at first glance, is not practical.

Comparison of Achievement with Effort Systems that compare achievement with effort are similar to those that compare achievement with aptitude. Students who get average test scores but have to work hard to get them are given high marks. Students who get average scores but do not have to work hard to get them are given lower grades.

Several problems plague marking systems that are based on effort. First, we have no known measure of effort. Unlike aptitude, for which reliable and valid measures exist, effort is at best estimated by informal procedures with unknown validity and reliability. Second, within such a system children are punished for being bright and catching on quickly, while other children are

TABLE 12.1 The Relationships among Aptitude, Achievement, and Marks in Marking Systems Based on Comparisons of Achievement with Aptitude

Aptitude Level	Achievement Level	Marks
High	High	High
	Average	Average
	Low	Low
Average	High	High
	Average	High
	Low	Average
Low	High	High
	Average	High
	Low	High

rewarded for taking a long time to master concepts. Third, there is the old problem of the marks not representing academic achievement. Effort may cover up academic attainment, making marks all the more difficult to interpret. Finally, record keeping is once again complex.

The advantage cited for grading based on effort is that it serves to motivate the slower or turned off students, but it may also serve to turn off the brighter students who would quickly see such a system as unfair. Whatever the case, the primary function of marking—to provide feedback about academic achievement—is not well served by such a system.

Comparison of Achievement with Improvement Marking systems may compare the amount of improvement, or growth, between the beginning (pretest) and end (post-test) of instruction. Students who show the most growth get the highest grades. An obvious problem occurs for the student who does well on the pretest. Improvement for such a student is likely to be less overall than for a student who does poorly on the pretest. In fact, some bright students have been known to "play dumb" on pretests when such systems are in force. Other shortcomings of these systems include the statistical problems we mentioned before in regard to comparisons with aptitude (i.e., unreliability of such comparisons and regression toward the mean) and unwieldy record keeping.

Which System Should You Choose? We have seen that each system has significant drawbacks as well as advantages. Which should you choose? In our opinion, comparisons with established standards would best suit the primary function of marking—to provide feedback about academic achievement. This would facilitate achievement comparisons across states that have adopted the Common Core State Standards (CCSS), or at least across schools within states that have not adopted the CCSS. It seems to us that such a system has the best chance of reducing misinterpretation of marks.

In reality, many schools and districts have adopted multiple marking systems, such as assigning separate grades for achievement and effort or for achievement, effort, and improvement. Others are now considering separate grades for paper-and-pencil tasks and performance and portfolio assessments, such as those we have considered in Chapters 9 and 10. As long as the achievement portion of the grade reflects only achievement, such systems seem to be reasonable. Two disadvantages of such systems are worth noting, however. First, they double or triple the number of grades to be assigned and interpreted, leading to an increase in record keeping and interpretation time. Second, unless the purpose of each grade is explained very clearly on the report card, marking systems are often difficult for parents to decipher.

Types of Symbols

Within marking systems, a variety of symbols have been used. Some of the more common types are discussed in this section.

Letter Grades Letter grades are the most common symbol system. Many U.S. schools use the letters A–F to report marks. Often, plus and minus symbols are used to indicate finer distinctions between the letter grades. This system, along with its variations (e.g., E, G, S, U for excellent, good, satisfactory, or unsatisfactory), has several advantages that have led to its widespread adoption and continuing popularity.

First, the letter system is widely understood. Students, teachers, parents, administrators, employers, and admissions committees understand, at least in a general sense, that grades of A represent excellent or exceptional performance and grades of D or F represent marginal or poor performance. Second, such a system is compact, requiring only one or two spaces to report a summary mark of an entire semester's work. Third, such a system has just about the optimal number of levels of judgment humans can effectively exercise (i.e., 5–15).

The limitations of the system are worth considering. First, the specific meaning of letter grades varies from class to class and from school to school. Different schools and districts tend to use different marking systems and, as will be discussed later in this chapter, also tend to combine and weight the components of a mark differently. Consequently, a grade of A in one school or district may represent performance similar to a grade of B or even C in another.

Second, letter grades fail to clearly indicate the student's actual level of mastery. There is often a considerable difference between the achievement of a "low-B" student and that of a "high-B" student. Finally, because of this, averaging of letter grades often results in a loss of information or misinterpretation of the student's actual achievement. When averaging letter grades, it is necessary to go back to the actual numerical grades to obtain the correct average.

Numerical Grades The numerical symbol system is another type of mark commonly used in the schools. Such systems usually employ 100 as the highest mark, and report cards often carry letter-grade equivalents for the range of numerical grades. For example,

Numerical Grade	Letter Grade
90–100	A
80–89	B
70–79	C
60–69	D
Below 60	F

Numerical grades have three main advantages. First, like letter grades, they provide a convenient summary mark for a semester's or year's work. Second, unlike letter grades, numerical grades are easily averaged to obtain the "correct" final marks. Third, they are widely understood—most pupils and parents realize that there are substantial differences between a mark of 95 and one of 75.

There are also disadvantages to such a system. First, the discriminations are finer than humans can really make. No one can make 40 reliable distinctions between grades from 61 to 100. Another way of saying this is that it is not possible to determine the real difference between a grade of 67 and a grade of 68 or between a grade of 95 and a grade of 96. Second, as with letter grades, we are never sure just what a grade means, since standards may vary considerably from school to school.

Other Symbols Pass–fail (P–F) grading is yet another way of indicating level of attainment. Although fairly popular about three decades ago, fewer schools exclusively employ this approach today because of its shortcomings. One shortcoming is that such symbols do not provide enough information: P could mean the student exhibited anywhere from exceptional to marginal performance in the class. This makes it difficult for employers and admissions officers to evaluate applicants. Students themselves have complained about the same lack of information—they really do not know how well they did. Finally, students tend to do the minimum necessary to earn a P under such systems. When used, pass–fail approaches should at least elaborate the strengths and weaknesses on which the mark was based.

Checklists A common adjunct to a letter, numerical, or pass–fail symbol system is a checklist. Since those symbol systems may fail to define just what a student can or cannot do, many report cards (and interim and summative tests reports) now include skill checklists to go along with their grade symbols for each subject. Checklists are also used to provide information about nonacademic aspects of the child. For example, checklists often are provided to identify problems in the areas of conduct, social skills, responsibility, and organization. Properly utilized checklists represent useful supplements to letter or numerical grades and can convey much more detailed information about the student without contaminating or confusing the interpretation of a student's overall achievement level.

As mentioned at the beginning of this chapter, districts and schools usually decide which symbol system teachers must use. In such situations, you have little choice but to employ the required system. It is more likely, though, that you will have some say about how the marks are actually assigned (i.e., what you will compare student achievement with). Now that you have been exposed to the pros and cons of various systems, you should be able to make better use of any marking or symbol system you are required—or choose—to use. However, a number of technical issues regarding the combining and weighting of the components of a mark must be considered before we leave this topic. The following discussion covers points that, unfortunately, most classroom teachers are unaware of regarding marks. Master the points and procedures covered, and you will have yet another important tool to add to your growing expertise in classroom measurement and evaluation.

COMBINING AND WEIGHTING THE COMPONENTS OF A MARK

As we mentioned, the classroom teacher seldom has control over the symbol system employed but may have latitude with regard to deciding on the type of comparison used to assign marks at the end of a marking period. But how does a teacher go about combining the grades from two quizzes, one major test, a performance assessment, several homework assignments, and a term paper into a mark without allowing one or more of these factors to influence the final mark too heavily or lightly? Recall the example at the beginning of this chapter. Mr. Stokes said that Jack's failure to turn in two homework assignments earned him "an automatic D," regardless of Jack's achievement on tests, oral reading, papers, and so on. While Mr. Stokes later contradicted himself on this point, there are some teachers who do adhere to such or similar practices. This is an example of allowing a component of a mark to influence that mark too heavily. Remember that the main purpose of marks is to provide feedback about student achievement.

Of course, such feedback is beneficial only if it is accurate. To attain this goal, each component of a final mark (tests, quizzes, homework assignments, papers, etc.) should affect the final mark *only to the appropriate extent*. At first glance, in computing the final mark, it might seem simple enough to weight components considered more important (e.g., a final test grade) more heavily than components considered less important (e.g., homework grades). However, while differential weighting of components is an important step in arriving at an accurate, fair, and just final mark, it is only one step of several that must be taken, and taken carefully, to prevent a final mark from misrepresenting student achievement. Unfortunately, failure to recognize this fact is widespread in classrooms today. As a result, feedback on student achievement provided through final marks is often distorted. It may be argued that distorted feedback is more troublesome than no feedback at all. To sensitize you to the complexity of what appears to be a simple issue, consider the following scenario.

Who Is the Better Teacher?

Mr. Nickels and Ms. Dimes, history teachers at different high schools in the same district, decided prior to the school year to collaborate in developing their instructional objectives, methods, tests, quizzes, and assignments for the upcoming school year. Since they always had similar students in the past, in terms of background and aptitude, they saw no problem in reducing their workload by using the same objectives, methods, and measurement instruments for both of their classes. They did have some concerns about students from the different schools "finding out" that they were using the same materials and sharing them, but they decided that this potential problem could be avoided by administering the quizzes and tests at the same time and by giving out assignments on the same day. Pleased that they had ironed out all the wrinkles, they agreed to meet at the end of the semester to compare marks. They expected that the marks would be about the same, on average, for both classes, since the marking symbols and the marking system they were required to use by the district were the same in both of their schools, and they both considered quizzes and test grades to be more important than homework or term paper grades. They agreed to weight their students' quiz and test grades twice as heavily in computing their final marks.

Both Mr. Nickels and Ms. Dimes prided themselves on their ability and dedication as teachers. They decided that this would be a good opportunity to determine who was the "better" teacher. Since their classes would be similar, and since they would both be using the same objectives, methods, measurement instruments, and weights for the various components that would go into their students' marks, they agreed that any significant difference in the marks earned by their classes must reflect differences in teaching ability and/or effectiveness. To spice things up a bit, they agreed to wager a cheeseburger on the outcome. The competition was on, and both Mr. Nickels and Ms. Dimes anticipated their own students earning the higher marks. Each teacher expected to earn a cheeseburger at the end of the semester.

At their end-of-semester meeting, however, Mr. Nickels was shocked to find that on the average Ms. Dimes's students earned marks that were one-half to a full letter grade higher than those earned by his students. Not panicking, he applied what he had learned in his college tests and measurements class. Mr. Nickels compared aptitude test scores for the two classes, hoping that by chance there would be some difference in aptitude between these two classes and their previous classes. He expected he would find significantly higher aptitude scores for Ms. Dimes's class, which would explain why their semester marks were higher than those of his class. After comparing aptitude scores for the two classes, however, Mr. Nickels found them to be quite comparable. "I could have told you that," responded Ms. Dimes somewhat haughtily.

Unwilling to concede and suspicious by nature, Mr. Nickels next suggested that Ms. Dimes must have "fixed" things by changing the curriculum—perhaps covering only two-thirds of the material he covered. This would have enabled her students to have more time to master the material and thereby earn higher grades. Offended by this challenge to her integrity, Ms. Dimes tossed her objectives, curriculum guide, and all the semester's assignments, quizzes, and tests to Mr. Nickels. "Read 'em and weep!" she exclaimed. And Mr. Nickels did ... at first. After comparing the materials piece by piece with his own, he found them to be identical. Next, however, he laboriously compared the test and quiz grades for both classes, since this is what both he and Ms. Dimes agreed would be the major basis for the marks of their students. To his relief, he discovered that the scores from both classes on the tests and quizzes *were about the same*.

"Look here, Ms. Dimes! The test and quiz grades for both classes are the same—you must have made a mistake in computing your marks," said Mr. Nickels. "Impossible, I triple-checked all my computations," stated Ms. Dimes firmly. However, when she compared the grades herself she agreed that Mr. Nickels was correct. The test and quiz grades were similar, yet she had assigned marks that on the average were one-half to a full letter grade higher than those assigned by Mr. Nickels.

Both teachers were confused. Not only were they unable to settle their bet, they were puzzled as to how such a situation could occur. They decided to review the procedures they used to combine and weight the marks their pupils had obtained. What they learned from this review is described in the following section.

Combining Grades into a Single Mark

Let's consider a set of grades earned by a typical student in Mr. Nickels's class, who earned a mark of B, and a set of grades of a typical student in Ms. Dimes's class, who also earned a B (see Table 12.2). Remember, both teachers used the same measurement instruments and applied the same scoring schemes to those instruments. Also, consistent with good measurement practice, they included only *achievement* factors in assigning their marks, not *nonachievement* factors such as attendance, conduct, appearance, effort, or other such factors.

Simply looking at the data in Table 12.2 indicates that student performance was different in an important way. Ms. Dimes's students obtained very low test and quiz grades but had very high homework and term paper grades, while Mr. Nickels's student displayed an opposite tendency. Yet both earned about the same number of overall points out of a possible 170, and both received B's. Since both teachers emphasize test and quiz grades over homework and term paper grades, this doesn't make sense, especially when one considers that Ms. Dimes's student had the lowest grade on one quiz and the second lowest grade on the final test—yet still earned a mark of B! To understand how this happened, we must consider how the teachers weighted and combined the obtained component scores.

Ms. Dimes, doing what most teachers commonly do in such situations, simply assigned double weight to the quiz and test scores and then added the scores:

$$(76 \times 2) + (5 \times 2) + (7 \times 2) + 25 + 25 = 226$$

Next, she divided this number by the total number of points possible, $(100 \times 2) + (10 \times 2) + (10 \times 2) + 25 + 25 = 290$, to arrive at the percentage of points earned by the student:

$$(226/290) \times 100 = 78\%$$

Since the district mandated that students who earn 78–88.99% of possible points be assigned a B, she assigned a mark of B to this student and followed the same procedure for all her students. Thus, even though Ms. Dimes herself believes that test and quiz performance is most important, and "weighted" those scores to reflect her belief, this student ended up with a grade of B in spite of having the lowest grade on one of the quizzes and close to the lowest grade on the final test! Unknowingly and unintentionally, Ms. Dimes is employing a combining and weighting procedure that contradicts her beliefs and her intent.

TABLE 12.2   Grades of Nickels's and Dimes's Students

	Student (Nickels's)	Student (Dimes's)
Semester test (75–100)	86	76
Quiz no. 1 (5–10)	9	5
Quiz no. 2 (5–10)	9	7
Homework (15–25)	18	25
Paper (15–25)	18	25
Total points earned	**140**	**138**

Note: The lowest and highest scores for each component are in parentheses.

Mr. Nickels assigned the *same weight* to the various components as did Ms. Dimes. However, he recalled that in his tests and measurements class, his instructor emphasized the importance of considering the *variation*, or *range*, of the scores, not just the scores themselves, in combining component scores into a *composite score*. Mr. Nickels also recalled that the reason for this is that *it is the extent of the variability of the scores of each component that largely determines the extent of the component's contribution to the composite score, NOT simply the weight attached to the component*.

Notice that each of the grade components was scored using scales of different ranges. The range is obtained by subtracting the lowest score from the highest score. A more accurate estimate of variation, called the *standard deviation* (covered in Chapter 14), is actually preferable to the range when combining component scores into a composite score. However, the range is an adequate estimate for most classroom purposes and is less time consuming and easier to compute than the standard deviation. Here are the ranges for the five score components:

Component	*Range*
Semester test	$100 - 75 = 25$
Quiz no. 1	$10 - 5 = 5$
Quiz no. 2	$10 - 5 = 5$
Homework	$25 - 15 = 10$
Paper	$25 - 15 = 10$

After determining the range for each of the components, Mr. Nickels decided to *equate the variability of each component before he could double the weights of the quizzes and the tests*. Since the semester test had the greatest range, 25 points, he did so by multiplying the quizzes by 5, the homework grade by 2.5, and the paper grade by 2.5. This procedure *equated* the variability of the scores (i.e., all components then had a range of 25 points). Only then did he *weight* the scores by multiplying the quiz and test scores by 2. Table 12.3 illustrates the procedure followed by Mr. Nickels. The maximum number of points possible, after equating and weighting, is $525(200 + 100 + 100 + 62.5 + 62.5 = 525)$. Dividing the points earned by the points possible gives us the student's percentage:

$$(442/525) \times 100 = 84.19\%$$

Recalling that the district's policy is to assign a B to all students who earn between 78% and 88.99% of possible points, Mr. Nickels assigned a mark of B to this student—the same mark assigned by Ms. Dimes to her student, in spite of this student's significantly better test and quiz performance.

Which procedure best achieved the teacher's goals, that is, to weight test and quiz performance *twice* as heavily as homework and term paper performance? Which procedure do you think is more fair? Which procedure is less likely to result in a storm of protest from the students, who will invariably compare their scores and marks?

TABLE 12.3 Weighting Procedure Followed by Mr. Nickels

	Score	×	Equating Factor	=	Equated Score	×	Weight	=	Weighted Score
Semester test	86	×	1		86	×	2		172
Quiz no. 1	9	×	5		45	×	2		90
Quiz no. 2	9	×	5		45	×	2		90
Homework	18	×	2.5		45	×	1		45
Paper	18	×	2.5		45	×	1		45
Total									**442**

TABLE 12.4 Effect of Mr. Nickels's Correct Procedure on Ms. Dimes's Student's Mark

	Score	×	Equating Factor	=	Equated Score	×	Weight	=	Weighted Score
Semester test	76	×	1		76	×	2		152
Quiz no. 1	5	×	5		25	×	2		50
Quiz no. 2	7	×	5		35	×	2		70
Homework	25	×	2.5		62.5	×	1		62.5
Paper	25	×	2.5		62.5	×	1		62.5
Total									**397.0**

Let's consider one more example. This time let's compare the effects of Mr. Nickels's correct procedure on the mark earned by Ms. Dimes's student, as shown in Table 12.4. Dividing the total points earned after equating and weighting (397) by the total points possible (525) gives us the percentage of points earned:

$$(397/525) \times 100 = 75.6\%$$

According to the district's policy, this student mark would be a C. Clearly, it is more fair that this student, who has such low test and quiz grades, be assigned a lower semester mark than a student whose test and quiz grades are significantly higher.

We hope that this example sensitizes you to a potential problem in assigning semester or grading period marks. When developing a composite mark from scores with different ranges or variation, remember to *equate before you weight* to avoid the problem encountered by Ms. Dimes.

However, in the face of the increasing demands placed on today's classroom teacher, finding the time to go through the outlined procedures may prove to be frustrating. Furthermore, in these examples, we have only considered a limited sample of mark components: test, quiz, homework, and paper. Today, most teachers also have to include marks for performance assessments, portfolios, and notebooks in their composite semester or other marking period summary marks. As important as it may be to accuracy in measurement, remembering to equate all these components before you weight may be lost in the face of the other important instructional, administrative, and legal considerations that today's classroom teacher faces. To guard against such an oversight, we will next present equating procedures that are less computationally complex, less time consuming, and more congruent with the typical teacher's intuitive marking practices.

PRACTICAL APPROACHES TO EQUATING BEFORE WEIGHTING IN THE BUSY CLASSROOM

The approaches we present in this section represent compromises between the equating approach taken by Mr. Nickels and the nonequating approach taken by Ms. Dimes. Technically, even Mr. Nickels's approach is a compromise since, from a statistical perspective, the standard deviation rather than the range is the preferred variability measure to be used in developing a composite score or mark. We believe that the following methods represent an efficient way for busy teachers to incorporate equating considerations (although they are approximations) into their marking procedures. By presenting these methods, we hope to minimize the likelihood that equating will be overlooked completely.

Performance and portfolio assessments require a substantial commitment of teacher time and learner-engaged time. Consequently, a teacher who decides to use them should ensure that the performance assessment has substantial weight in the 6-week or final report card grade. The following equating methods lend themselves well to the relatively straightforward inclusion of these important additional measures to the traditional test, quiz, homework, and paper components of a mark.

Front-End Equating

The front-end equating approach requires that you immediately convert all grades assigned into a 100-point scale (i.e., a percentage) by dividing the number of points obtained on every component by the total number of points possible and multiplying by 100. For example, a student who obtains 37 of 50 possible points on a performance assessment would be assigned a grade of 74:

$$(37/50) \times 100 = 74\%$$

This is a very common practice followed by many teachers. If all components (e.g., tests, quizzes) are similarly converted, then all grades will be on the same 100-point scale. Each component will then have the same potential range of 100 points; you have thereby equated the scores without having to go through Mr. Nickels's more time-consuming (but more technically correct) procedure.[1] Computing the composite mark, then, simply involves averaging the grades for each component, multiplying these averages by the weight assigned to the component, and adding the products to determine the final grade. Figure 12.1 provides examples of three formulas to accomplish this.

Back-End Equating

With the "back-end" approach, you decide how many points each component of your marking system is worth on a case-by-case basis. You may want some tests to be worth 40 points, some 75, some 14, and so on, since the total point value should depend on the complexity of the items and the number of discriminations you can reliably make, rather than a multiple of 5 or 10, as is common practice. Similarly, some homework assignments may be worth 10 points, or 7 points; portfolios may be worth 23 points, or 64 points, and so on. The front-end approach requires you to convert the scores into percentages before combining them. As we shall see, the next approach addresses this consideration at the back end rather than the beginning of the process. Both approaches will lead to the same outcome, so experiment with both until you find one that best fits your style. Here are the procedures involved in setting up a back-end marking scheme for a 6-week marking period.

Step 1: Identify the components of your marking system and assign each component a weight. Recall that a weight is the percentage of total points a particular component carries. For example,

Component	Weight
Homework	15%
Objective tests	20%
Performance tests	20%
Portfolio	20%
Classroom work	15%
Notebook	10%
	100%

[1] This approach and the following approach are intended to promote comparable variation in scale scores across components that will be combined into a final mark. They assume that the variation of actual scale scores for each component will be approximately the same, that is, that you use the full or comparable portions of the scale across components.

Marking Formula Example #1:

This formula is known as the "One, Two, Three Times Plan."

Homework and classwork:

All grades recorded for homework and classwork will be totaled and averaged.

The average grade will count once (one-sixth of the 6-week mark).

Example homework and classwork grades:

84, 81, 88, 92, 96, 85, 78, 83, 91, 79, 89, 94 = 1040/12 = 86.7 = 87 average

Quizzes:

All of the quizzes are totaled and averaged. This average grade will count two times (one-third of the 8-week mark).

Example quiz grades:

82, 88, 80, 91, 78, 86 = 505/6 = 84.2 = 84 average

Performance assessments:

All of the performance assessment grades will be totaled and averaged. This average grade will count three times (one-half of the 6-week mark).

Example performance assessment grades:

81, 91, 86 = 258/3 = 86 average

Then, the 6-week mark would be computed as follows:

87 (one time) + 84 + 84 (two times) + 86 + 86 + 86 (three times) = 513/6 = 85.5 = 86 as the 6-week mark.

Marking Formula Example #2:

This formula is known as the "Percentages Plan."

A teacher determines a percentage for each component. For example, homework and classwork will count for 20% of the grade, quizzes will count for 40% of the grade, and performance assessments will count for 40% of the grade. Using the same scores as previously listed, a student's mark would be computed as follows:

20% of the 86.7 for homework and classwork is 17.3,

40% of the 84.2 for quizzes is 33.7, and

40% of the 86 for performance assessments is 34.4

17.3 + 33.7 + 34.4 = 85.4 as the 6-week mark.

(This mark differs from the mark obtained from Example 1 because the weight put on each component differs in the two examples.)

Marking Formula Example #3:

This formula is known as the "Language Arts Plan." A language arts teacher determines that the publishing, goal meeting, journal, and daily process grades each count one-fourth (25%) of the 6-week mark. A language arts mark will be computed as follows:

The publishing grade, issued at the end of the 6-week period, is 88.

The goal-meeting grade, issued at the end of the 6-week period, is 86.

The journal grades are 82 + 92 + 94 + 90 + 88 + 86 = 532/6 = 88.7 = 89.

The daily process grades are 78 + 82 + 94 + 94 + 91 + 86 = 525/6 = 87.5 = 88.

The 6-week mark would be 88 + 86 + 89 + 88 = 351/4 = 87.75 = 88.

FIGURE 12.1   Three examples of different front-end ways to equate and weight a 6-week mark based on grades from a 100-point scale.

Step 2: Record the actual points earned out of the total possible in the grade book. Leave a row for totals. These scores are illustrated in Figure 12.2. As you can see, each component and each separate assignment have varying numbers of points possible to be earned. Assign possible points for each component based on the length of the assignment, your ability to make reliable distinctions, and so on.

Step 3: Total the actual points earned for each component and divide this by the possible points and multiply by 100. The results represent the percentage of points earned for each particular component. In our example from Figure 12.2, Cornell and Rosie earned the following total points:

	Cornell	*Rosie*
Homework	50/70 = 71	55/70 = 79
Objective tests	45/60 = 75	35/60 = 58
Performance tests	33/40 = 83	39/40 = 98
Portfolio	18/20 = 90	15/20 = 75
Classroom work	39/50 = 78	37/50 = 74
Notebook	5/10 = 50	8/10 = 80

Step 4: Multiply each of these percentages by the weights assigned, as shown here, and then sum the products.

Component	Dates	Cornell	Rosie
Homework	8/20	10/10	10/10
	9/7	8/10	5/10
	9/14	14/15	12/15
	9/20	10/10	8/10
	9/28	8/15	12/15
	10/6	0/10	8/10
	Total	**50/70**	**55/70**
Objective tests	9/17	20/30	15/30
	10/7	25/30	20/30
	Total	**45/60**	**35/60**
Performance tests	9/23	15/20	20/20
	10/8	18/20	19/20
	Total	**33/40**	**39/40**
Portfolio	**10/7**	**18/20**	**15/20**
Classwork	9/2	9/10	8/10
	9/6	7/15	14/15
	9/14	10/10	0/10
	9/23	9/10	10/10
	10/5	4/5	5/5
	Total	**39/50**	**37/50**
Notebook	**10/8**	**5/10**	**8/10**

FIGURE 12.2 Sample grade recording sheet, first 6 weeks.

	Cornell	*Rosie*
Homework	$71 \times 0.15 = 10.7$	$79 \times 0.15 = 11.9$
Objective tests	$75 \times 0.20 = 15.0$	$58 \times 0.20 = 11.6$
Performance tests	$83 \times 0.20 = 16.6$	$98 \times 0.20 = 19.6$
Portfolio	$90 \times 0.20 = 18.0$	$75 \times 0.20 = 15.0$
Classroom work	$78 \times 0.15 = 11.7$	$74 \times 0.15 = 11.1$
Notebook	$50 \times 0.10 = \;\,5.0$	$80 \times 0.10 = \;\,8.0$
Totals	**77.0**	**77.2**

Step 5: Record the 6-week mark either as a letter grade (e.g., A = 90–100, and B = 80–89.99) or as the total (i.e., percentage) for each student, depending on your district's policy.

Although the approaches we have presented involve a lot of manual calculation for a class of 25–30 students, use of a spreadsheet can speed up the process significantly. Simply create formulas in a spreadsheet and then input the scores. The program will then convert the scores you input into their equated and weighted scores, and the final mark or composite score. If you are not spreadsheet savvy, consult with someone who is—this can be a real-time saver at the end of the marking period!

SUMMARY

This chapter introduced you to various issues related to marks and marking systems. Its major points are as follows:

1. Marks are used to provide information about student achievement.

2. Marks should reflect academic achievement and nothing more. Grades for attitude, effort, improvement, conduct, and so on should be recorded separately from marks.

3. Marks often reflect factors other than achievement and are often assigned according to a variety of marking systems. This makes valid comparisons of marks across schools, and even across teachers, difficult at best.

4. Several types of marking systems are employed in the schools today. These involve comparison of a student with:
   a. Other students (grades depend on how well the student did compared with other students).
   b. Established standards (grades depend on how well a student's performance compares with preestablished standards).
   c. Aptitude (grades depend on how consistent a student's actual achievement is with his or her achievement potential).
   d. Effort (grades depend on how hard the student works).
   e. Improvement (grades depend on how much progress a student makes over the course of instruction).

5. Each system has its advantages and disadvantages, but marking based on comparisons with established standards seems to best fit the main function of marks—to provide feedback about academic achievement.

6. The symbols most commonly used in marking systems are letter grades (A–F, E–U) and numerical grades (0–100). Such symbol systems are often combined with checklists to provide specific information about factors such as skill level, conduct, and attitude.

7. When combining grades from quizzes, tests, papers, homework, and so on, that have different ranges or variation and that are not on 100-point scales, equate the variability of each component before weighting and computing the final mark.

8. A practical alternative to this technique is to use the front-end or back-end equating approaches. These approaches yield approximate but similar outcomes, and they are less time-consuming ways to equate scores from quizzes, tests, homework, performance assessments, portfolios, and notebooks.

FOR DISCUSSION AND PRACTICE

1. List the pros and cons of each of the following types of marking systems:

   a. Comparison with other students

   b. Comparison with established standards

   c. Comparison of achievement with one's own aptitude

   d. Basing grades on effort

   e. Basing grades on improvement

2. Create a numerical scale for measuring effort and another for measuring improvement. For each level of the scale, indicate the type of behavior(s) you are looking for. What might be another way of measuring these two qualities?

3. Choose the most appropriate marking system among the following pairs of symbol systems and give reasons for your choices.

   A–F and 0–100

   0–100 and P–F

   E–U and P–F

*Answer for question 5 appears in Appendix B.

4. The school in which you will teach will probably have an established marking system to report subject matter grades. With what behaviors might you augment this marking system to report to students and parents the additional information you think is important? How would you measure these additional behaviors?

*5.** Using the following scores obtained from a single student, use both the front-end and back-end methods to determine an overall mark: Quiz, 10 out of 15; test, 32 out of 50; paper, 8 out of 10; homework, 80 out of 100; and portfolio, 9 out of 10. You decided that the quiz, test, paper, homework, and portfolio would be weighted 15, 30, 30, 10, and 15% of the final mark, respectively. What is the final numerical mark? What letter grade would be assigned if A = 90–100, B = 80–89.99, C = 70–79.99, D = 65–69.99, and F = 64.99 and below? If both approaches yield the same numerical mark, explain why. If the procedures yield different numerical marks, explain why.

CHAPTER 13

SUMMARIZING DATA AND MEASURES OF CENTRAL TENDENCY

LEARNING OUTCOMES

After completion of this chapter, the student will be able to:

1. Define statistics.
2. Give examples of statistics that we all deal with in everyday life.
3. Explain why statistics are important to the classroom teacher.
4. Compare and contrast simple lists, simple frequency distributions, and grouped frequency distributions.
5. Compare the advantages and limitations of each approach to organizing and tabulating data.
6. Compute the appropriate number of intervals and interval width for a grouped frequency distribution.
7. Compare and contrast histograms, frequency polygons, and smoothed curves.
8. Apply text guidelines to construct histograms, frequency polygons, and smooth curves.
9. Compare and contrast positively skewed, symmetrical, and negatively skewed distributions.
10. Determine the mean, median, and mode, given a set of data.
11. Explain why the mean is influenced by extreme scores.
12. Correctly locate the relative positions of the measures of central tendency in various distributions represented by smooth curves.
13. Compute the median for an even and an odd number of scores.
14. Explain why the median is a special kind of percentile.
15. Compute values of the median and other percentiles in a distribution.
16. Identify the measure of central tendency that best represents the data in various distributions.
17. Explain why the mode is the least stable measure of central tendency.
18. Draw conclusions about data based on the measures of central tendency and/or smooth curves based on the data.
19. Compare and contrast the measures of central tendency.

FOR MANY, the term *statistics* forebodes evil. It is probably one of the most misunderstood terms in education. A statistician, or statistical expert, is stereotypically seen as a social isolate who lacks a sense of humor, speaks in strange tongues, and knows how to make numbers say whatever he or she desires them to say. Indeed, in some doctoral programs, courses in statistics are acceptable as substitutes for foreign languages! Having taught statistics courses, both authors are keenly aware of the anxiety and/or resentment many students feel when they are required or encouraged to take their first statistics course. As we mentioned in Chapter 1, however, fewer than 1% of the students we have taught fail courses in tests and measurement because of statistics. Then why are students so anxious about statistics?

The answer, we believe, lies in the misconceptions students have about statistics and statisticians. Let's clarify some things. We do not intend that you become full-fledged statisticians after completing this section of the text. In fact, a complete program of graduate study is usually necessary before one can call oneself a statistician. Perhaps you know students who suffered through an introductory statistics course. Will you have to undergo the trauma they may have undergone? Again, the answer is no. Even introductory courses treat statistics in much greater depth than is necessary for an introductory course in tests and measurement. If you did well on the self-test and review in Appendix A, you have little to fear. If you failed to do well, brush up on the fundamentals presented in Appendix A until you perform well. After you complete the review, it should be apparent that the four basic functions—addition, subtraction, multiplication, and division—will suffice for the statistics we will deal with. Master these operations, and with a little work (and an open mind), mastery of statistics at the tests and measurement level will soon follow.

WHAT ARE STATISTICS?

Thus far, we have been talking about statistics in general. In reality, there are two types of statistics: descriptive and inferential. For our purposes, we will deal entirely with the "easy" side of statistics, descriptive statistics. Inferential statistics are more complicated and are best taught in more advanced courses.

Descriptive statistics are simply numbers, for example, percentages, numerals, fractions, and decimals. These numbers are used to describe or summarize a larger body of numbers. For example, if you wanted to give someone an indication of how your grades have been in college, you could list all your courses and the grade you received in each course, or you could simply report your grade point average (GPA). Both approaches have advantages and disadvantages, of course, but we think you will agree that reporting your GPA would normally be the most useful approach. In this example, the GPA is a descriptive or summary statistic, since it describes or summarizes extensive data.

In the classroom, the typical teacher may have 25–30 pupils. When a test is administered to the class, 25–30 test scores result. If a teacher gives 10 tests over the year, 250–300 test scores result. Naturally, these scores would be recorded in the teacher's grade book or computer spreadsheet, but when it comes time to report grades to parents at the end of the year, are they all reported? Obviously not. Instead, teachers report descriptive or summary statistics—that is, grades—probably without realizing they are reporting statistics!

Any time you deal with averages (GPAs, batting averages), rates (death rates, birth rates), or other numbers used to describe or summarize a larger body of numbers, you are dealing with descriptive or summary statistics. All of us deal with statistics daily. One of our goals for this chapter is to make you better users and consumers of such information. We hope to do this by going a little beyond commonsense statistics and looking at statistics and its uses more systematically.

WHY USE STATISTICS?

As we said, the term *statistics* is frequently misunderstood. Although some people want nothing to do with statistics, statistics are important and appear to be an increasingly important aspect of our personal as well as professional lives. Any time you read, hear, or see "a 70% chance of rain" or "82% of doctors surveyed recommend" or "an EPA average of 32 miles per gallon," you are being exposed to statistics. Exposure to statistics will not go away. The ability to understand and profit from everyday descriptive statistics is well within your reach. You will become a better interpreter of educational data (and thus a better teacher) by mastering the statistical concepts presented in this section of the text.

You will also become a better consumer of everyday data presented in advertising, public relations, opinion polls, and so forth. Much of what you learn in teacher training may seem to have little application outside the classroom. This is not the case for statistics. Master the concepts in this chapter, and they will serve you throughout your personal and professional life.

With increasing calls for accountability, it will become all the more important that classroom teachers understand the statistics reported to them and the statistics they report to others. Needless to say, the teacher who understands the uses and limitations of various kinds of statistical data will have a decided advantage over the teacher who lacks such understanding. While your professional survival and development may not depend entirely on a working knowledge of statistics, they may certainly be enhanced by it.

TABULATING FREQUENCY DATA

The classroom teacher normally deals with a large amount of data, usually in the form of test scores. As more and more scores accumulate, it gets more and more difficult to make sense of the data. And it becomes more difficult to answer questions such as the following:

How many people are above average?

How many scored above the cutoff passing score?

Did most of the class do well on the test?

What is the highest or lowest score?

Keeping these questions in mind, consider the following set of scores obtained by 25 sixth-grade children on a math test:

36	63	51	43	93
54	48	84	36	45
57	45	48	96	66
54	72	81	30	27
45	51	47	63	88

Without doing anything to these test scores, are you able to answer the questions? You cannot answer the first two questions until you compute the average score and establish the cutoff or passing score. But what about the last two questions?

You can eventually answer these questions, but it takes a lot of time to do so. In arriving at answers to the last two questions, you probably resorted to some sort of strategy to organize the data so that they make sense. For example, to determine whether "most of the class did well," you may have crossed off and counted the number of scores in the 80s and 90s.

Whatever strategy you used, you used it because the 25 scores, as they stood, were difficult to make sense of or to interpret. Next, we will consider several systematic ways to make sense of an unwieldy group of numbers. We will be organizing and introducing some sort of order to unorganized, unordered test scores. The first method is to simply list the scores in ascending or descending numerical order.

The List

Let's list our set of 25 scores in descending order:

96	72	54	48	43
93	66	54	47	36
88	63	51	45	36
84	63	51	45	30
81	57	48	45	27

Introducing some order or "sense" into this group of scores makes trends, patterns, and individual scores easier to find and interpret. At a glance, we can now determine the highest score, lowest score, and even the middle score. We can easily see that only five students scored above 80 on the test. Listing has helped us organize this set of scores. But what if we had 50 scores, or 100 scores, or 1,000 scores?

As the number of scores increases, the advantage of simply listing scores decreases. Many scores will repeat themselves several times. It becomes more and more difficult to make sense of data when the number of scores would require a lot of paper. Also, when you list data, there are usually many missing scores (e.g., 95, 94, 92, 91, 90, 89, 87, and so on in the previous example). Failure to consider these missing scores can sometimes result in a misrepresentation of the data.

To sum up, a simple list summarizes data conveniently if N, the number of scores, is small. If N is large, however, lists become difficult to interpret. Trends are not always very clear, numbers tend to repeat themselves, and there are usually a lot of missing scores. Next we will consider a *simple frequency distribution*. This approach to tabulating data considers all scores, including those that are missing.

The Simple Frequency Distribution

Inspecting the simple frequency distribution in Table 13.1 may cause as much or more confusion as the original group of 25 unorganized scores. Usually, for classroom purposes, a simple frequency distribution is too unwieldy. Unless your tests yield a narrow spread of scores, simple frequency distributions tend to be so lengthy that it is difficult to make sense of the data, which is what we are trying to do. Seldom will a simple frequency distribution prove useful in the average classroom.

TABLE 13.1 Simple Frequency Distribution

X (Score)	f (Frequency)	X (Score)	f (Frequency)
96	1	61	0
95	0	60	0
94	0	59	0
93	1	58	0
92	0	57	1
91	0	56	0
90	0	55	0
89	0	54	2
88	1	53	0
87	0	52	0
86	0	51	2
85	0	50	0
84	1	49	0
83	0	48	2
82	0	47	1
81	1	46	0
80	0	45	3
79	0	44	0
78	0	43	1
77	0	42	0
76	0	41	0
75	0	40	0
74	0	39	0
73	0	38	0
72	1	37	0
71	0	36	2
70	0	35	0
69	0	34	0
68	0	33	0
67	0	32	0
66	1	31	0
65	0	30	1
64	0	29	0
63	2	28	0
62	0	27	1

In summary, a simple frequency distribution will summarize data effectively *only* if the spread of scores is small. If there is a large amount of variation in test scores, a simple frequency distribution usually results in a table similar to Table 13.1, full of zeros in the frequency column and with so many categories that it becomes difficult to interpret the data. Fortunately, a variation of the simple frequency distribution, called the *grouped frequency distribution*, eliminates these shortcomings and can be quite useful in the classroom. Let's consider this variation.

The Grouped Frequency Distribution

The grouped frequency distribution method of tabulating data is very similar to the simple frequency distribution, except that ranges or intervals of scores are used for categories rather than considering each possible score as a category. The following is a grouped frequency distribution for the 25 scores we've been talking about:

Interval	f
91–97	2
84–90	2
77–83	1
70–76	1
63–69	3
56–62	1
49–55	4
42–48	7
35–41	2
28–34	1
21–27	1

Compare this grouped frequency distribution with the simple frequency distribution and with the listing of scores. The grouped frequency distribution has two major advantages over the listing and the simple frequency distribution. It compresses the size of the table and makes the data much more interpretable. At a glance, it becomes apparent that most of the class (as indicated by the numbers in the frequency column) obtained scores of 55 or below. If we add the numbers in the f column, we can see specifically that 15 $(4 + 7 + 2 + 1 + 1 = 15)$ of the 25 students in the class scored 55 or below. That is, four students scored between 49 and 55, seven scored between 42 and 48, two scored between 35 and 41, one scored between 28 and 34, and one scored between 21 and 27.

Since most of the class scored 55 or lower, one interpretation that the grouped frequency distribution helps us make is that the test may have been too difficult. However, at least three other possible interpretations are suggested: Perhaps the students simply failed to prepare for the test; perhaps the students need more instruction in this area; or perhaps the instruction was ineffective or inappropriate.

Whichever of these interpretations is correct is irrelevant to us at the moment. What is important is that once we construct a grouped frequency distribution, it quickly becomes apparent that the class did not do well on the test. We may have arrived at the same conclusion after looking at the listing of scores or at the simple frequency distribution, but it certainly would take longer. Thus, a grouped frequency distribution helps us make sense of a set of scores. But there are also disadvantages to using a grouped frequency distribution.

The main disadvantage of a grouped frequency distribution is that information about individual scores is lost. As a result, the information we deal with becomes less accurate. Consider the interval of scores 49–55 in the previous grouped frequency distribution. We see that four scores fell in this interval. However, exactly what were these scores? Were they 49, 51, 53, and 55? Or were they 49, 50, 51, and 54? Or were all four scores 49? Or were two scores 52 and two scores 53? Or 51? The four scores could be any conceivable combination of scores. Without referring to the original list of scores, we cannot tell.

Although a grouped frequency distribution compresses table size and makes data easier to interpret, it does so at the expense of accuracy and information about individual scores. Usually, the advantages of constructing grouped frequency distributions are great enough to offset the disadvantages. Next, we will consider the five steps involved in actually constructing a grouped frequency distribution.

Steps in Constructing a Grouped Frequency Distribution

Step 1: Determine the range of scores (symbolized by R). The range (or spread) of scores is determined by subtracting the lowest score (L) from the highest score (H).

$$\textit{Formula} \qquad \textit{Application}$$
$$R = H - L \qquad R = 96 - 27 = 69$$

The range of scores for the 25 sixth graders is 69.

Step 2: Determine the appropriate number of intervals. The number of intervals or categories used in a grouped frequency distribution is somewhat flexible or arbitrary. Different authorities will suggest that you select from among 5, 10, or 15 intervals, or 8, 10, 12, or 15 intervals, and so on. In our example, we used 11 intervals. Well, then, what is "correct"?

As we said, this decision is somewhat arbitrary. In making such decisions, though, be sure to use as many categories or intervals as are necessary to demonstrate variations in the frequencies of scores. In other words, if you decide to use five intervals and find that for an N of 25 scores there are frequencies of five in each interval, the number of intervals is too small. Increasing the number of intervals to 10 in this case should result in different frequencies for each interval. Selecting too many intervals is also a possibility.

Step 3: Divide the range by the number of intervals you decide to use and round to the nearest odd number. This will give you i, the interval width:

$$\textit{Formula} \qquad\qquad \textit{Application}$$
$$i = \frac{R}{\text{number of intervals}} \qquad i = \frac{69}{10}$$

The width of the interval is 7. If we decided to use 8 for our number of intervals, we would arrive at a wider interval width.

$$\textit{Formula} \qquad\qquad \textit{Application}$$
$$i = \frac{R}{\text{number of intervals}} \qquad i = \frac{69}{8}$$
$$= 8.6 \text{ (rounded to nearest odd number} = 9)$$

If we decided to use 15 intervals, we would arrive at a narrower interval width than we would with 10 or 8 intervals.

$$\textit{Formula} \qquad\qquad \textit{Application}$$
$$i = \frac{R}{\text{number of intervals}} \qquad i = \frac{69}{15}$$
$$= 4.6 \text{ (rounded to nearest odd number} = 5)$$

You can see there is an inverse relationship between the number of intervals and the width of each interval. That is, as fewer intervals are used, the width of each interval increases; as more intervals are used, the interval width decreases. Also, keep in mind that as i, the interval width, increases, we lose more and more information about individual scores.

Step 4: Construct the interval column making sure that the lowest score in each interval, called the lower limit (LL), is a multiple of the interval width (i). The upper limit (UL) of each interval is one point less than the LL of the next interval. All this means is that the lowest score of each interval should be a value that is equal to the interval width times 1, 2, 3, and so on. With an interval width of 7, the LL of each interval could be 7, 14, 21, and so forth (7×1, 7×2, 7×3, etc.). However, we eliminate those intervals below and above the intervals that include or "capture" the lowest and highest scores. Consider the following sets of intervals for which the highest score was 96 and the lowest score was 27:

Lower Limit	Upper Limit	
112	118	
105	111	
98	104	
91	97	← Highest score captured;
84	90	eliminate all intervals above.
77	83	
70	76	
63	69	
56	62	
49	55	
42	48	
35	41	
28	34	
21	27	← Lowest score captured;
14	20	eliminate all intervals below.
7	13	

We retain only the intervals 21–27 through 91–97. Thus, the interval column of our grouped frequency distribution should look like this:

Intervals

91–97
84–90
77–83
70–76
63–69
56–62
49–55
42–48
35–41
28–34
21–27

Step 5: Construct the f, or frequency column by tallying the number of scores that are captured by each interval.

Intervals	Tally	f
91–97	||	2
84–90	||	2
77–83	|	1
70–76	|	1
63–69	|||	3
56–62	|	1
49–55	||||	4
42–48	|||| ||	7
35–41	||	2
28–34	|	1
21–27	|	1

Next, simply eliminate the tally column, and you have a grouped frequency distribution.

However, didn't we decide we wanted 10 intervals? How is it we ended up with 11? The answer to the first question is yes, but it is not unusual to end up with one more or one less interval than you intended. This happens because of what we often end up doing at Step 3.

At Step 3, we round to the nearest odd number. The inaccuracy we introduce by rounding to the nearest odd number is multiplied by the number of intervals (since in effect we do this for each interval). The result is that the range from the UL of the highest interval to the LL of the lowest interval is greater than the range from the highest score to the lowest score. In our example:

$$
\begin{array}{lr}
\text{Upper limit of highest interval} & 97 \\
\text{Lower limit of lowest interval} & \underline{-21} \\
& 76 \\
\\
\text{High score} & 96 \\
\text{Low score} & \underline{-27} \\
& 69
\end{array}
$$

Notice the difference between 76 and 69. The extra interval is needed to include the extra values. Fortunately, ending up with one more or one less interval than we intended is not a serious problem. We need only to be aware of it, not unduly concerned with it.

Before we leave grouped frequency distributions, let's clarify one more point. In Step 3, we said "round to the nearest odd number." There is no sound mathematical reason for this recommendation. Rather, it serves to simplify determining the midpoint of the interval. While the midpoint is of little importance for grouped frequency distributions, it is important in the construction of a frequency polygon, a graphical representation of a grouped frequency distribution, which we will consider next.

GRAPHING DATA

"A picture is worth a thousand words" is a well-worn expression, but it is especially applicable to statistics. Some of you may have the ability to extract meaning from groups of numbers, but others, the authors included, need to see graphical representations before such data can be meaningful.

In any case, a graph will almost always clarify or simplify the information presented in a grouped frequency distribution. We will consider three types of graphs: the *bar graph*, or *histogram*; the *frequency polygon*; and the *smooth curve*.

The Bar Graph, or Histogram

The bar graph, or histogram, is the type of graph used most frequently to convey statistical data. The histogram in Figure 13.1 is based on the grouped frequency distribution used earlier to represent the scores of 25 sixth graders.

In constructing a histogram, or bar graph, several guidelines, which are listed in Figure 13.2, should be followed. The interpretation of bar graphs is straightforward. The higher the column, the greater the number of scores falling in that interval. The lower the column, the fewer the number of scores falling in that interval.

The Frequency Polygon

Technically, a frequency polygon is best used for graphically representing what are called continuous data, such as test scores. Continuous data usually represent entities that can be expressed as fractions or parts of whole numbers, for example, achievement test scores and GPAs. Histograms are best used for graphically representing discrete or noncontinuous data. Discrete or noncontinuous data represent entities that usually cannot be expressed as fractionated parts of anything and, hence, signify different dimensions, for example, Catholics, Protestants, and Jews. However, we need not be overly concerned with discriminating between continuous and discrete data because much overlap exists in the actual ways these two types of graphs are used.

For our purposes, what is the critical difference between a histogram and a frequency polygon? The answer is that a frequency polygon is an alternative way of representing a grouped frequency distribution. It uses straight lines to connect the midpoint (MP) of each interval rather than bars or columns to show the frequency with which scores occur. The grouped frequency distribution with midpoints and the frequency polygon shown in Figure 13.3 represent the same group of scores we have been considering.

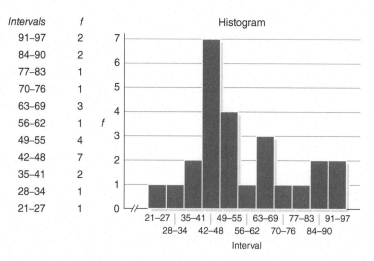

FIGURE 13.1   Histogram based on a grouped frequency distribution.

1. The vertical axis should be three-fourths as long as the horizontal axis to help prevent misrepresenting the data.
2. Scores are listed along the horizontal axis and increase from left to right. Frequencies are listed along the vertical axis and increase from bottom to top.
3. Double slash marks (//) are used to indicate breaks in the sequence of numbers (horizontal axis) or in the sequence of frequencies (vertical axis).
4. Points in the scales along the axes are expanded or compressed so that the range of scores and frequencies fit within the "three-fourths" guideline given above.
5. If an interval or intervals with frequencies of zero occur, these *must not* be omitted from the horizontal axis. To do so misrepresents the data. The following example illustrates this point.

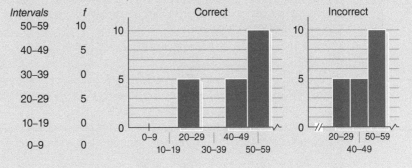

FIGURE 13.2 Guidelines for constructing a frequency histogram.

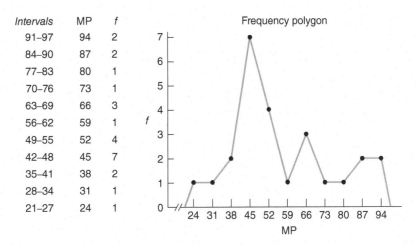

FIGURE 13.3 A grouped frequency distribution and frequency polygon.

Interpretation of the frequency polygon is similar to that of the histogram. The higher or lower the dots, the greater or lesser the number of scores in the interval.

Comparing the frequency polygon with the histogram demonstrates the same pattern of scores (see Figures 13.1 and 13.3). This is a perfectly logical finding, since they were both constructed from the same grouped frequency distribution, except that we add a midpoint column to construct a frequency polygon.

Determining the MP is straightforward and results in a whole number if the interval width is an odd number. Its determination results in a fractional number if the interval width is an even number. In either case, the midpoint is simply the middle score in each interval. If you mistrust your ability to determine the middle score in an interval, you can check yourself mathematically. Simply add the LL (lowest score in the interval) to the UL (highest score in the interval) and divide the sum of these two scores by 2 (see the examples that follow Fig. 13.4).

1. Construct the vertical axis three-fourths as long as the horizontal axis.
2. List scores along the horizontal axis and increasing from left to right, and list frequencies along the vertical axis, increasing from bottom to top.
3. Double slash marks (//) are used to indicate breaks in the sequence of numbers between scores and/or frequencies and zero points.
4. Points in the scales along the axes are expanded or compressed to fit the "three-fourths" guideline.
5. When intervals of zero frequency occur, the midpoints *must not* be omitted from the horizontal axis and the lines connecting the dots must be brought down to the baseline to represent zero frequencies.
6. The lines should also be brought down to the baseline halfway into the intervals above and below the highest and lowest intervals, as noted in the diagram below.

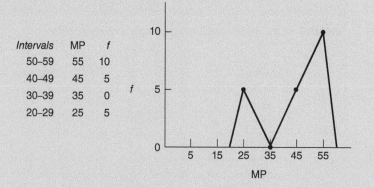

Intervals	MP	f
50–59	55	10
40–49	45	5
30–39	35	0
20–29	25	5

This guideline represents more of an aesthetic than a statistical consideration. A frequency polygon "tied" to the baseline has a better or more complete appearance, as shown below.

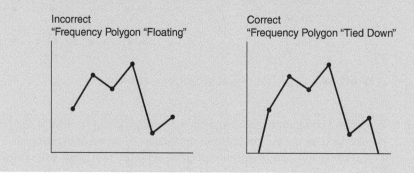

Incorrect
"Frequency Polygon "Floating"

Correct
"Frequency Polygon "Tied Down"

FIGURE 13.4   Guidelines for constructing a frequency polygon.

Formula   *Application*

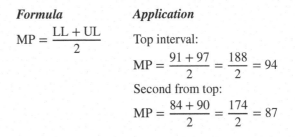

$$MP = \frac{LL + UL}{2}$$

Top interval:

$$MP = \frac{91 + 97}{2} = \frac{188}{2} = 94$$

Second from top:

$$MP = \frac{84 + 90}{2} = \frac{174}{2} = 87$$

Guidelines for constructing a frequency polygon appear in Figure 13.4. Notice that they are similar to those for histograms.

The Smooth Curve

Thus far, we have discussed two graphical ways of depicting data represented by a grouped frequency distribution: the histogram and the frequency polygon. Our topic for this section, the *smooth* or *smoothed* curve, is not really an appropriate way to represent data from grouped frequency distributions, since an accurate smooth curve requires that advanced mathematical calculations be computed. Nevertheless, we will make great use of a smooth curve as a general representation of groups of scores. An example of a smooth curve is provided in the following graph:

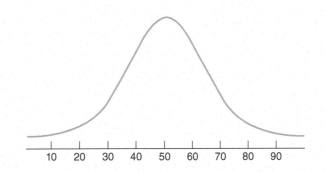

The curve represents a set of data. Note that it closely resembles a frequency polygon except that the *f*, or frequency, axis is omitted, and curved rather than straight lines are used. Although the *f* column is omitted, we can still make decisions about the frequency of occurrence of certain scores on the basis of the height of the curve. That is, scores in the 40–60 range were obtained by large numbers of students, while very few students obtained scores below 20 or above 80. With a histogram or frequency polygon, we could determine *exactly* how many students scored between 40 and 60 or above 80 or below 20 by referring to the *f* axis. However, we are willing to sacrifice this accuracy when dealing with smooth curves because we use these curves to depict the *shape* of a distribution rather than to accurately represent the data.

Smooth curves can easily be developed from existing histograms or frequency polygons by connecting the high points of the bars or midpoints of the intervals, as shown in Figure 13.5. Follow these two guidelines in constructing smooth curves:

1. Be sure your score axis increases from left to right.
2. Be sure the "tails" or ends of the curves come close to, but do not touch, the baseline.

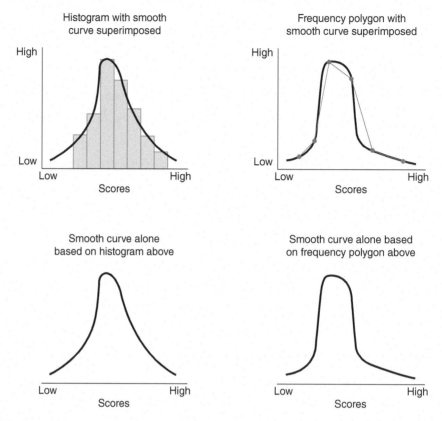

FIGURE 13.5   Smooth curves.

Remember, although we use smooth curves to give us an idea of the shape of a distribution, they also enable us to make general statements about the frequency of scores.

The higher the curve, the more frequently the same scores occur. The lower the curve, the less frequently the same scores occur. Next, let's consider two major characteristics of distributions: symmetry and skewness.

Symmetrical and Asymmetrical Distributions   There are two major types of distributions: symmetrical and asymmetrical. In a symmetrical distribution, each half or side of the distribution is a mirror image of the other side. An asymmetrical distribution, on the other hand, has nonmatching sides or halves. Both types of distributions are illustrated in the following graphs:

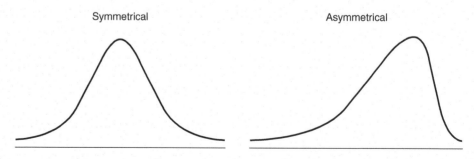

Symmetrical distributions can come in a variety of configurations. As illustrated, they may appear peaked, flattened, or somewhere in between:

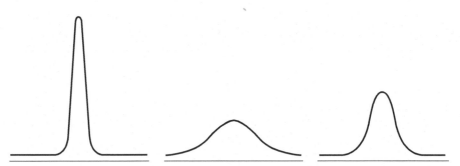

All three of these are symmetrical distributions. The distribution on the right, however, has special significance. It is a special kind of symmetrical distribution called a normal distribution. It has some unique characteristics that make it among the most important distributions in statistics. Practice drawing this distribution. You will be called on to draw it many times before leaving this section of the book. Technically, the normal distribution follows very precise mathematical rules, but as long as you can approximate the illustration you need not worry about its precise mathematical properties. We will have more to say about the normal curve later.

Positively and Negatively Skewed Distributions   There are also two types of skewness: positive skewness and negative skewness. A positively skewed distribution results from an asymmetrical distribution of scores. In this case, the majority of scores fall below the middle of the score distribution. There are many low scores but few high scores. A positively skewed distribution is illustrated as follows:

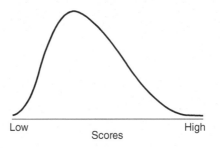

Low   High

Scores

In a classroom testing situation, a positively skewed distribution indicates that the class did poorly on the test (a majority of low scores and few high scores). The reasons for such poor performance could include these: The test was too difficult, teaching was ineffective, the students didn't study, or not enough time was allowed. A positively skewed distribution does not tell you why the class did poorly; it only informs you of the fact that they did poorly.

A negatively skewed distribution also results from an asymmetrical score distribution. In this type of distribution, the majority of scores fall above the middle of the score distribution. There are many high scores but few low scores. A negatively skewed distribution is illustrated as follows:

One interpretation attached to a negatively skewed distribution is that the class did well on the test (a majority had high scores and few had low scores). Again, there could be many reasons for this. The test may have been too easy, too much time may have been allowed, the class may be exceptionally bright, and so forth. Distributional shapes only describe data. They do not explain why the data take their shape.

We have discussed the what and why of statistics and have described methods for tabulating and depicting data. Next, we will discuss what are probably the most widely used (and frequently misunderstood) summary statistics, *measures of central tendency*.

MEASURES OF CENTRAL TENDENCY

There are three measures of central tendency: the *mean*, the *median*, and the *mode*. We will define each in turn, give an example or examples of its computation, and discuss its characteristics. The main point to remember about these measures is that they represent our best bet when we must rely on a single score to represent an entire distribution. Since we have three measures of central tendency, it may occur to you that each is more or less applicable in different situations. But before we go any further, test yourself to see if you are on top of the statistical jargon we have already presented. If you can define the terms listed in Figure 13.6, the jargon checklist, you are in good shape. If not, review these terms and commit them to memory to build your vocabulary and to prepare yourself to learn more terms later.

The Mean

Have you ever computed your grade average in elementary school, your GPA in college, your field goal average in basketball, or any other average? The mean is nothing more than the average of a group of scores:

$$\text{Average} = \text{mean}$$

Statistics	Frequency (f)
List	Midpoint (MP)
Simple frequency distribution	Histogram
Grouped frequency distribution	Frequency polygon
N	Smooth curve
Range (R)	Symmetrical distribution
Interval (i)	Normal distribution
Lower limit (LL)	Positively skewed distribution
Upper limit (UL)	Negatively skewed distribution

FIGURE 13.6 Jargon checklist.

The symbol we will use for the mean is M, the symbol that has been adopted in the American Psychological Association's style manual (American Psychological Association, 2004) to represent the mean. In previous editions of this text we have used $\overline{X}$ (pronounced "X bar") to represent the mean. Some texts continue to use $\overline{X}$ rather than M to symbolize the average or mean score, but most now use M, and so will we. Just in case you have forgotten how, we will compute a mean (our sneaky way of introducing a formula with, a couple of other unfamiliar symbols). The formula and its plain English interpretation appear here:

Formula	*Plain English Version*
$M = \dfrac{\Sigma X}{N}$	$\text{Average} = \dfrac{\text{sum of all the scores}}{\text{total number of scores}}$

The formula looks impressive. But as you can see, it (like all mathematical formulas) is only a shorthand way of describing the process you go through to compute an average. Let's have a closer look at the terms in the formula:

M = Symbol for the mean or arithmetic average

Σ = Sigma symbol used in mathematics that tells you to sum up whatever follows it

X = Symbol we will use from now on to represent a test score

N = Total number of scores in a distribution

Thus, Σ tells you to sum up the test scores, and $\Sigma X/N$ tells you to sum up the test scores and divide this value by the total number of scores in the distribution. Let's work an example for the following set of scores: 90, 105, 95, 100, and 110.

Example	*Application*
$M = \dfrac{\Sigma X}{N}$	$M = \dfrac{\Sigma X}{N}$
	$M = \dfrac{90 + 105 + 95 + 100 + 110}{5}$
	$M = \dfrac{500}{5}$
	$M = 100$

The mean has several characteristics that make it the measure of central tendency most frequently used. One of these characteristics is stability. Since each score in the distribution enters into the computation of the mean, it is more stable over time than other measures of central tendency, which consider only one or two scores.

Another characteristic is that the sum of each score's distance from the mean is equal to zero. Presently, this is probably quite meaningless to you. However, it is a key concept in more advanced statistical operations. We will discuss this characteristic and its importance shortly.

A third characteristic of the mean is that it is affected by extreme scores. This means that a few very high scores in a distribution composed primarily of low scores (a positively skewed distribution) or a few very low scores in a distribution composed primarily of high scores (a negatively skewed distribution) will "pull" the value of the mean down or up toward the extreme score or scores. Table 13.2 illustrates this point. Since the mean is affected by extreme scores, it is usually

TABLE 13.2 The Effect of Extreme Scores on the Mean

Original Set of Scores	Add an Extremely Low Score	Add an Extremely High Score
90	90	90
105	105	105
95	95	95
100	100	100
+110	110	110
$\Sigma X = 500$	+20	+200
	$\Sigma X = 520$	$\Sigma X = 700$
$M = \dfrac{\Sigma X}{N}$	$M = \dfrac{\Sigma X}{N}$	$M = \dfrac{\Sigma X}{N}$
$M = \dfrac{500}{5} = 100$	$M = \dfrac{520}{6} = 86.67$	$M = \dfrac{700}{6} = 116.67$

not the measure of choice when dealing with skewed distributions. In such cases, a measure that is more resistant to extreme scores is required. Our next topic for discussion, the median, represents such a measure.

The Median

The median is the second most frequently encountered measure of central tendency. The median is the score that splits a distribution in half: 50% of the scores lie above the median, and 50% of the scores lie below the median. Thus, the median (abbreviated MDN) is also known as the 50th percentile. You may also think of the median as the middle score, since it is the score or value, that falls in the middle of the distribution of scores.

For most classroom purposes, simple methods may be used to determine the median. When the score distribution contains an odd number of scores, the median is the score that has equal numbers of scores above and below it. We mentioned the median in Chapter 3. We noted that when curriculum-based measurement (CBM) is employed for progress monitoring under the response-to-intervention (RTI) model, the median of the three CBM probes is used. The following example describes the steps involved in determining the median when N, the total number of scores in the distribution, is odd.

EXAMPLE: *Determine the median for the following set of scores: 90, 105, 95, 100, and 110*

Steps

1. Arrange the scores in ascending or descending numerical order (don't just take the middle score from the original distribution).
2. Circle the score that has equal numbers of scores above and below it; this score is the median.

Application

110

105

(100) = MDN

95

90

When N is even, the procedure is a bit more complicated. In this case, select the *two* scores in the middle that have equal numbers of scores above and below them. Taking the average of these two scores will give you the median. These steps are illustrated in the following example.

EXAMPLE: *Determine the median for the following set of scores: 90, 105, 95, 100, 110, and 95*

Steps

1. Arrange the scores in numerical order.
2. Circle the *two* middle scores that have equal numbers of scores above and below them.
3. Compute the average of those two scores to determine the median.

Application

$$110$$
$$105$$
$$\boxed{100}$$
$$\boxed{95}$$

Two middle scores: $\dfrac{95 + 100}{2} = \dfrac{195}{2} = 97.5 = \text{MDN}$

$$95$$
$$90$$

In this example, the two middle scores are different scores, and the median is actually a decimal rather than a whole number (integer). This can be confusing unless you remember that the median is a value, not necessarily a score. In the classroom, test scores are almost always integers. So it is possible, in a situation like this, for the value of the median to be neither a score actually obtained by a student in the class nor a whole number!

Sometimes, when the number of scores is even, more than two students who are in the middle of a distribution obtain the same score. Which score do you use? In such cases keep in mind that it is only the values of the two middle scores that are important in determining the median, not who obtained them. For example, if Julio, Janelle, Joe, Jill, and Juanita all score in the middle of the classroom test distribution, it does not matter whether you use Julio and Janelle's scores, or Jill and Juanita's, to determine the median, because it is the score value that is relevant, not the student who obtained it.

For example:

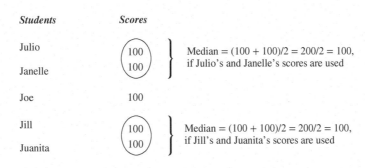

Students	*Scores*	
Julio	100	Median = (100 + 100)/2 = 200/2 = 100,
Janelle	100	if Julio's and Janelle's scores are used
Joe	100	
Jill	100	Median = (100 + 100)/2 = 200/2 = 100,
Juanita	100	if Jill's and Juanita's scores are used

Next, let's put all five of these scores into a distribution and compute the MDN when N is even.

EXAMPLE: *Determine the median for the following set of scores: 100, 90, 100, 105, 100, 95, 100, 110, 95, and 100*

Steps

1. Arrange the scores in numerical order.
2. Circle the two middle scores that have equal numbers of scores above and below them.
3. Compute the average of those two scores to determine the median.

Application

Students	Scores
Bo	110
Deanna	105
Julio	100
Janelle	100
Joe	100
Jill	100
Juanita	100
Thomas	95
Dara	95
Richard	90

Two middle scores: $\dfrac{100 + 100}{2} = \dfrac{200}{2} = 100 = \text{MDN}$

In this case, the median is a whole number and has the same value as the five middle, or tied, scores. Tied scores are a common occurrence, and when they are in the middle of a distribution the median will always be a whole number. When the middle scores are not tied, the median may be either a decimal or a whole number.

The median determination methods we have provided are useful for classroom purposes, although other computational methods also exist. For technical reasons that we do not need to be unduly concerned about, the method we just described to determine the median *when we have an even number of scores may, at times, overestimate or underestimate, by a fraction, the actual value of the median.* This can occur only when more than two scores around the center of the distribution are the same. (For those who are interested, an example of this more complex, but sometimes more accurate, approach to determining the median when there are multiple tied scores in the middle of the distribution can be found on the companion website for this text. There you can also find an updated list of introductory statistics and measurement textbooks that were previously included in Appendix E of the tenth edition (go to http://www.wiley.com/college/kubiszyn).

The main characteristic of the median is that it is not affected by extreme scores. This is because only the middle or two middle scores are considered in determining the median. Let's consider the following examples:

Original Set of Scores	Substitute an Extremely High Score	Substitute an Extremely Low Score
110	**600**	110
105	105	105
100	100	100
100	100	100
95	95	95
90	90	**5**
$\text{MDN} = \dfrac{100 + 100}{2} = 100$	$\text{MDN} = \dfrac{100 + 100}{2} = 100$	$\text{MDN} = \dfrac{100 + 100}{2} = 100$

Since the median is not affected by extreme scores, it represents central tendency better than the mean when distributions are skewed. In skewed distributions, the mean is pulled toward the extremes, so that in some cases it may give a falsely high or falsely low estimate of central tendency. Since the median, on the other hand, is the score above and below which half the scores lie, it always indicates the center of the distribution, as illustrated by the following diagrams:

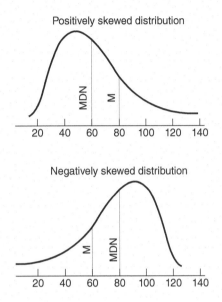

In the positively skewed distribution, the few scores of 100 or above pull M toward them. The mean presents the impression that the typical student scored about 80 and passed the test. However, the MDN shows that 50% of the students scored 60 or below. In other words, not only did the typical student fail the test (if we consider the middle student typical), but the majority of students failed the test (assuming that a score of 60 is failing, of course).

In the negatively skewed distribution, the few scores of 40 or below pull the mean down toward them. Thus, the mean score gives the impression that the typical student scored about 60 and failed the test. Again, the median contradicts this interpretation. It shows that 50% of the students scored 80 or above on the test and that actually the majority of students passed the test.

As you can see, it is important that the median be considered when skewed distributions are involved. Too often, however, only the average or mean is reported when statistics are presented, without regard for the shape of the distribution.

Percentiles Now that we have introduced the idea of the median as the 50th percentile, it is only a small step to finding out how to determine the score that represents any desired percentile in a frequency distribution. Although a percentile is not considered a measure of central tendency unless it is the 50th percentile, the calculation of other percentiles is very similar to that of the median. A percentile is a score below which a certain percentage of the scores lie. In the case of the median, we saw that 50% of the total number of cases were lower (and higher) than the median. Percentiles divide a frequency distribution into 100 equal parts. Percentiles are symbolized $P_1, P_2, ..., P_{99}$. P_1 represents that score in a frequency distribution below which 1% of the scores lie. P_2 represents that score in a frequency distribution below which 2% of the scores lie. P_{99} represents that score in a frequency distribution below which 99% of the scores lie.

A score can be calculated for each percentile from P_1 to P_{99} in a manner similar to the way the median—or 50th percentile (or P_{50})—was calculated for a distribution with an even number of scores. That is:

1. Arrange the scores in numerical order.
2. Counting up from the bottom, find the point below which the desired percentage of scores falls.
3. Circle the two scores that surround this point.
4. The average of this pair of scores will be the percentile of interest.

For example, for the following data, P_{75} and P_{25} would be determined in the following manner:

115
110
110
110     $P_{75} = (110 + 110)/2 = 220/2 = 110$
105
100
100
95

95
90     $P_{25} = \dfrac{95 + 90}{2} = 92.5$
90
85

As you can see from these examples, when the two scores used to determine a percentile are tied values, the percentile will be an integer, but if the two values are not tied, the percentile may be a decimal or an integer. If this is confusing, review the procedures for determining the median when the middle values are tied and untied for clarification. As we mentioned with regard to the methods, we used to determine the median, more complex, specific procedures exist to compute percentiles, but for classroom purposes this approach should be sufficient.

Finally, we will consider the last measure of central tendency—the mode.

The Mode

The mode is the least reported measure of central tendency. The mode, or modal score, in a distribution is the score that occurs most frequently. However, a distribution may have one score that occurs most frequently (unimodal), two scores that occur with equal frequency and more frequently than any other scores (bimodal), or three or more scores that occur with equal frequency and more frequently than any other scores (multimodal). If *each* score in a distribution occurs with equal frequency, the distribution is called a rectangular distribution, and it has *no mode*.

The mode is determined by tallying up the number of times each score occurs in a distribution and selecting the score that occurs most frequently. The following examples illustrate this:

EXAMPLE: *What is the mode of this score distribution: 90, 105, 95, 100, and 100?*

X	Tally	
105	I	
100	II	Mode = 100
95	I	This is a unimodal distribution.
90	I	

EXAMPLE: *What is the mode for this set of scores: 90, 110, 95, 100, 110, 90, 105, 100, 110, and 95?*

X	Tally	
110	III	
105	I	
100	II	Mode = 110
95	II	This is a unimodal distribution.
90	II	

EXAMPLE: *What is the mode for this set of scores: 6, 9, 1, 3, 4, 6, and 9?*

X	Tally	
9	II	
6	II	
4	I	Mode = 6 and 9
3	I	This is a bimodal distribution.
1	I	

The mode has the advantage of being easy to determine. If you know how to count, you can determine a mode! However, it is the least used of the measures of central tendency because of a serious shortcoming. The mode is the least stable measure of central tendency. A few scores can influence the mode considerably. Consider the following:

Original Set of Scores		*Add a Few Scores* *(e.g., 90, 70, 70, 70, and 90)*	
X	Tally	X	Tally
105	I	90	I
100	II	70	II
95	I	70	I
90	I	70	III
		90	III
Mode = 100		Mode = 70 and 90	

Because of this unfortunate characteristic, the mode usually is not used as the only measure of central tendency. An exceptional case, however, is the normal distribution because in a normal distribution all three measures of central tendency have the same value.

The Measures of Central Tendency in Various Distributions

As was mentioned, the mean, median, and mode all have the same value in a normal distribution, which is illustrated here:

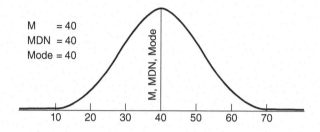

In a positively skewed distribution, the mean usually has the highest value of all the measures of central tendency, the mode the lowest, and the median the middle or intermediate value:

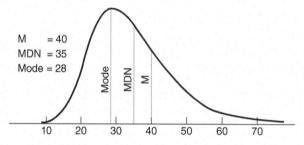

Just the opposite occurs in a negatively skewed distribution. In a negatively skewed distribution, the mean usually has the lowest value, the mode the highest, and the median the middle or intermediate value:

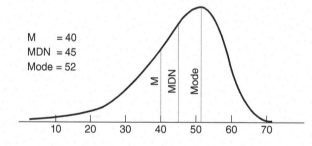

Knowing the relationships of the measures of central tendency to these distributions enables you to place these measures in their appropriate position when a distribution's shape is known. The opposite is also true. Knowing the values of the measures of central tendency enables you to determine the shape of the distribution. For example, if the mean = 47, median = 54, and mode = 59, what is the shape of the distribution? You know it is not normal (since the values are different). But before you guess at whether it's positively or negatively skewed, take the uncertainty or guesswork out of the question. How? The answer to this and many other questions concerning statistical principles is to draw a picture.

EXAMPLE: *What is the shape of a distribution with a mean of 47, median of 54, and mode of 59?*

Steps

1. Examine the relationship among the three measures of central tendency.
2. Draw a picture (baseline first); then mark the measures of central tendency in the appropriate spaces. Draw in the curve. Remember that the high point of the curve is the mode.
3. Evaluate the curve to arrive at the answer, in this case, negatively skewed.

Application

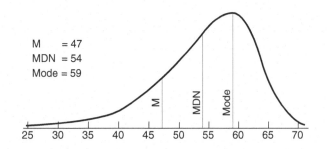

We've been discussing estimates of one important aspect of a distribution. Estimates of central tendency represent good bets about the single value that best describes a distribution. But some good bets are better than others. In the next chapter, we will consider statistics that indicate how adequate our good bets really are. These are estimates of variability.

SUMMARY

This chapter introduced you to various methods of tabulating and graphing data and to the measures of central tendency. Its major points are as follows:

1. Descriptive statistics are numbers used to describe or summarize a larger body of numbers.
2. Data are tabulated to introduce some order to the data and make them more interpretable. Three methods of tabulating data are listing, simple frequency distributions, and grouped frequency distributions.
3. While each method has its advantages and disadvantages, the grouped frequency distribution is usually most appropriate for classroom use.
4. The following steps are followed in constructing a grouped frequency distribution:
   a. Determine the range.
   b. Determine the number of intervals.
   c. Divide the range by the number of intervals and round to the nearest odd number to get the interval width (i).
   d. Develop the interval column, being sure the lower limit (LL) of each interval is a multiple of i.
   e. Tally the scores in each interval to get f, that the frequency column.

5. Data from grouped frequency distributions may be graphically represented by histograms or frequency polygons.

6. Histograms, or bar graphs, use columns of varying height to represent the frequencies in each interval.

7. Frequency polygons use straight lines to connect the midpoints of each interval, which vary in height depending on the frequency of scores in the interval.

8. The following general guidelines apply to the construction of both histograms and frequency polygons:
    a. Make sure that the vertical axis is three-quarters as long as the horizontal axis.
    b. List scores along the horizontal axis, frequencies along the vertical axis, and label the axes clearly.
    c. Use double slash marks (//) to indicate breaks in any number sequences.
    d. Do not omit intervals with frequencies of zero.

9. A smooth curve is usually drawn to represent a distribution's shape, although decisions about frequency of occurrence of scores or scores in intervals can be made by looking at the height of the curve. The f axis is omitted in a smooth curve.

10. In a symmetrical distribution, each half or side of the distribution is a mirror image of the other, unlike in an asymmetrical distribution.

11. A normal distribution is a special type of symmetrical distribution.

12. An asymmetrical distribution in which most scores are low is called a positively skewed distribution. The tail in such a distribution points toward the high scores.

13. An asymmetrical distribution in which most scores are high is called a negatively skewed distribution. The tail in such a distribution points toward the low scores.

14. One of the measures of central tendency (mean, median, and mode) is used to represent a distribution when a single value must be used. Such a measure is our "best bet" about the overall distribution.

15. The mean, or the arithmetic average, of a set of scores is determined by summing all the scores and dividing by the number of scores.

16. The mean has several important characteristics. Of the measures of central tendency it is the most stable, the sum of the differences of each score from the mean always equals zero, and it is affected by extreme scores.

17. Since the mean is affected by extreme scores, it is not the measure of central tendency of choice for skewed distributions.

18. The median is the score that splits a distribution in half. It is also known as the middle score or the 50th percentile.

19. The median is determined by finding the score or value that has equal numbers of scores above or below it. In certain cases when there are multiple tied scores in the middle of the distribution, the most accurate way of determining the median is through interpolation (see Appendix C, online chapter).

20. The most important characteristic of the median is that it is not affected by extreme scores. Thus, it is the measure of central tendency of choice in a skewed distribution. It is also the measure of choice when multiple curriculum-based measurement (CBM) probes are used for progress monitoring in the classroom.

21. The mode is the score in a distribution that occurs most frequently.

22. The mode is determined by counting the number of times scores occur and selecting the score(s) that occurs most frequently. A distribution may have more than one mode.

23. The major characteristic of the mode is its instability. Seldom is the mode, by itself, acceptable as a measure of central tendency.

24. In a normal distribution, the mean, median, and mode have the same value.

25. In a positively skewed distribution, the mean has the highest and the mode the lowest value of the measures of central tendency. The median has an intermediate value.

26. In a negatively skewed distribution, the mean has the lowest value and the mode the highest value of the measures of central tendency. Again, the median has an intermediate value.

FOR DISCUSSION AND PRACTICE

*1. An achievement test designed to measure the level of arithmetic achievement among students in the middle of the third grade is administered to three classes of equal size: one first-grade class, one third-grade class, and one fifth-grade class. The test is administered in the middle of the school year. Other things being equal, what sort of distribution would you predict for each of the three classes? Sketch a distribution of the shape you would expect for each grade. On each of your three sketches, indicate the probable location of the three measures of central tendency.

*2. Mr. Martin's best reading group obtained the following scores on an achievement test:

85, 90, 90, 92, 94, 94, 96, 97, 97, 98

Mr. Scott's best reading group obtained the following scores on the same achievement test:

61, 85, 90, 90, 92, 93, 94, 97, 97, 97

For each group, determine the following:

a. N

b. R

c. M

d. MDN

e. Mode

f. Why is there so much of a difference between means?

g. Which measure of central tendency should be used to compare these distributions?

*3. For the following group of 30 scores, construct three grouped frequency distributions with different numbers of intervals. Graph your data, using both a histogram and a frequency polygon. Decide which frequency distribution best represents the data.

60, 60, 63, 68, 70, 72, 75, 75, 75, 76, 76, 77, 78, 80, 83, 83, 84, 88, 93, 93, 93, 94, 94, 94, 94, 95, 97, 98, 100, 100

*Answers for these questions appear in Appendix B.

*4. Match the terms in Column B with the characteristics listed in Column A. The options from Column B may be used more than once.

Column A	*Column B*
1. Least stable measure of central tendency	**a.** Mean
2. More than one possible in the same distribution	**b.** Median
3. Most influenced by extreme scores	**c.** Mode
4. Also known as the 50th percentile	
5. Measure of choice in skewed distributions	

*5. Find P_{25} and P_{50} in the following distribution of scores:

115, 112, 110, 108, 106, 104, 100, 100, 98, 96, 96, 94, 93, 91, 90, 88

*6. Indicate the type of distribution to which each of these sets of data refer:

a. M = 78.37, MDN = 78.37, mode = 78.37

b. M = 374.3, MDN = 379.7, mode = 391.3

c. M = 109.5, MDN = 107.4, mode = 107.4

*7. For the following sets of data, which method of tabulating data would be most appropriate? Why?

a. 70, 70, 70, 71, 72, 72, 73, 73, 73, 73, 74

b. 39, 47, 67, 51, 92, 60, 75

c. 35, 88, 85, 45, 49, 52, 69, 71, 49, 50, 90, 72, 79, 36, 43, 52, 92, 81, 80, 47, 55, 60, 72, 94, 91, 53, 48, 72

8. Your study partner for this chapter says "I think we should just do away with two of the three measures of central tendency because they all mean the same thing." Explain why your study partner's conclusion is not correct. Give two examples of situations in which his suggestion would lead to different conclusion based on the central tendency measure chosen.

CHAPTER 14

VARIABILITY, THE NORMAL DISTRIBUTION, AND CONVERTED SCORES

LEARNING OUTCOMES

After completing this chapter, the student will be able to:

1. Explain what variability or score dispersion means.
2. Compute the range, semi-interquartile range, and standard deviation for a given set of data.
3. Compare and contrast the range, semi-interquartile range, and standard deviation.
4. Compute quartiles and percentiles for a given set of data.
5. Explain why the normal distribution is useful for statistical decision making.
6. Compare and contrast the approximate percentages of cases falling between standard deviation units in the normal curve.
7. Determine the percentage of cases falling above, below or between given scores in a distribution, when the distribution is assumed to approach normality.
8. Differentiate between raw and converted scores.
9. Apply the *z*-score concept to facilitate comparisons of scores from distributions with different means and standard deviations.
10. Compute equivalent raw scores, *z*-scores, *T*-scores, and percentile ranks.
11. Use the measures of central tendency, variability, converted scores, and the properties of the normal curve to make decisions about measurement data, both for individual students and for groups.

IN CHAPTER 13, we learned that measures of central tendency can be used to describe a distribution. However, an estimate of the variability, or spread, of scores is needed before we can compare scores within and between distributions. For example, suppose we have the following data: M = 160, MDN = 170, and mode = 180. After drawing a curve, we know that the distribution is negatively skewed. What we don't know is how spread out, dispersed, or variable the scores are. For this, we would at least need to know the range of obtained scores. Were all the scores between 100 and 200? 50 and 250? 150 and 190? Without an estimate of variability, we don't know which of the following three negatively skewed distributions best fits the data:

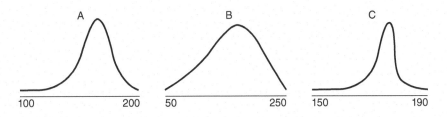

In A, the scores vary between about 100 and 200; in B between 50 and 250; and in C between 150 and 190. In other words, it's possible for two or more distributions to have the same values for the mean, median, and mode but be different in the way their scores are spread out around these measures. This is why we must have an estimate of variability. This estimate helps us determine the compression or expansion of the distributions.

THE RANGE

The easiest estimate of variability to compute is one we've already been exposed to: the range (R). The range is determined by subtracting the lowest score from the highest score.[1] This is what you did as the first step in constructing a grouped frequency distribution. Ease of computation does not offset the major drawbacks of the range as an estimate of variability, however. Since the range is dependent only on the low and high scores, it is often unstable and is useful only for gross ballpark estimates of variability. If an extreme score is present, R can be very misleading. Consider the following example.

EXAMPLE: *Compute the range for the following set of data: 11, 11, 11, 11, 12, 12, 13, 14, 14, 14, 15, 15, 15, 15, 16, 17, 18, 18, 18*

$$R = H - L$$
$$R = 18 - 11 = 7$$

Now substitute one extreme score, 96, for one of the scores of 18 and compute the range: 11, 11, 11, 11, 12, 12, 13, 14, 14, 14, 15, 15, 15, 15, 16, 17, 18, 18, 96.

$$R = H - L$$
$$R = 96 - 11 = 85$$

This single extreme score increased R by 78 points and gives the impression that there is a large spread of scores when, with the exception of the single extreme score, there is actually very little.

---

[1] Sometimes the range is defined as the lowest score subtracted from the highest score plus 1. This is called the inclusive range. It is the statistic most often referred to in introductory statistics texts and is based on mathematical concepts that need not concern us here.

THE SEMI-INTERQUARTILE RANGE (SIQR)

The semi-interquartile range (SIQR) compensates for the sensitivity of the range to extreme scores by preventing extreme scores from influencing its computation. The SIQR computation is determined by the middle 50% of the scores in a distribution. The lower 25% and upper 25% do not enter into its final computation. The formula for the SIQR is presented here:

$$SIQR = \frac{Q_3 - Q_1}{2}$$

In this formula, Q_3 stands for the third quartile and Q_1 stands for the first. Quartiles, like the median, are points in a distribution below which a certain percentage of scores lie. In fact, the median, or 50th percentile, is the same as Q_2 or the second quartile.

Q_1 is the point below which 25% of the scores lie, and Q_3 is the point below which 75% of the scores lie. The same process we used in Chapter 12 to determine a percentile is used to determine Q_1 and Q_3 (since Q_1 is the same as P_{25} and Q_3 is the same P_{75}), as illustrated by the following example.

EXAMPLE: *Determine the semi-interquartile range for the following set of scores: 85, 115, 90, 90, 105, 100, 110, 110, 95, 110, 95, 100*

Process

1. Determine Q_1 and Q_3 by employing the steps used to determine the median (Q_2) for a distribution with an even number of scores.
   a. Arrange scores in numerical order.
   b. Counting up from the bottom, find the points below which 25% of the score values and 75% of the score values fall (theoretically, that is, since we are talking about values rather than the actual scores).
   c. Circle the two scores that surround these points.
   d. The averages of each of these two pairs of scores are Q_1 and Q_3.

$$
\begin{array}{l}
115 \\
110 \\
Q_1 \cdots \left(\!\!\begin{array}{c}110 \\ 110\end{array}\!\!\right) \left.\begin{array}{c}\\ \\\end{array}\right\} \quad Q_3 = \frac{110 + 110}{2} = 110 \\
105 \\
\underline{100} \\
100 \\
95 \\
Q_1 \cdots \left(\!\!\begin{array}{c}95 \\ 90\end{array}\!\!\right) \left.\begin{array}{c}\\ \\\end{array}\right\} \quad Q_1 = \frac{95 + 90}{2} = 92.5 \\
90 \\
85
\end{array}
$$

2. Plug Q_1 and Q_3 into the formula and determine the SIQR.

   Formula

   $$SIQR = \frac{Q_3 - Q_1}{2}$$

   Application

   $$SIQR = \frac{110 - 92.5}{2}$$
   $$= \frac{17.5}{2}$$
   $$= 8.75$$

Although the SIQR has the advantage of not being influenced by extreme scores, it has the disadvantage of being determined ultimately by only *half* the scores in a distribution. Any time all scores in a distribution do not enter the computation of a statistic, an element of error is introduced. Although the SIQR is a better estimate of variability than the range, it is not as good or as stable as the estimate of variability known as the standard deviation (SD). The SD, like the mean, considers all scores in its computation. As a result, it is the most commonly used estimate of variability. When the SIQR is reported, it usually accompanies the median, which is not surprising since they share part of the same computational process. Next, we will consider the SD, which we will symbolize as SD.

THE STANDARD DEVIATION

The most accurate measure of variability is the SD, which includes all the scores in a distribution in its computation. The SD is normally reported as the estimate of variability that accompanies the mean in describing a distribution.

Remember, we said an estimate of variability tells us how poor our best bet is as a single value with which to describe a distribution. Consider the following three distributions:

A	*B*	*C*
38	20	25
34	20	24
26	20	23
24	20	22
20	20	21
20	20	19
16	20	18
14	20	17
6	20	16
2	20	15

$$\Sigma X = \overline{200} \qquad \Sigma X = \overline{200} \qquad \Sigma X = \overline{200}$$

$$M_A = \frac{\Sigma X}{N} \qquad M_B = \frac{\Sigma X}{N} \qquad M_C = \frac{\Sigma X}{N}$$

$$= \frac{200}{10} = 20 \qquad = \frac{200}{10} = 20 \qquad = \frac{200}{10} = 20$$

Although the distributions are composed of many different scores, they all have the same mean value. In distribution B, this best bet is right on the mark. Our mean value of 20 perfectly represents each and every score in the distribution, simply because each score in the distribution is 20. What about our best bets in A and C? How good or poor are they?

From these cases, we can easily see that the mean is a better estimate of the scores in distribution C than in distribution A. We know this because none of the scores in C is more than five points away from the mean. In distribution A, on the other hand, 6 of the 10 scores are six or more points away from the mean. Using this information, we can conclude that there is less variability, spread, or dispersion of scores in C. But just how much less variable is C than A? And what if there were less of a discrepancy in scores between A and C? How could we determine which was more or less variable?

With only this information, it would be difficult if not impossible to answer these questions. We need a reliable index of variability that considers all scores. Let's develop one by putting down on paper what we did when we compared A and C.

First, we looked at each distribution to see how far away each score was from the mean. We can do this more formally by subtracting the mean from each score (X − M). We'll call this distance the score's *deviation* from the mean and use the symbol x (lower case) to represent such deviation scores. Thus X − M = x, which is illustrated here:

	A			*C*	
X − M =		x	X − M =		x
38 − 20 =		18	25 − 20 =		5
34 − 20 =		14	24 − 20 =		4
26 − 20 =		6	23 − 20 =		3
24 − 20 =		4	22 − 20 =		2
20 − 20 =		0	21 − 20 =		1
20 − 20 =		0	19 − 20 =		−1
16 − 20 =		− 4	18 − 20 =		−2
14 − 20 =		− 6	17 − 20 =		−3
6 − 20 =		−14	16 − 20 =		−4
2 − 20 =		−18	15 − 20 =		−5

This is just what we did before, except it was done in our heads. Since we want a single number or index to represent the deviations, why don't we just sum the x column, being careful to note the sign of the number, and then average the result? Let's do this:

A	*C*
x	x
18	5
14	4
6	3
4	2
0	1
0	−1
−4	−2
−6	−3
−14	−4
−18	−5
$\frac{\Sigma x}{N} = 0$	$\frac{\Sigma x}{N} = 0$

Because the positive and negative numbers cancel one another out, the sum of both x columns is zero. Remember the characteristics of the mean? One of them is that the sum of the deviations from the mean always equals zero. Now you can see what is meant by this characteristic. This characteristic holds true for all shapes and sizes of distributions without exception. We cannot use Σx or even the average deviation, $\Sigma x/N$, as our index of variability, as promising as these two indices might appear at first glance.

Fortunately, mathematics provides us with a way out of this dilemma. An index of variability based on deviation scores that we can use is computed in much the same manner. There are two differences, however. First, let's square all the individual deviation scores and then sum them, as illustrated here:

	A				C		
X − M =	x	x^2		X − M =	x	x^2	
38 − 20 =	18	324		25 − 20 =	5	25	
34 − 20 =	14	196		24 − 20 =	4	16	
26 − 20 =	6	36		23 − 20 =	3	9	
24 − 20 =	4	16		22 − 20 =	2	4	
20 − 20 =	0	0		21 − 20 =	1	1	
20 − 20 =	0	0		19 − 20 =	−1	1	
16 − 20 =	−4	16		18 − 20 =	−2	4	
14 − 20 =	−6	36		17 − 20 =	−3	9	
6 − 20 =	−14	196		16 − 20 =	−4	16	
2 − 20 =	−18	324		15 − 20 =	−5	25	
		$1144 = \Sigma x^2$				$110 = \Sigma x^2$	

The next step is to find the average of the sum of the squared deviation scores:

$$\text{A} \qquad\qquad \text{C}$$
$$\frac{1144}{10} = 114.4 \qquad\qquad \frac{110}{10} = 11.0$$

The average of the sum of the squared deviation scores is called the *variance*. By themselves these estimates are not very useful because they represent squared units, not the units we started with. To return the values to units representative of our original data, we must extract their square roots:

$$\text{A} \qquad\qquad \text{C}$$
$$\sqrt{114.4} = 10.7 \qquad\qquad \sqrt{11.0} = 3.32$$

These values—10.7 for distribution A and 3.32 for distribution C—are the indices we've been looking for. They are based on all the scores in a distribution and are on the *same scale* of units as our original set of data. These values are the SDs for distributions A and C.

The following formula is simply a shorthand mathematical way of representing what we have just done for distributions A and C:

$$SD = \sqrt{\frac{\Sigma(X - M)^2}{N}}$$

or, since X − M = x,

$$SD = \sqrt{\frac{\Sigma x^2}{N}}$$

These formulas are equivalent. In other words, they tell you that to find the SD you must square each deviation score, sum the squares of the deviation scores, divide this value by the number of scores in the distribution, and find the square root of that final value. Just to be sure you understand the process, we will work one more example and follow each of the steps.

The Deviation Score Method for Computing the Standard Deviation

> **EXAMPLE:** *Determine the standard deviation for the following set of scores: 92, 100, 90, 80, 94, 96*

Process

1. Determine the mean.

$$100 \qquad M = \frac{\Sigma X}{N}$$
$$96$$
$$94$$
$$92 \qquad M = \frac{552}{6}$$
$$90$$
$$\underline{80}$$
$$\Sigma X = 552 \qquad M = 92$$

2. Subtract the mean from each raw score to arrive at the deviation scores. (As a check on your computations, sum the x column to see if it equals zero.)

X − M =	x
100 − 92 =	8
96 − 92 =	4
94 − 92 =	2
92 − 92 =	0
90 − 92 =	−2
80 − 92 =	−12
Σx =	0

3. Square each deviation score and sum the squared deviation scores.

X − M =	x	x^2
100 − 92 =	8	64
96 − 92 =	4	16
94 − 92 =	2	4
92 − 92 =	0	0
90 − 92 =	−2	4
80 − 92 =	−12	144
		$\Sigma x^2 = 232$

4. Plug the Σx^2 into the formula and solve for the SD.

$$SD = \sqrt{\frac{\Sigma x^2}{N}} = \sqrt{\frac{232}{6}} = \sqrt{38.67} = 6.22$$

The Raw Score Method for Computing the Standard Deviation

The following formula is another, quicker way of representing what we have just done for distributions A and C. It is called the raw score formula for the SD, since it uses only the raw scores and does not require the more laborious process of finding deviations from the mean. Here is the raw score formula for calculating SD:

$$SD = \sqrt{\frac{\Sigma X^2 - (\Sigma X^2)/N}{N}}$$

where

ΣX^2 = each raw score squared and then summed

(ΣX^2) = the square of the sum of the raw scores (i.e., add the scores, then square the total)

N = the number of pupils

Both the more cumbersome deviation method and the shorter raw score method of computing the SD will give you the same result; keep in mind that the raw score formula will be easier to use. Just to be sure you understand the process of obtaining an SD, we will use the raw score formula to work one more example.

EXAMPLE : *Determine the standard deviation for the following set of scores: 10, 12, 15, 13, 20, 14, 15, 14, 18, 13*

Process

1. Determine the square of each raw score.

X	X²
10	100
12	144
15	225
13	169
20	400
14	196
15	225
14	196
18	324
13	169

2. Sum both the raw scores (X) and the squared scores (X^2).

X	X^2
10	100
12	144
15	225
13	169
20	400
14	196
15	225
14	196
18	324
13	169
$\Sigma X = 144$	$\Sigma X^2 = 2{,}148$

3. Square the sum of the raw scores.

$$(\Sigma X)^2 = 144^2 = 20{,}736$$

4. Find N, the number of scores.

$$N = 10$$

5. Plug ΣX^2, $(\Sigma X)^2$, and N into the formula and solve for the SD.

$$
\begin{aligned}
SD &= \sqrt{\frac{\Sigma X^2 - (\Sigma X)^2/N}{N}} \\
&= \sqrt{\frac{2148 - (20{,}736)/10}{10}} \\
&= \sqrt{\frac{2148 - 2074}{10}} \\
&= \sqrt{\frac{74}{10}} \\
&= \sqrt{7.4} \\
&= 2.72
\end{aligned}
$$

Since the SD is an estimate of score variability or spread, it stands to reason that large SD values indicate greater score variability than do small SD values. In other words, when the SD is small, scores tend to cluster closely around the mean. Such a distribution is said to be homogeneous and tends to have a compressed shape, whether it is symmetrical or skewed. Three examples of homogeneous distributions with compressed shapes are pictured here:

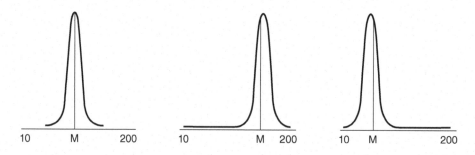

In those examples, the mean is a very good bet as the single value that best represents all the scores in each distribution. Our best bet is much poorer when distributions have large SDs. Such distributions have a lot of variability or spread of scores and all have an expanded appearance. These are called heterogeneous distributions. Three examples follow:

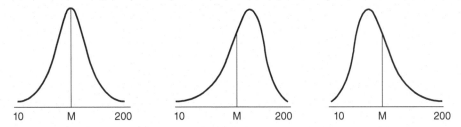

To sum up, measures of central tendency help us determine whether a distribution is symmetrical or skewed. Measures of variability help us determine more precisely whether these distributions appear compressed (small SD) or expanded (large SD). The SD also has a very important role in a special kind of symmetrical distribution. This is called the *normal distribution*, and it is to this topic that we now turn.

THE NORMAL DISTRIBUTION

The normal distribution is a special kind of symmetrical distribution that represents specific mathematical properties. This distribution has special importance for us because it is the model we most frequently use to make comparisons among scores or to make other kinds of statistical decisions. It is important, however, to note that the normal distribution is hypothetical. No distribution of scores matches the normal distribution perfectly. However, many distributions or scores in education come close to the normal distribution and herein lies its value. The following example shows a distribution of Stanford–Binet IQ scores for a large number of students:

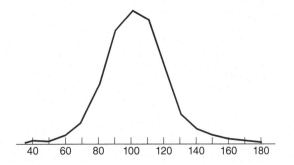

Looking at the figure, you can see that although the IQ distribution differs somewhat from the symmetrical, normal distribution, it is close enough that we do not lose too much accuracy by using the normal distribution as a model for the actual distribution. Many other characteristics of individuals also come close enough to the normal distribution for it to be used as a model for these distributions. Apart from IQ, examples of these include most kinds of achievement and physical characteristics (e.g., height and weight). The accuracy we sacrifice by employing a slightly inaccurate model is offset by the advantages of being able to make statistical and measurement decisions based on a *single* standard for comparison, the normal distribution. Before we can make such decisions, though, we must become familiar with the fixed properties of the normal distribution.

Properties of the Normal Distribution

The curve drawn here represents the normal distribution.

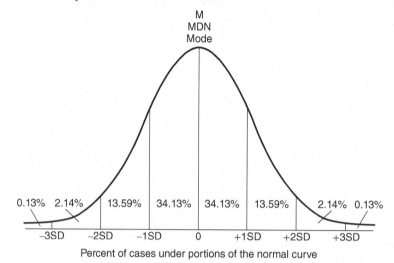

Percent of cases under portions of the normal curve

Notice in the curve that the mean, median, and mode all coincide. This, of course, will occur whenever a distribution is normal. The percentages show how many cases fall under portions of the curve.

Now add up the percentages you see above the baseline between three SD units below and three SD units above the mean. Notice that more than 99.7%, or almost all scores in the normal distribution, fall between three SD units below the mean and three SD units above the mean. Now look at the area of the curve between the mean and one SD above the mean. The 34.13% you see in this area indicates the percentage of cases that fall between the mean value and the value of the mean *plus* the value of one SD unit in a normal distribution of scores. For example, if we were using the normal curve as a model for a distribution with a mean of 61 and an SD of 7, we would expect 34.13% (about 34% or one-third) of the scores in this distribution to fall between 61 and 68, as the following illustration shows:

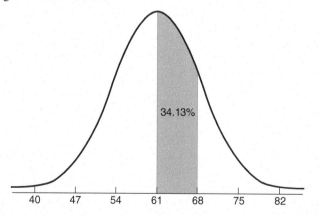

Notice also that for a distribution with a mean equal to 61 and an SD equal to 7, seven points are added for each SD unit above the mean (68, 75, 82) and seven points are subtracted from the mean for each SD unit below the mean (54, 47, 40). Thus, we can see that *about* 68% or *about* two-thirds of the scores in this distribution fall between 54 and 68, as shown here:

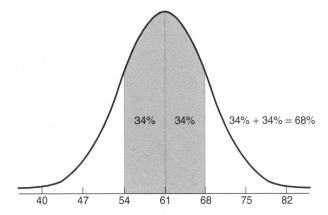

The interval between the mean and 75 represents what percentage of scores? We know what percentage of cases fall in each interval of the normal curve, so we can easily find the answer. The answer is about 48%, as shown in the following illustration:

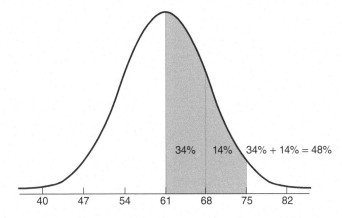

We can also use the normal curve to determine the percentage of scores above or below a certain score. The interval above 47 represents what percentage of scores? The answer, about 98%, is illustrated next:

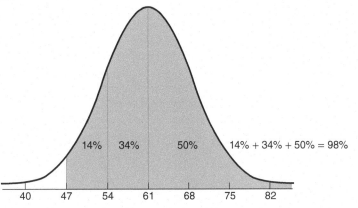

The interval below 68 represents what percentage of scores? The answer is about 84%, as shown in the following illustration:

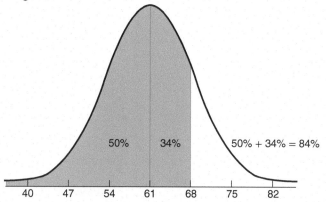

In other words, in a distribution with a mean of 61 and an SD of 7, a score of 68 is at the 84th percentile. Recall that a percentile, like a quartile, is the point below which a given percentage of scores lie. If you wanted to determine the score at the 16th percentile, you would find that score below which there is 16% of the area under the normal curve, as illustrated here:

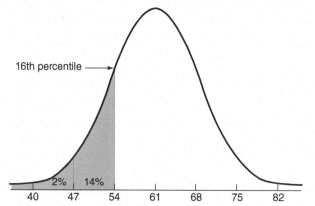

Assuming that test scores for a group of students were normally distributed—that is, if they conformed to a normal curve or close approximation of it—the SD of that group could be converted into numbers and percentages of students scoring above or below certain score points. Before illustrating this concept, however, we must know how to accomplish this conversion.

CONVERTED SCORES

Thus far, we have talked about scores that come directly from tests. These actual or obtained scores are called *raw* scores. Consider the following:

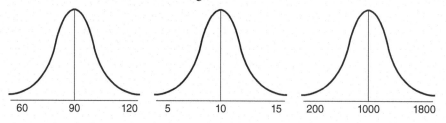

In these illustrations, all three distributions have the same shape, but their means and SDs are different, which is often what happens because tests have different ranges of scores. The example illustrates what we are up against when we try to compare scores from different tests.

The following example shows the process necessary to compare scores from distributions with different means and SDs.

John obtained a score of 85 on his psychology midterm and 90 on his history midterm. On which test did he do better compared to the rest of the class?

At first glance, you might say he did better in history. Well, this may be true, but how do you know? If you did say history, chances are you're treating the raw scores as percentages. Most of us are accustomed to test scores being converted into percentages before they are reported to us, but this is not always the case. John's score of 85 *may* mean he answered 85 out of 100 correctly, or it *may* mean he answered 85 out of 85 correctly, or 85 out of 217! Similarly, his history score may indicate he answered 90 out of 100, 90 out of 90, or 90 out of 329 items correctly. The point is that without additional information, we can't say which of these scores is higher or lower. With only raw scores reported, we *cannot* determine whether these scores are low, high, or intermediate. We need more information. Raw scores, by themselves, are *not* interpretable. This is an important but often overlooked point. Let's add some information.

The information we have—the raw scores—exists as part of two distributions: one for psychology and one for history. The distributions consist of the raw scores obtained by *all* the students who took these tests. If we can determine where John's scores fall in these distributions, we should be able to answer our question. First, we need information that describes each distribution. As we now know, the mean and SD are necessary to describe a distribution. If we have the mean and the SD for each distribution, we should be able to answer our question. Let's add the information we need, but one piece at a time. First, we will add the means. The mean in psychology was 75, and the mean in history was 140. Before we go any further, let's organize our data and examine them carefully.

Psychology	*History*
X = 85	X = 90
M = 75	M = 140

We see that John's score was 10 points above the class mean in psychology and 50 points below the class mean in history. Clearly, compared with the rest of the class, he performed better in psychology than in history. We have answered our question without even using the SD of these distributions. Well, then, of what value is the SD? As we will soon see, the SD will enable us to pinpoint the percentage of scores above or below each of these scores. At first glance, it may appear that John's history score is far below average, maybe even the lowest in the class. However, we don't know for sure because we have no idea how spread out or variable the history scores were.

Consider the following illustrations:

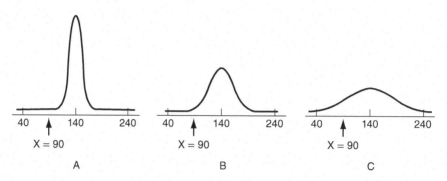

If the history scores are distributed as they are in the left-hand graph, then a score of 90 may indeed be among the lowest in the class. If the distribution looks like the middle graph, 90 will not be the lowest score. In the distribution in the right-hand graph, we can expect a fair percentage of scores to be lower than 90. Similarly, we don't know if John's psychology score of 85 is far above average or only a little above average, simply because we don't know how spread out the distribution is. We will now add the SDs and pinpoint the locations of John's scores in their respective distributions.

The SD in psychology was 10, and the SD in history was 25. Again, let's organize our data before we do anything else.

Psychology	*History*
X = 85	X = 90
M = 75	M = 140
SD = 10	SD = 25

Next, let's construct curves to represent these data, assuming that the scores are normally distributed.

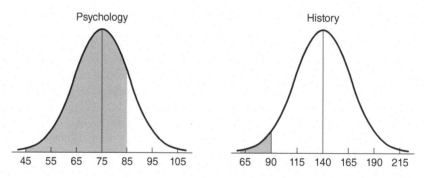

The shaded area in each distribution represents the proportion of scores below John's score. We can see that his psychology score is one SD above the mean, and his history score is two SDs below the mean. To determine exactly what percentage of scores is lower than John's scores, all we need to do is consult the normal curve diagram to determine the percentage of cases lower than one SD unit above the mean (for psychology) and lower than two SD units below the mean (for history).

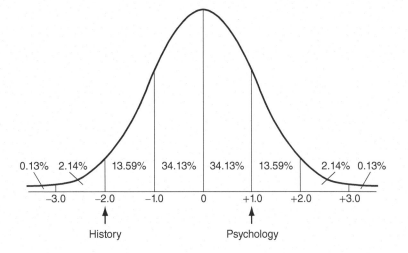

This diagram is identical to the normal curve presented in the section "Properties of the Normal Distribution." The normal curve is used when we need a common basis on which to compare scores from distributions with different means and SDs. Examining this distribution, we can see that about 84% of the class scored lower than John in psychology, while only about 2% scored lower in history. As compared with the rest of the class, his performance in psychology was far better than his performance in history. In psychology he scored at the 84th percentile, and in history he scored at the 2nd.

z-Scores

Now we have very specific information about John's performance. We had to collect the proper data (means and SDs for each distribution) and determine how far above or below the mean in SD units each score was in order to determine the percentage of scores below (or above) the obtained raw scores. It took a while, but we got there! Fortunately, there is a mathematical shortcut. A relatively simple formula enables us to determine a score's exact position in the normal distribution quickly. The formula is called the *z*-score formula, and it converts raw scores into what are called *z*-scores. These are scores that tell us how far above or below the mean in SD units raw scores lie:

$$z = \frac{X - M}{SD}$$

where

z = z-score

X = obtained raw score

M = mean score

SD = standard deviation

This formula enables us to convert raw scores from any distribution into a common scale, regardless of its mean or SD, so that we can easily compare such scores. This eliminates the confusion that would ordinarily result from such comparisons. As we mentioned, this formula is a shortcut method of doing what we just did in step-by-step manner.

In case you don't believe us, let's work through the same example, this time using the z-score formula.

John obtained a score of 85 on his psychology midterm and 90 on his history midterm. On which test did he do better compared to the rest of the class?

The first thing we should do is to organize the relevant information. We already have the raw scores, the mean, and the SD.

Psychology	*History*
X = 85	X = 90
M = 75	M = 140
SD = 10	SD = 25

Once we have all the necessary data—the obtained score, mean, and SD for each distribution—we are ready to plug the data into the z-score formula, obtain z-scores for each raw score, and compare these using the z-score distribution:

Psychology	*History*
$z = \dfrac{X - M}{SD}$	$z = \dfrac{X - M}{SD}$
$= \dfrac{85 - 75}{10}$	$= \dfrac{90 - 140}{25}$
$= \dfrac{10}{10}$	$= \dfrac{-50}{25}$
$= +1.0$	$= -2.0$

As you can see, we were quickly able to get the same results as before by using the mathematical formula (i.e., John's scores in psychology and history are +1 and −2 SDs from the mean, respectively). We can now use the properties of the normal curve to answer a variety of questions about these scores. For example,

What percentage of scores fall higher? Lower?

At what percentile do the scores lie?

How much better than average were the scores? How much poorer?

Just to make sure you understand the z-score concept, let's work through two examples.

EXAMPLE: *On a 70-item test, Mary obtained a score of 49. The test had a mean of 40 and a standard deviation of 3. What percentage of the class scored higher than Mary?*

Process

1. Organize the relevant information.

$$X = 49$$
$$M = 40$$
$$SD = 3$$

2. Convert to z-scores.

$$z = \frac{X - M}{SD}$$
$$= \frac{49 - 40}{3} = \frac{9}{3} = +3.0$$

3. Use the normal curve to answer questions about comparisons, percentages, or percentiles.

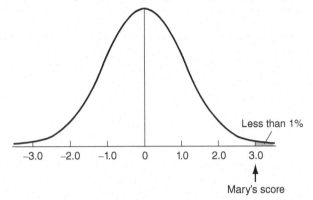

The shaded area in the z-score distribution indicates the percentage of obtained scores that were higher than Mary's. In other words, less than 1% (or, more accurately, 0.13% or less) of the individuals who took the test scored higher than Mary.

EXAMPLE: *On the verbal portion of the Scholastic Assessment Test (SAT), Pete obtained a score of 350. The mean of the SAT-V is 500, and its standard deviation is 100. The college Pete wants to go to will not accept applicants who score below the eighth percentile on the SAT-V. Will Pete be accepted by this college?*

Process

1. Organize data.

$$X = 350$$
$$M = 500$$
$$SD = 100$$

2. Compute the z-score.

$$z = \frac{X - M}{SD}$$

$$= \frac{350 - 500}{100} = \frac{-150}{100} = -1.5$$

3. Use the normal curve properties to draw conclusions.

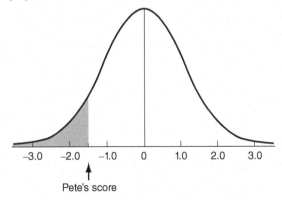

So far, we have not had to deal with z-scores containing decimals. We can see that the shaded area in the curve represents the percentage of scores below Pete's score. The question is, does this shaded area represent at least 8% of the scores obtained by others? If it does, Pete's score is at or above the eighth percentile, and he will be accepted. If it represents less than 8%, Pete's score is below the eighth percentile, and he will not be accepted.

In an introductory statistics course, you would learn to determine exactly what percentage of the z-score distribution falls below a z-score of 1.5, but we will settle for an estimate. Let's go ahead and estimate, considering the following illustration:

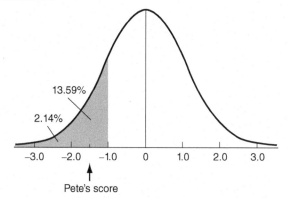

We know that about 2% of the scores fall below two z-score units below the mean and that about 14% fall between one and two z-score units below the mean. A common mistake is to erroneously assume that since -1.5 is halfway between -1.0 and -2.0, about 7% of the scores fall between -1.0 and -1.5 and another 7% fall between -1.5 and -2.0. This reasoning would be correct if the proportions of the curve between -1.0 and -1.5 and between -1.5 and -2.0 were the same. The following illustration shows, however, that a greater proportion of scores falls between -1.0 and -1.5 than falls between -1.5 and -2.0.

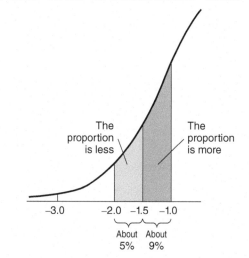

Remember, we are dealing with a curve, not with a histogram! If we were dealing with a histogram, splitting the percentage in half would be correct. Since we are not dealing with a histogram, we must estimate the proportions any time we have a z-score that results in a decimal number.

Now, returning to our example, we see that about 7% (2% below $z = -2$% and 5% between $z = -1.5$ and $z = -2.0$) of SAT-V scores fall below 350. Pete's score is below the eighth percentile. He will not be accepted by the college.

T-Scores

In working through this last example, at times you may have been confused about the negative numbers or may have forgotten that you were dealing with negative numbers. To avoid this difficulty, statisticians often convert z-scores into T-scores. T-scores are identical to z-scores, except that the T-score distribution has a mean of 50 and an SD of 10. Our z, or normal curve distribution, had a mean of 0 and an SD of 1.0. In the T-score distribution, negative numbers are eliminated except in those extremely rare cases where raw scores more than five SDs below the mean are obtained. To convert a raw score into a T-score, you must first convert into a z-score. The formula for a T-score is

$$T = 10z + 50$$

This formula says multiply the z-score by 10 and add 50 to this value to obtain the equivalent T-score. Let's convert John's psychology z-score of $+1.0$ and history score of -2.0 into T-scores.

<table>
<tr><td align="center">Psychology</td><td align="center">History</td></tr>
<tr><td align="center">$T = 10z + 50$</td><td align="center">$T = 10z + 50$</td></tr>
<tr><td align="center">$= 10(1.0) + 50$</td><td align="center">$= 10(-2.0) + 50$</td></tr>
<tr><td align="center">$= 10 + 50$</td><td align="center">$= (-20) + 50$</td></tr>
<tr><td align="center">$= 60$</td><td align="center">$= 30$</td></tr>
</table>

Thus, a z-score of 1.0 is equivalent to a T-score of 60, and a z-score of -2.0 is equivalent to a T-score of 30. Notice that the negative number has been eliminated. The following illustration shows the relationship between z-scores and T-scores:

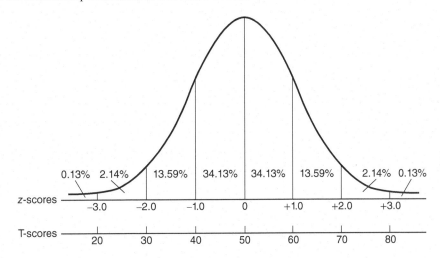

Thus far, we have considered statistical methods of tabulating and graphing data, the measures of central tendency and variability, the normal distribution, and converted scores. In the next chapter, we will consider another statistic, one that enables us to indicate how closely related or associated different sets of scores are.

SUMMARY

This chapter introduced you to the concept of score variability, methods to compute estimates of variability, the normal distribution, and converted scores. Its major points are as follows:

1. Variability is the term we use to describe how spread out or dispersed scores are within a distribution.

2. The range, a gross estimate of variability, is determined by subtracting the lowest score from the highest score in the distribution.

3. The semi-interquartile range (SIQR), which is usually reported along with the median, is determined by subtracting the value for the first quartile from the value for the third quartile and dividing the remainder by two.

4. The standard deviation (SD) is usually reported along with the mean and is our best estimate of variability. It is determined by subtracting the mean from each raw score to obtain a deviation score (x), squaring each deviation score, summing the squared deviation scores, dividing the total by the number of scores, and then determining the square root of this value.

5. Distributions with small standard deviations have a compressed appearance and are called homogeneous distributions.

6. Distributions with large standard deviations have a more expanded appearance and are called heterogeneous distributions.

7. The normal distribution is a specific type of symmetrical distribution that is mathematically determined and has fixed properties.

8. Although the normal distribution is hypothetical, it approximates the distribution of many test scores, enabling us to use it as a model on which to base statistical decisions.

9. We use the normal distribution as our basis for comparing scores from distributions with different means and standard deviations.

10. We do so by converting raw scores from different distributions to either z-scores or T-scores and using these converted scores as the baseline for the normal distribution. This enables us to compare scores from different distributions on a single distribution with a single mean and standard deviation.

11. Determine z-scores by subtracting the mean for the distribution from the raw score and dividing by the standard deviation of the distribution.

12. Determine T-scores by first computing the corresponding z-score for a raw score and then multiply the z-score by 10 and add 50 to the product.

13. The main advantage of the T-score over the z-score is the elimination of negative numbers.

14. Sometimes, the range is defined as the lowest score subtracted from the highest score plus 1. This is called the inclusive range. It is the statistic most often referred to in introductory statistics texts and is based on mathematical concepts that need not concern us here.

FOR DISCUSSION AND PRACTICE

*1. For this set of scores (5, 6, 6, 4, 5, 1, 2, 3, 5, 3), compute the following:

 a. N
 b. Mode
 c. Median
 d. Mean
 e. Standard deviation
 f. Variance
 g. Range

*2. Given M = 100 and SD = 10,

   a. Convert these raw scores into z-scores: 120, 132, 140, and 145.

   b. Convert these z-scores into raw scores: −2.5, 0.6, 1.25, and 2.15.

   c. Convert these T-scores into raw scores: 75, 38, 35, and 28.

   d. What percentages of scores lie between the following scores?

      75 − 90
      90 − 120
      100 − 110
      112 − 125

*3. A normal score distribution has a mean of 100 and a standard deviation of 15.

   a. What z-score is the equivalent of a raw score of 120?

   b. What raw score is most equivalent to a T-score of 33?

   c. Approximately what percentage of scores lies below a score of 85?

*4. A pupil obtains a raw score of 82 on a test with a mean of 100 and a standard deviation of 12. His score corresponds to what T-score?

*5. The mean for the following distribution is 80, and the standard deviation is 12. Assuming a normal distribution,

*Answers for these questions appear in Appendix B.

compute or determine the z-scores and T-scores for the following students:

Student	Score
John	68
Mary	104
Jim	86
Claire	62

*6. The following are the means and standard deviations of some well-known standardized tests, referred to as Test A, Test B, and Test C. All three yield normal distributions.

Test	Mean	Standard Deviation
Test A	500	100
Test B	100	15
Test C	60	10

   a. A score of 325 on Test A corresponds to what score on Test C? A score of 640 on Test A corresponds to what score on Test B?

   b. The counselor told Sally that she had scored so high on Test A that only 2 people out of 100 would score higher. What was Sally's score on Test A?

7. Your study partner for this course says he does not understand why both the concepts of central tendency and variability are necessary to describe and to compare distributions. Provide him with an explanation, and also include at least two real-world examples to illustrate your explanation.

CHAPTER 15

CORRELATION

LEARNING OUTCOMES

After completing this chapter, the student will be able to:

1. Explain what a correlation between two distributions means.
2. Provide examples of distributions that are highly or weakly correlated in everyday life.
3. Given a set of date from two distributions, develop a scatterplot and compute the correlation coefficient.
4. Interpret scatterplots and correlation coefficients as to strength, direction, and meaning.
5. Explain why the presence of even a very strong correlation does not imply causality.
6. Compare and contrast the correlation coefficient and the coefficient of determination.
7. Compare and contrast linear and curvilinear relationships.
8. Recognize a scatterplot depicting a curvilinear relationship.
9. Explain what the term "truncated range" means.
10. Explain why correlation coefficients computed from a truncated range of data will be weaker than if computed from the entire range of data.

OUR LAST statistical topic is correlation. Thus far, we have discussed statistics that are used to describe distributions and the position of individual scores within a distribution. There are times, however, when we are interested in the extent to which an individual's position or rank in one distribution is similar or dissimilar to his or her position or rank in a different distribution. That is, at times we want to determine how closely scores in *different* distributions are related to one another. Or, simply, we wish to know if individuals with high scores in distribution A also tend to obtain high scores in distribution B.

These and similar issues are concerned with the extent to which two different distributions of scores correlate. A statistic called a *correlation coefficient* (symbolized by r) helps us address general issues such as those just mentioned or answer specific questions such as those that follow:

Are athletes really poor scholars?

If you do poorly on the verbal portion of the SAT, are you likely to do poorly on the quantitative portion as well?

Do students with high grades in high school really tend to get high grades in college?

In this first question what is being asked is whether individuals who score high in a distribution of ratings pertaining to physical ability tend to score low in a distribution of ratings pertaining to intellectual ability. Using information gained from the previous chapter, we can illustrate this as follows:

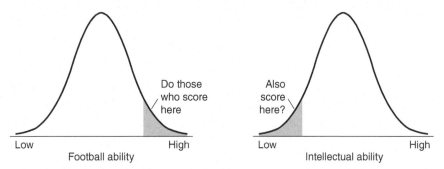

This question asks whether there is a *negative* correlation between the two. Are high scores in one distribution associated with low scores in the other?

The next question asks whether those who score low in the SAT-V distribution also score low in the SAT-Q distribution. Here, too, we can illustrate the question being asked, but note the difference from our previous illustration:

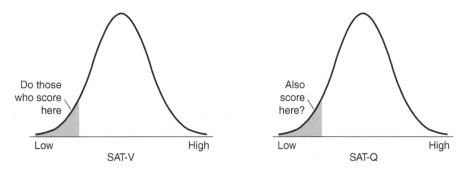

This question asks whether there is a *positive* correlation between the two distributions of scores.

Our last question asks whether students with high grades in high school also tend to receive high grades in college. This issue could be illustrated in the same manner as earlier:

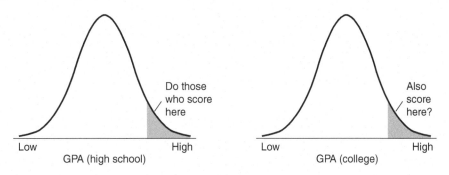

It asks whether there is a *positive* correlation between the two distributions. In other words, are high scores in one distribution associated with high scores in the other distribution?

THE CORRELATION COEFFICIENT

As we have seen, distributions can correlate positively or negatively. They may also not correlate at all! The correlation coefficient (r) tells us at a glance the strength and direction (positive or negative) of the relationship between distributions. Correlation coefficients range from -1.0 to $+1.0$. The closer a coefficient gets to -1.0 or to $+1.0$, the stronger the relationship. The sign of the coefficient tells us whether the relationship is positive or negative. The following examples are illustrative of correlation coefficients:

Coefficient	Strength	Direction
$r = -0.85$	Strong	Negative
$r = +0.82$	Strong	Positive
$r = +0.22$	Weak	Positive
$r = +0.03$	Very weak	Positive
$r = -0.42$	Moderate	Negative

Strength of a Correlation

The previous coefficients are described as ranging from very weak to strong. You may ask yourself, "How high must r be for it to be strong?" Well, there is no cut and dried answer to this question because an $r = 0.40$ may be considered strong for one set of data (e.g., correlation of IQ scores and "happiness") and very weak for another (e.g., correlation of scores from two standardized achievement tests intended to measure the same standards or objectives). In other words, we must always consider the distributions with which we are dealing before deciding whether an r is weak, moderate, or strong. If our distributions are composed of scores arrived at by fairly objective means, such as standardized achievement tests, we require r values to be fairly high (e.g., 0.80 or more) before we call them strong. When distributions are composed of scores arrived at by subjective means, such as ratings of happiness, job success, or maturity, we usually consider much lower r values (e.g., 0.50 to 0.60) as indicative of the presence of a strong relationship between the distributions in question.

Direction of a Correlation

The following illustrates the possible relationships between distributions that will result in positive or negative correlation coefficients. A positive correlation exists when:

1. High scores in distribution A are associated with high scores in distribution B.
2. Low scores in distribution A are associated with low scores in distribution B.

   A negative correlation exists when:

1. High scores in distribution A are associated with low scores in distribution B.
2. Low scores in distribution A are associated with high scores in distribution B.

A common example of a positive correlation is the relationship between height and weight. As people *increase* in height, they tend to *increase* in weight, and vice versa. A real-life example of negative correlation is the relationship between the number of cigarettes smoked per day and life expectancy. As the number of cigarettes smoked per day *increases*, life expectancy *decreases*, and vice versa. Fortunately, for those who are smokers, the correlation is not very strong.

When there is no systematic relationship between two distributions, correlation coefficients around .00 are found. These indicate that high scores in distribution A are likely to be associated with *both* high and low scores in distribution B, and vice versa. In other words, there is no consistent pattern.

Scatterplots

As we have noted, the strength and direction of a relationship between two distributions can be determined by a correlation coefficient. Scatterplots also enable us to determine the strength and direction of a correlation but in a less formal manner. A scatterplot is nothing more than a graphical representation of the relationship between two variables representing the scores in two distributions.

Suppose we are interested in determining whether there is a relationship between number of touchdowns scored and academic achievement. To do so, we randomly select five running backs from past football teams, count up the number of touchdowns they scored, and obtain copies of their transcripts. Although it is not necessary to do so, for illustrative purposes we will then rank each player on the two variables in question: touchdowns scored and GPA.[1] The results might look something like those in Figure 15.1, which is a scatterplot of the data for each individual player. This graph indicates that there is a *perfect negative* correlation ($r = -1.0$) between rank in touchdowns and rank in GPA. The player ranked highest in touchdowns is ranked lowest in GPA, and vice versa. There is a *perfect* correlation because all the plotted points can be connected by a straight line. We can tell that it is a *negative* correlation because the slope of the scatterplot descends from left to right.

Let's collect the same data from another school, one that emphasizes academics and not football. These data are shown in Figure 15.2. The scatterplot in Figure 15.2 indicates a *perfect*

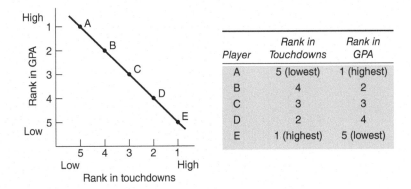

FIGURE 15.1   A scatterplot indicating a perfect negative correlation.

[1] We could also have used the unranked, or raw score, data. Our choice of data will determine the type of correlation coefficient that we compute and the symbol used to denote it, as we explain later.

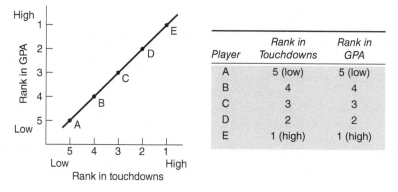

FIGURE 15.2 A scatterplot indicating a perfect positive correlation.

positive correlation ($r = 1.0$) between these variables. The player ranked lowest in touchdowns was also ranked lowest in GPA. The player ranked highest in touchdowns was also ranked highest in GPA. This is a *perfect* correlation because, again, the points are connected by a straight line. However, this time we can see the correlation is *positive* because the slope of the scatterplot ascends from left to right.

As you might have suspected, both of these examples are unrealistic. Perfect correlations, whether positive or negative, seldom occur. Normally, one ends up with r values somewhere between -1.0 and $+1.0$. Consider in Figure 15.3 the data collected from a third school. The scatterplot in this figure represents a *positive* correlation. However, it is not a perfect correlation because the points are "scattered" around the line rather than falling on the line. The line drawn through the points, called the regression line, is mathematically determined and is included here only to highlight the degree to which the data points slope upward or downward.

These data yield an r of 0.42. You can estimate the position of a regression line by drawing a straight line through the scattered points that best fits the movement of data upward (positive correlation) or downward (negative correlation). This movement is actually the rate at which rank in touchdowns changes relative to rank in GPA as we move from one individual to another. You may also enclose scattered data points with an ellipse, as we have done, to highlight the *strength* of the

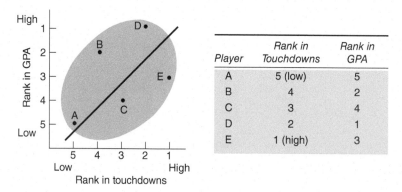

FIGURE 15.3 A scatterplot indicating a weaker positive correlation.

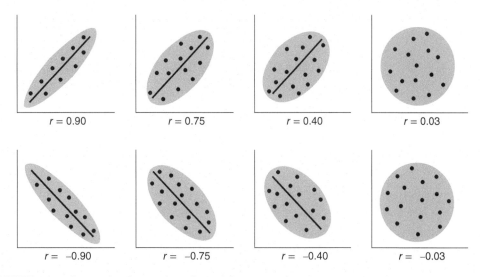

FIGURE 15.4 Scatterplots for a variety of correlations.

relationship. As the data points form a tighter and tighter ellipse, the correlation gets stronger. This is illustrated by the scatterplots in Figure 15.4. Notice that when r approaches zero, a circle rather than an ellipse may better capture all the data points. As these examples illustrate, we often deal with correlations less than $+1.0$ or -1.0 because people do not conform to strict rules governing relationships among their abilities and other characteristics. Instead, relationships occur according to general trends with lots of exceptions. For example, there is a positive relationship between height and weight. Tall people tend to weigh more than short people. However, there are reversals to this trend (or exceptions to the rule): tall, skinny folks and short, stout folks. The more reversals or exceptions present in relationships, the weaker the correlation between the variables.

Where Does *r* Come From?

The correlation is determined through any one of a variety of mathematical formulas. One of these formulas uses data that have been ranked, rather than raw scores—data like those shown in Figure 15.1. This type of correlation coefficient is called a rank difference correlation,[2] which has the following formula:

$$r_\rho = 1 - \frac{6\Sigma D^2}{N(N^2 - 1)}$$

where

r_ρ = rank difference coefficient of correlation

Σ = sum the terms that follow

D = difference between a pair of ranks

N = number of pupils

---

[2] The rank difference correlation is one of several different types of correlations. The Greek letter rho (ρ) is used to identify a rank difference correlation.

The results of this formula for the rank difference coefficient when applied to the data presented in Figure 15.1 are as follows:

Rank in Touchdown	Rank in GPA	Difference between Ranks	D^2
5	1	4	16
4	2	2	4
3	3	0	0
2	4	−2	4
1	5	−4	16
			$\Sigma D^2 = 40$

$$r_\rho = 1 - \frac{6(40)}{5(25-1)}$$
$$= 1 - \frac{240}{120} = 1 - 2 = -1.0$$

The calculation of another type of correlation coefficient, called the Pearson product–moment correlation coefficient, is illustrated with an example located on the companion website for this text (go to http://www.wiley.com/college/kubiszyn). The advantage of the rank difference correlation is that it can be used with small numbers of subjects, whereas the Pearson product–moment correlation must be used with larger numbers of scores, usually 30 or more pairs of scores. Generally, when this number of scores is obtained, the Pearson product–moment correlation (symbolized simply as r) is computed because it is easier to use and more accurate with more than 30 scores. However, since few teachers are ever called on to actually compute a correlation coefficient, especially on large numbers of students, we will not concern ourselves with computations for the Pearson product–moment correlation in this chapter. More important is your ability to understand and interpret correlation coefficients. Thus far, we have described what a correlation is, and we have considered the numerical and graphical representations of correlations. Next, let's consider a frequently misunderstood aspect of correlation.

Causality

Correlation does not imply causality. That is, a correlation only indicates that some sort of relationship or association exists between two distributions. It does not mean that one distribution of scores *causes* the other distribution of scores. This may seem perfectly logical and sensible to you. Yet, one of the most frequent misinterpretations in statistics (and in education) is to infer that because two variables are correlated with one another, one variable causes the other. It is possible that one variable may cause another, and thus account for the relationship between the two. However, it is just as possible, and usually more likely, that the two variables are correlated with each other because of the effects of some third unidentified variable. That is, a third variable is actually causing one or both conditions, thus making it appear as though the first variable is causing the second.

For example, there is a negative correlation between air temperature and frequency of colds. As air temperature decreases, the number of people who catch colds increases. Thus, one might infer, incorrectly, that a drop in air temperature will cause colds. While this is a possibility, it is much more likely that the effect is the result of the effects of a third variable. That is, rather than a drop in air temperature causing an increase in colds, it may be that a drop in air temperature causes people to stay indoors and come in contact with each other more frequently, which causes an increase in colds. Figure 15.5 illustrates the probable sequence of events.

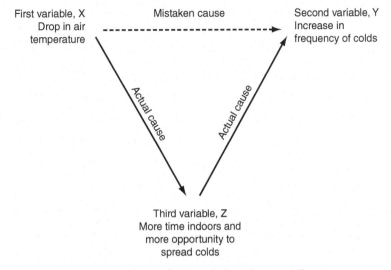

FIGURE 15.5 One way a third variable may affect conclusions about causality.

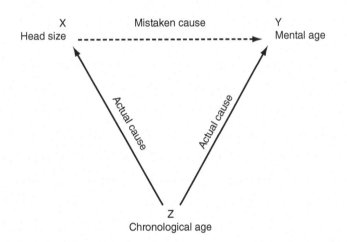

FIGURE 15.6 Another way a third variable may affect conclusions about causality.

Two variables may also correlate with one another because a third variable affects them both. For example, head size correlates with mental age. However, this does not mean that increases in head size cause increases in mental age. Both of these are affected by a third variable, chronological age, shown in Figure 15.6.

To sum up, in and of themselves, correlation coefficients alone can never be used to prove causality. Now that we are aware of this common misinterpretation, let's consider some other cautions.

Other Interpretive Cautions

Coefficient of Determination A correlation coefficient of 0.83 is referred to as "point eight three," *not* as 83%. Furthermore, to make comparative decisions about the relative strength of correlation coefficients, it is insufficient to simply compare the coefficients themselves. Instead, it is necessary to square the coefficient and multiply the result times 100. The result of this operation is called the *coefficient of determination*. The coefficient of determination is the percentage of variability (see Chapter 14) in one variable that is associated with or determined by the other variable. The following computations of the coefficient of determination demonstrate that a correlation coefficient of 0.80 is *4* times as strong as a coefficient of 0.40 and *16* times as strong as a coefficient of 0.20.

Correlation Coefficient (r)	r^2	$r^2 \times 100$	*Coefficient of Determination*
0.80	0.64	64	64%
0.40	0.16	16	16%
0.20	0.04	4	4%

The coefficient of determination is an important concept in more advanced statistical operations. For our purposes, we need to keep in mind only that correlation coefficients are not percentages and that we must convert correlation coefficients into the coefficient of determination *before* we can make decisions about their relative strength.

Curvilinearity All the scatterplots we have discussed thus far are plots of variables that have *linear* relationships with each other. In a linear relationship, scores on variables A and B either increase or decrease at approximately the same rate throughout the entire range of scores. That is, they progressively move up or down together in the same way regardless of whether they are at the low, middle, or high end of the score continuum. In a *curvilinear* relationship, scores on variables A and B may increase together at first and then decrease, or they may decrease at first and then increase, depending on whether the scores are at the low, middle, or high end of the score distribution. The curvilinear relationship between anxiety and test performance is depicted in the scatterplot here:

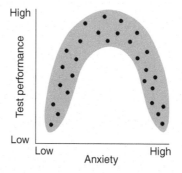

When data are related to each other in curvilinear manner, a curved regression line fits the data better than a straight regression line. This curvilinear relationship between anxiety and test performance indicates that increases in anxiety are positively associated with test performance up to a point, after which the association between anxiety and test performance is negative. When plotted, such data take on a boomerang shape. While it is possible to compute a correlation coefficient for such data, the coefficient is of a special type. For curvilinear data, computing a rank difference or Pearson coefficient like we would for linear data will yield an artificially low *r*. Thus, it is always a good idea to plot and inspect data before deciding on the type of correlation coefficient to compute or use.

Truncated Range Normally, we compute correlation coefficients across the range of all possible values for variables A and B. At times, however, we may desire or be forced to consider only a part of all the possible values (e.g., just low-ranked or high-ranked individuals). Here, we are dealing with a truncated or restricted range of scores. When only a portion of the entire range of scores is considered, the strength of the correlation coefficient goes down. The following scatterplots illustrate this phenomenon. The first scatterplot illustrates the relationship between IQ scores and standardized test scores.

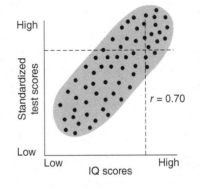

However, let's say that we are concerned only with the relationship between high scores on both tests (indicated by the broken lines demarcating the upper right-hand section of the scatterplot). The correlation between only the high scores is much weaker than the correlation between scores across the entire range. This is illustrated in the next scatterplot, which is an enlargement of the upper right-hand section of the previous scatterplot.

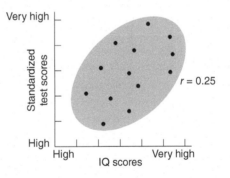

This completes our chapters on statistics. We trust you now have a good working knowledge of the concepts and methods presented. If so, you are ready to apply some of these concepts and methods in the following chapters. If not, now is the time to review. The remainder of the text will be a lot easier to understand if you take the extra time to master these concepts.

SUMMARY

In this chapter, you were introduced to a number of considerations related to the topic of correlation. The major points are as follows:

1. Correlation refers to the extent to which two distributions are related or associated. That is, it refers to the extent to which scores in one distribution vary depending on the variation of scores in the other distribution.

2. The extent of correlation is indicated numerically by a correlation coefficient (r) and graphically by a scatterplot.

3. When high scores in one distribution tend to be associated with low scores in another distribution, and vice versa, the correlation is negative.

4. When high scores in one distribution tend to be associated with high scores in another distribution (with the same being true for low and moderate scores), the correlation is positive.

5. Correlation coefficients may range from -1.0 (perfect negative correlation) to $+1.0$ (perfect positive correlation). A correlation of 0.00 indicates a complete absence of relationship or association.

6. The size of the number of the correlation coefficient indicates the strength of the correlation (higher numbers indicate stronger correlation), and the sign indicates the direction (positive or negative).

7. Scatterplots range from straight lines indicative of a perfect correlation to ellipses that approach circles. The tighter the ellipse, the stronger the correlation; the more circular the ellipse, the weaker the correlation.

8. The fact that two variables are correlated with one another does not necessarily mean that one variable causes the other. Often, the correlation is the result of the effects of a third variable.

9. To compare the relative strength of correlation coefficients, it is necessary to square the coefficients, resulting in coefficients of determination. Correlation coefficients are not percentages; coefficients of determination are.

10. When two distributions are linearly related, scores increase or decrease across the range of scores.

11. When two distributions have a curvilinear relationship, scores in one distribution may increase and then decrease, or vice versa, while scores in the other distribution consistently increase or decrease.

12. Since a linear correlation coefficient will underestimate the strength of a curvilinear relationship, it is wise to construct a scatterplot before computing a correlation coefficient to determine whether a linear correlation coefficient is appropriate.

13. When only a portion of the entire range of scores for a distribution is considered (e.g., only high or low scores) in computing a correlation coefficient, the strength of the correlation coefficient decreases. This effect is due to use of a truncated range of scores rather than the entire range of scores.

14. We could also have used the unranked, or raw score, data. Our choice of data will determine the type of correlation coefficient that we compute and the symbol used to denote it, as we explain later.

15. The rank difference correlation is one of several different types of correlations. The Greek letter rho (ρ) is used to identify a rank difference correlation.

FOR DISCUSSION AND PRACTICE

1. After pairing each X score with each Y score in the order given, construct a scatterplot of the data.

X: 15, 15, 15, 15, 30, 30, 30, 30, 45, 45, 45, 45, 60, 60, 60, 60, 75, 75, 75, 75

Y: 1, 2, 1, 3, 12, 10, 13, 15, 19, 18, 20, 21, 15, 11, 12, 12, 2, 3, 1, 2

*2. Does the scatterplot in Question 1 indicate that the data are linear or curvilinear? If X represents age and Y represents average annual income in thousands of dollars, describe this relationship in words.

*3. Using the formula given in Appendix D (online chapter), compute a Pearson product–moment correlation coefficient for the following data.

X: 10, 8, 14, 6, 4, 8, 7, 3, 7, 10

Y: 12, 7, 13, 8, 7, 6, 6, 4, 9, 11

How would you describe the direction and size of this relationship?

*4. Compute the coefficient of determination for the data in Question 3.

***5.** In the following matching exercise, Column A contains scatterplots and Column B contains correlation coefficients. Indicate which of the correlation coefficients in Column B most closely approximates the scatterplots in Column A by putting its number in the space to the left of the scatterplot. Each of the options may be used only once or not at all.

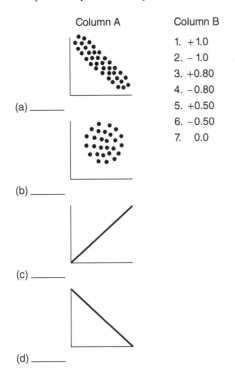

Column A

Column B

1. +1.0
2. −1.0
3. +0.80
4. −0.80
5. +0.50
6. −0.50
7. 0.0

(a) _____

(b) _____

(c) _____

(d) _____

*Answers for these questions appear in Appendix B.

***6.** A researcher finds a high positive correlation between shoe size and vocabulary size in elementary school pupils. The researcher concludes that big feet cause big vocabularies. Do you agree or disagree? If so, why? If not, why not?

***7.** Explain why the use of a truncated range of scores will result in a lower correlation between the variables in question than if the distribution were not truncated.

CHAPTER 16

VALIDITY EVIDENCE

LEARNING OUTCOMES

After completing this chapter, the student will be able to:

1. Explain why validity is the most important technical consideration for a test.
2. Define validity, reliability, and accuracy.
3. Compare and contrast content validity, concurrent validity, and predictive validity evidence.
4. Describe procedures used to establish the content validity evidence of a test.
5. Identify the most appropriate type of validity evidence when given different purposes for testing.
6. Identify the limitations of content validity procedures in appraising a test's validity.
7. Describe procedures used to establish the concurrent validity evidence of a test.
8. Describe procedures used to establish the predictive validity evidence of a test.
9. Describe procedures used to establish the construct validity evidence of a test.
10. Justify why content validity evidence is most important for achievement tests.
11. Apply the principles provided in the text to interpret validity coefficients.
12. Explain how group heterogeneity affects the size of a validity coefficient.
13. Select the most valid test for a given purpose when given different types of validity information.

IN THE PREVIOUS three chapters, we introduced you to the field of statistics. In this and subsequent chapters, we will show you how to use some of this newly acquired knowledge to evaluate tests. In short, we will show you how statistical tools are applied to test results to determine the degree of confidence we can place in the results.

WHY EVALUATE TESTS?

If a test shows that 60% of the students in our third-grade class are reading below grade level, should we be seriously concerned? Your initial response might be an unqualified yes, but we would say not necessarily. We would be worried only if we had confidence in the results of our test. We have such confidence only when we are reasonably sure a test measures the skill, trait, or attribute it is supposed to measure; when it yields reasonably consistent results for the same individual; and when it measures with a reasonable degree of accuracy. That is, we should seriously consider using test results only from tests that yield sufficient evidence that they are valid, reliable, and accurate for the purposes they are used for, and for the persons with whom they are used. As we discussed at some length in Chapter 1, a test may be used for more than one purpose and with people who have different characteristics, and the test may be more or less valid, reliable, or accurate when used for different purposes and with different persons. In general, we can define validity, reliability, and accuracy as follows:

1. *Validity:* Does the test measure what it is supposed to measure?
2. *Reliability:* Does the test yield the same or similar scores or rankings (all other factors being equal) consistently?
3. *Accuracy:* How closely does the test score represent an individual's true level of ability, skill, or aptitude?

To be a "good" test, a test ought to have adequate evidence for its validity, reliability, and accuracy for the purpose it is being used for and for the persons with whom it is being used. In this chapter, we will see how statistics help us determine the extent to which tests possess validity evidence.

TYPES OF VALIDITY EVIDENCE

A test has validity evidence if we can demonstrate that it measures what it says it measures. For instance, if it is supposed to be a test of third-grade arithmetic ability, it should measure third-grade arithmetic skills, not fifth-grade arithmetic skills and not reading ability. If it is supposed to be a measure of ability to write behavioral objectives, it should measure that ability, not the ability to recognize bad objectives. Clearly, if a test is to be used in any kind of decision making, or indeed if the test information is to have any use at all, we should be able to identify the types of evidence that indicate the test's validity for the purpose it is being used for.

Content Validity Evidence

There are several ways of deciding whether a test has sufficient validity evidence. The simplest is content validity evidence. The content validity evidence for a test is established by inspecting test questions to see whether they correspond to what the user decides should be covered by the test. This is easiest to see when the test is in an area such as achievement, where it is fairly easy to specify what the content of a test should include. It is more difficult if the concept being tested is a personality or an aptitude trait, as it is sometimes difficult to specify beforehand what a relevant question should look like. Another problem with content validity evidence is that it gives information about whether the test *looks* valid, but not whether the reading level of the test is too high or if the items are poorly constructed. A test can sometimes look valid but measure something entirely different than what is intended, such as guessing ability, reading level, or skills that may have been acquired before instruction. Content validity evidence is, therefore, more a minimum requirement for a useful test than it is a guarantee of a good test.

In the context of classroom testing, content validity evidence answers the question "Does the test measure the instructional objectives?" In other words, a test with good content validity evidence matches or fits the instructional objectives. In a high-stakes testing context, content validity evidence answers the question "Does the test align with state academic standards, or the Common Core State Standards (CCSS)?"

Criterion-Related Validity Evidence

A second form of validity evidence is criterion-related evidence. In establishing criterion-related validity evidence, scores from a test are correlated with an external criterion. There are two types of criterion-related validity evidence: concurrent and predictive.

Concurrent Criterion-Related Validity Evidence Concurrent criterion-related validity evidence deals with measures that can be administered at the same time as the measure to be validated. For instance, the *Stanford–Binet V* and the *Wechsler Intelligence Scale for Children–V* (WISC–V) are widely accepted well-known IQ tests. Therefore, a test publisher designing a short screening test that measures IQ might show that the test is highly correlated with the WISC–V or the Binet V and thus establish concurrent criterion-related validity evidence for the test. Unlike content validity evidence, criterion-related validity evidence yields a numeric value, which is simply a correlation coefficient. When used to illustrate validity evidence, the correlation coefficient is called a *validity coefficient.*

The concurrent validity evidence for a test is determined by administering both the new test and the established test to a group of respondents, and then finding the correlation between the two sets of test scores. If there exists an established test (criterion) in which most people have confidence, criterion-related validity evidence provides a good method of estimating the validity of a new test for this use. Of course, having a new test usually has some practical advantage—it is less expensive to give, or shorter, or it can be administered to groups. Otherwise, it would be easier simply to use the established test. The following example illustrates how concurrent validity evidence might be established for a new third-grade math test.

> *The Goodly Test of Basic Third-Grade Math has been around a long time, but it takes 60 minutes to administer. Being pressed for teaching time, you develop another test that takes only 20 minutes to administer and call it the Shorter and Better Test of Basic Third-Grade Math. With visions of fame and wealth you send it off to a test publisher.*
>
> *The publisher writes back to ask whether the test is as good as the Goodly Test: "No point marketing a test that isn't at least as good as the Goodly."*

To address this challenge, you would determine the test's concurrent validity evidence by giving both the Goodly and the Shorter and Better to the same group of students and calculating a correlation coefficient between scores on the two tests. If the same students rank similarly on both tests, indicated by a high correlation, the new test could be said to have concurrent validity evidence for this use. Consider the following hypothetical data:

Student	Score on Goodly	Score on Shorter and Better
Jim	88	37
Joan	86	34
Don	77	32
Margaret	72	26
Teresa	65	22
Victor	62	21
Veronica	59	19
Wilson	58	16

Since the correlation in this instance is likely to be very high (notice that, for the data shown, everyone maintains the same rank across tests), the concurrent validity evidence for the Shorter and Better Test has been established. The publisher will be impressed, and you will soon be famous.

Predictive Validity Evidence Predictive validity evidence refers to how well the test predicts some future behavior of the examinees. This form of validity evidence is particularly useful and important for aptitude tests, which attempt to predict how well test-takers will do in some future setting. The SAT, for instance, is frequently used to help decide who should be admitted to college. It would be desirable, therefore, for it to do a good job of predicting success in college. If a personality test is used to choose among various types of therapy for mental patients, it is desirable that it have good predictive validity evidence for that purpose. That is, it should predict who will do well with what kind of therapy. The predictive validity evidence of a test is determined by administering the test to a group of subjects, and then measuring the subjects on whatever the test is supposed to predict after a period of time has elapsed. The two sets of scores are then correlated, and the coefficient that results is called a *predictive validity coefficient.*

If a test is being used to make predictions, an effort should be made to find its predictive validity evidence for the setting in which it will be used. High-predictive validity evidence provides a strong argument for the worth of a test, even if it seems questionable on other grounds. In such a situation you might argue about whether it is being used to predict something worthwhile, but you can't argue about whether the test does a good job of predicting. The following example illustrates the concept of predictive validity evidence:

"Psychics predict blizzard for Houston on July 4th!" You have likely seen similar predictions in various tabloids while waiting in checkout lines at supermarkets. Are they valid? Initially, you'd probably say no, but how can you be sure? The only answer is to wait and see if the predictions come true. With a test, similar reasoning applies. Just because a test is named the Test to Predict Happiness in Life doesn't mean it can (or cannot). More likely than not, we would be inclined to say it can't. But again, the only way to be sure is to wait for a period of time and see if the individuals for whom the test predicts happiness are actually happy.

Both predictive and concurrent criterion-related validity evidence yield numerical indices of validity. Content validity evidence does not yield a numerical index, but instead yields a logical judgment as to whether the test measures what it is supposed to measure, based on a systematic comparison of the test to the domain it is intended to measure. However, all three of these indices—content, concurrent, and predictive—assume that some criterion exists external to the test that can be used to anchor or validate the test. In the case of content validity evidence for a classroom achievement test, it was the instructional objectives (or state academic standards, or the CCSS) that provided the anchor or point of reference; in the case of concurrent validity evidence, it was another well-accepted test measuring the same thing; and in the case of predictive validity evidence, it was some future behavior or condition we were attempting to predict. However, if a test is being developed to measure something not previously measured, or not measured well, and no criterion exists for anchoring the test, another kind of validity evidence must be obtained. This type of validity evidence is called *construct validity evidence.*

Construct Validity Evidence

A test has construct validity evidence if its relationship to other information corresponds well with some theory. A theory is simply a logical explanation or rationale that can account for the interrelationships among a set of variables. Many different kinds of theories can be used to help determine the construct validity evidence of a test. For instance, if a test is supposed to be a test of arithmetic computation skills, you would expect scores on it to improve after intensive coaching in arithmetic, but not after intensive coaching in a foreign language. If it is a test of mechanical aptitude, you might expect that mechanics would, on the average, do better on it than poets. You might also expect that it would have a *low* correlation with scores on a reading test, since it seems reasonable to assume that reading ability and mechanical ability are not highly related.

In general, any information that lets you know whether results from the test correspond to what you would expect (based on your own knowledge about what is being measured) tells you something about the construct validity evidence for a test. It differs from concurrent validity evidence in that there is no accepted second measure available of what you're trying to measure, and it differs from predictive validity evidence in that there is no available measure of future behavior.

Already in this chapter we have had to introduce some new terms and concepts. Before proceeding, be familiar with them, and if necessary, reread our presentation on validity evidence. Before you do, let's try to understand at a commonsense level what we've been saying.

WHAT HAVE WE BEEN SAYING? A REVIEW

A test should ideally do the job it's intended to do. It should measure what it's supposed to measure. In other words, we should be able to collect evidence of its validity for a particular use. The following three questions are equivalent:

1. Is the test valid for the intended purpose?
2. Does the test measure what it is supposed to measure?
3. Does the test do the job it was designed to do?

It makes no sense to prepare or select for the classroom a test designed to measure something other than what has been taught. If we want to measure someone's height, does it make sense to use a scale? A ruler, yardstick, or a tape measure would certainly be more appropriate. Similarly, if we are interested in knowing whether our students can multiply two-digit numbers, would it make sense to administer a test that focuses on the addition of two-digit numbers? The appropriate measure would be a test that includes items on two-digit multiplication. Such a test would *do the job it's supposed to do*. It would have content validity evidence.

For achievement tests, content validity evidence is most important because the "job" of an achievement test is to measure how well the content taught has been mastered. The best way to ensure that a test has content validity evidence is to be sure its items match or measure the instructional objectives. Recall that in Chapter 6 we discussed ways to check whether items match objectives. Now, let's review predictive validity evidence.

Consider a situation in which the purpose of a test is to identify those individuals who are likely to stay with a company for at least 3 years. A valid test in this case would accomplish this purpose. But just what is the purpose? Is it to measure how well certain concepts have been mastered? No, the purpose is to predict who will last 3 years and who won't. A different kind of validity evidence is necessary—predictive validity evidence.

In this situation, we are interested only in finding a measuring instrument that correlates well with length of time on the job. We don't care whether it is an IQ test, math test, reading test, vocational test, visual–motor integration test, or whatever. The purpose is to predict who will last 3 years. If the math test correlates 0.75 with length of time on the job and the vocational test correlates 0.40 with length of time on the job, which test has the better predictive validity evidence? The math test, of course, because it would provide us with the most accurate prediction of future behavior.

In the case of concurrent validity evidence, the purpose of a test is to approximate the results that would have been obtained had a well-established test been used. In other words, if the ranking of students with the new or shorter test *concurs* with the rankings of students on the older, standard test, then the new or shorter test has concurrent validity evidence. Remember, unless a new test does something more easily or better than an established measure, there is no point in constructing a new test!

Finally, let's think about construct validity evidence. Construct validity evidence is important in establishing the validity of a test when we cannot anchor our test either to a well-established test measuring the same behavior or to any measurable future behavior. Since we do not have these anchoring devices to rely on, we can only create verbal and mathematical descriptions or theories of how our test behavior (called a construct) is either likely to change following or during certain situations or likely to be related to other constructs. If a test of our theory reflects or demonstrates the relationships specified, the new measure has construct validity evidence. Unlike predictive and concurrent validity evidence, not one but many correlation coefficients emerge from a construct validation study. The actual process used to assess construct validity evidence can be lengthy and complex and need not concern us here. Figure 16.1 summarizes our discussion of the types of validity evidence most relevant in the classroom. Believe it or not, our presentation of test

	Ask the question:	*To answer the question:*
• Content Validity Evidence	Do test items match and measure objectives?	Match the items with objectives.
• Concurrent Criterion-Related Validity Evidence	How well does performance on the new test match performance on an established test?	Correlate new test with an accepted criterion, for example, a well-established test measuring the same behavior.
• Predictive Criterion-Related Validity Evidence	Can the test predict subsequent performance, for example, success or failure in the next grade?	Correlate scores from the new test with a measure of some future performance.

Remember: Predictive validity evidence involves a time interval. A test is administered and, after a period of time, a behavior is measured which the test is intended to predict. For example:

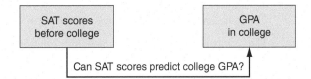

Remember: Concurrent validity evidence does not involve a time interval. A test is administered, and its relationship to a well-established test measuring the same behavior is determined. For example:

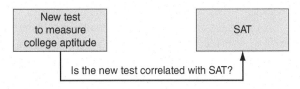

FIGURE 16.1 Review of validity evidence.

validity has been quite superficial as far as measurement theory goes. If you are interested in a more intensive discussion of any of these topics, you can consult one or more of the measurement texts listed in Appendix E (online chapter). Next, we will discuss the role of validity coefficients in evaluating tests.

INTERPRETING VALIDITY COEFFICIENTS

Now that we have discussed and reviewed the concepts of content, concurrent, and predictive validity evidence, we can begin to put these concepts to use in evaluating educational tests. Remember, validity coefficients enable us to estimate the extent to which a test measures what it is supposed to measure. Let's consider the role of validity coefficients in making decisions about tests.

Content Validity Evidence

If you are wondering why content validity evidence is included in this section, you are probably grasping more of what has been presented than you may realize. Procedures to determine a test's content validity evidence do *not* yield validity coefficients. Content validity evidence is established by comparing test items with instructional objectives (e.g., with the aid of a test blueprint, see Chapter 6) to determine whether the items match or measure the objectives. After such an examination takes place, a test is judged either to have or not to have content validity evidence for a particular use. No correlation coefficient is computed. Instead, human judgment is relied upon.

Concurrent and Predictive Validity Evidence

Concurrent and predictive validity evidence requires the correlation of a predictor or concurrent measure with a criterion measure. These types of validity evidence do yield numerical coefficients. Using our interpretation of these coefficients, we can determine whether a test is useful to us as a predictor or as a substitute (concurrent) measure. In general, the higher the validity coefficient, the better the validity evidence for the test is. However, several principles must be considered in evaluating validity coefficients.

> **PRINCIPLE 1.** Concurrent validity coefficients are generally higher than predictive validity coefficients. This does *not* mean, however, that the test with the higher validity coefficient is more suitable for a given purpose.

The rationale for this principle is that in establishing concurrent validity evidence, no time interval (or a very small time interval) is involved between administration of the new test and the criterion or established test. Thus, the chance that the behavior of individuals measured on both the new test and the criterion test has changed between testings is negligible. On the contrary, predictive validity evidence coefficients are by definition susceptible to such changes. Lifestyle, personality, and attitudinal or experiential changes may alter an individual's rank on a criterion measure 2 years from now from what it was at the initial testing. Thus, a *decline* in the size of the correlation between the test and a measure of future performance would be expected as the time interval between the two measurements increases.

Generally, concurrent validity coefficients in the 0.80 and higher range and predictive validity coefficients in the 0.60 and higher range are considered encouraging. However, judgments about the strength of a validity coefficient must consider the attributes being measured. If a new achievement test reports a concurrent validity coefficient of 0.60 with an established achievement test, we probably would not consider using the new achievement test; we would look for higher correlations because correlations between achievement tests are generally higher. On the other hand, if a new college selection test correlated 0.60 with college GPA, the new test might be considered suitable for use as a college selection test because correlations between such tests and GPA are generally much lower. In other words, the *purpose* of the test as well as the size of the validity coefficient must be considered in evaluating the test's validity evidence.

PRINCIPLE 2. Group variability affects the size of the validity coefficient. Higher validity coefficients are derived from heterogeneous groups than from homogeneous groups.

If the college selection test mentioned earlier was administered to *all* high school seniors in a district (a heterogeneous group) and if all these students went to the same 4-year college, the obtained validity coefficient would be higher for this group than if the test were administered only to high school seniors in the top 10% of their class (a homogeneous group). At first glance this may not seem to make sense. The picture becomes clear, however, if we think about how changes in the rankings of individuals on the two measures are affected by the variability of these distributions. In the heterogeneous group, students who are at the top of their high school class are likely to score high on the test and have high college GPAs. Students at the bottom of the class are likely to score low and have low college GPAs. That is, the likelihood of major shifting in ranks occurring is small. It's not likely that students who score low on the test will have high GPAs and vice versa, as is illustrated in Figure 16.2. Although some shifting in ranks or position might be expected,

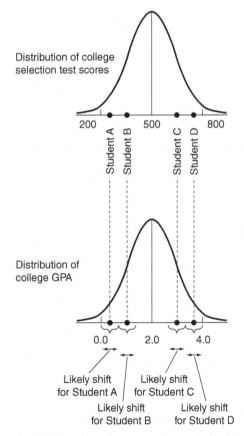

FIGURE 16.2 Comparison of probable rankings between college selection test scores and college GPA for four students from a heterogeneous group.

as indicated by the arrows in Figure 16.2, dramatic shifts would be unlikely. While it might be possible for our lowest scoring student on the selection test (Student A) to obtain a 3.5 GPA, it would be unlikely.

But what happens when the variability of the group is greatly reduced, creating a homogeneous group composed only of the top 10% of the high school seniors? Now we would expect a pronounced shifting of ranks or positions to take place. This is likely to occur because the students are all ranked so closely together on the selection test that even small differences between their ranks on GPA will lower the size of the validity coefficient. This is illustrated in Figure 16.3.

Compare the overlap, or possible shifting in ranks, for this group to the possible shifting in ranks for the heterogeneous group. The width of the arrows has not changed, but their significance has. There is much more likelihood of dramatic shifts occurring among the students in this homogeneous group. They are so much alike in ability that the test is unable to discriminate among those individuals in the high-ability group who will rank low, middle, or high in their GPAs, since the range of GPAs for this group is only about 3.5–4.0. When test scores or criterion measures are more heterogeneous; however, the test is able to discriminate among those who will rank low, moderate, or high in GPAs. In such a case, GPAs might range from 0.0 to 4.0.

In evaluating the adequacy of a test's validity coefficient, it is necessary to consider the variability of the group from which the coefficient was derived. For example, critics who discourage using the SAT-II as a criterion for college admission often point out that its predictive validity evidence coefficient is only about 0.40. What they may fail to consider, however, is that the coefficient

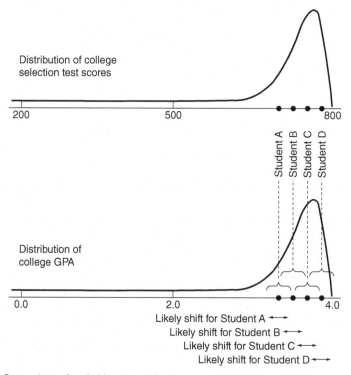

FIGURE 16.3 Comparison of probable rankings between college selection test scores and college GPA for students from a homogeneous group (upper 10% of senior class).

is not based on all high school students, but only on those who took the test and actually went to college. This is a far more homogeneous group than the entire body of high school students. Thus, its predictive validity evidence coefficient is smaller than would be expected if it were based on *all* high school students.

PRINCIPLE 3. The relevance and reliability of the criterion should be considered in the interpretation of validity coefficients.

Wherever predictive validity evidence is being considered, it is necessary to be aware that the size of the resulting coefficient is dependent on both the reliability of the predictor *and* the criterion measure. If you are using a test to predict whether someone will last for 3 years on a job, your criterion is easy to measure, and your criterion measure would be dependable. For this measure, you need simply to determine whether someone is employed after 3 years. Unfortunately, in many cases criterion measures are not so simple. For example, let's say you want to establish the predictive validity evidence of a test to predict job success rather than simply whether someone is employed after 3 years. What does job success mean? Herein lies the problem of selecting a criterion measure. Is it best measured by salary scale? Number of promotions? Amount of sales? Merchandise produced? Supervisor ratings? Peer ratings? All of these? We could probably go on and on, but the point is that criterion measures that are meaningful are often difficult to identify and agree upon.

Each of the criterion measures mentioned may be an important *aspect* of job success, but none is *equivalent* to job success. Ideally, you would want to collect many measures of job success and determine their relationship to the test. In reality, however, such a thorough approach might be impossible due to financial or time constraints. What typically happens in a predictive validity investigation is that one or two of what are considered to be relevant criterion measures are selected and correlated with the predictor. Naturally, such a compromise limits somewhat the weight that one might attach to predictive validity coefficients, since not all relevant aspects of the criterion are considered.

If a test has a predictive validity coefficient of 0.60 with salary after 3 years, but coefficients of 0.20 with supervisor ratings and 0.16 with peer ratings, we would question the test's validity evidence. Since salary typically increases from year to year, often independent of success on the job, the correlation with salary might not be very meaningful, since salary may not be all that *relevant*. On the other hand, supervisor and peer ratings may be more relevant measures. However, our test's correlation with those measures is little more than what might occur by chance. Since the test does not correlate highly with more relevant criteria, we might question its predictive validity evidence. However, to do so without considering the dependability of the criterion measure, we have chosen would be a mistake.

To correlate highly or even moderately with each other, measures must be dependable or fairly stable (i.e., *reliable*). If ratings by supervisors or peers vary greatly from rating period to rating period, then any attempt to correlate such ratings with a predictor will yield low correlation coefficients—even if the predictor is highly reliable. If an employee gets a high rating from one peer or supervisor and a low rating from another, how can the predictor possibly predict a rating? The answer is that it can't. Some evidence of stability or reliability in a criterion measure is necessary before we can conclude that a predictor that correlates poorly with a criterion measure is actually a poor predictor and not a reflection of an unreliable criterion measure.

We have intended this discussion to alert you to the importance of studying carefully any and all statistical data presented in test manuals. Where predictive validity coefficients are reported, check the adequacy (the relevance) of the criterion measure and its dependability (the reliability) before drawing any conclusions about the validity evidence for the predictor.

SUMMARY

This chapter introduced you to the major types of validity evidence and some principles to be considered in interpreting validity coefficients. The major points are as follows:

1. To be considered seriously, test results should have adequate validity evidence and be reliable.

2. A valid test measures what it is supposed to measure.

3. Content validity evidence is assessed by systematically comparing a test item with instructional objectives (or the CCSS or state academic standards) to see if they match. Content validity evidence does not yield a numerical estimate of validity.

4. Criterion-related validity evidence is established by correlating test scores with an external standard or criterion to obtain a numerical estimate of validity evidence.

5. There are two types of criterion-related validity evidence: concurrent and predictive.
   a. Concurrent validity evidence is determined by correlating test scores with a criterion measure collected at the same time.
   b. Predictive validity evidence is determined by correlating test scores with a criterion measure collected after a period of time.

6. Construct validity evidence is determined by finding whether test results correspond with scores on other variables as predicted by some rationale or theory.

7. In interpreting validity evidence, the following principles should be kept in mind:
   a. The adequacy of validity evidence depends on both the strength of the validity coefficient and the purpose of the test.
   b. Group variability affects the strength of the validity coefficient.
   c. Validity coefficients should be considered in terms of the relevance and reliability of the criterion or standard.

FOR DISCUSSION AND PRACTICE

*1. A teacher who is a friend of yours has just developed a test to measure the content in a social studies unit you both teach. His test takes 30 minutes less time to complete than the test you have used in the past, and this is a major advantage. You decide to evaluate the new test by giving it and the old test to the same class of students. Using the following data, determine if the new test has concurrent validity evidence.

   a. Scores on the new test: 25, 22, 18, 18, 16, 14, 12, 8, 6, 6.
   b. Scores for the same students on the old test: 22, 23, 25, 28, 31, 32, 34, 42, 44, 48.

*2. Indicate how and with what types of tests you would evaluate the predictive and construct validity evidence of the new social studies test in Question 1.

*3. Examine the validity coefficients of the following tests and, assuming that they have content validity evidence, determine which are suitable for use. State your reasons. What is unusual about Test C?

	Test A	Test B	Test C
Concurrent validity coefficients	0.90	0.50	0.75
Predictive validity coefficients	0.72	0.32	0.88

*4. Assuming that the following tests measure the same content and assuming that all other things are equal, rank them in terms of their overall acceptability for predicting behavior in upcoming years.

	Test A	Test B	Test C
Concurrent validity coefficient	0.90	0.80	0.85
Predictive validity coefficient (1-month interval)	0.50	0.65	0.60
Predictive validity coefficient (6-month interval)	0.40	0.10	0.55

*5. What types of validity evidence go with the following procedures?

    a. Matching test items with objectives.

    b. Correlating a test of mechanical skills after training with on-the-job performance ratings.

    c. Correlating the short form of an IQ test with the long form.

*Answers for these questions appear in Appendix B.

    d. Correlating a paper-and-pencil test of musical talent with ratings from a live audition completed after the test.

    e. Correlating a test of reading ability with a test of mathematical ability.

    f. Comparing lesson plans with a test publisher's test blueprint.

*6. The principal is upset. The results of the 4-year follow-up study are in. The correlation between the grades assigned by you to your gifted students and their college GPA is lower than the correlation between grades and college GPA for nongifted students. The principal wants to abandon the gifted program. How would you defend yourself and your program?

7. A colleague says that as long as a test is reliable it can be used. Apply what you have learned from the textbook so far to point out the flaws in your colleague's thinking.

CHAPTER 17

RELIABILITY

LEARNING OUTCOMES

After completing this chapter, the student will be able to:

1. Differentiate between test reliability and score reliability.
2. Define the three different methods of estimating score reliability.
3. Describe procedures used to estimate test–retest score reliability.
4. Describe procedures used to estimate alternate-forms score reliability.
5. Identify situations in which test–retest or alternate-forms score reliability is most appropriate.
6. Describe procedures used to compute split-half and Kuder–Richardson estimates of internal consistency.
7. Describe how the Spearman–Brown prophecy formula is used and its effect on the reliability coefficient.
8. Compare and contrast power and speeded tests and their relationship to score reliability.
9. Discuss the pros and cons of using only internal consistency score reliability estimates.
10. Apply the principles provided in the text to interpret score reliability coefficients.
11. Explain why group heterogeneity affects score reliability coefficients.
12. Explain why longer tests tend to be more reliable than shorter tests.
13. Explain why different estimates of reliability will yield different reliability coefficients for the same test.
14. Select the best test for a given purpose when provided with score reliability information for different tests.
15. Select the best test for a given purpose when given score reliability and validity evidence for several tests.
16. Identify the most appropriate type of score reliability when given different purposes for testing.

THE RELIABILITY of a test refers to the consistency with which it yields the same rank for individuals who take the test more than once. In other words, a test (or any measuring instrument) is reliable if it consistently yields the same, or nearly the same, ranks over repeated administrations during which we would not expect the trait being measured to have changed. For instance, a bathroom scale is reliable if it gives you the same weight after five weighings in a single morning. If the five weights differ by several pounds, the scale is not especially reliable. If the five weights differ by 25 pounds, it is extremely unreliable. In the same manner, scores from educational tests may be very reliable, fairly reliable, or totally unreliable. For instance, if a multiple-choice test given to a class were so difficult that everyone guessed at the answers, then a student's rank would probably vary quite a bit from one administration to another and the test would be unreliable.

If any use is to be made of the information from a test, it is desirable that the test results, or scores, be reliable (or consistent). If the test is going to be used to make placement decisions about individual students, you wouldn't want it to provide different rankings of students if it were given again the next day. If a test is going to be used to make decisions about the difficulty level of your instructional materials, you wouldn't want scores from the test to indicate that the same materials are too difficult one day and too easy the next. In testing, as in our everyday lives, if we have use for some piece of information, we would like that information to be stable, consistent, and dependable.

METHODS OF ESTIMATING SCORE RELIABILITY

There are several ways to estimate the reliability of scores from a test. It is common for reliability to be attributed to a test, as though it is a fixed characteristic of a test. As we will see in this chapter and Chapter 18, this is not accurate. Many factors can influence scores from the same test when administered to different groups or for different purposes (see Chapter 1). For example, the reliability of a test's score when administered to English language learners may differ from the reliability of its scores when administered to English-proficient students. Because the reliability of a test's scores varies, it is correct to refer to a test's *score* reliability rather than a *test's* reliability. The three basic methods most often used are called *test–retest*, *alternative form*, and *internal consistency*.

Test–Retest or Stability

Test–retest is a method of estimating score reliability that is exactly what its name implies. The test is given twice, and the correlation between the first set of scores and the second set of scores is determined. For example, suppose a math test given to six students on Monday is given again on the following Monday without any math having been taught in between these times. The six students make the following scores on the test:

Student	*First Administration* *Score*	*Second Administration* *Score*
1	75	78
2	50	62
3	93	91
4	80	77
5	67	66
6	88	88

The correlation between these two sets of scores is 0.96. It could be concluded that scores from this test are quite reliable. Or, if you prefer, the coefficient indicates that the scores are very consistent or stable.

The main problem with test–retest reliability data is that there is usually some memory or experience involved the second time the test is taken. That means that the scores may differ not only because of the unreliability of the test but also because the students themselves may have changed in some way. For example, they may have gotten some answers correct on the retest by remembering or finding answers to some of the questions on the initial test. To some extent this problem can be overcome by using a longer interval between test administrations, to give memory a chance to fade. However, if the interval is too long, the students may have changed on the trait being measured because of other factors, for example, reading in the library, instruction in other courses, seeing a film, and so on. So, in considering test–retest reliability coefficients, the interval between testings must also be considered. In general, the longer the interval between test and retest, the lower the reliability coefficient will be. Test–retest reliability is illustrated in Figure 17.1.

Alternate Forms or Equivalence

If there are two equivalent forms of a test, these forms can be used to obtain an estimate of the reliability of the scores from the test. Both forms are administered to a group of students, and the correlation between the two sets of scores is determined. This estimate eliminates the problems of memory and practice involved in test–retest estimates. Large differences in a student's score on two forms of a test that supposedly measures the same behavior would indicate an unreliable test. To use this method of estimating score reliability, two equivalent forms of the test must be available, and they must be administered under conditions as nearly equivalent as possible. The most critical problem with this method of estimating score reliability is that it takes a great deal of effort to develop *one* good test, let alone two. Hence, this method is most often used by test publishers who are creating two forms of their test for other reasons (e.g., to maintain test security). Figure 17.2 illustrates alternate-forms reliability.

Internal Consistency

If the test in question is designed to measure a single basic concept, it is reasonable to assume that people who get one item right will be more likely to get other similar items right. In other words,

To determine test–retest score reliability, the same test is administered twice to the same group of students, and their scores are correlated. Generally, the longer the interval between test administrations, the lower the correlation. Since students can be expected to change with the passage of time, an especially long interval between testings will produce a "reliability" coefficient that is more a reflection of student changes on the attribute being measured than a reflection of the reliability of the test.

This time interval reflects the reliability of the test.	January 1 Test A	February 1 Test A
	Correlation, $r = 0.90$	
This time interval reflects the reliability of the test plus unknown changes in the students on the attribute being measured.	January 1 Test A	June 1 Test A
	Correlation, $r = 0.50$	

FIGURE 17.1 Test–retest reliability.

To determine alternate-forms reliability of a test, two different versions of the same test are administered to the same group of students in as short a time period as possible, and their scores are correlated. Efforts are made to have the students complete one form of the test in the morning and another equivalent form of the test in the afternoon or the following day.

June 1, morning   June 1, afternoon
Test A (Form X)   Test A (Form Y)

Correlation, $r = 0.80$

FIGURE 17.2 Alternate-forms reliability.

items ought to be correlated with each other, and the test ought to be internally consistent. If this is the case, the reliability of the scores for the test can be estimated by the internal consistency method. One approach to determining a test's internal consistency, called *split halves*, involves splitting the test into two equivalent halves and determining the correlation between them. This can be done by assigning all items in the first half of the test to one form and all items in the second half of the test to the other form. However, this approach is only appropriate when items of varying difficulty are randomly spread across the test. Frequently, they are not; easier items are often found at the beginning of the test and difficult items at the end. In these cases, the best approach would be to divide test items by placing all odd-numbered items into one half and all even-numbered items into the other half. When this latter approach is used, the reliability data are called *odd–even reliability*.

Split-Half Methods To find the split-half (or odd–even) reliability, each item is assigned to one half of the test or the other. Then, the total score for each student on each half is determined and the correlation between the two total scores for both halves is computed. Essentially, a single test is used to make two shorter alternative forms. This method has the advantage that only one test administration is required and, therefore, memory or practice effects are not involved. Again, it does not require two tests. Thus, it has several advantages over test–retest and alternate-form estimates of reliability. Because of these advantages, it is the most frequently used method of estimating the reliability of classroom tests. This method is illustrated in Figure 17.3.

Internal consistency calculated by this method is actually a way of finding alternate-form reliability for a test half as long as the original test. However, since a test is usually more reliable if it is longer, the internal consistency method *underestimates* what the actual reliability of the full test would be. The split-half (or odd–even) reliability coefficient should be corrected or adjusted

The internal consistency of a test is determined from a single test administration. Hence it does not involve a time interval as do the test–retest and alternate-form methods. The test is split into two equal parts and the total scores for each student on each half of the test are correlated. The internal consistency method of determining reliability is appropriate only when the test measures a unitary homogeneous concept (e.g., addition or finding the least common denominator) and not a variety of concepts.

Half of Test A   Half of Test A
(e.g. even-numbered items)   (e.g. odd-numbered items)

Correlation, $r = 0.75$

FIGURE 17.3 Internal consistency reliability (odd–even method).

upward to reflect the reliability that the test would have if it were twice as long. The formula used for this correction is called the Spearman–Brown prophecy formula.

$$r_w = \frac{2r_h}{1 + r_h}$$

It is where r_w is the correlation for the *whole* test and r_h is the correlation between the two *halves* of the test. The result of applying this formula gives the predicted split-half (or odd–even) reliability coefficient for a test twice as long as either of its halves. In almost all cases, it will increase the size of the reliability coefficient from that computed for the two half-tests.

Kuder–Richardson Methods

Another way of estimating the internal consistency of a test is through one of the Kuder–Richardson (KR) methods. These methods measure the extent to which items within one form of the test have as much in common with one another as do the items in that one form with corresponding items in an equivalent form.

The strength of this estimate of reliability depends on the extent to which the entire test represents a *single*, fairly consistent measure of a concept. Normally, KR techniques will yield estimates of reliability somewhat lower than those of split halves, but higher than test–retest or alternate-form estimates. These procedures are sometimes called item–total correlations.

There are several ways to determine the internal consistency of a test using KR procedures. Of these, two ways are frequently seen in test manuals. The first is more difficult to calculate since it requires that we know the percentage of students passing each item on the test. It is, however, the most accurate and has the name KR20 (Kuder–Richardson formula 20). The resulting coefficient is equal to the average of all possible split-half coefficients for the group tested. The second formula, which is easier to calculate but slightly less accurate, has the name KR21. It is the least cumbersome of the KR formulas and requires knowledge only of the number of test items (n), the mean of the test (M), and its variance (SD^2). The variance is simply the square of the standard deviation (see Chapter 14). The formula for KR_{21} is

$$KR_{21} = \frac{n}{n-1}\left(1 - \frac{M(n-M)}{nSD^2}\right)$$

We know, this formula looks intimidating, but it really isn't. Let's work an example to show you how it's done. Let's say we have a 100-item test, with a mean score of 70 and a standard deviation of 10. Plugging in the numbers, we can determine KR_{21}:

$$KR_{21} = \frac{100}{99}\left(1 - \frac{70(100-70)}{100(10)^2}\right)$$

$$KR_{21} = 1.01\left(1 - \frac{2,100}{10,000}\right)$$

$$KR_{21} = 1.01(0.79) = 0.80$$

KR_{21} tends to produce a smaller (less accurate) coefficient than KR_{20} but has the advantage of being easier to calculate. Test publishers often report a KR coefficient, so it is important that you recognize it and know something about it.

Before leaving the topic of internal consistency, we need to mention one other coefficient because of its frequent use. This coefficient, called coefficient Alpha, is closely related to KR procedures but has the advantage of being applicable to tests that are multiply scored, that is, that are not scored right or wrong or according to some other all-or-none system. For example, on attitude or personality surveys, the respondent may receive a different numerical score on an item depending on whether the response "all," "some," "a little," or "none" is checked. In such cases, our previous methods of determining internal consistency would not be applicable, and the coefficient Alpha should be used. Coefficient Alpha is laborious to compute, so its computation is best left to a computer program or the test publisher. Its interpretation is not difficult, however, because it is interpreted the same way as the KR methods and therefore may be taken as an index of the extent to which the instrument measures a single, unified concept.

Problems with Internal Consistency Estimates Internal consistency techniques are useful and popular measures of reliability because they involve only one test administration and are free from memory and practice effects. However, there are some cautions to consider when using these methods. First, they should only be used if the entire test consists of similar items measuring a single concept. Thus, they *would* be appropriate for use on a spelling test, but *not* for a language test involving a spelling section, a reading comprehension section, and a composition section.

A second caution is that measures of internal consistency yield inflated estimates of reliability when used with *speeded* tests. A speeded test consists entirely of easy or relatively easy item tasks with a strict time limit. On such a test, test-takers are expected to correctly answer most items attempted. Ranks or grades are usually assigned mostly on the basis of the number of items attempted (since the items are easy, most attempts are successful), rather than on mastery of the subject areas, written expression, and so forth. Examples of speeded tests are typing tests or such manual dexterity tests as screwing nuts on bolts or putting square pegs in square holes.

Speeded tests may be thought of in contrast to *power tests*. Power tests have difficult items, or items varying in difficulty, but have such generous time limits that most students have an opportunity to attempt most or all of the items. With a power test, ranks or grades are assigned based mostly on the quality or "correctness" of answers, rather than on the number of items attempted. Examples of power tests are essay tests, word problems, and reasoning tasks. In reality, most tests are a combination of power *and* speed tests. The typical classroom or standardized achievement test is partially a speeded test (e.g., some easy items and fairly strict time limits) and partially a power test (e.g., items range in difficulty, and most students are expected to attempt most items in the allotted time).

Why is this important? Recall that we said that measures of internal consistency yield inflated estimates of reliability when used with speeded tests. Since most achievement tests are partially speeded, estimates of internal consistency reliability that are computed for such tests will also be somewhat inflated. Naturally, they will not be as falsely high as they would be for a *pure* speeded test, but they will be high enough to suggest that the test scores are more reliable than they actually are. For this reason, it is always preferable to look for a second estimate of reliability (e.g., test–retest or alternate form) rather than relying on the internal consistency method to evaluate the reliability of a test's scores. In Chapter 18, we will also see that internal consistency measures are not as sensitive to errors in test construction, administration, and scoring as are other types of reliability data.

INTERPRETING RELIABILITY COEFFICIENTS

In Chapter 16, we discussed several principles relevant to the interpretation of validity coefficients. These were provided to give you some guidelines with which to consider the validity evidence of a test. In this chapter, we will discuss several principles related to the interpretation of reliability coefficients, which should prove useful as guidelines in evaluating the reliability of scores from a test.

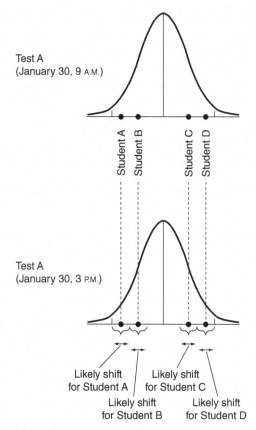

FIGURE 17.4 Comparison of probable rankings for repeated administrations of the same test (or alternate forms of the same test) for four students from a heterogeneous sample.

Our first principle relates to the effect of group variability on the size of the reliability coefficient. It should sound familiar, since we considered this concept in discussing the interpretation of validity coefficients.

> **PRINCIPLE 1.** Group variability affects the size of the reliability coefficient. Higher coefficients result from heterogeneous groups than from homogeneous groups.

Rather than present our rationale for this principle, we suggest that you might want to refresh your memory by reviewing principle 2 from Chapter 16. The concept applied here is exactly the same, except that it refers to repeated administrations of the same test, or to alternate forms of the same test, rather than predictor and criterion measures. Figures 17.4 and 17.5 illustrate principle 1 applied to test–retest reliability.

> **PRINCIPLE 2.** Scoring reliability limits test score reliability. If tests are scored unreliably, error is introduced that will limit the reliability of the test scores.

Recall that in Chapters 8–10 we emphasized how important it is to make essay, performance, and portfolio scoring as reliable as possible. If there is little agreement among scorers about the "correctness" of an answer, scores for an otherwise good test or assessment may not have sufficient reliability. Stated another way, if scoring reliability is 0.70, then 0.70 becomes the *maximum*

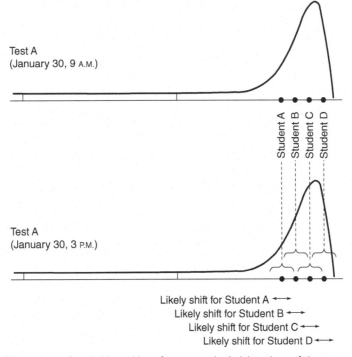

FIGURE 17.5 Comparison of probable rankings for repeated administrations of the same test (or alternate forms of the same test) for four students from a homogeneous sample.

possible reliability of the test scores. In reality, it would be even lower since other sources of error would add to the unreliability of the test scores. This is why objectivity in scoring and clerical checks is important. Before dismissing a test as yielding scores that are too unreliable for your purposes, check its scoring reliability. It may be that improvements in scoring procedures will result in a reliability increment large enough to make the test usable.

> **PRINCIPLE 3.** All other factors being equal, the more items included in a test, the higher the reliability of the scores.

There are several reasons for this principle. First, the number of items increases the potential variability of the scores (i.e., group variability will increase). According to principle 1, this will lead to an increase in the stability of ranks across administrations and increased reliability. Second, when more items are added to a test, the test is better able to sample the student's knowledge of the attribute being measured. For example, a 10-item test about the presidents of the United States will provide a more reliable and representative sample of student knowledge of U.S. presidents than a two-item test. With a two-item test, a student might get lucky and guess correctly twice, earning a perfect score. Furthermore, such a limited sample may penalize better prepared students since its narrow focus may miss much of what they have mastered. It should be noted that principle 3 is the basis of the Spearman–Brown prophecy formula we introduced earlier. A caution is in order, however. Simply increasing the number of items on a test will not *necessarily* increase the reliability of the test's scores. For example, if the extra items are ambiguous or otherwise poorly written items, then score reliability will likely *decrease*. Only if the added items are at least the equivalent of those in the original, test will score reliability increase.

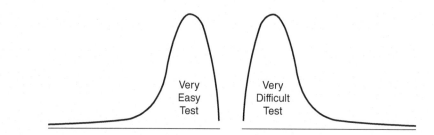

FIGURE 17.6 Score distributions for very easy and very difficult tests.

In interpreting the reliability of a test's scores, always consider its length. A very short test with a score reliability of 0.80 may, with only a few more items added, turn out to measure some trait just as well as or better than a longer test with a score reliability of 0.90.

> **PRINCIPLE 4.** Reliability of test scores tends to decrease as tests become too easy or too difficult.

As tests become very easy (nearly everyone answers all of the items correctly) or very difficult (nearly everyone answers all of the items incorrectly), score distributions become homogeneous, which is illustrated in Figure 17.6. By referring to principle 1, we can conclude that when distributions are homogeneous, significant shifting of ranks and a lowering of the correlation coefficient will occur. Another factor worth considering is that when tests are made very difficult, guessing is encouraged. This is another source of error that serves to lower test score reliability even further. Hence, both very easy and very difficult tests will have low score reliabilities. Because of error due to guessing, score reliability for very difficult tests will be even less than for very easy tests.

SUMMARY

This chapter introduced you to the concept of reliability, various methods of estimating reliability, and several principles to be considered in interpreting reliability coefficients. Its major points are as follows:

1. Reliability refers to the stability of a test score over repeated administrations. A test with good score reliability will yield stable scores over repeated administrations, assuming that the trait being measured has not changed.

2. Test–retest estimates of score reliability are also called measures of stability. They are obtained by administering the same test twice to the same group of individuals, with a small time interval between testing, and correlating the scores. The longer the time interval, the lower test–retest estimates will be.

3. Alternate-form estimates of score reliability are also called measures of equivalence. They are obtained by administering two alternate or equivalent forms of a test to the same group and correlating their scores. The time interval between testings is as short as possible.

4. Internal consistency estimates of score reliability fall into two general categories: split-half or odd–even estimates and item–total correlations, such as the Kuder–Richardson (KR) procedures. These estimates should be used only when the test measures a single or unitary trait.

5. Split-half and odd–even estimates divide a test into halves and correlate the halves with one another. Because these correlations are based on half-tests, the obtained correlations underestimate the score

reliability of the whole test. The Spearman–Brown prophecy formula is used to correct these estimates to what they would be if they were based on the whole test.

6. KR methods determine the extent to which the entire test represents a single, fairly consistent measure of a concept.

7. Internal consistency estimates tend to yield inflated score reliability estimates for speeded tests.

8. Since most achievement tests are at least partially speeded, internal consistency estimates for such tests will be somewhat inflated.

9. In interpreting reliability coefficients, the following principles should be considered:
   a. Group variability affects test score reliability. As group variability increases, score reliability goes up.
   b. Scoring reliability limits test score reliability. As scoring reliability goes down, so does the test's score reliability.
   c. Test length affects test score reliability. As test length increases, the test's score reliability tends to go up.
   d. Item difficulty affects test score reliability. As items become very easy or very hard, the test's score reliability goes down.

FOR DISCUSSION AND PRACTICE

*1. All other things being equal, which test—A, B, or C—would you use?

Type of Reliability	Test A	Test B	Test C
Split-half reliability coefficient	0.80	0.90	0.85
Test–retest reliability coefficient	0.60	0.60	0.75
Alternate-forms reliability	0.30	0.60	0.60

*2. If the unadjusted odd–even reliability for a test's scores is 0.60, what is its true reliability?

*3. What reliability coefficient would be least appropriate in each of the following situations?

   a. The test is speeded.

   b. The test measures heterogeneous topics.

   c. Students can easily learn the answers from taking the test.

*4. Assuming that the scores for the following tests all had exactly the same internal consistency reliability coefficient of 0.75, and assuming all other things are equal, which test—A, B, or C—would you use?

Aspect of Test	Test A	Test B	Test C
Content	Homogeneous	Heterogeneous	Homogeneous
Test length	50 items	25 items	100 items
Difficulty	Average	Difficult	Average
Speed/power	Speeded	Speed and power	Power

*5. For each of the following statements indicate which type of reliability is being referred to from among the four alternatives that follow:

   Test–retest   Alternate-forms (long interval)
   Alternate forms   Split-half

   a. "Practice effects" could most seriously affect this type of reliability.

   b. This procedure would yield the lowest reliability coefficient.

   c. This approach requires the use of a formula to adjust the estimate of the reliability to that for a total test.

   d. This approach should be used by teachers who want to give comparable (but different) tests to students.

   e. Changes due to item sampling will not be reflected.

*6. Both Test A and Test B claim to be reading achievement tests. The technical manual for Test A reports a test–retest reliability of 0.88, and the technical manual for Test B reports split-half reliability of 0.91. Test B has good content validity evidence with Mr. Burns's classroom objectives. Test A has good concurrent validity evidence with a recognized reading test, but measures several skills not taught by Mr. Burns. If Mr. Burns wishes to evaluate progress over his course of instruction, which test should be used for both his pretest and posttest?

*7. Both Test A and Test B claim to be reading readiness tests for use in placing children in first-grade reading groups.

*Answers for these questions appear in Appendix B.

Neither test reports validity data. The technical manual for Test A reports an internal consistency reliability of 0.86, and the technical manual for Test B reports a test–retest reliability of 0.70. If a first-grade teacher came to you for advice on test selection, what would be your recommendation?

8. Your instructor's test includes the following statement: "A test that has high score reliability may or may not also yield good validity evidence." Do you agree or disagree with this statement? Take a stand and defend your position based on what has been covered in this chapter and Chapter 16.

CHAPTER 18

ACCURACY AND ERROR

LEARNING OUTCOMES

After completion of this chapter, the student will be able to:

1. Explain what the authors mean by accuracy as it applies to test scores.
2. Define and give examples of error in testing.
3. Explain how error can operate to both increase and decrease test scores.
4. Compare and contrast obtained, true, and error scores.
5. Describe the error score distribution.
6. Explain why the standard deviation of the error scores is important in test interpretation.
7. Compare and contrast the standard deviation and the standard error of measurement.
8. Apply the standard error in interpreting test scores when provided with test data.
9. Compute the standard error when given data about a test's standard deviation and reliability.
10. Compute 68%, 95%, and 99% confidence bands around obtained scores when given the standard error.
11. Explain why the standard error should always be used in interpreting test scores.
12. Identify the four sources of error in testing.
13. Give examples of each of the four sources as they apply to classroom testing.
14. Describe the extent to which the various estimates of score reliability are differentially affected by the sources of error.
15. Compare and contrast real and chance differences between scores.
16. Explain how band interpretation can help us differentiate between real and chance differences among subtest scores in a test battery.
17. Given subtest scores and standard errors construct a band interpretation table.
18. Interpret differences as real or chance at both the 68% and 95% confidence levels.

WHEN IS A test score less than completely accurate? Almost always. Surprised? If you are, you have reason to be. We have learned (or have been programmed) to put a great deal of faith in test scores. In fact, to some individuals, test results represent the ultimate truth. Our position is that tests and the scores they yield are useful, and also fallible. They come with varying degrees of "goodness," but no test or score is completely valid or reliable. Furthermore, as we discussed in Chapters 1 and 4, a test's reliability and validity will vary depending on the purpose of the test and the population with which it is used. In other words, all tests and scores are imperfect and are subject to error.

If most or all test scores were perfectly reliable, we could put a great deal of confidence in a person's score from a single test. If Student A scores 75 on a test with perfectly reliable scores, then 75 is his or her "true" score. However, most test scores are not perfectly reliable—in fact, most test scores are a long way from being perfectly reliable. Therefore, when Student A scores 75 on a test, we only hope that his or her true score—his or her actual level of ability—is somewhere around 75. The closer the score reliability of a test is to perfect, the more likely it is that the true score is very close to 75.

Later in this chapter, we will introduce a special statistic that will enable you to estimate the *range* of scores within which lies an individual's true score or true level of ability. This is the extent of the precision we can realistically arrive at in interpreting test scores. In other words, a score from any test is our best guess about an individual's true level of knowledge, ability, achievement, and so forth, and, like all guesses, the guesses we make can be wrong.

All tests are subject to various sources of error that impair the reliability of their scores and, consequently, the accuracy with which they represent an individual's true score. Logically, if we understand the sources of error in test scores, we should be able to minimize them in constructing administering and scoring tests and thereby improve test score reliability. But just what is "error" in testing?

ERROR—WHAT IS IT?

"I've made a mistake." We have all said this aloud or to ourselves at one time or another. In other words, we've made an error—we have failed to do something perfectly, or as well as we would like to have done it. The notion of error in testing is very similar. No test measures perfectly, and many tests fail to measure as well as we would like them to. That is, tests make "mistakes." They are always associated with some degree of error. Let's look at a test score more closely.

Think about the last test you took. Did you obtain exactly the score you thought or knew you deserved? Was your score higher than you expected? Was it lower than you expected? What about your *obtained* scores on all the other tests you have taken? Did they *truly* reflect your skill, knowledge, or ability, or did they sometimes underestimate your knowledge, ability, or skill? Or did they overestimate? If your obtained test scores did not always reflect your true ability, they were associated with some error. Your obtained scores may have been lower or higher than they should have been. In short, an *obtained score* has a *true* score component (actual level of ability, skill, and knowledge) and an *error* component (which may act to lower or raise the obtained score).

Can you think of some concrete examples of a type of error that lowered your obtained score? Remember when you couldn't sleep the night before the test, when you were sick but took the test anyway, when the essay test you were taking was so poorly constructed it was hard to tell what was being tested, when the test had a 45-minute time limit but you were allowed only 38 minutes, or when you took a test that had multiple defensible answers? Each of these examples illustrates various types of error. These and perhaps other sources of error prevented your "true" score from equaling your obtained score. Another way of saying this is simply that your obtained score equaled your true score *minus* any error.

Now, what about some examples of situations in which error operated to *raise* your obtained score above your actual or "true" level of knowledge, skill, or ability? In short, what about the times you obtained a higher score than you deserved? Never happened, you say! Well, what about the time you just happened to see the answers on your neighbor's paper, the time you got lucky guessing, the time you had 52 minutes for a 45-minute test, or the time the test was so full of unintentional clues

TABLE 18.1   The Relationship among Obtained Scores, Hypothetical True Scores, and Hypothetical Error Scores for a Ninth-Grade Math Test

Student	Obtained Score	True Score[a]	Error Score[a]
Donna	91	88	+3
Jack	72	79	−7
Phyllis	68	70	−2
Gary	85	80	+5
Marsha	90	86	+4
Milton	75	78	−3

[a]Hypothetical values.

that you were able to answer several questions based on the information given in other questions? Each of these examples illustrates error. Again, because of this error your obtained score was not a completely accurate reflection of your true score. You received a higher score than you deserved! In these cases, your obtained score equaled your true score *plus* any error.

Then how does one go about discovering one's true score? Unfortunately, we do not have an answer. The true score and the error score are both theoretical and hypothetical values. We never actually know an individual's true score or error score. Why bother with them then? They are important concepts because they allow us to illustrate some important points about test score reliability and test score accuracy. For now, simply keep in mind the following:

$$\text{Obtained score} = \text{true score} \pm \text{error score}$$

Table 18.1 illustrates the relationship among obtained scores, true scores, and error. In considering the table, remember that the *only* value in the table we are sure about is the obtained score value. We *never* know what the exact true scores are or what the exact error scores are. This is probably one of the most abstract and challenging concepts you have to master.

According to Table 18.1, Donna, Gary, and Marsha each obtained higher scores than they should have. These students had error work to their advantage in that their obtained scores were higher than their true scores.

On the other hand, Jack, Phyllis, and Milton each obtained lower scores than they should have. These students had error work to their disadvantage in that their obtained scores were *lower* than their true scores. Unfortunately, as noted earlier, we never actually know what an individual's true and error scores are. The values shown in our table are hypothetical values used to impress on you the fact that *all* test scores contain error. If you understand the notion of test error, you already have an intuitive understanding of our next topic, the standard error of measurement.

THE STANDARD ERROR OF MEASUREMENT

The standard error of measurement of a test (abbreviated S_m) is the standard deviation of the *error scores* of a test. In the following calculations, S_m is the standard deviation of the error score column. It is determined in the same manner you would determine a standard deviation of any score distribution (see Chapter 14). Review the following calculations to confirm this. We will use error scores from Table 18.1: 3, −7, −2, 5, 4, −3.

Step 1: Determine the mean.

$$M = \frac{\Sigma X}{N} = \frac{0}{6} = 0$$

Step 2: Subtract the mean from each error score to arrive at the deviation scores. Square each deviation score and sum the squared deviations.

$$
\begin{array}{rrr}
\text{X} - \text{M} = & x & x^2 \\
+3 - 0 = & 3 & 9 \\
-7 - 0 = & -7 & 49 \\
-2 - 0 = & -2 & 4 \\
+5 - 0 = & 5 & 25 \\
+4 - 0 = & 4 & 16 \\
-3 - 0 = & -3 & 9 \\
& & \overline{\Sigma x^2 = 112}
\end{array}
$$

Step 3: Plug the sum x^2 into the formula and solve for the standard deviation.

$$
\text{Error score SD} = \sqrt{\frac{\Sigma x^2}{N}} = \sqrt{\frac{112}{6}} = \sqrt{18.67} = 4.32 = S_m
$$

The standard deviation of the error score distribution, also known as the standard error of measurement, is 4.32. If we could know what the error scores are for each test we administer, we could compute S_m in this manner. But, of course, we never know these error scores. If you are following so far, your next question should be, "But how in the world do you determine the standard deviation of the error scores if you never know the error scores?"

Fortunately, a rather simple statistical formula can be used to estimate this standard deviation (S_m) without actually knowing the error scores:

$$
S_m = SD\sqrt{1 - r}
$$

where r is the reliability of the test and SD is the test's standard deviation.

Using the Standard Error of Measurement

Error scores are assumed to be random. As such, they cancel each other out. That is, obtained scores are inflated by random error to the same extent as they are deflated by error. Another way of saying this is that the mean of the error scores for a test is zero. The distribution of the error scores is also important since it approximates a normal distribution closely enough for us to use the normal distribution to represent it. In summary, then, we know that error scores (1) are normally distributed, (2) have a mean of zero, and (3) have a standard deviation called the standard error of measurement (S_m). These characteristics are illustrated in Figure 18.1.

Returning to our example from the ninth-grade math test depicted in Table 18.1, we recall that we obtained an S_m of 4.32 for the data provided. Figure 18.2 illustrates the distribution of error scores for these data. What does the distribution in Figure 18.2 tell us? Before you answer, consider this: The distribution of error scores is a normal distribution. This point is an important one since, as you learned in Chapter 14, the normal distribution has characteristics that enable us to make decisions about scores that fall between, above, or below different points in the distribution. We are able to do so because fixed percentages of scores fall between various score values in a normal distribution. Figure 18.3 should refresh your memory.

In Figure 18.3, we listed along the baseline the standard deviation of the error score distribution. This is more commonly called the *standard error of measurement* (S_m) of the test. Thus, we can see that 68% of the error scores for the test will be no more than 4.32 points higher or

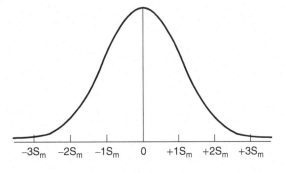

FIGURE 18.1 The error score distribution.

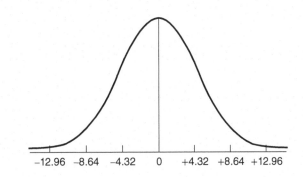

FIGURE 18.2 The error score distribution for the test depicted in Table 18.1.

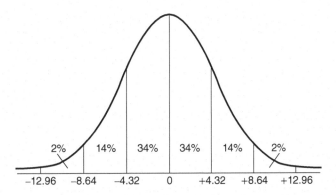

FIGURE 18.3 The error score distribution for the test depicted in Table 18.1 with approximate normal curve percentages.

4.32 points lower than the true scores. That is, if there were 100 obtained scores on this test, 68 of these scores would *not* be "off" their true scores by more than 4.32 points, plus or minus the obtained score. The S_m then tells us about the distribution of obtained scores around true scores. By knowing an individual's true score, we can predict what his or her obtained score is likely to be.

The careful reader may be thinking, "That's not very useful information. We can never know what a person's true score is, only their obtained score." This is correct. As test users, we work

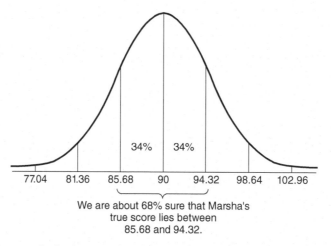

We are about 68% sure that Marsha's
true score lies between
85.68 and 94.32.

FIGURE 18.4 The error distribution around an obtained score of 90 for a test with S_m = 4.32.

only with obtained scores. However, we can follow our logic in reverse. If 68% of obtained scores fall within 1 S_m of their true scores, then 68% of true scores must fall within 1 S_m of their obtained scores. Strictly speaking, this reverse logic is somewhat inaccurate when we consider individual test scores. However, across all test scores, it would be true 99% of the time (Gullikson, 1987). Therefore, the S_m is often used to determine how test error is likely to have affected individual obtained scores.

Let's use the following number line to represent an individual's obtained score, which we will simply call X:

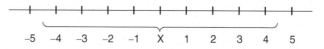

That is, X plus or minus 4.32 (±4.32) defines the range or band, which we are about 68% sure contains this individual's true score. Extending this reasoning, we can construct a similar band around *any* obtained score to identify the range of scores that, at a certain level of confidence, will capture or span an individual's true score. Stated another way, if a student obtains a score of X on a test, the student's true score on the test will be within ±1S_m of X about 68% of the time. We know this to be the case since error (the difference between obtained and true scores) is normally distributed. We can conceptualize what we have been describing by considering error to be normally distributed around any obtained score. Returning once again to our ninth-grade math test (Table 18.1), we see that Marsha had an obtained score of 90. We also know that the S_m for the test was 4.32. Knowing the data, and that error is normally distributed, we can graphically depict the distribution of error around Marsha's obtained score of 90 as shown in Figure 18.4. Figure 18.5 illustrates the distribution of error around an obtained score of 75 for the same test.

Why all the fuss? Remember our original point. All test scores are fallible; they contain a margin of error. The S_m is a statistic that estimates this margin for us. We are accustomed to reporting a single test score. Considering the S_m, that is, reporting a range of scores that spans or captures an individual's true score, helps us present a more realistic picture of someone's obtained scores. From our last two examples, we could conclude with 68% certainty that for a distribution with a standard error of measurement of 4.32, each student's true score would be captured by a

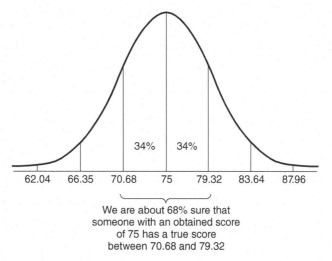

We are about 68% sure that
someone with an obtained score
of 75 has a true score
between 70.68 and 79.32

FIGURE 18.5   The error distribution around an obtained score of 75 for a test with $S_m = 4.32$.

range of scores 4.32 points, plus or minus, from his or her obtained score. Left unsaid was the fact that we would probably be wrong in drawing such a conclusion 32% of the time! Even though we report a band of scores 8.64 points wide around a single score, we will still draw an incorrect conclusion 32% of the time.

This is *not* an exceptional case. Even the *best* tests often have S_m of 3–5 points (more or less, depending on the scale). In education we have long had a tendency to *overinterpret* small differences in test scores since we too often consider obtained scores to be completely accurate. Incorporating the S_m in reporting test scores greatly minimizes the likelihood of overinterpretation and forces us to consider how fallible our test scores are. After considering the S_m from a slightly different angle, we will show how to incorporate it to make comparisons among test scores. This procedure is called *band interpretation*. First, however, let's sew up a few loose ends about S_m.

More Applications

Let's look again at the formula for the standard error of measurement:

$$S_m = SD\sqrt{1 - r}$$

We know that an obtained score, X, $\pm 1S_m$ will span or capture the true score 68% of the time. Extending this thinking further, we know that the range of scores covered by $X \pm 2S_m$ will capture the true score 95% of the time. Finally, we know that the range of scores covered by $X \pm 3S_m$ will capture the true score more than 99% of the time. Figure 18.6 illustrates these relationships.

Let's work an example. Scores for a test have a standard deviation of five points and a reliability of 0.75. The standard error of measurement of the test is

$$S_m = 5\sqrt{1 - 0.75} = 5\sqrt{0.25} = 2.5$$

If a student obtains a score of 80 on the test, you know that his or her true score lies between

77.5 and 82.5 ($X \pm 1S_m$) 68% of the time

75 and 85 ($X \pm 2S_m$) 95% of the time

72.5 and 87.5 ($X \pm 3S_m$) 99% of the time

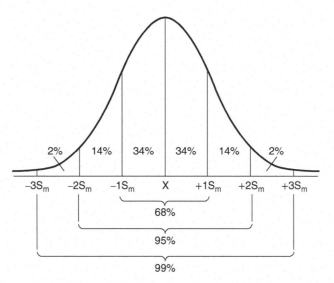

FIGURE 18.6 The area or bands for a given obtained score that are 68%, 95%, and 99% sure to span the true score.

The expressions "68% of the time," "95% of the time," and so on refer to the hypothetical situation in which the student is given the test many times. In this case, the student could expect that his or her true score would be within the interval a certain percentage of the total number of times the test was taken.

Here's another example. A teacher gets back the results of class IQ tests. The IQ test given to the students has a standard deviation of 15, and the scores have a test–retest reliability of 0.84. Therefore, the test has a standard error of measurement of 6. The teacher then knows that of the children who made an IQ score of 100, about 68% have a true score between 94 and 106; 95% have a true IQ score between 88 and 112; and 99% have a true IQ score between 82 and 118. For one particular child with an IQ of 100, the teacher knows that probably the true IQ is between 94 and 106, but 32% of the time ($100 - 68 = 32$) it will be even further than that from 100. Thus, the teacher has some idea of just how much confidence to place in the score. That is, the teacher has an idea about the accuracy of the score.

If test scores are perfectly reliable ($r = 1.0$), a student will always get exactly the same score. In this case, the S_m is zero, as can be seen by substituting a coefficient of 1.0 in the formula for S_m. If test scores are very close to perfectly reliable, the S_m will be very small, and we can assume that the student's obtained score is very close to his or her true score. If test scores are not reliable (i.e., r near 0.00), the S_m will be nearly as large as the standard deviation, and we can assume that the student's obtained score is not a good approximation of his or her true score. The relationships among true scores, error scores, obtained scores, and score reliability are illustrated next.

Scores from Test K Are Perfectly Reliable ($r = 1.00$) In other words, a student's ranking on repeated administrations of Test K *never changes*. There is no error, and as a result the student's true score equals the obtained score *and* there is *no* error score distribution. Thus, S_m is zero.

Proof

$$S_m = SD\sqrt{1 - r}$$
$$= SD\sqrt{1 - 1.0}$$
$$= SD\sqrt{0}$$
$$= 0$$

Scores from Test L are Totally Unreliable (r = 0.00) In other words, a student's ranking on repeated administrations of Test L is *likely to vary across the range of possible rankings*. If the student is ranked first on one administration, he or she could easily be ranked last on the next administration. Because *so much error* is present, the S_m will be the same as the SD of the test.

Proof

$$S_m = SD\sqrt{1 - r}$$
$$= SD\sqrt{1 - 0.00}$$
$$= SD\sqrt{1}$$
$$= SD(1)$$
$$= SD$$

In reality, neither of the examples presented here actually occurs. So, the S_m typically takes on a value greater than zero and smaller than the test's standard deviation. As score reliability increases, S_m decreases, and as score reliability decreases, the S_m increases. In summary, the S_m can be thought of as a measure of the accuracy of a test score. The larger the S_m, the less accurately the obtained score reflects the true score. The smaller the S_m, the more accurately the obtained score reflects the true score.

Standard Deviation or Standard Error of Measurement?

Until you have a working familiarity with these concepts, you can expect to confuse the standard deviation (SD) with the standard error of measurement (S_m). Don't despair! The two have some similarities, but they are very different. Both are measures of score variability, but of different kinds of scores. The standard deviation is a measure of variability of raw scores for a *group* of test-takers. It tells you how spread out the scores are in a distribution of raw scores. You learned to compute and interpret standard deviations in Chapter 14. The standard error of measurement, however, is the standard deviation of the hypothetical *error* scores of a distribution. This is what you learned to compute and interpret in *this* chapter. Think about what you have just read:

Standard deviation (SD) is the variability of *raw* scores.

Standard error of measurement (S_m) is the variability of *error* scores.

The standard deviation is based on a group of scores that *actually exist*. The standard error of measurement is based on a group of scores that is *hypothetical*.

WHY ALL THE FUSS ABOUT ERROR?

In reality, an individual's obtained score is the best estimate of an individual's true score. That is, in spite of the foregoing discussion, we usually use the obtained score as our best guess of a student's true level of ability. Well, why all the fuss about error then? For two reasons: First, we want to make you aware of the fallibility of test scores, and, second, we want to sensitize you to the factors that can affect scores. Why? So they can be better controlled so that obtained scores better represent true scores. Now you know how to determine how wide a range of scores around an obtained score must be to be 68% sure that it captures the true score. Controlling error can help narrow this range, thereby increasing the accuracy of test results. Let's consider error more closely.

The sources of error can be classified into the following categories:

1. Test-takers.
2. The test itself.
3. Test administration.
4. Test scoring.

Error Within Test-Takers

The source of error within test-takers could be called intraindividual error. Earlier, we talked about several within-student factors that would likely result in an obtained score lower than a student's true score. The examples we used were fatigue and illness. We also noted that accidentally seeing another student's answer could be a factor that might result in an individual's obtained score being higher than his or her true score. Situations such as these are undesirable since they have unpredictable effects on test performance, and as a result the validity, reliability, and accuracy of the scores yielded by the test suffer. They are usually temporary situations, affecting a student on one day but not on another. Any temporary and unpredictable change in a student can be considered intraindividual error or error within test-takers. Remember, we are *not* saying anything about actual errors or mistakes test-takers make in responding to test items. Rather, we are talking about factors that change unpredictably over time and, as a result, impair consistency and accuracy in measurement.

Error Within the Test

We may refer to error within the test as an intratest or within-test error. The poorly designed essay test that results in an obtained score lower than a true score and the poorly written test replete with clues that results in an obtained score higher than a true score are both examples of this source of error.

Many factors *increase* error within a test. The following is only a partial list:

Trick questions.

Reading level that is too high.

Ambiguous questions.

Items that are too difficult.

Poorly written items.

To the extent that test items and tests are poorly constructed, test score reliability and accuracy will be impaired.

Error in Test Administration

Misreading the amount of time to be allotted for testing is an example of error in test administration that could raise or lower obtained scores in relation to true scores. However, a variety of other direct and indirect test administration factors are to be considered, including physical comfort, distractions, instructions and explanations, and test administration attitudes.

Physical Comfort Room temperature, humidity, lighting, noise, and seating arrangement are all potential sources of error for the test-taker.

Instructions and Explanations Different test administrators provide differing amounts of information to test-takers. Some spell words or provide hints, or tell whether it's better to guess or leave blanks, while others remain fairly distant. Naturally, your score may vary depending on the amount of information you are provided.

Test Administrator Attitudes Administrators will differ in the notions they convey about the importance of the test, the extent to which they are emotionally supportive of students, and the way in which they monitor the test. To the extent that these variables affect students differently, test score reliability and accuracy will be impaired.

Error in Scoring

With the advent of computerized test scoring, error in scoring has decreased significantly. However, even when computer scoring is used, error can occur. The computer, a highly reliable machine, is seldom the cause of such errors. But teachers and other test administrators prepare the scoring keys, introducing possibilities for error. And students sometimes fail to use No. 2 pencils or make extraneous marks on answer sheets, introducing another potential source of scoring error. Needless to say, when tests are hand scored, as most classroom tests are, the likelihood of error increases greatly. In fact, because you are human, you can be sure that you will make some scoring errors in grading the tests you give.

These four sources of error—the test-takers, the test, the test administration, and the scoring—are factors that can increase the discrepancy between an individual's obtained score and his or her true score. To the extent that these sources of error are present, individual and group scores will be prone to error, and therefore less accurate. We can take measures to minimize error within the test, the test administration, and the scoring, but we can never eliminate such error completely. Generally, error due to within-student factors is beyond our control.

These sources of error also affect the different types of reliability coefficients we have discussed. Next we consider the extent to which our four sources of error influence the test–retest, alternate-forms, and internal consistency methods of estimating reliability.

SOURCES OF ERROR INFLUENCING VARIOUS RELIABILITY COEFFICIENTS

Test–Retest

If test–retest reliability coefficients are determined over a short time, few changes are likely to take place *within students* to alter their test scores. Thus, short-interval test–retest coefficients are not likely to be affected greatly by within-student error. However, as the time interval involved increases, it becomes more and more likely that significant changes will occur in the test-takers.

Correspondingly, test scores will be increasingly affected by those changes, and the test–retest reliability coefficient will be lowered. This lowered score reliability may be more a result of new learning on the part of the students than it is an indication of the unreliability of the test items.

Since the *same* test is administered twice in determining test–retest reliability, error within the test itself (e.g., from poorly worded or ambiguous items) does not affect the strength of the reliability coefficient. Any problems that do exist in the test are present in both the first and second administrations, affecting scores the same way each time the test is administered. As long as similar administration and scoring procedures are followed, administration and scoring errors are likely to contribute only minimally to error. However, if there are significant changes in either or both, these can contribute significantly to error, resulting in a lower estimate of test–retest score reliability.

Alternate Forms

Since alternate-forms reliability is determined by administering two different forms or versions of the same test to the same group close together in time, the effects of within student error are negligible. Students usually do not change significantly between morning and afternoon or from 1 day to the following day. Granted, students may be more fatigued when taking Form B of a test immediately after taking Form A. However, those factors can be controlled by splitting the test administration across groups of students, as suggested in Table 18.2.

TABLE 18.2   Splitting Same-Day Alternate-Form Administrations across Groups

a.m. Group	p.m. Group
Students whose last names begin with A–K get Form A.	Students whose last names begin with A–K get Form B.
Students whose last names begin with L–Z get Form B.	Students whose last names begin with L–Z get Form A.

Error within the test, however, has a significant effect on alternate-forms reliability. Unlike test–retest reliability, error within the test is *not* the same between test administrations. Error within Form A combines with error within Form B to have an effect on alternate-forms reliability. By now you are aware of how difficult it is to construct one good test, much less two! Yet, this is just what is necessary for acceptable alternate-forms score reliability to be established.

As with test–retest methods, alternate-forms score reliability is not greatly affected by error in administering or scoring the test, as long as similar procedures are followed. Since within-test error is considered by alternate-forms estimates, these estimates normally have the lowest numerical index of score reliability.

Internal Consistency

With test–retest and alternate-forms reliability, within-student factors affect the method of estimating score reliability, since changes in test performance due to such problems as fatigue, momentary anxiety, illness, or just having an "off day" can be doubled because there are two separate administrations of the test. If the test is sensitive to those problems, it will yield different scores from one test administration to another, lowering the reliability (or correlation coefficient) between them. Obviously, we would prefer that the test not be affected by those problems. But if it is, we would like to know about it.

With internal consistency reliability, neither within-student nor within-test factors affect score reliability. Since there is a single test administered, no changes in students should occur, and any errors within the test will occur only once. Similarly, since there is but a single administration and scoring procedure, administration and scoring errors are held to a minimum.

Measures of internal consistency, then, are influenced by the *fewest* of the four sources of error affecting test score reliability. Thus, we would expect such measures to yield *higher* reliability coefficients than test–retest or alternate-forms estimates. Stated differently, internal consistency estimates are less sensitive to the sources of error than are test–retest or alternate-forms reliability estimates. This is important in evaluating test data presented in standardized test manuals. If a test publisher presents only internal consistency estimates of score reliability, the publisher has failed to indicate how consistent the obtained scores from the test are likely to be over time. Also unknown is whether any parallel or alternative forms being offered are equivalent to one another. Simply saying, the two alternate, equivalent, or parallel forms are not sufficient. To evaluate their equivalence, there must be an estimate of alternate-forms reliability.

By itself, then, an internal consistency reliability coefficient—high though it may be—does not provide sufficient evidence of a test's score reliability. When you must have an estimate of a test's score reliability and can give only a single administration (such as with a typical teacher-made test), measures of internal consistency can be useful. However, any well-constructed standardized test must provide more than just information on the test's internal consistency. A measure of the test's score reliability over time (i.e., test–retest reliability) and, if the test advertises alternate forms, an estimate of the equivalence of the forms being offered (i.e., alternate-forms reliability) must be provided.

The influence of the four sources of error on the test–retest, alternate-forms, and internal consistency methods of estimating test score reliability are summarized in Table 18.3.

TABLE 18.3 Extent of Error Influencing Test–Retest, Alternate-Forms, and Internal Consistency Methods of Score Reliability

Reliability Measure	Type of Error			
	Within Student	Within Test[a]	Administration	Scoring
Test–retest, short interval	Minimal	Minimal	Minimal[b] or moderate[c]	Minimal[d] or moderate[e]
Test–retest, long interval	Extensive	Minimal	Minimal[b] or moderate[c]	Minimal[d] or moderate[e]
Alternate forms, short interval	Minimal	Moderate[b] or extensive[c]	Minimal[b] or moderate[c]	Minimal[d] or moderate[e]
Alternate forms, long interval	Extensive	Moderate[b] or extensive[c]	Minimal[b] or moderate[c]	Minimal[d] or moderate[e]
Internal consistency	Minimal	Minimal	Minimal	Minimal

[a] Assuming test is well constructed.

[b] If test is standardized.

[c] If test is teacher-made.

[d] If test is objective.

[e] If test is subjective.

BAND INTERPRETATION

We have learned how to use the standard error of measurement, S_m, to more realistically interpret and report single test scores. In this section, we will show you how to use the standard error of measurement to more realistically interpret and report groups of test scores.

Let's consider the following example: John obtained the following scores on an end-of-year achievement test:

Subtest	*Score*
Reading	103
Listening	104
Writing	105
Social Studies	98
Science	100
Math	91

Note: M = 100 and SD = 10 for all subtests.

Suppose you have a parent conference coming up, and John's parents want you to interpret his scores to them. What would you say? Would you say that he did best in Writing and poorest in Math? Would you say that the differences among the scores are likely due to measurement error, or do they represent actual differences in achievement?

It seems likely that John's parents would know from looking at the scores what John did best in and what he did poorest in. If they had some statistical sophistication, as you now have, they might even be able to conclude that his Math score is at about the 19th percentile and that his Reading score is at about the 69th percentile—a difference between the two tests of 50 percentile points. This appears to be a rather dramatic difference indicating a real difference in achievement. But how can we be sure that the difference is not due to error? Granted, it seems to be so large a difference that it probably is a "real" difference rather than a "chance" (i.e., due to error) difference. But what about the difference between Writing (69th percentile) and Science (50th percentile)? Is this difference a "real" or a "chance" one? In short, how large a difference do we need between test scores to conclude that the differences represent real and not chance differences? As you might have guessed, we can employ the standard error of measurement to help us answer these questions. The specific technique we will be discussing is called *band interpretation*. This technique lends itself quite well to the interpretation of scores from test batteries. Here is a step-by-step approach to band interpretation.

Technically, the approach we will be describing fails to consider the problem of the *reliability of the difference scores*. That statistical concept basically states that in comparing scores from two tests (or subtests), the reliability of the difference between the two scores will be less than the reliability of each of the two scores. Thus, less confidence should be placed in the difference score than in either of the individual scores. For those who may be interested, the formula to compute the reliability of the difference score is as follows:

$$r_{\text{Diff}} = \frac{(r_{11} + r_{22})/2 - r_{12}}{1 - r_{12}}$$

where r_{11} is the reliability of one measure, r_{22} is the reliability of the other measure, and r_{12} is the correlation between the two measures.

Our approach, band interpretation, represents a practical compromise between that statistically correct approach and the all-too-common acceptance of difference scores as being reliable.

Steps: Band Interpretation

List Data List subtests and scores and the M, SD, and reliability (*r*) for each subtest. For purposes of illustration, let's assume that the mean is 100, the standard deviation is 10, and the score reliability is 0.91 for all the subtests. Here are the subtest scores for John:

Subtest	*Score*
Reading	103
Listening	104
Writing	105
Social Studies	98
Science	100

Determine S_m Since SD and *r* are the same for each subtest in this example, the standard error of measurement will be the same for each subtest.

$$S_m = SD\sqrt{1 - r}$$
$$= 10\sqrt{1 - 0.91} = 10\sqrt{0.09} = 3$$

Add and Subtract S_m To identify the band or interval of scores that has a 68% chance of capturing John's true score, add and subtract S_m to each subtest score. If the test could be given to John 100 times (without John learning from taking the test), 68 out of 100 times John's true score would be within the following bands:

Subtest	*Score*	*68% Band*
Reading	103	100–106
Listening	104	101–107
Writing	105	102–108
Social Studies	98	95–101
Science	100	97–103
Math	91	88–94

Graph the Results On each scale, shade in the bands to represent the range of scores that has a 68% chance of capturing John's true score (see example above).

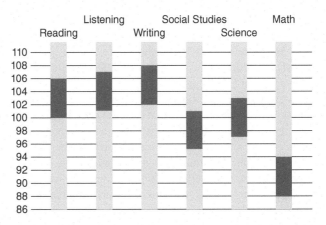

Interpret the Bands Interpret the profile of bands by visually inspecting the bars to see which bands overlap and which do not. Those that *overlap* probably represent differences that likely occurred by *chance*. For example, scores in Reading, Listening, Writing, and Science may differ from one another only by chance, in spite of the fact that John's Science score of 100 was five points lower than his Writing score of 105, a difference of half a standard deviation. We arrive at this conclusion because there is at least some overlap among the bands for each of these subtest scores. Thus, we could say John's level of achievement is similar in each of these subjects.

However, we can see a large difference in John's Math achievement compared to these same four subtests. Since there is no overlap, we will consider this difference a *real*, not a chance, difference. Social Studies shows a *real* difference compared to Writing (again, no overlap), but only a *chance* difference compared to Reading, Listening, and Science (again, because there is overlap).

Getting the hang of it? Band interpretation is one of the most realistic and appropriate ways to interpret scores from test batteries, since it considers the error that is always present in testing. Work with it and you will reduce the natural tendency to put too much weight on small or chance differences among scores.

So far we have used the subtest score plus and minus the standard error of measurement to identify whether a real difference exists among subtest scores. We have constructed ranges of scores around each obtained score in which we are 68% sure the individual's true score lies. Recall from our earlier discussion of S_m, though, that by adding and subtracting twice the value of S_m to the obtained subtest score, we can construct an interval or range of scores within which we are 95% sure the individual's true score lies. Naturally, this would create a much wider band for each obtained score, which has the effect of making overlap much *more* likely. This means "real" differences would be less likely to appear. That is, if we use the 95% rule by adding two S_m to and subtracting two S_m from each score instead of adding and subtracting only one standard error of measurement, we may have very different interpretations of the same test scores. Let's see what kind of difference this makes. Figure 18.7 compares and contrasts the 68% and 95% approaches.

Now let's compare conclusions. At the 68% level, we concluded that there was a significant discrepancy between John's Math achievement and all his other subjects (there is no overlap between his Math score interval and any other subtest score interval). We also concluded that there was a real difference (i.e., no overlap) between John's Social Studies achievement and his Writing achievement. All other differences were attributed to chance (i.e., there was overlap).

Now look at the 95% profile in Figure 18.7. In essence, we have doubled the width of each band in order to become more confident that we have really captured John's true score within each subtest interval. With this more conservative approach to test interpretation, the real differences decline sharply. We use the word "conservative" with the 95% approach since the odds of John's true score falling outside the band are only 1 in 20 or a probability of 0.05 with the 95% approach, but 1 in 3 or a probability of about 0.32 with the 68% approach. We are, therefore, *more confident* that John's true score is within the band with the 95% approach. Since the bands will be larger, the only real differences we find at the 95% level are between John's Math achievement and his achievement in Listening and in Writing. All the other bands overlap, suggesting that at the 95% level the differences in obtained scores are due to chance. If we employ the more conservative 95% approach, we would conclude that even though the difference between John's obtained Reading and Math scores is 12 points ($103 - 91 = 12$, a difference of 1.2 standard deviations), the difference is due to chance, not to a real difference in achievement.

Why bother with the 95% level, then? Well, if you are going to make important decisions about a student, a conservative approach appears warranted. In short, if you are concerned about the effects of a "wrong" decision (i.e., saying a real difference in achievement exists when it is really due to chance), take the conservative approach. On the other hand, if little is at risk for the

Subtest	Score*	68% range (X ± 1S_m)	95% range (X ± 2S_m)
Reading	103	100–106	97–109
Listening	104	101–107	98–110
Writing	105	102–108	99–111
Social Studies	98	95–101	92–104
Science	100	97–103	94–106
Math	91	88–94	85–97

*M = 100, SD = 10

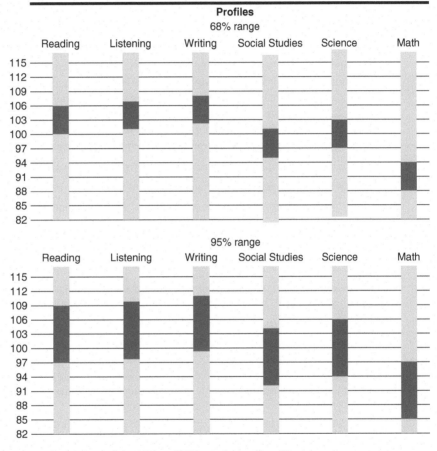

FIGURE 18.7 Comparison of the 68% and 95% methods of band interpretation.

student (or yourself), then the less conservative 68% approach is probably warranted. To make it simpler yet, let differences at the 68% level be a signal to you; let differences at the 95% level be a signal to the school and to the parents.

In Chapter 19, we will describe an application of band interpretation in which we believe the more conservative 95% approach should typically be employed. This will be in relation to determining real differences between a student's potential for achievement, called *aptitude*, and actual achievement. This approach, known as the severe discrepancy model, was the primary basis for determining whether students are eligible for special education under the Specific Learning

Disability (SLD) category from the mid-1970s. With the passage of the Individuals with Disabilities Education Improvement Act (IDEIA) in 2004, Congress clearly indicated that the use of the aptitude–achievement discrepancy model alone for SLD determination could no longer be required. The discrepancy model could continue to be used in conjunction with a response-to-intervention (RTI) model in some states, whereas other states mandated the use of RTI only, or other approaches to SLD determination (see Chapter 3 and the textbook's companion website for further discussion of this controversial issue. Go to http://www.wiley.com/college/kubiszyn and click on the link to the Student Companion Site).

A FINAL WORD

Technically, there are more accurate statistical procedures for determining real differences between an individual's test scores than the ones we have been able to present here. Those procedures, however, are time consuming, complex, and overly specific for the typical teacher. Within the classroom, band interpretation, properly used, makes for a practical alternative to those more advanced methods and is superior to simply comparing individual scores.

Before we complete this chapter, answer the questions—using the 95% approach—that we raised at the beginning of the last section. To refresh your memory, here they are as follows:

Is there a real difference between John's Reading score and his Math score?

Is there a real difference between John's Writing score and his Science score?

(Note: Answers to these questions may be found in Appendix B)

SUMMARY

This chapter presented the concepts of accuracy and error, the statistic used to represent error (the standard error of measurement), and the four sources of error in measurement. Its major points are as follows:

1. No test is perfectly reliable, and therefore no test is perfectly accurate. All tests are subject to error.

2. Error is any factor that leads an individual to perform better or worse on a test than the individual's true level of performance.

3. An obtained score for a test contains two components: One reflects the individual's true level of performance, and the other reflects the error associated with the test that prevents the individual from performing at exactly his or her true level of ability.

4. An individual's true score and error score are hypothetical. We can never be sure exactly what they are.

5. The standard error of measurement (S_m) is the standard deviation of the error score distribution of a test.

6. The standard error of measurement for a test can be determined mathematically if we know the test's standard deviation and reliability.

7. The error distribution is normally distributed and has a mean of zero, and its standard deviation is the standard error of measurement.

8. We can be 68% sure an individual's true score lies in the range between one S_m above and one S_m below that individual's obtained score.

9. We can be 95% sure a true score lies in the range of scores between two S_m above and two S_m below the obtained score.

10. We can be 99% sure a true score lies in the range of scores between three S_m above and three S_m below the obtained score.

11. Using the S_m in interpreting scores helps us avoid overinterpreting small differences among test scores.

12. Accuracy increases and the S_m decreases as reliability increases.

13. The S_m refers to the variability of error scores; the SD refers to the variability of raw scores.

14. We can improve test accuracy by controlling the sources of error in testing.

15. Error is classified into four categories:
    a. Error within test-takers.
    b. Error within the test.
    c. Error within the test administration.
    d. Error within scoring.

16. Error within the test-takers refers to changes in the student over which the test administrator has no control.

17. Error within the test refers to technical problems in the test. The test developer has considerable control over this source of error.

18. Error within the test administration refers to physical, verbal, and attitudinal variables that vary from administration to administration and affect test scores. The administrator can minimize this source of error by standardizing administration procedures.

19. Error in scoring typically refers to clerical errors that influence test scores. The test administrator can control this source of error by using objective items and clerical checks or by using computer scoring.

20. Different estimates of score reliability are differentially affected by the various sources of error.

21. Test–retest score reliability is most susceptible to error within test-takers.

22. Alternate-forms score reliability is most affected by error within the two forms of the test. As a result, it usually yields lower score reliability estimates than test–retest or internal consistency estimates.

23. Since only one administration and one test are necessary for internal consistency estimates, this approach is least affected by error. As a result, internal consistency estimates of score reliability typically will be higher for the same test than for test–retest or alternate-forms score reliability estimates.

24. Band interpretation is a technique that the teacher can use to help separate real differences in student achievement from differences due to chance. This approach helps prevent overinterpretation of small differences among subtests in achievement test batteries.

FOR DISCUSSION AND PRACTICE

*1. Calculate the standard error of measurement for a test with a standard deviation of 10 and a score reliability of 0.84. Draw a normal curve picturing the error score distribution in units of the standard error of measurement.

*2. Suppose an individual received a score of 16 on the test in Question 18.1. Calculate the range or band within which we could be 95% sure that this individual's true score is contained. What would this range or band be if we wanted to be 99% sure this individual's true score is contained within it? To be 68% sure?

*3. What are the four sources of error that increase the discrepancy between an individual's obtained score and his or her true score? Give a specific example of each.

*4. Indicate the extent to which (a) within-student, (b) within-test, (c) administration, and (d) scoring error affects each of the following methods of determining reliability:

a. Test–retest, short interval

b. Test–retest, long interval

c. Alternate forms, short interval

d. Alternate forms, long interval

e. Internal consistency

*5. Construct a subtest profile with bands for each of the following subtests taken by a particular student. Assume that the mean is 50, the standard deviation is 8, and the reliability is

0.91 for all the tests. Construct your bands so that they have a 68% chance of capturing this individual's true scores. How would you interpret the differences between subtests to this student's parents?

Subtest	Score
Reading	56
Listening	50
Writing	61
Social Studies	35
Science	60
Math	56

*6. The following table lists the scores obtained by Tom and Mary on five different tests. At the 99% level, indicate which tests showed real differences in performance between Tom and Mary.

Test	S_m	Tom	Mary
A	5.5	80	60
B	16.0	150	165
C	3.4	32	35
D	30.0	620	679
E	8.0	89	103

*Answers for these questions appear in Appendix B.

*7. The following score reliability coefficients were reported for a test administered to a single class. How do you account for the differences?

Test–retest (30 days)	$r = 0.90$
Alternate forms	$r = 0.84$
Split-half (corrected using the Spearman–Brown formula)	$r = 0.93$

*8. Consider the following information from two tests:

Test	Mean	Reliability	SD
A	100	0.91	20
B	100	0.75	10

On which test would an individual's score fluctuates the most on repeated test administrations? Explain why.

9. In the teacher's lounge, Mr. Blinders, who never took a tests and measurements course, emphatically states that "Including the standard error in interpreting test scores is counterproductive. All it does is give parents more ammunition to argue with us about when they are not happy with our test based decisions." Knowing that you completed a tests and measurements class, the other teachers all look at you for a response. How would you reply to Mr. Blinders?

CHAPTER 19

STANDARDIZED TESTS

LEARNING OUTCOMES

After completion of this chapter, the student will be able to:

1. Describe why standardized tests are called "standardized."
2. State the purpose(s) of summative standardized tests.
3. Differentiate between teacher-made and standardized tests.
4. Describe "high-stakes" educational decisions.
5. Explain why standardized administration and scoring procedures must be followed.
6. Describe the effects of accommodations on standardized tests.
7. Explain why test accommodations and alternative assessments may compromise the utility of standardized assessment for the progress of special education students in the general educational curriculum.
8. Explain why standardized testing will continue even if performance and portfolio-based assessment becomes more prevalent.
9. Identify two impediments to the widespread adoption of performance and portfolio-based assessments.
10. Compare and contrast standardized and teacher-made tests.
11. Differentiate among the sources of error controlled or minimized by standardized tests.
12. Describe the effects of controlling or minimizing error through standardized tests.
13. Identify acceptable reliability coefficients for standardized achievement tests.
14. Compare and contrast grade-equivalent scores, age-equivalent scores, percentile ranks, converted scores, stanines, and standard scores.
15. Describe how grade- and age-equivalent scores are obtained.
16. Explain how stanines differ from other converted scores.
17. Recall the major interpretive cautions identified by the author in using converted scores.
18. Given an appropriate norms table, convert raw scores to percentile ranks, standard scores, and other converted scores.
19. Differentiate among the test-related factors that must be considered in interpreting standardized test results.
20. Explain why close correspondence between the make-up of the norm group and the make-up of your class is important.
21. Develop a local norms table given a set of test scores.
22. Describe student-related factors that must be considered in interpreting standardized test scores.
23. Give examples of the ways that student-related factors can affect standardized test scores.

24. Compare and contrast the terms underachiever, overachiever, and achievement at expectancy.

25. Identify aptitude–achievement discrepancies when provided with tabular data depicting aptitude and achievement test scores for a group of students.

26. Interpret norm-referenced individual score reports, considering test- and student-related factors.

27. Interpret criterion-referenced individual score reports, considering test- and student-related factors.

28. Explain why it is useful for publishers to include percentile bands for each subtest on individual score reports.

29. Describe the types of resources available on test publisher websites, including the Smarter Balanced and PARCC Common Core test consortia.

T**HUS FAR,** most of the text has focused on the development, administration, scoring, and interpretation of teacher-constructed tests and assessments—and with good reason. Teacher-made tests are used regularly and frequently for most classroom testing and decision making. However, teachers are also required at least once each year to administer commercial or state-developed summative *standardized* tests, evaluate the results of such tests, and interpret the results to interested and sometimes concerned parents. Although there is some overlap between teacher-made and standardized tests, these types of tests also differ in several important ways. We will describe and remind you about the differences throughout this chapter.

Today, awareness of the issues that surround standardized testing is more critical than ever for teachers. Standardized summative tests, or test batteries (i.e., that measure learning in multiple subject areas), have been at the heart of the high-stakes testing (HST) movement (see Chapter 2). The results from these lengthy standardized test batteries have been used to meet the accountability requirements of the No Child Left Behind (NCLB) Act. In Chapter 2, we noted that the recent Race to the Top (RTT) initiative awarded funding for the development of two multistate assessment consortia, the Smarter Balanced Assessment Consortium (Smarter Balanced), and the Partnership for Assessment of Readiness for College and Careers (PARCC). Both consortia were provided with funding to develop online standardized tests that were closely aligned with the Common Core State Standards (CCSS) and that were to be used by all states that were members of each consortium. As a result, summative standardized tests today may be those developed traditionally by standardized test publishers (see Chapter 20), education agencies for use in specific states (often in collaboration with standardized test publishers), or the Smarter Balanced or PARC tests aligned with the CCSS that are to be used in states that are members of those consortia. Over the last several years, test publishers, state educational agencies, and both the Smarter Balanced and PARCC consortia have developed and included on their websites a variety of helpful resources to facilitate understanding and interpretation of standardized tests. These resources include videos, sample questions, sample reports, scoring rubrics, and the objectives and standards that the tests are intended to measure.

We probably do not need to remind you that high-stakes standardized test results can affect (or in some states even determine) student promotion and graduation; teacher and principal evaluation, contract extensions, and cash incentives; public recognition or humiliation for schools and districts; real estate values; and other noneducational issues! With so much riding on standardized test results today, it is increasingly important for teachers to know about the development, purposes, advantages, limitations, and uses of standardized tests, and to learn how to interpret their results appropriately. This is what we will cover in this chapter.

Before we do so, it is important to clarify that this chapter and the next focus on the lengthy, *summative* (i.e., administered at the end of instruction) standardized tests and test batteries that are administered annually to assess what students have learned and for accountability purposes. Even though they too can be standardized, we will not focus on the brief, *formative* progress-monitoring assessments (e.g., CBM, see Chapters 1 and 3) that we introduced you to in the context of the response-to-intervention (RTI) model (see Chapter 3). Nor will we focus on the increasingly common standardized formative assessments that have been developed for use in the states that are members of the Smarter Balanced and PARCC consortia, or the formative standardized assessments that have been developed by standardized test publishers since the development of the CCSS (Cavanagh, 2013). We will not focus on these formative assessments (i.e., administered to inform day-to-day instructional decision making) because their purpose and interpretation differ from the purpose and interpretation of the *summative* instruments that is the focus of this chapter.

WHAT IS A STANDARDIZED TEST?

Standardized achievement tests often take years to construct as opposed to a few days for a teacher-made test. They are called *standardized* because they are administered and scored according to *specific* and *uniform* (i.e., standard) procedures. In other words, a standardized achievement test administered and scored in Buffalo, New York, would be administered and scored in exactly the same manner in New York City, Chicago, Los Angeles, Mobile, Alabama, or anywhere else in the United States. Because of these standardization procedures, measurement error due to administration and scoring is reduced, which increases score reliability (as we know from Chapter 18).

Standardized tests are constructed by test construction specialists, usually with the assistance of curriculum experts, teachers, and school administrators. They may be used to determine a student's level of performance relative to (1) the performance of other students of similar age and grade or (2) a criterion, such as state academic standards, or the CCSS (see Chapter 2). When standardized tests are used to compare a student's performance to the performance of students in the normative sample they are called standardized norm-referenced tests, and when they are used to determine whether performance meets or exceeds criteria like state standards, they are called standardized criterion-referenced tests.

All states and the District of Columbia now employ some form of summative HST to meet the requirements of the federal NCLB Act. Those tests are standardized in terms of their administration and scoring, and they are usually carefully constructed. However, some high-stakes tests are primarily norm-referenced (e.g., the *Terra-Nova, Third Edition*; the *Stanford Achievement Test, Tenth Edition*) while others are primarily criterion-referenced (e.g., the State of Texas Assessment of Academic Readiness, or STAAR; the *Massachusetts Comprehensive Assessment System of Skills*, or MCAS). As we will see, however, some standardized tests intended to be primarily criterion-referenced can also be used to compare student performance to school, district, or state norms, as we will describe later in this chapter. Although much of what we discuss in this chapter applies to both norm- and criterion-referenced standardized tests, our primary focus will be on norm-referenced standardized tests.

Scores for students taking a nationally norm-referenced standardized test are determined by comparing their obtained scores to a nationally representative sample, or norm group, which also took the test under standardized conditions. Thus, scores for standardized, norm-referenced test-takers are determined by comparing their scores to a norms table based on the performance of the norm group, or normative sample. Standardized testing is not limited to achievement measurement. Other standardized tests include tests of academic and general aptitude, personality, interest, and other characteristics. We will review each category and examples of each type of test in Chapter 20.

Do Test Stimuli, Administration, and Scoring Have to Be Standardized?

An edition of the television news program *Nightline* entitled "Cheating Teachers" (Koppel, 2001) began a series of media accounts that have documented multiple, ongoing examples of inappropriate and unethical standardized test practices intended to inflate standardized test scores on summative, high-stakes standardized tests. These actions have included principals, teachers, and others "helping" some students taking standardized, high-stakes achievement tests by suggesting or directly telling students to change incorrect answers, or by physically changing incorrect answers to correct answers on scoring sheets.

Such practices may also prove to be illegal, rather than simply inappropriate or unethical. For example, in Fall 2014, a trial began for 12 Atlanta school administrators, principals, test administrators, and teachers who were charged with being part of a widespread conspiracy to increase summative test scores in hopes of increasing their salaries. The trial ended with the conviction of 11 of 12 educators on racketeering charges, and they were sentenced to 1–7 years in prison, fines of $1,000 to $25,000 and probation after prison terms were completed. Prior to the trial, 21 others accepted plea bargains for obstruction or making false statements (Faucet, 2014).

The criminal convictions in the Atlanta case illustrate the seriousness with which adherence to standardized administration and scoring procedures must be followed. Although some of the perpetrators may have thought that what they were doing was actually helpful to students by raising their scores, they failed to understand that altering administration and scoring procedures seriously compromised the utility and validity of test results for all students. Furthermore, the Atlanta debacle was not an isolated case. Faucet (2014) reported that the National Center for Fair and Open Testing, or Fair Test, substantiated that manipulation of standardized high-stakes test scores took place in at least 39 states and the District of Columbia. As we learned in Chapter 18, variation in administration and scoring procedures increases error, thereby decreasing score accuracy and reliability, and test validity. Did the actions of the educators in question really "help" these students by invalidating their test results? We hope you understand that the answer to that question must be a resounding "No!"

When standardized achievement tests are appropriately administered and scored, test results from different students, classes, schools, and districts can be more easily and more confidently compared to one another, or to state standards or the CCSS, than would be the case with different teacher-made tests. Imagine the difficulty in comparing teacher-made test results from Ms. Smith's fifth-grade class in Orlando with results from Ms. Wilson's fifth-grade class in Seattle. Not only would the test items be different, but also the length of the test, the amount of time allowed, the instructions given by the teacher, and the scoring criteria would also be different. In short, there would be little or no basis for comparison. Standardization of achievement test stimuli and administration and scoring procedures reduces measurement error (see Chapter 18) and enables students evaluated with the same test under the standardized conditions to be compared with one another, or state standards, over time and across classes, schools, districts, and states.

Standardized Testing: Effects of Accommodations and Alternative Assessments

Under the 2004 reauthorization of the Individuals with Disabilities Education Improvement Act (IDEIA) and the NCLB Act, students with disabilities must participate in annual state- and district-wide achievement assessments. Prior to passage of the previous version of the IDEA in 1997, students with disabilities often were excluded from annual achievement assessments. Congress was concerned that the exclusion of children with disabilities from annual achievement assessments impeded assessment of the educational progress of children with disabilities and the development of an accountability system to ensure their achievement. Congress's intent in requiring that children with disabilities participate in these annual assessments was to increase accountability by enabling comparisons to be made for individual students to state standards over time and across students, schools, and districts. By enabling such comparisons, Congress also intended to enhance educational outcomes for children with disabilities.

Congress recognized that the very disabilities that qualify students for special education services may interfere with standardized achievement test performance (e.g., visual or hearing impairments, learning disabilities, and health or emotional conditions). Thus, IDEIA allows students with disabilities to (1) take the same annual state tests that regular education students take, (2) take the tests with appropriate alterations to the test stimuli and administration procedures (i.e., through accommodations that limit or eliminate the impact of disabilities on test performance), or (3) take an alternative assessment approved by the state, but only if that option is specified in the student's Individualized Educational Plan (IEP).

The requirement for appropriate accommodations and alternative assessments was well intended and a seemingly appropriate effort to ensure fairness for special learners. Requiring a visually impaired special learner to take the test under the same conditions as a nonvisually impaired student likely would limit the performance of the visually impaired student by comparison. The allowance for accommodations and alternate assessments was included in IDEIA to "level the playing field" for children with disabilities during annual assessments. However, studies of the impact on accommodations have been inconclusive regarding the fairness of the impact of accommodations (Cawthon et al., 2009).

Although Congress was well intentioned in encouraging accommodations and alternate assessments, some test modifications and alterations can preclude the very comparisons Congress wanted to enable! Without ongoing, systematic evaluation, no one can be certain how alteration of test stimuli, changes in administration procedures, or alternate assessments may affect test performance. Thus, the performance of children with disabilities evaluated under nonstandardized conditions (e.g., additional time and access to other resources) may not be directly comparable with (1) their own past or future performance, (2) the performance of other students with disabilities, or (3) students evaluated under standardized conditions.

The point is that even when decision makers have good intentions, the purposes and procedures related to standardized testing continue to be misunderstood and misapplied at local, state, and national levels. When this happens, the potential for misuse and abuse of the potentially useful tool called a standardized test increases, and often it is the test that ends up being blamed for any confusion or controversy that results. For further discussion of the IDEIA and its broad implications for general education teachers, testing, and assessment, please review the special education assessment chapters now located on this textbook's companion website (go to http://www.wiley.com/college/kubiszyn and click on the link to the Student Companion Site).

Fortunately, learning to use standardized test results appropriately is not an overwhelming task. In this chapter, we will present the principles that comprise good practice with standardized tests. Learn them and follow them (even if others do not!), and you will find that appropriately used standardized tests can be valuable measurement tools and can be helpful in educational decision making. Again, although our primary focus is on the interpretation of standardized norm-referenced test scores, much of what we discuss also applies to standardized criterion-referenced tests.

USES OF STANDARDIZED ACHIEVEMENT TESTS

In Chapter 4, we discussed educational decision making. We concluded that teacher-made measurement instruments are useful for most day-to-day educational decisions. Historically, standardized tests were used to compare test scores over time or across students, classes, schools, or districts. Today, standardized tests are also used to make high-stakes decisions (e.g., promotion, graduation, teacher and principal ratings and incentives, and school and district evaluations). In some cases, standardized achievement tests are also used diagnostically to help educators identify student strengths and weaknesses or to evaluate specific programs and curricula. Group-administered standardized achievement tests are most useful for comparative purposes. This is quite different from the main uses of teacher-made tests, which are to determine pupil mastery or skill levels, assign grades, and provide students and parents with feedback. Why, then, would the classroom teacher administer a standardized test? To compare this year's students with last year's? To compare class A with class B? Yes, but the most accurate answer is more likely that the classroom teacher administers standardized achievement tests because he or she is required to do so under NCLB and by state HST laws. This is the case in all school districts in the country today. It should be noted, however, that the trend toward increased standardized testing predates the 2002 enactment of NCLB. Cizek (1998) estimated that standardized tests were administered to 140 million to 400 million students worldwide. Nevertheless, standardized testing may be increasing more rapidly than ever today. Reingold (2015) reported that the revenue generated by standardized testing increased by 57% to $2.5 billion between 2011 and 2014 alone.

A large part of the reason for the sustained increase in standardized testing over the last two decades has been accountability requirements related to HST. As teacher salaries and school taxes increase, taxpayers demand more justification for how their tax dollar is spent. By and large, taxpayers tend to support higher teacher salaries if teacher effectiveness increases, or at least remains constant (often as measured by standardized test results). As long as the public and policy makers want standardized achievement tests administered in the schools, the public will elect school board members who feel similarly, who will in turn choose school administrators who feel similarly, and those administrators will, in turn, require teachers to administer standardized achievement tests in their classrooms.

Accountability also includes evaluation of various federal and state programs. Most, if not all, such programs require that standardized achievement tests be administered as part of the program's evaluation requirement. Further funding may depend on the results of these tests.

What this boils down to is that citizens, school administrators, special project personnel, and administrators of federal and state programs want to be able to compare students, schools, and districts with one another, and over time, in order to make judgments concerning the effectiveness of school-wide, district-wide, or state-wide programs and practices. Indeed this desire was the driving force behind the NCLB, IDEIA, CCSS, and RTT initiatives we discussed in Chapter 2. As long as this goal remains, standardized test administration and interpretation will be a necessary part of teaching. Hence, the classroom teacher must learn to administer and interpret these tests.

WILL PERFORMANCE AND PORTFOLIO ASSESSMENT MAKE STANDARDIZED TESTS OBSOLETE?

As we noted in Chapters 1, 9, and 10, pressure has been mounting to use performance and portfolio assessments (sometimes called authentic assessments) to supplement traditional tests, both standardized and teacher-made. And pressure to increasingly use performance and portfolio assessments to evaluate students and programs is being felt at all levels—local, state, and national. This is reflected in the inclusion of performance assessments in both of the CCSS-aligned tests developed by the Smarter Balanced and PARCC consortia. The PARCC refers to performance assessment as performance-based assessment (PBA), and examples of its third- and seventh-grade PBAs may be viewed at http://www.parcconline.org/ela-types/performance%E2%80%93based-assessment-pba. Smarter Balanced sample performance tasks can be reviewed at their website (http://www.smarterbalanced.org/sample-items-and-performance-tasks/). Does all this mean that the utility and usage of traditional or even online standardized tests will decrease? While some would say yes, we do not think so.

First, administering standardized performance and portfolio assessments to all pupils would be extremely time consuming and demanding on teachers, and far more expensive than traditional standardized testing (although time and expense may be reduced through online administration and scoring). Second, for performance and portfolio assessment to be useful in comparing schools or districts on a state or national level, procedures will need to be developed that meet appropriate psychometric standards. Since standards for performance and portfolio assessments are not yet universally accepted, it is likely to be some time until procedures can be established that adhere to them. The performance assessments included in the Smarter Balanced and PARCC assessments may represent progress in this direction. And third, performance and portfolio procedures provide a different kind of information than that provided by traditional standardized tests; they do not replace the information provided by standardized tests.

Thus, there will almost certainly be the room and the need for both assessment approaches—traditional and online standardized and performance- and portfolio-based—in the schools of the future. In the meantime, a primary need facing the new teacher will be to learn how to use and interpret traditional standardized tests. This skill in interpretation will also put you a step ahead if standardized performance and portfolio assessment systems become a widespread requirement.

ADMINISTERING STANDARDIZED TESTS

Recall our discussion of reliability and error in Chapters 17 and 18. We identified four major sources of error associated with measurement:

1. Factors within the student (illness, fatigue).
2. Factors within the test (poor items, poor content validity).
3. Factors in administration (too little time, too many hints).
4. Factors in scoring (miskeyed items, clerical errors).

ARITHMETIC TEST

Ask students to place their test booklets on their desks next to the blank sheet of paper you provided. Once they have done so, check to ensure that each student has his or her own test booklet.

Then say: "Open your test booklet and turn to page 4. Page 4 says Arithmetic Test at the top of the page." Show students what page 4 looks like using your sample test booklet. Once the students have finished turning to page 4 again, check to make sure that they are on the proper page.

Then say: "Please read the directions for the Arithmetic test to yourself while I read them out loud." Look around the room to see if any of the students are confused, and provide any direction that is needed to ensure that everyone is on the same page.

Then say: "For the arithmetic test, you are to fill in the oval to indicate which of the four options is the best answer for each question. Be sure to make your marks heavy and dark within the oval, and do not make any additional marks in your answer booklet. If you want to change your answer, erase the mark in the oval as completely as you can. Be sure to fill in all the ovals, even if you are not sure about your answers. You can use the blank sheet of paper that was provided for your computations. Again, do not make any marks on the test booklet other than filling in the ovals to indicate your answer. Are there any questions?"

FIGURE 19.1 An example of the directions that are to be read aloud to students completing a standardized Arithmetic test.

Because a standardized test has been carefully prepared over several years, it generally will have carefully constructed items, thereby minimizing error within the test. This is certainly the case for standardized norm-referenced tests, although some state standardized criterion-referenced tests may not be as carefully constructed. Since such tests usually are machine scored, clerical errors in scoring are minimized. Little can be done in standardized test situations to minimize error attributable to within-student factors, but standardized tests do minimize error in test administration. Figure 19.1 provides an example of how a standardized test minimizes error in test administration. Notice the specific directions that are given to the test administrator as to what to say and what to do during the test. The best way to guard against error in test administration is to instruct *everyone* to administer the test in exactly the same way. Instructions such as these attempt to promote uniformity in how the test is administered across teachers, schools, and districts. If performance and portfolio assessment are used for comparisons between students in different localities, similar standardized instructions and conditions under which performances and portfolios must be demonstrated will be necessary. Figure 19.2 also provides some helpful hints to keep in mind when administering standardized tests.

The last point in Figure 19.2 bears further emphasis. It is not uncommon for well-intentioned classroom teachers to "individualize" the test administration by helping slower students or by pushing faster students. As we discussed earlier in this chapter, this is a violation of standardized testing procedure, and in certain circumstances may even rise to the level of criminal activity, such as the Atlanta case we described earlier. Regardless of whether the teacher or administrator is naive or well intentioned, such violations compromise the very reason the tests are administered, which is to allow reliable and valid comparisons of pupil achievement to be made. The test and its administration and scoring are called *standardized* because everyone gets the same treatment. This sameness is what helps reduce error and allows reliable comparisons to be made.

Do
• Read the manual *before* test administration day.
• Be sure you have been given the correct form for your grade level.
• Adhere strictly to the administration instructions, unless accommodations that may modify the instructions have been authorized.

Don't
• Try to minimize the achievement nature of the test.
• Deviate from the standardized administration instructions (i.e., do *not* allow more time, give hints, spell words, define words), unless accommodations that may modify the instructions have been authorized.

FIGURE 19.2   Dos and don'ts in administering standardized tests.

TYPES OF SCORES OFFERED FOR STANDARDIZED ACHIEVEMENT TESTS

In this section, we will consider the advantages and disadvantages of the types of converted scores publishers usually offer for standardized norm-referenced tests. Converted scores include grade equivalents, age equivalents, percentiles, and standard scores.

Grade Equivalents

Grade-equivalent scores are among the most widely used vehicle to report test results. They are also likely to be those *most often misinterpreted*. Grade equivalents are deceptively simple to interpret on the surface. Consider the following statement:

> *Danielle obtained a Math Computation grade-equivalent score of 7.6 (seventh grade, sixth month) on the California Achievement Test (CAT). That means that even though she's only in fourth grade, she can do math at the seventh-grade level.*

Do you agree with this statement? If you do, you have fallen victim to the most common kind of misinterpretation regarding grade-equivalent scores. Danielle's obtained score is the score that the publisher *estimates* would be obtained by the average seventh grader during the sixth month of school. It does not necessarily mean that Danielle is ready for seventh-grade math! She may not necessarily have mastered the prerequisites for success in seventh grade or even sixth grade! All we know for sure is that a fourth grader who obtains a math grade equivalent of 7.6 is *well above average* in math. This is not the same as saying the student is ready for seventh-grade math work. In fact, we don't even know how seventh graders would do on this test since it is unlikely that any seventh grader took the test! To understand the statement, we must consider the way in which grade-equivalent scores are determined.

Usually, a test is administered to the targeted grade (e.g., fourth grade) plus the grades immediately below and above the targeted grade (e.g., third and fifth grades). Thus, grade equivalents are based on obtained scores only for students one grade level below to one grade level above the grade being tested. Scores appearing in grade-equivalent norms tables that are more than one grade level below or above the grade being tested are *estimated*—they are extrapolated from the obtained scores. This is where the problem lies. Much higher or lower grade equivalents than average represent only relative degrees of performance. They say nothing about specific skills mastered or about deficiencies.

Unfortunately, the problems related to grade equivalents do not end there. Others are listed here:

1. Equal differences in scores do not necessarily reflect equal differences in achievement. For example, growth in reading comprehension from 2.6 to 3.6 will likely not mean the same degree or amount of growth as growth in reading comprehension from 7.6 to 8.6. It is likely that the 1-year's improvement is attributable to different factors in each case.

2. Grade equivalents are meaningless unless a subject is taught across all grades. Why report a physics grade equivalent of 6.2 when physics is taught only during the twelfth grade? What does it mean to say your performance in physics is equivalent to that of a beginning sixth grader?

3. Grade equivalents are often misinterpreted as *standards* rather than norms. That is, teachers (and parents and others!) often forget that grade equivalents are averages—about half the students will score above and half below grade placement (depending on aptitude, of course!).

4. Grade equivalents may not be directly comparable across school subjects. That is, a fifth grader who is 1 year behind grade placement in reading is not necessarily as far behind in reading as he or she may be in math, even though he or she is 1 year behind in math, too. This is because growth in different subjects occurs at different rates. Equal levels of growth or deficiency, as indicated by grade-equivalent scores, may mean quite different things.

In spite of these shortcomings, grade equivalents continue to be popular. Our recommendation is that if you use them, you should carefully consider the cautions we have outlined. In general, they are more useful for the elementary grades, where they can be used to compare growth across a common core of subjects. In spite of this, remember that we cannot be very confident in the equality of the units, their equivalence across subjects, or their meaningfulness when grade equivalents far above or below grade placement are obtained.

Age Equivalents

Age-equivalent scores are very similar to the grade-equivalent scores just discussed. And they are just as frequently misinterpreted. Age-equivalent scores are determined in a manner similar to that described for grade equivalents. That is, samples of 7-, 8-, and 9-year-olds might be tested and average scores for each age determined. Scores for younger or older students would then be estimated or extrapolated from those scores. Problems similar to those affecting grade equivalents affect age equivalents, as outlined here:

1. Equal differences in scores may not reflect equal differences in achievement. In other words, does growth from age 6 to age 7 represent the same amount of growth as from age 10 to 11? It may or may not, depending on the trait being measured. Furthermore, growth in most traits slows down or stops during the teens or early twenties. In other words, a year's growth in reading after age 17 is likely to be very different from a year's growth in reading at age 7.

2. Age equivalents are only meaningful if subjects are taught across all grades. It makes little sense to say someone has an age equivalent of 16.9 in subtraction.

3. Age equivalents may be misinterpreted as standards, rather than as averages or norms.

4. Growth across subjects may vary greatly, even if age equivalents show equal growth. A year's increase in language age equivalent does not necessarily mean the same thing as a year's increase in science age equivalent.

Unlike grade equivalents, age equivalents have *not* attracted widespread acceptance in the schools. Like grade equivalents, they are most useful in the elementary grades to compare growth across a common group of subjects. These shortcomings should always be considered in interpreting age equivalents.

Percentile Ranks

With grade- and age-equivalent scores, we indicate the grade or age group in which a student's test performance would be considered average. That is, if a student obtains a grade-equivalent score of 4.5, we can say the student did as well on the test as an average fourth grader during the fifth month of school. At times, however, we are not interested in making such comparisons. In fact, we would go so far as to say that in most cases we are more interested in determining how a student's performance compares with that of students in his or her own grade or of the same age. Percentile ranks enable us to make such comparisons.[1]

Percentile ranks are a substantial improvement over grade- and age-equivalent scores in that they do not suffer from the many limitations of grade and age equivalents. Since comparisons are within grade, it does not matter whether subjects are taught across grades, and since growth is only relative to others in the grade, the problem of growth being unequal at different grade levels is avoided. In addition, percentile ranks are less likely to be considered as standards for performance. However, percentile ranks do have two major shortcomings:

1. Percentile ranks are often confused with *percentage correct*. In using percentile ranks, be sure you are communicating that a percentile rank of 62, for example, is understood to mean that the individual's score was higher than 62% of the people who took the test or, conversely, that 62% of those taking the test received scores lower than this individual. Commonly, a score at the 62nd percentile is misinterpreted to mean the student answered only 62% of the items correct. A score at the 62nd percentile might be equivalent to a B or a C, whereas a score of 62% would likely be an F.

2. Equal differences between percentile ranks do *not* necessarily indicate equal differences in achievement. To refresh your memory, review the section on percentiles in Chapter 13. Briefly, in a class of 100 pupils, the difference in achievement between the 2nd percentile and 5th percentile is substantial, whereas the difference between the 47th and 50th is negligible, assuming a normal distribution. Interpretation of percentile ranks has to consider that units toward the tails of the distribution tend to be spread out, while units toward the center tend to be compressed, as illustrated in Figure 19.3. As long as these limitations are considered, percentiles represent a useful type of score to employ in interpreting standardized test results.

---

[1] You may be wondering what the difference is between percentiles and percentile ranks. Percentiles and percentile ranks have slightly different meanings. In finding *percentiles*, one starts with the percentile desired (e.g., P_{25}, P_{50}, and P_{75}) and then finds the score value below which there is that percentage of cases (e.g., 25 percent of the class scored below a score of 70). In finding *percentile ranks*, the reverse direction is taken: One starts with all the score values and then finds the percentage of cases falling below each value. Percentile ranks are generally determined by all the scores in a distribution at the same time.

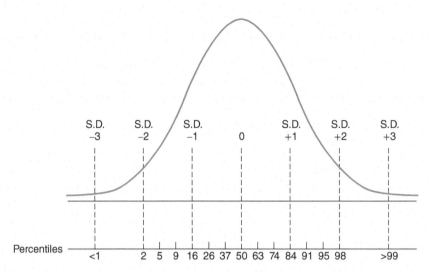

FIGURE 19.3 Normal curve with approximate percentile ranks indicated along the baseline.

Standard Scores

Like percentile ranks, standard scores compare a student's performance to that of other students at the same grade level. Often standard scores are called scale scores. The problem of equal differences between units not representing equal differences in achievement is overcome through the use of standard scores. Computation of such converted scores was discussed in Chapter 14, and you might want to review the relevant sections of that chapter. Recall that the z-score is the basic type of standard or scale score, and all other standard scores are derived from it (e.g., T-scores, GRE scores, SAT scores, ACT scores, and NCE scores). This is an important consideration to keep in mind since many test publishers create new types of standard scores with various means and standard deviations when they publish new tests (e.g., Developmental Standard Scores on the *Iowa Tests of Basic Skills*, or Expanded Standard Scores on the *Comprehensive Tests of Basic Skills*). You need not be overwhelmed by such scores since conceptually they are identical to z-scores.

Stanines Similar to, but different from, z-scores is a special type of standard score called *stanines*. Unlike all other standard scores, stanines are ranges or bands within which fixed percentages of scores fall. They are determined by dividing the normal curve into nine portions, each being one-half standard deviation wide. Stanines and the percentage of cases within each stanine are indicated here:

Stanine	Percentage of Cases
1	4 (lowest)
2	7
3	12
4	17
5	20
6	17
7	12
8	7
9	4 (highest)

Stanines have a mean equal to 5 and a standard deviation equal to 2. Each stanine is one-half standard deviation wide. Interpreting stanines is straightforward in that a student is simply described as being "in" the second stanine, ninth stanine, and so on. A major advantage of stanines is that, since they are intervals or bands, they tend to minimize overinterpretation of data. Also, since they only require single-digit numbers, they are useful for situations where recording space is limited.

Advantages and Disadvantages of Standard or Scale Scores From a technical perspective, standard scores represent the ultimate in standardized test score interpretation. However, there is one factor that limits their widespread adoption: Most educators, parents, and students do not understand how to use standard scores. As a result, schools or districts may not request standard scores from test publishers. As we will demonstrate, however, standard scores can save time and effort in determining aptitude–achievement discrepancies, which can help determine whether students are achieving at, below, or above their potential, based on aptitude. They also allow for easy comparison of scores both within and across pupils, either over time or across subjects (assuming standardized test administration and scoring procedures have been followed!).

Having had a course in tests and measurements, you will be better able to make use of standard scores to make sense out of standardized test scores. Keep in mind that such scores are not understood by most parents and students and as a result may not be the best choice for reporting standardized test results. What should you use, then? In our opinion, grade and age equivalents lend themselves too easily to misinterpretation and have too many limitations. As we mentioned, standard scores would be our choice but may be too complicated for use by the general public. We recommend, therefore, that you use percentile ranks when reporting and interpreting standardized test results to parents. Be sure, however, to consider the limitations we mentioned regarding percentile ranks in making such interpretations.

Next, we will show you how you can convert raw scores into various converted scores using the norms table provided for a standardized test. We complete this chapter by discussing the many test and student-related factors that should be considered in test interpretation, and then provide examples of standardized test score reports to familiarize you with the kinds of reports available today.

THE NORMS TABLE

A standardized test's printed or web-based administrative or technical manual provides you with the information you need to convert raw scores to converted scores, and back again, into enable accurate performance comparisons. For example, norms tables like the sample norms table in Table 19.1 from a fictitious standardized test (the Best of All Tests, or BOAT) can enable you to determine the proportion of test-takers who scored above, at, or below the various scores on a test or what scores met state performance standards. In addition, norms tables enable you to convert raw scores to percentiles and a variety of scale scores, or standard scores.

One important thing to keep in mind in using norms tables is the nature of the standardization sample, which may be nationally representative or not, depending on the intended use of the test (remember that we discussed that important issue in Chapter 1, and review this concept if necessary). With the rise of the HST movement over the last few decades, many states developed tests (and norms tables) based on state-specific instructional objectives or standards and for state-specific curricula. Using a norms table from a state-specific test to measure achievement in a different state with different standards and criteria would *not* be appropriate. This is one reason why it is critically important to clarify the representativeness of the normative sample *before* you begin using a norms table to convert scores or compare performances.

For our purposes, we can consider the BOAT English Language Arts tenth-grade norms table in Table 19.1 to be nationally representative. Table 19.1 enables you to convert BOAT raw scores into scale scores, percentile ranks, and Lexile measures. Regardless of what they may be called, scale scores conform to the *z*-score interpretations presented in Chapter 14, albeit with different means and standard deviations. The mean scale score for the BOAT is 900 and the standard deviation is 200 (review these concepts from Chapters 13 and 14 to maximize your comprehension of what follows). Table 19.1 also includes Lexile measures that correspond to raw, scale scores, and percentile ranks on this BOAT subtest. Not all standardized tests provide Lexile measures, which are intended to enhance matching of a student's instructional reading level (based on a scale score) to textbooks and other instructional materials with a comparable Lexile level of reading ability. Table 19.1 also provides cutoff scores that identify whether students scored at or above Proficiency or Exemplary levels on the BOAT English Language Arts test (i.e., whether they met performance standards or not, see Chapter 2 if you are unclear about this concept).

TABLE 19.1   The Fictitious Best of All Tests (BOAT) Raw Score Conversion Table English Language Arts—Spring 2015 Administration Grade 10

Raw Score*	Scale Score	Percentile	Lexile Measure	Raw Score*	Scale Score	Percentile	Lexile Measure
50	1,400	99	1500L	24	880	45	955L
49	1,380	99	1500L	23	860	41	925L
48	1,360	99	1500L	22	840	37	895L
47	1,340	99	1440L	21	820	34	880L
46	1,320	98	1395L	20	800**	31	870L
45	1,300	98	1395L	19	780	28	855L
44	1,280	97	1355L	18	760	24	840L
43	1,260	96	1355L	17	740	21	810L
42	1,240	95	1320L	16	720	18	785L
41	1,220	94	1320L	15	700	16	755L
40	1,200	93	1285L	14	680	15	715L
39	1,180	92	1285L	13	660	12	675L
38	1,160	90	1255L	12	640	10	625L
37	1,140	88	1230L	11	620	8	595L
36	1,120	86	1200L	10	600	6	560L
35	1,100***	84	1180L	9	580	5	545L
34	1,080	81	1155L	8	560	4	545L
33	1,060	78	1135L	7	540	3	545L
32	1,040	75	1110L	6	520	2	545L
31	1,020	72	1095L	5	500	2	545L
30	1,000	69	1075L	4	480	1	545L
29	980	66	1035L	3	460	1	545L
28	960	63	1020L	2	440	1	545L
27	940	59	1005L	1	420	1	545L
26	920	55	985L	0	400	1	545L
25	900	50	975L				

*Number of multiple-choice and short answer score points.

**Met minimum proficiency standard.

***Met minimum exemplary standard.

Interpreting a Norms Table

A norms table like the one shown in Table 19.1 can be confusing and intimidating at first glance. The key to successfully maneuvering through a norms table is to first understand how the table is organized. Table 19.1 lists the tenth-grade BOAT English Language Arts raw scores in the first and fifth columns. The asterisks next to the "Raw Score" headings in the first and fifth columns refer you to the note at the bottom of the page that explains how the raw scores are determined.

To convert a raw score into a scale score or a percentile, find the student's raw score in either the first or the fifth columns, and look along a straightedge (e.g., a ruler) to find the scaled score or percentile that corresponds to the raw score in question (or the Lexile measure if that is of interest). For example, a student with a raw score of 35 would have a scale score of 1,100 and a percentile rank of 84 (and a Lexile measure of 1180L), a student with a raw score of 14 would have a scale score of 680 and a percentile rank of 15 (and a Lexile measure of 715L), and a student with a raw score of 44 would have a scale score of 1,280 and a percentile rank of 97 (and a Lexile measure of 1355L). Note that the scale score of 800 has a double asterisk next to it. The note at the bottom of the table indicates that this is the "Met Minimum Proficiency Standard" score, the minimum score set by the state for "acceptable" performance on this BOAT subtest. Similarly, the triple asterisk next to the scale score of 1,100 indicates that this was the minimum score necessary to meet the "Minimum Exemplary Standard" performance level on this BOAT subtest. Standardized tests include similar, but somewhat different, approaches to converting raw scores into various converted and scale scores, so always be sure to read the explanations that accompany norms tables to minimize misinterpretations.

Specialized Norms Tables   In recognition of our nation's increasing cultural, linguistic, and academic diversity, standardized test publishers may offer specialized norms tables to supplement the nationally representative norms tables they have always offered. Specialized norms may be found in some standardized test manuals or may be available on request from the test publisher. Specialized norms tables for students for whom English is a second language, for students in low-achieving schools, for students from low socioeconomic backgrounds, and for others may be available, depending on the publisher. It is important to note, however, that the sizes of the samples for these specialized norms tables will be smaller than the size of the nationally representative sample and may be substantially smaller. Therefore, we must not be overconfident about the accuracy of any comparisons we may make that are based on specialized norms tables.

Local Norms   When a class, school, or district is substantially different from the normative sample, local norms may enable better use of test results. It should be noted, however, that we are not suggesting that local norms should be substituted for national, regional, state, or district norms. We are suggesting that local norms are useful tools that can, in some situations, increase the interpretability of test scores. They do so by enabling more meaningful comparisons to be made among and within unique students, classes, and schools. Since such norms are established on relatively homogeneous groups, they enable better comparisons within such groups, but they do not allow broader or national comparisons to be made. Table 19.2 compares and contrasts national and local norms.

Establishing Local Norms   Although establishing norms generally will be the responsibility of the school district's support staff, they are fairly easy to develop. To construct a local norms table, use the following procedures:

1. Collect scores for all individuals in the local group.
2. Tally all the obtained scores.

TABLE 19.2 A Comparison and Contrast of National and Local Norms

	National Norms	Local Norms
Composition	Large numbers of students of various ethnicity and income selected to represent U.S. population.	All students in a specific school or district.
Use	Compare local performance to a national norm.	Compare local performance to a local norm.
Advantage	Allows broad, general comparisons in areas of broad concern (e.g., college entrance, scholarships).	Allows comparisons in areas of local or immediate concern (e.g., academic gain within homogeneous groups, placement in local classes).
Disadvantage	Not useful in comparisons when relatively homogeneous groups are involved.	Not useful for making broad comparisons at a national level.

3. Construct a simple frequency distribution (refresh your memory by rereading this procedure in Chapter 13).

4. Compute percentile ranks for each score in the table (see Chapter 13).

5. Refer to the table as you would do a national norms table.

Let's turn to the final question addressing test-related factors that influence standardized test interpretation:

Were standardized administration procedures followed?

Here, the teacher needs to think back to the day the test was administered. Were any required procedures or wording altered or omitted? Was extra time or too little time afforded? Was help made available above and beyond what was permissible according to the test manual? If no such violations occurred, no more need be done about this consideration. If one or more violations did occur, the teacher must realize that reliability and validity have been affected to some unknown extent. Obviously, this reduces the confidence you can place in the test results. Since you will never be sure how reliability and validity have been affected by such violations, or be certain the violations resulted in increased or decreased scores, there is little you can do to correct for such errors—except, of course, to prevent them.

INTERPRETING STANDARDIZED TESTS: TEST AND STUDENT FACTORS

Standardized tests, though less useful for day-to-day instructional decision making than teacher-made tests, can be very useful for selection, placement, and diagnostic decisions and for providing feedback to parents, students, and decision makers. As we know, standardized tests are now also widely used for accountability purposes. Unfortunately, standardized test interpretation is by no means a straightforward task. Standardized or not, tests are fallible and require thoughtful and considerate use. To acquire the skill of properly using standardized tests, you must consider certain factors. These factors can be classified into two categories: test-related and student-related.

Test-Related Factors

Test-related factors can limit the interpretability of the test's results due to problems inherent in the test itself, its use, or its administration or scoring. They can be addressed by asking the following questions:

Does the test have acceptable score reliability and criterion-related validity evidence?

Does the test have content validity evidence for my instructional objectives or for the CCSS or my state's academic standards?

Was the test's norm group composed of students similar to my class (for standardized norm-referenced tests)?

Were the standardized administration and scoring procedures followed?

Let's consider each of these questions.

Does the test have acceptable score reliability and criterion-related validity evidence?

This question highlights the need to know how valid, reliable, and accurate a test is. In Chapters 16–18, we discussed validity evidence, score reliability, and accuracy. We can review the evidence for a test's score reliability, accuracy, and validity from information contained in the administrator's manual or the technical manual accompanying the standardized test. Let's consider this information.

Reliability An acceptable standardized test should have approximately the following score reliability coefficients:

0.95 for internal consistency,

0.90 for test–retest, and

0.85 for alternate forms.

If your test has coefficients this high, you can feel confident that scores from the test are reliable. Of course, there is nothing sacred about these particular coefficients. If your test scores have coefficients of 0.92 for test–retest reliability, 0.93 for internal consistency, and 0.82 for alternate forms, it will still have good score reliability. Keep in mind though that a good standardized test should report score reliability with more than just an estimate of internal consistency (see Chapters 17 and 18).

Accuracy Obtained results will be close to an individual's true level of achievement when the test demonstrates evidence of its validity (i.e., that it measures what it is intended to measure). Under the section "Standard Error of Measurement" in the administrator's or technical manual, you will find a numerical value that will enable you to determine the range of scores within which an individual's true score is likely to lie. Recall from Chapter 18 that this range of scores can be determined at the 68%, 95%, and 99% levels of confidence.

Criterion-Related Validity Evidence Recall that criterion-related validity evidence may be of two types: predictive and concurrent. Since standardized achievement tests are used to assess past learning, it makes little sense to report predictive validity coefficients for them. However, concurrent validity coefficients are often reported. These are numerical estimates of the extent to which a test correlates with another established test or tests. However, using such coefficients to determine an achievement test's validity is difficult. Since the content and specificity of the different tests will vary, a valid achievement test may yield concurrent validity coefficients of 0.60 with Test X and 0.90 with Test Y and still be a good achievement test. The reason for the discrepancy may reflect a closer match in content and specificity between your test and Test Y, and less of a match with Test X. For this reason, it is *most* important to evaluate the content validity evidence of standardized achievement tests. This is the same as the concept of a high-stakes test's alignment with state standards or the CCSS, as was discussed in Chapters 2 and 16. Concurrent validity evidence is of secondary importance. Of course, one would be very suspicious of an achievement test that yielded a concurrent validity coefficient of less than 0.50 with an established standardized achievement test that measures the same objectives, CCSS, or state standards.

Does the test have content validity evidence for my instructional objectives or for state academic standards or the Common Core State Standards?

A numerical estimate of validity showing that Test A correlates highly with Test B is not evidence that either test has content validity for your instructional objectives. Only by matching items with your objectives, or with state standards or the CCSS, can you determine whether a standardized achievement test has content validity evidence. If the test has several items covering dictionary skills and you have not taught such skills, the case for content validity evidence of the test for your class has been weakened. That is, if the test does not measure or match your objectives and your instruction, the test's results will be ambiguous and challenging to interpret, regardless of score reliability or accuracy.

Was the test's norm group composed of students similar to my class?

When the pilot or preliminary version of a standardized test is constructed, it is often administered to a test or pilot group of students. Revisions are made as indicated, and then it is administered to a *norming group* or *normative sample*. A norms table (essentially a frequency distribution; see Chapter 13) for the test is then compiled based on the performance of this sample of the test.

Most standardized test publishers are careful to select norm groups that are representative of the general U.S. population. This means that the sample is scientifically chosen to be as similar to the general U.S. population as possible in terms of sex, ethnicity, education level, state, region, income, and other such factors. A nationally representative sample increases the usefulness of the test for making comparisons between your class and the performance of other classes in other schools, cities, or states. Often, a compromise must be reached in creating a norms table. In trying to closely represent the U.S. norm, we create a norms table that may not represent the unique characteristics of any individual classroom, school, city, state, or region. So, depending on how similar or dissimilar your class is to the U.S. population in general, the comparisons you make you make to a nationally representative norm will be more useful or less useful.

One of the factors to consider when considering a test's appropriateness for your situation is regional diversity. Historically, education has been largely controlled by the states, with educational goals, objectives, tests, and target or criterion scores, and test performance often differing significantly across the states (Finn, Petrilli, & Winkler, 2009). If your goal is to compare local student performance to national student performance be sure to check your test's norms table to ensure the test's norms table is *nationally* representative and not based on performance in a single state. On the other hand if you are comparing student performance to that of other students in your state, a state-wide norms table would be appropriate.

Knowing the socioeconomic composition of the norm group is also important. If the test you administer to your upper-income class was normed on a sample of low-income children from impoverished backgrounds, and your class scored somewhat higher than 50% of the norm group, would you interpret the findings to mean that your class had exceptional performance?

Hopefully not. Since children who were raised in impoverished, low-income families tend to score low on standardized tests, we would expect children from upper-income families to score considerably higher regardless of instructional method or the academic potential of the children involved. Similarly, it would be inappropriate to compare the performance of low-income children to a norm group composed entirely of upper-income children. The low-income group would be expected to fare poorly in comparison, again, regardless of instructional methods or academic potential.

How well the educational achievement of the norm group matches your class or student is also important to consider. Trying to assess progress in a class for the talented and gifted (e.g., TAG, or GT) by comparing test scores to a national norm would not be appropriate. All or most students would score high in comparison because the educational attainment of the majority of the norm group would be substantially lower than the TAG students in your class. In this case, a more appropriate norm group might be one composed of nationally representative TAG students instead.

A similar case could be made for the inappropriateness of comparing a class composed entirely, or mainly, of low-achieving students to a norm group representative of the national population. Such a class would score very low by comparison, and a comparison to a norm group of other low-achieving students may be a better choice. Most teachers, however, do not have uniformly high- or low-achieving students in their classes. How, then, can teachers in such classes tell how appropriate are the comparisons they make? Fortunately, there is an answer.

The teacher knows approximately what his or her class composition is with respect to income and ethnicity. The teacher can then find the composition of the norm group by reading the "Norm Group" description section in the manual accompanying the standardized test (or posted on the test publisher's website). An example of such a description is presented in Figure 19.4. After studying the description, you can compare your class to the norm group. The closer the correspondence

The norms for this test are derived from a sample of 13,000 students in grades K-12. Approximately 1,000 students were included for each grade level (K-12). Only students who never repeated or skipped a grade were included. Their ages ranged from 5 to 19. The test was administered to the sample in spring 2000. The sample was stratified to be representative of the U.S. population according to gender, parental income, parental education, ethnicity, and geographic region. The actual composition of the standardization sample is described next.

Gender: Approximately equal numbers of males and females were included (6,432 boys and 6,568 girls) in the overall sample. At each grade level, the number of males and females in the grade samples did not differ by more than 50.

Parental Income: Approximately 10% of the sample had parental income of $80,000 or more, 60% had incomes ranging from $30,000 to $79,999, and 30% had incomes under $30,000. These proportions (plus or minus 1.5%) were maintained at each grade level.

Parental Education: 28% of the parents whose children were included in the sample completed 4 or more years of college, 16% had some college, 32% completed high school or had a high school equivalency diploma, and 24% did not complete high school.

Ethnicity: 66% of the sample was Caucasian, 15% African American, 13% Hispanic American, and 4% Asian American, with other ethnic groups comprising the remaining 2%.

Region: 26.5 of the sample came from the Northeast, 23% from the southeast, 24.5% from the northwest, and 26% from the southwest regions of the United States.

FIGURE 19.4 An example of a norm group description that would be found in a standardized test manual.

between the class and the norm group, the more confidence you can have in interpreting the norms table. The more discrepant the norm group and your class, the less confidence you can place in interpretations based on the norms table. This is a judgment that one gets better at with time and practice. But what if you decide there is a large discrepancy between the norm group and your class? Is there any way to better interpret the standardized test results? There are other options. Today, on request some test publishers will provide specialized norms tables that enable comparisons broken down by school, district, state, or region as well as the nation as a whole. And one can always consider the option of establishing local norms, following the process we described earlier in this chapter.

This completes our discussion of test-related factors to be considered in interpreting standardized tests. Now let's consider several equally important student-related factors.

Student-Related Factors

The variety of student-related factors that can affect test score interpretation can be divided into several categories: linguistic and cultural; age, gender, and developmental; motivational; emotional state on the test day; disabilities; and aptitude.

Linguistic and Cultural For decades, there has been a steady flow of immigrants from non-English-speaking countries into the United States. Most would agree that there are legal, moral, and practical reasons why non-English-speaking children of these immigrants should be educated in our schools. Thus, we have seen considerable growth in the language and cultural diversity of our classrooms over the last several decades. Although immigration trends may change, there is no reason to believe immigration to the United States will abate (e.g., the number of immigrants from Asian countries has increased in recent years, as have the number of immigrants from Mexico and Latin American countries).

In Chapters 1, 3, and 5, we discussed the importance of considering a student's language proficiency and sociocultural context in relation to norm- and criterion-referenced test selection and the interpretation and assessment process. We asked whether Svetlana, a recent Russian immigrant with limited English proficiency, or Diana, a recent immigrant from England with excellent proficiency in English, would be expected, all other factors being equal, to score higher on a standardized test in English. Our obvious conclusion was that Diana would score higher simply because she could read and comprehend the test questions far more easily, accurately, and quickly than Svetlana.

Yet, there have been many instances where well-intentioned, but unthinking or naive, individuals have administered standardized and teacher-made tests in English to students with limited English proficiencies. Worse, when students with limited English proficiency obtain scores on tests in English that are below national norms, or fail to meet proficiency criteria, they have at times been labeled as slow learners, learning disabled, or intellectually disabled.

Sociocultural factors beyond language factors can also negatively affect a child's performance on a standardized test. In our culture, competitiveness, assertiveness, frequent testing, and the use of tests to determine entry into schools, trades, and professions have been accepted and are valued. As a result, parents and students raised in our culture have learned to recognize the "demands" of the typical testing situation. Another way of saying this is that they have become "acculturated" into our competitive, test-oriented culture.

Immigrants may lack this acculturation if their native culture places less emphasis and importance on competitiveness and testing. For example, parents and students from our majority culture realize that students must prepare for a test, concentrate and work quickly and accurately during the test, and insist on equitable treatment from the test administrator. Children from other cultures may not even be aware of these expectations, much less agree with or be prepared to accomplish them. Thus, their behavior during important testing situations may be discrepant with expectations based on children who have been acculturated to testing and may be interpreted negatively by educators. Other factors may also affect test behavior and performance among students who are not from the majority culture. Some examples include hunger and poor nutrition, poverty, the importance placed on achievement in the family, and a variety of other behavioral differences across cultures (e.g., assertiveness, competitiveness, and compliance with authority figures).

In summary, language proficiency and a variety of sociocultural factors can negatively affect test behavior and standardized test performance. Language proficiency and sociocultural differences from the majority culture should always be considered in planning for selecting, administering, and interpreting standardized test results (Basterra, Trumbull, & Solaro-Flores, 2010).

Age, Gender, and Development An awareness of individual differences has influenced educational practice for many years. We read and hear about students being visual or auditory learners, high or low IQ, advanced or delayed, and so forth. Yet we sometimes fail to consider three of the most obvious of the individual differences among children—age, gender, and stage of development.

Typically, norms tables are broken into three or four sections to correspond to various times of the year. Students are expected to know more, and therefore answer more items correctly, in May than in October, due to the effects of schooling. This makes sense, of course, but what about the case of a first grader who turns 6 the day before school starts, compared to the first grader who turns 7 the day after school starts? Should both students, all other factors except age being equal, be expected to improve their test scores equally? If you are familiar with younger elementary-age children, your answer would likely be a firm no. Five-, six-, and seven-year-olds show very different rates of development in different areas. Furthermore, there are differences that correlate with gender. Girls tend to master verbal skills and reading earlier than boys. Norms tables for achievement tests may not take such factors into account. The reasons for academic performance are complex and, of course, involve more than just age, gender, and stage of development. Do not treat them as though they alone determine test performance and do not neglect those factors in interpreting standardized test scores.

Motivational Ever find it hard to be "up" for a test? If you are like most of us, it happens from time to time. At those times, your performance is less likely to reflect your actual level of achievement than if you were up for the test. Most pupils have little trouble getting ready for a teacher-made achievement test—they know that their grades depend on it. With standardized tests, however, motivation can be a problem.

Both pupils and their parents have made more sophisticated use of standardized tests over the last few years. Many parents realize that such tests do not affect a child's grades in school, but at the same time, they may not realize that such results may be used for instructional grouping and high-stakes decisions that will affect their child later. Believing standardized tests are not important may lead pupils to take a "who cares?" attitude toward standardized tests. Teachers sometimes unintentionally transmit such an attitude in an effort to minimize the anxiety some pupils experience over tests. The result can be a decline in motivation and a consequent decline in performance.

Emotional State on the Test Day Just as teachers get emotionally upset from time to time, so do their students. This does not simply refer to students who are nervous about the test, but also to students who may be undergoing severe stress for personal reasons, such as an argument before the test, a dispute at home, or some destabilizing event within the family. One cannot function at one's best when depressed, angry, or very nervous. When you find these characteristics exhibited by a student before or during the test, make a note of it and consider it when you interpret the student's test performance at a later date.

Disabilities   Physical and/or emotional challenges hinder academic achievement for a sizable percentage of students in the public schools. In the past, children with disabilities were often excluded from annual state- and district-wide standardized assessments. As we mentioned at the beginning of this chapter, beginning with passage of the 1997 Amendments to the *Individuals with Disabilities Education Act* (IDEA–97), and reinforced by NCLB in 2002 and in 2004 by IDEIA, students with disabilities must now participate in annual academic assessments, albeit with accommodations or through alternate assessments. This well-intended participatory requirement attempted to minimize disability-related impediments to performance on annual assessments by encouraging appropriate accommodations (i.e., intended to eliminate or reduce the limiting effects of a student's disability on test performance) and various kinds of alternative assessments to standardized tests. However, some accommodations and modified or alternative assessments will limit comparability of scores for children with disabilities with one another, with themselves over time, and across classes, schools, districts, and states, as we mentioned at the beginning of this chapter.

Aptitude   Aptitude and potential can be considered synonymous for our purposes. They refer to the maximum we can expect from a student, as indicated by a student's score on a test of academic aptitude or potential. Such tests are often referred to as IQ tests, intelligence tests, or cognitive ability tests. IQ tests will be discussed in more depth in Chapter 20. The academic aptitude, or IQ, test provides us with an estimated ceiling for a student's academic performance. The achievement test, on the other hand, measures actual academic performance.

Traditionally, students have been labeled overachievers or underachievers when achievement scores are discrepant with academic aptitude scores. Figure 19.5 illustrates an underachiever, an overachiever, and a student achieving at expectancy. Student A in Figure 19.5 is a student with considerable potential who is not achieving at his or her potential. Student B is a student with moderate potential who is achieving above his or her potential. More accurately, this "overachiever" is a student whose obtained aptitude score (not necessarily true score) is lower than his or her obtained achievement score. Student C represents a student achieving at the level we would expect, given his or her aptitude score. The obtained aptitude score is equivalent to the obtained achievement score.

Obviously, it is necessary to have an aptitude score to enable you to determine whether a student is achieving at *expectancy* (the level you would expect, given the student's aptitude) or

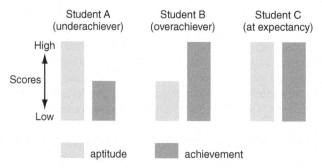

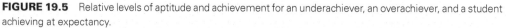

FIGURE 19.5   Relative levels of aptitude and achievement for an underachiever, an overachiever, and a student achieving at expectancy.

whether a *discrepancy* exists between aptitude and achievement. However, school district policies vary in requiring the administration of aptitude tests. Depending on your district, you may have aptitude tests administered to students every few years, or only in the fourth and ninth grades, or not at all. If you find aptitude test scores in your students' folders, you can use them to enhance your achievement test interpretation.

Most aptitude tests yield more than one overall IQ score. Many yield a *verbal* and a *nonverbal* score, or a *language* and a *nonlanguage* score, or a *verbal* and a *quantitative* score. Quantitative scores represent general math or number ability. When the aptitude or IQ test yields a verbal score and a nonverbal score or a quantitative score, more relevant comparisons are possible than when only one overall score is reported. Consider the following example.

Donna, a new fifth grader, obtained the following scores on the Cognitive Abilities Test, or CogAT (an aptitude test) at the beginning of fourth grade (note: M = 100, SD = 15).

Verbal = 100
Quantitative = 130

Donna's scores on the California Achievement Test (CAT) given at the end of fourth grade are as follows:

Subtest	Percentile Rank
Reading vocabulary	66
Reading comprehension	60
Reading total	63
Math concepts	99
Math computation	99
Math total	99

Donna's parents have requested a conference with you. They want you to push her harder in reading until her reading scores match her math scores, which have been superior.

What would you do? How would you interpret Donna's scores? Would you push her in reading? Before you answer those questions, let's make Donna's data interpretable. We can do so by using bar graph comparisons to illustrate the concepts of underachievement and overachievement.

We know that an obtained IQ score of 100 is at the 50th percentile on an IQ test with a mean of 100 and a standard deviation of 15. We also know that on the same test an IQ score of 130 is at the 98th percentile, two standard deviations above the mean. In the graphs in Figure 19.6 our percentile scales do not correspond directly to each other, but that is of little consequence since we are not interested in comparing reading with math. Rather, we are interested in comparing verbal aptitude with reading total, both of which are on the same scale, and quantitative aptitude with math total, which are also on a common scale.

From the graphs, we would conclude that Donna's obtained math achievement score actually *exceeds* the obtained math aptitude score. According to our popular but somewhat misleading terminology, she is "overachieving" in math. Unless she is paying a high price socially or emotionally for working so hard at math, we see no problem here. Hence, the qualifier "over" in the word *overachiever* should not imply a negative valuation of what this student has accomplished. But Donna's parents are not concerned with her math achievement; they are concerned with her reading achievement. They want her pushed, which suggests that they feel she can do better than she has in the past. That is, Donna's parents feel she is underachieving in reading. Is she?

On the basis of a comparison of her obtained verbal aptitude score and her obtained reading achievement score, our conclusion would have to be no. In fact, Donna is "overachieving" in reading, too. That is, her obtained reading achievement score exceeds her obtained verbal aptitude score; she is actually performing above expectancy. Would you agree that she needs to be pushed?

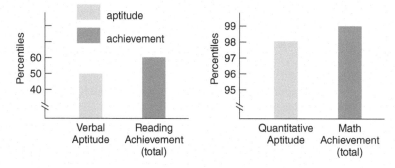

FIGURE 19.6 A comparison of Donna's aptitude and achievement scores.

By now, we should hope not. In fact, you might suggest to Donna's parents that they ease up, using your skills in the interpretation of standardized test results to substantiate your suggestion.

APTITUDE–ACHIEVEMENT DISCREPANCIES[2]

What we have been doing is making a general or global decision about whether Donna is achieving at her expected level, as indicated by her aptitude score. In other words, are there any differences between her aptitude and her achievement? When these differences are large enough to indicate substantial variation in the traits being measured, we call them *aptitude–achievement discrepancies.*

But when is a difference a discrepancy? How large must the gap be before we call a difference a discrepancy? Does this begin to sound familiar? We hope so, but if it does not, this next question should help: How large a difference do we need between an aptitude score and an achievement score before we can conclude that the difference is due to a "real" discrepancy rather than a "chance" difference? In Chapter 18, we learned how to use the standard error of measurement (S_m) and band interpretation to discriminate real from chance differences among subtests in an achievement test battery. This same principle can be applied to discriminate real discrepancies from chance differences when dealing with aptitude and achievement test scores.

We will consider an example in a moment, but first let's review one aspect of band interpretation. Recall that we can use the 68% (score $\pm$ 1 S_m) or 95% (score $\pm$ 2 S_m) methods, depending on how conservative we want to be regarding the educational decisions to be made. If such findings are kept within the classroom and little of consequence is to follow from a band interpretation, or if comparisons are limited to those among subtests on an achievement battery, the 68% approach may be appropriate.

Beyond the confines of your own classroom, however, important educational decisions or conclusions may be based on comparisons between achievement and aptitude. Indeed, for

[2] The following discussion assumes high difference score reliability. Unfortunately, difference scores often are less reliable than the reliability of the aptitude or achievement tests that are used to determine them. The formula for determining reliability of difference scores is presented in the section on band interpretation of scores in Chapter 18. The procedures described in the section are intended to provide the regular classroom teacher with an easy-to-use standard for identifying students who may be in need of further testing or diagnosis. They are not intended to classify a student solely on the basis of aptitude–achievement discrepancy.

individual students, demonstration of a *severe* aptitude–achievement discrepancy was required by federal law since 1977 until the IDEIA was passed in 2004 to qualify a student to receive special educational services as a child with a Specific Learning Disability (SLD). Under the IDEIA, states can no longer require schools to use the discrepancy approach for SLD determination. Instead they must permit a response-to-intervention (RTI) approach (see Chapter 3), combine the discrepancy and RTI approaches, or use an alternative approach. The special education chapters on this textbook's companion website provide more detail (go to http://www.wiley.com/college/kubiszyn and click on the link to the Student Companion Site).

Regardless of the SLD determination method used in your state or district, the special education referral process often begins with a teacher suspecting that a student is not achieving at an average rate, or up to his or her potential. Thus, we would strongly encourage you to consider using the more conservative 95% approach any time you consider making a special education referral based on aptitude–achievement discrepancies you have observed.

Let's turn to an example that illustrates how aptitude–achievement discrepancies are determined. Table 19.3 lists scores obtained by three students on the *California Achievement Test* and an aptitude test, the *Cognitive Abilities Test*. Inspect the table. Are there any aptitude–achievement discrepancies? Are you having trouble answering?

Before going any further, let's try to make some sense out of the table. Provided are three types of scores for the *California Achievement Test*: grade equivalents, percentile ranks, and standard scores. It is more often the case than not that several scores are reported for each student. However, aptitude scores, such as those in our table from the *Cognitive Abilities Test*, are typically reported in standard scores only. The first step in determining aptitude–achievement discrepancies is to be sure both sets of scores are on the same scale. If for some reason standard scores are not included on your score report, request or download a copy of the test manual and convert the scores you do have (e.g., either grade or age equivalents, or percentiles) to standard scores. Instructions on how to perform the necessary operations will be provided in the manual, and they likely will differ somewhat from test to test.

After you have converted all scores into standard scores, the remaining steps are very similar to those we followed in the section on band interpretation in Chapter 18. Once our scores are all on the same scale, determine the S_m for each subtest. This is important because each subtest will have a somewhat different S_m values. Do not use the S_m for the whole test, as this would give an inaccurate or misleading interpretation in many cases. In Table 19.3, the S_m is listed under each subtest. While the S_m is usually not included in score reports, you can find the S_m for each

TABLE 19.3 Scores for Max, Betty, and Robert Reported in Standard Scores (SS), Percentile Ranks (%), and Grade Equivalents (GE)

| | California Achievement Test | | | | | | | | | | | | | | | | | | Cognitive Abilities Test | |
| | Reading Recognition | | | Reading Comprehension | | | Reading Total | | | Math Concepts | | | Math Computation | | | Math Total | | | | |
Name	GE	%	SS[a]	GE	%	SS[a]	GE	%	SS[a]	GE	%	SS[a]	GE	%	SS[a]	GE	%	SS[a]	Verbal[a]	Quantitative[a]
Max	2.2	13	82	2.3	15	83	2.2	14	82	1.9	9	79	2.5	17	85	2.2	13	85	81	89
Betty	2.9	25	89	3.3	34	94	3.1	30	92	3.2	32	93	3.6	42	97	3.4	37	95	112	120
Robert	5.4	84	116	5.8	89	121	5.6	87	118	4.6	68	107	4.8	73	109	4.7	70	108	114	118
	$S_m = 3.5$			$S_m = 3.0$			$S_m = 3.3$			$S_m = 3.5$			$S_m = 2.5$			$S_m = 3.0$			$S_m = 3.5$	$S_m = 3.5$

[a]M = 100, SD = 15.

Note: S_m is in standard score units. The values provided are illustrative estimates only. Actual values will differ somewhat.

subtest in the test manual. You could also compute the S_m for each subtest, using the formula from Chapter 18: ($S_m = SD\sqrt{1-r}$). To do so, you would need to look up the reliability of each subtest in the manual.

After determining the S_m for each subtest, add and subtract 2 S_m to each obtained score. This gives us the range of scores for each subtest within which we are 95% sure the student's true score lies. Remember, we are advising the use of the more conservative 95% approach in determining aptitude–achievement discrepancies. Using Table 19.3, here are the data for Betty's reading and verbal IQ scores:

Name	Subtest	Obtained Score	S_m	95% Range
Betty	Verbal IQ	112	3.5	105–119
	Reading recognition	89	3.5	82–96
	Reading comprehension	94	3.0	88–100
	Reading total	92	3.3	85.4–98.6

Now we are ready to complete our band interpretation and identify any aptitude–achievement discrepancies. Transfer your data to a table like the one used in Chapter 18, as shown in Table 19.4. Inspection of the bands in Table 19.4 reveals that there are real differences between Betty's verbal aptitude or IQ and her reading achievement, even though we used the conservative 95% approach (there is no overlap between her verbal aptitude and her reading achievement). We could state with considerable confidence that the differences indicates real discrepancies, even at the 95% level.

Keep in mind, however, that when an aptitude–achievement discrepancy is found, the teacher's task is only beginning. Why the discrepancy exists must be determined, and then appropriate steps taken to remediate it.

This concludes our discussion of aptitude–achievement discrepancies. Recall why we began this discussion: to consider comparing actual student achievement to individual potentials, not just to one another or to a local or national norm. Students have differing levels of potential, and searching for aptitude–achievement discrepancies helps sensitize you to these differences. Instructional planning and standardized score interpretation are facilitated and aided when student achievement

TABLE 19.4   Band Interpretation of Betty's Verbal IQ and Reading Scores (95% Level)

is considered in relation to potential, not simply in relation to norms. The beneficiaries of such an approach to standardized test interpretation are likely to be both you and your students.

Do I really have to consider test- and student-related factors in standardized test interpretation?

Yes! We have discussed several test-related and student-related factors in this chapter that can affect the usefulness of standardized tests (i.e., their validity evidence, score reliability, and accuracy). And because the consideration of these factors may be omitted when highly visible HST results are released, you may believe that they are not important or not applicable to high-stakes tests! This is simply not true. All tests provide only estimates of performance, and all are affected by test-related and student-related factors such as those we have covered in this chapter.

It may seem as though these factors are too many and too complex to deal with every time you have to interpret standardized test scores. However, with time and practice, they become second nature—if you make yourself consider them in your initial attempts at standardized test interpretation. We will present a dialogue in the next section that illustrates this point. The dialogue will provide examples of how these factors can be vital to sound educational decision making in what sometimes can become emotion-laden parent conferences. They also demonstrate how these factors can be integrated with marks or grades from teacher-made tests, performance-based assessments, and background information to clarify your students' performance to parents. We consider this to be best practice, and an illustration of the assessment process that we described in Chapter 1, rather than just testing or assessment.

INTERPRETING STANDARDIZED TESTS: PARENT–TEACHER CONFERENCES AND EDUCATIONAL DECISION MAKING

We have defined what standardized tests are; described their various uses; and discussed important considerations in administering standardized tests, the types of scores reported for standardized tests, and various test-related and student-related factors that can affect the validity, score reliability, and accuracy of standardized tests. If it seems as though we have covered a lot of territory in this chapter, your perceptions are correct. In this section, we will integrate and apply this information to an actual, real-world situation. A second application example can be found on the companion website for this text (go to http://www.wiley.com/college/kubiszyn). Our intent in including these dialogues is to provide you with examples of the way information gathered during the assessment process, and the principles presented in this chapter can help the teacher use test data effectively, and not misuse it, or ignore it. Keep in mind our main point. Tests are tools that may be used correctly or incorrectly and should only be used in conjunction with other relevant information when important educational decisions must be made. The following example and the second on the website show how test data and the thoughtful incorporation of background and other contextual data can enhance your understanding of student achievement and better inform educational decision making.

An Example: Pressure to Change an Educational Placement

(Miss Garza, the seventh-grade math teacher, is grading papers in her office when Jackie, one of the students in her Introductory Algebra class, walks in. Looking sad and forlorn, Jackie asks Miss Garza if she can speak with her.)

JACKIE:	Miss Garza, can I transfer out of Introductory Algebra and get into Fundamentals of Math? (*Introductory Algebra is the standard-level mathematics class for seventh grade; Fundamentals of Math is a remedial math class designed for students with limited mathematical aptitude and achievement.*)
MISS GARZA:	You want to switch out of Algebra and into Fundamentals! Why, Jackie?
JACKIE:	Well, you know that I barely passed Algebra for the first 6 weeks, and I'm failing it for the second 6 weeks. I just don't get it. It's too hard for me. I'm not good in math.
MISS GARZA:	Well, Jackie, why is that? You have always done well in math in the past, as your record indicates, and that's on both standardized achievement tests and your grades in math up to this point. Are you studying? It sure doesn't look it from your test performance, and as you know, you failed to turn in most of the assignments.
JACKIE:	The reason I don't turn in the assignments is because they are too hard. That's my whole point. I just can't understand algebra. It's too hard for me. It's really making me depressed. If I can't get out of algebra, I'm going to fail it. That means I'll not only be ineligible to play volleyball for the school, but I'll also be grounded until I bring my grades back up.
MISS GARZA:	Jackie, how do you think transferring into Fundamentals is going to help you?
JACKIE:	Well, I'll be able to play volleyball, I won't be grounded, and then I won't feel depressed.
MISS GARZA:	Well, Jackie, this is an important decision, and I think your parents should be involved. This decision has a big potential impact on your future, not just in terms of sports and whether you're grounded but on whether you take the right courses needed in high school and to get into college. So I'm going to give your parents a call and set up a conference to review this with them.
JACKIE:	Why do you have to do that?
MISS GARZA:	This decision is one that you and I should not make until we consult with your parents and review your entire record.
JACKIE:	Well, I thought teachers were supposed to be here to help students. If you get my parents involved in this, it's not going to help at all. They're probably going to say they want me to stay in Algebra because they don't care whether I pass or fail anyway. They just want something to complain about.
MISS GARZA:	Well, that may or may not be the case, but the bottom line is that we're not making any decisions about transferring you out of Algebra until all the information is reviewed with your parents.

(Jackie grabs her books quickly and storms out of Miss Garza's room without saying good-bye. Miss Garza then contacts Mrs. Williams, Jackie's mother, and lets her know that she would like to set up a conference as soon as possible to review Jackie's math performance. A parent conference is arranged, and the next dialogue describes the interchange between Miss Garza and Mr. and Mrs. Williams.)

(After exchanging pleasantries, Miss Garza informs the parents about Jackie's request to switch from Algebra to Fundamentals.)

MR. WILLIAMS:	Oh, why does she want to do that?
MRS. WILLIAMS:	She's failing, isn't she?
MISS GARZA:	Well, I'm afraid so. For the first 6 weeks she barely passed, and this 6 weeks her grades are well below passing. Unless she really gets to work, gets her

| | homework completed and turned in, and prepares properly for the tests, she's not likely to pass for this 6 weeks. |

MR. WILLIAMS: Well, let's go ahead and transfer her into Fundamentals, then. As you know, with the present school policy, if she fails she'll be ineligible to play volleyball.

MISS GARZA: I realize that, Mr. Williams. However, I'm concerned that if we take this step, we may send her the wrong message for the future.

MRS. WILLIAMS: What do you mean? You want her to fail? She just loves to play sports, and it would kill her to have to sit out because of ineligibility.

MISS GARZA: Well, Mr. and Mrs. Williams, you're Jackie's parents, and I think you should have the final say on this matter. My concern is that Jackie has worked herself into a corner and is trying to take the easy way out, rather than putting together an effective plan to solve the problem herself. If this is the way she solves her problem now, I'm concerned she'll continue to do the same in the future.

MR. WILLIAMS: Maybe you just don't like Jackie. Is that it?

MISS GARZA: Mr. Williams, if I didn't like Jackie and if I wasn't concerned for her future, I wouldn't have called you, I wouldn't have set up this conference, and I wouldn't have collected all the information I've gotten for us to review. My hope is that we can review her records, including her report cards and standardized test results, and make an informed decision that is most likely to benefit Jackie in the long run, rather than a hasty and impulsive one based on emotion rather than reason.

MRS. WILLIAMS: Are you saying Jackie has emotional problems?

MISS GARZA: No, Mrs. Williams. I'm not qualified to make a diagnosis or decision about emotional problems. However, I have taught middle school for a number of years, and situations like this come up frequently. Adolescence is a difficult time for both students and their parents, and the patterns that we put in place early in adolescence tend to repeat themselves later on. My concern is that Jackie has more than ample ability to handle Introductory Algebra, but she currently is unwilling to put in the time and effort required. If she lacked the mathematical or intellectual aptitude, or if it were evident that other factors might be contributing to her academic difficulties, I would not have suggested a conference.

MR. WILLIAMS: Okay, let's see what information you have. I know what her report card says, but I don't know anything about the standardized test scores she brought home.

(Miss Garza then describes how standardized tests are constructed and what their scores are designed to represent. Subsequently, she reviews scores from the group IQ test that Jackie took in fifth grade, as well as the year-end standardized test scores from first through sixth grade. Miss Garza then indicates these scores on a piece of paper, as illustrated in Figure 19.7).

(After reviewing the data, Miss Garza points out that almost all the scores are at or above the 80th percentile. This, she says, indicates that Jackie's mathematical aptitude and achievement are well above average. Thus, there is no evidence that suggests that she should be unable to handle the Introductory Algebra course because of a lack of aptitude or ability.)

MR. WILLIAMS: Wait a minute! What about her scores in fourth grade? They're not at the 80th percentile; they're way down at the 24th percentile. How do you explain that? If she has such great aptitude and achievement, how could she do so badly on that test?

Grade	Test	Percentile Scores		
		Math Computation	**Concepts**	**Math Total**
1	ITBS	91	81	86
2	ITBS	94	90	93
3	ITBS	85	83	84
4	ITBS	32	14	24
5	CogAT	—	—	88
5	ITBS	90	85	87
6	ITBS	88	82	85

FIGURE 19.7 Jackie Williams: Test scores from first through sixth grades.

MISS GARZA: I really don't know, Mr. Williams. However, there are any number of reasons why a student may do poorly on a standardized test administration. (*She then shares with Jackie's parents a copy of Figure 19.8.*)

Test-related factors

1. Does the test have acceptable reliability and criterion-related validity evidence?

2. Does the test have content validity evidence for my instructional objectives?

3. Was the test's norm group composed of students similar to my class?

4. Were standardized procedures followed?

Student-related factors

1. Language and sociocultural

2. Age, sex, and development

3. Motivation

4. Emotional state on the test date

5. Disabilities

6. Aptitude

FIGURE 19.8 Factors to consider in interpreting standardized test scores.

MISS GARZA: As you can see, interpreting standardized tests is not as simple as it might first appear. The reliability and validity of any score or group of scores depends on a number of factors related to the test and a variety of factors related to the student. Since the test was the fourth-grade version of the *Iowa Test of Basic Skills*, the same test that she took before and after fourth grade, we can pretty well rule out test-related factors as being contributory to her poor performance. If, on the other hand, for some reason the district had administered a completely different test, which may have had less direct applicability to the district's instructional objectives, that factor might explain the decline. I would conclude that some factor other than her ability was probably the cause.

MRS. WILLIAMS: Aren't these the tests that are administered over a 3-day period in April?

MISS GARZA: Yes, that's right.

MR. WILLIAMS: (*Looking empathically at his wife*) Wasn't it in April of Jackie's fourth-grade year that your mother died?

MRS. WILLIAMS: Yes, it was. And you know how devastated Jackie was when her grandmother died. (*Looking at Miss Garza*) They were very close.

MR. WILLIAMS: Miss Garza, do you think that could explain why she did so poorly that year?

MISS GARZA: Well, I can't be sure, but it sounds reasonable.

MRS. WILLIAMS: Yes, it does. What other information do you have?

(*Miss Garza then reviews with the parents Jackie's grades in math from her previous report cards. These range from straight A's from first through fourth grade, through A's and B's in fifth and sixth grades. Jackie's first D in math was in her first 6 weeks of seventh-grade Algebra. Miss Garza points out that, with the exception of the D, these grades are completely consistent with what would be expected from an individual with standardized test scores at the 80th percentile.*)

MISS GARZA: So, from all the evidence we have available, we have a consistent pattern except for the fourth-grade standardized test. So you see why I'm concerned that we may be allowing Jackie to avoid responsibility and take the easy way out by transferring into Fundamentals. More important, this will put her behind her peers and make it difficult for her to have the same advantages they have in high school and college.

MR. WILLIAMS: What! How can that be? How can what you take in seventh grade affect you in college?

MISS GARZA: Well, if Jackie goes into Fundamentals now, that means she'll take Introductory Algebra or Consumer Math next year. As a result, during her first year in high school she will be enrolled in one of the lower or remedial math classes, such as Beginning Algebra or Math in Life, rather than Algebra 1.

MRS. WILLIAMS: This is confusing. Are you telling me that ninth-grade Beginning Algebra is a remedial class rather than the beginning or entry-level algebra class?

MISS GARZA: That's right, Mrs. Williams. Students who pass Introduction to Algebra in seventh grade will go on to Geometry in eighth grade, Algebra I in ninth grade, Geometry in tenth grade, Algebra II in eleventh grade, and either Trigonometry, Calculus, or one of the other options during twelfth grade.

MR. WILLIAMS: So if she gets off this track, she would end up basically being a year behind in math when she graduates.

MISS GARZA: That's right, Mr. Williams.

MR. AND MRS. WILLIAMS: (*Together*) We'll talk to her!

The situation described is not designed to provide a complete and detailed diagnosis or intervention plan for Jackie. Rather, it is to illustrate what has been presented in this and other chapters. Without examining the cumulative record of test scores, report cards, and the factors identified in Figure 19.8, neither Miss Garza, the parents, nor Jackie would be likely to make an informed decision. An individual grade, such as Jackie's grade in Algebra, or a standardized test score, such as her test score in fourth grade, should not be the basis on which important educational decisions are made. Instead, defensible educational decisions require that all sources of data be considered, including standardized test scores, report cards, classroom grades, and relevant background information. This is an example of using data collected through the *assessment process* (see Chapter 1) to inform educational decision-making. It is also your best safeguard to ensure an informed parent–teacher conference.

Obviously, Jackie will not be happy with the decision. However, Jackie is also a seventh grader who is unaware of the long-term ramifications of transferring into the remedial class at this point. In her mind the transfer would clearly be the best option, since it would lead to resolution of all her problems and would require very little in the way of commitment on her part. All too often, educators find themselves in the position of making decisions in order to please parents or students, without considering the appropriateness of all the data on which the decisions are based as well as the short- and long-term consequences of those decisions. In a case such as this, it is likely that if Jackie's parents sit down with her and discuss the short- and long-term consequences of their decision and provide the proper support, the outcome will be a positive one. A second example illustrating similar principles for a student considered for a TAG program is available on the companion website for this text (go to http://www.wiley.com/college/kubiszyn).

INTERPRETING STANDARDIZED TESTS: SCORE REPORTS FROM PUBLISHERS

Test publishers today, including state education agencies and the Smarter Balanced and PARCC consortia, offer a wide variety of reports for test users. These can range from the small press-on labels that are designed to be affixed to report cards or cumulative folders to provide a concise record of achievement, to more comprehensive reports such as those illustrated in Figures 19.9 and 19.10–19.12. We have reproduced three sample reports from the TerraNova3, a widely used standardized norm-referenced test, and a sample report from the New York (NY) State Common Core Mathematics tests (NY State is part of the PARCC consortium) to familiarize you with these reports. Reports from other test publishers may look somewhat different, so be sure to take the time to thoroughly understand how they are structured. The sample reports illustrate how standardized tests can be used to compare individual or overall classroom performance to national norms (Figures 19.9 and 19.11), to criteria like objectives or standards (Figure 19.10), or to both norms and standards (Figure 19.12).

Comprehensive individual score reports are designed to provide norm-referenced and/or criterion-referenced information. The norm-referenced sample Home Report in Figure 19.9 enables us to compare the individual student's performance in the major content areas on the TerraNova3 to national norms. The criterion-referenced sample Individual Skills Report in Figure 19.10 compares the individual student's performance on the TerraNova 3 to several more specific objectives within each content area and can help teachers diagnose a student's specific strengths and weaknesses. The sample Group List report in Figure 19.11 enables the teacher, Ms. Jones, or a principal or school board member to compare the performance of her class to national norms. The Your Child's Tests Results sample report in Figure 19.12 compares the student's performance to others in NY State (state percentile rank) and uses both a Scale Score and a Performance Level from the PARCC-developed test to assess achievement of the Common Core Standards that were adopted by NY State.

Notice that various sections of each of the sample reports include large, indexed letters or numbers. The letters or numbers refer you to explanations for each report section. The explanations are found below the summary graphical or numerical portions of the report. Review these carefully to minimize confusion in reviewing or interpreting such reports. Of course, actual score reports may not include similar referencing guides, but the publisher's or consortium's websites will always provide clarification, if needed.

Any questions parents have about their student's performance in various subject areas compared to national norms should be fairly easy to answer based on the information in Figure 19.9. Similarly, Figure 19.10 can help you answer questions about subskills in each subject area based on

Home Report

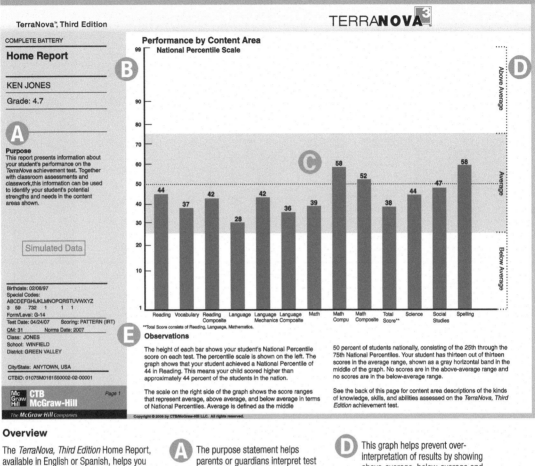

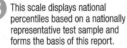

Overview

The *TerraNova, Third Edition* Home Report, available in English or Spanish, helps you inform parents or guardians about their student's academic progress, allowing them to become more involved in the learning process. This easy-to-understand report is particularly useful for parent-teacher conferences. The second page of the Home Report describes the content measured by each test and provides the student's level of content understanding.

The primary audience for the Home Report is parents or guardians, followed by teachers and students.

Equivalent Reports

TerraNova, The Second Edition:
Home Report

TerraNova:
Home Report

SUPERA:
Home Report

A The purpose statement helps parents or guardians interpret test results.

B This scale displays national percentiles based on a nationally representative test sample and forms the basis of this report.

C The height of each bar shows student performance compared with students nationally. This profile helps identify relative strengths and weaknesses.

D This graph helps prevent over-interpretation of results by showing above-average, below-average and average performance based on national percentiles.

E The Observations section is written in terms everyone can understand and helps parents or guardians interpret their student's test results.

Page 2 of the Home Report (not shown) describes the tests and provides a description of the student's performance on each test.

To see an interactive version of this report, go to **CTB.com/TerraNova3/Reports**

FIGURE 19.9 CTB McGraw-Hill. A sample Home Report for a fourth-grade student from the TerraNova3. *Source*: Reproduced with permission of McGraw-Hill Education CTB. TerraNova3 and TerraNova are registered trademarks of McGraw-Hill Education.

Individual Profile Report

TerraNova™, Third Edition

TERRA**NOVA**³

COMPLETE BATTERY

Individual Profile Report

GARY JONES

Grade: 3.7

Purpose
This report presents information about this student's performance on *TerraNova*. Page 1 describes achievement in terms of performance on the objectives. Together with classroom assessments and classwork, this information can be used to identify potential strengths and needs in the content areas shown.

Simulated Data

Birthdate: 02/08/97
Special Codes:
ABCDEFGHIJKLMNOPQRSTUVWXYZ
3 59   732 1   1   1
Form/Level: G-13

Test Date: 04/15/07   Scoring: PATTERN (IRT)
QM: 31   Norms Date: 2007
Class: JONES
School: WINFIELD
District: GREEN VALLEY
City/State: ANYTOWN, USA
CTBID: 01075M0161550002-02-00001

Mc Graw Hill **CTB McGraw-Hill**   Page 1
The McGraw-Hill Companies

A Performance on Objectives

National Reference group grade 3.8

*OPI is an estimate of the number of items that a student could be expected to answer correctly if there had been 100 items for that objective.

Obj. No.	Objective Titles	Student OPI	Nat'l OPI	Diff	Moderate Mastery Range
	Reading				
02	Basic Understanding	91	79	12	48–70
03	Analyze Text	92	84	8	52–75
04	Evaluate/Extend Meaning	65	66	-1	50–70
05	Identify Rdg. Strategies	70	74	-4	45–73
	Language				
07	Sentence Structure	63	68	-5	45–70
08	Writing Strategies	59	74	-15	50–75
09	Editing Skills	78	63	15	55–75
	Mathematics				
10	Number & Num. Relations	71	69	2	47–77
11	Computation & Estimation	83	72	11	45–75
13	Measurement	66	86	-20	45–60
14	Geometry & Spatial Sense	71	72	-1	50–78
15	Data, Stats., & Prob.	61	83	-22	52–78
16	Patterns, Func., Algebra	77	88	-11	44–73
	Science				
19	Science Inquiry	47	74	-27	50–75
20	Physical Science	49	69	-20	52–77
21	Life Science	46	83	-37	45–78
22	Earth & Space Science	52	84	-32	48–73
23	Science & Technology	48	78	-30	52–69
24	Personal & Social Persp.	52	56	-4	50–73

Obj. No.	Objective Titles	Student OPI	Nat'l OPI	Diff	Moderate Mastery Range
	Social Studies				
26	Geographic Perspectives	79	91	-12	48–70
27	Historical & Cultural	84	92	-8	52–75
28	Civics & Government	66	65	1	50–70
29	Economic Perspectives	74	70	4	45–73

Key
Moderate Mastery Range
Low Mastery ○
Moderate Mastery ◐
High Mastery ●

Continued on next page →

Copyright © 2008 by CTB/McGraw-Hill LLC. All rights reserved.

Overview

The Individual Profile Report is one of many assessment reports that CTB offers.

The report helps you identify a student's strengths and weaknesses in both norm- and criterion-referenced terms. Data are presented in an attractive, understandable format of numeric, graphic, and narrative elements that describe student performance on each content area and objective. The Individual Profile Report is a valuable tool for parent-teacher conferences.

The primary audiences for the Individual Profile Report are teachers and counselors, followed by parents or guardians and principals.

Equivalent Reports

TerraNova, The Second Edition:
Individual Profile Report

TerraNova:
Individual Profile Report

SUPERA:
Individual Profile Report

A The first page, Performance on Objectives, shows the student's mastery of each objective measured by the test.

B The Objectives Performance Index is an estimate of the number of items a student could be expected to answer correctly had 100 such items been taken.

C The objectives measured by *TerraNova, Third Edition* are listed for each content area. Each objective is measured by at least four items.

D A graph for each objective shows the student's Objectives Performance Index (represented by a small circle) and the associated confidence band (represented by a line extending to either side of the circle). A fully darkened circle indicates High Mastery, a half-darkened circle indicates Moderate Mastery, and an open circle represents Low Mastery.

To see an interactive version of this report, go to **CTB.com/TerraNova3/Reports**

FIGURE 19.10 CTB McGraw-Hill. A sample Individual Skills Report for a third grader from the TerraNova3. *Source*: Reproduced with permission of McGraw-Hill Education CTB. TerraNova3 and TerraNova are registered trademarks of McGraw-Hill Education.

Group List Report

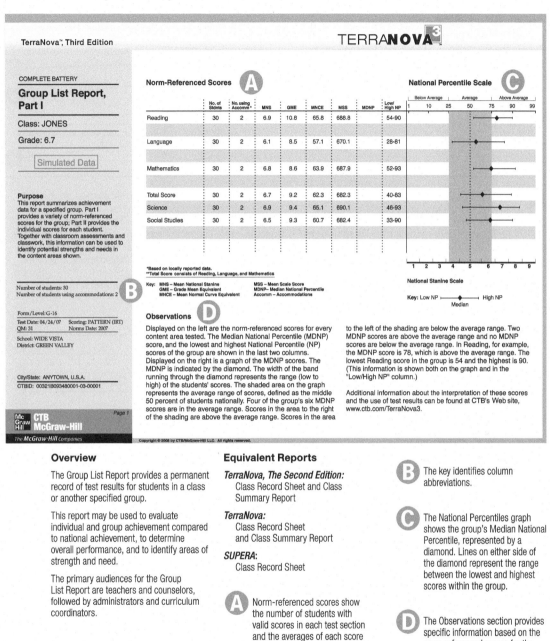

FIGURE 19.11 CTB McGraw-Hill. A sample Group List Report for Ms. Jones' sixth-grade class from the TerraNova3.

Source: Reproduced with permission of McGraw-Hill Education CTB. TerraNova3 and TerraNova are registered trademarks of McGraw-Hill Education.

Page 1 – Front Side

Your Child's Test Results

2013–14 Mathematics Scale Score Ranges:

NYS Level 4: 340–394

NYS Level 3: 314–339

NYS Level 2: 285–313

NYS Level 1: 139–284

CHART

2013–14 Test Results Grade 4 Mathematics

1

Scale Score (316)

Performance Level (NYS Level 3)

2

Overall State Percentile Rank* (73)

3

*Your child's score on the test was the same or higher than 73 percent of all students statewide who took this test.

2012-13 Test Results: Grade 3 Mathematics

Performance Level (NYS Level 1)

4

---

1 **_Scale Score (2013–14):_** The *Scale Score* is determined by the number of points your child earned on the test in 2013–14. The number of points have to be on a scale so that the test results mean the same thing year after year even though different students are taking the test with different questions. The higher the number of points your child earned, the higher his or her scale score. Scale scores are most meaningful when they are associated with a performance level. Table 1 provides the range of scale scores for each grade in 2013–14, as well as the scale score your child would need to meet their grade level performance expectations and to be on track for college and career readiness. Note that the 2013–14 scale score may be absent from the report if a student completed an insufficient number of items on the exam, was medically excused from the exam, or there was an administrative error.

Table 1: Range and Proficiency Level of Scale Scores Across Grades

	Grade					
	3	**4**	**5**	**6**	**7**	**8**
Range of Scale Scores	139–394	126–402	126–405	119–399	133–401	119–403
Scale Scores Greater than or Equal to this Value are Proficient	314	314	319	318	322	322

2 **_Performance Level (2013–14):_** Students are assigned a *Performance Level* based on how they perform on the test. There are four possible performance levels: NYS Level 1, NYS Level 2, NYS Level 3, and NYS Level 4. Each student is assigned to a performance level based on the scale score earned. For example, the student in the score report achieved a NYS Level 3. This level of performance indicates the student demonstrated proficiency of the grade level standards. For a full description of each performance level, please refer to the bottom of page 1 on the score report. For a detailed description of the skills, knowledge, and practices that are typical of students at each performance level, please visit
    http://www.engageny.org/resource/performance-level-descriptions-for-ela-and-mathematics

3 **_Overall State Percentile Rank (2013–14):_** *Overall State Percentile Rank* compares your child's score to the rest of the students who took the same subject area test in 2013–14. Percentile ranks are reported on a scale of 1–99. If your child has an *Overall State Percentile Rank* of 73, it means that your child's scale score was the same or higher than 73% of all students who took the same test. The higher the *Overall State Percentile Rank*, the better your child did compared to other students.

4 **_Performance Level (2012–13):_** The 2012–13 performance level indicates the performance level your child achieved on 2012–13 test. The 2012–13 performance level can be compared to the 2013–14 performance level to determine whether your child has demonstrated improvement between years. If your child achieved a NYS Level 1 in 2012–13 and then achieves a NYS Level 3 in 2013–14, then your child has gone from performing well below proficient to demonstrating grade level proficiency in the grade level standards. Note that students taking the 3rd grade exam will not have a 2012–13 performance level as there is no assessment in 2nd Grade.

FIGURE 19.12 A sample Your Child's Test Results report from the PARCC fourth-grade mathematics test adopted by NY state.
Source: New York State Education Department (2015). Retrieved January 27, 2015, from http://www.p12.nysed.gov/assessment/ei/eiscorereports14.html.

the pupil's performance compared to the relevant criterion. Although the comparison of the classroom to national norms in Figure 19.11 may not be of interest to parents most concerned with their child's performance, similar reports can clarify how a teacher's class compares to national norms in various subjects areas. The sample report in Figure 19.12 allows you to compare a student's performance to state norms and enables you to compare the current scale score with prior year scores and to compare a student's current performance level (a measure proficiency on the Common Core Standards) with the performance level the previous year. Figure 19.12 only includes the first page of the actual report. A second page breaks down performance by specific standards to enable more specific skills or standards analysis, similar to what we see in Figure 19.10.

With proper interpretation, summative score reports like these provide a wealth of information that can help educators, parents, students, and others understand how well a child has achieved in the many content and skill areas that are part of the child's curriculum and academic standards. Today, standardized test publishers and state education agencies also include a wide variety of other reports. As we discussed in Chapter 2, the Smarter Balanced and PARCC assessment consortia also have produced sample test reports specific to their CCSS-aligned tests that are available to the public. These can be found on their respective web pages, or the web pages of the state education agencies that have adopted a CCSS-aligned test, such as New York State for the PARCC and Washington State for the Smarter Balanced (e.g., https://www.engageny.org/ and https://www.k12.wa.us/assessment/StateTesting/default.aspx).

Beyond sample reports, many test publishers and the CCSS consortia and state websites include a wealth of resources that include listings of the instructional objectives and standards their tests are aligned with, instructional guidance, sample test questions, videos, recommended readings and references, and a variety of other helpful resources. We highly recommend reviewing the website of the publisher of the test used in your school in advance of parent–teacher conferences to familiarize yourself with the reports and other resources. In our increasingly web-savvy world, you can be sure that some of the parents of your students will have done the same!

By now, you should be prepared to deal with parent questions based on the reports shown. However, just to be sure, let's consider a couple of possible situations. Try responding to the following interpretive scenarios before looking at the authors' responses. After you have responded, compare your reactions with the authors' responses. If you have difficulty determining why the authors respond the way they did, review the relevant sections of this text before proceeding farther, and before you attempt to interpret standardized test results in the future!

Report-Based Interpretive Scenarios

Scenario #1: based on Figure 19.9

Ken Jones' distressed parents insisted on a face–face meeting with the classroom teacher (Mr. Jones, who is not related) after the TerraNova3 reports came out. Here is what they said at that meeting.

> *Our son, Ken Jones, has not received a grade lower than a C all year, and almost all his grades have been B's or C's. So, as a parent yourself, Mrs. Jones, and as Ken's fourth grade teacher all year, you might imagine how shocked we were to get his TerraNova3 Home Report and see that he failed every one of the subtests. In fact, his highest grades were only 58 on both Math Computation and Spelling, and the rest are almost all below 50! Please explain to us how he can get average to above grades all year and then fail this end of year test so miserably? Or, should we talk to the principal about it?*

How would you respond if you were Mr. Jones, the fourth-grade classroom teacher?

Scenario #2: Based on Figure 19.10

Following the release of the third-grade Terra Nova3 reports, Gary Jones' parents requested a meeting. Here is what they said:

> Gary has been in reading tutoring 3 days a week for the entire school year. We were very disappointed to see that his scores on the Reading section of the Individual Profile Report have only improved from last year on the objectives that measure the Reading Understanding and Analyzing Text objectives, and not on the other two objectives. Those continue to be average. You're his teacher, should we be worried about this? I seem to remember something about real and chance differences from my tests and measurements class in college, but I'll be darned if I can recall what that means. We just do not know whether the differences between the two objectives he did well on are really that much better than his performance on Evaluating/Extending Meaning and Identifying Reading Strategies. We are thinking of firing his tutor. Can you help us understand please? Should we fire the tutor?

How would you respond if you were Gary Jones' third-grade classroom teacher?

Authors' Responses

In Scenario #1, Ken Jones's parents commit a common error, interpreting percentile ranks as though they are classroom grades or standards for performance. Our response might go something like this:

> Thank you for asking to set up the conference today. Of course you are free to also meet with the principal if you wish, but I think we can clear up what I think is a common misunderstanding. First of all, you are correct about his grades. They have ranged between C's and B's all year. Because we tend to think of 65 or 70 as passing it is easy to see why it looked he failed every subtest on the TerraNova3. However, that is not the case! The TerraNova3 is a standardized test and the test scores you see on the report are what are known as national percentile ranks. National percentile ranks show how a student's performance compared to the performance of the national sample of students on which the test was based. In other words, his score at the 44th percentile on the Reading scale indicates that he scored higher than 44% of children in the national sample that took the test, which is very different than saying he failed that test. On the other hand, a grade of 44 on a test administered in my class would likely mean that he failed most of the items on the test, which would equate to a grade of F. Because all his scores were between the 28th percentile in Language and the 58th percentile in Science, we can see from the shaded horizontal Average section of the report that all his scores were in the average range, consistent with his grades in class.

In Scenario #2, a different Mr. and Mrs. Jones also asked for a parent teacher conference after Gary Jones's TerraNova3 reports were released.

> I understand that you are concerned, and we appreciate that you have supported classroom instruction by taking Gary for tutoring all year. Thank you. Although I cannot decide for you whether to continue with tutoring or not, I can say that you are right to recall the concept of real and chance differences from your tests and measurements class. In fact, this report provides us with an opportunity to apply that concept to Gary's TerraNova3 test results. Let's do that together and see what we

can conclude. The Individual Profile Report column that is titled the Objectives Performance Index (OPI) is what enables us to determine whether variations in scores are likely due to real differences in skill acquisition among the objectives, or whether the differences are more likely to be attributable to chance or measurement error. To evaluate the score differences, we look to see whether there are any gaps between the lines that extend from both sides of the circles for each of the 23 objectives listed in the OPI column. The circles in that column indicate where Gary's actual test score fell. The lines on both sides of the circles represent the margin of error associated with each score. You might recall that the technical term for the margin of error is the standard error of measurement. If you used Educational Testing and Measurement by Kubiszyn & Borich in your tests and measurements class, you can review the Band Interpretation section in Chapter 18 to refresh your memory about all this.

If the lines overlap with each other when we compare subtests we conclude that score differences are due to chance, but if there are gaps we would conclude there are real differences. So, when we look at the Reading objectives, we see that there is no overlap between both of the first two objectives, Basic Understanding and Analyze Text, and both of the last two Reading objectives, Evaluate/Extend Meaning and Identify Reading Strategies. This means that there are real differences in Gary's performance between the first two Reading objectives and the last two. Of course I would not know, but it may be that his tutor has been focusing on reading for understanding and text analysis, which would explain why they are so much higher, and it may be useful to show the tutor the report and ask her to increase her focus on evaluating and extending meaning and identifying reading strategies, if you decide to continue tutoring.

Regardless of the type of feedback your district provides to parents, you will be asked to interpret various types of test scores for parents and students. When these questions come up, be sure to consider what we have covered in the text. Your considerations should include referring to Figure 19.8 to help you consider the test- and student-related factors that may influence standardized test scores, using whatever individualized score reports are available to fine-tune and personalize your interpretation, and using the standard error measurement and band interpretation to minimize the tendency to overinterpret chance or apparent score differences as real differences. If you consider these factors, we are confident you will join the ranks of informed, intelligent test users.

SUMMARY

This chapter introduced you to the use, administration, and interpretation of standardized tests. Its major points are as follows:

1. Standardized tests are carefully constructed by specialists, and they carry specific and uniform, or standardized, administration and scoring procedures; they may be both norm-referenced and criterion-referenced. Although standardized tests are typically summative assessments, there has been a surge of interest in standardized formative assessments in recent years.

2. Standardized tests may be achievement, aptitude, interest, or personality tests.

3. Standardized norm-referenced achievement tests facilitate comparisons across students, classrooms, schools, districts, states, and regions because of uniformity of content, administration, and scoring and

a common basis for comparison—the nationally representative norms table. Recently, developed tests from the Smarter Balanced and PARCC assessment consortia provide assessments aligned with the CCSS, to facilitate comparisons among the states within each consortium.

4. Standardized achievement tests are frequently used to make comparisons over time or across students, schools, or districts. IDEIA and NCLB now require that all children with disabilities participate in annual assessments, but they encourage accommodations and alternate assessments that may compromise the comparisons that the IDEIA and NCLB intended to enable for children with disabilities.

5. Although standardized norm-referenced achievement tests may not be as useful to the classroom teacher as teacher-made tests, NCLB accountability requirements, high-stakes testing, and the CCSS-aligned tests have made it necessary for teachers to administer and interpret them. And with participation of children with disabilities in annual assessments now required, classroom teachers may also have to interpret standardized test results to parents of children with disabilities.

6. When administering standardized tests, all administrators should uniformly follow instructions in order to minimize error in test administration (there may be exceptions to this rule when appropriate accommodations have been authorized).

7. Since standardized tests have become requirements under NCLB and state high-stakes testing programs, and in states that have adopted the CCSS, incidents of teachers and administrators violating standardized test administration procedures (when appropriate accommodations have not been authorized) have increased to the point that they have been verified in most of the states. In some cases, educators who have violated the procedures have been convicted of crimes.

8. Although grade-equivalent scores are commonly used to compare scores, they have several limitations, including the following:
   a. They tend to be misinterpreted as indicative of skill levels, rather than relative degrees of performance.
   b. Equal differences in units do not reflect equal changes in achievement.
   c. They have limited applicability except where subjects are taught across all grade levels.
   d. They tend to be seen as standards rather than norms.
   e. Comparability across subjects is difficult.

9. Age equivalents are much less commonly used and suffer from limitations similar to those of grade equivalents.

10. Percentile scores compare a student's performance with that of his or her peers. Although percentiles are superior to grade and age equivalents, they suffer from the following two disadvantages:
    a. They are often confused with percentage correct.
    b. Equal differences in units do not reflect equal changes in achievement.

11. Standard scores also compare a student's performance with that of his or her peers. In addition, equal differences in units do reflect equal differences in achievement. Standard scores are superior to percentile ranks for test interpretation, but they tend to be not well understood by many educators and by much of the general public.

12. Percentiles are recommended for interpreting standardized test results to the public. However, their limitations must be kept in mind.

13. Both test-related and student-related factors should be considered in interpreting standardized test results.

14. Test-related factors require the teacher to assess the test's score reliability and validity evidence, the appropriateness of the norm group, and the extent to which standardized procedures were followed.

15. When a class is considerably different in composition from the norm group, the appropriateness of comparison to the norm group becomes questionable. In such situations, specialized norms tables now available from some test publishers may be used, or local norms may be established.

16. Differences in student-related factors require the teacher to consider the following in interpreting standardized test scores: the child's language proficiency and cultural background; age, gender, and development; motivation; emotional state on the test day; disabilities; and aptitude.

17. Students whose obtained achievement scores are lower than their obtained academic aptitude scores are said to be below expectancy.

18. Students whose obtained achievement scores are higher than their obtained academic aptitude scores are said to be above expectancy.

19. Students whose obtained achievement and academic aptitude scores are equivalent are said to be achieving at expectancy.

20. Students whose obtained achievement scores show "real" differences when compared with their obtained academic aptitude scores have aptitude–achievement discrepancies. Band interpretation using 95% levels is recommended for such comparisons.

21. Interpreting standardized test scores by comparing students to their individual potential or aptitude can sometimes lead to more effective educational decision making than comparing students to the norms.

22. Under the 2004 IDEIA, the previous requirement that a student must demonstrate a significant discrepancy between aptitude and achievement to be eligible for special education under the Specific Learning Disability (SLD) category has been made optional and cannot be required as the sole method of SLD identification by any state.

23. Consider the various test- and student-related factors that can affect performance on standardized tests, along with other available information (e.g., grades, cumulative folders), in consulting with parents about important educational decisions. Considering all sources of data before making a decision decreases the likelihood that test results will be over- or underinterpreted.

24. Standardized test publishers provide a wide variety of score reports. Depending on district policy, students and parents may receive reports that are fairly straightforward or are complex and require careful scrutiny. In any case, the classroom teacher who is skilled in their interpretation will be the one most likely to use these reports in the best interests of the students.

25. Today, the websites of commercial test publishers, state education agencies, and the Common Core-aligned multistate test consortia (i.e., Smarter Balanced and PARCC) are populated with a wealth of resources related to their particular tests. These include, but are not limited to, suggestions for relevant instructional activities, the test's objectives or standards the test measures, a variety of technical information, samples of score reports, and videos to assist with administration and interpretation.

26. Both the Smarter Balanced and PARCC consortia now include standardized performance assessments as part of their CCSS-aligned tests. Increasingly, standardized test publishers also have begun to market standardized performance assessment systems. The teacher skilled in standardized test theory, application, and interpretation will have little difficulty incorporating standardized performance and portfolio assessment tools into the decision-making process.

FOR DISCUSSION AND PRACTICE

1. "Our principal is so insensitive," said Donna. "He knows Billy Brown has trouble reading, but he won't let me help him read the test questions when we give the TerraNova3 test next week." Should the principal allow Donna to read the questions to Billy? Support your decision with arguments based on points made in this chapter.

2. "I'm so glad Congress passed NCLB," beamed Mr. A. D. Vocate. "Now we'll finally be able to see just how well the students in each of our special ed classes is learning because they will all have to take the annual standardized achievement tests, just like the regular ed kids do, although accommodations for their disabilities will be made." Will NCLB enable Mr. Vocate

and others to more accurately compare scores for special ed kids with each other and regular ed kids? Why or why not?

3. "Blanketiblank Public Schools Again Score Below National Average on TerraNova3—Mayor Calls for Freeze on Teacher Pay Until Scores Reach National Average." As a teacher in the Blanketiblank Public Schools, how would you respond to such a newspaper headline? In your response, critique the assumption underlying the headline and suggest an alternative way to measure student progress.

*4. Consider the following data obtained from the Wechsler Intelligence Scale for Children–V (WISC–V) and the Stanford Achievement Test at the end of fourth grade.

Student	Verbal IQ	Reading Vocabulary		Reading Comprehension	
	GE	G.E.	SS	G.E.	SS
Bonnie	107	5.9	113	6.5	119
Chris	94	4.5	93	4.0	88
Jack	125	5.8	112	5.6	110
	$S_m = 3.0$	$S_m = 2.5$		$S_m = 3.5$	
	M = 100, SD = 15				

After inspecting the data, answer the following questions:

a. Is each student's achievement about what we would expect? If not, who is not achieving at expectancy?

b. Are there any aptitude–achievement discrepancies?

*Answers for these questions appear in Appendix B.

*5. Check your work in Question 4 by constructing a table like Figure 18.7 and subject the scores to band interpretation at the 95% level. Now answer the same questions again.

*6. *Modify the scores provided in the small table in Question 4 so that the data indicate underachievement aptitude–achievement discrepancies for each student at the 68% level, but no such discrepancies at the 95% level. How would you explain this apparent contradiction?

7. Mr. Simpson "simply can't understand" why his third-grade son can't skip fourth grade. "After all," he says, "your own test scores show he's reading and doing math at a fifth-grade level." Tactfully explain to Mr. Simpson why his son may not really be ready for fifth-grade reading and math.

8. Distinguish among raw scores, percentile ranks, converted scores, standard scores, stanines, and scale scores.

9. Mr. Gregg, fresh out of college (and having taken a tests and measurements course), is constantly extolling the virtues of standard scores over other types of converted scores. Parent conferences are coming up, and he is confident that the parents he meets with will "finally get a clear and precise interpretation of their children's test results" because he will interpret the tests using standard scores, not grade or age equivalents or percentiles. As a "seasoned veteran," what advice would you give to Mr. Gregg?

CHAPTER 20

TYPES OF STANDARDIZED TESTS

LEARNING OUTCOMES

After completing this chapter, the student will be able to:

1. Compare and contrast various types of standardized tests, including achievement test batteries, single-subject achievement tests, and diagnostic achievement tests.

2. Recognize the names of commonly used survey batteries and single-subject achievement tests.

3. Explain how detailed information about achievement tests, including Common Core-aligned tests, can be obtained.

4. Describe how the purpose of diagnostic achievement tests differs from other tests reviewed in this chapter.

5. Explain why the authors are reluctant to call IQ tests intelligence tests.

6. Describe the history of IQ testing.

7. Explain how the stability of IQ scores changes for different ages and across different time spans.

8. Describe the relationship between IQ scores and academic achievement and between IQ scores and job success.

9. Recognize the names of commonly administered individual and group IQ tests.

10. Explain why there is no universally accepted definition of personality.

11. Compare and contrast objective and projective personality assessment techniques, being sure to consider the major advantages and disadvantages of each approach.

IN THIS CHAPTER, we will describe various types of standardized, typically norm-referenced, tests classroom teachers may come into contact with. First, we will consider achievement test survey batteries, single-subject achievement tests, and diagnostic tests. Next, we will consider individual and group tests of academic aptitude. Finally, we will describe various personality tests that sometimes appear in student records. Our intention is *not* to evaluate or recommend any of these tests. Each of the tests we describe is simply an "accepted" test with satisfactory technical adequacy (i.e., score reliability and validity evidence) for the test's intended purpose and population. At the same time, we do not mean to imply that the tests we have selected are the only tests with acceptable technical adequacy for a particular purpose or population. With any test, how useful or appropriate a test is depends importantly on the purpose of testing, and the population the test will be used with (see Chapter 1). With the rapid spread of the high-stakes testing phenomenon to all the states, and the annual accountability requirements of the No Child Left Behind (NCLB) Act (described in detail in Chapter 2), teachers will also be certain to be exposed to their state's high-stakes test, which may be either norm-referenced or criterion-referenced. If you are interested in learning more about what these specific tests are like, most state education agencies now carry extensive information about their state's high-stakes tests on their web pages. If you work in a state that has adopted the tests aligned with the Common Core State Standards (CCSS) by the Smarter Balanced or Partnership for the Assessment of Readiness for College and Careers (PARCC) multistate consortia (see Chapter 2), you can also find extensive resources to help you understand, administer, and interpret those tests on their respective websites (http://www.smarterbalanced.org/ or http://parcconline.org/), in addition to information your state education agency may provide. If your state is using one of the achievement test we review briefly in this chapter, their respective websites also provide resources to assist you with understanding, administering, and interpreting those tests.

STANDARDIZED ACHIEVEMENT TESTS

The first standardized tests came into existence around 1900. These tests were tests of a single achievement area, such as spelling. Single-subject achievement tests are still used today, although they are largely confined to the secondary grades.

A variation of the single-subject achievement test is the diagnostic achievement test. However, use of the diagnostic test is normally limited to those elementary and secondary school pupils who are experiencing academic difficulty. These tests are administered to "diagnose" or indicate the specific cause or causes of a problem (e.g., faulty letter identification) in some general academic area (e.g., reading comprehension). Seldom are such tests administered to an entire class or grade. Students are typically selected for diagnostic testing after a single-subject test, or an achievement battery has indicated a problem in some general academic area.

The most frequently used type of achievement test is the *summative* achievement test battery or survey battery. Such batteries are widely used, often beginning in the first grade and administered each year thereafter, and often to meet state high-stakes testing and NCLB accountability requirements. Variations of these summative survey batteries have also been increasingly used as *interim* or *benchmark* assessments. In those cases, the interim assessments may be administered two to three times per year to identify students in need of additional academic assistance. When interim assessments are used to identify students who may not meet criterion levels on the annual summative tests they are called benchmark tests. However, these tests are not diagnostic tests because they may only identify students who need extra attention, but not diagnose why they are not progressing as well as others.

There are several reasons survey batteries are more popular than single-subject achievement tests. The major advantages of survey batteries over single-subject achievement tests are as follows:

1. Each subtest is coordinated with every other subtest, resulting in common administration and scoring procedures, common format, and minimal redundancy.

2. Batteries are less expensive and less time consuming to administer than several single-subject tests.

3. Each subtest is normed on the same sample (if it's a norm-referenced standardized test, of course!), making comparisons across subtests, both within and between individuals, easier and more valid.

This last point is probably the major reason survey batteries have had widespread use. Recall that we often use standardized tests to compare students, classes, or schools for high-stakes and accountability purposes. It takes less time to make these comparisons when a single norm group is involved than when several are involved. Furthermore, the likelihood of clerical errors is minimized when single, comprehensive score reports from a battery are used to make comparisons, as opposed to several single-subject score reports. Of course, batteries have their disadvantages, too:

1. The correspondence (content validity) of various subtests in the battery may not be uniformly high.
2. The battery, which emphasizes breadth of coverage, may not sample achievement areas in as much depth as a single-subject achievement test.

Nonetheless, many districts conclude that these limitations are offset by the advantages of a summative achievement battery. Next, we will briefly describe some of the more popular summative achievement test batteries. Those working in states that are part of the Smarter Balanced Assessment Consortium (http://www.smarterbalanced.org/) or the Partnership for the Assessment of Readiness for College and Careers (PARCC) (http://parcconline.org) are referred to those websites and their state education agencies for information about the consortium assessments. Those assessments are aligned with the CCSS and also include formative assessments and a wealth of supporting resources.

Achievement Test Batteries, or Survey Batteries

TerraNova, Third Edition (Terra Nova 3) The TerraNova, Third Edition, is a major revision of the CAT/6, or Terra Nova CAT-2 battery. It is published by CTB/McGraw-Hill and is appropriate for students in grades K–12. The Third Edition includes a Common Core battery for grades 3–8 that is aligned with the Common Core State Standards (CCSS). The Common Core includes Reading, Math, and English Language Arts subtests for grades 3–8. The Third Edition also includes a Survey Battery for Reading, Math, Science, and Social Studies for grades 2–12 and Language for grades 3–12; a Complete Battery for Reading, Math, and Language for grades K–12 and Science and Social Studies for grades 1–12; and Multiple Assessments for Reading, Math, Science, and Social Studies for grades 1–12 and Language for grades 3–12.

Iowa Tests of Basic Skills (ITBS), Forms A, B, and C The ITBS battery is published by the Riverside Publishing Company. It is appropriate for students in grades K–8. Scores are provided for Vocabulary, Word Analysis, Listening, Reading, Comprehension, Language (spelling, capitalization, punctuation, and usage), Mathematics (concepts, problem solving, and computation), Social Studies, Science, Sources of Information, and Basic and Total Battery. We were not able to determine whether the ITBS has been aligned with the CCSS.

Metropolitan Achievement Tests, Eighth Edition (MAT 8) Pearson Assessments publishes the MAT battery, which is appropriate for students in grades K–12. Thirteen levels span the various grades, and two alternate forms are available. The Primer level includes scores for Listening for Sounds, Language, and Mathematics. The next level, Primary, includes scores for Sounds, Reading Vocabulary and Reading Comprehension, Mathematics Computation, and

Mathematics Concepts, Language Spelling, Science, and Social Studies. The remaining levels eliminate the Sounds subtest. The MAT-8 was normed with the *Otis-Lennon School Abilities Test, 7th Edition*, to facilitate identification of aptitude–achievement discrepancies. We were not able to determine whether the MAT-8 has been aligned with the CCSS.

Stanford Achievement Test Series, Tenth Edition (SAT-10) Like the MAT, the SAT-10 battery is published by Pearson Assessments. It is appropriate for grades K through 12. Thirteen levels are provided for the various grades, and two alternate forms are available. Subtests for Reading, Mathematics, Language Arts, Spelling, Study Skills, Listening, Science, and Social Science are available, with open-ended writing tests available for grades 3–13. The SAT-10 was co-normed with the *Otis–Lennon School Abilities Test, Eighth Edition* (OLSAT 8), to facilitate aptitude–achievement discrepancy identification. The SAT-10 was recently made available as an online version for grades 3–12. We were not able to determine whether the SAT-10 has been aligned with the CCSS

Single-Subject Achievement Tests

Gates–MacGinitie Reading Tests, Fourth Edition (GMRT 4) The Gates–MacGinitie Reading test is published by Riverside Publishing Company. It is appropriate for grades K–12 and uses nine levels to cover these grades. Two alternate forms, S and T, are available for the six highest levels. The upper seven levels include subtests measuring Vocabulary and Comprehension. The formats vary across the levels, with stimuli ranging from pictorial at the lower levels to increasingly complex prose at the higher levels. Items measure recognition rather than recall.

KeyMath 3 Diagnostic Assessment The KeyMath 3 is published by Pearson Assessments. It is designed for students in grades K–12. The KeyMath 3 must be administered individually. It includes two parallel forms (A and B) and 10 subtests that measure three general math content areas: Basic Concepts (conceptual knowledge), Operations (computational skills), and Applications (problem solving).

Nelson–Denny Reading Test, Forms G and H The Nelson–Denny Reading tests are designed for high school, college, and adult populations and are published by Riverside Publishing. Forms G and H are appropriate for grades 9–16 and adults. A CD-ROM version of Forms G and H is appropriate for grades 9–14 and adults. Each form includes a Vocabulary and a Reading Comprehension subtest. Norms are available for high school and for 2-year and 4-year colleges. Special norms are also available for extended time administrations and law enforcement academies.

Diagnostic Achievement Tests

Group Reading Assessment and Diagnostic Evaluation (GRADE) The GRADE was designed to replace the Stanford Diagnostic Reading Test, Fourth Edition (SDRT-4), and was first sold in late 2013. The GRADE is published by Pearson Assessments and is appropriate for Pre-K through grade 12 and for adults. There are two parallel forms for each of 10 test levels, and it is reported to be better aligned with the CCSS than was the SDRT-4 that it replaced. It takes 50–90 minutes to complete. It is designed to identify the reading skills that have been mastered and those that are in need of further instruction or remediation.

Group Mathematics Assessment and Diagnostic Evaluation (G-MADE) The G-MADE was designed to replace the Stanford Diagnostic Mathematics Test, Fourth Edition (SDMT-4), and was first sold in late 2013. The G-MADE is published by Pearson Assessments and is appropriate for students in K through 12 and for adults. Two parallel forms are available for each of the 10 test levels provided, and it is reported to be better aligned with the CCSS than was the SDMT-4 that it replaced. It takes 50–90 minutes to complete. It is intended to identify the mathematics skills that have been mastered and those that are in need of further instruction or remediation.

STANDARDIZED ACADEMIC APTITUDE TESTS

Thus far in this chapter, we have discussed tests that are used to measure past achievement. The intent of these tests is to identify what students have learned. At times, however, we are also interested in measuring an individual's potential for learning or an individual's academic aptitude. Such information can be useful in making selection and placement decisions and in determining whether students are achieving up to their potential, that is, to indicate aptitude–achievement discrepancies. In short, aptitude tests are used to predict *future* learning. Achievement tests are used to measure *past* learning.

The History of Academic Aptitude Testing

The development of tests to predict school achievement began in France at the beginning of the twentieth century. France had embarked on a program of compulsory education, and the minister of public instruction realized that not all French children had the cognitive or mental potential to be able to benefit from instruction in regular classes. "Special" classes were to be established for the instruction of such children. Admission to these classes was to be dependent on the results of a medical and psychological evaluation. However, at the time no tests were available that could be used to identify children who had the cognitive or mental potential to benefit from instruction in regular classes. In 1905, Alfred Binet and his assistant, Theo Simon, were commissioned to develop such a test. The aim of their test was to develop a series of tests to measure mental or cognitive traits that would predict school achievement.

They revised their test in 1908 and again in 1911. The concept of mental age (as opposed to chronological age) as an index of mental development was introduced with the first revision and refined with the second. The concept of mental age eventually become known as the intelligence quotient, or IQ. Since Binet was commissioned to develop a test that would predict school achievement, he was concerned with the predictive validity of his scale and repeatedly studied its validity for use in the public schools.

By the time of his death in 1911, Binet's scale was widely used and heralded as an "intelligence" test. English translations of the 1908 and 1911 revisions were made, and in 1916 a Stanford University psychologist, Louis Terman, standardized the Binet test on American children and adults. That version of the test became known as the Stanford–Binet Intelligence Scale or IQ test, and it was revised and/or restandardized again in 1937, 1960, 1972, 1985, and 2003. What had begun as an academic aptitude test designed to predict *school achievement* evolved into a test of intelligence.

Since Binet's seminal work, several other intelligence or IQ tests have been developed. Some, like the Stanford–Binet, are designed to be administered individually (e.g., *Wechsler Intelligence*

Scale for Children–V, Wechsler Adult Intelligence Scale–IV, Kaufman Assessment Battery for Children–II, Slosson Intelligence Test); others are designed for group administration (e.g., *Cognitive Abilities Test, Otis–Lennon Mental Ability Test, Kuhlmann–Anderson Intelligence Tests*). Although each of these tests differs from the Binet, each also has similarities and correlates strongly with the Binet. Recall that tests that correlate strongly measure much the same thing. Since Binet's test predicts school achievement, it is no surprise that both individually and group-administered intelligence tests also predict school achievement.

But do we know that these tests *actually* measure intelligence? We *do* know they predict academic achievement. To answer the question, we first need to define intelligence and then determine whether people who score high on intelligence tests possess more of these elements than people who score low on intelligence tests. Unfortunately, we can't agree on what the "stuff" of intelligence is. For example, one of the recent conceptions of intelligence (Sternberg, 2008) is that it can be defined by its underlying components and altered through instruction. Thus, traits previously thought to be inherited and unalterable could be taught, according to this conceptualization. However, there is no universally accepted definition of intelligence, and therefore there is no single accepted measure of intelligence. Theorists have been hypothesizing and arguing for decades about what intelligence is, and the debate will likely go on for decades or centuries more. Consequently, since we do not agree on what intelligence is, we cannot be sure we are measuring it.

Discussions of definitions and theories of intelligence may be found in most graduate-level measurement tests. For our purposes, we will conclude that the tests mentioned here, and others like them, do predict school achievement. We are not at all sure, however, that they are measuring intelligence. Since we are not sure that they are measuring intelligence, we are reluctant to call them intelligence tests. We can use such tests intelligently, though, by restricting their application to what we know they can do—predict school achievement. Before we review some of the more common of these tests, we will consider two important aspects of the scores such tests yield, namely, their stability and other characteristics they predict.

Stability of IQ Scores

In general, IQ scores tend to increase in stability with increases in age. In other words, IQ scores for younger children are less reliable or more subject to error than are IQ scores for older children and adults. Furthermore, test–retest reliabilities tend to decline as the time interval between test and retest increases. Table 20.1 illustrates these relationships.

As Table 20.1 indicates, little is gained in terms of predicting later performance by administering IQ tests to children less than 4 years of age. Once children reach the age of about 6, their IQ scores tend to remain fairly stable. An individual's obtained score can still change beyond this age, but changes are likely to be small and not greatly affect the individual's overall percentile rank in the general population.

TABLE 20.1 Approximate Correlations between Individual IQ Tests and Retests

Age at First Test	Age at Second Test	Approximate Correlation
2	14	0.20
4	14	0.55
6	14	0.70
8	14	0.85
10	14	0.90

What Do IQ Tests Predict?

In this section, we review the research to see the extent to which what we now call IQ tests or intelligence tests can predict a variety of outcomes. We consider the following outcomes: academic achievement, job success, emotional adjustment, and happiness.

Academic Achievement We have said that IQ tests or tests of academic aptitude predict school achievement. But just how well they predict school achievement depends on what we use as an outcome measure. Correlations between IQ tests and standardized achievement tests generally range from 0.70 to 0.90. However, correlations between IQ tests and grades generally range from 0.50 to 0.60. Standardized achievement tests tend to be carefully constructed and measure outcomes similar to those measured by academic aptitude tests, as the strong correlations between IQ scores and standardized achievement tests scores reflect. By keeping this in mind and realizing that grades tend to be considerably more subjective, and often based on teacher-made tests rather than tests constructed by professional test developers, it is no surprise that the correlation with grades is somewhat lower. As might be expected, IQ scores also correlate highly with the highest level of schooling completed. However, the reader should keep in mind that other factors apart from IQ also predict academic achievement. For example, Duckworth and Seligman (2005) found that group-administered IQ scores predicted grade-point average in adolescents less well than did a measure of self-discipline.

Job Success In any criterion-related validity study, the size of the obtained correlation will depend on the particular outcome measure or criterion measure employed. Gottfredson (1997) reported that when completion of a training program is considered as a criterion for job success, moderately strong correlations are found between IQ and job success, especially if the job requires complex skills (i.e., $r = 0.35$ to 0.45). Several studies have also reported weaker to moderate correlations with self-help skills, independent living skills, driving ability, academic success, vocational skills, and employment status (Kubiszyn et al., 2000). In short, the predictive validity evidence for IQ test results is stronger for academic achievement than for job success and most other outcomes. Part of the reason for this may be the often subjective nature of the criteria used to rate job success or other outcomes (e.g., supervisor's ratings, employee ratings). Just as subjectivity in teacher-assigned grades may lead to a lower correlation between IQ and school performance, subjectivity in determining job success may be responsible for the lower correlation between ratings of job success and IQ test scores.

Emotional Adjustment No firm conclusion may be drawn about the relationship between IQ and emotional adjustment. At the beginning of the twentieth century, it was commonly held that very high-IQ individuals tended to have more severe emotional and adjustment problems than did individuals with more "normal" IQs. However, a long-term follow-up (over 35 years) study of high-IQ individuals begun by Terman in 1921 did much to dispel this myth (Terman, 1959). Current thinking suggests that high-IQ individuals have emotional difficulties about as frequently as low-to-moderate IQ individuals.

Happiness Perhaps in part because we do not have a suitable definition or measure of happiness, we do not really know the extent to which IQ scores may predict happiness. Since they do predict school achievement and to a lesser extent job success, we might infer there would be a positive correlation between IQ and happiness. However, such a position is not supported by research data (Veenhoven & Choi, 2012) and assumes that school and job success are themselves correlated with happiness.

In summary, the characteristic that IQ tests predict most strongly is school achievement. Recall that the first IQ test was developed to predict school achievement. More than a century later, in spite of repeated attempts to modify and improve on the IQ test, we find that it still does best just what it was designed to do. Although it has been used in a variety of ways, the IQ test remains, first and foremost, a good predictor of school achievement. Whatever else it measures or predicts, it does so less effectively and efficiently, or not at all. Our recommendation is to recognize IQ tests for what they are—predictors of school achievement—and avoid the tendency to make them into something they are not. In the next section, we will briefly describe some of the commonly used group and individually administered IQ tests.

Individually Administered Academic Aptitude Tests

Stanford–Binet Intelligence Scale, Fifth Edition The Stanford–Binet V, published by Houghton Mifflin, is appropriate for ages 2 through adult. As mentioned, it was originally developed in France in 1905 and revised for American use in 1916. The Fifth Edition appeared in 2003 and represents a significant revision and renorming effort. It is a substantial improvement over previous editions. Stimuli are now more contemporary, and the test now has 15 subtests organized into five areas: Fluid Reasoning, Knowledge, Quantitative Reasoning, Visual–Spatial Processing, and Working Memory, which provides a more complete assessment of individual intelligence. Subtest scores are standard scores with a mean of 10 and a standard deviation of 3, and overall IQ scores have means of 100 and standard deviations of 15. The Fifth Edition has considerably more utility than the previous version, but it may take longer to administer than the Wechsler scales and other individually administered IQ tests.

Wechsler Intelligence Scale for Children–V (WISC–V) The WISC–V was revised in 2014, and it is published by Pearson Assessments. It is appropriate for students between 6 and 16 years of age. Along with its companion tests, the *Wechsler Preschool and Primary Scale of Intelligence–IV* (WPPSI–IV), appropriate for ages 2–7, and the *Wechsler Adult Intelligence Scale–IV* (WAIS–IV), appropriate for ages 16–adult, the Wechsler scales are the most popular individually administered IQ tests. The WISC–V includes both a paper and pencil and a digital format that requires tablet computers. It has also been substantially changed from the WISC-IV. The WISC-IV IQ model was based on four statistically validated indices but the WISC-V is based on five validated indices. The WISC-V also includes several new and revised subtests and new Primary, Ancillary, and Complementary Index Scales.

Group-Administered Academic Aptitude Tests

Cognitive Abilities Tests (CogAT), Form 7 The CogAT test is published by the Riverside Publishing Company. There are two age-designated levels in Form 7, a change from Form 6, which used letters and numbers instead of age designations. Levels 5/6–8 are known as primary-level subtests and are appropriate for students in kindergarten through grade 2. Levels 9–17/18 are appropriate for grades 3–12. The primary-level subtests were revised to make them more accessible to English language learners (ELLs), and the complete test can be administered with Spanish administration directions for students whose native language is Spanish. All levels of test now include three independent batteries, Verbal, Quantitative, and Nonverbal, and each battery has subtests that utilize multiple-item formats rather than a single format. An ELL-friendly CogAT 7 Screening Form is also available for screening of students for talent development programs.

Otis–Lennon School Ability Tests, Eighth Edition (OLSAT-8)   The OLSAT-8 is published by Pearson Assessments and is appropriate for grades K–12, with seven grade-based levels of materials available. Earlier versions of this test were called the *Otis Quick-Scoring Mental Ability Test* and the *Otis–Lennon Mental Ability Test*. The test requires 60–75 minutes to administer. The OLSAT-8 includes scores to characterize a student's Total, Verbal, and Non-Verbal performance, and a School Ability Index (SAI). Tasks include detecting likenesses and differences, recalling words and numbers, defining words, following directions, classifying, establishing sequence, solving arithmetic problems, and completing analogies. The OLSAT-8 was normed with the *Stanford Achievement Test, Tenth Edition*, to facilitate identification of aptitude–achievement discrepancies.

Primary Test of Cognitive Skills (PTCS)   Published by CTB/McGraw-Hill, the *Primary Test of Cognitive Skills* (PTCS) is a group-administered series of four tests designed to measure the cognitive skills of early learners in Kindergarten and first grade. When used with *TerraNova, Third Edition*, anticipated-achievement scores for individual students and groups can be generated to facilitate early identification of aptitude–achievement discrepancies.

STANDARDIZED PERSONALITY ASSESSMENT INSTRUMENTS

Of the types of standardized tests with which the classroom teacher comes in contact, personality tests are probably the least used and the least understood. Perhaps this is the way it should be, since teachers are mainly concerned with academic development and are not trained in personality development or assessment. Nonetheless, teachers cannot help but have some impact on and ideas about personality development, and results from such tests do show up in pupil folders. Interpretation of such tests is beyond the scope of this text and the training of classroom teachers. Thus, we will limit ourselves to briefly considering what personality is, discussing the two major approaches to personality assessment, and briefly describing several examples of personality tests.

What Is Personality?

As in the case of intelligence, no one has yet arrived at a definitive, universally accepted definition of personality. We do know that people tend to behave in certain relatively fixed ways across various situations. One such pattern of typical and expected behavior may be considered to be a personality *trait*. For example, individuals who tend to become nervous or anxious when speaking in front of groups tend to become anxious in any public speaking situation, large or small. A personality trait for such individuals would be anxiety. All of an individual's traits or characteristics, taken together, make up an individual's personality. Thus, perhaps we can define personality as the typical or characteristic ways individuals behave. This is a deceptively simple definition, however. Allport and Odbert (1936) estimated that the number of typical ways individuals behave is in the *thousands*. If we accept this definition, then, we must admit that the task of measuring these traits would be an enormous one. Nevertheless, the task has been approached with considerable success over the last 90 years or so. Essentially, the efforts to measure personality have moved in two directions: objective personality assessment and projective personality assessment. We will describe both of these assessment instruments and then present some examples of each type.

Objective Personality Assessment   Objective personality assessment usually employs self-report questionnaires. Items are often based on questions used in psychiatric interviews. The first instrument of this type appeared during World War I. Since then, they have gained considerable popularity among psychologists, the military, and industry. This approach provides a lengthy list of statements, adjectives, or questions to which examinees respond. A variety of formats have been employed, including checklists, true–false, and multiple choice. Some items are obviously indicative of serious psychopathology; others are much more subtle. In most cases, *individual* responses are not that meaningful in the interpretation. Instead, *patterns* of responses or a *profile of scores* is relied on for interpretation.

Objective personality instruments have the advantage of being economical to administer. They can be group administered and monitored by a clerk rather than requiring the time and training of a psychiatrist or psychologist for valid administration. Major disadvantages include their sometimes questionable validity, their dependence on reading comprehension, a tendency for examinees to mark answers in a safe or socially desirable manner (thereby perhaps masking certain traits), or examinee attempts to fake a normal or pathological response pattern. This last point has received extensive attention by personality test developers, and validity scales have been built into some instruments to inform the examiner that responses have been faked or that reading comprehension may be suspect.

Projective Personality Assessment Projective personality assessment involves requiring examinees to respond to unstructured or ambiguous stimuli (e.g., incomplete sentences, inkblots, and abstract pictures). The basic theory underlying projective personality testing can be summarized as follows:

1. With the passage of time, response tendencies in various situations tend to become resistant to change and to reproduce themselves in the presence of various stimuli.

2. When presented with suggestive or ambiguous stimuli, examinees will respond to them in ways that relate to conscious or unconscious motives, beliefs, or experiences.

3. Projective tests will elicit responses in ways that reflect test-takers' conscious or unconscious motives, beliefs, or experiences by presenting stimuli that are suggestive of various aspects of the individual's life (e.g., mother–father relationships, the need for achievement) or are ambiguous.

An advantage of projective over objective tests is that the stimuli are often sufficiently abstract to allow scoring criteria to detect a variety of appropriate and inappropriate behaviors. Such techniques may uncover a broader range of psychopathology and allow for the use and interpretation of unique responses. Although projective measures have been criticized for what some consider to be a lack of validity, they can compare favorably with objective measures when used to predict clearly identified outcomes (Meyer et al., 2001). Disadvantages of projective techniques include the level of training necessary to administer and score them due to their often-complex administration and scoring rules. Projective personality tests always require administration and scoring by an appropriately trained psychologist or psychiatrist.

Objective Personality Tests

Adjective Checklist Published by the Consulting Psychologists Press, the Adjective Checklist is appropriate for individuals in ninth grade through adults. It consists of an alphabetical list of adjectives and is usually completed in about 15 minutes. The subject checks those adjectives that are applicable. Scores can be obtained in 24 variables, including self-confidence, self-control, counseling readiness, and various needs and aspects of personal adjustment.

Edwards Personal Preference Schedule (EPPS) The EPPS is published by the Psychological Corporation and is appropriate for college students and adults. It is normally completed in 45–50 minutes. Subjects respond by choosing one of a pair of statements that apply to them. Each statement represents a need, and each of these needs is assessed by nine pairs of statements.

Minnesota Multiphasic Personality Inventory–2 (MMPI-2) The MMPI-2 is appropriate for individuals over 18 years of age and is published by Pearson. It generally takes about 1 hour to complete. The MMPI-2 is the most widely used of the objective personality tests and has been in use for over 60 years. It requires individuals to respond to 567 statements presented in true–false format. Responses are scored on several scales, including validity scales and scales measuring concern for bodily functioning, depression, hysteria, psychopathological tendencies, paranoia, anxiety, schizophrenia, level of mental activity, and social comfort. In 2003, several additional scales known as the Restructured Clinical (RC) scales were developed to enhance the interpretive utility of the clinical scales. The MMPI-2 is widely used as a screening instrument in psychiatric, educational, military, industrial, and government institutions. A modified version of the MMPI-2, called the MMPI-A, was published in 1992 and is appropriate for adolescents.

Minnesota Multiphasic Personality Inventory-2-RF (MMPI-2-RF) The MMPI-2-RF was released in 2008 as an alternative to the MMPI-2, not a replacement, and it is also published by Pearson. It is shorter than the MMPI-2 (338 instead of 567 items) and reportedly takes 35–50 minutes to complete. Like the MMPI-2, the MMPI-2-RF includes several validity scales. It also includes three Higher Order (H-O) scales (Emotional/Internalizing Dysfunction, Thought Dysfunction, and Behavioral/Externalizing Dysfunction) and the same RC scales as the MMPI-2.

Myers–Briggs Type Indicator (MBTI) The Myers–Briggs Type Indicator (MBTI) is published by the Educational Testing Service. It is appropriate for ninth grade through adult and requires about 1 hour to complete. The format is forced-choice, and scores are provided for introversion versus extroversion, sensation versus intuition, thinking versus feeling, and judgment versus perception. The MBTI has been in use for over 50 years and enjoys widespread popularity.

Projective Personality Tests

Rorschach Inkblot Technique The Rorschach test is published by Hans Huber Medical Publisher, Berne, Switzerland. It consists of 10 cards or plates. Each card contains an inkblot, some black and white, some colored. Examinees are asked to describe what they "see" in the ambiguous blot. Responses are scored according to location, content, and a variety of other factors, including whether form or color was used to construct the image, whether movement is suggested, and whether shading or texture was considered. Scoring is complex, but acceptable validity is evident when properly trained scorers are used. The Rorschach has been one of the most popular projective tests used by clinical psychologists. In the hands of a skilled clinician, it can yield a surprising variety of information.

Thematic Apperception Test (TAT) The Thematic Apperception Test (TAT) is published by the Harvard University Press and is designed for individuals aged 10 through adult. Adaptations of the test for younger children (*Children's Apperception Test*) and senior citizens (*Senior Apperception Test*) are also available. The subject is presented with a series of pictures (usually 10 or 12 of the total of 30) and asked to make up a story to fit each picture. The pictures vary in degree of structure and ambiguity. The record of stories is then examined to determine the projection of the subject's personality, as indicated by recurrent behavioral themes, needs, perceived pressures, and so on. Interpretation is often complex and requires an appropriately trained psychologist or psychiatrist.

This concludes our discussion of the types of standardized tests. By no means all inclusive, our presentation of various types of tests has focused on those tests that the average classroom teacher is most likely to come into contact with.

SUMMARY

This chapter has described various types of standardized tests and briefly reviewed examples of each type. Its major points are as follows:

1. The survey battery is the type of achievement test most frequently used today.

2. The main advantages of a survey battery over several single-subject tests are the following:
   a. Coordinated subtests are provided.
   b. Savings in time and expense are realized.
   c. A common norm group is used.

3. The disadvantages of a survey battery over single-subject tests are the following:
   a. Content validity may vary across subtests.
   b. Depth of coverage may be less than that obtained with a single-subject test.

4. Single-subject achievement tests are mainly used in the secondary grades.

5. Diagnostic achievement tests are usually administered only to selected students who have already exhibited difficulties in achievement.

6. Detail about standardized tests may be available on test publisher websites, state education association websites, or on the Smarter Balanced and PARCC websites for the Common Core-aligned tests. Instructional and interpretive resources, including videos, sample questions, scoring rubrics and objectives, and standards may also be found on those sites.

7. Academic aptitude or IQ tests are used to predict future learning; achievement tests measure past learning.

8. Academic aptitude tests were initially developed over 100 years ago to predict school performance but came to be known as intelligence tests. Today, they still do a good job of predicting school performance and have moderate to limited ability to predict a variety of other variables.

9. After about age 6, IQ scores tend to be fairly stable for the remainder of an individual's life. Prior to age 6, and especially during the first few years of life, they tend to be unstable.

10. One definition of personality is the typical and characteristic ways people behave.

11. The objective approach to personality assessment relies on self-report questionnaires that are economical but suffer from questionable validity, test-takers' perception of the social desirability of answers, and faking.

12. Projective personality assessment is based on the theory that when individuals are presented with suggestive or ambiguous stimuli, these stimuli will elicit responses that are fairly rigid and reflective of conscious or unconscious motives, beliefs, or wishes.

13. Projective tests are more flexible than objective personality tests but suffer from questionable validity and greater expense.

FOR DISCUSSION AND PRACTICE

1. Identify two advantages and two disadvantages of standardized tests.

2. Compare and contrast single-subject achievement tests and survey batteries.

3. Discuss some of the ways IQ scores should be used and some of the ways they should not be used. Give specific examples.

4. The TerraNova, Third Edition, is aligned with the Common Core State Standards.

What does that mean? How would you determine how well the Terra Nova3, or any other standardized test is, aligned with the CCSS, or with you state's specific academic standards?

5. Describe the advantages and disadvantages of objective versus projective personality tests. If your personality were being measured, which would you choose?

CHAPTER 21

IN THE CLASSROOM: A SUMMARY DIALOGUE

TO GIVE you an idea about how what we have presented in the text applies to the "real world," we encourage you to read this chapter before you put the text aside for future reference! The following dialogue between Ms. Wilson, a sixth-grade teacher, and some of the school staff with whom she works illustrates many of the concepts and topics we have covered. Ms. Wilson is 3 months into her first teaching assignment at a middle school in a medium-sized metropolitan school district. We begin our dialogue with Ms. Wilson on a Friday afternoon as she wraps up the final class session before a quarterly testing period is to begin.

MS. WILSON: I know you all feel we've covered a tremendous amount this year. Well, you're right. We have. And now it's time to find out how much you've learned. It's important for you to know how well you're doing in each subject so you can work harder in the areas where you might need improvement. It's also nice to know in what areas you might be smarter than almost everyone else. So, next week, I want you to be ready to take tests over all the material we have covered so far. (*A few students groan in unison.*) Remember, this will be your chance to show me how smart you are. I want you to get plenty of sleep Sunday night so you'll be fresh and alert Monday. (*As the bell rings, Ms. Wilson shouts over the commotion of students leaving the classroom.*) Don't forget, I'll be collecting homework on Monday! Oh yeah! Keep in mind that these tests will also help you prepare for the state PAG test (*NOTE: The PAG Test is the Promotion and Graduation Test—the state high-stakes test that recently was aligned with the Common Core State Standards, or CCSS*) that you will have to pass to be promoted to the seventh grade.

(*As Ms. Wilson collapses into her chair, Ms. Palmer, an experienced teacher, walks in.*)

MS. PALMER: Glad this grading period is just about over. Next week will be a nice break, don't you think? Just reviewing and giving tests. It'll sure be nice to have this weekend free without any preparations to worry about. Except of course we have to start getting the kids fired up for the PAG test. I'm on the pep rally committee this year. Are you on the tee-shirt committee?

MS. WILSON: You mean you won't be making up tests this weekend?

MS. PALMER: No. I have tests from the last 3 years that I've been refining and improving. They align with the PAG so with only a few modifications, they'll do fine.

MS. WILSON: You're awfully lucky. I'm afraid I haven't had a chance to even think about how I'm going to test these kids. All these subjects to make tests for, and then all the scoring and grading to do by next Friday. I think I'm going to have an awful weekend. And I really hate even thinking about the PAG test committees right now. It seems that PAG testing is all we care about these days.

MS. PALMER: Well, it is important that kids get promoted and graduate, isn't it? I think it's good that we have the PAG. It is aligned with the Common Core State Standards and our scores on the PAG have gone up for several years in a row now, so we have continued to make AYP. Back to your class though … Will you be giving criterion-referenced or norm-referenced tests?

MS. WILSON: Umm … well … I don't know. I remember hearing those terms in a tests and measurement class I once took, but I guess I just haven't had time to worry about those things until now. I suppose I'm going to have to get my old textbook out tonight and do some reviewing. Gosh! I hope I can find it.

MS. PALMER: Well, if you use norm-referenced tests, there are some available in Ms. Cartwright's office. You know, she's the counselor who is always so helpful with discipline problems. In fact, she has a whole file full of tests.

MS. WILSON: Will *you* be using norm-referenced tests next week?

MS. PALMER: Not really. For these mid-semester grades, I like to make my tests very specific to what I've been teaching, and my teaching is aligned with the Common Core. It seems to provide better feedback to the kids and parents—especially the parents of the fully included kids with disabilities. Anyway, the parents aren't really interested in where their kid scores in relation to other students until later in the school year, when I've covered more content and the kids have had a chance to get their feet on the ground. The norm-referenced tests also don't cover the Common Core State Standards very well, so they don't really identify the kids who need more attention to pass the PAG.

MS. WILSON: You mean these norm-referenced tests don't cover specifically what you've taught?

MS. PALMER: (*Trying to be tactful*) Well, no. Not exactly. I guess you have forgotten a few things since you took that tests and measurement course. If we're going to raise PAG scores, we've got to teach to the Common Core State Standards; otherwise we may be teaching things to the kids that the PAG doesn't measure because it's aligned with those Standards.

MS. WILSON: I guess so. I just thought that all tests were pretty much the same. You know, I thought we could use any test and get the same results.

MS. PALMER: Well, you *might* find a norm-referenced test that happens to be aligned with the Common Core, but I doubt it. Why don't you make a test blueprint and then you can compare it to the test items in the norm-referenced tests in Ms. Cartwright's test file?

MS. WILSON: A test *what* print?

MS. PALMER: A test blueprint. You know, where you take the objectives from your lesson plans and construct a table that shows the content you've been teaching and the level of complexity—knowledge, comprehension, and application—that you're shooting for. Then, see how Ms. Cartwright's tests match the test blueprint, making accommodations for the students with disabilities, of course.

MS. WILSON: But what if I didn't write down all my objectives? I had objectives, of course, but I just didn't write them down all the time, or when I did, I usually didn't keep them for long. You know what I mean? (*No comment from Ms. Palmer.*) And I don't think I wrote them so they included levels of complexity according to that taxonomy of objectives thing I think you're referring to. And I haven't even thought about accommodations!

Ms. PALMER: But I'm afraid that without specific classroom objectives, you don't know whether you're teaching to the Common Core Standards! And without objectives that are linked to those Standards, you won't know if the items on Ms. Cartwright's tests match what you've taught. Would you believe that last year a teacher in this school flunked half his class using a test that didn't match what he taught? Boy, what a stir that caused! And now that the PAG is being used for promotion decisions, as well as AYP, you can bet there will be lots of people looking over our shoulders to be sure we're teaching what kids need to know to pass that test! And with IDEIA and NCLB, you better be aware of any authorized accommodations and use them appropriately!

Ms. WILSON: (*Looking worried*) I guess I'll have to start from scratch, then. It looks like a very long weekend.

Ms. PALMER: Of course, you might consider giving some essay items.

Ms. WILSON: You mean long-answer questions, not multiple-choice questions?

Ms. PALMER: Yes, but you'll have to consider the time it will take to develop a scoring guide for each question and the time you'll spend grading all those answers. And, then, of course, only some of your objectives may be suited to an essay format, and some children with disabilities may not be able to use them at all.

Ms. WILSON: (*Trying to sort out all of what Ms. Palmer just said without sounding too stupid*) By scoring guide, do you mean the right answer?

Ms. PALMER: Well, not quite. As you know, essay items can have more than one right answer. So, first you will have to identify all the different elements that make an answer right and then decide how to weight or assign points to each of these elements, depending on what percentage of the right answer they represent.

Ms. WILSON: How do you decide that?

Ms. PALMER: (*Trying to be polite and being evasive for the sake of politeness*) Well ... very carefully.

Ms. WILSON: I see. (*Long pause*) Well, maybe my old tests and measurement book will have something about scoring essays

Ms. PALMER: Well, I'm sure it will, but it probably won't have anything on high-stakes tests like the PAG or the Common Core State Standards. They are such recent developments that high-stakes testing and the Common Core State Standards have only recently been addressed in testing textbooks. I mean ... I hate to sound judgmental, but it sounds like you don't really understand how the PAG fits in with your classroom tests, the Common Core, and your instructional objectives.

Ms. WILSON: I ... I ... I guess you're right. It's just that this is all so new to me. It sounds as though I have my work cut out for me. I guess I'll just have to organize my time and start to work as soon as I get home.

(*Ms. Palmer and Ms. Wilson leave the classroom and meet Mr. Smith, another teacher.*)

Mr. SMITH: You won't believe the meeting I just had with Johnny Haringer's parents!

Ms. PALMER AND Ms. WILSON: What happened?

Mr. SMITH: Well, they came to see me after Johnny missed an A by two points on one of my weekly math tests. It was the first time that he had missed an A the entire semester.

Ms. WILSON: Were they mad?

MR. SMITH: They were at first. But I stayed calm and explained very carefully why two points on the test really should make a difference between an A and a B.

MS. WILSON: What kinds of things did you tell them?

MR. SMITH: Well, luckily I keep student data from past years for all my tests. This allows me to calculate reliability and validity coefficents for my tests using a computer program on one of the PCs in the math lab. I simply explained to Johnny's parents, in everyday, commonsense language, what score reliability and validity evidence of a test meant, and then gave them some statistical data to support my case. I also explained the care and deliberation I put into the construction of my tests—you know, all the steps you go through in writing test items and then checking their content validity and doing qualitative and quantitative item analyses. I think they got the idea of just how much work it takes to construct a good test.

MS. WILSON: And?

MR. SMITH: And after that they calmed down and were very responsive to my explanation. They even commented that they hadn't realized the science of statistics could be so helpful in determining the score reliability and validity evidence for a test. They even commended me for being so systematic and careful. Can you believe that?

MS. WILSON: Umm … score reliability and validity? Do you mean we have to know the score reliability and validity for every test we use?

MR. SMITH: Yep! Ever since that lawsuit by the parents of some kid over at Central for unfair testing, the school board has made every teacher individually responsible for using reliable tests and for identifying evidence of the validity of the test for the specific purpose it's being used for. And don't forget, now that promotion as well as graduation decisions will be made based solely on PAG scores, we need to ensure that our teacher-made tests measure the same State Standards that the PAG is aligned with. It's just a matter of time before someone gets sued over that!

(*Looking surprised, Ms. Wilson turns to Ms. Palmer, and Ms. Palmer slowly and painfully nods to indicate her agreement with what Mr. Smith has been saying.*)

MS. WILSON: Boy! I don't think I could explain reliability and validity that well—at least not to parents—and I know I wouldn't have the slightest idea of how to compute a reliability coefficient or identify validity evidence. And Ms. Palmer can tell you that I need to brush up on the PAG test and the State Standards too.

MR. SMITH: Well, that I don't know about, but I'm sure glad we won't have any preparations to worry about this weekend … nothing but review and testing next week. You have a nice weekend.

MS. PALMER: Well, it may not be all that bad. You've got that tests and measurement text at home, and next quarter, who knows? You may have time to plan for all this ahead of time. As for the PAG and Common Core, if you go to the state education agency's website you can find a lot of helpful information there. You can also go to the Smarter Balanced and PARCC websites. Even though our state is not using either of the tests developed by those consortia, they provide lots of helpful resources that will help you prep for the PAG, because it is aligned with the Common Core.

MS. WILSON: (*Being purposely negative*) That's if I have any time left after I try to learn about reliability and validity, construct a test blueprint, learn the difference between norm-referenced and criterion-referenced tests, develop appropriate accommodations for special learners, make a scoring key for an essay test, and, of course, compute some test item statistics I probably can't even pronounce!

MS. PALMER: Let's get to our cars before the roof falls in. (*To Ms. Wilson under her breath*) Speaking of the roof.

(*The principal approaches them.*)

PRINCIPAL: Ah, Ms. Wilson. I'm glad I ran into you. How'd things go for you this quarter? Which PAG committee are you on? We really need to keep up the push to raise PAG test scores. Never can settle for what you have.

MS. WILSON: Very well, thank you. I really like my classroom, and the parents I've met have been very nice. All my students—well, almost all—have made me feel at home. I'm on the PAG tee-shirt committee.

PRINCIPAL: Good. I've had good reports about your teaching, and your classroom discipline and management seem to be improving. I suppose you're all set for the end of this grading period. It's only a week away, you know. (*The principal looks at Ms. Wilson for some kind of response.*)

MS. WILSON: (*After a brief pause, she responds almost inaudibly*) Yes.

PRINCIPAL: Well, that's excellent, because you know how much emphasis our parents place on grades. All of our teachers spend a lot of time on grading. We've never had a serious incident in this regard like they've had over at Central. I'd like to think it was because of my policy that every teacher be responsible for using reliable tests with adequate evidence of their validity, for making accommodations for special learners, and for interpreting test scores to parents. I only wish that all teachers in the state would have to prove themselves competent in tests and measurement to be certified, like they do in some other states. I'm sure there would be a lot fewer angry students and parents if this were the case. Well, Ms. Wilson, glad things are going so well. Of course, the final test will be whether scores go up for your class on the PAG. I am counting on you to make that happen. In fact, we are all counting on you to make the PAG scores go up. You wouldn't want to be the one responsible for the school losing its "exemplary" rating, would you? Gotta run … have a nice weekend. You too, Ms. Palmer.

MS. WILSON: Thank you.

MS. PALMER: You too.

MS. WILSON: (*On the verge of tears*) I don't think I've had a more miserable Friday afternoon. I can only guess what the weekend will be like.

MS. PALMER: Maybe I can help. (*Ms. Wilson looks directly at her.*) I have the new, eleventh edition of a tests and measurement book called *Educational Testing and Measurement: Classroom Application and Practice*, which covers the kinds of things that might be helpful in preparing your tests for next week. It talks a lot about the Common Core, the Smarter Balanced and PARCC consortia that developed Common Core-aligned tests with funding from the Race to the Top. They also provide a lot of help with developing instructional objectives, writing test items, and interpreting test results. They even give you examples of how to interpret results to parents. If you're not busy, why don't I bring it over and help you with those tests?

MS. WILSON: (*Straining to be reserved and matter of fact*) I guess that would be … okay. (*Then, with a sigh of relief*) Yes, I think that would be fine.

Ms. PALMER: That sounds good. Listen, there's a silver lining to this. As long as you are going to review it, the eleventh edition of Kubiszyn and Borich also includes a chapter on the response-to-intervention, you know, RTI, approach that we started to implement this year. It does a nice job of comparing and contrasting the differences between the formative assessment approach we have adopted under RTI to the traditional summative assessments we've been using. It also explains what interim or benchmark assessments are and how they fit into RTI and continuing to improve our performance on the PAG so that we continue to improve on our AYP. If you start learning about RTI now, you will be way ahead of the game when we fully implement it next year.

Ms. WILSON: (*wincing a bit*) Well, you may be right. If there's one thing I've learned so far this year, it's that new teachers really do need to have competency in all kinds of testing and measurement issues and that things have really changed a lot in the last few years.

Ms. PALMER: Not just new teachers, Ms. Wilson, all teachers!

You might think that this scenario is a bit far-fetched. It may come as a surprise, but we are willing to bet that something like this will happen to you long before the end of your first grading period. The incidents we have described repeat themselves thousands of times each school day in schools across the country.

Unless you are confident that you fully understood all aspects of this dialogue, we encourage you to go the text's companion website (go to http://www.wiley.com/college/kubiszyn). There we provide a review of the issues we have raised in this dialogue. Once you have done so, unless you are very confident that you comprehend all the issues we discuss in the website supplement for Chapter 21, we strongly encourage you to review carefully the relevant sections of the text. If you do, we believe you will be much better prepared to survive and successfully navigate through the sometimes turbulent (but navigable!) waters that can swirl around educational testing and measurement.

After reading this book and engaging with the wealth of information we have provided, you should have a good understanding of the practical side of testing and some insights into how to handle yourself professionally in the face of the many challenging situations that are part and parcel of the realm of real-life educational testing. But real life is not easily portrayed on the pages of a book. For you, the reader, and for us, the authors, it occurs only in classrooms, and this of course is why we have chosen to spend the better part of our lives in those classrooms. Our advice is to use this book to prepare for that real world. Review its contents often and keep this book close at hand for future reference. Combine the skills you have learned with your own good judgment and experience and you will be sure to continue to learn as you teach.

MATH SKILLS REVIEW

THIS REVIEW of math skills covers all operations necessary to complete the calculations in this text. The Self-Check Test and answer key that appear at the end of the appendix can help you determine which skills you may need to review.

ORDER OF TERMS

The order of terms in addition is irrelevant.

$$2 + 3 = 3 + 2 = 5$$

The order of terms in subtraction is important.

$$3 - 2 \neq 2 - 3$$

The order of terms in multiplication is irrelevant.

$$3(2) = 2(3) = 6$$

There are several ways to write "multiplied by."

$$3 \times 2 = 3(2) = 3 \cdot 2 = 6$$

The order of terms in division is important.

$$6/2 \neq 2/6$$

There are several ways to write "divided by."

$$4 \div 2 = 4/2 = 2\overline{)4} = 2$$

ORDER OF OPERATIONS

When multiplying (or dividing) the sum (or difference) of several numbers by another number, you may either multiply (divide) or add (subtract) first.

$$2(3 + 4) = 2(7) = 14 \quad \text{or} \quad 2(3 + 4) = 6 + 8 = 14$$
$$3(5 - 1) = 3(4) = 12 \quad \text{or} \quad 3(5 - 1) = 15 - 3 = 12$$

$$\frac{6+4}{2} = \frac{10}{2} = 5 \quad \text{or} \quad \frac{6+4}{2} = \frac{6}{2} + \frac{4}{2} = 3 + 2 = 5$$

$$\frac{9-6}{3} = \frac{3}{3} = 1 \quad \text{or} \quad \frac{9-6}{3} = \frac{9}{3} - \frac{6}{3} = 3 - 2 = 1$$

The operations within parentheses are completed first. Within the parentheses, multiplication and division are completed before addition and subtraction. After math in the parentheses is finished, other multiplications and divisions are completed before additions and subtractions.

$$(3 - 2) - 4(6 + 1) + 8 = 1 - 4(7) + 8 = 1 - 28 + 8 = -19$$

$$(6 + 4) - 6(3 - 2) + 11 = 10 - 6(1) + 11 = 10 - 6 + 11 = 15$$

$$(4/2) + 3(2 + 6) - 3 = 2 + 3(8) - 3 = 2 + 24 - 3 = 23$$

FRACTIONS

For addition and subtraction, fractions must have the same denominator. If a common denominator is not obvious, multiply the two denominators to get a common denominator. In order to keep the value of the new fractions equal to that of the original fractions, multiply each numerator by the denominator of the other fraction (cross-multiplying).

$$\frac{1}{2} + \frac{1}{4} = \frac{4}{8} + \frac{2}{8} = \frac{6}{8} = \frac{3}{4}$$

$$\frac{2}{3} - \frac{2}{5} = \frac{10}{15} - \frac{6}{15} = \frac{4}{15}$$

$$\frac{1}{5} + \frac{1}{2} = \frac{2}{10} + \frac{5}{10} = \frac{7}{10}$$

This could also be accomplished by multiplying both the numerator and the denominator of each fraction by the denominator of the other fraction.

$$\frac{1}{2} + \frac{1}{4}$$

$$\frac{1}{2} \times \frac{4}{4} = \frac{4}{8} \quad \text{and} \quad \frac{1}{4} \times \frac{2}{2} = \frac{2}{8} \quad \text{so} \quad \frac{4}{8} + \frac{2}{8} = \frac{6}{8} = \frac{3}{4}$$

$$\frac{2}{3} - \frac{2}{5}$$

$$\frac{2}{3} \times \frac{5}{5} = \frac{10}{15} \quad \text{and} \quad \frac{2}{5} \times \frac{3}{3} = \frac{6}{15} \quad \text{so} \quad \frac{10}{15} - \frac{6}{15} = \frac{4}{15}$$

$$\frac{1}{5} + \frac{1}{2}$$

$$\frac{1}{5} \times \frac{2}{2} = \frac{2}{10} \quad \text{and} \quad \frac{1}{2} \times \frac{5}{5} \quad \text{so} \quad \frac{2}{10} + \frac{5}{10} = \frac{7}{10}$$

To multiply two fractions, simply multiply across the numerators and across the denominators.

$$\frac{3}{4} \times \frac{1}{2} = \frac{3}{8} \qquad \frac{2}{7} \times \frac{1}{3} = \frac{2}{21} \qquad \frac{3}{6} \times \frac{1}{3} = \frac{3}{18} = \frac{1}{6}$$

To divide two fractions, invert the divisor and then multiply.

$$\frac{3}{8} \div \frac{1}{2} = \frac{3}{8} \times \frac{2}{1} = \frac{3}{4} \qquad \frac{2}{3} \div \frac{3}{4} = \frac{2}{3} \times \frac{4}{3} = \frac{8}{9}$$

$$\frac{1}{2} \div \frac{3}{5} = \frac{1}{2} \times \frac{5}{3} = \frac{5}{6} \qquad \frac{3}{4} \div \frac{4}{5} = \frac{3}{4} \times \frac{5}{4} = \frac{15}{16}$$

To simplify multiplication and division of fractions, you may cancel out equal amounts in the numerators and denominators.

$$\frac{1}{2} \times \frac{2}{3} \div \frac{1}{9} = \frac{1}{2} \times \frac{2}{3} \times \frac{9}{1} = \frac{1}{\cancel{2}_1} \times \frac{\cancel{2}^1}{\cancel{3}_1} \times \frac{\cancel{9}^3}{1} = \frac{3}{1} = 3$$

$$\frac{3}{24} \times \frac{8}{9} \div \frac{1}{2} = \frac{3}{24} \times \frac{8}{9} \times \frac{2}{1} = \frac{\cancel{3}^1}{\cancel{24}_3} \times \frac{\cancel{8}^1}{\cancel{9}_3} \times \frac{2}{1} = \frac{2}{9}$$

$$\frac{1}{32} \div \frac{1}{16} \times \frac{3}{4} = \frac{1}{32} \times \frac{16}{1} \times \frac{3}{4} = \frac{1}{\cancel{32}_2} \times \frac{\cancel{16}^1}{1} \times \frac{3}{4} = \frac{3}{8}$$

MIXED NUMBERS

In addition and subtraction, it is necessary to have only the denominators of the fractions the same.

$$2\frac{1}{4} + 3\frac{1}{3} = 2\frac{3}{12} + 3\frac{4}{12} = 5\frac{7}{12}$$

$$8\frac{2}{3} - 3\frac{2}{7} = 8\frac{14}{21} - 3\frac{6}{21} = 5\frac{8}{21}$$

$$6\frac{2}{3} + 4\frac{1}{4} = 6\frac{8}{12} + 4\frac{3}{12} = 10\frac{11}{12}$$

In subtraction it is sometimes necessary to "borrow" from the whole number in order to subtract the fractional part.

$$4\frac{1}{2} - 2\frac{2}{3} = 4\frac{3}{6} - 2\frac{4}{6}$$

You cannot subtract the fractions, but since $1 = \frac{6}{6}$ you can convert $4\frac{3}{6}$ to $3\frac{9}{6}$, so

$$3\frac{9}{6} - 2\frac{4}{6} = 1\frac{5}{6}$$

An easier way to convert mixed numbers to fractions is to multiply the whole number by the denominator of the fraction, then add the numerator.

$$3\frac{1}{2} = \frac{(3 \times 2) + 1}{2} = \frac{6 + 1}{2} = \frac{7}{2}$$

$$2\frac{3}{4} = \frac{(2 \times 4) + 3}{4} = \frac{8 + 3}{4} = \frac{11}{4}$$

$$8\frac{1}{3} = \frac{(8 \times 3) + 1}{3} = \frac{24 + 1}{3} = \frac{25}{3}$$

DECIMALS

To convert a fraction to a decimal number, perform simple division.

$$\frac{3}{8} = 8\overline{)3.000} = 0.375 \quad \frac{1}{2} = 2\overline{)1.0} = 0.5 \quad \frac{3}{4} = 4\overline{)3.00} = 0.75$$

The number of decimal places is not changed by addition or subtraction.

0.2	0.68	0.374	0.949
+0.5	−0.32	−0.234	+0.055
0.7	0.36	0.140	1.004

In multiplication, the number of decimal places in the answer is equal to the total of the number of places in the numbers you are multiplying.

0.42	0.81	0.5	0.24
×0.003	×0.2	×0.5	×0.02
0.00126	0.162	0.25	0.0048

In division, the divisor is converted to a whole number by moving the decimal point to the right as many places as necessary. The decimal point in the number you are dividing into must be moved the same number of places to the right.

$$0.25\overline{)1.000} = \quad \text{becomes} \quad 25\overline{)100.0} = 4.0$$

$$0.32\overline{)6.4} = \quad \text{becomes} \quad 32\overline{)640} = 20$$

$$0.482\overline{)14.46} = \quad \text{becomes} \quad 482\overline{)14460} = 30$$

SQUARES AND SQUARE ROOTS

Squaring a number is multiplying it by itself.

$$3^2 = 3(3) = 9 \qquad 4^2 = 4(4) = 16$$

Taking a square root is finding a number that, when multiplied by itself, equals the number from which you are taking the square root.

$$\sqrt{4} = +2 \text{ or} -2 \quad \text{since} \quad 2(2) = 4 \quad \text{and} \ -2(-2) = 4$$

$$\sqrt{16} = +4 \text{ or} -4 \quad \text{since} \quad 4(4) = 16 \quad \text{and} \ -4(-4) = 16$$

$$\sqrt{9} = +3 \text{ or} -3 \quad \text{since} \quad 3(3) = 9 \quad \text{or} \ -3(-3) = 9$$

ALGEBRA

To solve equations, you must get the unknown (usually symbolized by x) on one side of the equation and all other numbers on the other side. This is done by adding, subtracting, multiplying, or dividing both sides of the equation by the same number.

$$2x = 4$$

Divide both sides by 2

$$\frac{2x}{2} = \frac{4}{2}$$

$$x = 2$$

$$\frac{x}{6} = 3$$

Multiply both sides by 6

$$\frac{6x}{6} = 3(6)$$

$$x = 18$$

$$x + 3 = 9$$

Subtract 3 from both sides

$$(x + 3) - 3 = 9 - 3$$

$$x = 6$$

$$x - 4 = 6$$

Add 4 to both sides

$$(x - 4) + 4 = 6 + 4$$

$$x = 10$$

This procedure can also be done in combinations of the above.

$$2x + 4 = 10$$

Subtract 4 from both sides

$$(2x + 4) - 4 = 10 - 4$$

$$2x = 6$$

Divide both sides by 2

$$\frac{2x}{2} = \frac{6}{2}$$

$$x = 3$$

$$3x + 15 = 75$$

Subtract 15 from both sides

$$(3x + 15) - 15 = 75 - 15$$

$$3x = 60$$

Divide both sides by 3

$$\frac{3x}{3} = \frac{60}{3}$$

$$x = 20$$

$$4x + 10 = 110$$

Subtract 10 from both sides

$$(4x + 10) - 10 = 110 - 10$$
$$4x = 100$$

Divide both sides by 4

$$\frac{4x}{4} = \frac{100}{4}$$
$$x = 25$$

SELF-CHECK TEST

Directions: Solve the following problems.

_____ **1.** $13^2 =$ _____

_____ **2.**   Convert $\frac{1}{4}$ to a decimal _____

_____ **3.** $\sqrt{144} =$ _____

_____ **4.** $24(380 + 20) =$ _____

_____ **5.** $\frac{2}{5} + \frac{3}{15} =$ _____

_____ **6.** $144 \div 0.048 =$ _____

_____ **7.** $16x + 10 = 330 =$ _____

_____ **8.** $\frac{2}{3} \div \frac{7}{10}$ _____

_____ **9.** $1.32 \times 0.07 =$ _____

_____ **10.** $2\frac{2}{3} + 6\frac{1}{12} =$ _____

_____ **11.**   Convert $\frac{1}{5}$ to a decimal _____

_____ **12.** $\frac{2}{3} \div \frac{14}{15} \times \frac{2}{5} =$ _____

_____ **13.** $(24 - 15) - 2(17 + 4) + 32 =$ _____

_____ **14.** $1.375 + 0.139 =$ _____

_____ **15.** $9x + 72 = 342$ $x =$ _____

Answers:

1. $13 \times 13 = 169$	**6.** 3,000	**11.** 0.2
2. 0.25	**7.** $x = 0.20$	**12.** $\frac{2}{7}$
3. 12 or −12	**8.** $\frac{20}{21}$	**13.** −1
4. 9,600	**9.** 0.0924	**14.** 1.514
5. $\frac{3}{5}$	**10.** $8\frac{3}{4}$	**15.** 30

ANSWERS FOR DISCUSSION OR PRACTICE QUESTIONS

CHAPTER 1

3. Responses should consider the five factors noted in the text. These include tests are only tools that can be used correctly or not, tests can be well or poorly designed, poorly trained users can misuse even good tests, tests must be used for their designed purpose and population, and tests only provide *some* information that should be considered along with background and contextual information to make decisions.

4. The same factors listed in Answer #3 should be applied to this question.

5. The specific purposes of educational testing refer to the various academic content areas (e.g., spelling, math, language arts, and biology). The general purposes refer to the timing of testing: during instruction (formative), two to three times per year to gauge progress and identify students who may be at-risk for failure on annual high-stakes tests (interim or benchmark), and after teaching has been completed at the end of the year or semester (summative).

8. Testing/assessment involves selection administration and scoring of selected measures but testing/assessment is only one part of the assessment process, which also includes of those results with relevant and background information. That process should also include consideration of the five factors that affect the usefulness of a test.

CHAPTER 2

4. A state-developed test is more likely to be aligned than a national test when the state has established clear academic standards, or has adopted the CCSS, and the state's test is designed specifically to measure state standards or the CCSS, and where the national test measures more general objectives across many states.

5. Some states may have been pressured into utilizing a test before they had time to develop academic standards and/or a specific test to measure them.

6. The CCSS initiative was an attempt to establish uniform standards for all the states. It was sponsored by the National Governors' Association and the Council of Chief State School Officers, not the federal government or President Obama, in response to the widely varying academic and proficiency standards and tests across the states that interfered with meaningful growth comparisons across and within states. The RTT was a federal grant competition that was open to all the states. It was sponsored by President Obama and Secretary Duncan and was intended to support adoption of the CCSS and the development of two uniform assessments to measure states on the CCSS. For that reason, advocates of state control of education branded the RTT as an attempt by the federal government to take over state control. The CCSS was also characterized as a step toward federal

control over the states. There were other reasons as well, but state or federal control of education was primary.

CHAPTER 3

2. (a) Formative assessment occurs during instruction to give teachers rapid feedback about student achievement about the unit of instruction, interim or benchmark assessments are administered two to three times per year to gauge student progress and identify students who may be at-risk for failure on annual high-stakes tests, and summative assessments are administered after teaching has been completed at the end of the year or semester.
   (b) The implementation of RTI has grown over the years since IDEIA was enacted but remains uneven, with some states fully implementing RTI and others only partially.

4. After respectfully acknowledging their experience, you should explain that until fairly recently their perception was correct. However, the requirements of IDEA in 1997, NCLB in 2002 and IDEIA in 2004 have functioned to merge education and special education reform. As a result of those reforms, special education students, with few exceptions, are now engaged with the regular curriculum and are subject to the same annual assessments as regular education students, although with accommodations and alternate assessments, when necessary.

CHAPTER 5

10. (a) B (b) E (c) E (d) E (e) B (f) B (g) E (h) B
12. (1) c (2) d (3) d (4) e

CHAPTER 6

4. (1) d (2) a (3) b (4) e (5) f
5. (a) 2 comprehension, 1 application (b) 30% multiplication, 30% division

CHAPTER 7

3. (a) The "a" should be "a/an."
   (b) National origin of the names in the stem provides a clue to the answer.
   (c) Contains an absolute; opinionated.
   (d) Multiple defensible answers; lacks specificity.
   (e) Begins with a blank; lacks specificity.
   (f) Lists should be titled and arranged in some logical order. Too wide a variety of concepts being measured, making some answers obvious (i.e., nonhomogeneous lists).

CHAPTER 9

1. Conventional tests are given to obtain data on which to base grades, indicate how much has been learned, make decisions about instructional placement, talk to parents about, and help others make employment decisions. Performance assessments are given to stimulate higher-order thinking in the classroom and simulate real-world activities.

2. By refocusing the curriculum on thinking, problem solving, and student responsibility for learning.

3. An indirect measure, such as knowledge shown in a multiple-choice test, will only suggest that something has been learned. A direct measure, such as a problem-solving activity, requires that acquired

knowledge can be applied and exhibited in the context of a real-world problem.

5. For example, the Darwin School records percentage of words read accurately during oral reading, number of sentences read with understanding, and number of story elements learners can talk about on their own. The West Orient School requires portfolios of poetry, essays, biographies, and self-reflections.

8. Scoring rubrics are model answers against which a learner's performance is compared. They can be a detailed list of what an acceptable answer must contain or a sample of typical responses that would be acceptable.

CHAPTER 11

1. (a) $p = 0.22$ (a difficult item)
   (b) $p = 0.64$ (a moderately easy item)
2. (a) $D = 0.40$ (a good discriminating item)
   (b) $D = -0.33$ (a poor discriminating item)
3. (a) ambiguity, (b) miskeyed, (c) ambiguity, (d) guessing, (e) miskeyed
4. $p = 0.25$; $D = 0.10$. The key discriminates positively, but not all distracters discriminate negatively. Probably some guessing and/or ambiguity.

CHAPTER 12

5. Numerical mark = 74.75, letter grade = C; both approaches yield the same result because they differ only in the point at which the equating procedure is applied.

CHAPTER 13

1. Grade 1, positively skewed; grade 3, normal; grade 5, negatively skewed

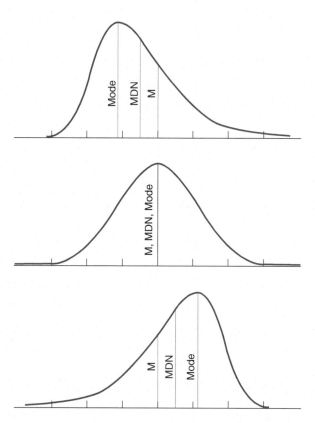

2. Group 1: N = 10, R = 13 (inclusive R = 14), M = 93.3, MDN = 94.0, mode = 90, 94, and 97
   Group 2: N = 10, R = 36 (inclusive R = 37), M = 89.6, MDN = 92.5, mode = 97
   The difference in means is caused by the score of 61 in Group 2. For Group 1, the mean would be the best measure of central tendency. For Group 2, the median would be the best measure of central tendency.
3. Use from 8 to 10 intervals. Choose the number that best demonstrates variations in the frequency of scores.
4. (1) c (2) c (3) a (4) b (5) b
5. $P_{25} = 93.5$; $P_{50} = 99$
6. (a) Normal; (b) negatively skewed; (c) positively skewed
7. (a) Simple frequency distribution; small number and range of scores

(b) List, small number but large range

(c) Grouped frequency distribution; large number and range of scores

CHAPTER 14

1. (a) N = 10; (b) mode = 5; (c) median = 4.5; (d) mean = 4.0; (e) standard deviation = 1.61; (f) variance = 2.6; (g) range = 5 (inclusive R = 6)

2. (a) 2.0, 3.2, 4.0, 4.5
   (b) 75, 106, 112.5, 121.5
   (c) 125, 88, 85, 78
   (d) About 15%; 82%; 34.13%; about 11%

3. (a) 1.33 (b) 74.5 (c) about 16%

4. 35

5. John, −1.0, 40; Mary, +2.0, 70; Jim, +.5, 55; Claire, −1.5, 35

6. (a) 42.5, 121 (b) 700

CHAPTER 15

2. Curvilinear. Income goes up until age 60, then income decreases with age.

3. 0.844; positive and strong

4. 71.2%

5. (a) 4 (b) 7 (c) 1 (d) 2

6. Disagree. A third variable, yet unmeasured, could cause both big feet and large vocabularies in the same individuals, making the relationship only appear causal. More likely, however, since such a variable probably could not be identified, it would be appropriate to regard the high correlation as erroneously caused by insufficient N or sampling.

7. Truncation restricts the variability of scores and, hence, cannot reveal the covariation of X and Y scores in the larger distribution of scores.

CHAPTER 16

1. The concurrent validity coefficient is −0.97. The test has no concurrent validity evidence when compared with the old test.

2. Predictive validity evidence: Correlate the test scores with scores on a subsequent test in social studies or with end-of-quarter grades in social studies. Construct validity evidence: Correlate the test scores with ratings on citizenship, scores on a test of social awareness, or any test that measures a part of what the new test measures. Conversely, it could also be correlated with the exact opposite of what the test measures.

3. Both Test A and Test C would be acceptable. Test C is unusual because predictive validity evidence is higher than concurrent. Normally, the opposite is true.

4. Test C is most acceptable, followed by Test A and Test B.

5. (a) Content   (d) Predictive
   (b) Predictive   (e) Concurrent
   (c) Concurrent   (f) Content

6. A lower correlation is expected since your gifted group is homogeneous. Therefore, the strength of the correlation is limited due to the truncated range of scores involved.

CHAPTER 17

1. Test C

2. $r_w = 0.75$

3. (a) Internal consistency; (b) internal consistency; (c) test–retest

4. Test C

5. (a) Test–retest
   (b) Alternate forms (long interval)

(c) Split–half

(d) Alternate forms

(e) Test–retest

6. Test B

7. Use neither test, unless acceptable validity can be established

CHAPTER 18

In the problem at the end of Chapter 18, there is a real difference between John's reading and math scores, but not between his writing and science scores.

1. $S_m = 4.00$

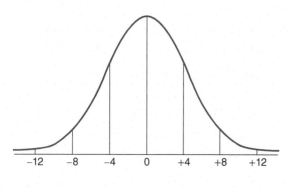

2. $95\% = 8–24$; $99\% = 4–28$; $68\% = 12–20$

3. Within student (illness); within test (poor items); within administration (timing); within scoring (miskeys)

4. (a) Least subject to within-student error

   (b) Most subject to within-student; least subject to within-test

   (c) Most subject to within-test; least subject to within-student

   (d) Most subject to all sources

   (e) Least subject to all sources

5. The following subtest profile shows bands for 68% certainty

Subtest	Band	
Reading	53.6–58.4	$S_m = SD\sqrt{1-r}$
Listening	47.6–52.4	$= 8\sqrt{1-0.91}$
Writing	58.6–63.4	$= 8\sqrt{0.09}$
Social Studies	32.6–37.4	$= 8(.3)$
Science	57.6–62.4	$= 2.4$
Math	53.6–58.4	

Social Studies is significantly lower than all others. Listening is significantly lower than all but Social Studies. Writing is significantly higher than all but Science. Other differences are due to chance.

6. None shows real differences.

7. Differences of this size and direction are expected since each method is affected by different sources of error.

8. S_m for A = 6 and S_m for B = 5; scores from A would fluctuate most.

CHAPTER 19

4. (a) Jack is achieving below expectancy, Bonnie is above, and Chris is at expectancy.
   (b) There is an aptitude–achievement discrepancy between Jack's Verbal IQ and his Vocabulary and Comprehension achievement.

5. At the 95% level, we continue to see a discrepancy between Jack's Verbal IQ and his Vocabulary and Comprehension achievement.

6. Real differences at the 68% level may disappear at the 95% level because the confidence intervals at the 95% level are twice as large as they are at the 68% level. As a result, score differences must be even more discrepant to show real differences at the 95% level than at the 68% level.

SUGGESTED READINGS

CHAPTER 1

American Educational Research Association, American Psychological Association, National Council on Measurement in Education. (2014). *Standards for Educational and Psychological Testing* (4th ed.). Washington, DC: Author.

Deno, S. L., Fuchs, L. S., Marston, D., & Shin, J. (2001). Using curriculum-based measurement to establish growth standards for students with learning disabilities. *School Psychology Review*, **30**, 507–524.

Haladyna, T. M. (2002). *Essentials of Standardized Achievement Testing*. Boston: Allyn & Bacon.

Holmes Group. (1986). *Tomorrow's Teachers*. East Lansing, MI: The Holmes Group, Michigan State University.

Individuals with Disabilities Education Act Amendments of 1997, 20 U.S. Code, Sec. 101.

Individuals with Disabilities Education Improvement Act of 2004, 20 U.S. Code 1400 et. seq., Sec. 101.

Lissitz, R. W., & Schafer, W. D. (2002). *Assessment in Educational Reform*. Boston: Allyn & Bacon.

National Commission on Excellence in Education. (1983). *A Nation at Risk: The Imperative for Educational Reform*. Washington, DC: Author.

No Child Left Behind Act (2002). Public Law 107–110.

Rhodes, R., Ochoa, H. & Ortiz, S. (2005). *Assessing Culturally and Linguistically Diverse Students*. New York: Guilford Press.

Spitzer, S., Cupp, R., & Parke, R. D. (1995). School entrance, age, social competence and self-perception in kindergarten and first grade. *Early Childhood Research Quarterly*, **10**, 433–450.

Stecker, P. M., & Lembke, E. S. (2007). *Advanced Applications of CBM in Reading (K–6): Instructional Decision-Making Strategies Manual*. U.S. Department of Education. Office of Special Education Programs. Available at http://www.studentprogress.org/summer_institute/2007/Adv%20Reading/AdvRdgManual_2007.pdf

CHAPTER 2

American Psychological Association. (2001). *Test User Qualifications: A Data-based Approach to Promoting Good Test Use*. Washington, DC: Author.

Common Core State Standards Initiative. (2010). The common core state standards (CCSS). Retrieved April 2, 2012 from http://www.corestandards.org

Fordham Institute. (2011). Our review of the common core standards. Retrieved January 22, 2012 from http://standards.educationgadfly.net/commoncore/ela

Haladyna, T. M. (2002). *Essentials of Standardized Achievement Testing*. Boston: Allyn & Bacon.

Hout, M., & Elliot, S. W. (Eds.) (2011). *Incentives and Test-Based Accountability in Education*. Washington, DC: National Academies Press.

Hursh, D. (2008). *High Stakes Testing and the Decline of Teaching and Learning*. New York: Rowman & Littlefield.

Lissitz, R. W., & Schafer, W. D. (2002). *Assessment in Educational Reform*. Boston: Allyn & Bacon.

National Research Council. (2000). *Tests and Teaching Quality: Interim Report*. Washington, DC: National Academies Press.

Nichols, S. L., & Berliner, D. C. (2005, March). *The Inevitable Corruption of Indicators and Educators through High-Stakes Testing*. East Lansing, MI: The Great Lakes Center for Education Research & Practice. http://www.greatlakescenter.org/g_l_new_doc/EPSL-0503-101-EPRU-exec.pdf

Nichols, S. L., & Berliner, D. C. (2007). *Collateral Damage: How High-Stakes Testing Corrupts America's Schools*. Cambridge MA:, Harvard University Press. Collateral Damage: How High-Stakes Testing Corrupts America's Schools

RAND Corporation. (2000, October 24). *What Do Test Scores Tell Us?* Santa Monica, CA: Author.

CHAPTER 3

Amato, J. M., & Watkins, M. W. (2011). The predictive validity of CBM writing indices for eighth-grade students. *Journal of Special Education*, **44**, 195–204.

Brown-Chidsey, R. & Steege, M. (2010). *Response to Intervention: Principles and Strategies for Effective Practice*. New York, NY: Guilford Press.

Burns, M. K., Vanderwood, M., & Ruby, S. (2005). Evaluating the readiness of pre-referral intervention teams for use in a problem-solving model: Review of three levels of research. *School Psychology Quarterly*, **20**, 89–105.

Burns, M. K., Wiley, H. I., & Viglietta, E. (2008). Best practices in facilitating problem-solving teams. In A. Thomas & J. Grimes (Eds.), *Best Practices in School Psychology* (5th ed.). Bethesda, MD: National Association of School Psychologists.

Christ, T. J., & Ardoin, S. P. (2009). Curriculum-based measurement of oral reading: Passage equivalence and probe-set development. *Journal of School Psychology*, **47**, 55–75.

Fuchs, D., Mock, D., Morgan, P. L., & Young, C. L. (2003). Responsiveness-to-intervention: Definitions, evidence, and implications for the learning disabilities construct. *Learning Disabilities Research and Practice*, **18**, 157–171.

Global Scholar/Spectrum K12 School Solutions (2011). Response to intervention (RTI) adoption survey 2011. Retrieved March 2, 2012 from http://www.spectrumk12 .com/rti/the_rti_corner/rti_adoption_report

Haager, D. (2007). Promises and cautions regarding using response to intervention with English language learners. *Learning Disability Quarterly*, **30**, 213–218.

Hoover, J. J., Baca, L., Wexler-Love, E., & Saenz, L. (2008). *National Implementation of Response to Intervention (RTI): Research Summary*. Boulder: University of Colorado, Special Education Leadership and Quality Teacher Initiative, BUENO Center-School of Education.

Hosp, M. K., & Hosp, J. (2003). Curriculum-based measurement for reading, math, and spelling: How to do it and why. *Preventing School Failure*, **48**, 10–17.

Individuals with Disabilities Education Improvement Act of 2004, 20 U.S. Code 1400 et seq., Sec. 101.

Jenkins, J. R., Hudson, R. F., & Johnson, E. S. (2007). Screening for service delivery in an RTI framework: Candidate measures. *School Psychology Review*, **36**, 560–582.

Jimerson, S. R., Burns, M. K., & VanDerHeyden, A. M. (2007). Response to intervention at school: The science and practice of assessment and intervention. In S. R. Jimerson, M. K. Burns, & A. M. VanDerHeyden (Eds.), *Handbook of Response to Intervention: The Science and Practice of Assessment and Intervention* (pp. 3–9). New York: Springer.

Johnson, E., Mellard, D. F., Fuchs, D., & McKnight, M. A. (2006). *Responsiveness to Intervention (RTI): How to Do It*. Lawrence, KS: National Research Center on Learning Disabilities.

National Center for Research on Learning Disabilities. (2007). What is RTI? Retrieved July 12, 2008 from http://www. nrcld.org/topics/rti.html

Zirkel, P. A. & Thomas, L. B. (2010, January–February). State laws for RTI: An updated snapshot. *Teaching Exceptional Children*, **42**, 56–63.

CHAPTERS 4 AND 5

Borich, G., & Tombari, M. (2004). *Educational Assessment for the Elementary and Middle School Classroom*. Columbus, OH: Merrill.

Collier, M. (1986). A specific investigation of relative performance of examination markers. *Assessment and Evaluation in Higher Education*, **11**(2), 130–137.

Cronbach, L. J. (1990). *Essentials of Psychological Testing* (5th ed.) (Chapter 2). New York: HarperCollins.

National Research Council. (2000). *Tests and Teaching Quality: Interim Report*. Washington, DC: National Academy Press.

Smith, C. W. (1987). 100 ways to improve and use teacher-made tests. *Illinois Schools Journal*, **66**(3), 20–26.

CHAPTER 6

Anderson, L., & Krathwohl, D. (Eds.) (2001). *Taxonomy for Learning, Teaching, and Assessing: A Revision of Bloom's Taxonomy of Educational Objectives*. New York: Longman.

Ball, D. W., et al. (1986). Level of teacher objectives and their classroom tests: Match or mismatch. *Journal of Social Studies Research*, **10**(2), 27–31.

Bloom, B., Englehart, M., Hill, W., Furst, E., & Kratwohl, D. (1984). *Taxonomy of Educational Objectives: The Classification of Educational Goals. Handbook I: Cognitive Domain*. New York: Longmans, Green.

Green, K. E., & Stager, S. F. (1987). Differences in teacher test and item use with subject, grade level taught, and measurement coursework. *Teacher Education and Practice*, **4**(1), 55–61.

Gronlund, N. E. (2000). *How to Write and Use Instructional Objectives*. Upper Saddle River, NJ: Merrill, Prentice-Hall.

Gullickson, A. R., & Ellwein, M. C. (1985). Post hoc analysis of teacher-made tests: The goodness-of-fit between prescription and practice. *Educational Measurement: Issues and Practice*, **4**(1), 15–18.

Mager, R. (1975). *Preparing Instructional Objectives* (2nd ed.). Palo Alto, CA: Fearon.

White, J. D. (1988). Who writes these questions, anyway? *College Composition and Communication*, **39**(2), 230–235.

Wiggins, G. (1998). *Educative Assessment: A Practical Guide for Designing Assessment Instruments*. San Francisco: Jossey-Bass.

Zeidner, M. (1987). Essay versus multiple-choice type classroom exams: The student's perspective. *Journal of Educational Research*, **80**(6), 352–358.

CHAPTER 7

Frisbie, D. A. (1988). Instructional module on reliability of scores from teacher-made tests. *Educational Measurement: Issues and Practice*, **7**(1), 25–33.

Gronlund, N. E. (1998). *Assessment of Student Achievement* (6th ed.). Boston: Allyn & Bacon.

Karras, R. (1985). A realistic approach to thinking skills: Reform multiple-choice questions. *Social Science Record*, **22**(2), 38–43.

Royer, J. M., et al. (1987). The sentence verification technique: A practical procedure for testing comprehension. *Journal of Reading*, **30**(5), 414–422.

White, J. D. (1988). Who writes these questions, anyway? *College Composition and Communication*, **39**(2), 230–235.

Zeidner, M. (1987). Essay versus multiple-choice type classroom exams: The student's perspective. *Journal of Educational Research*, **80**(6), 352–358.

CHAPTER 8

Baker, S., & Hubbard, D. (1995). Best practices in the assessment of written expression. In A. Thomas & J. Grimes

(Eds.), *Best Practices in School Psychology-III*. Bethesda, MD: National Association of School Psychologists.

Braun, H. I. (1988). Understanding scoring reliability: Experiments in calibrating essay readers. *Journal of Educational Statistics*, **13**(1), 1–18.

Dansereau, D. F. (1988). Cooperative learning strategies. In C. E. Weinstein, E. T. Goetz, & P. A. Alexander (Eds.), *Learning and Study Strategies: Issues in Assessment, Instruction, and Evaluation* (pp. 103–120). San Diego: Academic Press.

Gronlund, N. E. (1998). *Assessment of Student Achievement* (6th ed.). Boston: Allyn & Bacon.

Kemerer, R., & Wahlstrom, M. (1985). An alternative to essay examinations: The interpretive exercise, how to minimize test time and save dollars. *Performance and Instruction*, **24**(8), 9–12.

Smith, C. W. (1987). 100 ways to improve and use teacher-made tests. *Illinois Schools Journal*, **66**(3), 20–26.

Zeidner, M. (1987). Essay versus multiple-choice type classroom exams: The student's perspective. *Journal of Educational Research*, **80**(6), 352–358.

CHAPTER 9

Bransford, J. D., & Vye, N. J. (1989). A perspective on cognitive research and its implications for instruction. In L. B. Resnick and L. E. Klopfer (Eds.), *Toward the Thinking Curriculum: Current Cognitive Research* (pp. 173–205). 1989 ASCD Yearbook. Alexandria VA:, Association for Supervision and Curriculum Development.

Fuhrman, S. (1988). Educational indicators: An overview. *Phi Delta Kappan*, **2**, 486–487.

Gardner, H. (1990). Assessment in context: The alternative to standardized testing. In B. R. Gifford & M. C. O'Connor (Eds.), *Future Assessments: Changing Views of Aptitude, Achievement and Instruction*. Boston: Kluwer Academic Publishers.

Marzano, R., Pickering, J., & Heflebower, T. (2010). *The Highly Engaged Learner*. Denver, CO: Marzano Research Laboratory.

Resnick, L., & Resnick, D. (1990). Assessing the thinking curriculum: New tools for educational reform. In B. R. Gifford & M. C. O'Connor (Eds.). *Future Assessments: Changing Views of Aptitude, Achievement and Instruction*. Boston: Kluwer Academic Publishers.

CHAPTER 10

Borich, G. (2013). *Effective Teaching Methods* (8th ed.) (Chapter 13). Upper Saddle River, NJ: Pearson Education.

Borich, G., & Tombari, M. (1997). *Educational Psychology: A Contemporary Approach* (2nd ed.) (Chapter 13). New York: Addison-Wesley Longman.

Johnson, R., Mims-Cox, J. & Doyle-Nichols, A. (2009). *Developing Portfolios in Education: A Guide to Reflection, Inquiry and Assessment*. Thousand Oaks, CA: Sage.

Marzano, R. J., Pickering, D. and McTighe, J. (1993). *Assessing Student Outcomes*. Alexandria, VA: ASCD.

Nolet, V. (1992). Classroom-based measurement and portfolio assessment. *Diagnostique*, **18**, 5–26.

Reynolds, N. & Rich, R. (2006). *Portfolio Keeping: A Guide for Teachers*. New York; Bedford; St. Martin's Press.

Shavelson, R. J., & Baxter, G. (1992). What we've learned about assessing hands-on science. *Educational Leadership*, **49**(8), 20–25.

Swicegood, P. (1994). Portfolio-based assessment practices: The uses of portfolio assessments for students with behavioral disorders or learning disabilities. *Intervention in School and Clinic*, **30**, 6–15.

Tombari, M., & Borich, G. (1999). *Authentic Assessment in the Classroom: Applications and Practice*. Upper Saddle River, NJ: Prentice-Hall/Merrill.

CHAPTER 11

Anastasi, A., & Urbina, S. (1997). *Psychological Testing* (7th ed.) (Chapter 8). Upper Saddle River, NJ: Prentice-Hall.

Kolstad, R., et al. (1984). The application of item analysis to classroom achievement tests. *Education*, **105**(1), 70–72.

Secolsky, C. (1983). Using examinee judgments for detecting invalid items on teacher-made criterion-referenced tests. *Journal of Educational Measurement*, **20**(1), 51–63.

Smith, C. W. (1987). 100 ways to improve and use teacher-made tests. *Illinois Schools Journal*, **66**(3), 20–26.

CHAPTER 12

Ornstein, A. C. (1994). Grading practices and policies: An overview and some suggestions. *NASSP Bulletin*, **78**, 55–64.

Polloway, E. A., Epstein, M. H., Bursuck, W. D., Roderique, T. W., McConeghy, J. L. and Jayanthi, M. (1994). Classroom grading: A national survey of policies. *Remedial and Special Education*, **15**, 162–170.

Strein, W. (1997). Grades and grading practices. In G. Bear, K. Minke, & A. Thomas (Eds.), *Children's Needs-II*. Bethesda, MD: National Association of School Psychologists.

CHAPTERS 13–18

See Chapter 13 Supplement: "STATISTICS AND MEASUREMENT TEXTS" on the Book Companion website at www.wiley.com/

CHAPTER 19

Anastasi, A., & Urbina, S. (1997). *Psychological Testing* (7th ed.) (Chapter 4). Upper Saddle River, NJ: Prentice-Hall.

Dreher, M. J., & Singer, H. (1984). Making standardized tests work for you. *Principal*, **63**(4), 20–24.

Flanagan, D. P., Ortiz, S. O., & Alfonso, V. C. (2007). *Essentials of Cross-Battery Assessment* (2nd ed.). New York: Wiley.

Hadebank, L. (1995). Developing local norms for problem solving in schools. In A. Thomas & J. Grimes (Eds.), *Best Practices in School Psychology-III*. Bethesda, MD: National Association of School Psychologists.

Hills, J. R. (1983). Interpreting stanine scores. *Educational Measurement: Issues and Practice*, **2**(3), 18–27.

Lopez, E. C. (1995). Working with bilingual children. In A. Thomas & J. Grimes (Eds.), *Best Practices in School Psychology-III*. Bethesda, MD: National Association of School Psychologists.

Lopez, E. C., & Gopaul-McNicol, S. (1997). English as a second language. In G. Bear, K. Minke, & A. Thomas (Eds.), *Children's Needs-II*. Bethesda, MD: National Association of School Psychologists.

Stone, B. J. (1995). Use of standardized assessments. In A. Thomas & J. Grimes (Eds.), *Best Practices in School Psychology-III*. Bethesda, MD: National Association of School Psychologists.

Thorndike, R. M. & Thorndike-Christ, T. M. (2011). *Measurement and Evaluation in Psychology and Education* (7th ed.). New York: Pearson Education.

CHAPTER 20

Anastasi, A., & Urbina, S. (1997). *Psychological Testing* (7th ed.) (Chapter 14). Upper Saddle River, NJ: Prentice-Hall.

Cronbach, L. J. (1990). *Essentials of Psychological Testing* (5th ed.) (Chapter 7). New York: HarperCollins.

Flanagan, D., Ortiz, S., Alfonso, V. & Dynda, A. (2008). Best practices in cognitive assessment. In A. Thomas & J. Grimes (Eds.), *Best Practices in School Psychology-V*. Bethesda, MD: National Association of School Psychologists.

McConaughy, S. & Ritter, D. (2008). Best practices in multimethod assessment of emotional and behavioral disorders. In A. Thomas & J. Grimes (Eds.), *Best Practices in School Psychology-V*. Bethesda, MD: National Association of School Psychologists.

Sternberg, R. (1988). *The Triarchic Mind*. New York: Viking Penguin.

REFERENCES

Adams-Bullock, A., & Hawk, P. (2010). *Developing a Teaching Portfolio: A Guide for Preservice and Practicing Teachers* (3rd ed.) Boston: Pearson.

Allen, J. (2011). *A race to nowhere. Education Experts* (a *National Journal* blog). Retrieved February 10, 2013 from http://education.nationaljournal.com/2011/02/race-to-the-top-does-it-work.php#1883860

Allport, G. W., & Odbert, H. S. (1936). Trait-names: A psycho-lexical study. *Psychological Monographs*, **47**, 1–171.

Amato, J. M., & Watkins, M. W. (2011). The predictive validity of CBM writing indices for eighth-grade students. *Journal of Special Education*, **44**, 195–204.

American Educational Research Association, American Psychological Association, National Council on Measurement in Education. (1999). *Standards for Educational and Psychological Testing* (3rd ed.). Washington, DC: Author.

American Federation of Teachers. (2001). *Making Standards Matter 2001: A fifty state report on efforts to implement standards-based reform*. Retrieved March 1, 2002 from http://www.aft.org/pubs-reports/downloads/teachers/msm2001.pdf

American Federation of Teachers. (2006). *Smart testing: Let's get it right: How assessment-savvy have states become since NCLB?* Policy Brief No. 19. Retrieved January 26, 2009 from http://www.aft.org/presscenter/releases/2006/smarttesting/Testingbrief.pdf

American Psychological Association. (2000). *Report of the task force on test user qualifications*. Retrieved April 16, 2002 from http://www.apa.org/science/tuq.pdf

American Psychological Association. (2004). *Publication Manual of the American Psychological Association* (5th ed.). Washington, DC: Author.

American Statistical Association. (2014). ASA *statement on using value-added models for educational assessment*. Retrieved December 14, 2014 from https://www.amstat.org/policy/pdfs/ASA_VAM_Statement.pdf

Amrein, A. L., & Berliner, D. C. (2002). High-stakes testing, uncertainty, and student learning. *Education Policy Analysis Archives*, **10**, 18. Retrieved May 29, 2002 from http://epaa.asu.edu/epaa/v10n18

Anderson, L., & Krathwohl, D. (Eds.) (2001). *Taxonomy for Learning, Teaching, and Assessing: A Revision of Bloom's Taxonomy of Educational Objectives*. New York: Longman.

Banks, J., & Banks, C. (2013). *Multicultural Education: Issues and Perspectives* (8th ed.). Hoboken, NJ: Wiley.

Basterra, M. R., Trumbull, E., & Solano-Flores, G. (Eds.) (2010). *Cultural Validity in Assessing Linguistic and Cultural Diversity*. New York: Routledge.

Blair, J. (2001). Teacher tests criticized as single gauge. *Education Week on the Web*. Retrieved March 6, 2003 from www.edweek.com/ew/ewstory.cfm?slug=29teach.h20

Bloom, B., Englehart, M., Hill, W., Furst, E., & Kratwohl, D. (1984). *Taxonomy of Educational Objectives: The Classification of Educational Goals. Handbook I: Cognitive Domain*. New York: Longmans, Green.

Borich, G., & Tombari, M. (1997). *Educational Psychology: A Contemporary Approach* (2nd ed.). New York: Addison-Wesley Longman.

Borich, G., & Tombari, M. (2004). *Educational Assessment for the Elementary and Middle School Classroom*. Columbus, OH: Merrill.

Borich, G. (2015). *Effective Teaching Methods: Research Based Practice* (9th ed.). Boston, MA: Pearson.

Boser, U. (2012). *Race to the top: What have we learned from the states so far? A state-by-state evaluation of race to the top performance*. Center for American Progress. Retrieved December 12, 2014 from http://cdn.americanprogress.org/wp-content/uploads/issues/2012/03/pdf/rtt_states.pdf

Braden, J. P., Kubiszyn, T., & Ortiz, S. (2007, March). *Response to intervention (RTI) and assessment standards: Ensuring a reliable, valid and fair process*. Continuing education workshop conducted at the 39th Annual Convention of the National Association of School Psychologists, New York, NY.

Brown-Chidsey, R., & Steege, M. (2010). *Response to Intervention: Principles and Strategies for Effective Practice*. New York: Guilford Press.

Burke, K. (2010). *From Standards to Rubrics in Six Steps*. Thousand Oaks, CA: Corwin.

Burns, M. K., & Symington, T. (2002). A meta-analysis of pre-referral intervention teams: Student and systemic outcomes. *Journal of School Psychology*, **40**, 437–447.

Burns, M. K., Vanderwood, M., & Ruby, S. (2005). Evaluating the readiness of pre-referral intervention teams for use in a problem-solving model: Review of three levels of research. *School Psychology Quarterly*, **20**, 89–105.

Burns, M. K., Wiley, H. I., & Viglietta, E. (2008). Best practices in facilitating problem-solving teams. In A. Thomas & J. Grimes (Eds.), *Best Practices in School Psychology* (5th ed.). Bethesda, MD: National Association of School Psychologists.

Camera, L. (2014, November 25). Tennessee teachers chafe at Common-core uncertainty. *Education Week*. Retrieved on November 29, 2014 from http://www.edweek.org/ew/articles/2014/11/24/13thr_tennessee.h34.html

Cavanagh, S. (2013, October 1). Demand for testing products, services on the rise. *Education Week*. Retrieved on October 13, 2014 from http://www.edweek.org/ew/articles/2013/10/02/06testing_ep.h33.html

Cawthon, S. W., Ho, E., Patel, P. G., Potvin, D. C., & Trundt, K. M. (2009). Multiple constructs and effects of accommodations on accommodated test scores for students with disabilities. *Practical Research, Assessment and Evaluation*, **14**, 1–9.

Christ, T. J., & Ardoin, S. P. (2009). Curriculum-based measurement of oral reading: Passage equivalence and probe-set development. *Journal of School Psychology*, **47**, 55–75.

Cizek, G. J. (1998). *Filling in the Blanks: Putting Standardized Tests to the Test*. Washington, DC: Thomas B. Fordham Foundation.

Common Core State Standards Initiative (2010). *The Common Core State Standards (CCSS)*. Retrieved April 2, 2012 from http://www.corestandards.org

Costa, A. L., & Kallick, B. (Eds.). (2008). *Learning and Leading with Habits of Mind; 16 Characteristics for Success*. Alexandria, VA: Association for Supervision and Curriculum Development.

Costa, A. L., & Kallick, B. (2014). *Dispositions: Reframing Teaching and Learning*. Thousand Oaks, CA: Corwin.

Dansereau, D. F. (1988). Cooperative learning strategies. In C. E. Weinstein, E. T. Goetz, & P. A. Alexander (Eds.), *Learning and Study Strategies: Issues in Assessment, Instruction, and Evaluation* (pp. 103–120). San Diego: Academic Press.

Dave, R. H. (1970). Psychomotor levels. In R. J. Armstrong (Ed.), *Developing and Writing Behavioral Objectives*. Tucson, Arizona: Educational Innovators Press.

Deno, S. L., Fuchs, L. S., Marston, D., & Shin, J. (2001). Using curriculum-based measurement to establish growth standards for students with learning disabilities. *School Psychology Review*, **30**, 507–524.

Deno, S. L., Mirkin, P. K., & Chiang, B. (1982). Identifying valid measures of reading. *Exceptional Children*, **49**(1), 36–45.

Doherty, K. M. (2002, February 27). Assessment. *Education Week on the Web*. Retrieved May 1, 2002 from www.edweek.org/context/topics/issuespage.cfm?id=41

Duckworth, A. L., & Seligman, M. E. (2005). Self-discipline outdoes IQ in predicting academic performance of adolescents. *Psychological Science*, **16**, 939–944.

Fairbairn, S. B., & Fox, J. (2009). Inclusive achievement testing for linguistically and culturally diverse test takers: Essential considerations for test developers and decision makers. *Educational Measurement: Issues and Practice*, **28**, 10–24.

FairTest (2009, August). *Critical comments on U.S. Education Department's 'Race to the Top Fund' guidelines*. Retrieved August 13, 2012 from http://fairtest.org/fairtest-critical-comments-us-education-department

Faucet, R. (2014, September 29). Trial opens in Atlanta school cheating scandal. *New York Times*. Page A17, New York edition.

Finn, C. E., Petrilli, M. J., & Julian, L. (2006). *The State of State Standards 2006*. Washington, DC: Thomas B. Fordham Foundation.

Finn, C. E., Petrilli, M. J., & Winkler, A. M. (2009). *The Accountability Illusion*. Washington, DC: Thomas B. Fordham Foundation.

Flanagan, D. P., Ortiz, S. O., & Alfonso, V. C. (2013). *Essentials of Cross-Battery Assessment* (3rd ed.). Hoboken, NJ: Wiley.

Fletcher, J. (2008). Identifying learning disabilities in the context of response-to-intervention: A hybrid model. *RTI Action Network*. Retrieved March 12, 2009 from http://www.rtinetwork.org/Learn/LD/ar/HybridModel

Fletcher, J. M., Denton, C., & Francis, D. J. (2005). Validity of alternative approaches for the identification of learning disabilities: Operationalizing unexpected underachievement. *Journal of Learning Disabilities*, **38**, 545–552.

Fordham Institute. (2011). *Our review of the Common Core Standards*. Retrieved January 22, 2012 from http://standards.educationgadfly.net/commoncore/ela

Fordham Institute (2014). *The State Education Agency: At the Helm, not the Oar*. Retrieved Jun15, 2014 from http://edex.s3-us-west-2.amazonaws.com/publication/pdfs/State-Education-Agency-Helm-Not-Oar-FINAL.pdf

Francis, D. J., Fletcher, J. M., Stuebing, K. K., Lyon, G. R., Shaywitz, B. A., & Shaywitz, S. E. (2005). Psychometric approaches to the identification of learning disabilities: IQ and achievement scores are not sufficient. *Journal of Learning Disabilities*, **38**, 98–108.

Fuchs, L. S. (2003). Assessing intervention responsiveness: Conceptual and technical issues. *Learning Disabilities: Research and Practice*, **18**, 172–186.

Fuchs, L. S., & Fuchs, D. (2002). Curiculum-based measurement: Describing competence, enhancing outcomes, evaluating treatment effects, and identifying treatment nonresponders. *Peabody Journal of Education*, **77**, 64–84.

Fuchs, D., Mock, D., Morgan, P. L., & Young, C. L. (2003). Responsiveness-to-intervention: Definitions, evidence, and implications for the learning disabilities construct. *Learning Disabilities Research & Practice*, **18**, 157–171.

Global Scholar/Spectrum K12 School Solutions (2011). *Response to intervention (RTI) adoption survey 2011*. Retrieved March 2, 2012 from http://www.spectrumk12. com/rti/the_rti_corner/rti_adoption_report

Goetz, E. T., Alexander, P. A., & Ash, M. J. (1992). *Educational Psychology: A Classroom Perspective*. Upper Saddle River, NJ: Merrill/Prentice Hall.

Goldhaber, D. (2007). *Teacher Pay Reforms: The Political Implications of Recent Research*. Washington, DC: Center for American Progress.

Gottfredson, L. S. (1997). Why g matters: The complexity of everyday life. *Intelligence*, **24**, 79–132.

Great Schools Partnership. (2014, August 26). Hidden curriculum. In S. Abbott (Ed.), *The Glossary of Education Reform*. Retrieved January 4, 2015 from http://edglossary. org/hidden-curriculum

Gullikson, H. (1987). *Theory of Mental Tests*. Hillsdale, NJ: Erlbaum.

Harrow, A. (1977). *A Taxonomy of the Psychomotor Domain: A Guide for Developing Behavioral Objectives*. New York: David McKay.

Holmes Group. (1986). *Tomorrow's Teachers*. East Lansing, MI: The Holmes Group, Michigan State University.

Hursh, D. (2008). *High Stakes Testing and the Decline of Teaching and Learning*. New York: Rowman and Littlefield.

Individuals with Disabilities Education Act Amendments of 1997, 20 U.S. Code, Sec. 101.

Individuals with Disabilities Education Improvement Act of 2004 20 U.S. Code 1400 et seq., Sec. 101.

Jenkins, J. R., Hudson, R. F., & Johnson, E. S. (2007). Screening for service delivery in an RTI framework: Candidate measures. *School Psychology Review*, **36**, 560–582.

Jimerson, S. R., Burns, M. K., & VanDerHeyden, A. M. (2007). Response to intervention at school: The science and practice of assessment and intervention. In S. R. Jimerson, M. K. Burns, & A. M. VanDerHeyden (Eds.), *Handbook of Response to Intervention: The Science and Practice of Assessment and Intervention* (pp. 3–9). New York: Springer.

Johnson, R., Mims-Cox, J., & Doyle-Nichols, A. (2009). *Developing Portfolios in Education: A Guide to Reflection, Inquiry and Assessment*. Thousand Oaks, CA: Sage.

Joint Committee on Testing Practices (2004). Code of fair testing practices in education. Available from http://www. apa.org/science/programs/testing/fair-testing.pdf

Keller-Margulis, M. A., Shapiro, E. S., & Hintze, J. M. (2008). Long term diagnostic accuracy of curriculum-based measures in reading and mathematics. *School Psychology Review*, **37**, 374–390.

Kelly, D., Xie, H., Nord, C.W., Jenkins, F., Chan, J.Y., & Kastberg, D. (2013). *Performance of U.S. 15-Year-Old Students in Mathematics, Science, and Reading Literacy in an International Context: First Look at PISA 2012* (NCES 2014-024). U.S. Department of Education. Washington, DC: National Center for Education Statistics. Retrieved March 6, 2014 from http://nces.ed.gov/pubsearch

Klein A., & Camera, L. (2015, January 9). NCLB rewrite could target mandate on annual tests. *Education Week*. Retrieved on January 11, 2015 from http://www.edweek. org/ew/articles/2015/01/09/nclb-rewrite-could-target-tests.h34.html

Koppel, T. (2001, June 6). Cheating teachers. *Nightline*. New York: American Broadcasting Company.

Kowaleski, T., & Mahoney, J. (2008). *Data-Driven Decisions and School Leadership*. Boston: Allyn & Bacon.

Krathwohl, B., Bloom, B. S., & Masia, B. B. (1999). *Taxonomy of Educational Objectives. Handbook 2: Affective Domain*. New York: Longman.

Kubiszyn, T. & Borich, G. (2013). Educational Testing & Measurement: Classroom Application and Practice. Hoboken, NJ: John Wiley & Sons.

Kubiszyn, T., Meyer, G. J., Finn, S. E., Eyde, L. D., Kay, G. G., Moreland, K. L., et al. (2000). Empirical support for psychological assessment in clinical health care settings. *Professional Psychology: Research and Practice*, **31**, 119–130.

Layton, L. (2014, May 12). Good teaching, poor test scores: downcast grading teachers by student performance. *Washington Post*. Retrieved on August 6, 2014 from www.washingtonpost.com/local/education/good-teaching-poortestscores

Lightfoot, P. (2006). *Student Portfolios: A Learning Tool*. Bloomington, IN: BookSurge Publishing.

Malda, M., van de Vijver, F., & Temane, Q. M. (2010). Rugby versus soccer in South America: Content familiarity contributes to cross-cultural differences in cognitive test scores. *Intelligence*, **38**, 582–595.

Martinez, M. (2002, January 9). District fined for altering test data: Austin school district pleads no contest to tampering with TAAS reports, fined $5,000. *Austin American Statesman*, p. A1.

Marzano, R., Pickering, J., & Heflebower, T. (2010). *The Highly Engaged Learner*. Denver, CO: Marzano Research Laboratory.

Masterson, J. J. (2009). Curriculum-based measurement procedures for writing meet minimal reliability and validity standards: More complex measures offer promise for secondary students. *Evidence-Based Communication Assessment and Intervention*, **3**, 4–7.

McNeil, M. (2012, March 7). 26 states, D.C. join bid for NCLB waivers. *Education Week*, **31**, 24–26.

Meyer, G. J., Finn, S. E., Eyde, L. D., Kay, G. G., Moreland, K. L., Dies, R. R., Eisman, E. J., Kubiszyn, T., & Reed, G. M. (2001). Psychological testing and psychological assessment: A review of evidence and issues. *American Psychologist*, **56**, 128–165.

Miller, M. J. (1992). Model standards for beginning teacher licensing and development: A resource for state dialogue. Retrieved September 21, 1999 from http://www.ccsso.org/intascst.html

Mitchell, R. (2006). *Research Review: Effects of High-Stakes Testing on Instruction*. Center for Public Education. Retrieved August 3, 2007 from http://www.centerfor publiceducation.org/site/c.kjJXJ5MPIwE/b.1536671

Molnar, M. (2014, October 17). Educators evaluate array of formative testing products. *Education Week*. Retrieved October 30, 2014 from http://www.edweek.org/ew/articles/2014/10/22/09pl-formative.h34.html

Moore, K. (1992). *Classroom Teaching Skills* (2nd ed.). New York: McGraw Hill.

Murray, C. S., Woodruff, A. L., & Vaughn, S. (2010). First-grade student retention within a 3-tier reading framework. *Reading and Writing Quarterly*, **26**, 26–50.

National Center for Research on Learning Disabilities. (2007). What is RTI? Retrieved July 12, 2008 from http://www.nrcld.org/topics/rti.html

National Center on Response to Intervention (2012, June). *RTI Implementer Series: Module 1: Screening—Training Manual*. Washington, DC: U.S. Department of Education, Office of Special Education Programs, National Center on Response to Intervention.

National Joint Committee on Learning Disabilities. (2005). *Responsiveness to intervention and learning disabilities*. Retrieved February 2, 2009 from http://www.ncld.org/index.php?option=content&task=view&id=497

National Research Council. (2000). *Knowing What Students Know: The Science and Design of Educational Assessment*. Washington, DC: National Academies Press.

National Research Council. (2001). *Building a workforce for the information economy*. Committee on Workforce Needs in Information Technology. Board on Testing and Assessment; Board on Science, Technology, and Economic Policy; and Office of Scientific and Engineering Personnel. Washington, DC: National Academy Press.

Newsweek (1998, June 22). Chicago's last hope. *Newsweek*, **30**.

No Child Left Behind Act (2002). Public Law 107–110.

Orosco, M. J., Almanza de Schonewise, E., de Onis, C., Klingner, J. K., & Hoover, J. J. (2007). Distinguishing between language acquisition and learning disabilities among English language learners: Background information. In J. J. Hoover, L. M. Baca, & J. K. Klinger (Eds.), *Why Do English Language Learners Struggle with Reading: Distinguishing Language Acquisition from Learning Disabilities*. Thousand Oaks, CA: Sage Publications.

Polikoff, M. S., & Porter, A. C. (2014). Instructional alignment as a measure of teaching quality. *Education Evaluation and Policy Analysis*, **20**, 1–18.

Quellmalz, E. S. (1991). Developing criteria for performances assessments: The missing link. *Applied Measurement in Education*, **4**(4), 319–332.

Quellmalz, E. S., & Hoskyn, J. (1997). Classroom assessment of reasoning strategies. In G. Phye (Ed.), *Handbook of Classroom Assessment: Learning, Adjustment, and Achievement* (pp. 103–130). San Diego: Academic Press.

Ravitch, D. (2010). Obama's race to the top will not improve education. *Huffington Post*, Retrieved February 10, 2013 from http://www.huffingtonpost.com/diane-ravitch/obamas-race-to-the-top-wi_b_666598.html

Ravitch, D. (2014). *Reader: Another Liberal Who Questions the Overreach of the Common Core*. Retrieved April 30, 2014 from http://dianeravitch.net/2014/04/22/reader-another-liberal-who-questions-the-overreach-of-common-core/

Reingold, J. (2015, February 1). Everybody hates Pearson. *Fortune*, **171**, 74–84.

Reynolds, N., & Davis, E. (2013). *Portfolio Keeping: A Guide for Teachers*. New York; Bedford/St. Martin's Press.

Rhodes, R., Ochoa, H., & Ortiz, S. *Assessing Culturally and Linguistically Diverse Students*. New York: Guilford Press.

Richards, C., Pavri, S., Golez, F., Canges, R., & Murphy, J. (2007). Response to intervention: Building the capacity of teachers to serve students with learning difficulties. *Issues in Teacher Education*, **16**, 55–64.

Robelen, E. (2012). More states retaining struggling 3rd graders. *Education Week*, **31**, 1, 15.

RTI Action Network (2008). What is RTI? Retrieved February 22, 2009 from http://www.rtinetwork.org/Learn/What

Sawchuck, S. (2012, January 31) Analysis raises questions about rigor of teacher tests. *Education Week*, **31**, 1, 14.

Sax, G. (1989). *Principles of Educational and Psychological Measurement and Evaluation* (3rd ed.). Belmont, CA: Wadsworth.

Shapiro, E. (2009) The two models of RTI: Standard protocol and problem solving. Retrieved May 20, 2010 from http://www.doe.virginia.gov/VDOE/studentsVCS/RTI

Shapiro, E. S., Keller, M. A., Edwards, L., Lutz, G., & Hintze, J. M. (2006). General outcome measures and performance on state assessment and standardized tests: Reading and math performance in Pennsylvania. *Journal of Psychoeducational Assessment*, **42**(1), 19–35.

Shavelson, R., & Baxter, G. (1992). What we've learned about assessing hands-on science. *Educational Leadership*, **49**(8), 20–25.

Shavelson, R., Gao, X., & Baxter, G. (1991). *Design Theory and Psychometrics for Complex Performance Assessment*. Los Angeles: UCLA.

Spears, A. (2015). *TNReady … Already?* Tennessee Education Report: Education and Politics in the Volunteer State. Retrieved March 23, 2015 from http://tnedreport.com/?p=1310

Sternberg, R. (2008). *Wisdom, Intelligence, and Creativity Synthesized*. New York: Cambridge University Press.

Stiggins, R. J. (2011). *Introduction to Student-Involved Classroom Assessment* (6th ed.). Upper Saddle River, NJ: Prentice Hall.

Straus, V. (2015, May 3). *Why the movement to opt out of Common Core tests is a big deal*. Washington Post. Retrieved May 5, 2015 from http://www.washingtonpost.com/blogs/answer-sheet/wp/2015/05/03/why-the-movement-to-opt-out-of-common-core-tests-is-a-big-deal/

Szetela, W., & Nicol, C. (1992). Evaluating problem-solving in mathematics. *Educational Leadership*, **49**(8), 42–45.

Terman, L. (1959). *The Gifted Group at Mid-Life: Thirty-five Years Follow-up of the Superior Child*. Stanford University Press.

The Waco Experiment (1998, June 12). *The Austin American-Statesman*. p. A14.

Thorndike, R. M. (2004). *Measurement and Evaluation in Psychology and Education*. New York: Macmillan.

Tomlinson, C. (2004). *How to Differentiate Instruction in Mixed Ability Classrooms* (2nd ed.). Alexandria, VA: Association for Supervision and Curriculum Development.

Tomlinson, C. (2014). *The Differentiated Classroom: Responding to the Needs of All Learners* (2nd ed.). Alexandria, VA: Association for Supervision and Curriculum Development.

Tomlinson, C., & McTighe, J. (2006). *Integrating Differentiated Instruction and Understanding by Design*. Alexandria, VA: Association for Supervision and Curriculum Development.

U. S. Department of Education (2014, December). *ESEA flexibility*. Retrieved January 24, 2015 from http://www2.ed.gov/policy/elsec/guid/esea-flexibility/index.html

Veenhoven, R., & Choi, Y. (2012). Does intelligence boost happiness? Smartness of all pays more than being smarter than others. *International Journal of Happiness and Development*, **1**, 5–27.

White House (March, 2014). *Setting the Pace: Expanding Opportunity for American Students under Race to the Top*. Retrieved August 12, 2014 from http://www.whitehouse.gov/sites/default/files/docs/settingthepacerttreport_3-2414_b.pdf

Wright, R. (2007). *Educational Assessment: Tests and Measurements in the Age of Accountability*. Thousand Oaks, CA: Sage.

Zabala, D., Minnici, A., McMurrer, J., & Briggs, L. (2008). State high school exit exams: Moving toward end-of-course exams. Center for Education Policy. Retrieved January 4, 2009 from http://www.cepc.org/index.cfm?fuseaction=document_ext.showDocumentByID&nodeID=1&DocumentID=244

Zirkel, P. A., & Thomas, L. B. (2010, January–February). State laws for RTI: An updated snapshot. *Teaching Exceptional Children*, **42**, 56–63.

CREDITS

FIGURE 3.1: National Center on Response to Intervention (June 2012). *RTI Implementer Series: Module 1: Screening—Training Manual.* Washington, DC: U.S. Department of Education, Office of Special Education Programs, National Center on Response to Intervention.

TABLE 3.1: IRIS Center for the National Association of State Directors of Special Education's IDEA Partnership (2007). *Comparing Problem Solving and Standard Protocol Approaches to RTI.* Sponsored by the U.S. Department of Education.

FIGURE 19.9: CTB McGraw-Hill (2015). A sample *Home Report* for a fourth grade student from the TerraNova3. Reproduced with permission of McGraw-Hill Education CTB. TerraNova3 and TerraNova are registered trademarks of McGraw-Hill Education.

FIGURE 19.10: CTB McGraw-Hill (2015). A sample *Individual Skills Report* for a third grader from the TerraNova3. Reproduced with permission of McGraw-Hill Education CTB. TerraNova3 and TerraNova are registered trademarks of McGraw-Hill Education.

FIGURE 19.11: CTB McGraw-Hill (2015). A sample *Group List Report* for Ms. Jones' sixth grade class from the TerraNova3. Reproduced with permission of McGraw-Hill Education CTB. TerraNova3 and TerraNova are registered trademarks of McGraw-Hill Education.

FIGURE 19.12: New York State Education Department (2015). A sample *Your Child's Test Results* report from the PARCC 4th grade mathematics test adopted by NY State. Reproduced with permission of New York State Education Department (2015). Retrieved January 27, 2015 from http://www.p12.nysed.gov/assessment/ei/eiscorereports14.html.

INDEX